JAUNE CHROME MOYEN Medium chrome yellow	JAUNE CHROME FONCÉ Deep chrome yellow	J. CHROME ORANGÉ Chrome yellow orange	JAUN Lem
JAUNE D'OR Golden yellow	JAUNE INDIEN (imit.)	JAUNE MONACO Monaco yellow	JAUNE DE NAPLES (imit.)
JAUNE PERSAN CITRON Lemon persian yellow	JAUNE PERSAN CLAIR Light persian yellow	JAUNE PERSAN MOYEN Medium persian yellow	JAUNE PERSAN FONCÉ Deep persian yellow
LAQUE CARMINÉE Crimson lake	L. GARANCE BLEUE Blue madder lake	L. GARANCE BRUNE Brown madder L.	L. GARANCE CLAIRE Light pink madder
L. GARANCE FONCÉE Deep madder L.	L. GARANCE GRENAT Garnet madder	L. GARANCE ORANGÉE Orange madder L.	L. GARANCE POURPRE Purple madder
GARANCE VERT BLEU Blue green madder L.	GARANCE VERT OLIVE Olive green madder L.	GARANCE VERT CLAIR Light green madder	GARANCE VERT FONCÉ Deep green madder
GARANCE VIOLET BLEU Blue violet madder L.	GARANCE VIOLET ROUGE Red violet madder L.	LAQUE GÉRANIUM Geranium lake	LAQUE GRENAT Garnet lake
LAQUE INDIENNE Indian lake	LAQUE JAUNE CLAIR Light yellow lake	LAQUE JAUNE FONCÉ Deep yellow lake	LAQUE MORDORÉE Reddish brown lake
LAQUE NOIRE Black lake	LAQUE DE PERSE Persian lake	MARYLAND Maryland	MINE D'ORANGE Orange lead
NOIR D'IVOIRE Ivory black	NOIR INTENSE Deep black	NOIR VELOURS Velvet black	OCRE CITRON Lemon ochre

Henri Matisse

The Cut-Outs

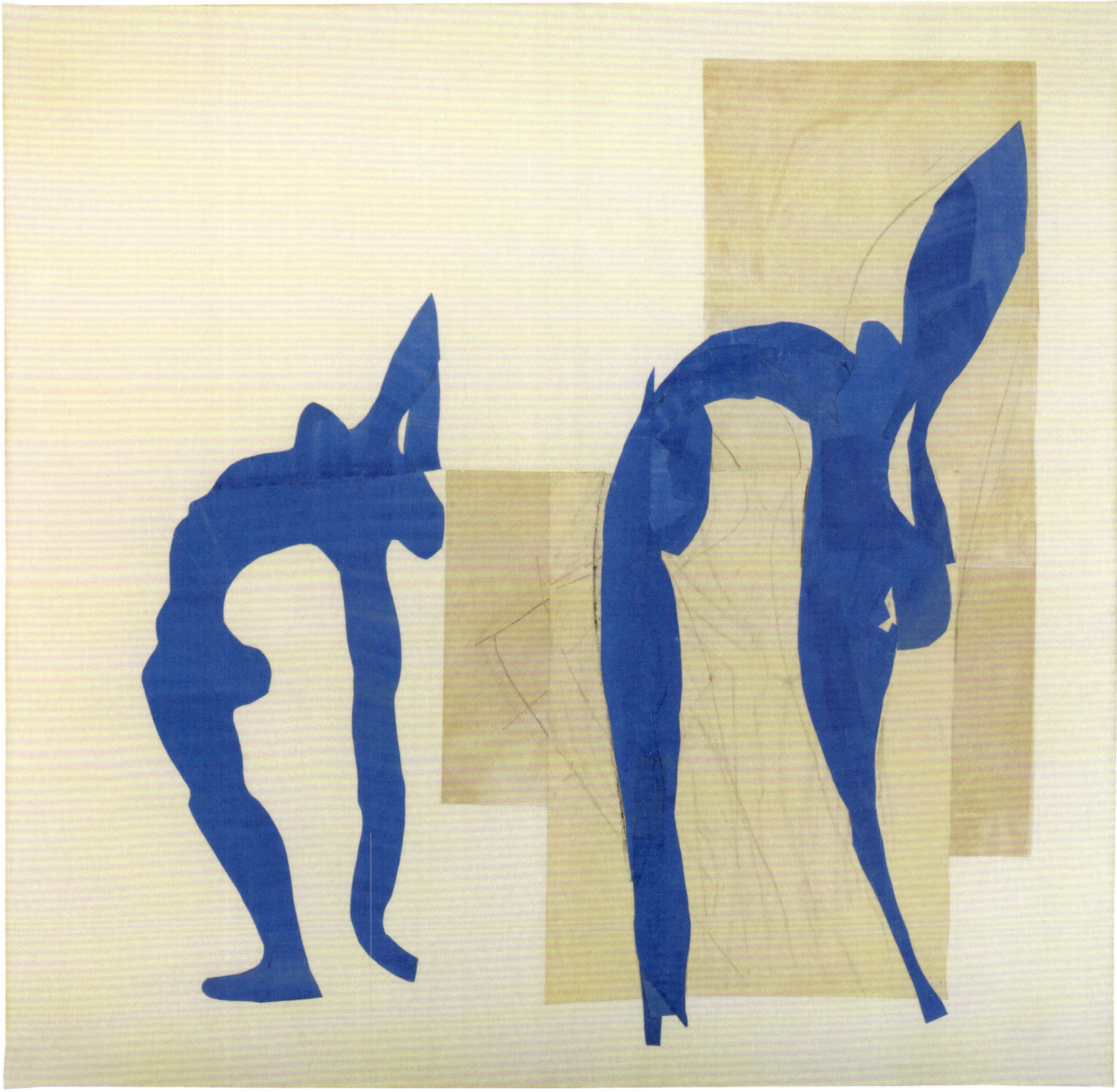

Henri Matisse
The Cut-Outs

Edited by
Karl Buchberg, Nicholas Cullinan,
Jodi Hauptman and Nicholas Serota

With essays by
Karl Buchberg, Nicholas Cullinan,
Samantha Friedman, Flavia Frigeri,
Markus Gross, Jodi Hauptman,
Stephan Lohrengel and
Nicholas Serota

Tate Publishing

First published 2014 by
order of the Tate Trustees
by Tate Publishing, a division
of Tate Enterprises Ltd,
Millbank, London SW1P 4RG
www.tate.org.uk/publishing

on the occasion of the exhibition
Henri Matisse: The Cut-Outs

Exhibition organised by
Tate Modern in collaboration with
The Museum of Modern Art, New York

Tate Modern, London
17 April – 7 September 2014

The Museum of Modern Art, New York
25 October 2014 – 9 February 2015

Bank of America Merrill Lynch

HANJIN SHIPPING

Supported by the Henri Matisse Exhibition
Supporters Group and Tate Patrons

A catalogue record for this book is
available from the British Library

ISBN 978-1-84976-129-1 (hbk)
ISBN 978-1-84976-130-7 (pbk)

Designed by Fraser Muggeridge studio
Colour reproduction by DL Imaging Ltd,
London
Printed by Graphicom SPA, Italy

Front cover: Henri Matisse, *Blue Nude II*
spring 1952 (see no. 110)
Back cover: Tetsuo Abe, Hôtel Régina, Nice,
28 September 1952 (see p. 81)
Frontispiece: Henri Matisse, *Acrobats*
spring–summer 1952 (see no. 113)

Measurements of artworks are given
in centimetres, followed by inches,
height before width.

FSC
www.fsc.org
MIX
Paper from
responsible sources
FSC® C013123

Director's Foreword

Henri Matisse is surely one of the leading figures of twentieth-century art, most widely recognised for his extraordinary and innovative use of colour. Matisse's artistic journey has been illustrated in recent decades by major exhibitions focusing primarily on his pictorial output. We now feel extremely privileged to have the opportunity to present this landmark exhibition exploring in depth the final chapter of Matisse's career, in which he fused drawing, painting and sculpture into the spectacular series of paper cut-outs.

During the final fifteen years of his life, until his death in 1954, Matisse dispensed with the limits of easel painting and developed a new technique of gouached, cut, and glued paper. This manifested itself through a prolific series of designs for stained-glass windows, ceramic tile murals, book illustrations, church vestments and other textiles. Cutting directly into colour, often with large scissors for tailors, Matisse infused his gouached sheets with sculptural forms. The result is an extraordinary body of bold and exuberant compositions, in which colour and form are carefully balanced. At the same time Matisse radically rethought the process of creation, and overcame the limits of painting by working directly on the walls of his studio. The cut-outs were thus conceived as mutable and contingent compositions, curling off the walls and shifting in position over time. Ultimately these 'impromptu' works were made permanent through mounting and framing.

The present exhibition and this publication seek to reconsider the cut-outs' double lives as mutable and permanent works, as well as their role and function within Matisse's practice. Arranged in broadly chronological sequence, this project follows the development of the cut-outs from design aids on an intimate scale, into more complex and self-standing compositions increasingly monumental in size.

Exhibitions are collaborative by their very nature and I am delighted that Tate Modern, in collaboration with The Museum of Modern Art, has been able to present such a comprehensive exhibition and, in doing so, stimulate a new perspective on Matisse's cut-outs.

The success of this project is due in no small part to the excellent curatorial collaboration between Nicholas Cullinan and Nicholas Serota at Tate Modern and Jodi Hauptman and Karl Buchberg at MoMA. I am deeply grateful to them for their vision, enthusiasm and the extensive research they have undertaken in bringing this exhibition to fruition. Their ability to develop the thesis for the exhibition, select and locate artworks and negotiate the loans was matched by Flavia Frigeri in London and Samantha Friedman in New York, who have both worked tirelessly on the exhibition research and organisation. I should also like to thank each of them for the illuminating essays they have written for this catalogue.

I am most grateful to the Matisse family and estate who joined in the organisation with great generosity. Their support from the earliest days of the project has encouraged and helped us assemble this exceptional exhibition offering new insights on Matisse's late work. The many lenders, museum staff members and others who played important roles in bringing this exhibition and catalogue to fruition are acknowledged elsewhere in this publication, and I join in saluting their contributions.

The ambitious nature of this exhibition was matched by the generosity of its global sponsor, Bank of America Merrill Lynch, for which we express our sincere appreciation. We are particularly grateful for the additional support from Hanjin Shipping, as well as the committed group of individuals who have contributed to the exhibition through the Henri Matisse: The Cut-Outs Exhibition Supporters Group, including Thomas Gibson Fine Art Ltd and those donors who wish to remain anonymous.

This exhibition has been made possible by the provision of insurance through the Government Indemnity Scheme. Tate Modern would like to thank HM Government for providing Government Indemnity and the Department for Culture, Media and Sport and Arts Council England for arranging the indemnity.

Chris Dercon, Director, Tate Modern

Acknowledgements

An exhibition of this scale and complexity owes its existence to the very generous assistance and collaboration of many individuals and lenders in museums and private collections. Their willingness to part with such fragile works of art – many of which have never been brought together since they left Matisse's studio over fifty years ago – is extraordinary and we are ever so grateful for their enthusiastic support.

We acknowledge our deepest gratitude to the Matisse family and estate, but most especially to Georges Matisse and Wanda de Guébriant in Paris, who have provided sound orientation through the, sometimes labyrinthine, preparations for the exhibition. Their generous support and advice in many matters relating to loans and research has contributed substantially to the success of the project.

We would also like to acknowledge the role that three seminal exhibitions devoted to the cut-outs have played in helping us to appreciate the development of this novel medium: *Henri Matisse: Paper Cut-Outs* (National Gallery of Art, Washington DC; Detroit Institute of Arts and Saint Louis Art Museum, 1977–8); *Henri Matisse: Drawing with Scissors: Masterpieces from the Late Years* (Schirn Kunsthalle, Frankfurt, and Nationalgalerie, Sammlung Berggruen, Berlin, 2002–3); and *Matisse: La Couleur découpée, une donation révélatrice* (Musée départemental Matisse, Le Cateau-Cambrésis, 2013). These exhibitions undoubtedly paved the way for this one.

For their generosity in agreeing to lend their works for the period of the exhibition we would like to thank both institutions and private individuals: The Ascher Family Collection; Fondation Beyeler, Reihen/Basel; Carnegie Museum of Art, Pittsburgh; La Cinémathèque française, Paris; Colección Patricia Phelps de Cisneros; Dallas Museum of Art, Dallas; Designmuseum Danmark, Copenhagen; Hammer Museum, Los Angeles; Hilti Art Foundation, Schaan; Hirshhorn Museum and Sculpture Garden, Washington DC; Ikeda Museum of 20th Century Art, Shizuoka; Kunstmuseum Basel; Kunstsammlung Nordrhein-Westfalen, Düsseldorf; Los Angeles County Museum of Art; Fondation Maeght, Saint-Paul-de-Vence; Howard and Nancy Marks; Mr. and Mrs. Donald B. Marron; The Pierre and Tana Matisse Foundation, New York; The Menil Collection, Houston; The Metropolitan Museum of Art, New York; The Mourlot Archives; Frederick Mulder; Musée départemental Matisse, Le Cateau-Cambrésis; Musée Matisse, Nice; Musée d'Orsay, Paris; Musée national d'art moderne, Centre Pompidou, Paris; Museum Ludwig, Cologne; The Museum of Modern Art, New York; National Gallery of Art, Washington DC; The Perl Collection; Pushkin State Museum of Fine Arts, Moscow; Louisa Riley Smith, 20th Century Art Archives, Cambridge; Mr. Julian Robertson; Scottish National Gallery of Modern Art, Edinburgh; Skissernas Museum – Museum of Artistic Process and Public Art, Lund; Staatliche Museen zu Berlin, Museum Berggruen; Statens Museum for Kunst, Copenhagen; Stedelijk Museum, Amsterdam; Fondation Louis Vuitton, Paris; and those who wish to remain anonymous. It is very difficult to release these beautiful works, even for a few months, and we hope the lenders will enjoy seeing them in the context of the exhibition.

An exhibition of this kind often requires the aid of individuals outside the museum who can broaden our knowledge of the subject, as well as help us trace and secure crucial loans. We are deeply obliged to: Rosamond Bernier, Olivier Berggruen, Paule Caen-Martin, Patrice Deparpe, Jacqueline Duhême, Françoise Gilot, Ulf Küster, Adrien Maeght, Jules Maeght, Carrie Pilto, Marie-Thérèse Pulvénis De Seligny, Hilary Spurling, Jonas Storsve, Dominique Szymusiak, Verane Tasseau and Sheena Wagstaff. Additionally, we would like to thank Lily Galef, Charlotte Mitchell at Sotheby's, Giulia Omodeo-Sale, Suzanne Pennings, Fanny Saulay, Tim Schmelcher, and Jay Vincze at Christie's for their assistance in securing loans.

The exhibition has been realised in collaboration with The Museum of Modern Art, where we have been lucky enough to work with extraordinary colleagues, Jodi Hauptman, Senior Curator, Department of Drawings and Prints, Karl Buchberg, Senior Conservator and Samantha Friedman, Assistant Curator, Department of Drawings and Prints. This fruitful collaboration throughout the long period of the exhibition's development has been characterised by a shared vision, enthusiasm and extensive research, which has informed all aspects of the exhibition. Glenn D. Lowry has supported the project in important ways, and our thanks are also extended to his colleagues, including Ramona Bannayan, Carla Caputo, David Frankel, Katie Hanson, Christopher Hudson, Chul R. Kim, Allison Needle, Erik Patton and Carlos Yepes.

At Tate, we are indebted to the numerous colleagues who focused their expertise towards the project's realisation. Helen Sainsbury and Rachel Kent have overseen the discussions between the venues, and Chris Dercon, Achim Borchardt-Hume and Matthew Gale have supported the organisation of the exhibition in other important ways. Juliette Rizzi provided valuable research assistance, Priyesh Mistry and Helen O'Malley tackled a variety of tasks with efficiency, as did former curatorial intern, Micola Clara Brambilla. Neil Casey, Helen Craggs and Angela Green provided admirable back-up throughout. Carol Burnier Magno deftly coordinated the loan of works and all the logistical details of transportation and insurance with the help of Lucy Fisher. Phil Monk has led the art installation team with support from Rhona O'Brien, while Ryszard Lewandowski has ably overseen the art handling team. Patricia Smithen, Georgina Whiteley and Kevin Miles have given considerable conservation expertise to the project, assisted by other members of Tate's conservation department. We are grateful to Clare Gill, Emily Magnuson, Scott Walker and Chelsea Williams who have been instrumental in securing financial support for the exhibition. The exhibition's marketing has been masterminded by Elli Cartwright and Livia Ratcliffe, while Jeanette Ward and Cecily Carbone have supervised press coverage. Learning colleagues Simon Bolitho, Anna Murray, Minnie Scott and Sandra Sykorova have assisted with the exhibition interpretation and events programme. We would also like to thank Tate Library and Archive who have assisted in numerous ways and especially Krzysztof Cieszkowski for his contribution to the bibliography.

Tate's outstanding publishing department, led by Roger Thorp, worked diligently to accomplish the successful realisation of this catalogue. We are grateful to the entire team, especially Alice Chasey, project editor, who has skilfully overseen every aspect with her characteristic efficiency and dedication. Our thanks also to Roanne Marner, Roz Young and Deborah Metherell for their handling of production and picture research. We are extremely grateful to Sarah Newitt and Fraser Muggeridge of Fraser Muggeridge studio for their thoughtful design for the catalogue, which elegantly captures the spirit of Matisse's late work. We would also like to thank all of our authors, Karl Buchberg, Samantha Friedman, Markus Gross, Jodi Hauptman and Stephan Lohrengel for their insightful contributions.

The exhibition is supported by Bank of America Merrill Lynch and we owe them a huge debt of thanks for enabling us to bring Matisse's cut-outs to the large audience that Tate Modern commands. Hanjin Shipping who have supported this project from the outset are also commended, as well as the committed group of individuals who have contributed to the exhibition through the Henri Matisse: The Cut-Outs Exhibition Supporters Group including Thomas Gibson Fine Art Ltd and those donors who wish to remain anonymous. Ultimately it is only through the collaboration of so many individuals and supporters that an exhibition of ambition can be achieved.

Nicholas Serota, Director, Tate
Nicholas Cullinan, Curator, Modern and Contemporary Art, The Metropolitan Museum of Art
Flavia Frigeri, Assistant Curator, Tate Modern

Sponsors' Forewords

Global Sponsor
Bank of America Merril Lynch

Continuing our long tradition of support for the arts, Bank of America Merrill Lynch is pleased to be the sponsor of *Henri Matisse: The Cut-Outs*. We are delighted to once again partner with Tate Modern to bring to London this groundbreaking reassessment of Henri Matisse's innovative final works.

As a company serving clients in more than 100 countries around the world, Bank of America Merrill Lynch believes that the arts have a unique capability to educate and enrich societies, connect individuals, and foster thriving economies. We support a wide range of organisations, from local, community-based arts education programmes to leading, world-class arts institutions. We do this through sponsorships to arts organisations, sharing our collection through our Art in Our Communities® programme, providing grants for the restoration of artworks with historical and cultural significance, and through outreach and public access initiatives.

We hope you are inspired by *Henri Matisse: The Cut-Outs* to consider how art can transcend time and create meaningful human connections. Please share this rich cultural experience with family and friends, so that they too may enjoy one of the most talented artists of our time.

Brian T. Moynihan
Chief Executive Officer
Bank of America

Bank of America
Merrill Lynch

Hanjin Shipping

Hanjin Shipping is delighted to sponsor *Henri Matisse: The Cut-Outs* at Tate Modern and to share this unique exhibition with Tate's diverse audience. We hope that Tate's many visitors from around the world will be inspired by Henri Matisse and his artworks. We have enjoyed working with Tate tremendously and are proud of the relationship we have established with them over the years. Hanjin Shipping sponsors many major exhibitions around the world, and it is our priority to partner with museums in order to bring awareness to the arts and to support their development around the world. We are committed to continuing these activities with conviction and passion, and with the full organisation's support we shall continue to pursue this goal. As the scope of our business extends to every corner of the world, we believe that art can be an excellent means for communicating with the global community.

Hanjin Shipping is Korea's largest shipping company, and ranks among the top ten major shipping carriers in the world. Hanjin operates a fleet of over 200 containerships, bulk and LNG carriers with an extensive global network and yearly freight revenue of US $10 billion. The company has a comprehensive global business network with four regional headquarters, 200 overseas branch offices, and 30 local corporations, earning about 90% of its total revenue overseas.

Eunyoung Choi
Chairwoman and CEO
Hanjin Shipping

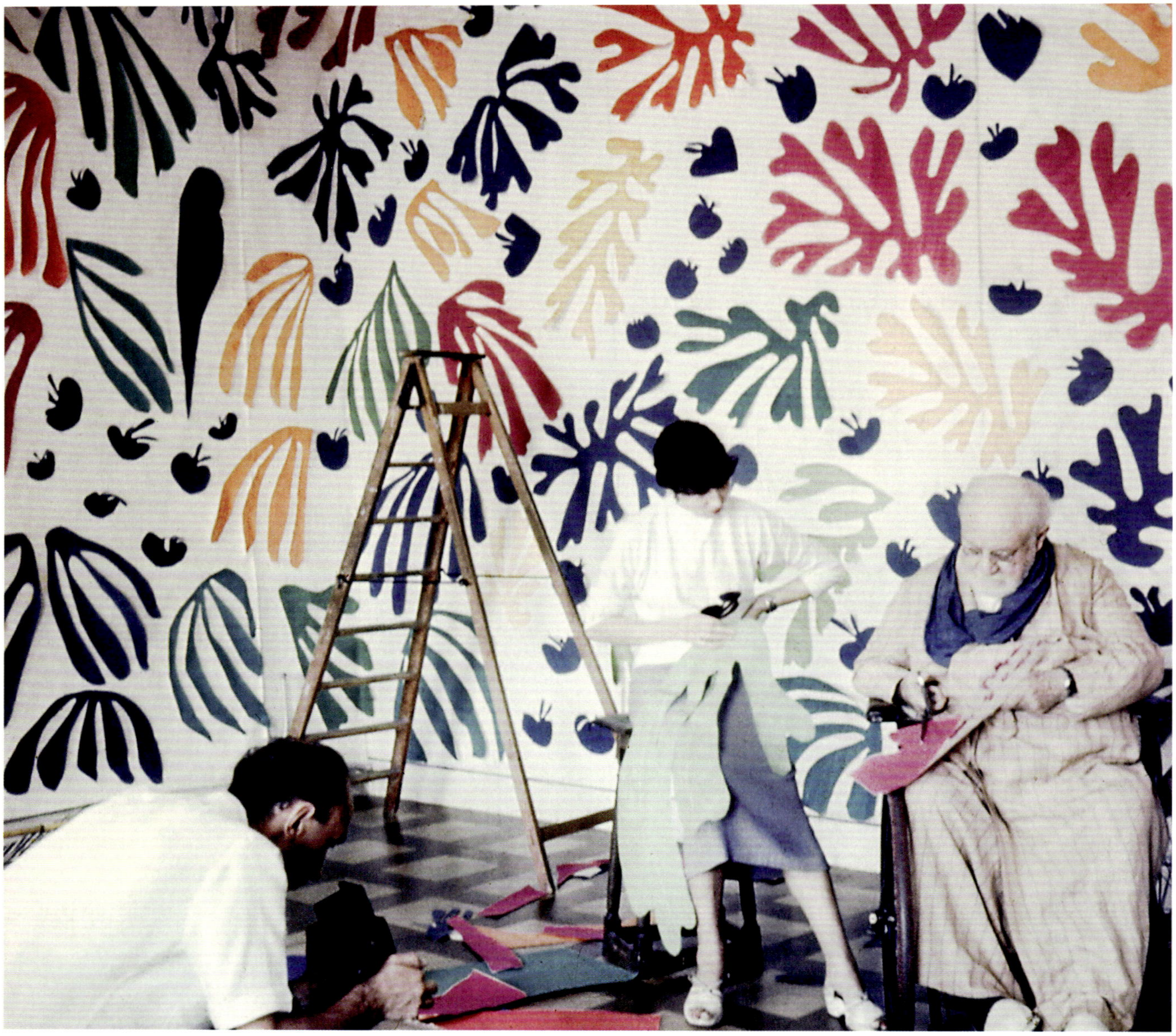

Fig. 1 Walter Carone, Matisse working at the Hôtel Régina, Nice, c. 1952

The STUDIO as SITE and SUBJECT

Karl Buchberg, Nicholas Cullinan, Jodi Hauptman and Nicholas Serota

In a 1952 interview with the writer André Verdet Henri Matisse describes a cluster of colourful cut-paper forms pinned to his studio walls as a 'little garden'. 'You see,' he explains, 'as I am obliged to remain often in bed because of the state of my health, I have made a little garden all around me where I can walk ... There are leaves, fruits, a bird.' As Matisse speaks, he points to 'a large mural composition of cut paper that encompassed half the room'.[1] Leaves in hues of green, red, blue, yellow and orange – heavy with finger-like tendrils or extended with limbs radiating outwards – and ultramarine pomegranates of varying sizes cover two adjoining walls. Arrayed across the walls and into the corner, the forms are pinned, some with multiple pins, but not too firmly or flatly, allowing each leaf or fruit to follow the force of its own materiality, weight and position: drooping, bending, relaxing, fluttering, reacting to a breath of air, making shadows. The meeting of the two walls at a ninety-degree angle creates a small plot – a space for planting – around which the artist and the interviewer can walk.

Though Matisse is referring to a specific group of cut-paper forms still then in progress – what ultimately became the work known as *The Parakeet and the Mermaid* (no. 118) – his description of this composition and by extension the studio in which it was made as a garden is particularly instructive in elucidating the extraordinary work of his last decade, when he turned to painted paper as his primary medium and scissors as his chief implement. His efforts – giving coloured sheets the radiance of stained glass, infusing contour with sculptural form, simplifying shapes into pure signs – resulted in an entirely new form called *papier découpé*, or cut-out.

Matisse had always treated his garden as an extension of his studio, observing differences in chromatic 'precision', 'intensity' and 'luminosity', studying the way 'seeds, spindly and pale, suck strength and color from the sun day by day' or, for comparison, setting flowers 'right alongside' his paintings and worrying at 'how poor and dull all my colors seem!'[2] In this period, at the end of his life, the studio took on the very features of a garden: in its organisation, at once organic and controlled; in its unceasing flux and metamorphosis; in its mix and melding of colour and texture; and in its environmental aspect, a three-dimensional space that could be physically experienced, a place where one 'can walk'. Cut-paper flora sprouted and spread across the walls of his living and work space; the artist literally lived within the works.[3] Verdet evocatively describes the scene: 'A limpid scattering of color bathes the whole room, glowing like a rainbow, flaring like lightning, becoming soft and supple, then iridescent again like a rainbow ... blue, orange, violet, almond green, leaf green, orderly, organised, each finding its own shape and place in an ensemble of forms.'[4] These features – organic growth, proliferation, perpetual flux and spatial expansion – are at the heart of Matisse's cut-out practice and reflect both a renewed commitment to investigating problems of colour and contour and an inventiveness directed at the very status of the work of art, whether as a unique object, ornament or environment.

By about 1947 Matisse began to work intensively with cut paper, creating over 200 works in less than a decade. Studio assistants painted large sheets with gouache colours of Matisse's choosing. Once they were dry, Matisse would select a sheet from a range of colours and finishes spread on the floor in front of him. He cut forms of varying shapes and sizes. These were then arranged into compositions and fastened into place with pins.[5] Initially, he would compose on a board small enough to fit on his lap, but as his ambitions and the size of the shapes and the compositions expanded, he worked directly on his studio walls with the help of assistants; balanced on ladders, they managed the positioning and pinning at his direction. What we see of these works today is of course very different from how they were first manifested in the studio. For the sake of permanence and protection, once it was decided that a work was finished or when space was required in the studio, the composition was transferred from the wall through an elaborate tracing process, the pins were ultimately removed and the shapes were eventually glued into place. This discrepancy between how they appeared in the studio and how they look today raises an intriguing set of questions about their material nature.

Matisse's cut-outs were hybrid from the start: not exactly painting, but with painting's scale and chromatic intensity; not exactly sculpture, but with three-dimensional presence; and not quite drawing, though the scissors make a contour as precise as a pen. Without the vocabulary at hand to designate and define this new process, Matisse turned to the practices he knew, famously describing his approach as 'drawing with scissors' – which allowed him, he explains, to link 'line with color, contour with surface' – or 'cutting directly into vivid color', which 'reminds' him 'of the direct carving of sculptors'.[6] In these terms, the cut-outs did seem to solve the conundrum Matisse had faced throughout his career: the tension between drawing and colour. By cutting directly into the coloured paper, 'the contour of a shape and its internal area were formed simultaneously', offering a solution to what had always seemed a challenging impasse.[7] Such possibilities became clear to Matisse during work on his first sustained cut-out project, *Jazz* (nos. 18–39), in which the artist deployed cut paper to make one of the century's greatest illustrated books, begun in 1943 but not published until 1947. He had used cut paper before in ballet projects like *Rouge et Noir* (nos. 6–7) and most notably in composing the Barnes *Dance* (no. 3), but it was in *Jazz* that a process for expediency became what Matisse called 'a cut-out operation'.[8]

This procedure for 'creating new combinations of color' was deployed over the next decade – which turned out to be his last – on a host of projects, following an arc from small scale to large murals and including free-standing works as well as maquettes for a host of decorative projects: cover designs for books and periodicals, textiles, stained glass, ceramics.[9] For the maquettes, Matisse not only used paper cut-out compositions to simulate the material they would eventually be translated into – whether this meant paper itself, cloth, stained glass or ceramic – but he quickly realised in the process that these paper maquettes had their own distinctive character and intrinsic worth as autonomous works of art. At the centre of these efforts was the Dominican Chapel of the Rosary in Vence (Chapelle du Rosaire de Vence), on which Matisse worked from 1948 to 1951, a project that allowed him to combine his interests in colour and light at the scale of an architectural environment. He used cut paper to design the chapel's stained-glass windows, extracting from paper the luminosity of sunlight, and made rough black and white drawings, eventually fired onto tile, to balance out the glass's bright hues. His thinking extended to how the chapel would be experienced: he used cut-outs to create the priest's vestments, which when worn would animate his designs and colourfully enliven the space. The Vence chapel allowed Matisse to think with paper on an all-enveloping scale and to craft a comprehensive decorative scheme.[10]

From almost the very beginning, the cut-outs evolved directly on the walls of the studio. In this respect, we might see the cut-outs in the context of Matisse's career-long engagement with depicting his own quarters, of regarding his studio as a subject. Consider, for example, his monumental canvas *The Red Studio* or the related *The Pink Studio*, both 1911. Without artist or models to populate them, these canvases show Matisse concentrating on the accoutrements of the studio, artist's tools and still-life elements, along with an elaborate gallery of his own painting and sculpture.[11] Similarly, in the Nice interiors of 1917–30, with their depictions of sumptuous fabrics, rugs and wall coverings, the working and living space is also the primary subject. In his Nice studio Matisse

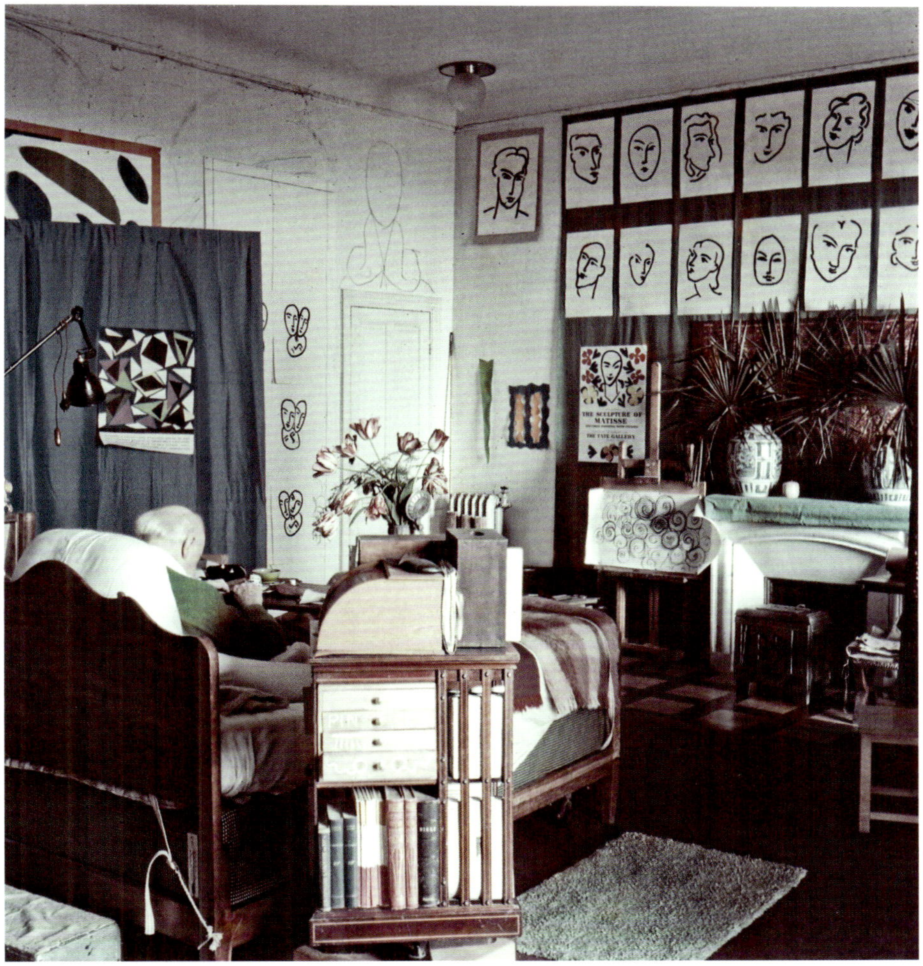

Fig. 2 Lydia Delectorskaya, Matisse at the Hôtel Régina, Nice, c. 1953

altered his environment, setting it up like a still life to be painted. 'It is as if Matisse, having theorized about the decorative, now decided to take an interest in interior decoration,' Isabel Monod-Fontaine suggests. 'Fabrics could be arranged and rearranged at will using a series of curtain rods and uprights, a platform covered with additional fabrics and rugs, a mattress or couch, cushions, folding screens, lights.'[12] Where painting the studio once meant painting a picture of the studio, in the case of the cut-outs it meant applying coloured paper to the walls of the studio. The studio went from being the subject to being the support.[13]

In trying to understand Matisse's approach, to get at the multivalent meanings of the cut-outs, our aim and challenge is to return to that lively and ever-changing garden that was his studio, where the walls often served as a blank canvas for Matisse's increasingly prolific and all-encompassing inventions.[14] This goal is based on our conviction that the cut-outs have two lives. The first was in the studio, where, pinned to the walls, contingent and mutable, their painted surfaces exhibited intense colour, texture and materiality, curled off the walls and shifted in position over time; where forms and groups of forms related to each other; where the walls facilitated pictorial expansion beyond the confines of an easel picture's frame; where they challenged the rules of architecture, sometimes ignoring structural guideposts like moulding, panelling, doors, mantels, heaters and windows, and paid little attention to distinctions between wall and floor; and where they were lived in and among, resulting in something closer to installation than painting. Their second life began when they left the studio: when they were made permanent and given a final form, via gluing and mounting, framing and glazing.

A collaboration between curators and conservators, this investigation focuses squarely on the physicality of Matisse's work in his last decade and the process of making: what exactly is this thing we call a 'cut-out'? What is the nature of the particular materials and how are they used?[15] On that score, we believe that the lessons of the cut-outs rest not only in their finished product or state but also, and even more, in their making. How can we return to the studio, to its impermanence and change, its experimentation, its liveliness? Can we imagine time running in reverse – un-mounting, un-gluing, un-transferring, re-pinning, un-pinning, un-cutting, un-painting – straight back to the original white sheet?[16]

Our trip back in time is made possible by the many photographs taken of Matisse's studio, including those that show the artist at work within it. Some of these photographs were made by Lydia Delectorskaya – Matisse's assistant, model, muse – to document the stages or progress of an individual work (called *états*[17]), allowing Matisse to study where he had been in order to determine where he would go; numerous others were taken by an array of visitors with cameras, some professional, some not, but all of whom were clearly fascinated by the work space as an intensely vibrant living organism. This trove (see pp. 30–83) includes informal snapshots, posed or carefully staged portraits, and those in which it appears that the photographer waited for a telling moment.[18] By putting these diverse photographs into chronological order (as best as we can), mapping their locations within and across Matisse's three primary studios of this period, wall by wall – Boulevard Montparnasse in Paris, Villa le Rêve in Vence, and the Hôtel Régina in Nice – and carefully reading their contents, the activities of the work space come into focus, even after more than seventy years. Paper elements cover any and all surfaces, from complicated large-scale compositions in mid-process to wall-size assemblages organised into patchworks and mosaics; from surfaces covered with individual works of varied size, texture and subject (recognisable, simplified or abstracted), and seemingly randomly installed, to a single form that dangles alone for no apparent compositional purpose; from work tables piled high with rolls of paper to assistants posing in their overalls, hammer and pins at the ready, like markers offering a sense of scale; from squares of coloured paper, arranged in a palette and hung for consideration, to bits of paper left on the floor in piles, a colourful negative of what we see on the wall. In those without people, evidence of a life lived, the blending of studio and bedroom, is everywhere: Matisse's bed carefully made with his brown plaid blanket, coffee pots, shells, travel souvenirs and other favourite items (many of which can be found in his paintings), bookcases and glass cabinets, plants in vases. In others Matisse is seen at work: settled into a wheelchair surrounded by colourful bits of paper; upright in a custom-built chair, at his side a specially designed cabinet with a roll-top desk, drawers labelled 'pins' and slots for books and papers; or seated in his bed, drawing directly on the walls and ceiling with a long stick.

What is common to and striking in all of these photographs is the way the pinned cut papers are fastened in groups so that they relate to one another and are mixed in with the architecture of the space and a myriad other works: ink drawings on paper; charcoal sketched on the wall; posters, paintings, textiles. In the studio, the cut-outs were never seen alone, demonstrating that Matisse's understanding of them is based on how they relate to each other and works in other media. Importantly, this was always true of how he approached colour. 'It is not enough to place colors, however beautiful, one beside another,' he argued, 'colors must also react with one another. Otherwise you have cacophony.'[19] And though each photograph tells its own story about the activities of the studio, it is the chronicle they tell together that is perhaps most enlightening. Looking from image to image, we see that individual works migrate from place to place, that elements are removed or adjusted and reappear back where they started or in absolutely new works, and that compositions are rotated or shift entirely – all of which speaks to the studio's flux.

This return to the studio leads us to understand the cut-outs in a particular way, not just as finished, framed objects that address the conceptual and formal problems of colour and line, but as records of a process, laboured over and revised in a way that long-standing myths about Matisse's ease of cutting and creating do not allow. From today's perspective, with the benefit of decades of art-making that extends the work into the space of the viewer, the cut-outs' first life may be seen as proto-installation or proto-environment – installation, environment or new media similarly challenge the necessity and propriety of finish and completion (what has sometimes been termed 'de-skilling'), and make the activities of the studio their subject (think, for example, of the studio practice of Bruce Nauman or William Kentridge). Even without those labels (and it may be better to avoid anachronism and leave them aside), the life of the cut-outs in the studio and their material logic mount a radical and wholesale rethinking of the temporality and physicality of the work of art.

Though this body of work was significant for young artists of Matisse's day struggling to find themselves – the excellent exhibition catalogue *Ils ont regardé Matisse* maps that impact[20] – and continues to resonate with contemporary practice, the cut-outs must also be seen in the context of a particular time: in the events of the mid-twentieth century and in Matisse's own life. The cut-outs emerged as a fully fledged practice on the precipice of, during, and in the wake of war, raising questions about the ways in which Matisse managed to negotiate invention with tragedy: how, under such extraordinarily difficult circumstances, did Matisse devise new solutions to long-studied pictorial problems?[21] How did the work inside the studio continue when the world seemed to be collapsing around it? In the midst of the war Matisse offered his own take on the urgency of work: 'Each one of us must find his own way to limit the moral shock of this catastrophe. For myself ... in order to prevent an avalanche overwhelming me, I'm trying to distract myself from it as far as possible by clinging to the idea of the future work I could still do, if I don't let myself be destroyed.'[22] Though Matisse himself did not suffer a loss of basic creature comforts, he was keenly aware of his compatriots who did, organising the delivery of food and supplies to friends and colleagues. Throughout the occupation he endured treacherous travel, as he made his way from Paris south, and deep worry over the arrest of his daughter Marguerite and his estranged wife for their work with the Resistance.[23] In *Jazz*, the key cut-out project of the war, a sense of the conflict and its resulting deprivation seeped in: Louis Aragon described the yellow bursts in *Icarus* as 'exploding shells' and Tériade 'was convinced that the earliest *Jazz* plates – Toboggan, Icarus, Burial of Pierrot – reflected the tragic ambiance of the time in which they were made'.[24] Later commentators found other references, from the reading by Riva Castleman of *The Wolf* as a stand-in for the Gestapo to the 'acts of aggression' noted by Rebecca Rabinow in *The Knife Thrower*, *The Sword Swallower* and *The Cowboy*.[25] The cut-outs also developed during a time of great physical trial for Matisse when he underwent surgery, a difficult rehabilitation and, finally, a sense of living on borrowed time. As he recovered, he wrote to his son Pierre: 'It's like being given a second life, which unfortunately can't be a long one.'[26]

The impact of these conditions – the war and his brush with death, along with his ongoing physical deterioration (Matisse continued to suffer bouts of pain, weakness and insomnia during his final thirteen years following surgery) – may be seen in the cut-outs' excessive proliferation on the walls of the studio and his constant reworking of them. Matisse's wartime focus on the studio's activities might be interpreted as unyielding creativity under difficult and deficient conditions – or taking advantage to the fullest extent of time that he should not have had. Similarly, though remaking and delays in completion were always hallmarks of Matisse's work, can the incessant rearranging in those last years be seen as a means of warding off the most absolute of terminations, that is death? The profusion and lack of finish of the cut-outs, then, were not solely the product of wartime, but might be described as the central features of what some call 'late style', a set of practices based on the artist's understanding that one's working life is rapidly nearing its end.[27]

As rich a metaphor as the garden is, given the revolutionary activities of the studio, perhaps it is not enough. The studio, we will see in this volume, served many other functions: bedroom, chapel, factory, tailor shop, concert hall, photography studio, aviary, infirmary, stage set, swimming pool, laboratory, subject and, most of all, ground.[28] As Matisse explained: 'There was a time when I never left my paintings hanging on the wall [of my studio] because they reminded me of moments of overexcitement and I did not like to see them again when I was calm.'[29] In the three studios of his final decade the walls did not undermine him, but were the fertile ground for an exceptional body of work.

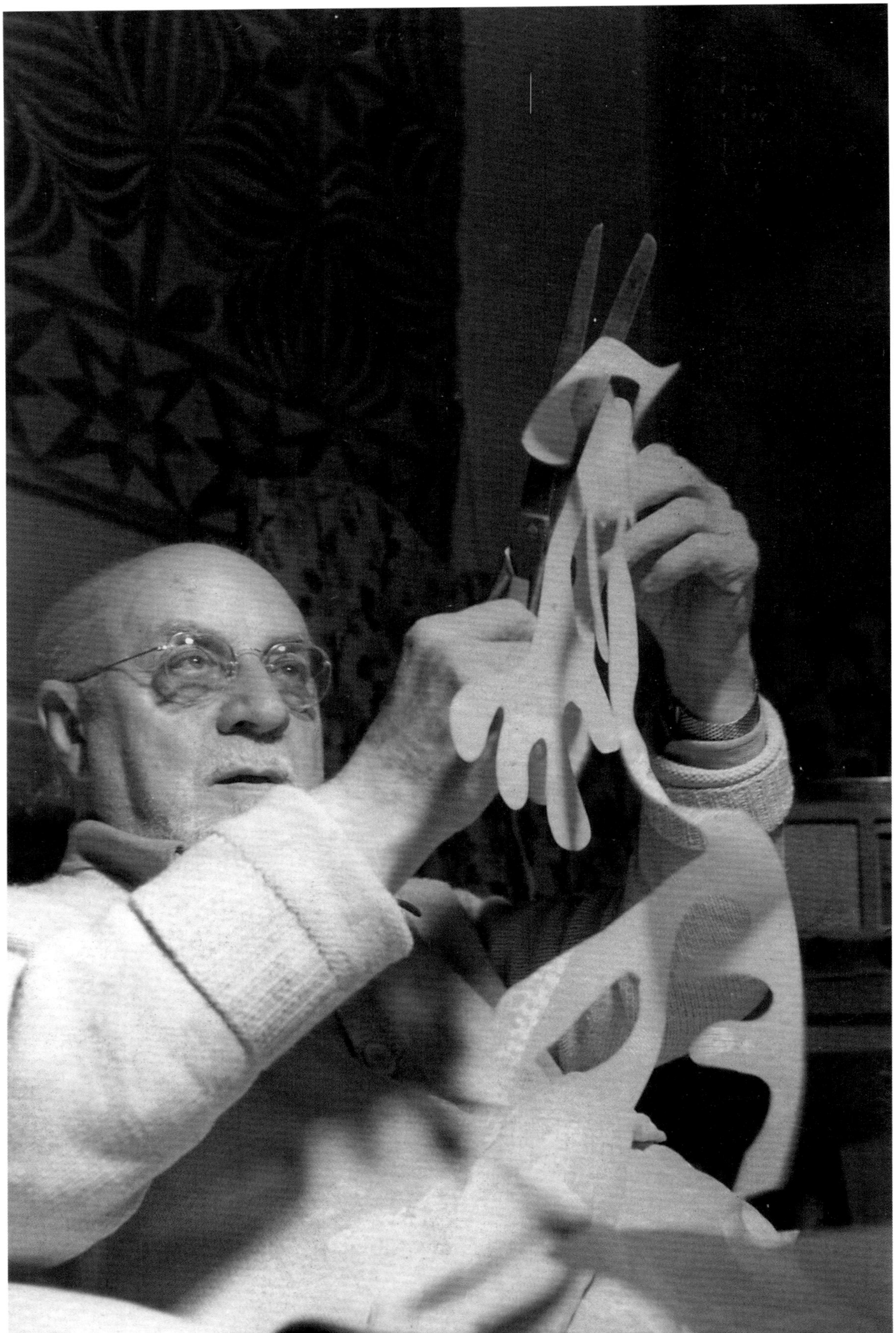

Fig. 3 Photographer unknown, Matisse at Villa le Rêve, Vence, c. 1946–7

INVENTING a NEW OPERATION

Jodi Hauptman

In a letter to André Rouveyre, dated 22 February 1948, Matisse writes: 'The walls of my bedroom are covered with cut-outs.' 'I do not yet know what I shall do with these new cut-outs,' he wonders, but with confidence announces: 'The result is of more importance than it would seem.'[1] Matisse's prediction turned out to be spot on: his cut-outs, though denigrated by some observers when they were first exhibited, have been enormously influential. Their 'importance', to borrow his word, can be seen in myriad ways. Their economy of means, their graphic geometries, their play with colour and contrast, their exploitation of decorative strategies all showed the artist, late in his career, continuing to advance the compositional and chromatic aspects of picture making.[2]

Matisse's positive assessment, it should be noted, was made when the cut-outs were still pinned to the walls, stretched around him from floor to ceiling, around doorways and against mouldings, and undulating into space. Matisse saw as yet unidentifiable potential in their tentative, sculptural and environmental conditions – in their very making. Looking back at photographs of his work pinned to the walls of his bedroom/studio at that time (pp. 36–41; fig. 22), we are awestruck not only by the cut-outs' sheer visual excitement, their colliding shapes and colour, their boundless – and gorgeous – contamination of surface, but even more in the revelation of a radically new form.[3] Matisse's invention of this new form – his distinctive approach to a basic set of tools and materials (especially the ways in which their particular qualities helped mould the results), the process by which the works were physically constructed in the studio, and the groundbreaking implications of his methods of cutting, pinning and composing on the wall – is our subject here.

Cutting

In a blurred and scratchy black and white film, an amateur production shot in 1952, Henri Matisse is seen in his studio cutting paper.[4] Using an oversized pair of shears – perhaps the kind used to cut fabric – Matisse cuts into a large sheet, so large in fact, that an assistant helps manipulate it. As Matisse cuts through the paper, the assistant turns and rotates the sheet so that the artist's hand and the scissors can keep to its course. The cut shape comes to life at the same time as its negative appears, dancing through space while it splits away from the blade. As the sheet is turned to the path and rhythm of the cut, we glimpse its unpainted back, a hint at the potential reversals and rotations of each cut form. The cut creates a positive and a negative, each offering equal potential to the user. In their making the negative and opposite of each shape can be perceived, launching an iterative vocabulary of forms: one geometry leads to another and still another in an ever-lengthening chain.

As low resolution as this film is, it nonetheless offers a strikingly clear window onto what Matisse called his 'cutting out operation' and the nature of the forms produced.[5] For Matisse, cutting was not a simple technique – though it may have started

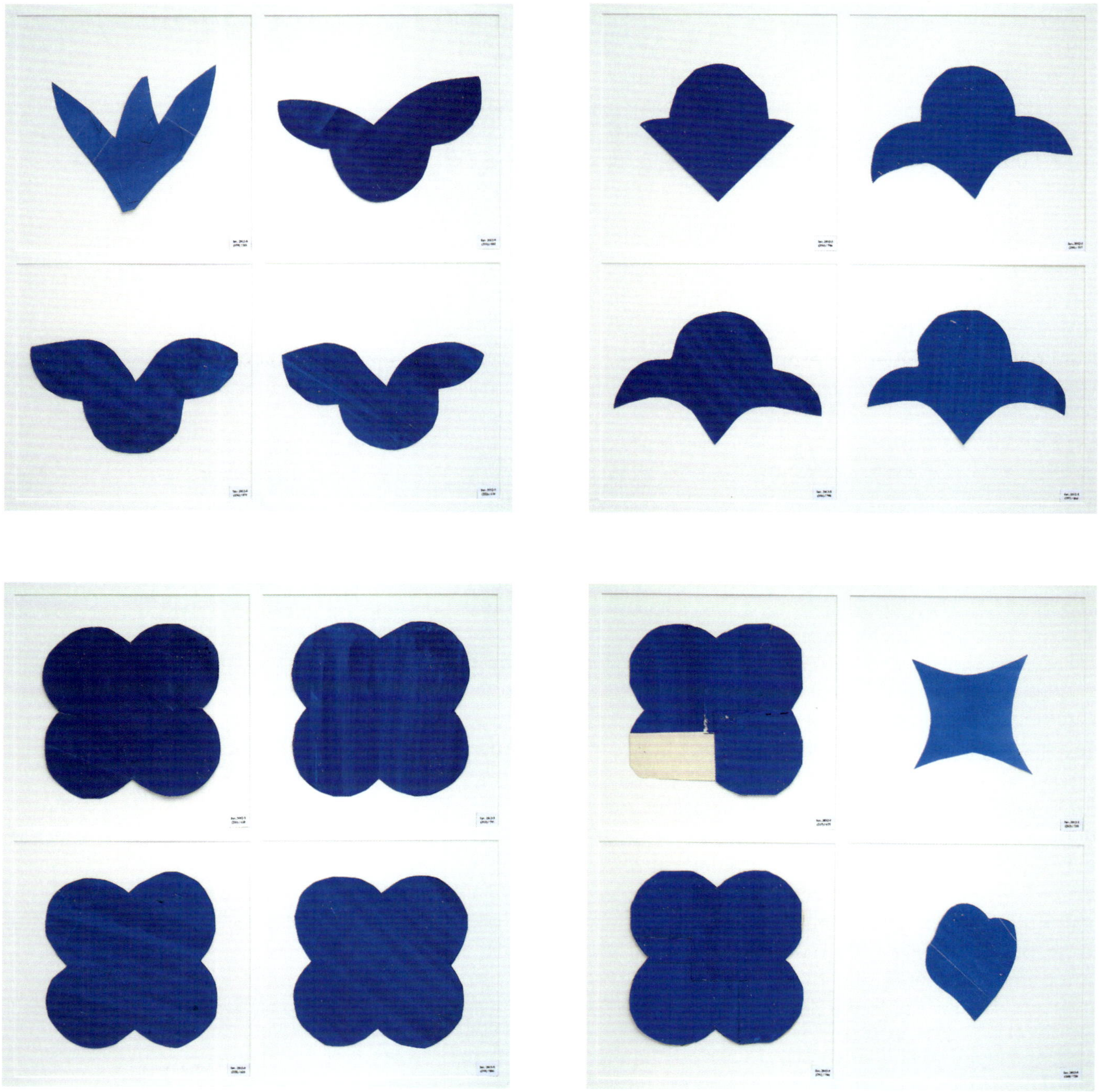

Fig.4 Ensemble of unused gouache cut-out elements, 1945–54
Musée départemental Matisse, Le Cateau-Cambrésis
Gift of the Matisse family

that way – but provided a system for thinking about and expanding the possibilities of shape and composition (fig. 3). Distinguishing this operation from painting, Matisse explains:

> It is no longer the brush that slips and slides over the canvas, it is the scissors that cut into the paper and into the colour. The conditions of the journey are 100 per cent different. The contour of the figure springs from the discovery of the scissors that give it the movement of circulating life. This tool doesn't modulate, it doesn't brush *on*, but it incises *in*, underline this well, because the criteria of observation will be different.[6]

What the scissors discover are the positives and negatives, reversals and inverses, the organic relations between shapes, their generation of one from another. Consider, for example, a group of blue clovers and related bat wings, leaves and other organic forms (fig. 4) that were not ultimately used by Matisse but were likely cut in the context of composing the chasubles for the Vence chapel; notice the way one shape seems to spawn another, finding its validity in any direction, its usefulness as a part or whole, and its transformation via the attachment of another cut form or juxtaposition with smaller pieces. Patrice Deparpe explains: 'Indeed, one can clearly identify "series" in which Matisse, starting with a shape that he composes, modifies, and associates, reaches a different shape that, in turn, will give birth through various new additions to yet another element, which will, subsequently, take on its own meaning.'[7] Similarly, such 'serial' cutting partly accounts for *Jazz*'s vibrant syncopation (nos. 18–39). Positives and negatives – though often it is impossible to tell which Matisse would have considered the original positive – are distributed throughout, sometimes on the same page, but not always. Observant viewers can engage in a game of perceptual gymnastics to reverse and invert forms in order to put the pieces back together. Other fully finished cut-outs – take *Screen Panel, Beige Background* (no. 67), for example – make ample use of cut forms that could be considered negatives or cast-offs, demonstrating that all cut shapes play equal roles in Matisse's formal lexicon.

Given that both positives and negatives were equally regarded by Matisse, we might conclude that the term used in English to name this technique – 'cut-out' – is flawed, as it implies that the cut thing is removed from something else and that what is left behind is inconsequential. In fact, cutting let Matisse see all possibilities of form, encouraging a vast, if not unending, proliferation of combinations and re-combinations.[8]

Pinning

The iterative nature of the cut-outs – the variety of forms and the resultant multiplicity of potential compositions made possible by cutting – is extended and enriched by pinning, which itself allows the works to remain in a tentative or contingent state, all the better to compose and recompose. Pins of course had a functional purpose: they were used by Matisse and his assistants to temporarily secure pieces of cut paper to each other and to boards when he worked on a small scale, or to the walls of his studio as his work grew larger (fig. 5). Eventually, when works were ready to leave the studio and after an elaborate method of tracing to ensure that the forms remained in the correct location, the elements were glued to a paper support that was then sometimes mounted on canvas. In the studio, however, the pins allowed the compositions to remain alive: assemblies were pinned and re-pinned, made on one wall and then moved to another; forms were pinned into one grouping and then removed to join another; works were composed in one orientation and rotated or inverted. Photographs of the studio demonstrate that these activities were continuous, that Matisse constantly reviewed, rethought and reconfigured his work. While artists typically aim for finality and finish, the cut-outs often remained in a state of perpetual deferral, sometimes for months or even years.

It is true that Matisse may have had a unique familiarity with pins (and other materials of the textile trade). Matisse's ancestors, Hilary Spurling reminds us, 'had been weavers for generations' and the village of his birth, Le Cateau-Cambrésis in the north of France, 'made its fortune from proliferating woollen mills. St-Quentin, where he went to school, was famous for its expanding lace industry and Bohain, where he grew up, for its luxury fabrics.'[9] Moreover, his wife was a milliner. Matisse's use of pins may be rooted in his access to textiles from his childhood, an interest, it should be noted, that he maintained throughout his adult life as a collector of fabrics from across the globe. Spurling explains

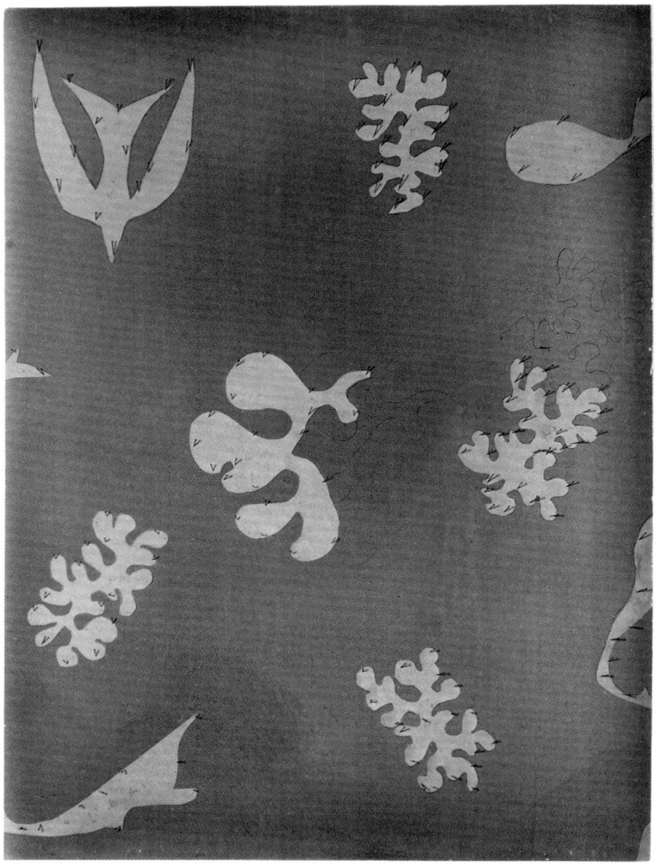

Fig. 5 *Oceania, the Sky* (no.52) in progress

that 'fellow painters were baffled to find Matisse experimenting with classic weavers' techniques like pinning tracing paper to his canvases' and argues that 'painted paper patterns' were 'regularly employed to test equations of form and color in his paintings, including *Periwinkles / Moroccan Garden*, 1912, *Pink Nude*, 1935, and *Still Life with Shell*, 1940 (no. 9).[10]

As deployed in the cut-outs, pins served a practical function, but they also have radical implications for the work's material logic, as Jeffrey Weiss has brilliantly laid out in the context of Picasso's *papiers collés*.[11] Making possible a part-by-part assembly different from that of painting and drawing, the pins indicate that one thing is attached to another, that the work is made from multiple pieces or that a shape is attached to a ground. Most important, Weiss's analysis helps us to see that pinning's ability to be undone – unpinned – reveals a tentativeness and contingency, flux and change, at the heart of the cut-out's practice. He writes:

> Pinning [is] a means through which a given part – a fragment of paper [or, in our case, a cut-out form] is affixed. Fixed, yes, but in principle only temporarily so: the work is made such that it could be unfixed. This is increasingly unlikely over time, of course (in that we are not apt to take it apart). But what matters is that the potential exists: pins could be removed and parts thereby set loose. In being fixed, the work punctuates its own contingency with a device that brings the mobility of its parts to momentary or suspended rest.[12]

Thus, something that is pinned can be unpinned, foregrounding the idea of what Weiss calls 'mobility and deferral'. Such works remain 'quasi-provisional due to the constitutional property of something like variable or unstable integrity: the degree to which things are apt to – or can, at least, be made to – come apart'.[13] Moreover, only fastened here and there, the pins allowed the paper to retain its flexibility and pliability; the paper could curl away from where it was pinned or move with a breeze, thus fostering a kinetic or sculptural sensation, another way of expressing a lack of fixity or finish. And though many of the pins were ultimately removed when the works left the studio and were mounted, the abandoned pinholes not only continue to suggest their once tentative existence but offer both a tangible record of the labour required to make them and the myriad compositional paths not taken.[14] Look closely, for example, at the profusion of pinholes in *Apollinaire*, a visceral testimony of the numerous campaigns such a seemingly simple work – white letters on a blue background – demanded (no. 103).

The cut-outs' contingency dovetails with Matisse's long-standing penchant for reworking, redoing, redrawing. As early as 1908, he writes, 'I do not repudiate any of my paintings but there is not one of them that I would not redo differently, if I had it to redo. My destination is always the same, but I work out a different route to get there.'[15] By facilitating the development of an anthology of spatial possibilities – removal, addition, inversion, rearranging, reordering, transposing – cutting and pinning suggest that potential and contingency are pervasive themes.

Composing

While the essential qualities and material logic of the cut-outs – the scissors' generation of multiple forms and the pins' allowance for contingency and deferral – were evident even early on when Matisse composed on his lap making intimate creations of book scale, their transfer to his studio walls marked an important shift, resulting in work that was environmental, sculptural, relational, boundless. Reconfiguring the relationship between object and viewer, they were no longer solely to be looked at but were also to be lived in.

For an endlessly iterative compositional practice, the studio walls offered a welcome surface, allowing the artist to expand his images vertically and horizontally. It also encouraged Matisse to consider his compositions in relation to each other. Certain combinations of cut-paper elements may have been thought out individually, but once they went up on the wall, they were seen in dialogue with other works already installed. In the Vence studio small compositions were put up cheek by jowl, together forming total wall installations. Compositions that we know today as individual objects crept into and onto one another, making it difficult to distinguish one from its neighbour. In one photograph, for example, we see the small floral shapes of *Two Masks (The Tomato)* (no. 62) reaching up into the composition above (fig. 22). So integrated were these works, in fact, that one visitor hoped to buy an entire wall composition and install it as a single environmental work.[16] On a wall, without a frame, the cut-outs also take on the physicality of sculpture, clearly visible in contemporary photographs. Layered and buckled sheets and straight pins create shadows; overlapping shapes build up a sense of three-dimensionality; loosely pinned forms move with the breeze; and ornament made as part of large-scale compositions relates to the room's architecture. Over time Matisse made work that functioned architecturally, using cut-outs to design the interior of the Vence chapel or to create a room environment, *The Swimming Pool* (no. 121, pp. 63–7), in his dining room. Perhaps no work, however, displays the sculptural potential of the cut-outs better than *La Négresse*, whose paper legs step off the wall onto the floor pp. 74–6).[17]

Matisse's engagement with the wall is crucial to his thinking, the fulfilment of a lifelong quest to 'give the impression of vastness in a limited space'.[18] This interest in expanding the experience of painting beyond the limits of its frame emerged as early as 1906 with the painting *Le Bonheur de vivre* (fig. 6), as Yve-Alain Bois has persuasively argued, and is seen at different points in the artist's career from the frenzied circulation of large canvases like *The Dance (I)*, 1909, to the creation of what he called 'architectural painting' in the Barnes mural (fig. 12).[19] Matisse's desire to work big may be seen in the context of his compatriots' efforts to create large-scale public works in the 1940s and 1950s, including tapestries and murals.[20] In his own aspiration to limitlessness and his deployment of patterning to fuel the expansion of his later wall-sized cut-outs, Matisse's interest in the decoration of Islamic art – from calligraphy to tiles and textiles – should also be considered. 'This art', he wrote in 1947, on the brink of turning to the cut-outs in force, 'suggests a greater space, a truly plastic space. This helped me to find my way out of intimate-scale painting.'[21] By working directly on the surfaces of his studio, Matisse accessed this 'greater space', allowing him to dispense with the limits of the frame and spread his coloured forms across his walls. With time, his cut-outs grew into monumental immersive works. Matisse writes: 'The role of painting, I think, the role of all decorative painting, is to enlarge surfaces to work so that one no longer senses the size of the wall.'[22]

'I know that these things should remain as they are'

Many observers of Matisse's work recognised the cut-outs' unique liveliness in the studio. One of his most perceptive interlocutors, Rouveyre, writes to Matisse expressing brutal honesty about what is lost when the cut-outs come off the studio walls:

> These paper cut-outs have a very pure existence when they escape from your hands, your scissors. Their papery material, with subtle plays of light on their flexibility, the very physicality of this flexibility, all of this contributes to making something miraculous that loses its essence when laid out flat. But it retains its essence when stuck up on the wall with pins by Lydia. For doing that preserves the vitality of the paper I mentioned, by subjecting it to constant changes.[23]

Rouveyre was especially conscious of the cut-outs' material and temporal qualities, how their physicality contributes to the experience of the work.

Aimé Maeght, gallerist and publisher, was even more visionary. Meditating on a recent visit to the studio, Maeght notes in particular the cut-outs' chromatic rhythm on the wall, what he senses as an almost synesthetic effect.[24] He suggests that the work could be 'a starting point for the realization of an interesting film, where rhythm, colors, forms and sounds would come together/respond to each other' along the lines of – but better than – Walt Disney's *Fantasia*: 'It is not my idea to animate the forms of your decoupages, but to see colored form and colored images materialize on the screen by apparition or by superimposition that is spontaneous and rhythmic/flowing.' As fascinating as this idea is – and what Matisse might have made of it – Maeght makes an even more surprising proposal. He suggests that the cut-outs remain pinned:

> I wonder, having thought long and hard about it, if we shouldn't consider a presentation in a frame under glass, which would form a 'box' and permit mounting with pins?
>
> After trying it out, I feel that imperfect collages without pins give the thing a strange quality. The

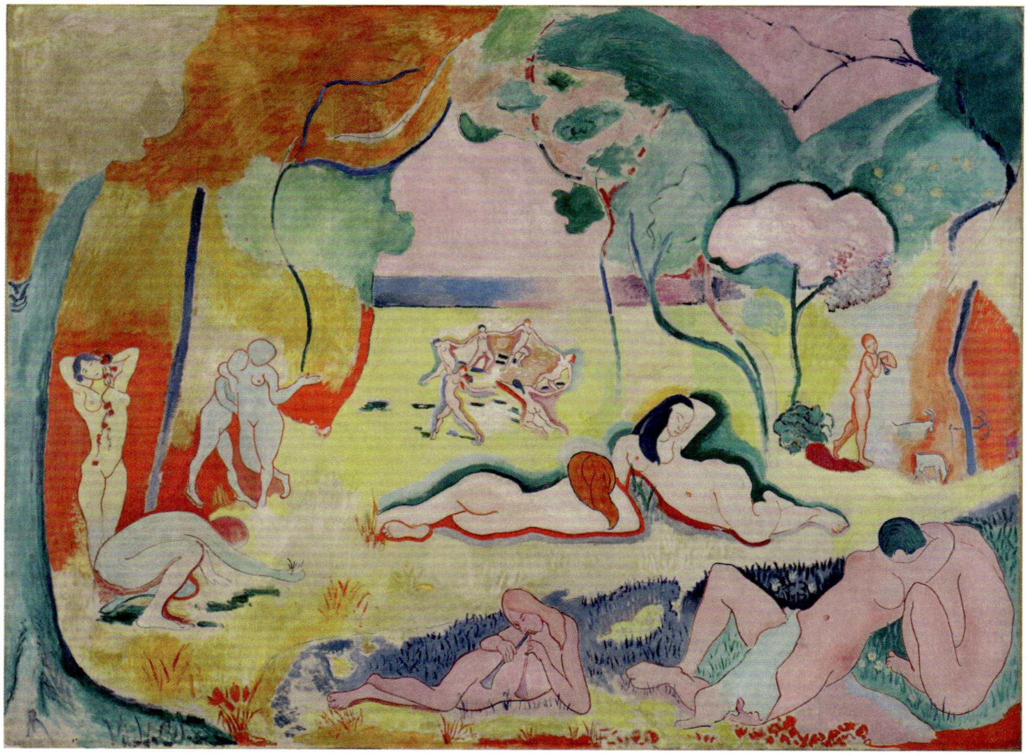

Fig. 6 Henri Matisse, *Le Bonheur de vivre*, between October 1905 and March 1906
Oil on canvas, 176.5 × 240.7 (69½ × 94¾). The Barnes Foundation, Philadelphia

pins are the manifestation of the fixing point. Without this element visible, the spirit of the spectator is too absorbed in discovering the means of the collage.

To avoid an excessively deep frame, it is possible to use phonograph needles.

We could use plywood, previously soaked in citric acid, as a support. Once it has dried, the parts of the needles buried in the wood will rust in a few days, and thus anchor themselves solidly in the wood. A piece of wax paper placed between the paper and the wood will prevent the paper from touching the acid-soaked wood. An experiment at my house seems conclusive at present.

For Maeght it is crucial to remind the viewer that the cut-outs are made from attached parts, and as we have seen, keeping them pinned would also signal their temporary and sculptural status. Unfortunately, there is no rejoinder from Matisse to Maeght's tantalising suggestion and its acknowledgment of the important role of the pins. We will never know exactly what the artist thought of the idea. We can surmise, however, that he did reflect on the cut-outs' physical status. Regarding *Jazz*, for example, Matisse 'know[s] that these things should remain as they are, originals – just gouaches'.[25] He laments their loss of 'charm' when translated into the stencilled *pochoir* prints of the finished book, while accepting that 'for someone who has not seen the originals it is the impression that is given by the book that is the main thing'.[26] Some of the earliest works to leave the studio during Matisse's lifetime – *The Eskimo*, for example – are only spot-glued; no longer pinned, they nonetheless retain their sculptural form (no. 57). But Matisse was also concerned about the cut-outs' longevity and permanence. For example, he expresses his distress to Pierre Berès about the gouache's potential loss of intensity when exposed to sunlight.[27] So while some of the smaller cut-outs retain their pins – the weaving in and out of straight pins and their flash of metal in *The Fall of Icarus* create a magical sense of the work's assembly from cut bits and a particular poignancy in the fastening of the bright red flash of a heart to the figure's chest – it is difficult to believe that Matisse could have envisaged the larger works remaining precariously pinned (no. 17).

It is fair to say that the implications of Matisse's means and materials went beyond what he could have imagined in his own day (this is not due to a lack of imagination, but a limit to what was considered possible then). The process, the outcome and the residue of cutting, pinning and composing on the wall resulted in a form that was contingent and impermanent; unbounded and environmental; assembled and relational; positive and negative. Given the pervasiveness since the 1960s of installation, environments and time-based practices, which allow viewers to be in and among works of art, to encounter art over time and to experience art that is forever unfinished or always in process, if the cut-outs were made today, the suggestions of Rouveyre and Maeght would probably be considered, if not accepted. From this perspective Matisse's compositions would not be mounted, but instead, the cut-paper forms could be unpinned, stored in archival boxes and re-pinned each time they were displayed. In these circumstances the cut-outs' contingency and flux, their sculptural presence, their process, their existence on the wall would no longer only be implied by the residue of their production, but would be tangible aspects of the current conditions of the work. Matisse may not have seen the enormous implications and applications of his own invention, but he had an inkling that the cut-outs – their materials and methods – would speak clearly to the future. He reasons:

> By creating these colored, paper cutouts, it seems to me that I am happily anticipating things to come. I don't think that I have ever found such balance as I have in creating these paper cut-outs. But I know that it will only be much later that people will realise to what extent, the work I am doing today is in step with the future.[28]

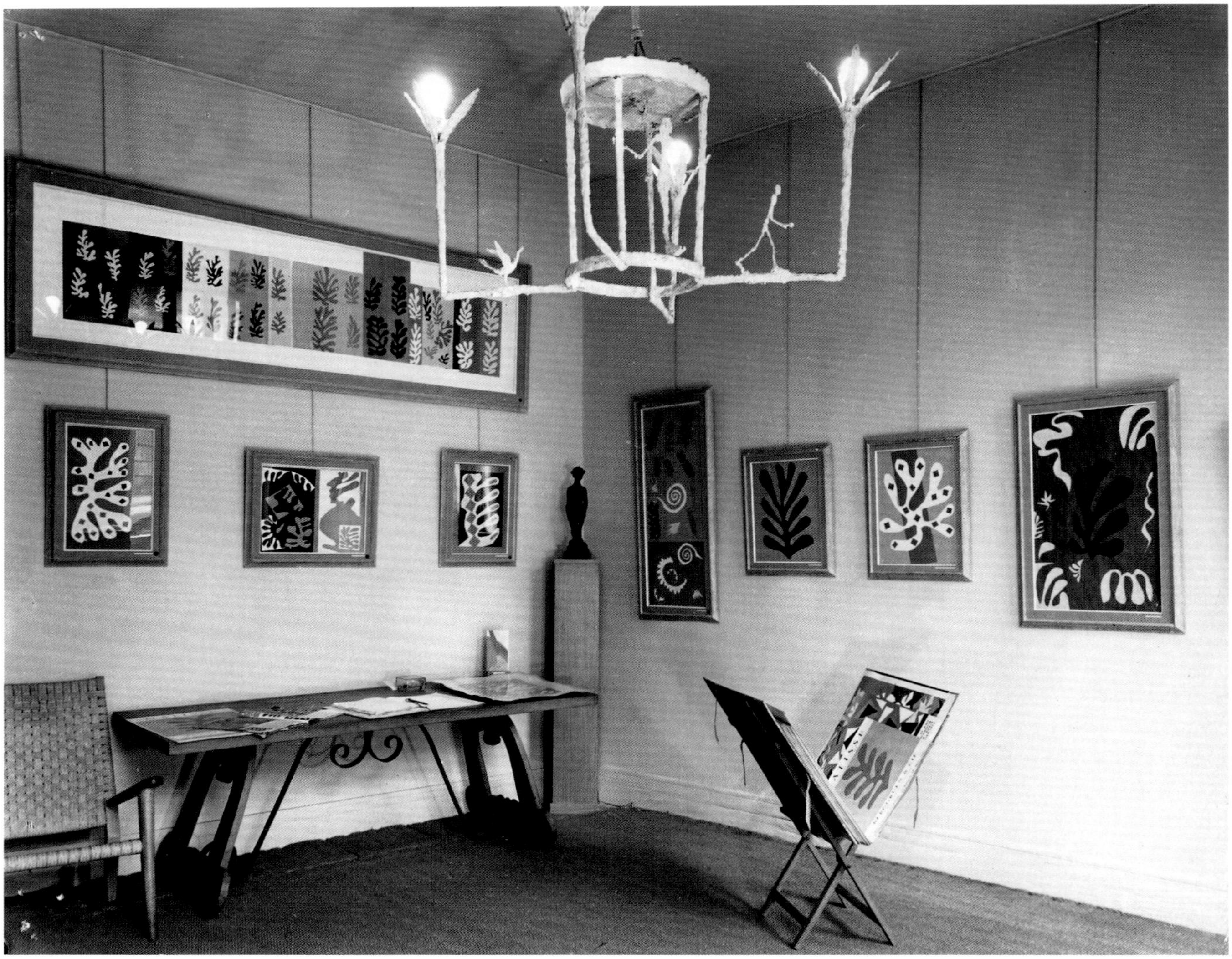

Fig. 7 *Henri Matisse: Papiers Découpés*, Galerie Berggruen et Cie, Paris, 1953

'An AGREEABLE DISTRACTION'

Nicholas Cullinan

The Early Reception of Matisse's Cut-Outs

It is an irony when surveying the copious literature on Henri Matisse's cut-outs, not to mention the rest of his long and prolific career, that one of the first things he ever spoke about cutting out was his own tongue.[1] This was his advice to young painters seeking to command their *métier*.[2] While this volume takes the activity inside Matisse's studio as he was making the cut-outs as its main focus, it is also important to consider how these utterly radical works were first exhibited, published, disseminated and discussed outside of the confines of these walls, both in the period that Matisse was experimenting with them and in the pivotal decade following his death, during which time his overall body of work was posthumously evaluated. As we shall see, if Matisse was largely confined to his house and studio during his final years, this in no way impeded the reception of his *gouaches découpées*, which were widely seen and much written about almost from the moment they were first made.

The reception of Matisse's work in the 1950s and 60s has been documented very thoroughly by Lucile Encrevé, in a chronology that covers a wider territory than is addressed in the present summary; much of what follows draws from and comments on her 2009 publication.[3] The earliest unveiling and reception of the cut-outs, however, began before Encrevé's writing starts – with illustrated books and periodicals in the mid-1930s. Perhaps the first independent cut-out was produced as the maquette for the cover of the journal *Cahiers d'Art* nos. 3–5 in 1936 (no. 10) and this design initiated not just Matisse's engagement with the cut-out method but also the initial critical scepticism extended towards these works in Matisse's home country of France. As Christian Zervos, the co-founder and director of *Cahiers d'Art*, and the person who had therefore commissioned Matisse to make his first cut-out work, would write retrospectively and in rather grudging terms in an article in 1949: 'I'm willing to admit that Matisse, having entered the game of the paper cut-outs as if by chance with the coloured cover done for *Cahiers d'Art* in 1936, later converted it into an agreeable distraction which would ease his long hours of insomnia!'[4] The implication of this decidedly faint praise was clear: such a 'game' was perhaps a permissible indulgence for an artist in his dotage, but no real substitute for the main task of painting. This initial design by Matisse for the cover of a periodical using the new technique of paper cut-outs was quickly followed by others: the first issue of Tériade's rival new publication *Verve* in 1937 (no. 11); a revisiting of his celebrated painting *La Danse* of 1910 (State Hermitage Museum, St Petersburg), partially using cut-outs to create a lithograph for another issue of *Verve* in 1938 (no. 12); a further cover maquette for *Verve*, vol. II, no. 8, in 1940 (no. 13); and another for *Verve*, vol. IV, no. 13, in 1945 (no. 15). These early projects for *Verve* of course fed directly into Matisse's thinking behind *Jazz*, his first masterpiece in the cut-out medium, which was published by Tériade in 1947 and is discussed in greater detail elsewhere in this volume (see pp. 88–9, 126–9).

A parallel initial public life for the cut-outs, beyond their role as the catalyst for lithographic designs for periodical covers, was as another decorative project – the thirty fabric screen prints of *Oceania, the Sea* and *Oceania, the Sky* created for Zika Ascher in 1946 (nos. 52–3), the two related

Ascher scarves from the same year each produced in an edition of 275 (no. 50–1), and the tapestries *Polynesia, the Sea* and *Polynesia, the Sky*, also from 1946 and made the following year. The cut-outs therefore seemed to have existed initially largely as compositional aids to Matisse's more decorative designs in either paper or fabric. But this proliferation of Matisse's cut-outs in the early years of their publication and reception as maquettes for journals or fabric designs seems to have had a double effect: it introduced them to the public as a striking and novel development in Matisse's work, but it also reconfirmed them, even if inadvertently, as design or decoration rather than as works of art per se.[5]

One notable tendency was that early critical responses to the cut-outs seem to have been more favourably disposed in America than in France. A case in point was when Pierre Berès, the distributor of Matisse's book *Jazz*, exhibited the twenty stencil-printed plates that Matisse designed to illustrate the text at his gallery in the Librairie Pierre Berès in Paris from 3 to 20 December 1947, which marked an exhibition debut of sorts for the cut-outs (it should also be noted that the plates for *Jazz* were simultaneously exhibited in Rio de Janeiro at the Galerie Europa, Arte Antiga e Moderna Ltd, from 3 to 20 December 1947).[6] The critics in response to the Paris show in publications such as *Arts* and *Le Figaro Littéraire* were somewhat apprehensive about Matisse's new work and direction.[7]

A month later, Berès exhibited *Jazz* in his gallery in New York from 20 January to 3 February 1948. The positive initial impact of *Jazz* in New York was confirmed later that same year, when it was included in the Philadelphia retrospective (discussed next) and when the The Museum of Modern Art staged the exhibition *Henri Matisse:* Jazz *– Gift of the Artist* from 1 to 31 October 1948 to commemorate the donation of a copy of the book to the museum by Matisse. During these years, however, the cut-outs were largely absent as stand-alone works from the exhibitions organised about Matisse in the United States, which instead focused more on his work in other media. For example, at the largest exhibition in America surveying Matisse's career to that date, *Henri Matisse – Retrospective Exhibition of Paintings, Drawing and Sculpture* at the Philadelphia Museum of Art from 3 April to 9 May 1948, the *pochoir* plates for *Jazz* were shown again, listed at the back of the catalogue along with other 'Books Illustrated by Matisse' and after his paintings, sculpture, drawings and graphic work (in that order), but the cut-out maquettes were not included.[8] If the cut-outs were still therefore understood only as a means to an end, even in such a comprehensive retrospective, the foreword by Henry Clifford, the curator of the exhibition, seemed to predict through its discussion of Matisse's most recent painting the direction his work would adopt through the cut-outs:

> These later years have been surprisingly productive when one thinks of a painter in his seventies. There is a new dash of almost unbridled color, an audacity and daring going further perhaps than in any former period. What seems at first glance line uncontrolled almost to abandon, is later seen to be the *désinvolture* of a master. This brilliant palette of the very latest pictures augurs well for future periods.[9]

However, in the press about the Philadelphia exhibition the new and still surprising (if not perplexing) stylistic development spurred by the paper cut-outs in Matisse's career was given prominence. In an article in *Time* magazine dated 5 April 1948 four pages from Matisse's *Jazz* were reproduced, while in a 'Matisse Special' published by *Art News* that same month, *The Clown* (no. 18) from *Jazz* was given pride of place on the cover of the magazine, and Thomas B. Hess's essay 'A Life of Color' began with one of the earliest published accounts of Matisse making the cut-outs in his studio by André Breton.[10]

That same month the critic Clement Greenberg's essay 'The Crisis of the Easel Picture' was published.[11] Here Greenberg, like Clifford, wrote of Matisse's painting in terms that would now seem to anticipate the development of the cut-outs, contributing to 'the reduction of the easel picture's fictive depth' and to the 'all-over picture ... with a surface knit together of a multiplicity of identical or similar elements'.[12] Greenberg continued: 'This sort of painting comes closest of all to decoration – to wall paper patterns capable of being extended indefinitely.'[13] His words were prescient, foreshadowing, as they did, Matisse's gradual mastery of the cut-out technique and its application to wall-size compositions and all-enveloping environments, as well as the dialogue this had with the increasingly more mural-like paintings in terms of scale and structure of younger artists such as Jackson Pollock.[14] Greenberg made many other references to the importance and influence of Matisse's painting for younger artists throughout the 1940s.[15] Also in 1948 Matisse's project for the Vence chapel began to be publicised, the stained-glass windows for which originated in the innovations Matisse was making with his cut-outs, now, unlike the early maquettes for periodicals, applied to the large scale demanded by the architecture, as discussed in depth on pp. 153–63. This international attention on the Vence chapel would grow considerably over the next three years until its completion.[16] Finally, in the autumn of 1948 a rapprochement of sorts between Matisse's parallel developments in different media was effected by a special issue of *Verve* (no. 14) that was dedicated to Matisse's paintings of the period 1944–8, consisting mostly of the view outside Matisse's window at the Villa le Rêve in Vence (nos. 72–3), and that featured a cover design using paper cut-out shapes to spell the title of the periodical (no.14).[17]

On 1 February 1949 the exhibition *Henri Matisse: Paintings, Papiers Découpés, Drawings 1945–1948* (fig. 26) opened at the Pierre Matisse Gallery in New York and ran until 28 February. Alongside thirteen recent paintings and at least six ink drawings were ten paper cut-outs, all dating from 1947, which marked the exhibition debut of Matisse's work in this medium as autonomous works themselves rather than as just tools towards a composition in another medium.[18] The reviews of the exhibition were positive, but they focused primarily on Matisse's paintings as opposed to the cut-outs.[19] This position was exemplified by Clement Greenberg in his review of the exhibition for *The Nation*.[20] In the summer of 1949 the exhibition *Henri Matisse: Oeuvres Récentes, 1947–1948* (fig. 23) opened at the Musée national d'art moderne, Paris, running from 9 June to 25 September.[21] The exhibition featured twenty-one paper cut-outs in addition to the *Oceania* screen prints, the *Polynesia* tapestries and illustrated books such as *Jazz*, while the cover of the catalogue was a reproduction of *Negro Boxer* of 1947 (no. 63). If the different states and functions of the cut-outs were now being more fully understood, with original maquettes, textiles and designs for publications shown alongside each other, again in France the reception of them was largely negative or at least uncomprehending.[22] The same year, Georges Duthuit's book *Les Fauves: Braque, Derain, van Dongen, Dufy, Friesz, Manguin, Marquet, Matisse, Puy, Vlaminck* was published, with a cover designed by Matisse (no.99), before being translated and published in English the following year, 1950, as *The Fauvist Painters*. In this book even Matisse's son-in-law expressed some misgivings about the cut-outs.

Matisse's *Zulma* (no. 84) was first shown at the Salon de Mai in Paris from 9 to 31 May 1950, where it made a marked impression on Ellsworth Kelly, then a young artist living in Paris.[23] At the 25th Venice Biennale, from 8 June to 15 October 1950, Matisse exhibited numerous works but no cut-outs, and was accorded the Gran Premio for painting.[24] Three of Matisse's cut-outs, in addition to works relating to the Vence chapel, were also seen that summer in the exhibition *Henri Matisse: chapelle, peintures, dessins, sculptures* at the Communist-sponsored Maison de la Pensée Française in Paris from 5 July to 24 September 1950. This exhibition included three larger cut-outs from 1950, *Zulma*, *The Thousand and One Nights* and *Creole Dancer* (nos. 85-6, 99), conceived and displayed as freestanding works in their own right and more commensurate with the scale, format and compositional structure of painting; the last two of these are dated to June 1950, only days before the exhibition opened (nos. 85–6). The reviews and reception of the cut-outs in France that attended this exhibition were again negative.[25]

On 25 June 1951 the inauguration of the Vence chapel brought much international press attention in publications such as *Art News Annual*, *Vogue*, *Art* and *Paris Match,* which is explored in detail elsewhere in this volume.[26] On 13 November 1951 the Matisse retrospective opened at the The Museum of Modern Art in New York curated by Alfred H. Barr, Jr, and ran until 13 January 1952.[27] The exhibition, spanning Matisse's career, included nine cut-outs, of which six were maquettes for the chasubles of the Vence chapel, and the catalogue cover was designed by Matisse in *gouaches découpées* (no. 100). The exhibition travelled across North America and attracted a great deal of press.[28] To coincide with it, Barr also published (New York) his magisterial monograph, *Matisse: His Art and his Public*, which surveyed Matisse's career up to the Vence chapel, including a short entry on Matisse's 'Cut-and-Pasted papers' from the period 1947–50 and once more featured a cover employing cut-outs (no. 101).[29]

The following year one of Matisse's masterpieces of the *papiers découpés* technique, *Sorrow of the*

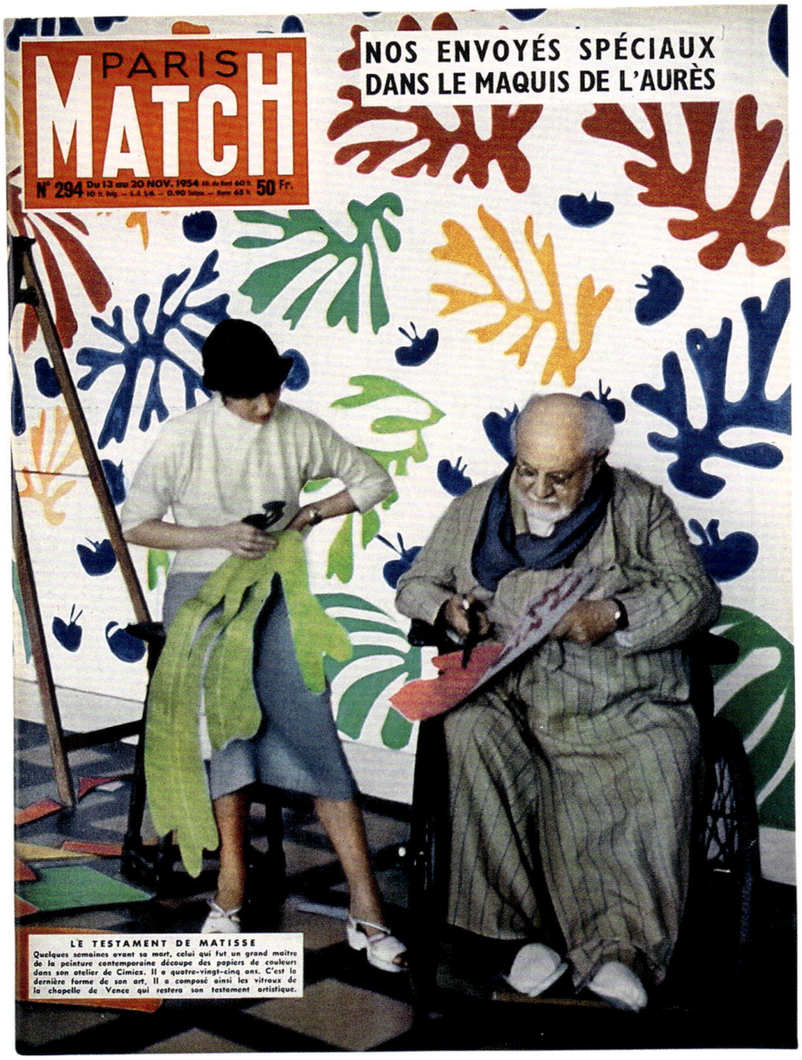

Fig. 8 Cover of *Paris Match* magazine, November 1954

King, was exhibited at the Salon de Mai in Paris from 9 to 29 May 1952. The same month saw the publication of André Verdet's *Prestiges de Matisse*, with a cover based on the cut-outs designed by Matisse.[30] Indeed, this is only one example (albeit one of the most lengthy and insightful, along with his text in *Jazz*), among many public statements, that Matisse made while he was working on the cut-outs, as he sought to explain them and perhaps frame their reception.[31] On 8 November 1952 the Musée Matisse opened in the town hall of Le Cateau-Cambrésis in Picardy, northern France, where Matisse was born, with a display that included *Jazz*.[32]

In 1953 the first exhibition devoted to the cut-outs, *Henri Matisse: papiers découpés*, was staged at Galerie Berggruen et Cie in Paris from 27 February to 28 March 1953.[33] The exhibition featured eighteen works, all of which had vegetal forms (fig. 7). Reviews now engaged more with the cut-outs, and noted their adjacency to abstraction.[34] Two of the *Blue Nudes* from 1952 were also shown at the Salon de Mai in Paris in 1953. The following year, 1954, Matisse's *The Sheaf* (no. 136) was included in the Xe (10th) Salon de Mai, which ran from 7 to 30 May, and was featured on the catalogue cover. *Sorrow of the King* was also acquired by the Musée national d'art moderne and exhibited frequently thereafter. After Matisse died on 3 November 1954, there was widespread press coverage of his life and work, during which time the late cut-outs began to be reappraised. For example, only a week after Matisse's death, an issue of the magazine *Paris Match* dedicated six pages to Matisse with a cover photograph of him working on *The Parakeet and the Mermaid* (fig. 8).[35]

After this, Matisse's posthumous reputation, in part perhaps spurred on by the frenetic pace of his work on the cut-outs during the last few years of his life and attendant public notice for projects such as the Vence chapel, steadily grew, along with the importance of the cut-outs as part of his overall body of work. A Matisse retrospective at the Salon d'automne in Paris took place in November 1955. The Museum of Modern Art also acquired maquettes for the chasubles from the Vence chapel, along with the actual robes by Matisse, in 1955 and then mounted the exhibition *Vestments by Matisse in the Collection of the MoMA* from 20 December 1955 to 15 January 1956. The year 1955 also brought the publication (in Paris) of the books *Les Chapelles du Rosaire à Vence par Matisse et de Notre-Dame-du-Haut à Ronchamp par Le Corbusier* and *Henri Matisse: Carnet de dessins préparatoires à La Perruche et la Sirène* by Jean Cassou. The next year, 1956, Pierre Courthion published 'Les Papiers découpés d'Henri Matisse' in *XXe Siècle*.[36] Later that year saw *Henri Matisse: exposition rétrospective* at the Musée national d'art moderne in Paris from 28 July to 18 November.[37] This exhibition included nine *gouaches collées*, including large-scale ones such as *The Parakeet and the Mermaid* (no. 118), and again attracted widespread press coverage.[38]

In an issue of *Verve* in 1958 dedicated to the cut-outs Georges Duthuit discussed Matisse's works from the last four years of his life and offered his first positive assessment of the cut-outs.[39] On 25 July 1959 the exhibition *Henri Matisse, 1950–1954: les grandes gouaches découpées* – the first museum exhibition dedicated to Matisse's cut-outs – opened at the Kunsthalle, Bern, before closing on 20 September that year.[40] As the exhibition title indicated, it gathered together many of Matisse's large, late cut-outs, many of which had not been seen before. In the catalogue essay Franz Meyer argued that the cut-outs had to be apprehended not just as aids to making work in other media or as analogous to painting, but as an entirely new and distinct medium – a view that was picked up in a more nuanced and thoughtful critical reception.[41] The exhibition included thirty cut-outs, eight drawings and two books, including *Jazz*. Focusing on the larger, mural- or painting-scaled cut-outs, the exhibition toured to the Stedelijk Museum, Amsterdam, from 29 April to 20 June 1960. Also in 1960, *Jazz* was once again the subject of an exhibition at the The Museum of Modern Art from 17 June to 19 September.

In 1961 the exhibition *Henri Matisse: les grandes gouaches découpées* opened at the Musée des Arts Décoratifs, Paris, running from 22 March to 15 May and was extensively reviewed.[42] It included more than forty cut-outs, including larger ones like The *Parakeet and the Mermaid,* while the accompanying catalogue featured photographs of some of the cut-outs in progress in Matisse's studio. *The Last Works of Henri Matisse: Large Cut Gouaches* ran at The Museum of Modern Art in New York from 17 October to 3 December 1961 before travelling to The Art Institute of Chicago (10 January – 13 February 1962) and the San Francisco Museum of Art (12 March – 22 April 1962).[43] Curated by Monroe Wheeler, the exhibition was intended as a 'sequel' to Barr's 1951 retrospective at MoMA, and one that could now address more fully 'this last chapter of [Matisse's] lifework'.[44]

Finally, a fitting conclusion of sorts is provided by the opening of the Musée Matisse in Nice on 5 January 1963, less than a decade after the artist's death. Housed in the Villa des Arènes, the museum is situated in the neighbourhood of Cimiez, not very far from where Matisse made his transcendent cut-outs in the final years of his life in the Hôtel Régina. But to end with this would imply a conclusion, while the reality is that Matisse's cut-outs only grew in stature and influence over the ensuing years, and came to be regarded as less 'an agreeable distraction' in the words of Christian Zervos, which lends this essay its title, and rather as the absolute summation of Matisse's work and a life spent exploring the expressive possibilities of both contour and colour, not to mention one of the most unique and indeed greatest late periods in any artist's career.[45]

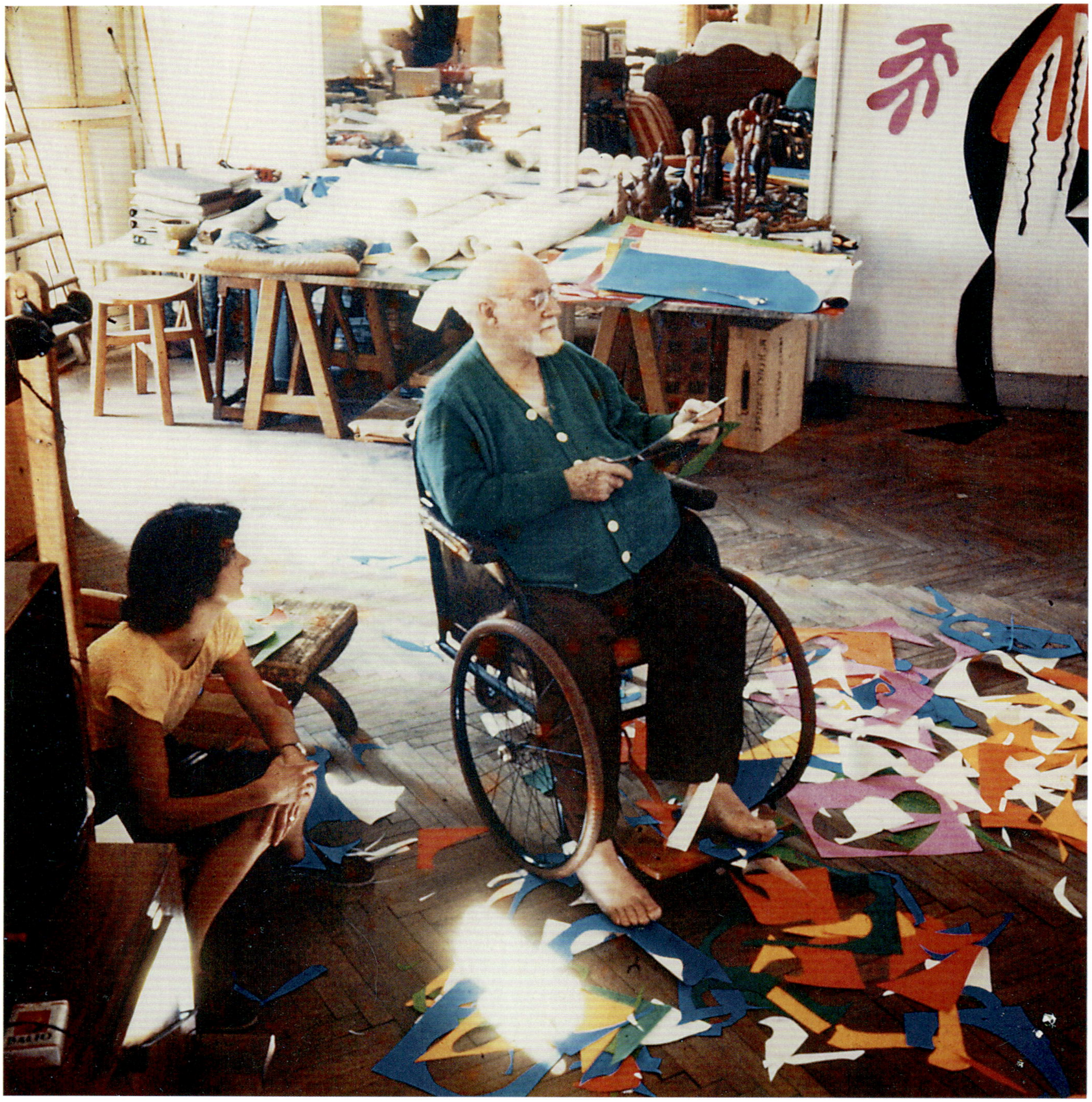

Lydia Delectorskaya, Matisse at the Hôtel Régina, Nice, c. 1952

In the Studio

A Photo Essay

Matisse created his cut-outs in three different studios. In 1946 he developed *Oceania, the Sky* and *Oceania, the Sea* on the walls of an apartment at 132 Boulevard Montparnasse, Paris. Towards the end of his time at the Villa le Rêve, in Vence, where he lived and worked between 1943 and 1948, Matisse covered its walls with vibrantly coloured cut-paper forms. From 1949 until his death in 1954 Matisse's cut-outs grew in ambition, expanding throughout the interiors of the Hôtel Régina, Nice. With this body of work, the studio changed from being a subject – as it had been in numerous paintings throughout Matisse's long career – to a support; the walls of his residences became the grounds for the cut-outs.

The selection of photographs that follows offers a glimpse into the three studios in which the cut-outs were made, allowing the reader to witness the evolution of Matisse's approach to his new medium. We see the metamorphosis of compositions and the constant migration of forms from one grouping to another, from one wall to another, from one studio to another. The images were taken by a variety of photographers, both professional and amateur: Matisse's secretary Lydia Delectorskaya and her cousin Hélène Adant; photographers on assignment for *Vogue* or *Paris Match*, like Clifford Coffin or Walter Carone; or scholars such as John Rewald, who interviewed Matisse for Alfred H. Barr, Jr's 1951 volume *Matisse: His Art and his Public*. The corresponding catalogue numbers for works included in the exhibition accompany each photograph, inviting the reader to compare the cut-outs' creation in the studio to their subsequent, independent lives and finished states.

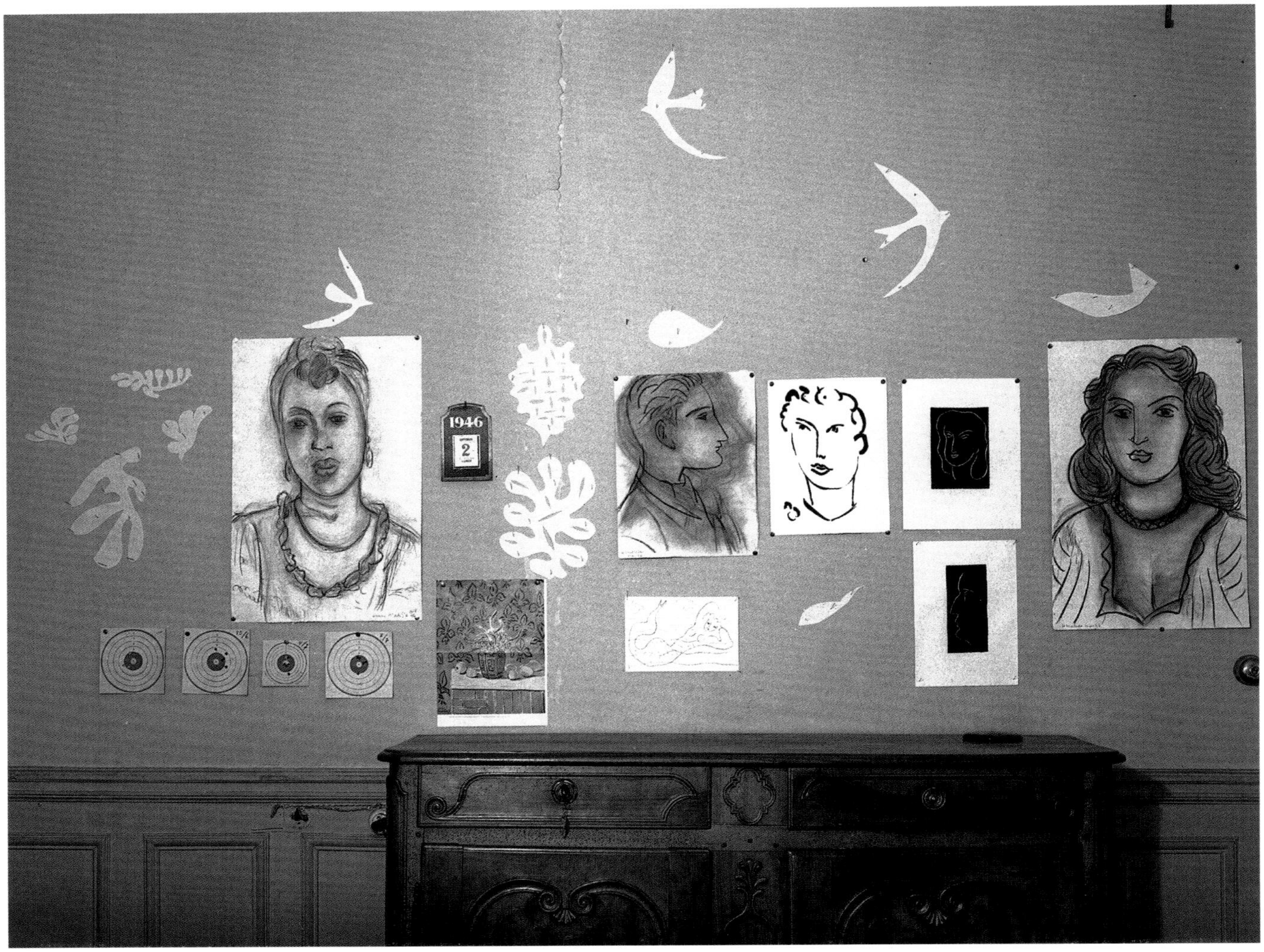

Hélène Adant, Boulevard Montparnasse, Paris, July/August 1946 (no. 52)

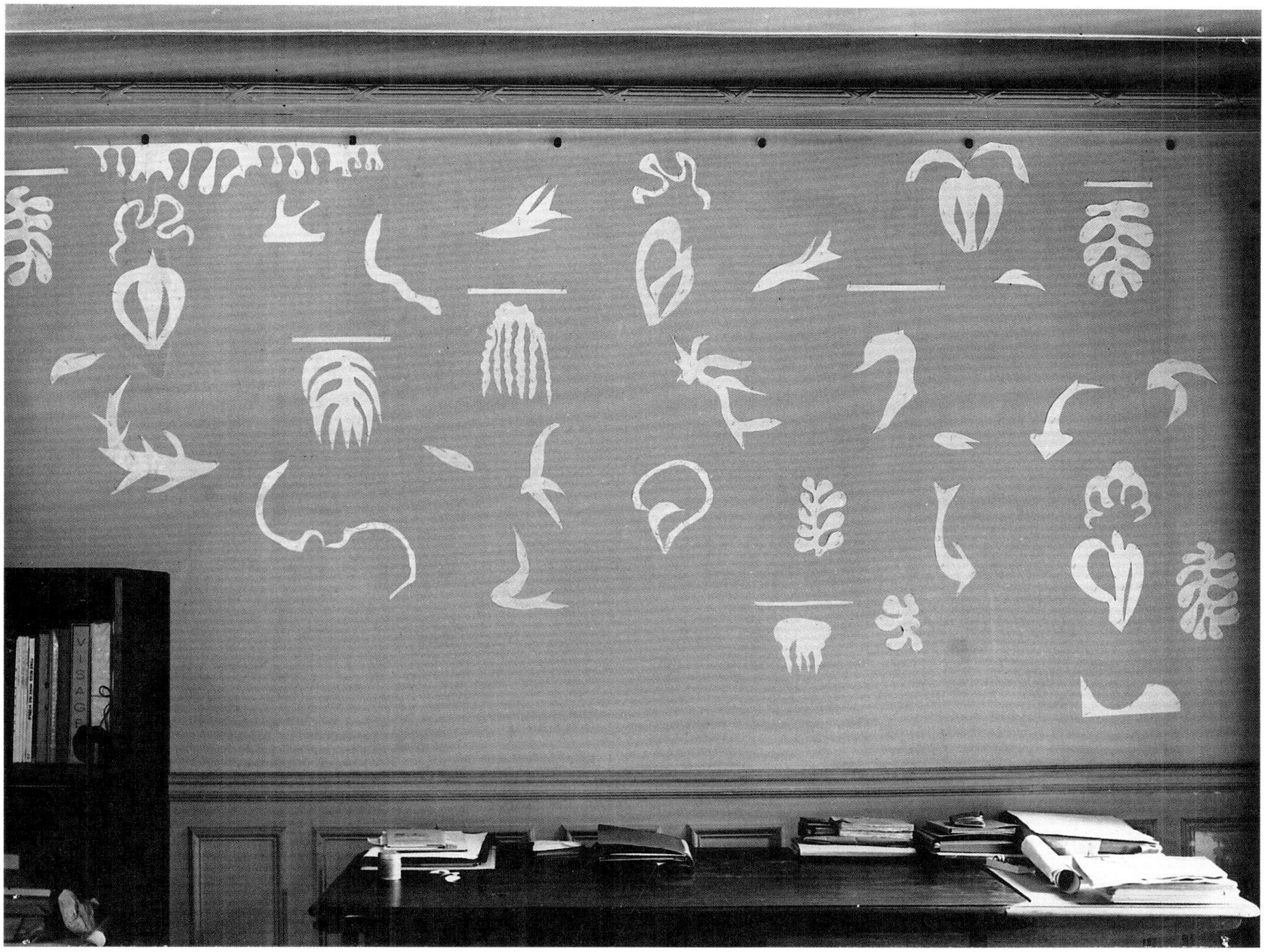

Hélène Adant, Boulevard Montparnasse, Paris, c.1946 (no. 53)

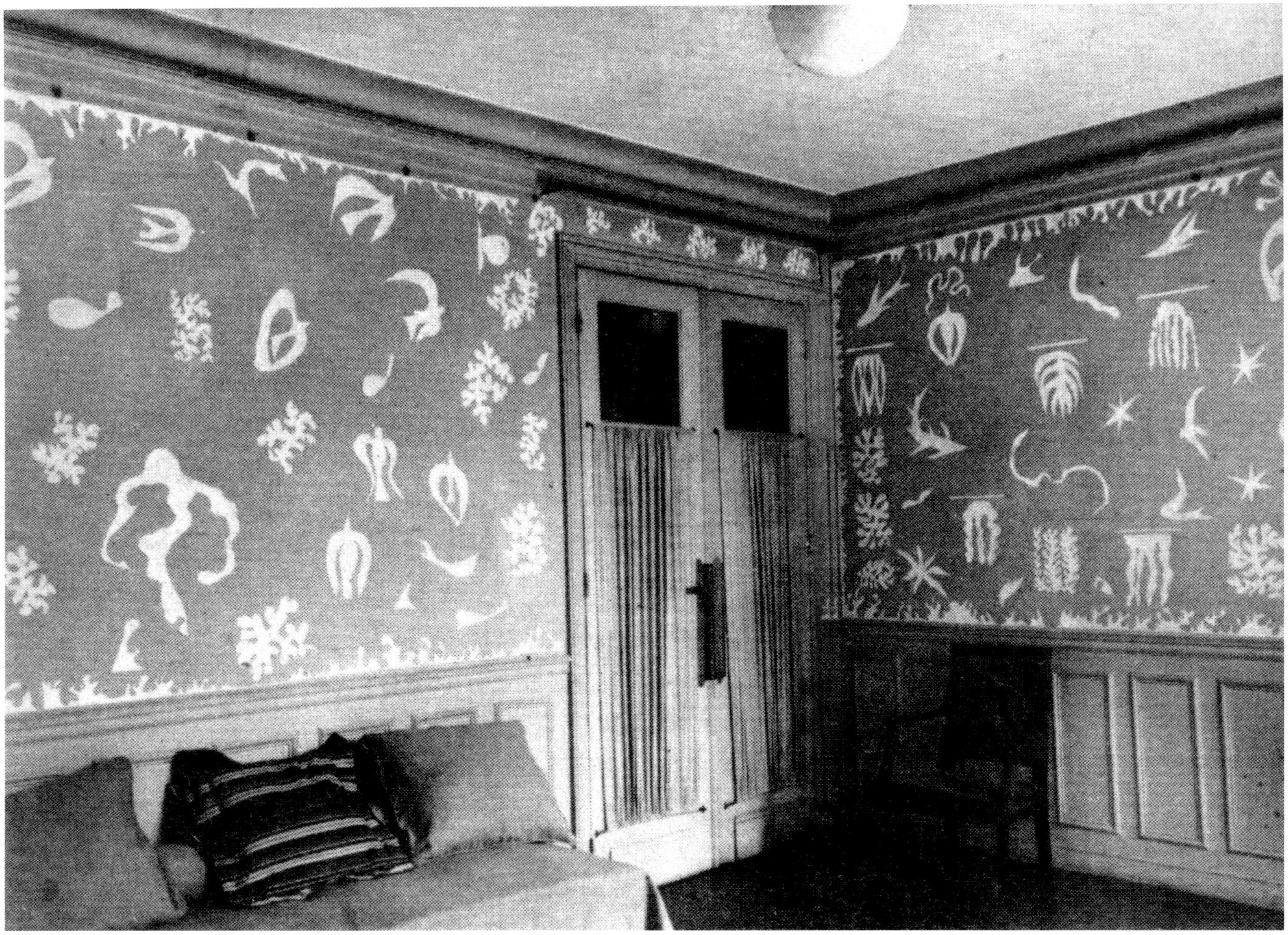

Hélène Adant, Boulevard Montparnasse, Paris, October 1946 (nos. 52–3)

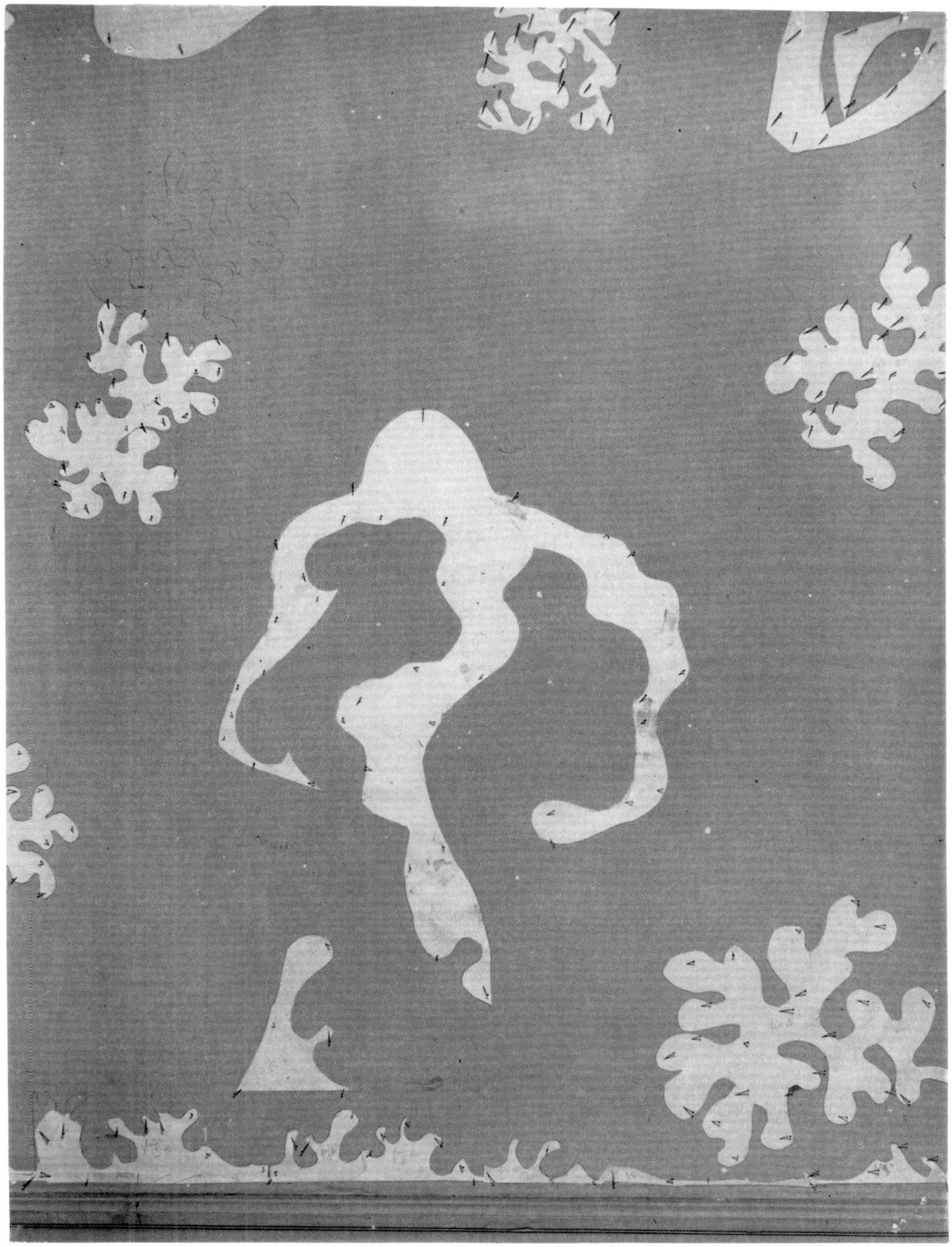

Hélène Adant, Boulevard Montparnasse, Paris, c.1946 (no. 52)

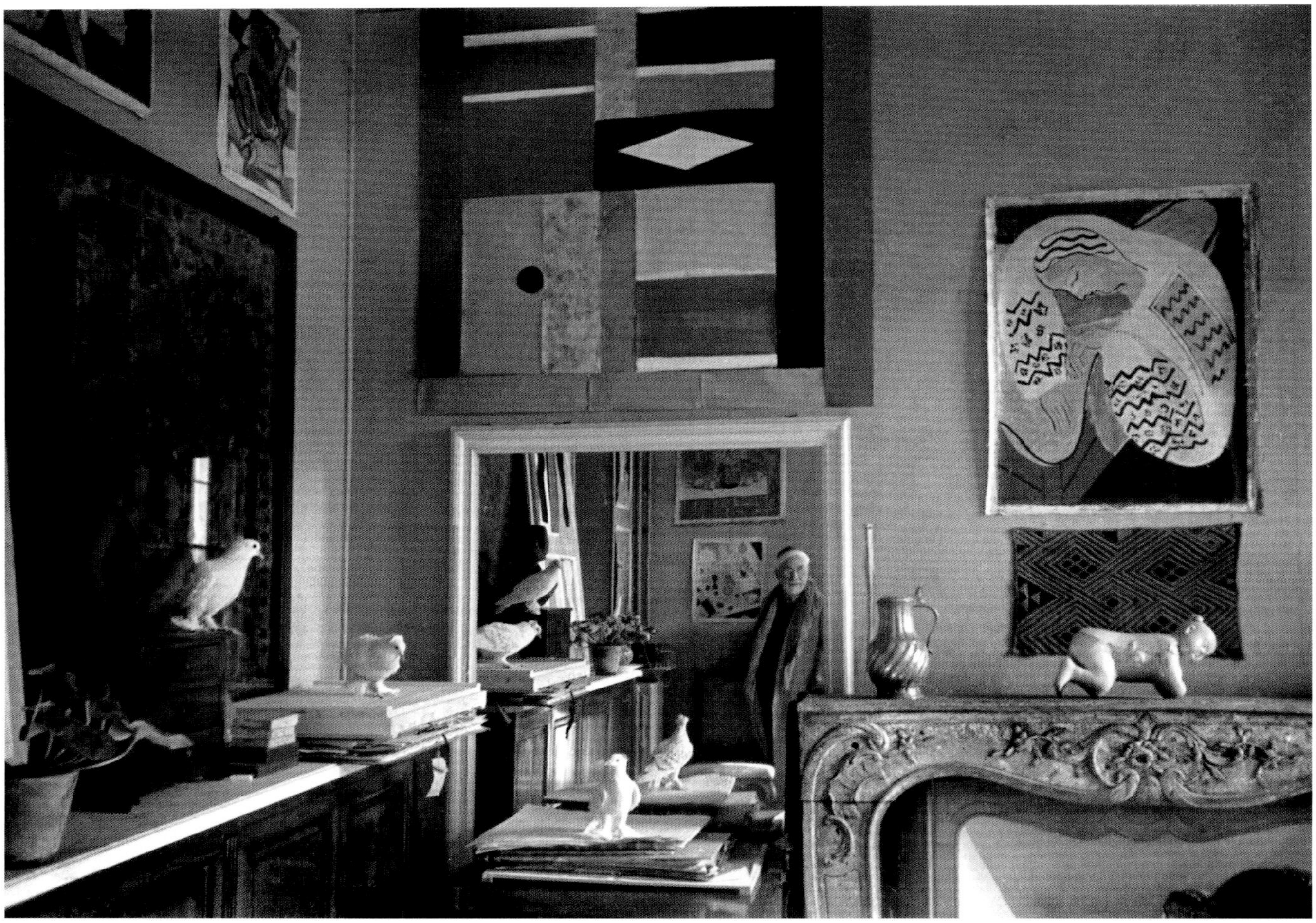

Henri Cartier-Bresson, Villa le Rêve, Vence, c. 1944

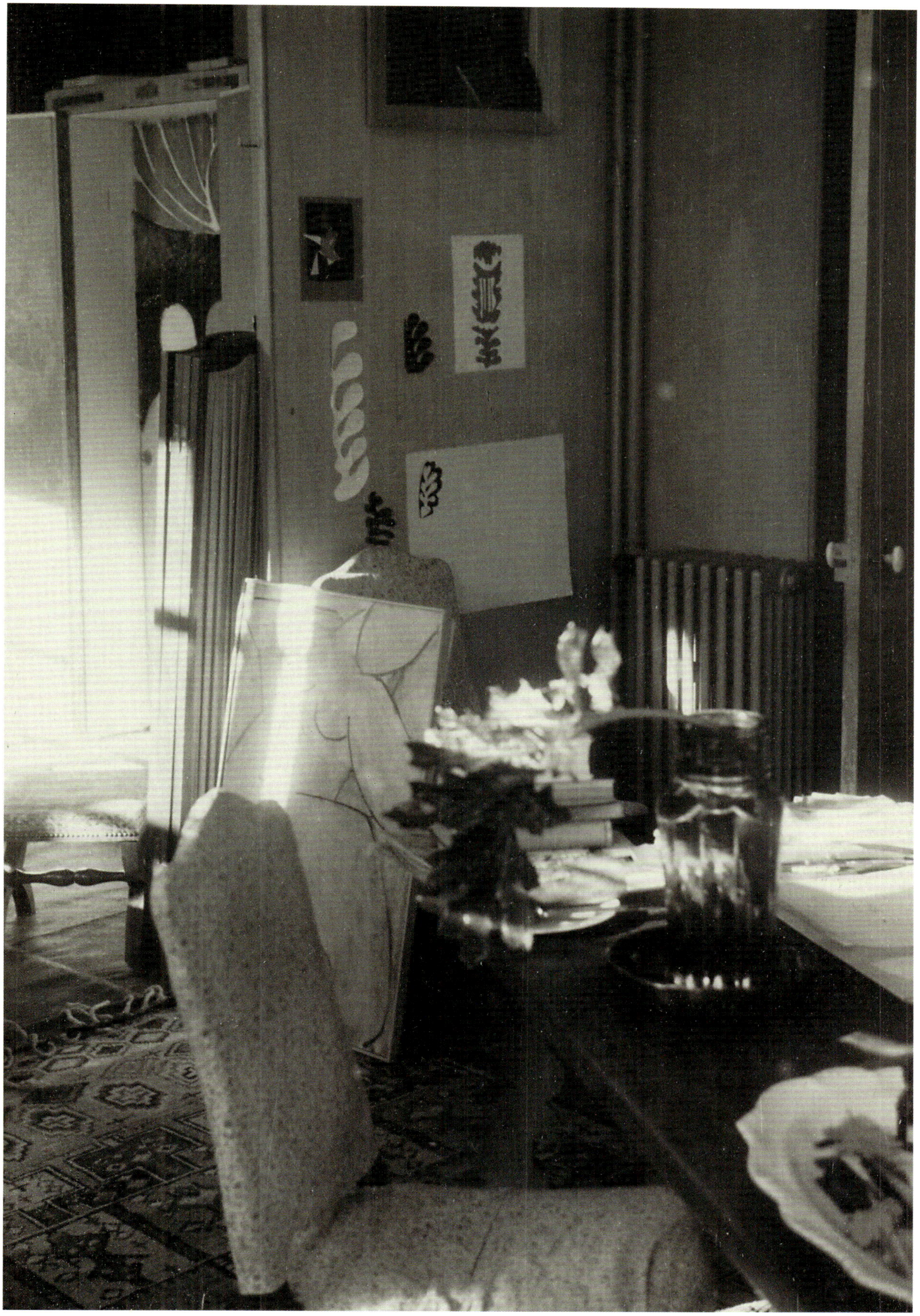

Unknown photographer, Villa le Rêve, Vence, c. 1946 (no. 49)

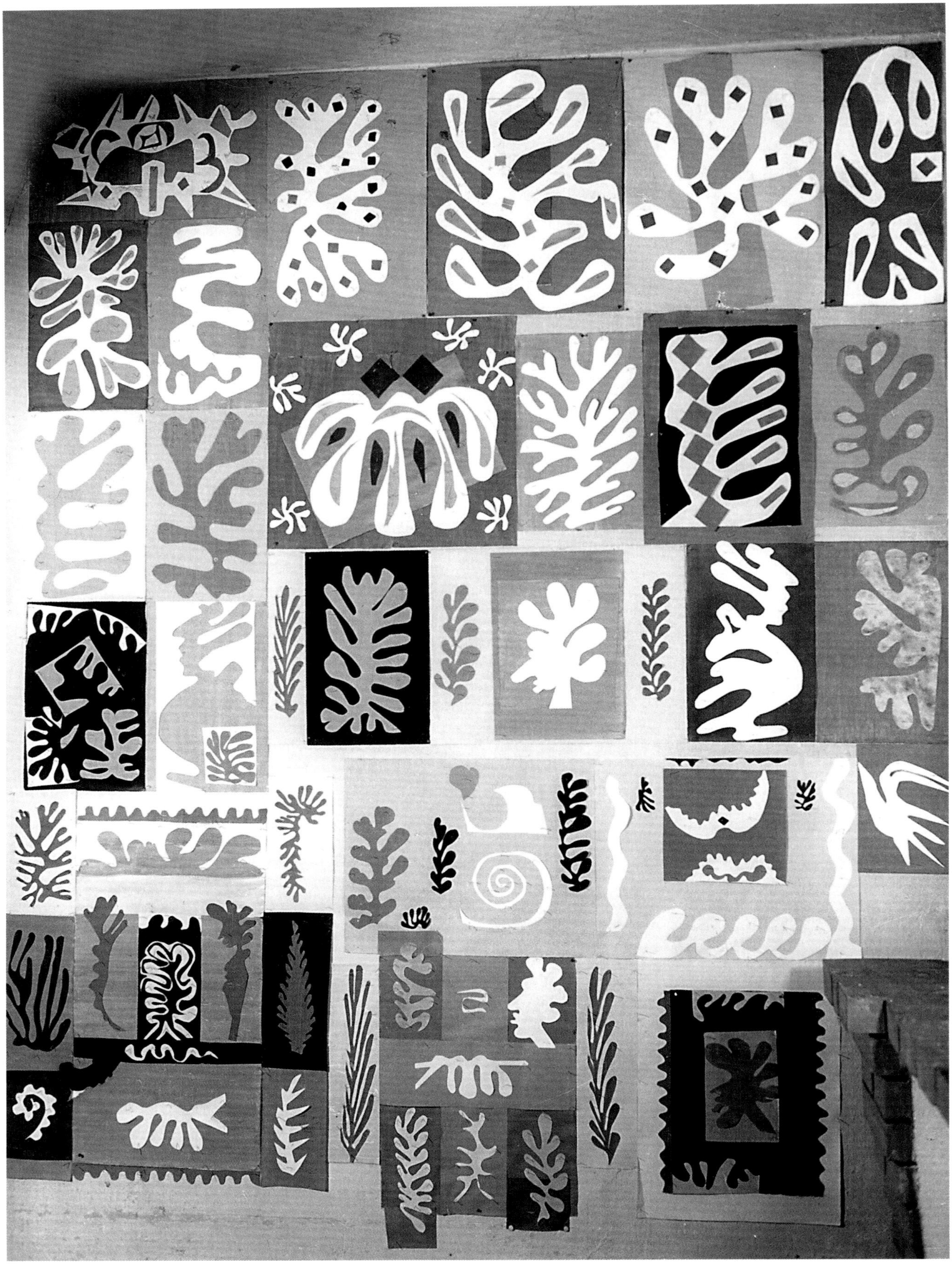

Michel Sima, Villa le Rêve, Vence, 22 May 1948 (nos. 54–62, 64)

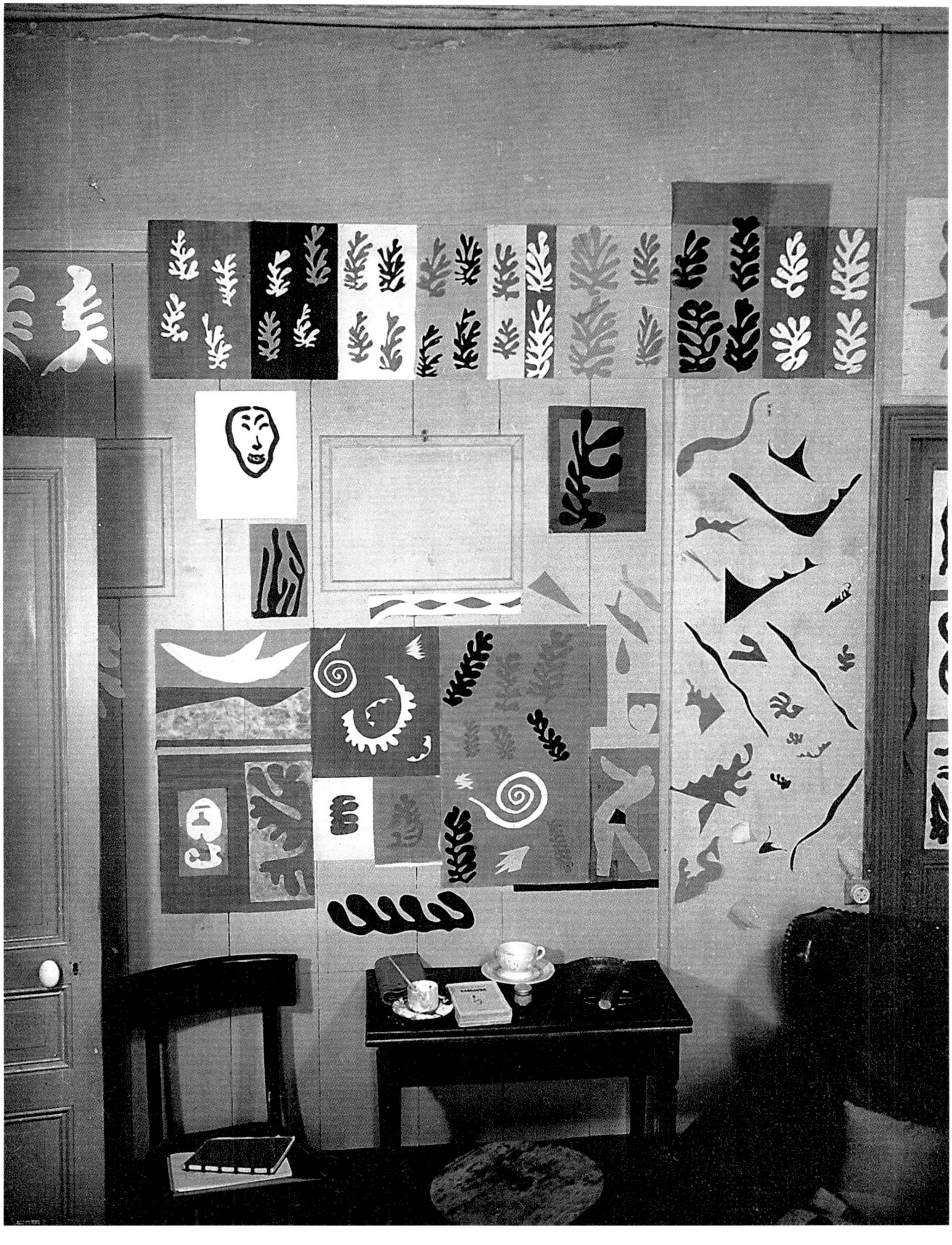

Michel Sima, Villa le Rêve, Vence, 22 May 1948 (nos. 4, 63, 65–7, 70)

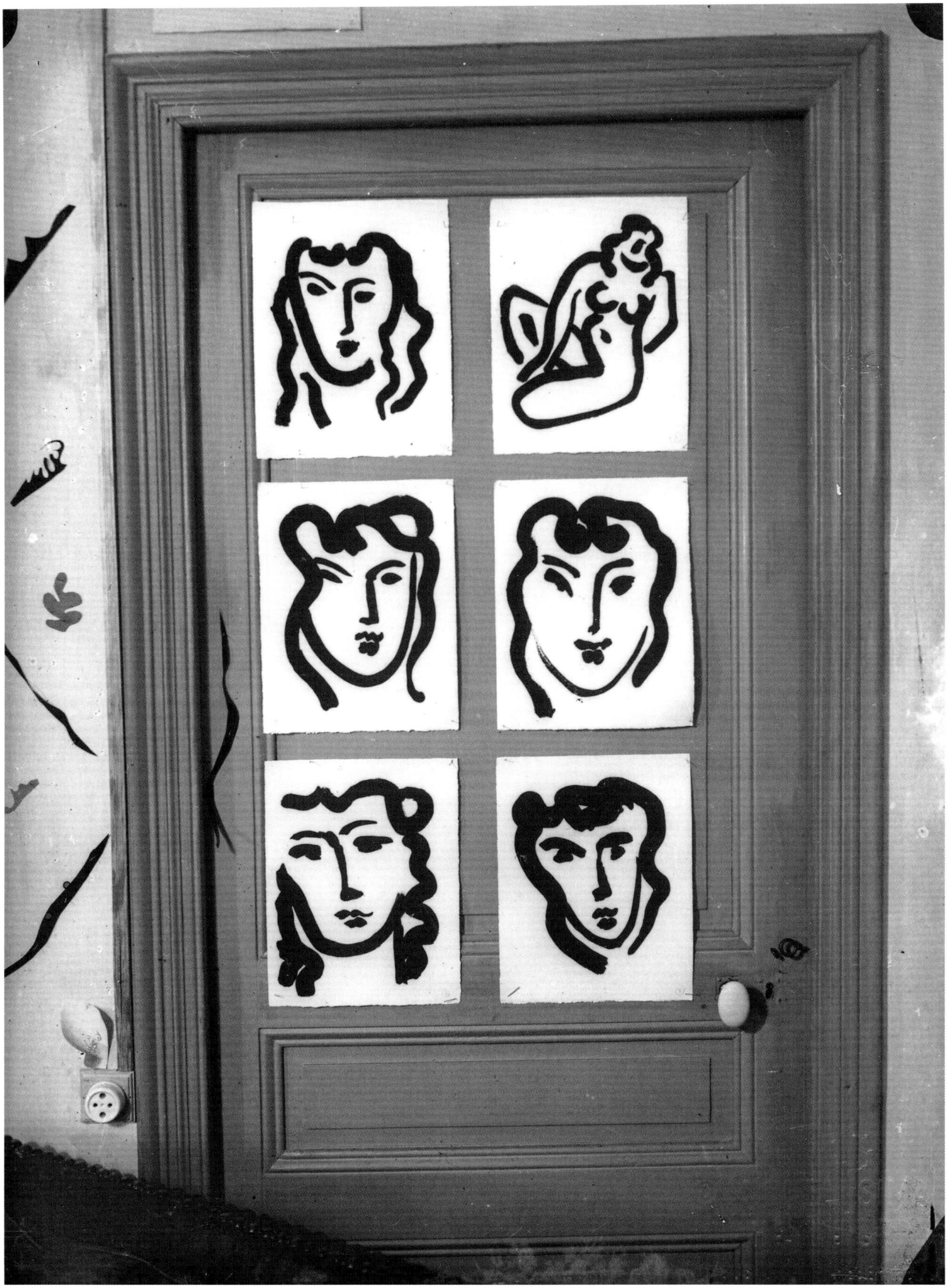

Michel Sima, Villa le Rêve, Vence, 22 May 1948 (no. 67)

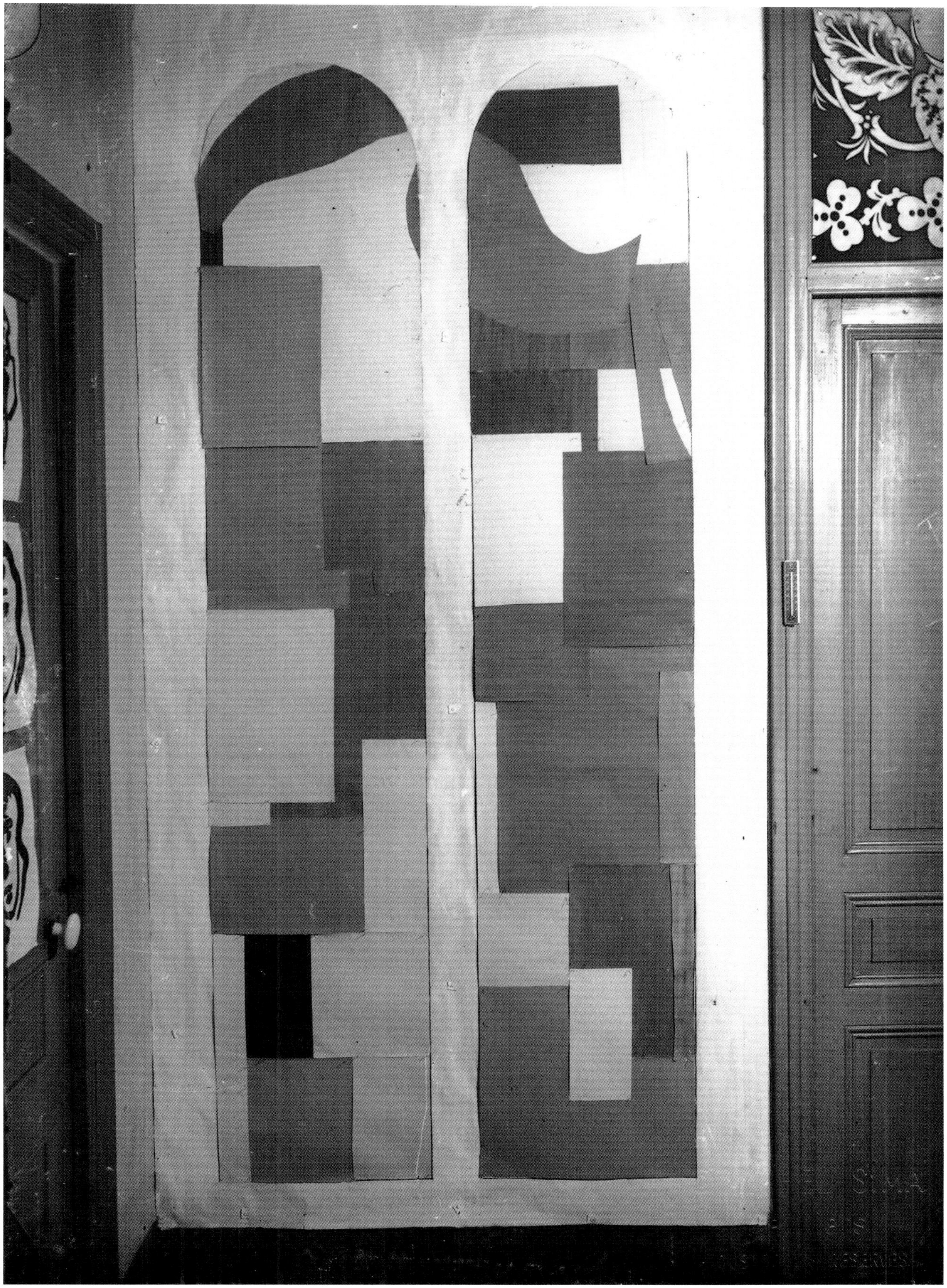

Michel Sima, Villa le Rêve, Vence, 22 May 1948 (no. 75)

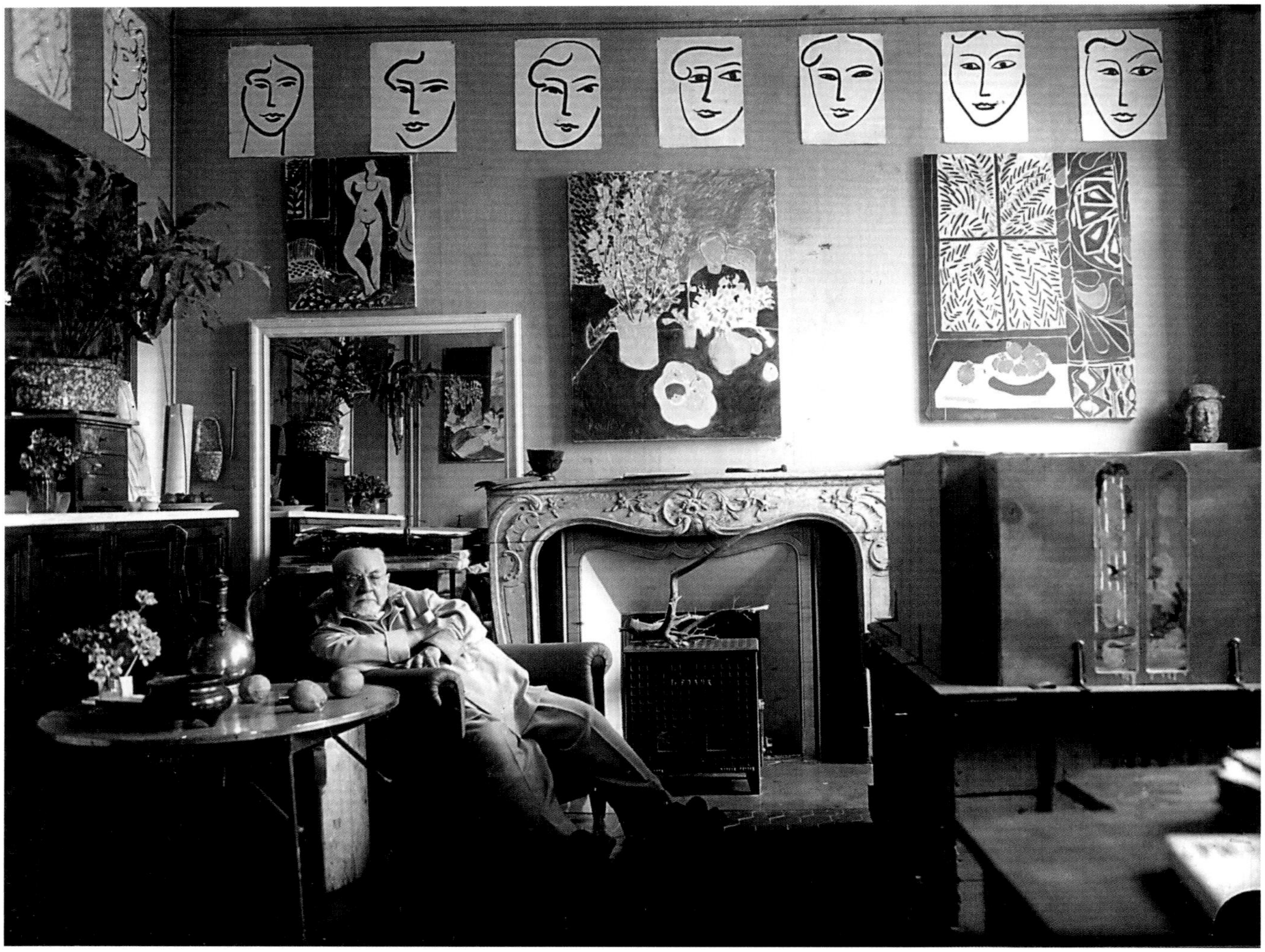

Michel Sima, Villa le Rêve, Vence, 22 May 1948

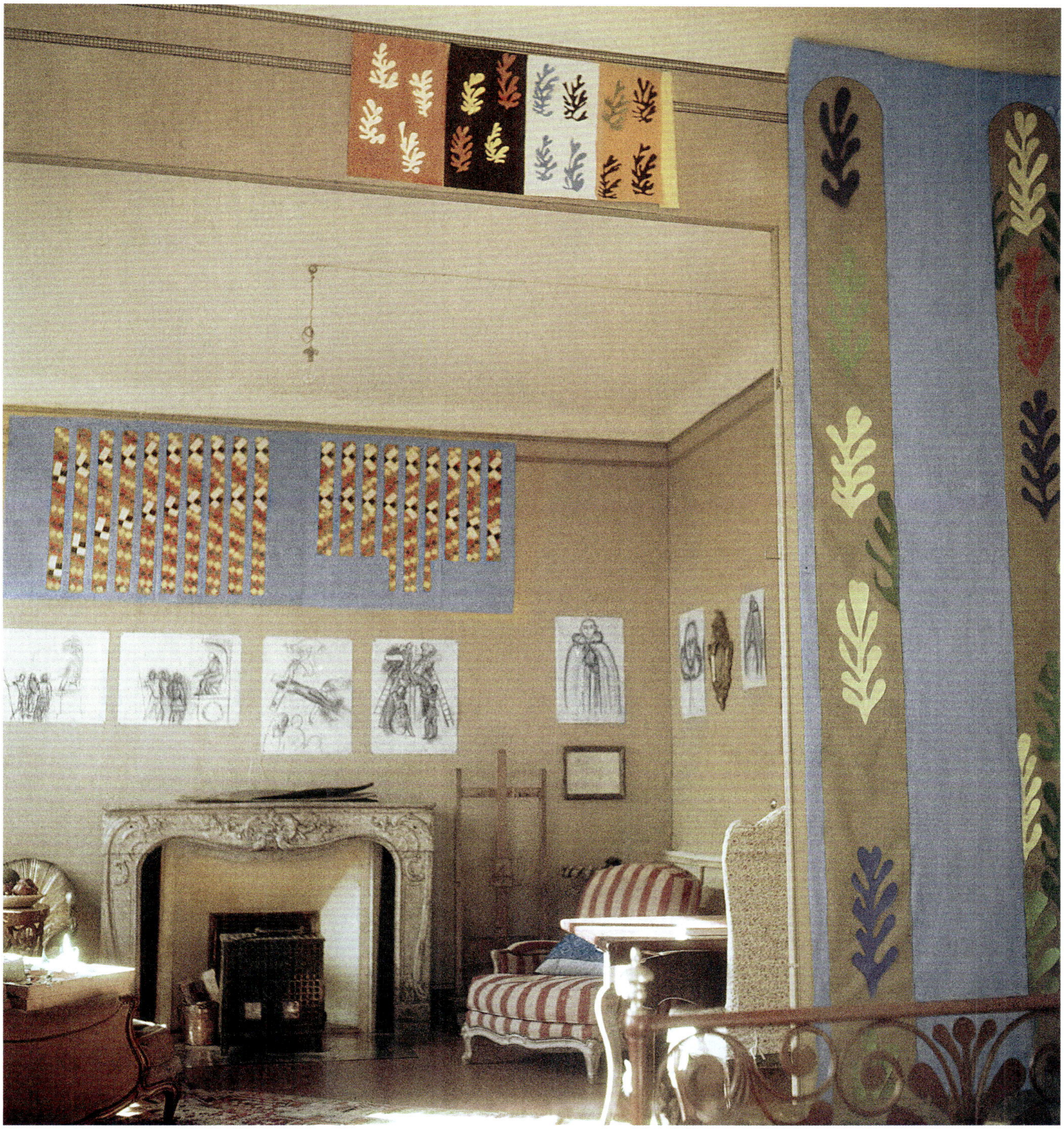

Clifford Coffin, Villa le Rêve, Vence, c. 1948 (nos. 65, 74)

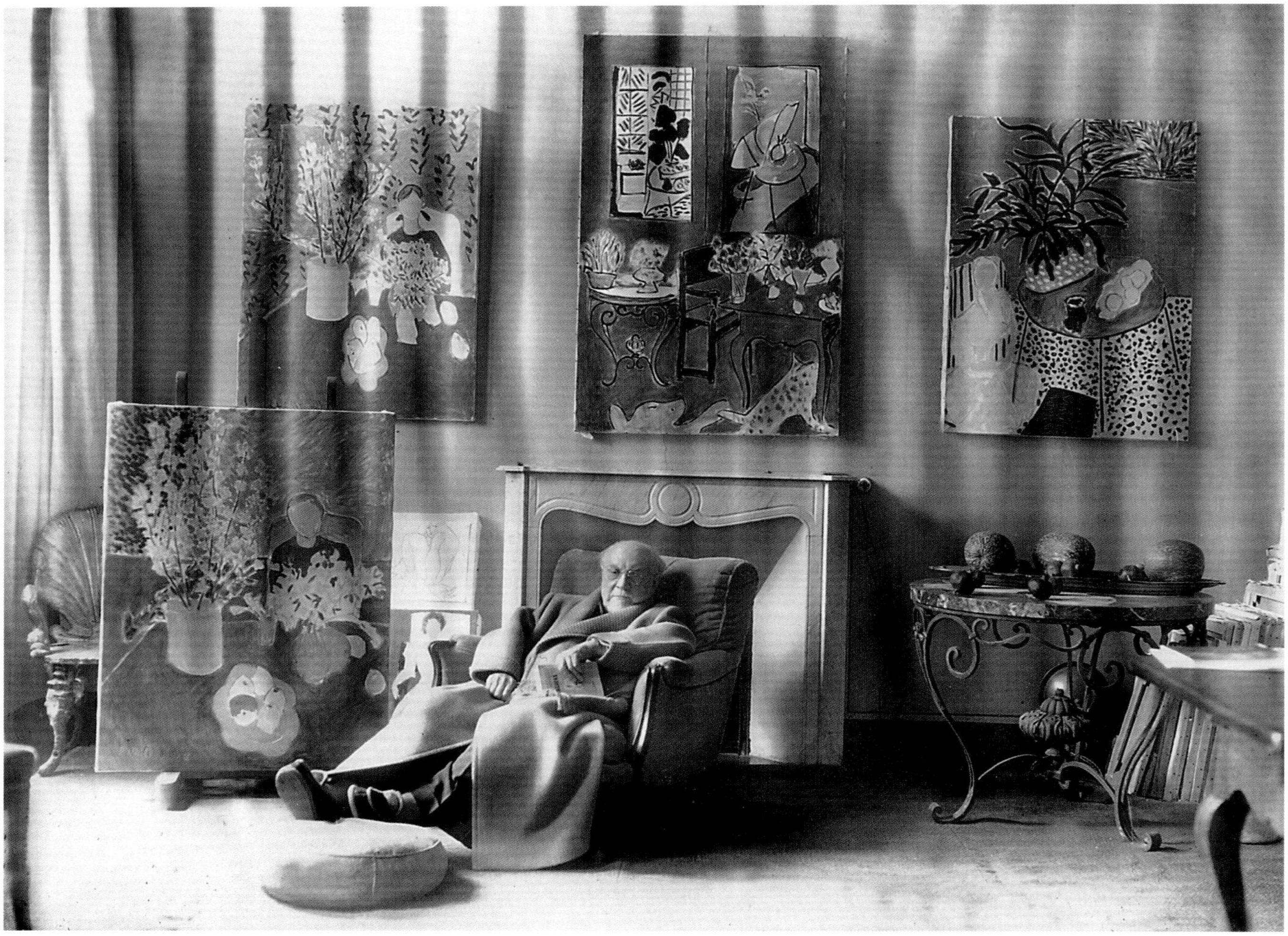

Michel Sima, Villa le Rêve, Vence, 22 May 1948 (no. 72)

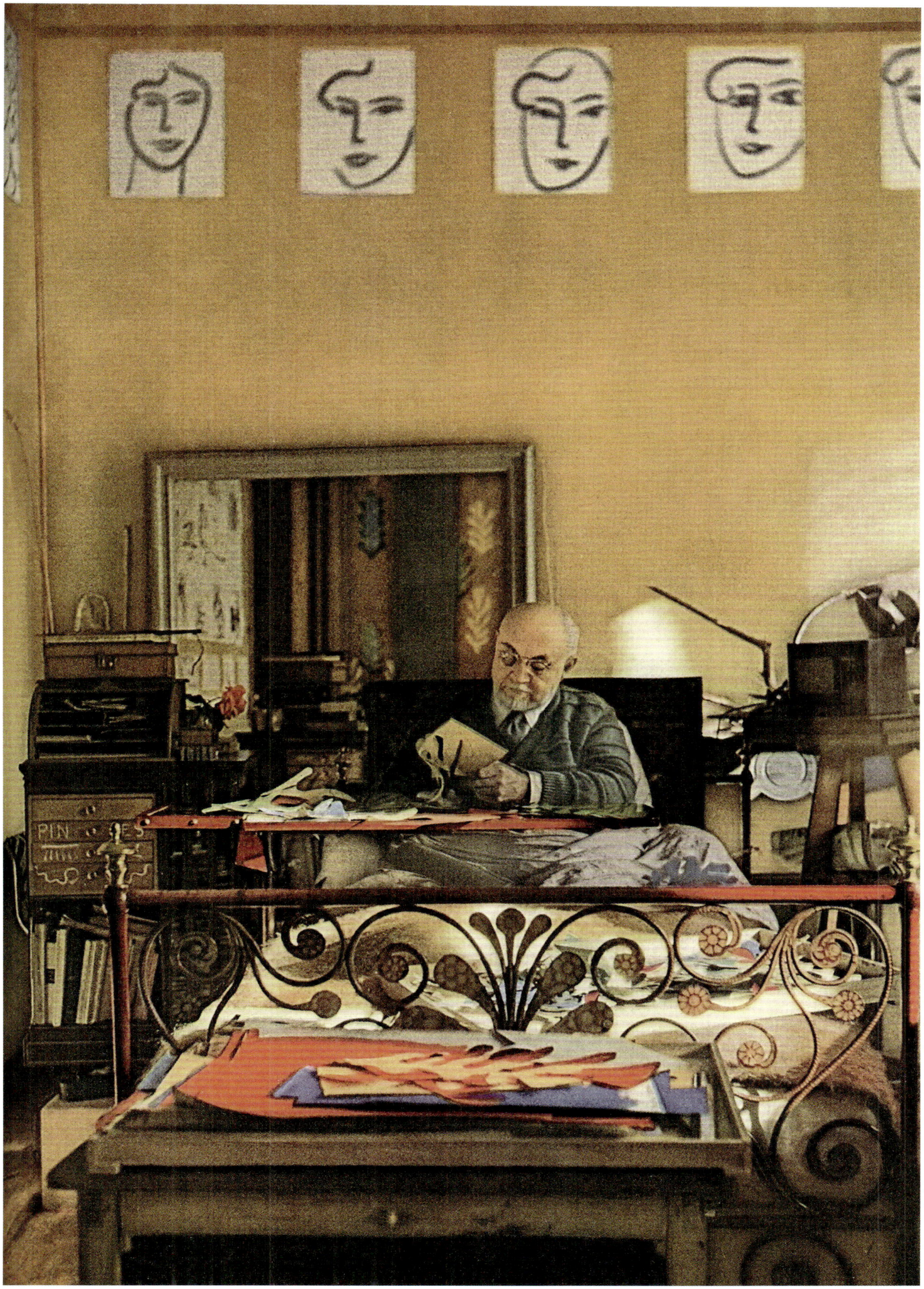

Clifford Coffin, Villa le Rêve, Vence, c. 1948

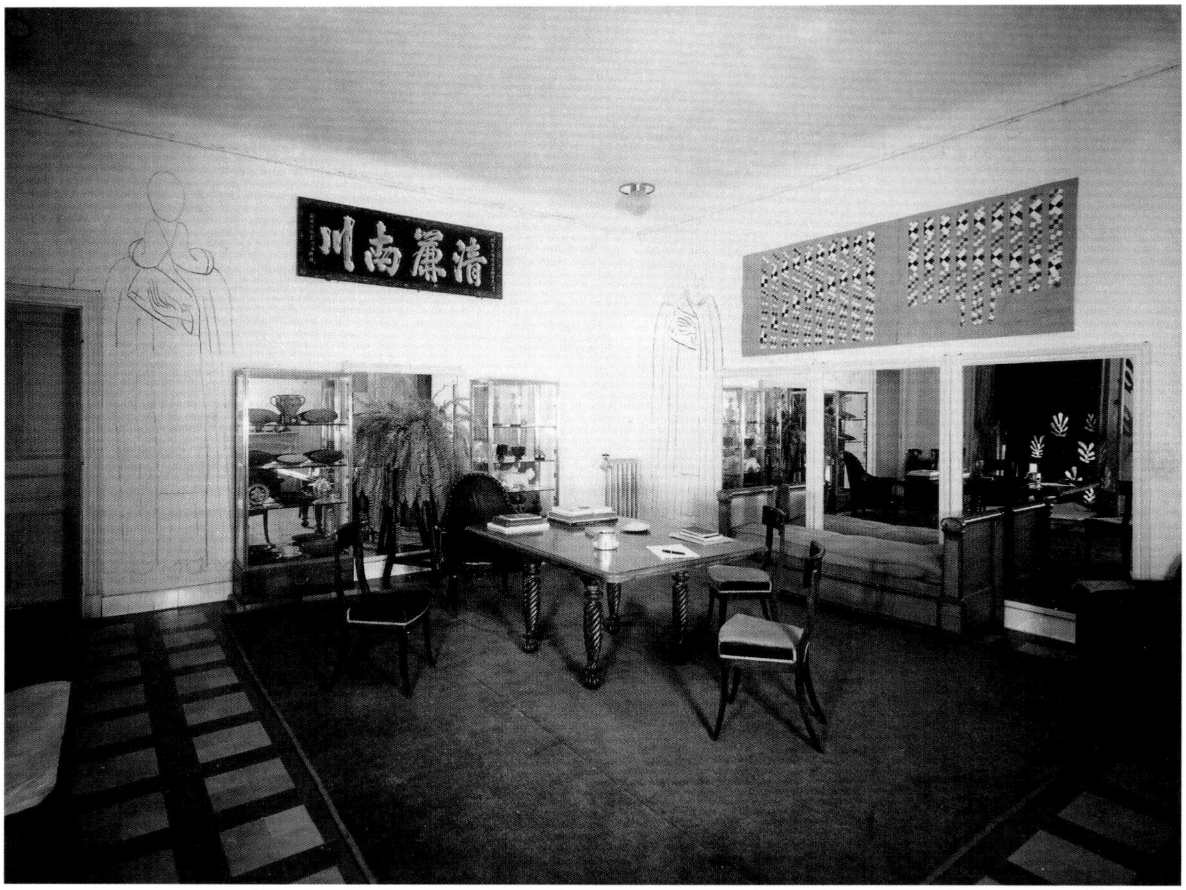

Mr Berard, Hôtel Régina, Nice, 1949 (no. 74)

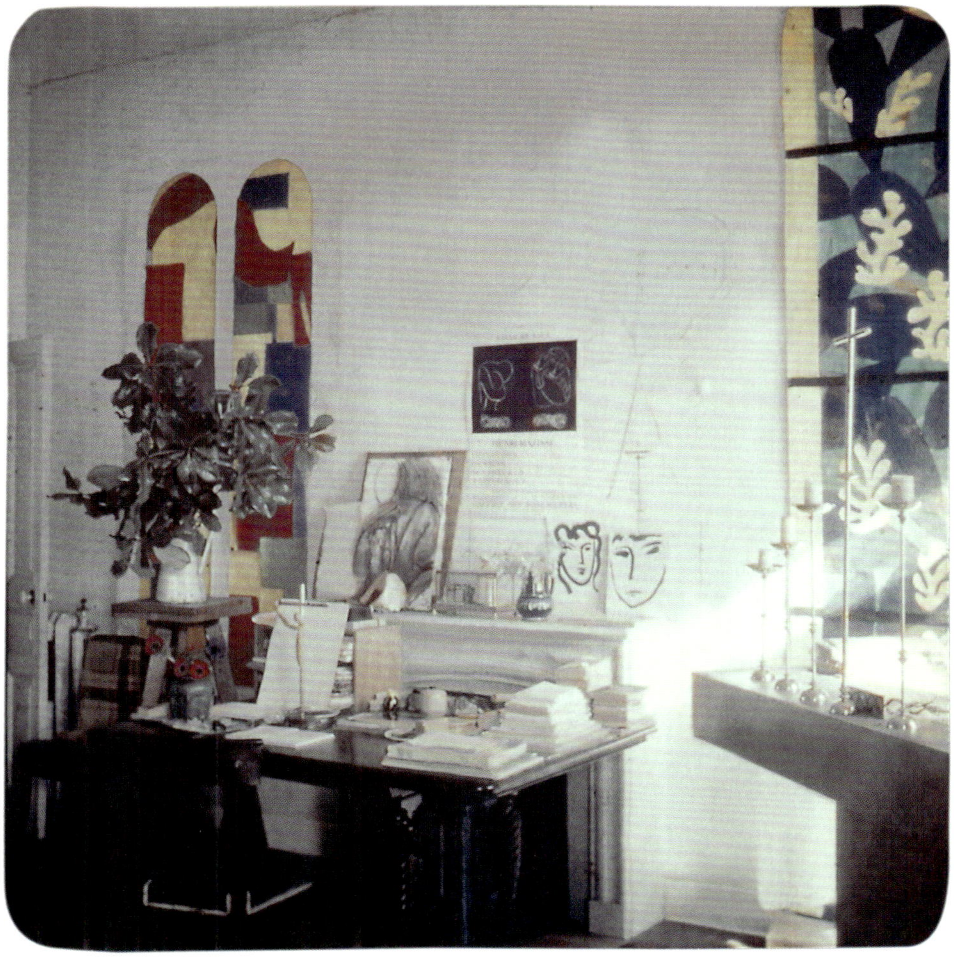

Lydia Delectorskaya, Hôtel Régina, Nice, 1949 (no. 75)

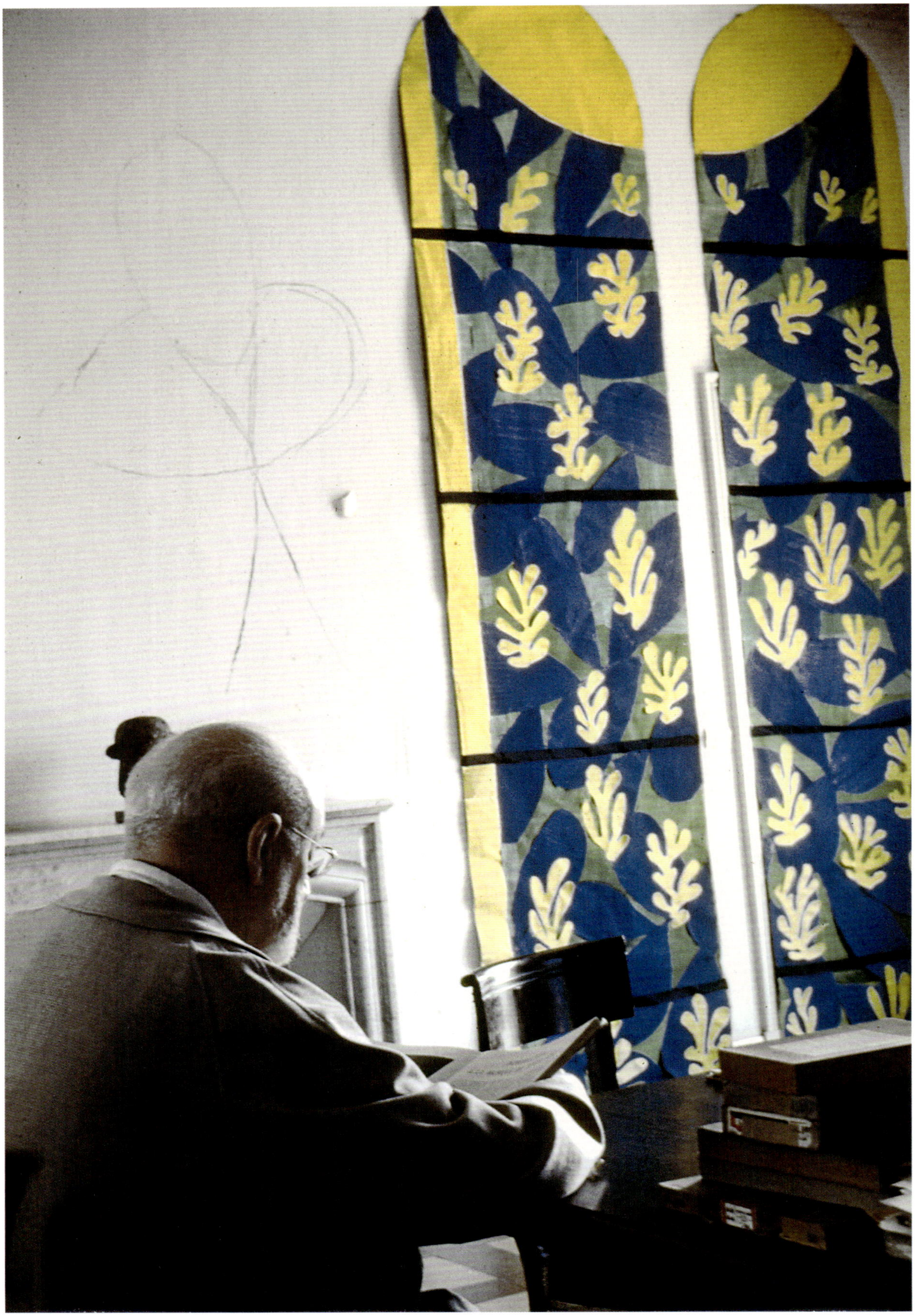

Lucien Hervé, Hôtel Régina, Nice, 1949

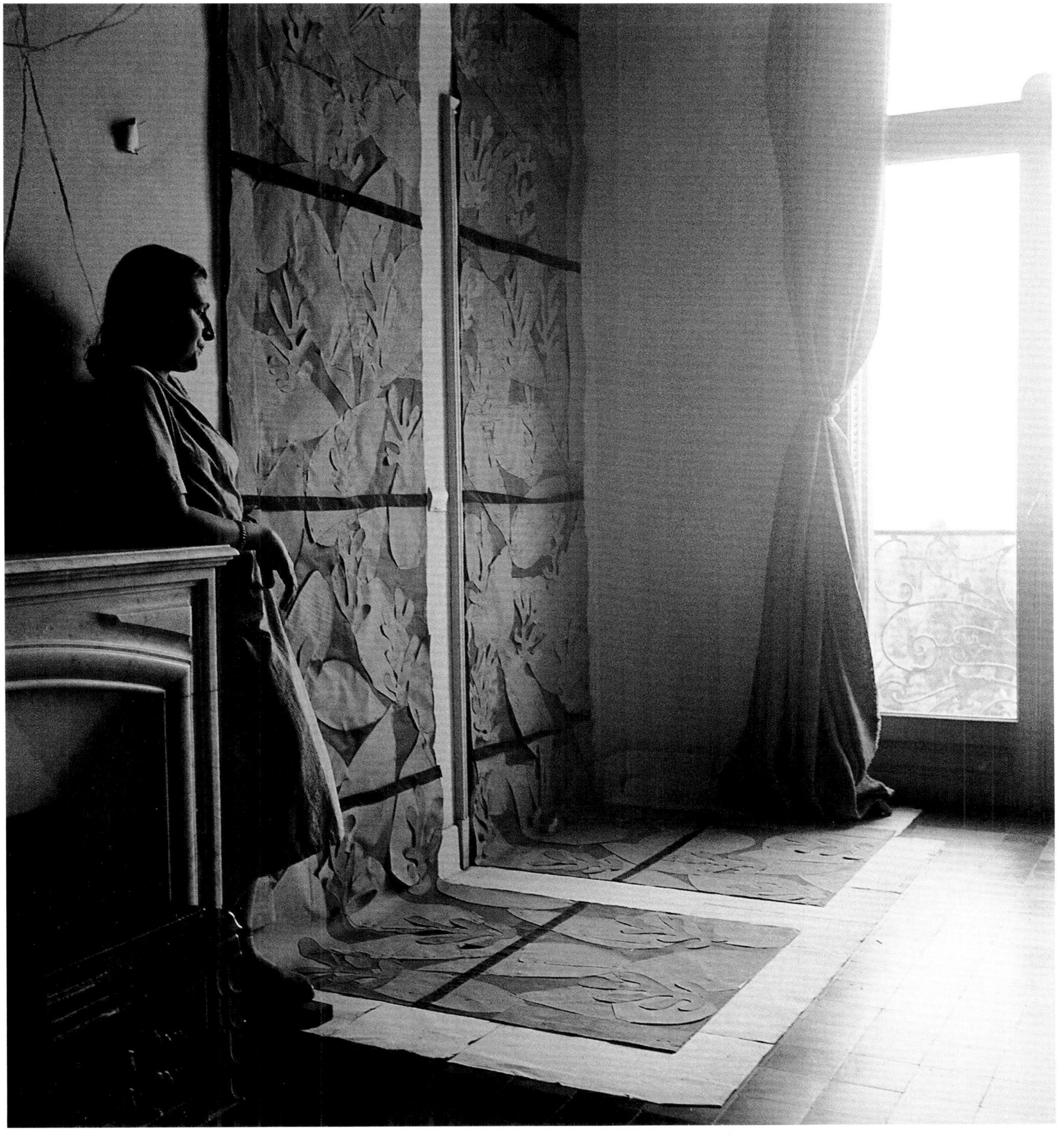

Lucien Hervé, Lydia Delectorskaya at the Hôtel Régina, Nice, 1949

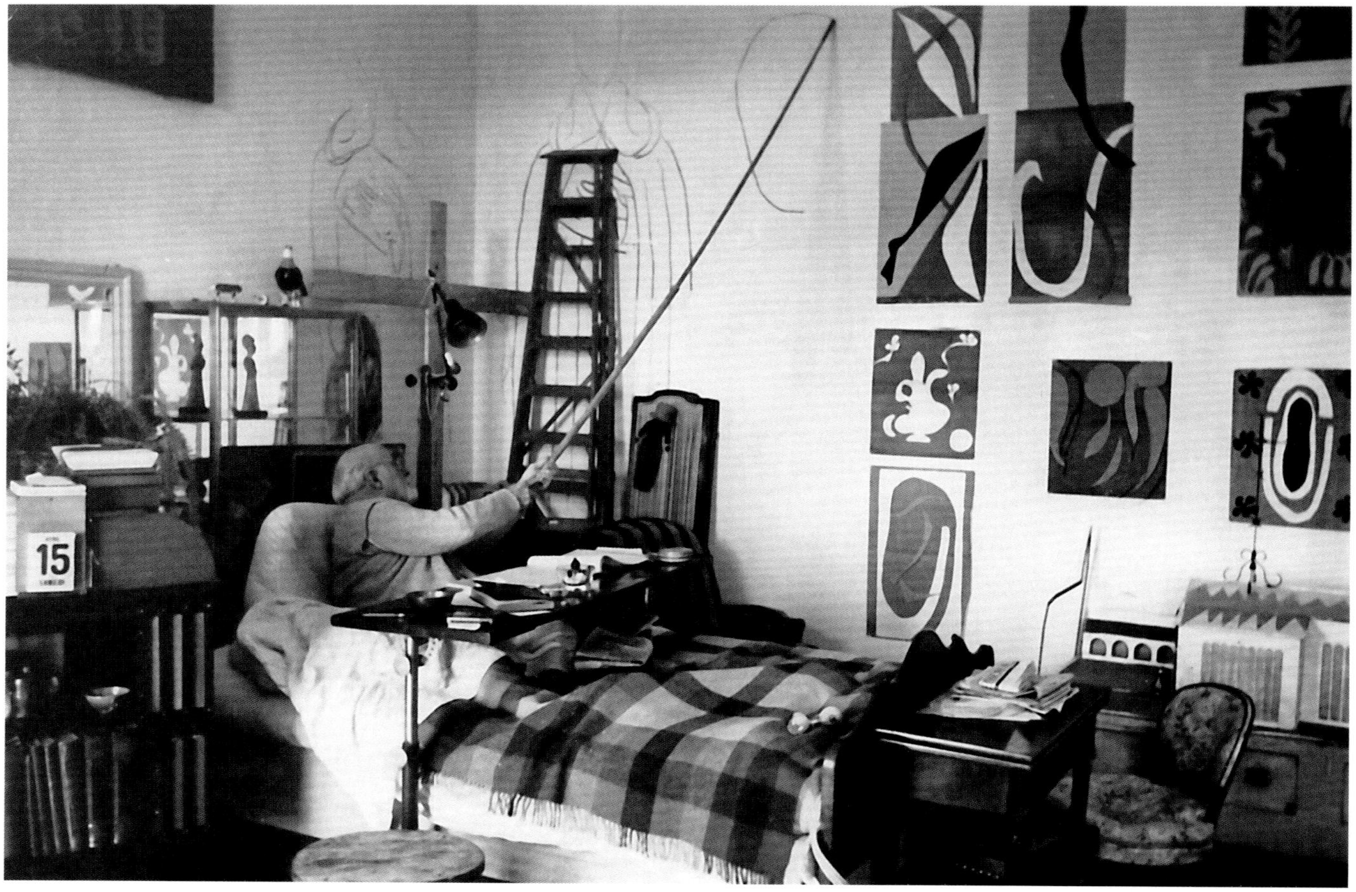

Walter Carone, Hôtel Régina, Nice, 15 April 1950 (nos. 86, 88)

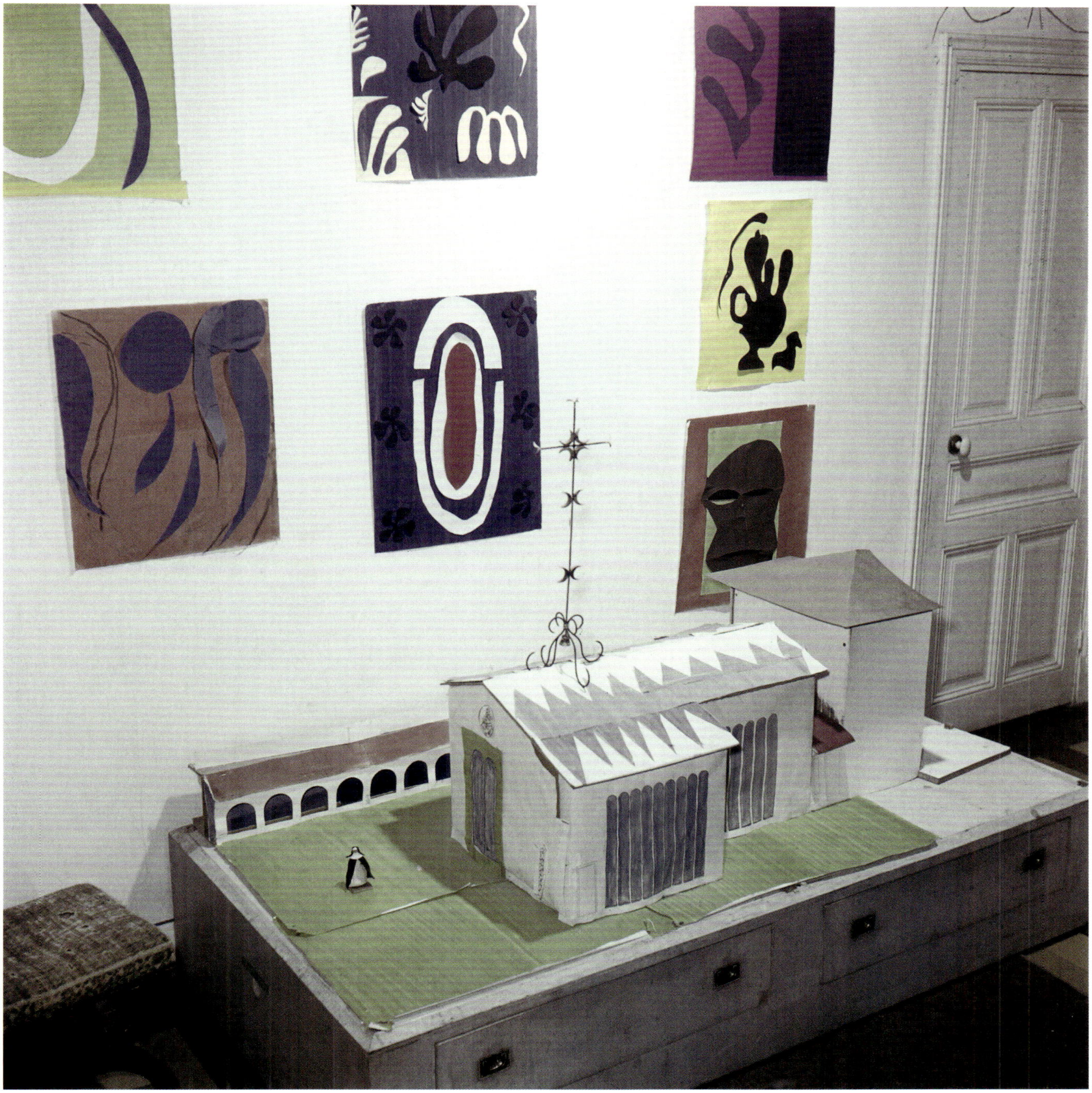

Walter Carone, Hôtel Régina, Nice, 15 April 1950 (no. 86)

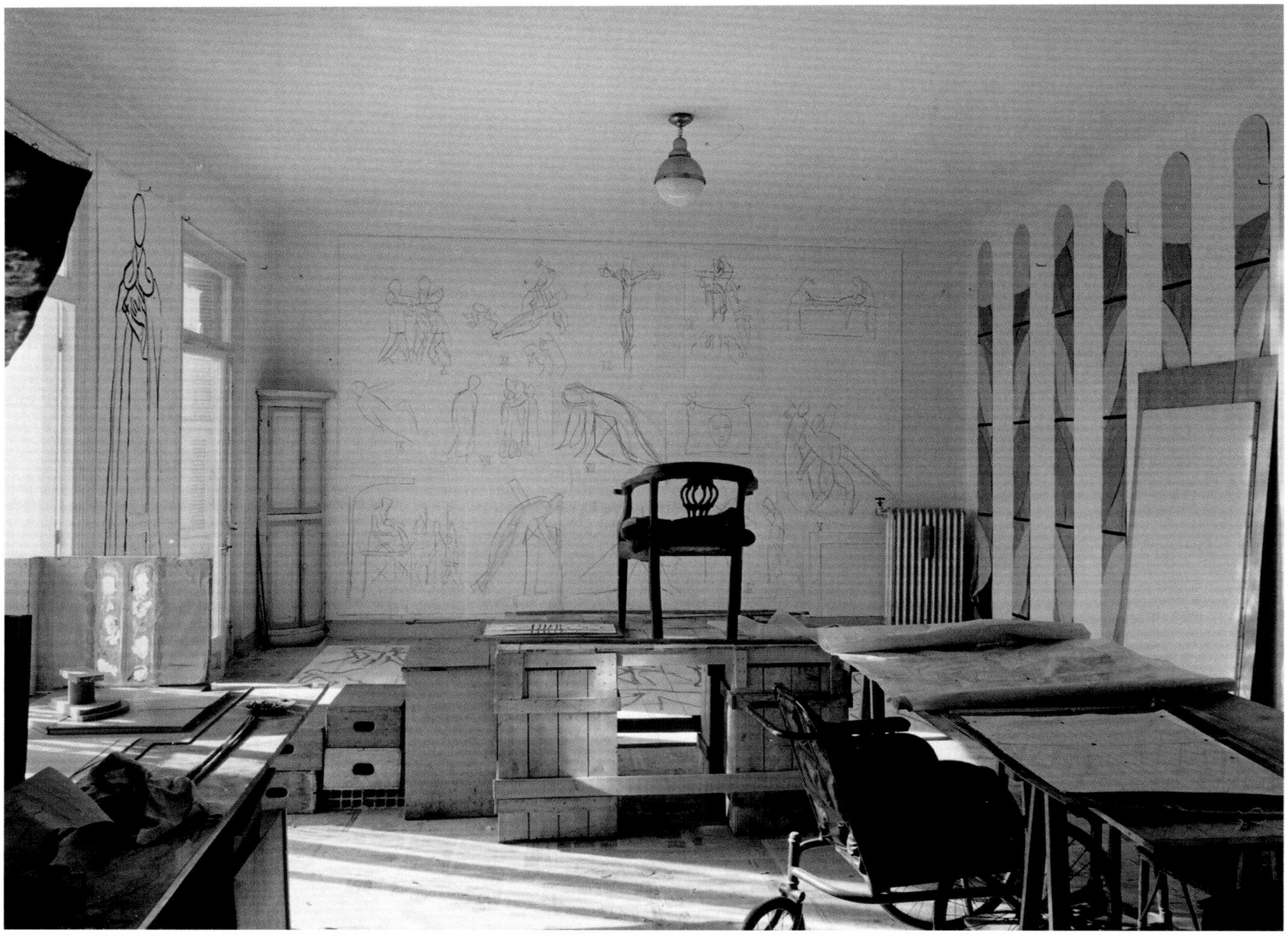

Hélène Adant, Hôtel Régina, Nice, 1950

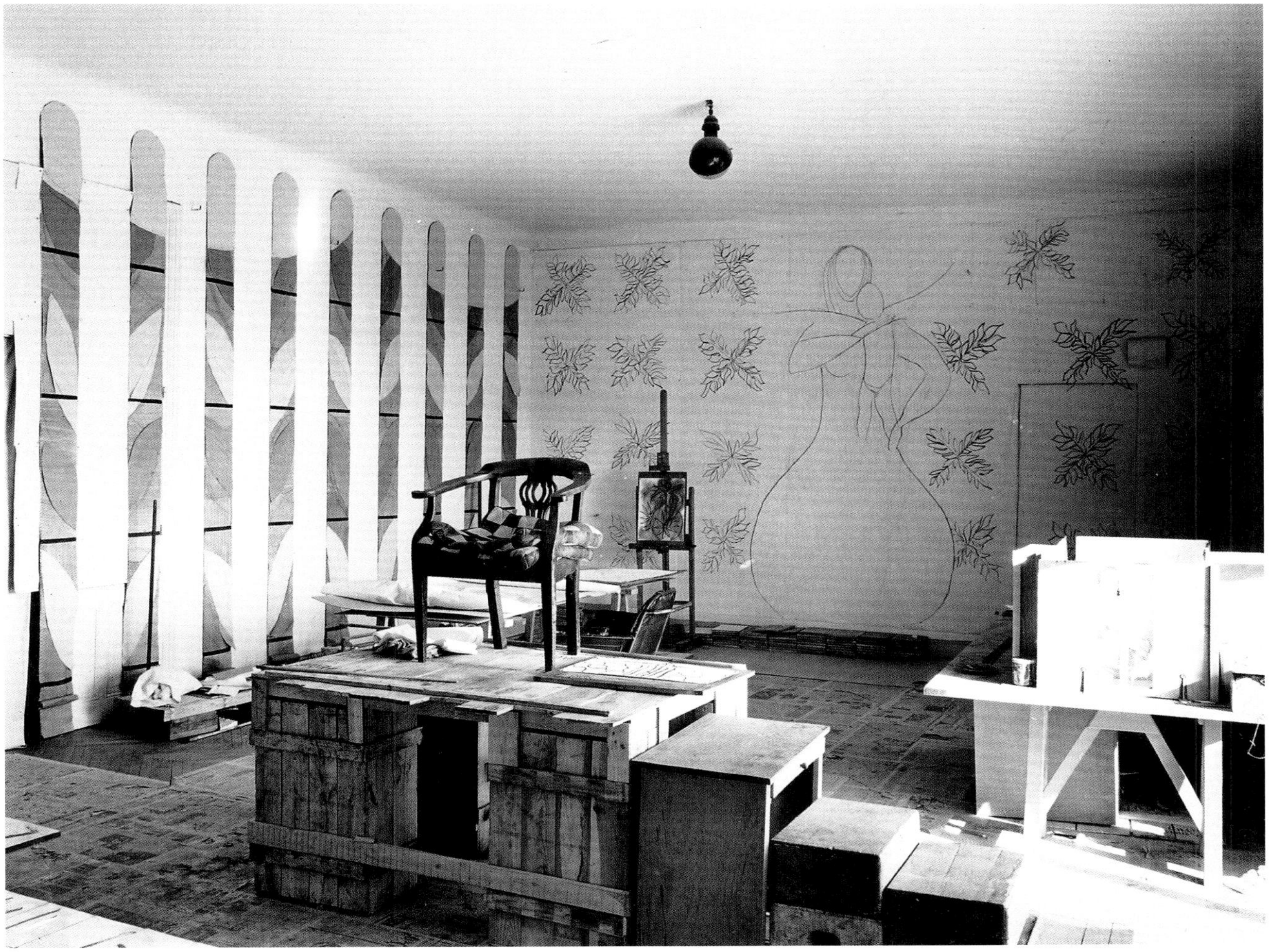

Hélène Adant, Hôtel Régina, Nice, 1950 (no. 76)

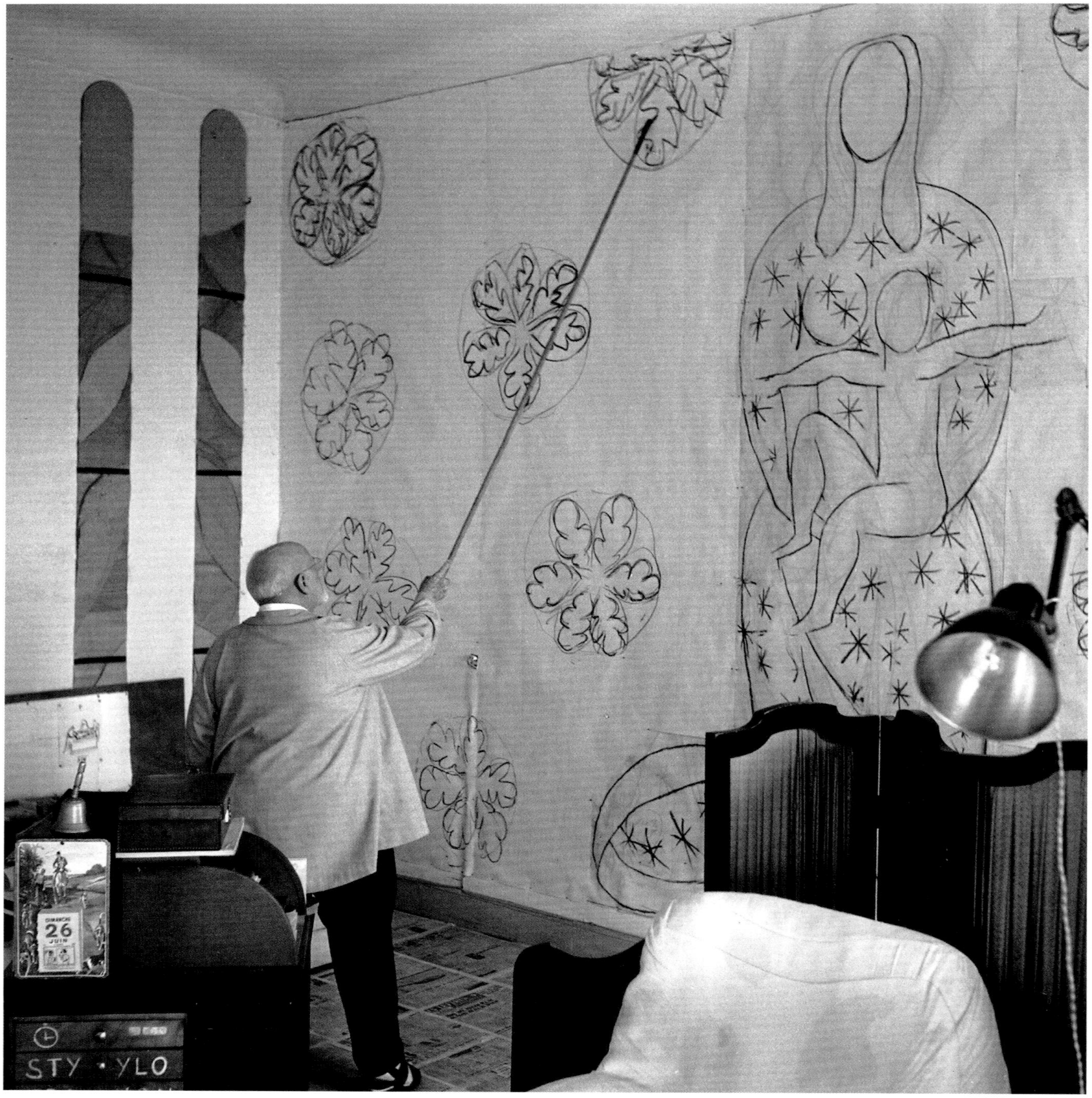

Lucien Hervé, Hôtel Régina, Nice, 1949 (no. 76)

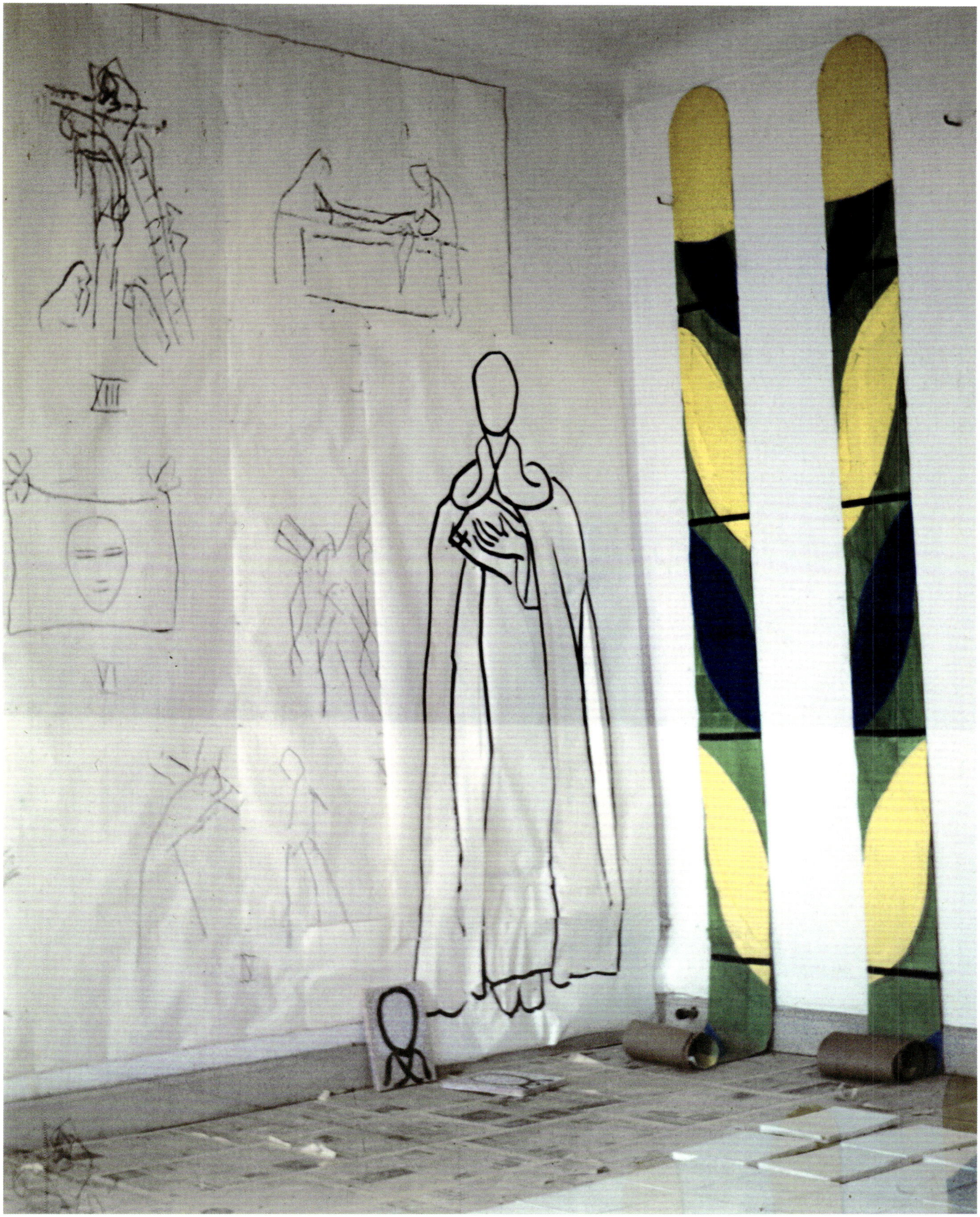

Lucien Hervé, Hôtel Régina, Nice, 1949

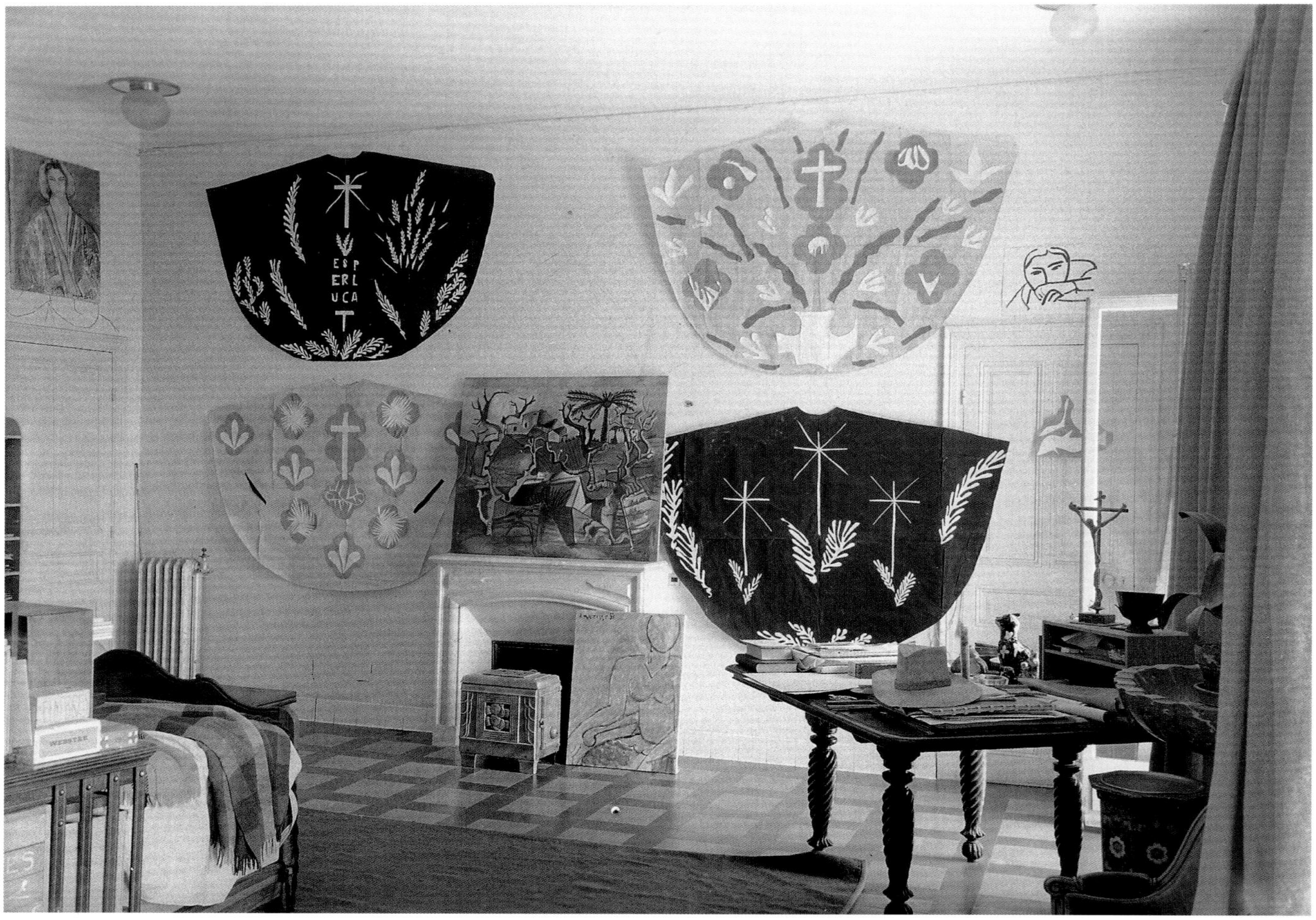

Hélène Adant, Hôtel Régina, Nice, c. 1951 (nos. 80–1)

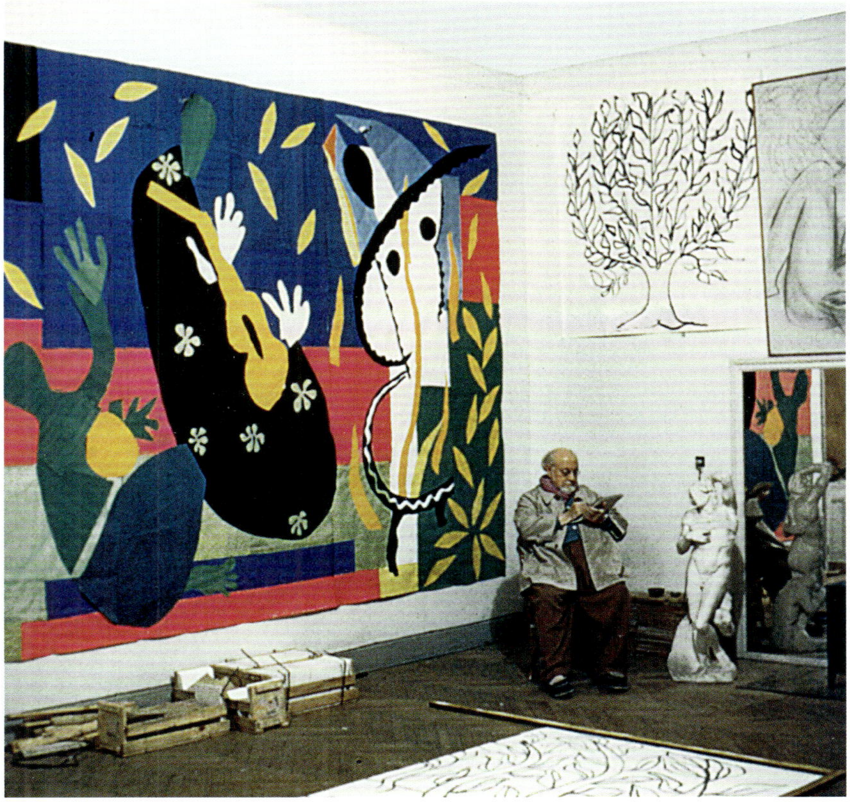

Unknown photographer, Henri Matisse at the Hôtel Régina, Nice, March or April 1952

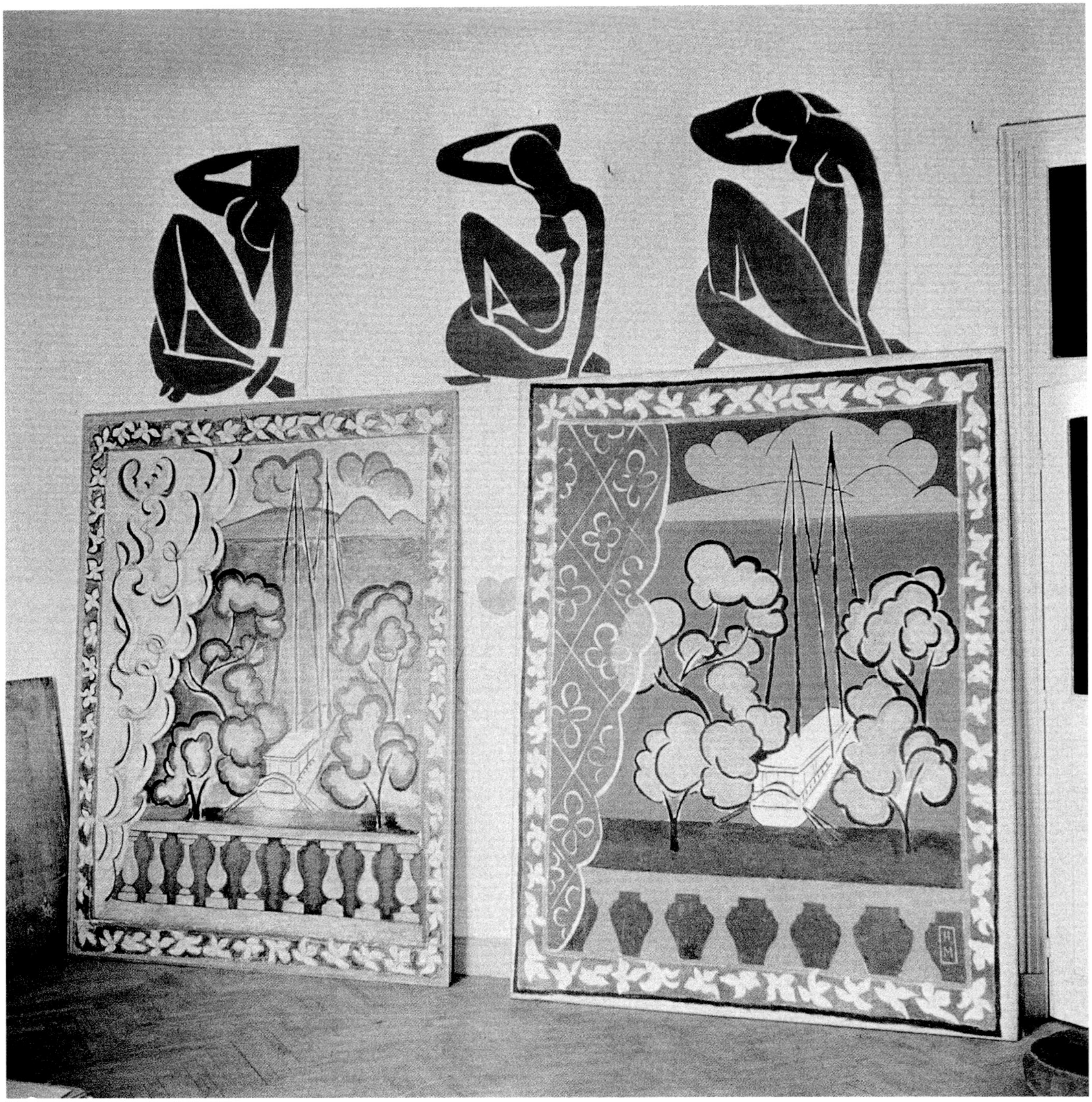

Hélène Adant, Hôtel Régina, Nice, 1952 (nos. 109–11)

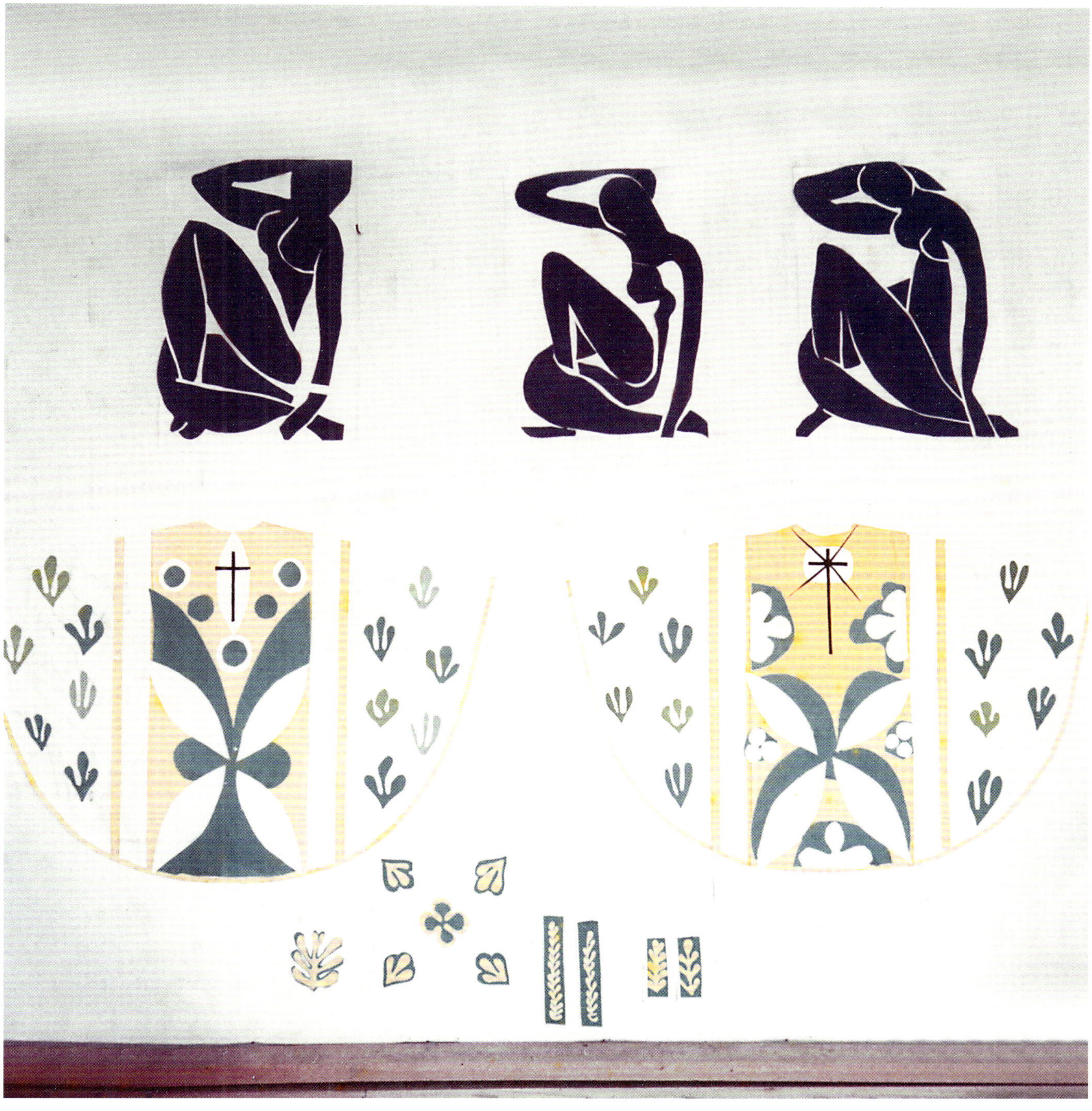

Lydia Delectorskaya, Hôtel Régina, Nice, 1952 (nos. 109–11)

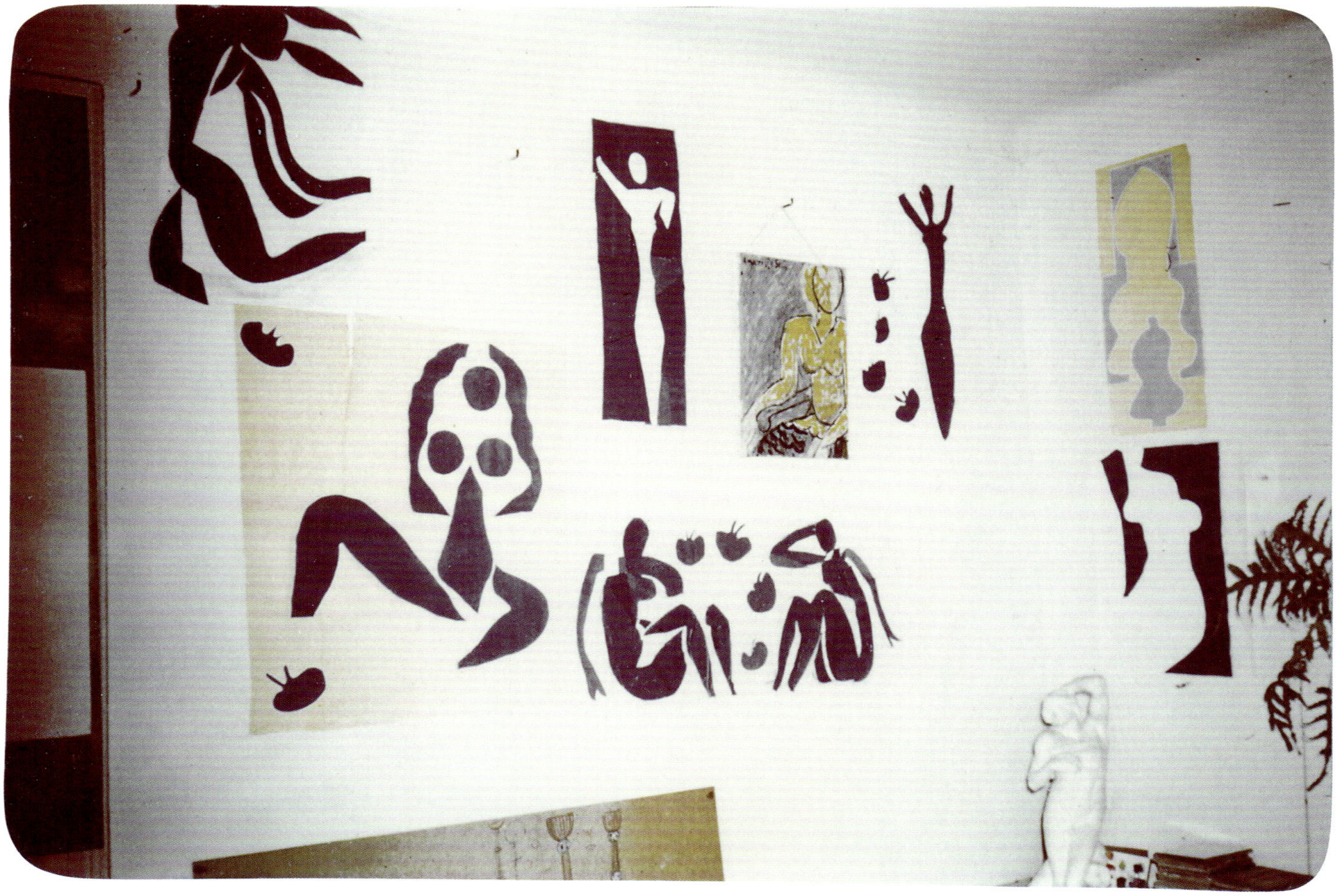

Lydia Delectorskaya, Hôtel Régina, Nice, 1952 (nos. 89, 115–16, 120, 123–4)

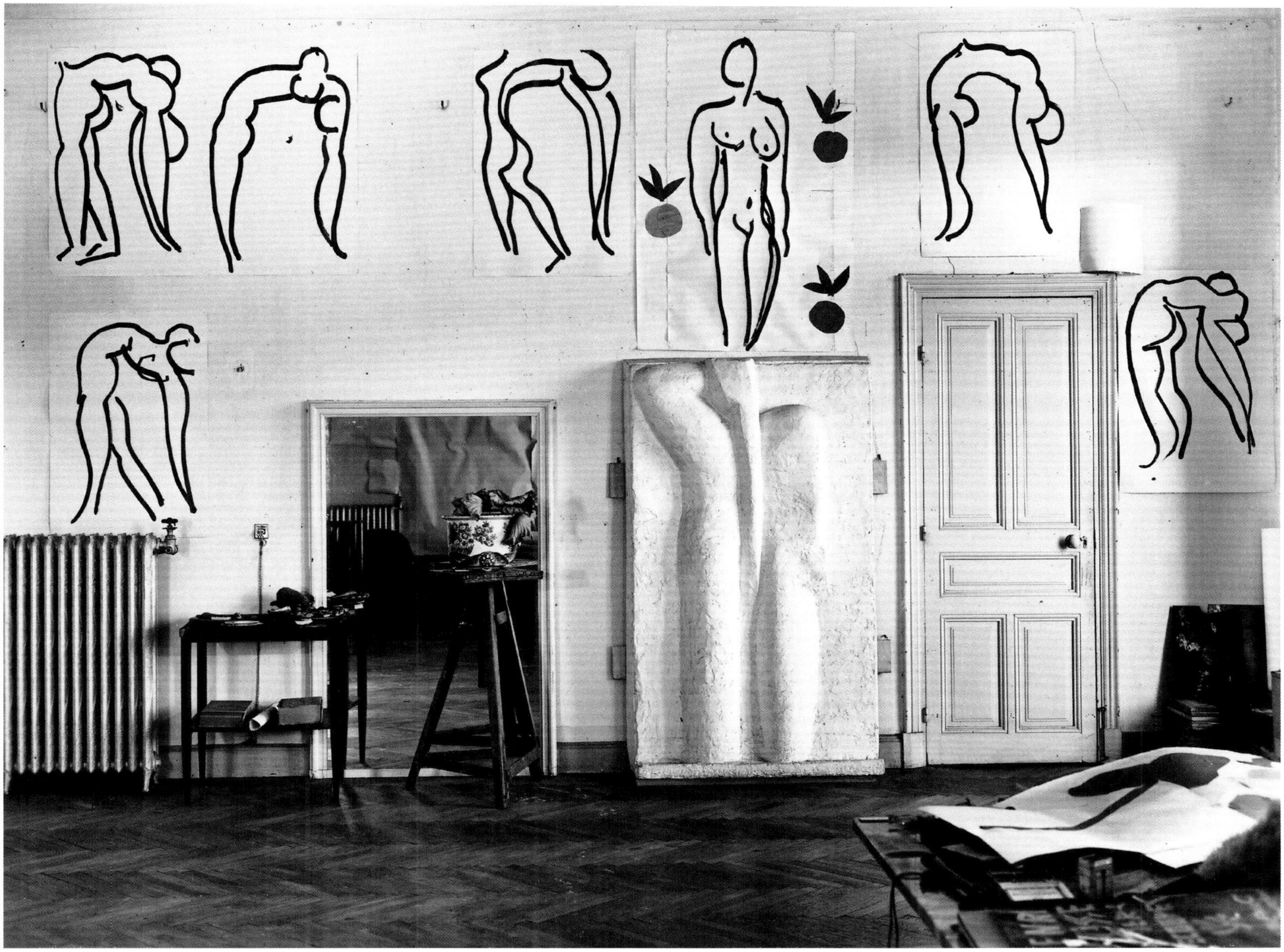

Unknown photographer, Hôtel Régina, Nice, 1953 (fig. 44)

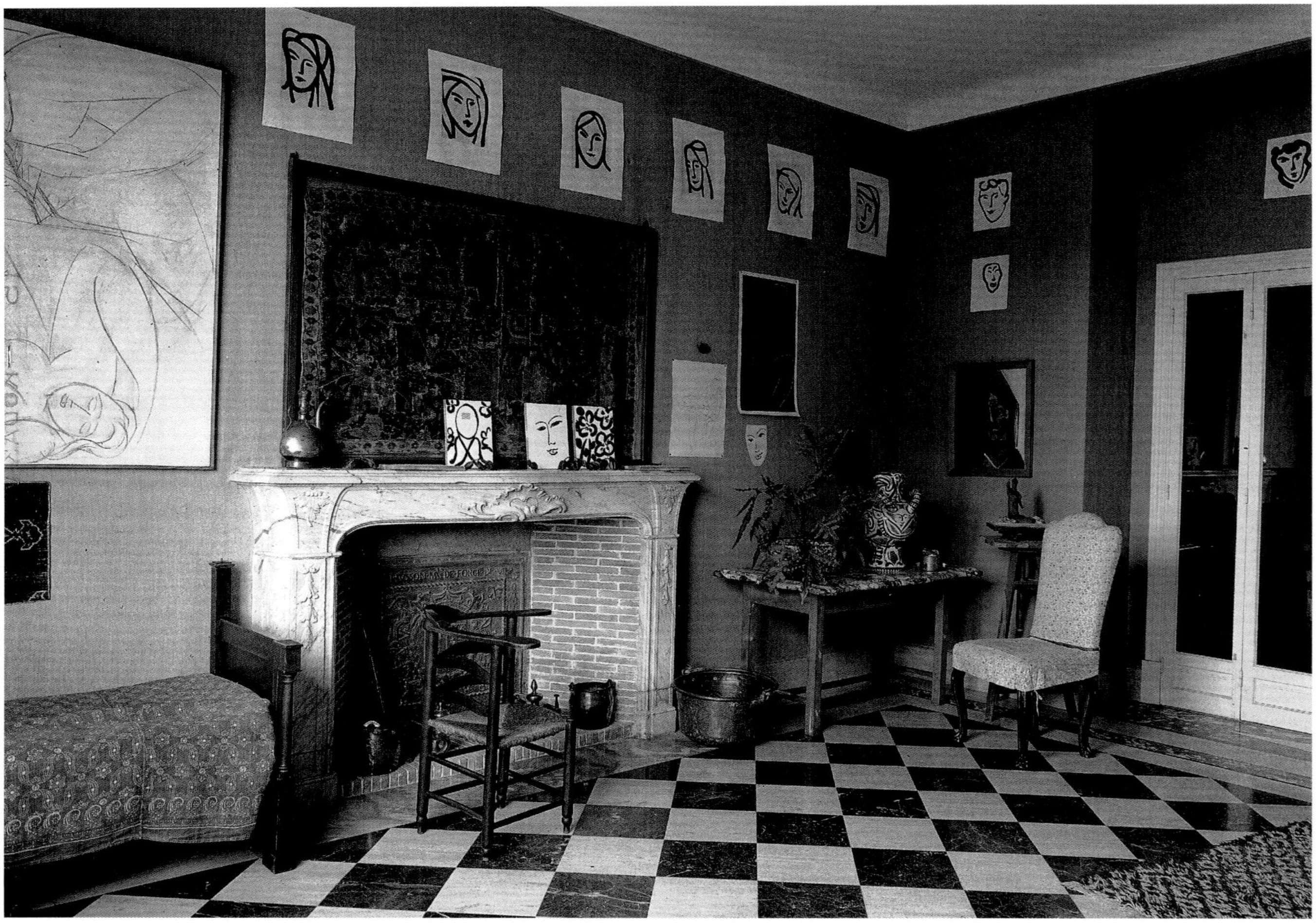

Hélène Adant, Hôtel Régina, Nice, 1949–50

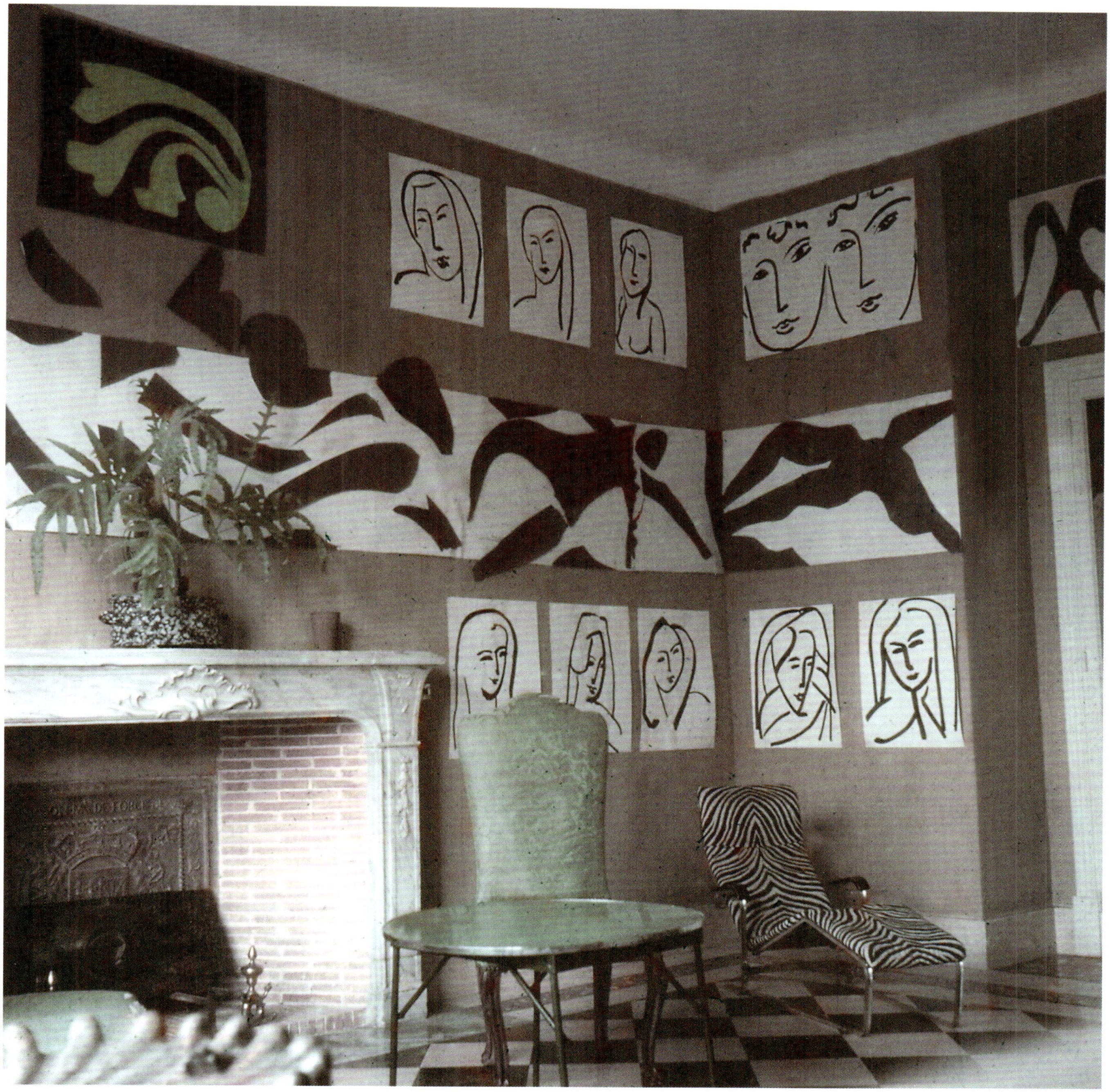

Lydia Delectorskaya, Hôtel Régina, Nice, 1952 (nos. 120–1)

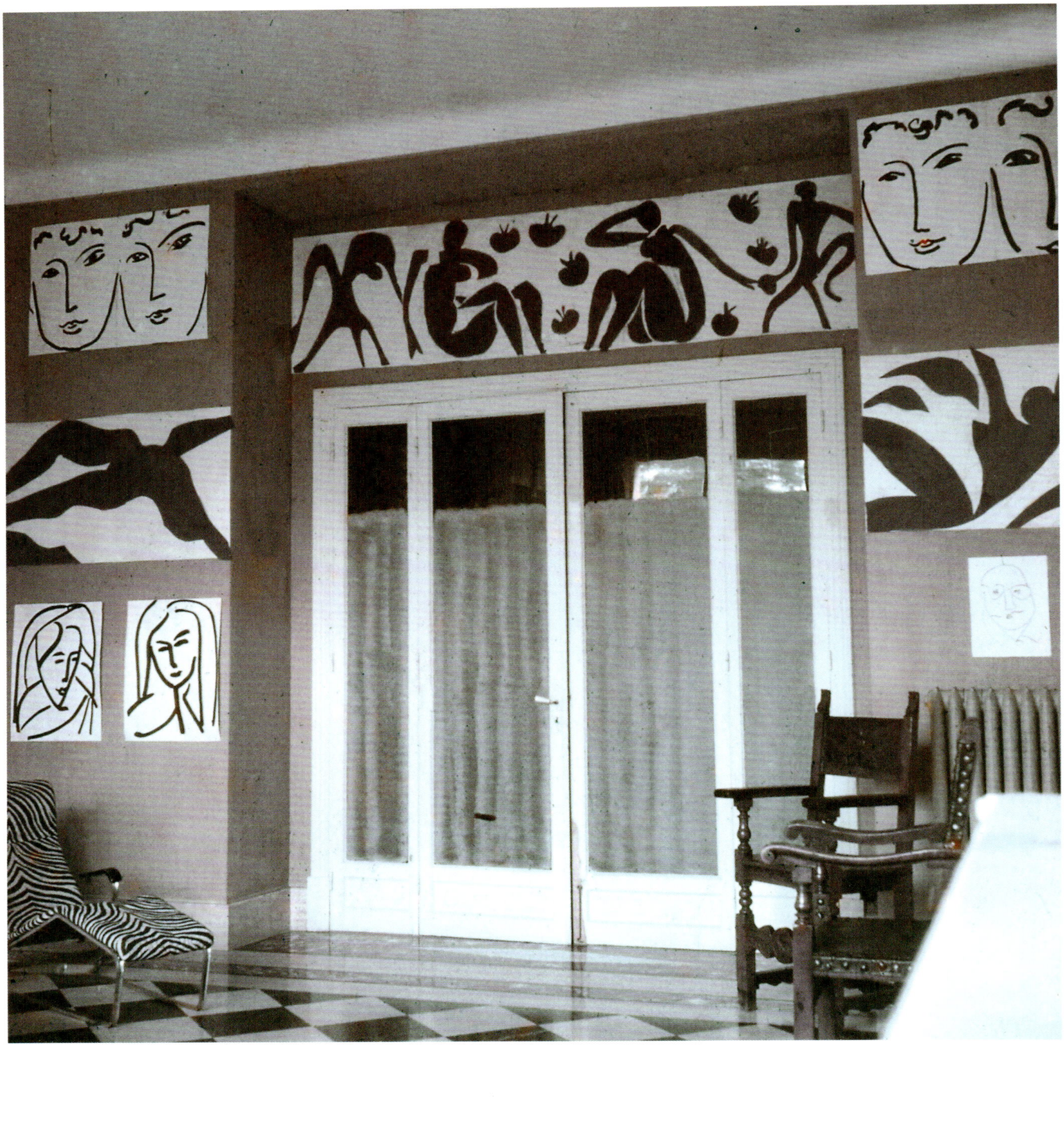

Lydia Delectorskaya, Hôtel Régina, Nice, 1952 (nos. 120–1)

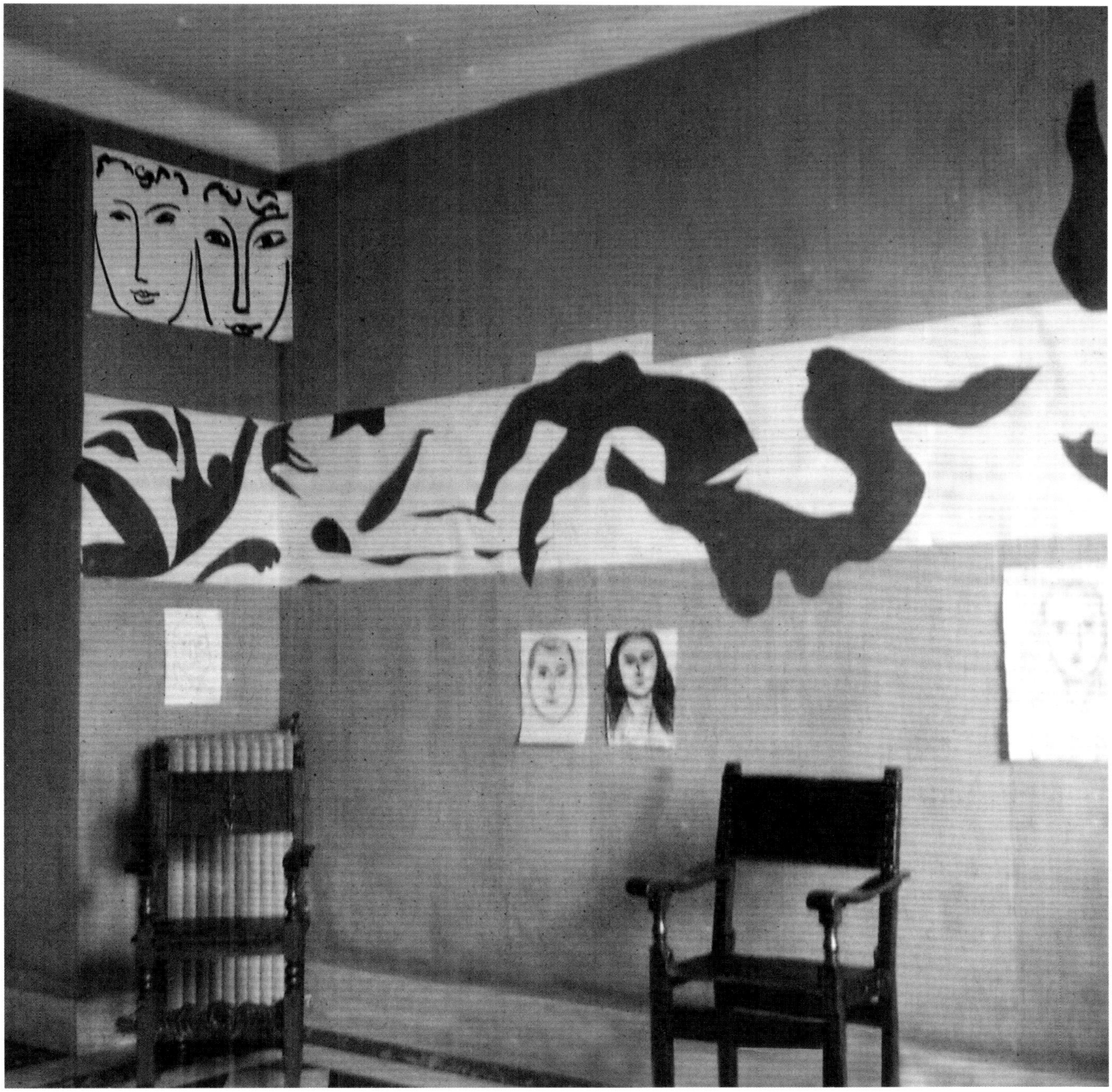

Lydia Delectorskaya, Hôtel Régina, Nice, 1952 (no. 121)

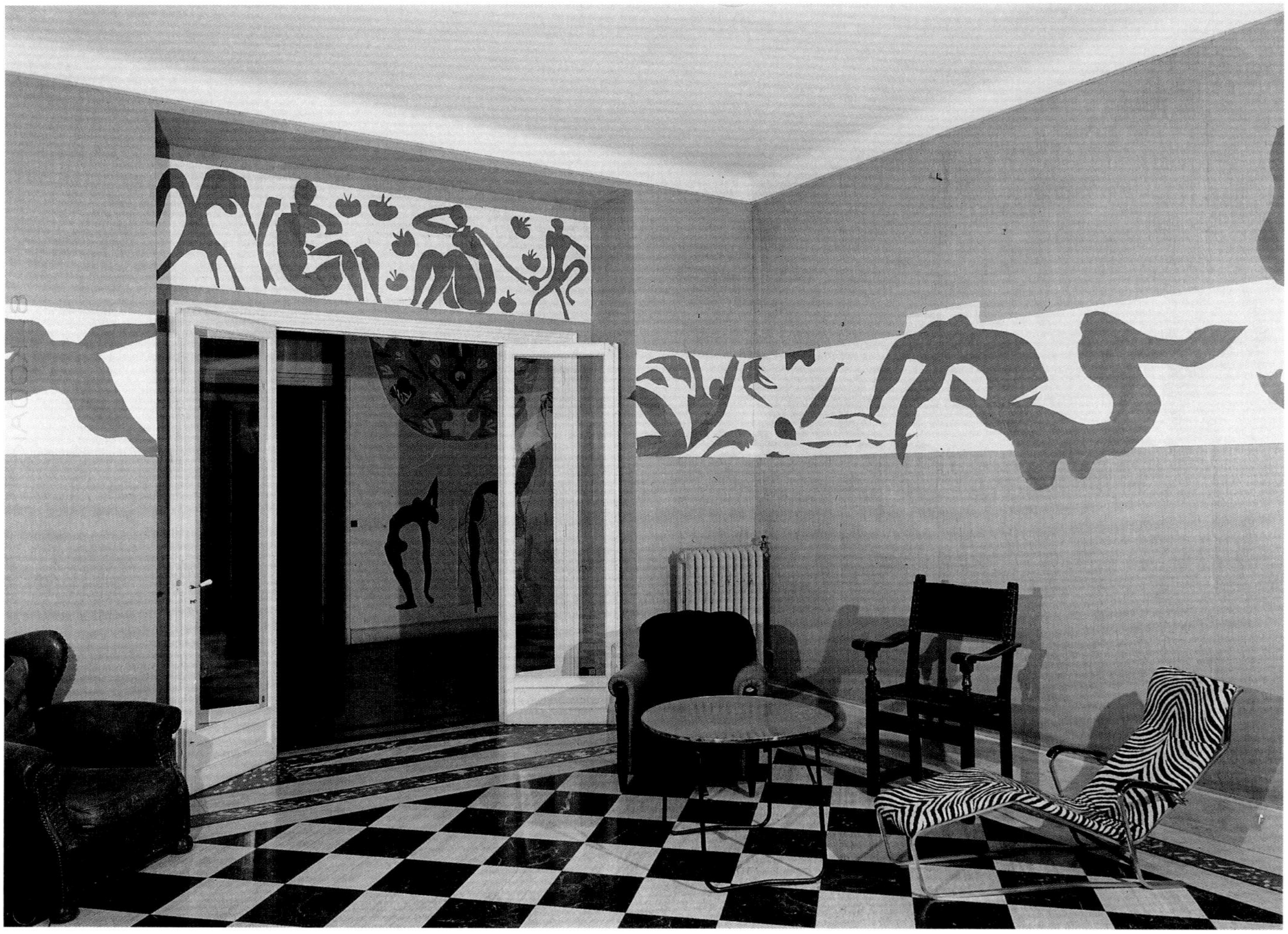

Hélène Adant, Hôtel Régina, Nice, 1953 (nos. 113, 120–1)

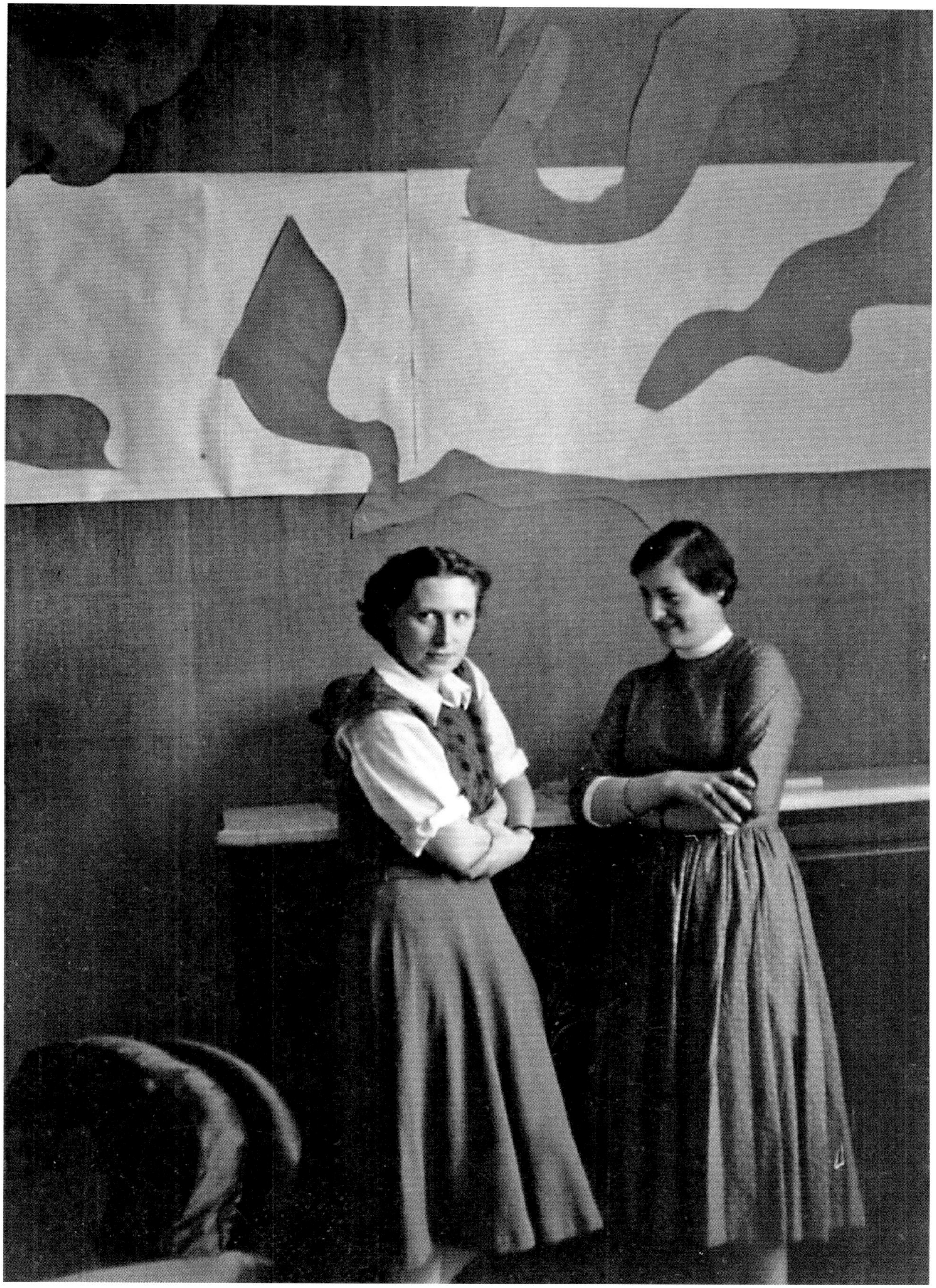

Unknown photographer, Lydia Delectorskaya and Angela Rosengart at the Hôtel Régina, Nice, c. 1952 (no. 121)

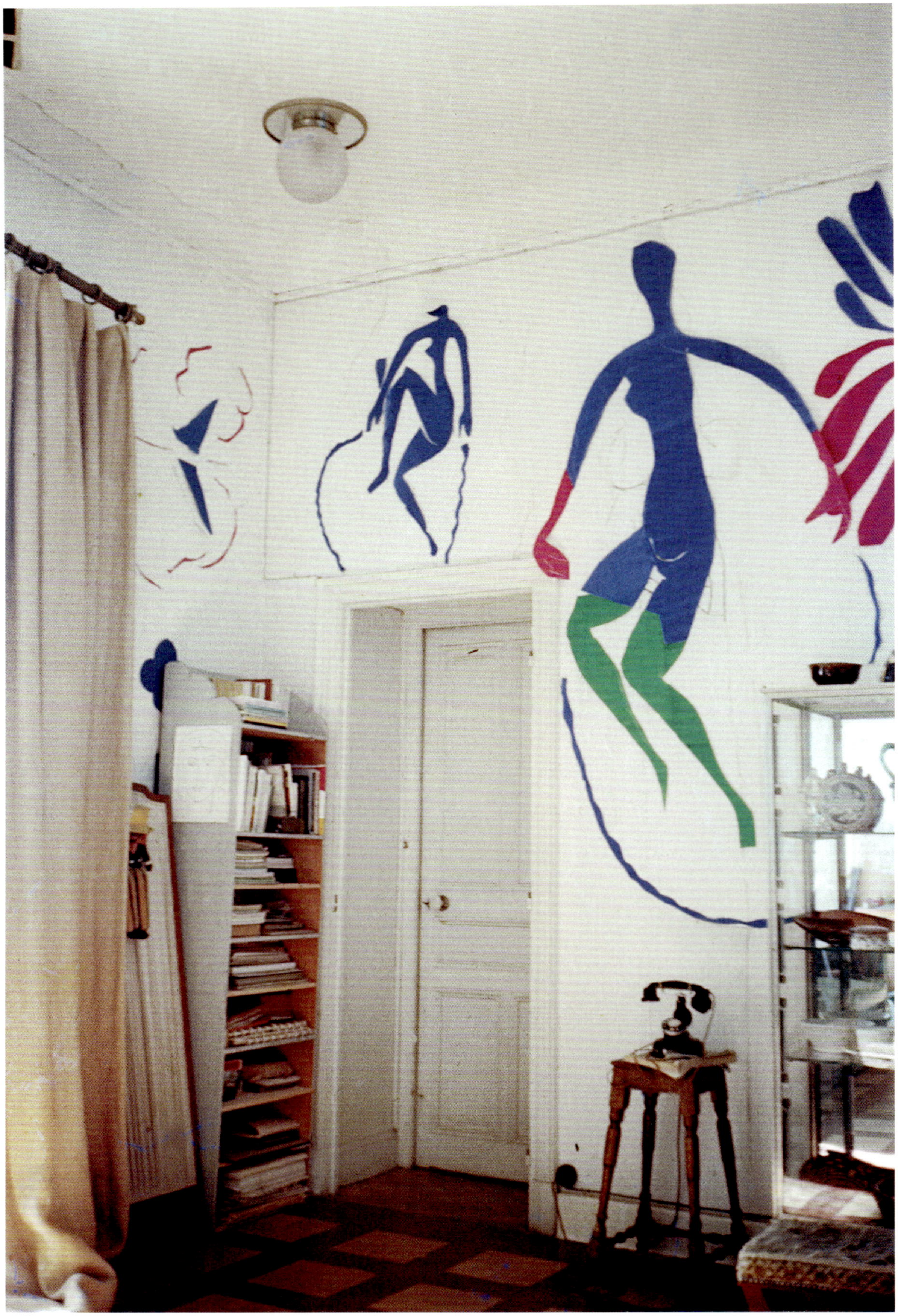

Tetsuo Abe, Hôtel Régina, Nice, 28 September 1952 (no. 117)

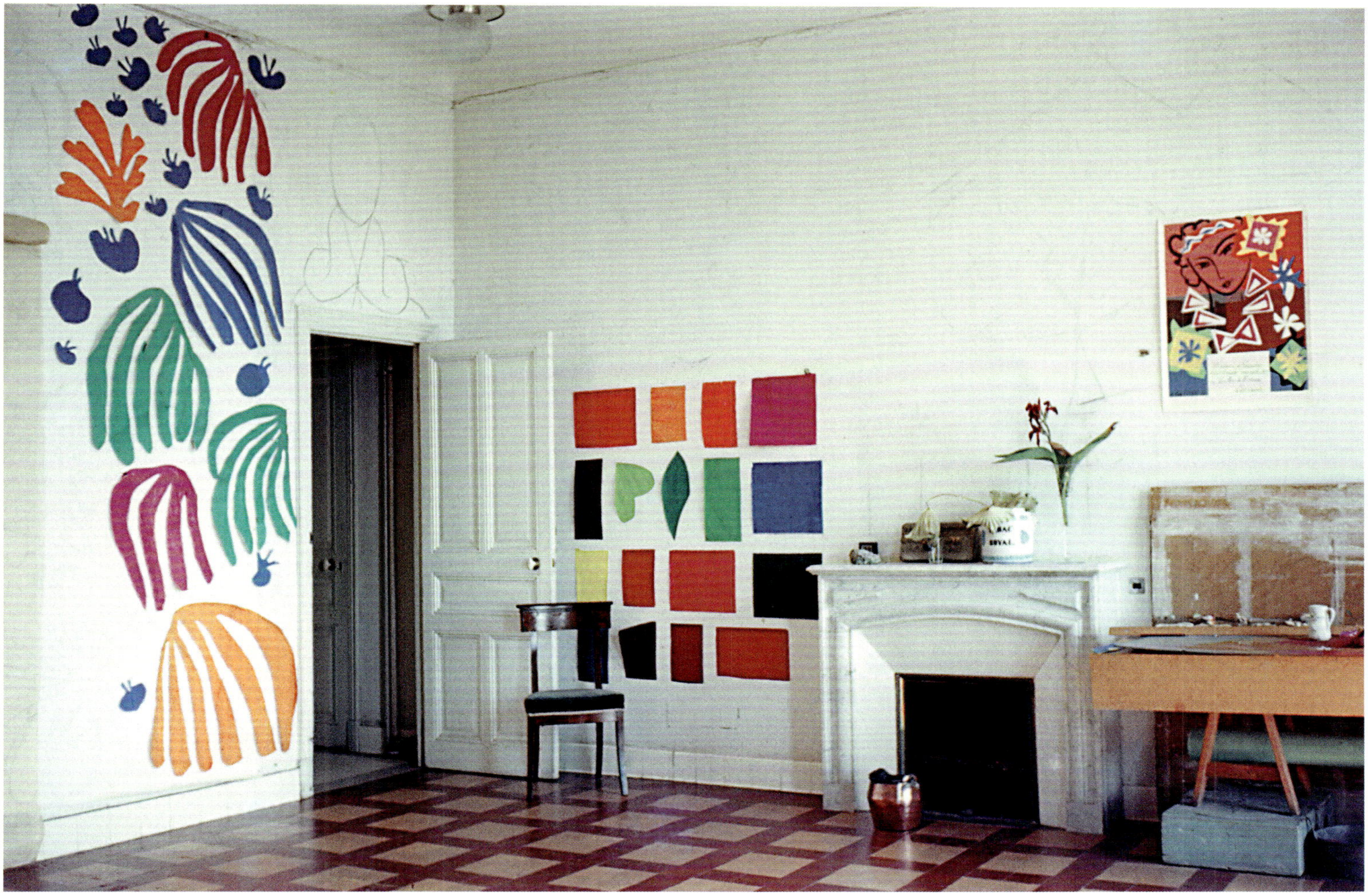

Tetsuo Abe, Hôtel Régina, Nice, 28 September 1952 (no. 118)

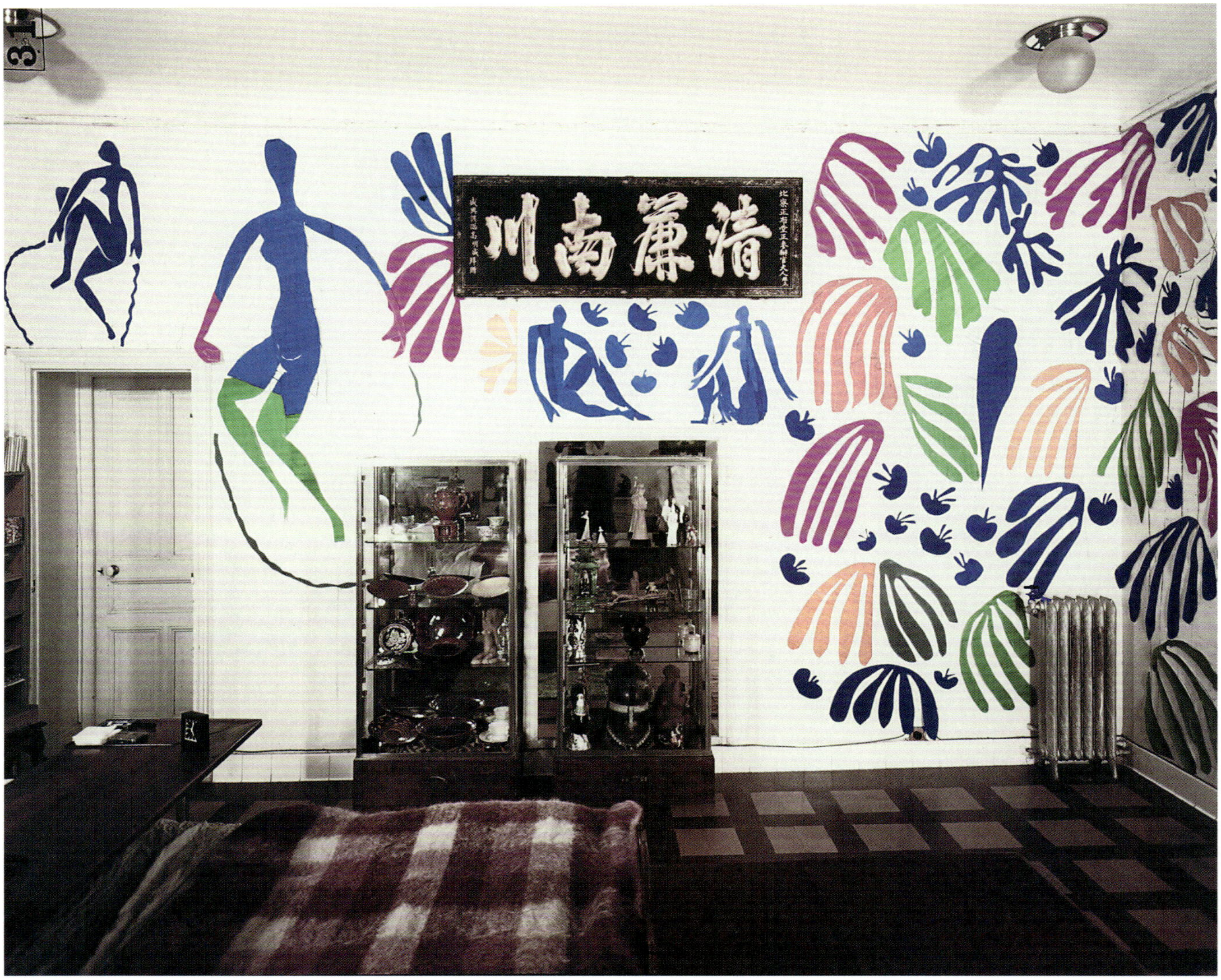

Lydia Delectorskaya, Hôtel Régina, Nice, 1952 (nos. 117–18, 120)

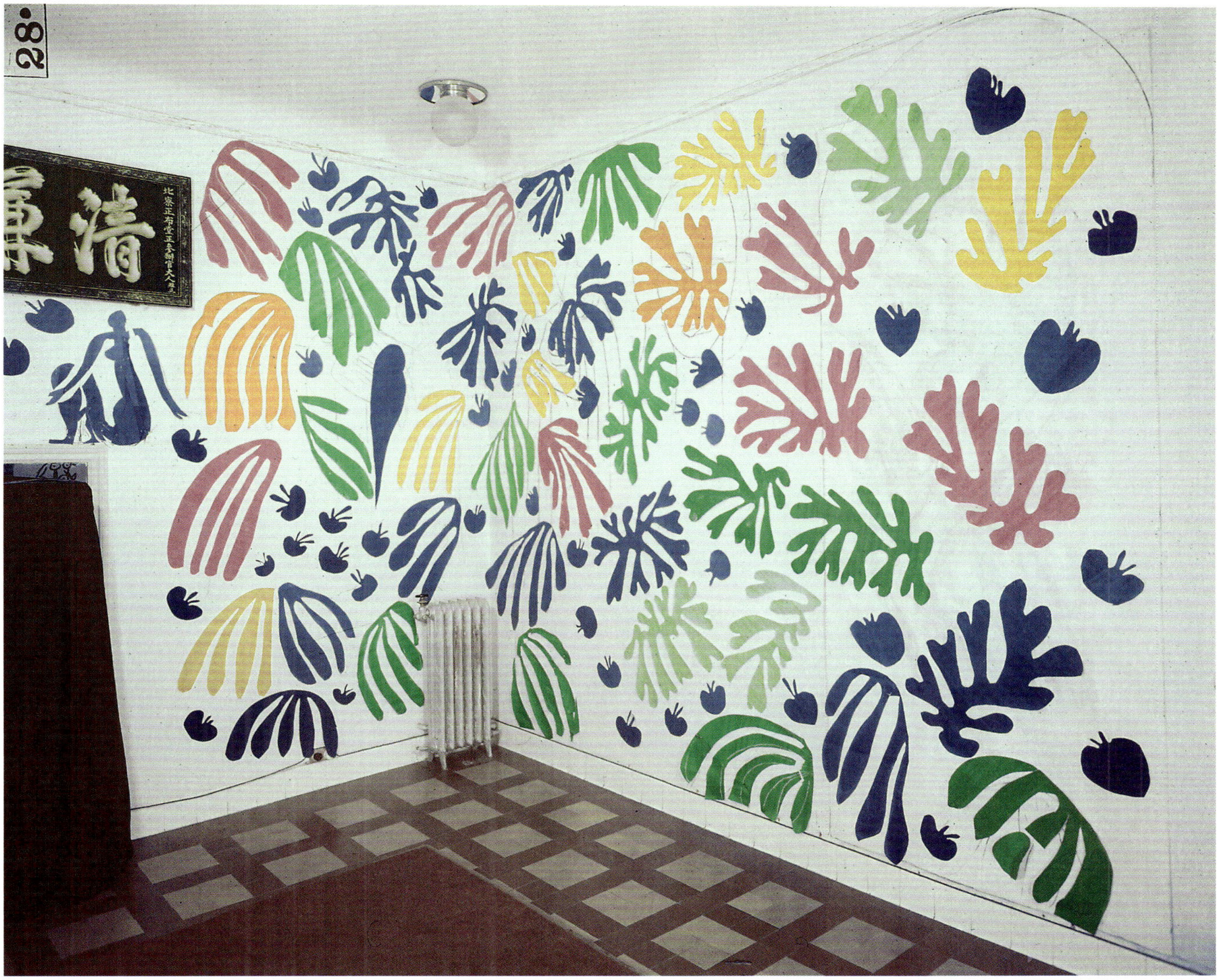

Lydia Delectorskaya, Hôtel Régina, Nice, 1952 (nos. 118, 120)

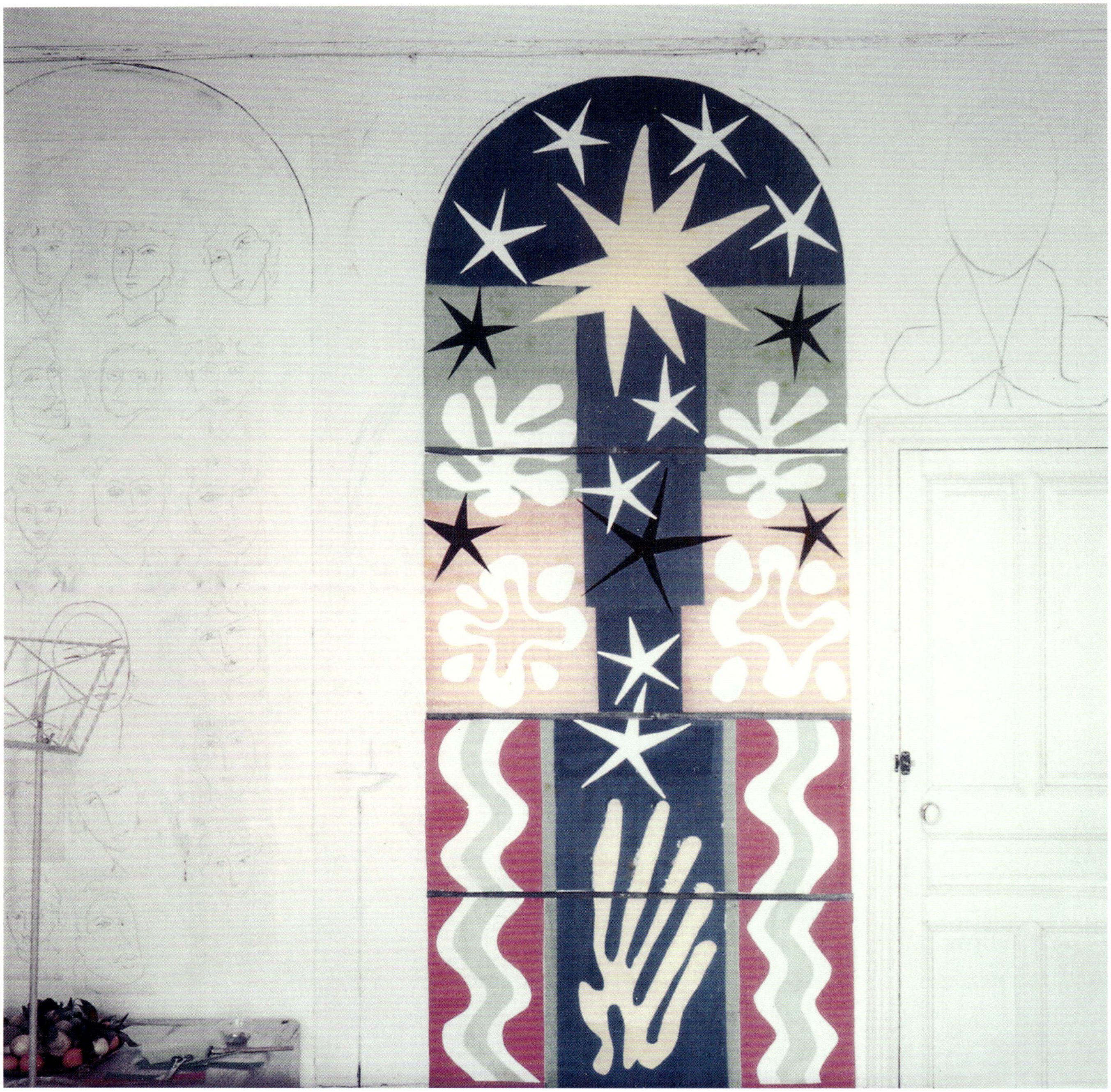

Lydia Delectorskaya, Hôtel Régina, Nice, c. 1952 (no. 98)

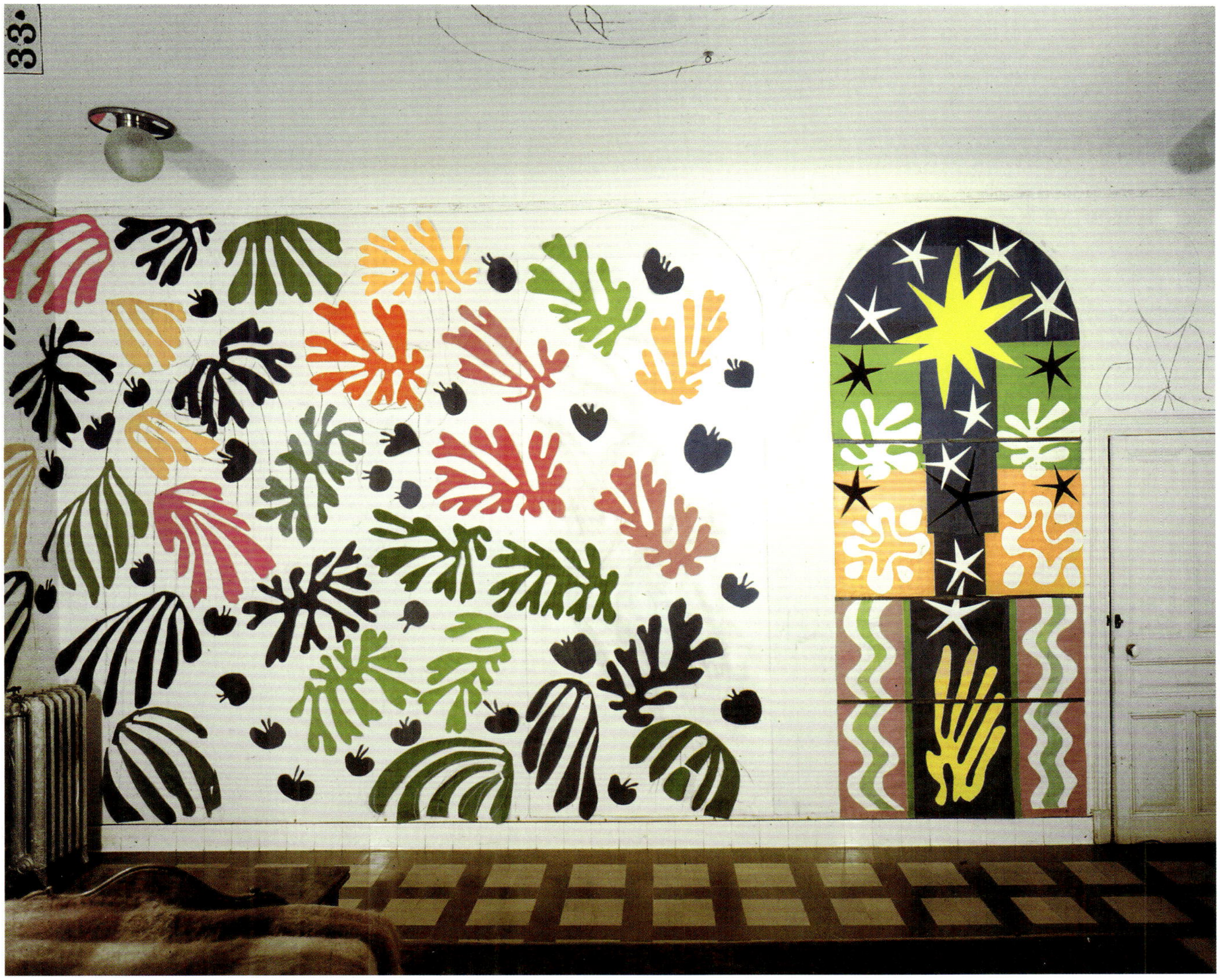

Lydia Delectorskaya, Hôtel Régina, Nice, 1952 (nos. 98, 118)

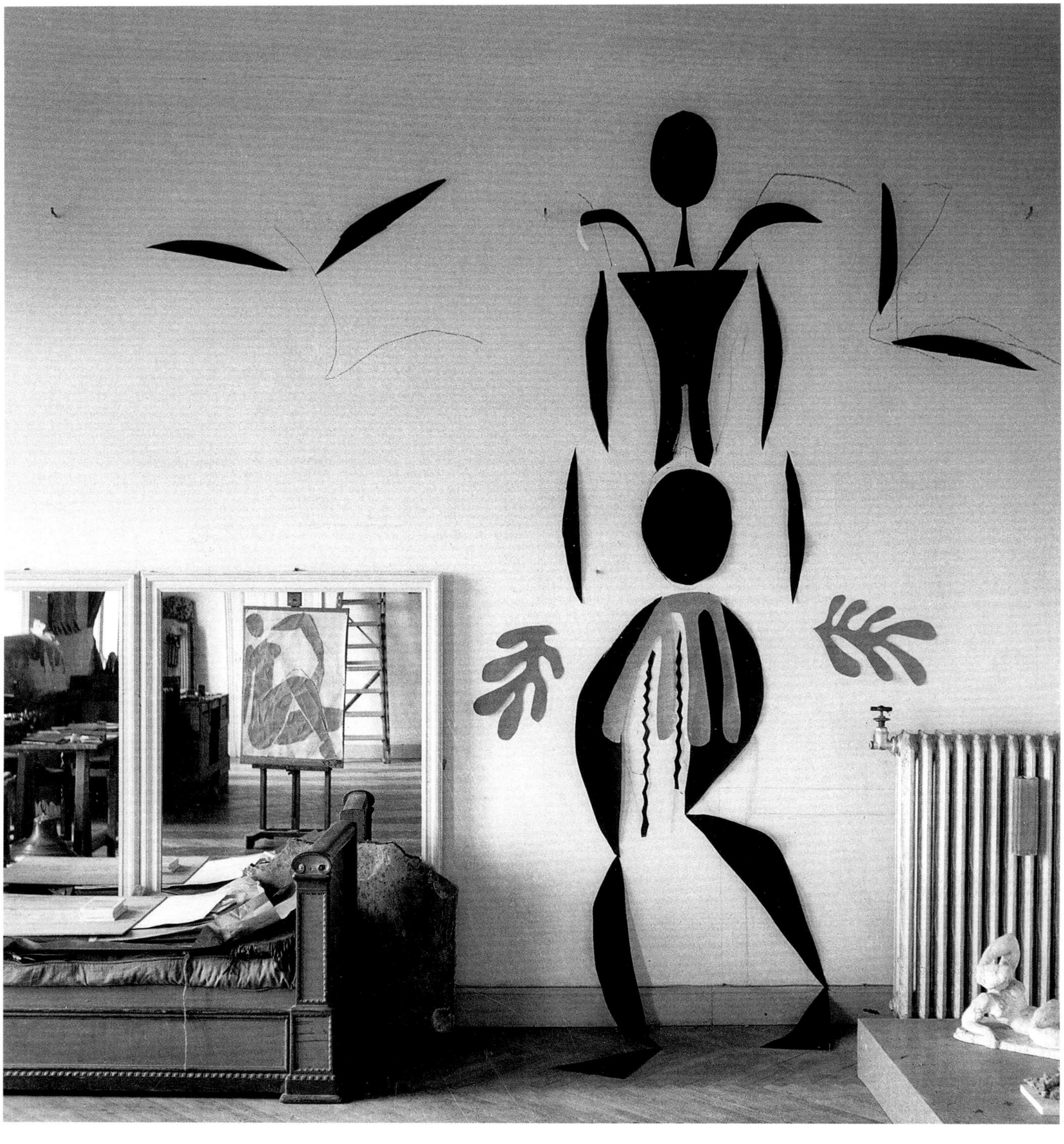

Hélène Adant, Hôtel Régina, Nice, 1952 (no. 107)

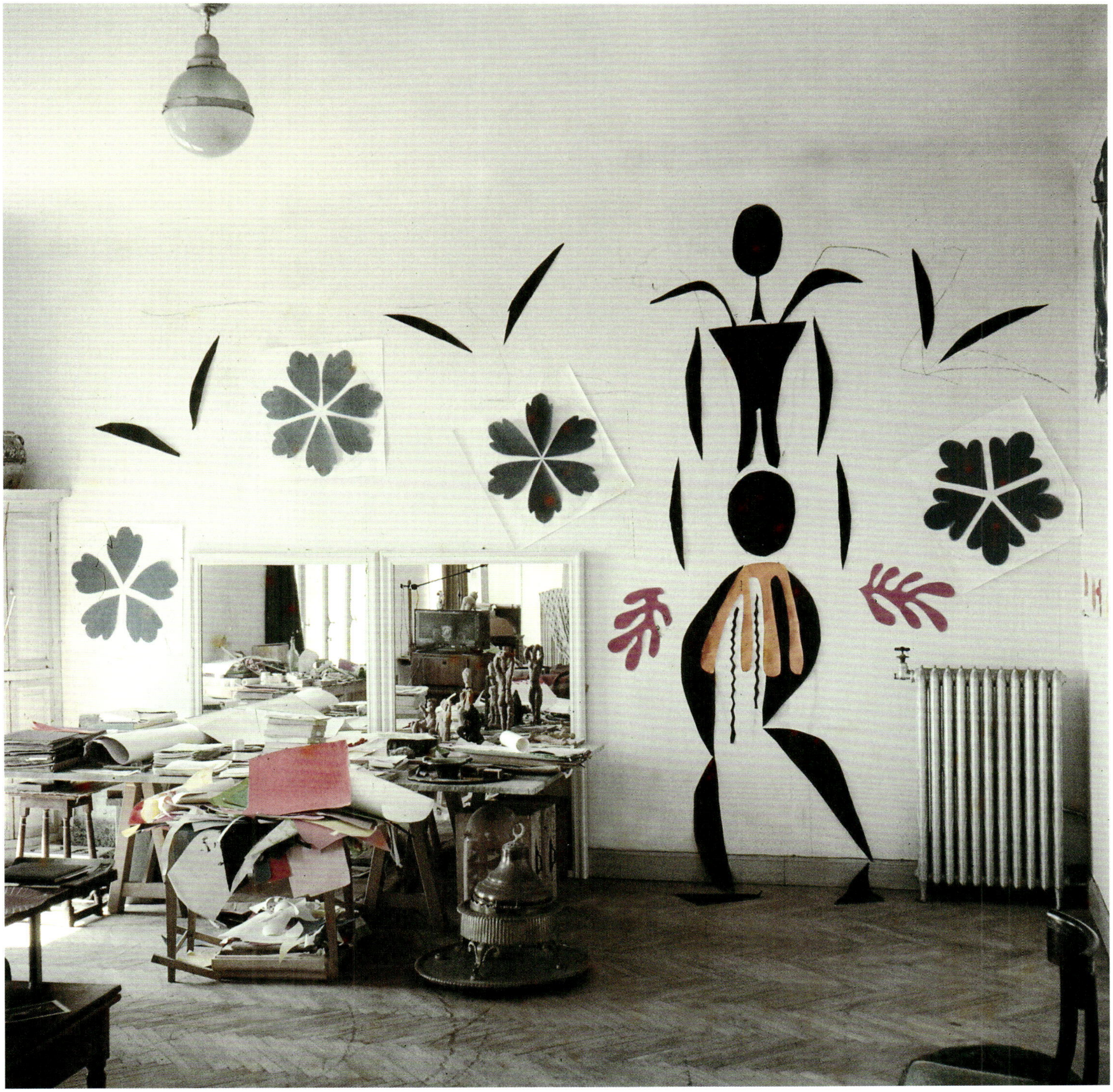

Lydia Delectorskaya, Hôtel Régina, Nice, c. 1952

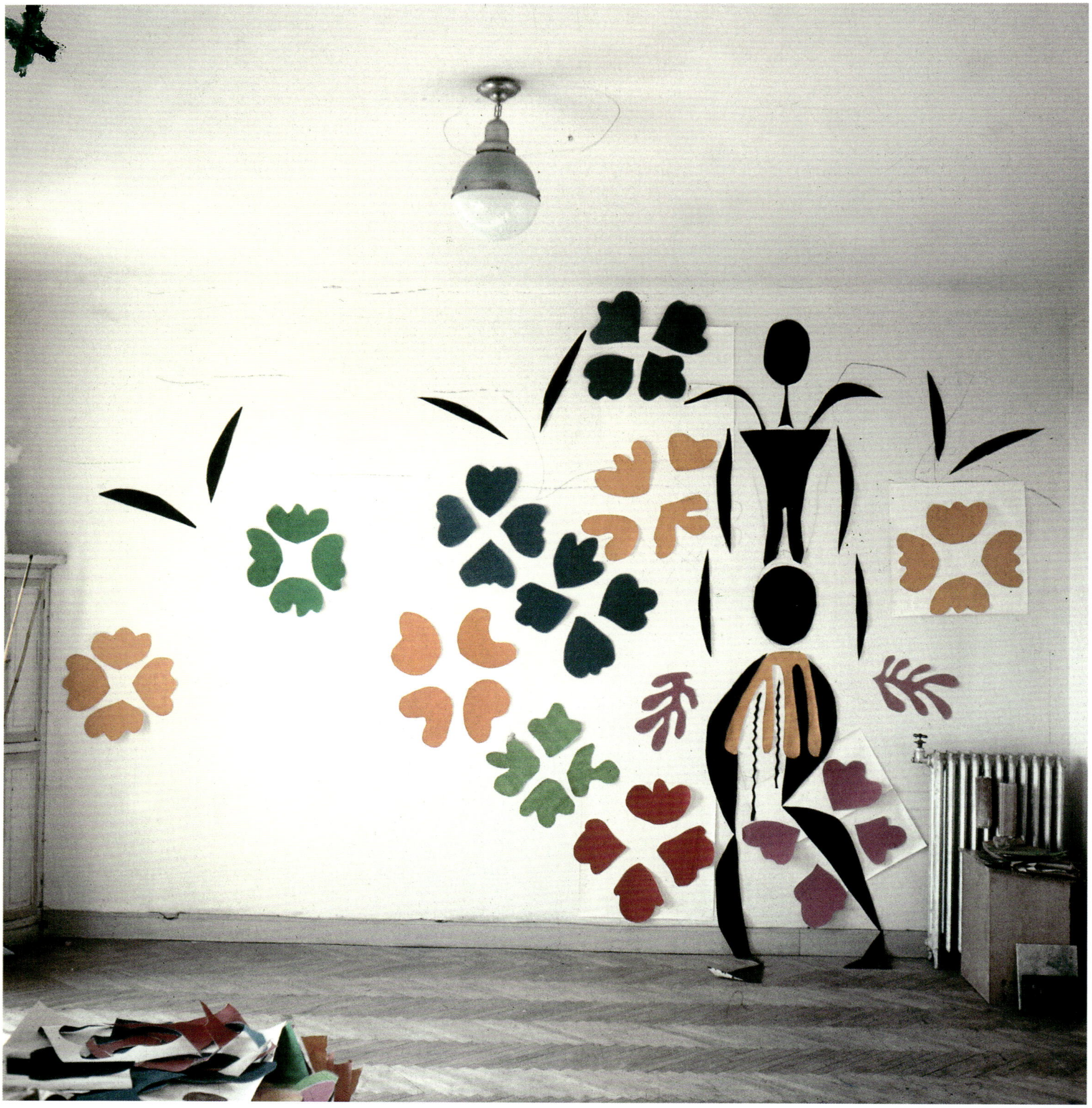

Lydia Delectorskaya, Hôtel Régina, Nice, c. 1952

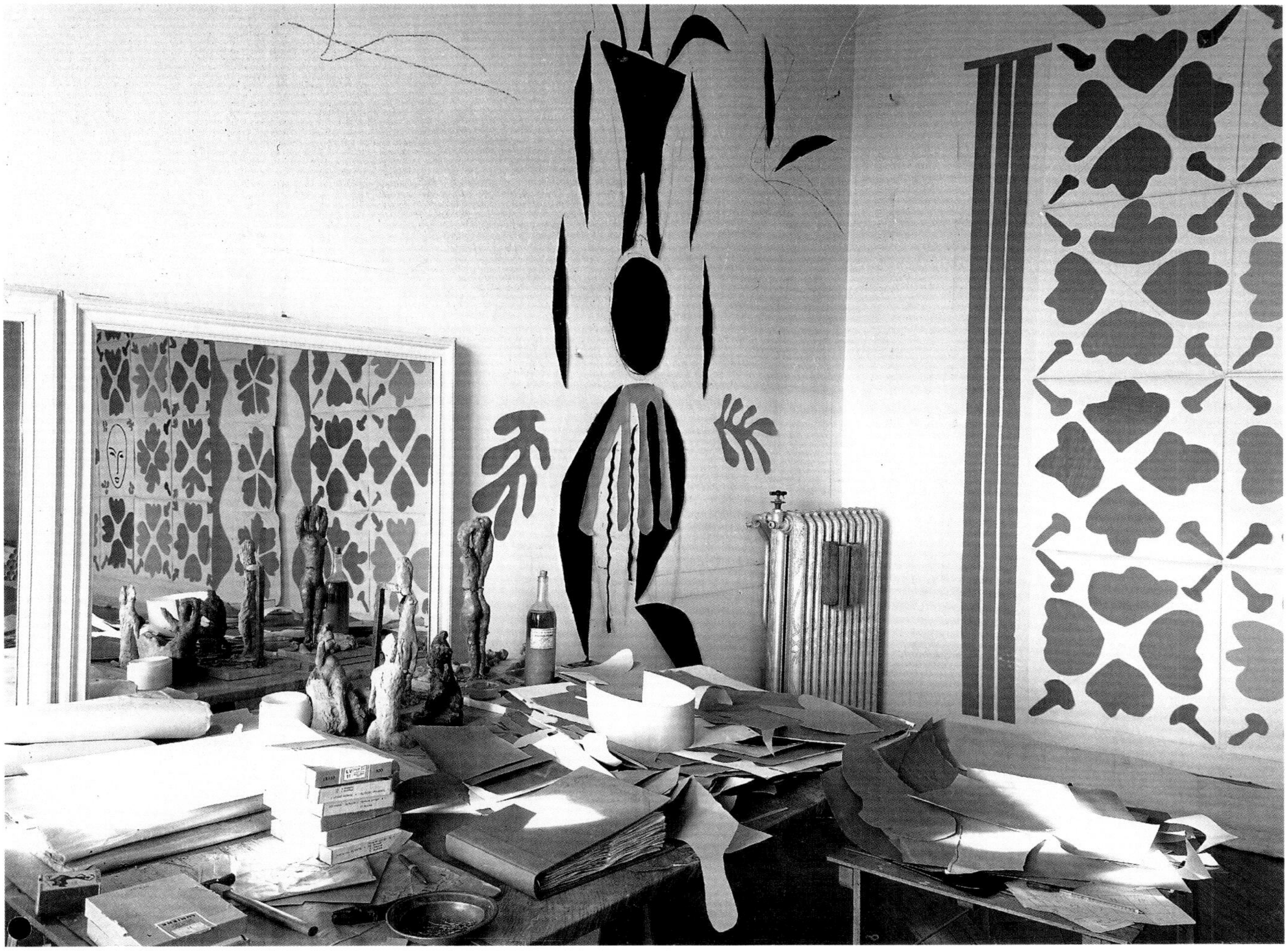

Hélène Adant, Hôtel Régina, Nice, 1952 (no. 131)

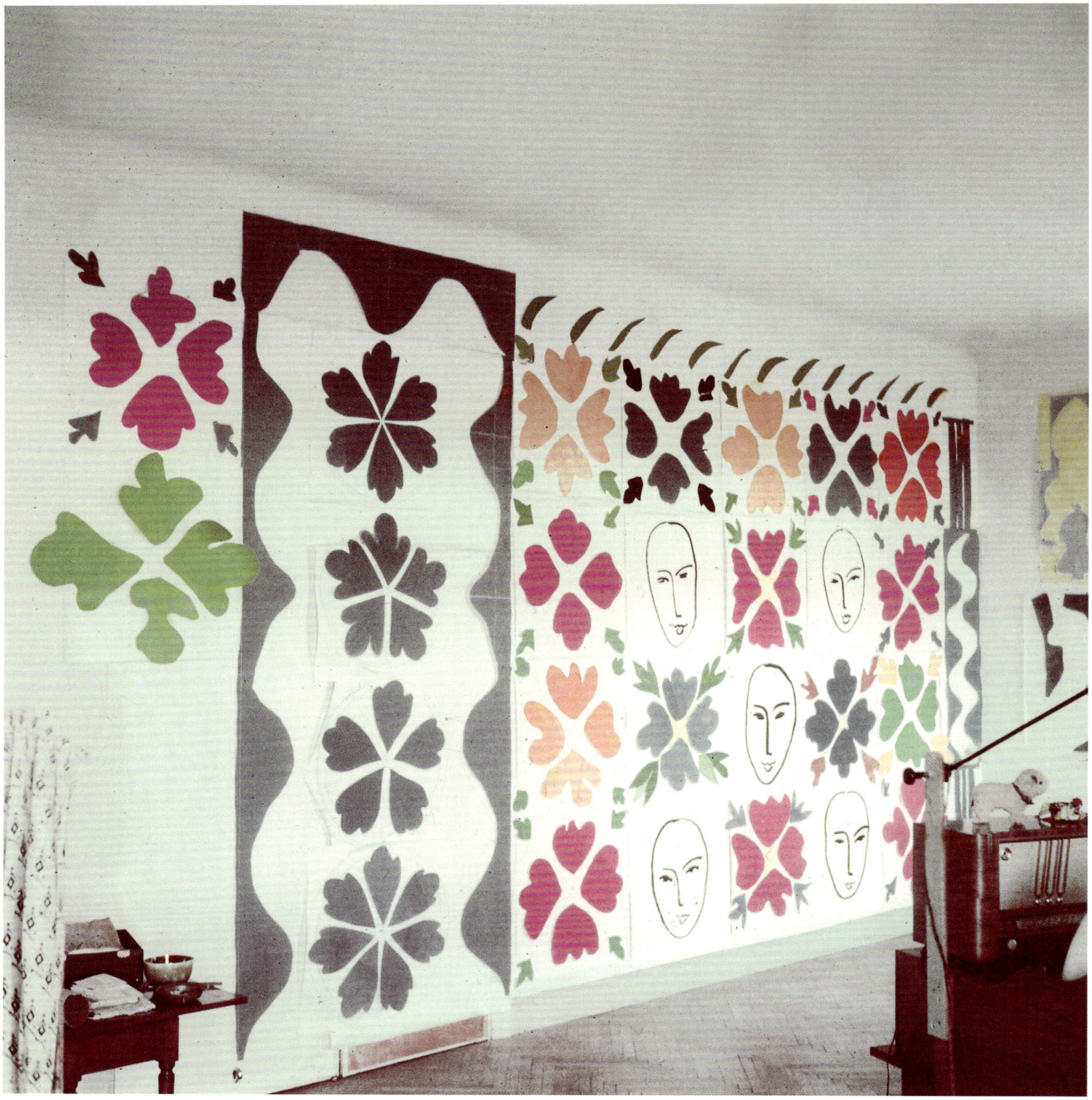

Lydia Delectorskaya, Hôtel Régina, Nice, c. 1952 (nos. 89, 115, 122, 131)

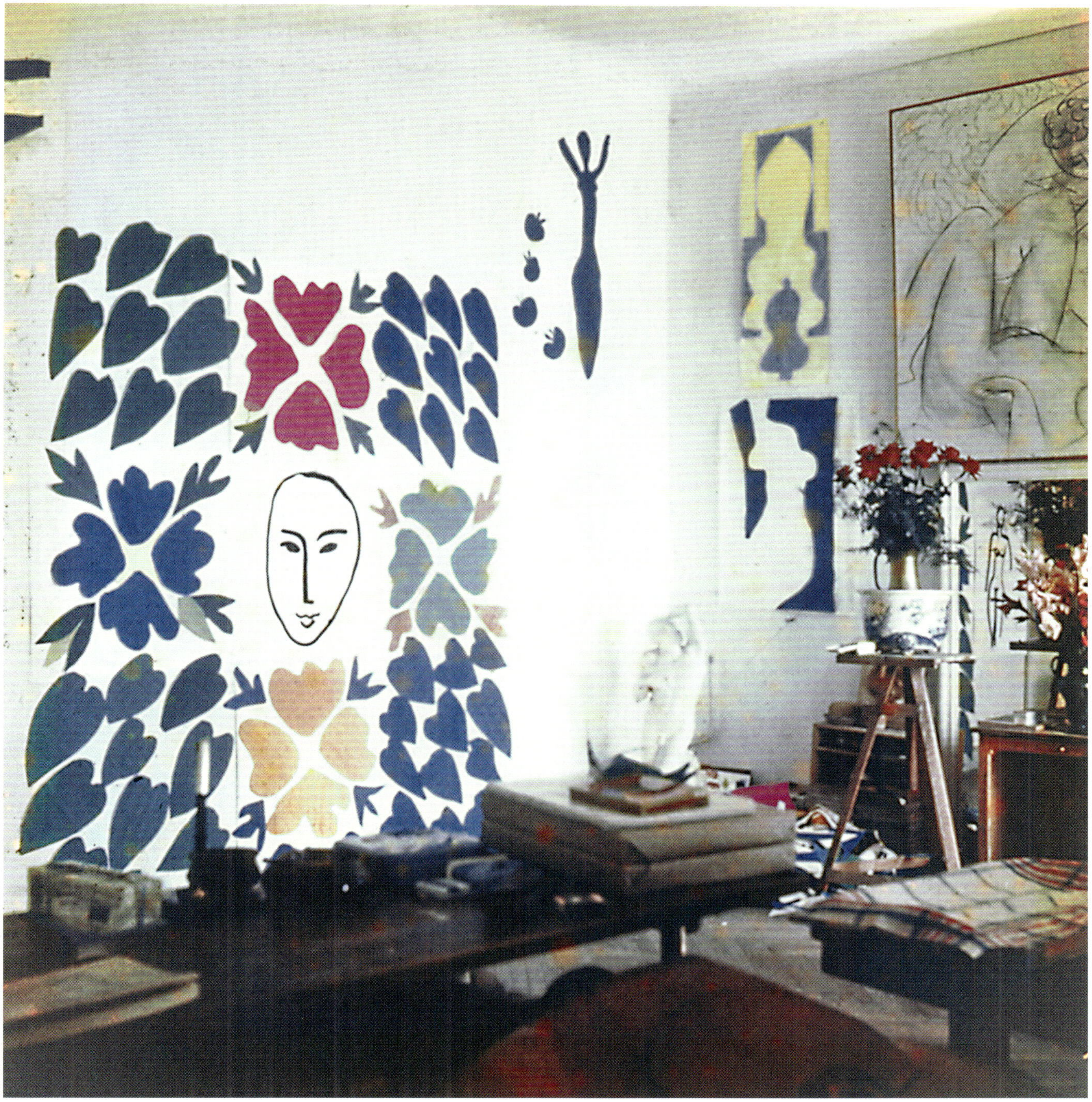

Lydia Delectorskaya, Hôtel Régina, Nice, c. 1952 (nos. 89, 115, 123, 131)

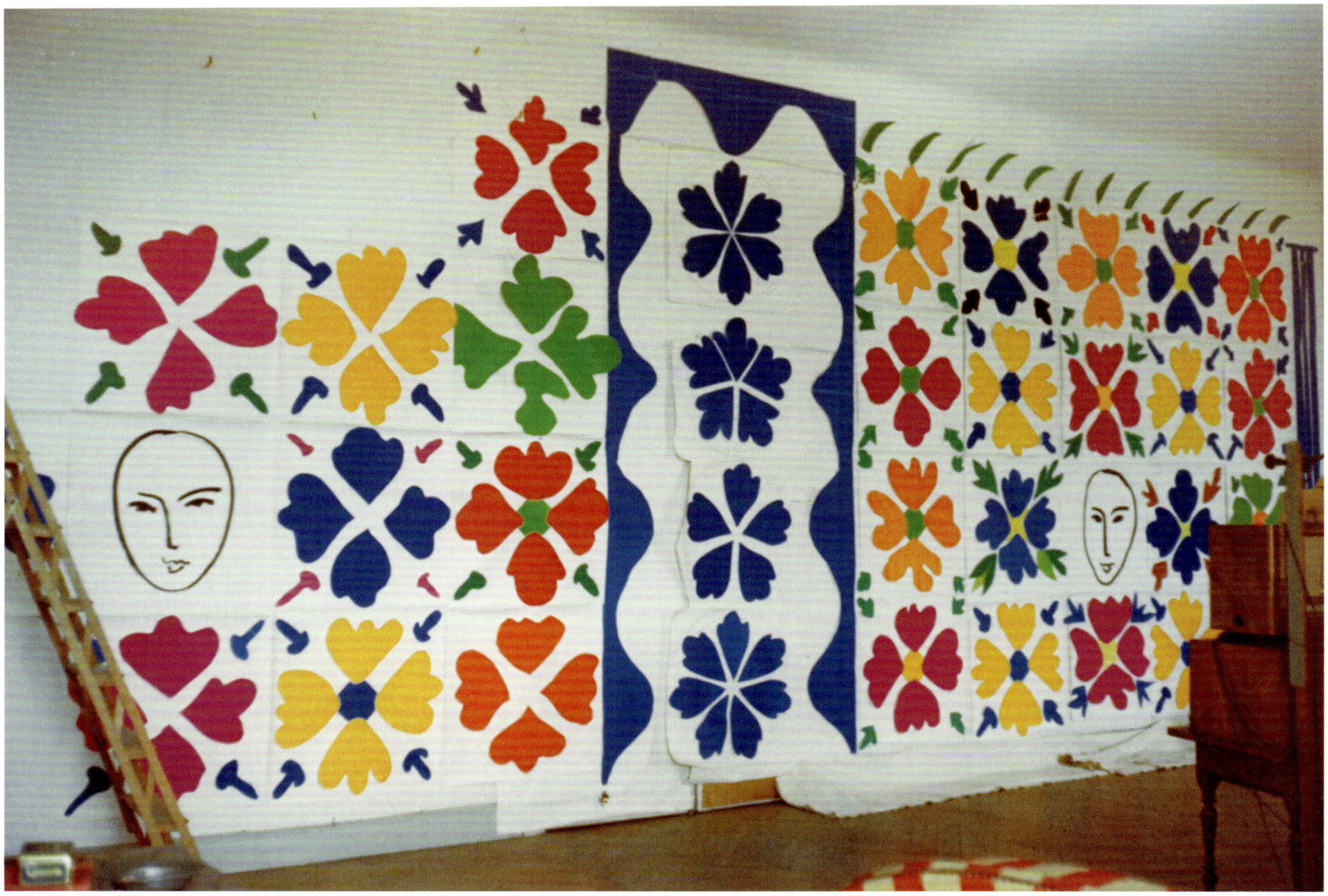

Tetsuo Abe, Hôtel Régina, Nice, 28 September 1952 (no. 131)

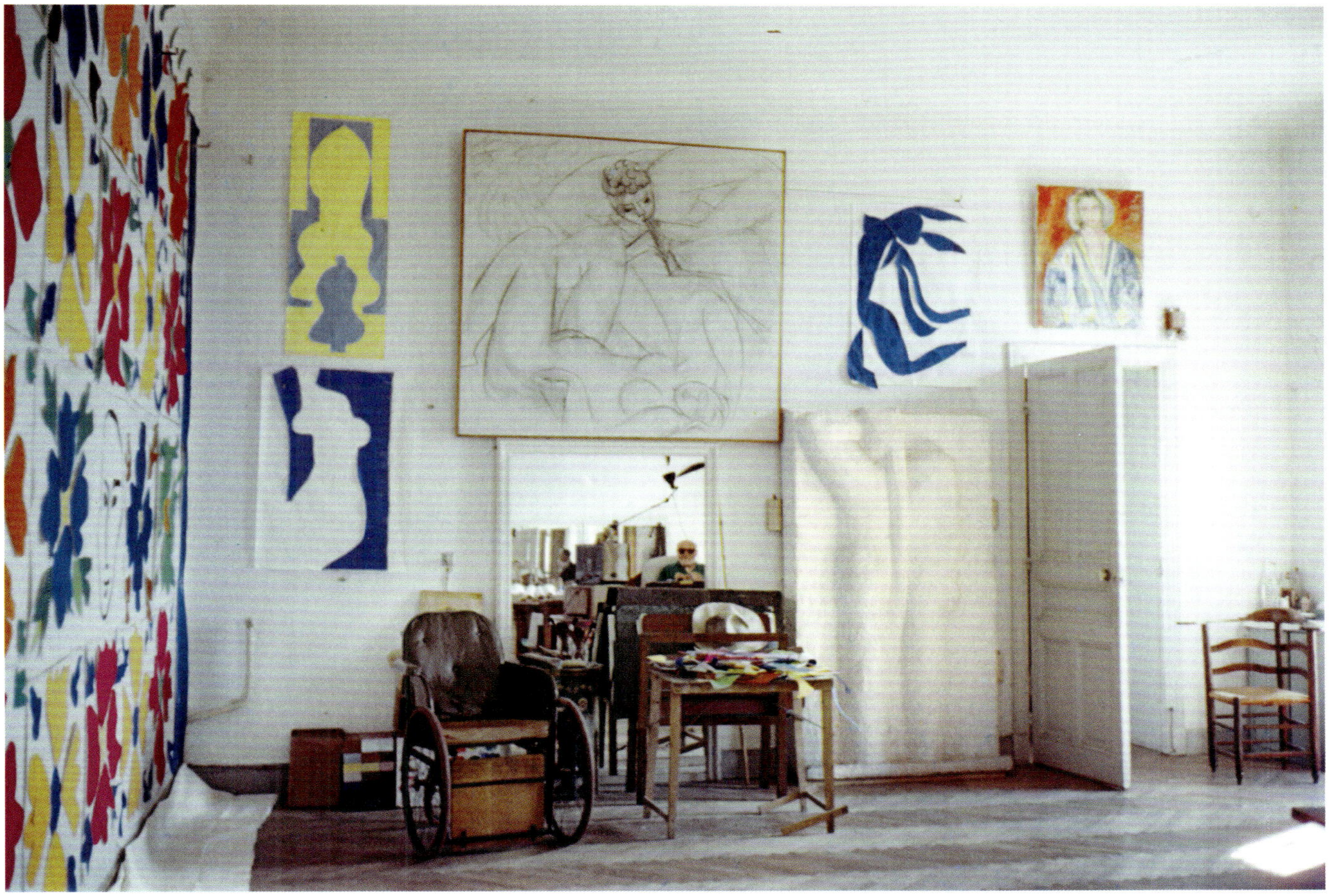

Tetsuo Abe, Hôtel Régina, Nice, 28 September 1952 (nos. 89, 115, 131)

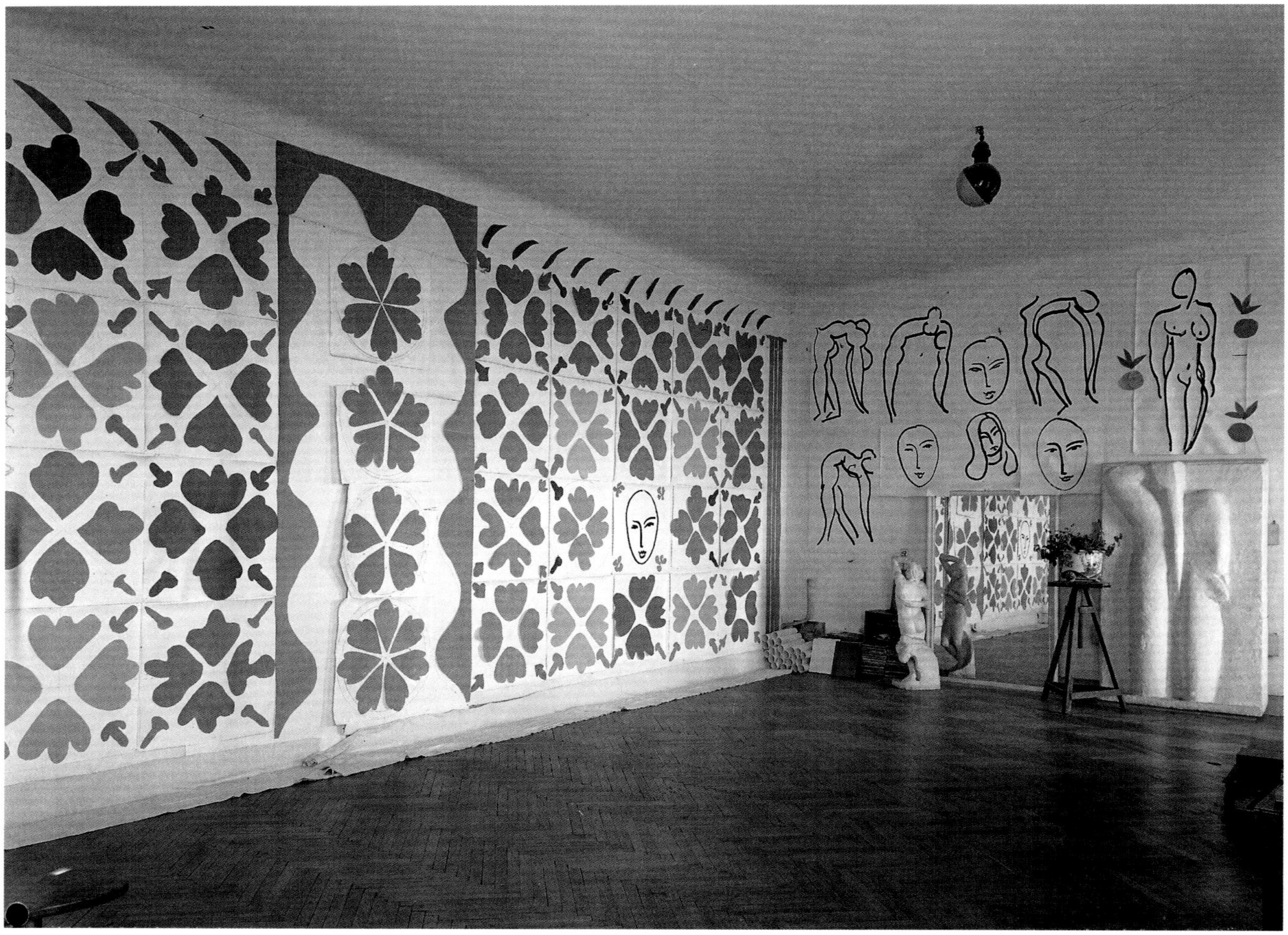

Hélène Adant, Hôtel Régina, Nice, c. 1953 (no. 131)

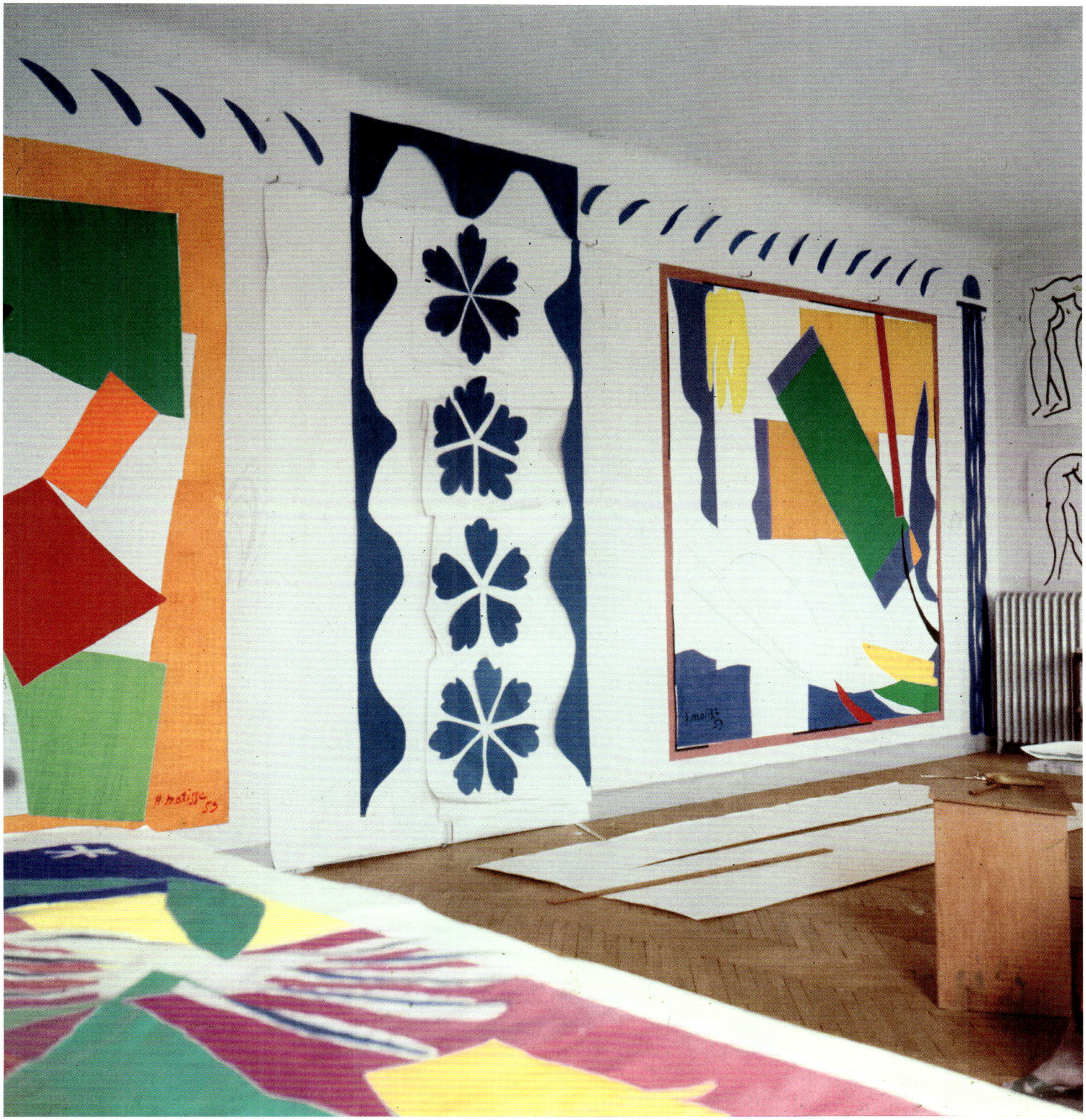

Lydia Delectorskaya, Hôtel Régina, Nice, c. 1953 (nos. 85, 129–31)

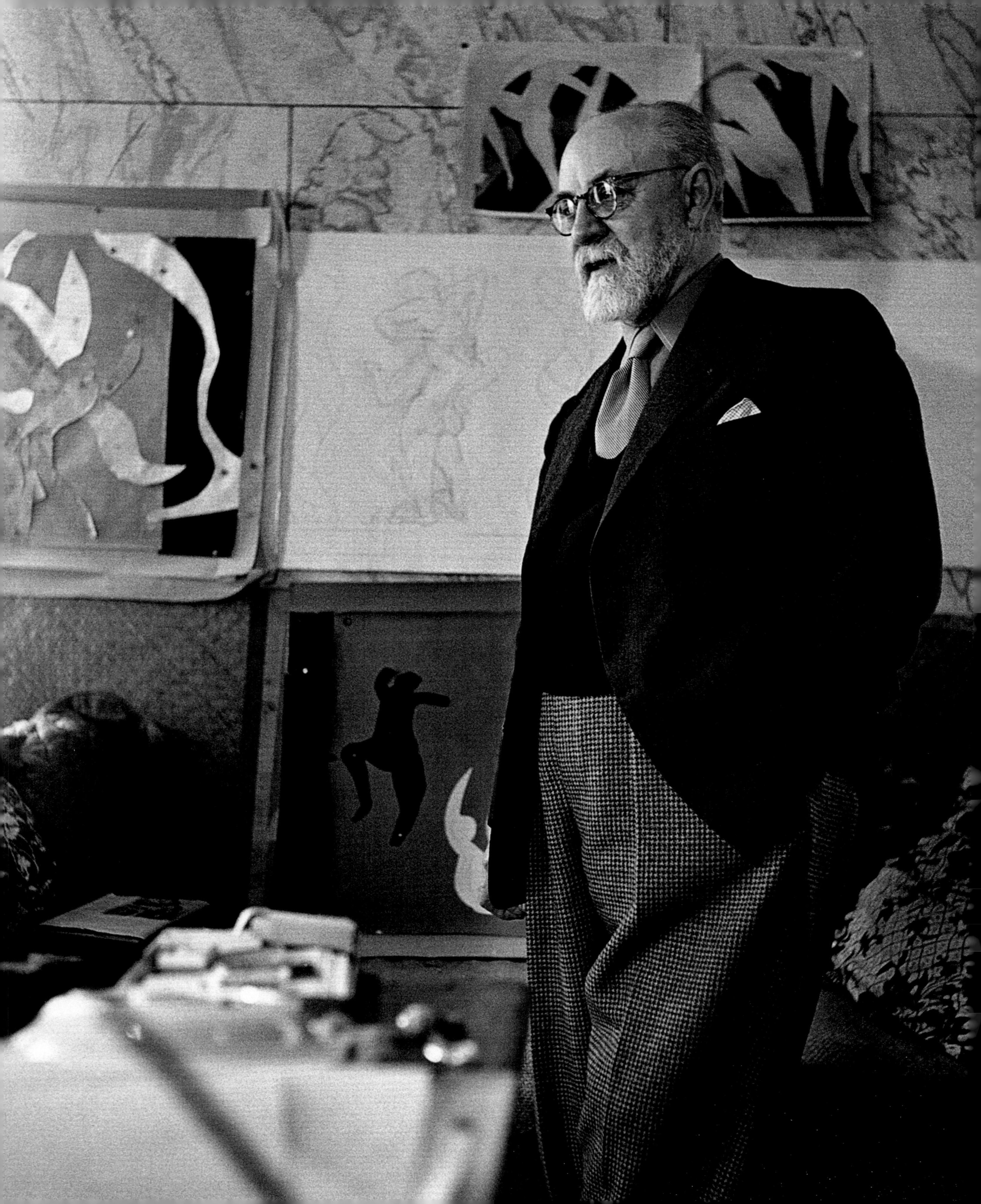

AVANT la LETTRE

Samantha Friedman

In 1938 the photographer Roger Schall visited Matisse on the fourth floor of 1 Place Charles-Félix in Nice to take pictures of the artist and his studio for a piece in *Vogue*. Though shot during this visit, the photograph seen here (fig. 9) was not among those that ultimately illustrated the article when it appeared in that year's June 15th issue; Schall's shot of the artist silhouetted against the cages of his aviary took full-page precedence instead. Two additional, smaller photographs (fig. 10) capture artwork *in situ*, though seemingly more to convey the interior's ambience than to record the artist's process. These images serve the accompanying prose's claim that 'the studio is far more like a salon, with plants, beautiful old pieces of furniture, charcoal studies of works in progress, and a mannequin's stand, left in place, with the posing dress thrown over a chair'.[1]

The main purpose of the piece was to publicise Matisse's designs for an upcoming Ballet Russe de Monte Carlo production, choreographed by Léonide Massine to a symphony by Dmitri Shostakovich. The ballet would premiere in Monte Carlo on 11 May 1939 with the title *Rouge et Noir*, though by the time it opened in Paris on 5 June of that year, its name had been changed to *L'Étrange Farandole*.[2] A large colour reproduction of 'Matisse's own sketch of monumental dancing figures for the backdrop of "La Farandole"' leads the article (fig. 11).[3] Though if the sketch's relationship to the ballet project were not clearly stated in its caption and the date of '38' not plainly inscribed, one might easily mistake it for a study relating to Matisse's large mural decoration for Albert Barnes's home

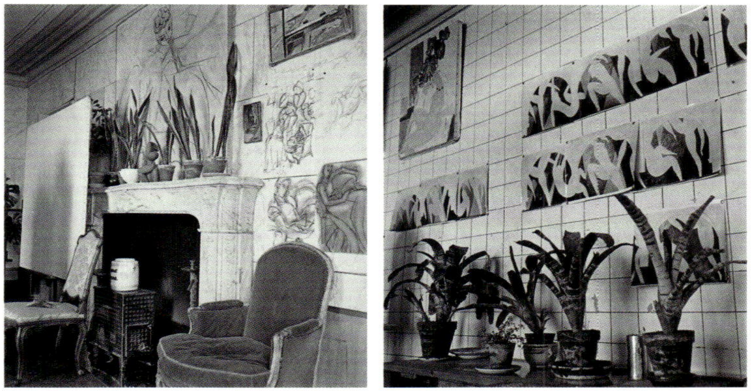

Fig. 10 Two photographs by Roger Schall ('The Studio – Paintings in Prospect on the Wall' and 'The Aviary – Ballet Studies on the Wall') as laid out in *Vogue*, 15 June 1938, p. 30

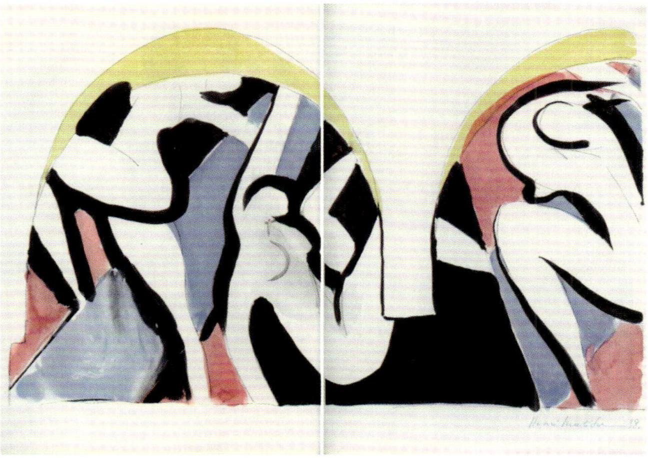

Fig. 11 'Matisse's own sketch of monumental dancing figures for the backdrop of "La Farandole"', as laid out in *Vogue*, 15 June 1938, pp. 28–9

Opposite: Fig. 9 Place Charles Félix, Nice, 1938

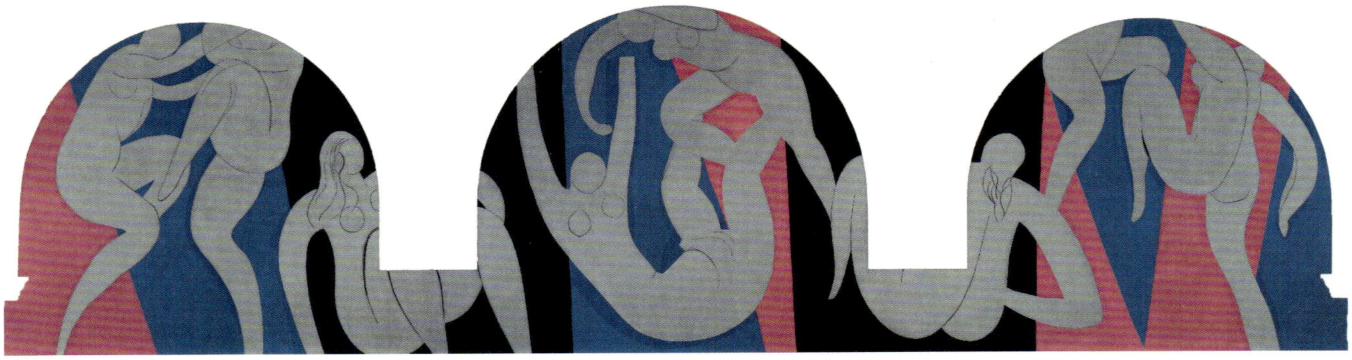

Fig. 12 *The Dance* (Merion Dance Mural), 1932–3. Oil on canvas, left panel: 339.7 × 441.3 (133¾ × 173¾); centre panel: 355.9 × 503.2 (140⅛ × 198⅛); right panel: 338.8 × 439.4 (133⅜ × 173). The Barnes Foundation, Philadelphia

in Merion, Pennsylvania. Its composition and palette relate more closely to that commission, completed in 1933 (fig. 12), than to the final designs for Massine's ballet.

This colour study represents just one example of visual evidence for an acknowledged connection between the Barnes and Ballet Russe projects. On visiting the Nice garage where the mural was under way, Matisse remembered, Massine 'was captivated by the great dancing movement, the grand rhythm of my composition: "That's the kind of dance I hope to see one day! Wouldn't you care to help me by redoing it as a ballet set?"'[4] Lydia Delectorskaya, Matisse's principal studio assistant and secretary during this period, remembered Massine's response to the work in progress as having been even more direct: '"Give us this for the décor!"'[5] Whatever the tenor of the request, Matisse satisfied it, adopting the lunettes of Merion's architecture for the ballet's set and replacing the painted dancers with live ones. Consequently, studies for the two projects can be nearly indistinguishable, and *Vogue*'s caption, 'The Aviary – Ballet Studies on the Wall', becomes crucial for identifying the compositions in the shot at the article's lower left, as they equally resemble a series of photographs taken of the Barnes commission in progress.

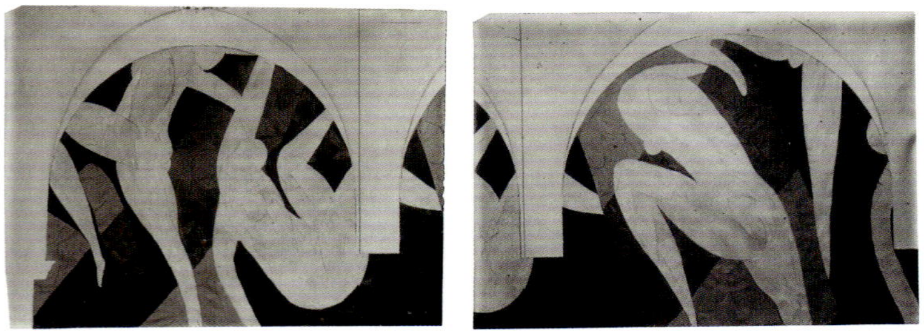

Fig. 13 Photographs of Cut Paper Composition for the *Paris Dance Mural*, 8 March 1932. The Barnes Foundation Archives, Merion

As Matisse developed this mural – with the help of a new technique of pinning, moving and cutting pieces of painted paper – he had photographs made regularly throughout its multiple phases (see no. 3).[6] This record of the mural's evolution not only enabled the artist to keep his transatlantic client abreast of developments,[7] and had the happy side effect of preserving the process for posterity, it also helped Matisse to *see* the composition – to visualise its possible end and revise it accordingly. A pair of these photographs (fig. 13) hang behind Matisse's head in Schall's ultimately unused shot. Documenting their presence among a cluster of works made between 1935 and 1938, this image demonstrates how a visual cue of the Barnes mural's development allowed Matisse not only to clarify that project's final composition but also to imagine future works – and future methods. If we know already, from both testimony and result, that Matisse's work on the Barnes decoration directly informed the design for *Rouge et Noir*, this photograph reveals *how* the translation took place. More crucially, it also suggests how a cut-paper working method that served as a means for realising various decorative commissions ultimately became an independent and radical end in itself.

From April 1931, when he first began to sketch out the Barnes mural on three full-scale canvases, to the end of that summer, Matisse developed the composition in charcoal and oil paint.[8] But after returning to Nice from a September trip to Italy, stimulated by the monumental possibilities of Giotto's Paduan frescoes, he adopted a new system of working. In order to cover large areas of the composition more quickly, and to make changes more efficiently, Matisse began to compose by pinning cut pieces of paper, pre-painted by a housepainter in the colours of the mural's palette, directly onto the canvas.[9] A visitor to the garage recalled how changes were made: 'Matisse, armed with a piece of charcoal at the end of a long stick, would walk up and down in front of the cartoon and draw outlines of the changes he wished to make and a young woman whom one had not noticed before would step out, climb a ladder and rearrange the coloured papers.'[10] When a mistake in the dimensions, discovered in February 1932, required Matisse to start over on new canvases, he enlisted the cut-out method once again.[11]

The process that would become the basis for the mature cut-out practice of Matisse's last decade was thus established, though the technique remained, for the time being, purely a means to an end. The artist was sufficiently aware of Dr Barnes's difficult reputation to be generally nervous about his client's reaction, but he was particularly sensitive about his new method. 'I have now "worked" with some blue paper for the background and gray for the figures in a way to be able to have it painted when all will be well fixed', Matisse wrote to his son and dealer Pierre, '*(but it is necessary not to say anything about this)*.'[12] The wording of Pierre's response suggests that the desire to hide this technique was implicit: 'I have naturally said nothing about the fashion in which Papa is working, I mean the cuttings of paper.'[13]

If Matisse regarded his new method as a kind of shameful secret, he nonetheless sensed its potential. Just as he had affixed studies for his 1909–10 *Dance* to the wall when he was starting the Barnes mural,[14] he now pinned studies for this latter decoration to the wall to help him design *Rouge et Noir*. Crucially, Matisse chose a photograph of a cut-paper version – rather than a drawn or painted stage – to think through his ballet designs. Perhaps the idea of employing cut paper to design for dance seemed natural to him, as he had used this method as early as 1919 for the ballet *Le Chant de Rossignol*, his first collaboration with Massine.[15] For this project Matisse built a scale model of the stage from a wooden crate, and 'all my décor, my accessories, and my characters [were] represented by little pieces of coloured paper which I moved around inside it'.[16] In an image that prefigures later descriptions of Matisse at work on his cut-outs, Vladimir Polunin, the scene painter who would execute Matisse's designs for *Le Chant*,

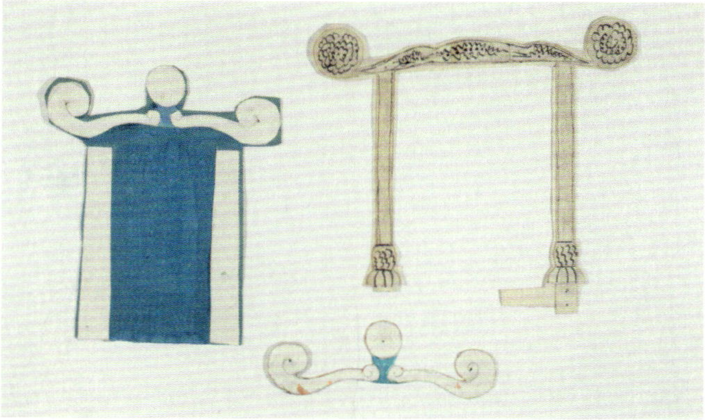

Fig. 14 Studies for the back wall in the ballet *Le Chant de Rossignol*, 1919. Gouache on paper, cut and pasted, and pencil, dimensions variable. Private collection

described how 'he set to work in the studio, scissors in hand, cutting out and piecing together a model'.[17] A small cut-out study for the set's back wall, presumably from this model, may represent the artist's earliest known work in the medium (fig. 14).

The photographs of the Barnes mural in progress not only provided Matisse with a prompt to use the cut-paper medium for his *Rouge et Noir* studies, they also offered a visual reminder of the formal possibilities for which that medium allowed. The method encouraged a compression of space that would inform the final painted mural and would also become a defining characteristic of the subsequent cut-out oeuvre's distinctive visual language. We can witness an example of this flattening taking place across four of the mural's successive stages, by watching the progression of the figure in the far-right lunette. In a charcoal rendering (fig. 15) the dancer twists in a classic contrapposto: her left leg extends in front of the right, while her torso counter-coils to face out.[18] Once Matisse begins to fill in the composition with bits of coloured paper, however (see no. 3), the interior lines that define a buttock or a neck are sacrificed in favour of the exterior line that bounds the figure's overall shape.[19] Consequently, what was initially the exterior of the dancer's left leg, stretched across her body, has become the interior of her lifted right leg. This now splayed body, the result of the artist responding to his new medium, can be seen as the origin of a form like the far-left figure in *Women and Monkeys* (1952), carved two decades later from a single sheet (no. 120).

These four views represent just a brief excerpt in the evolution of the Barnes mural, whose three

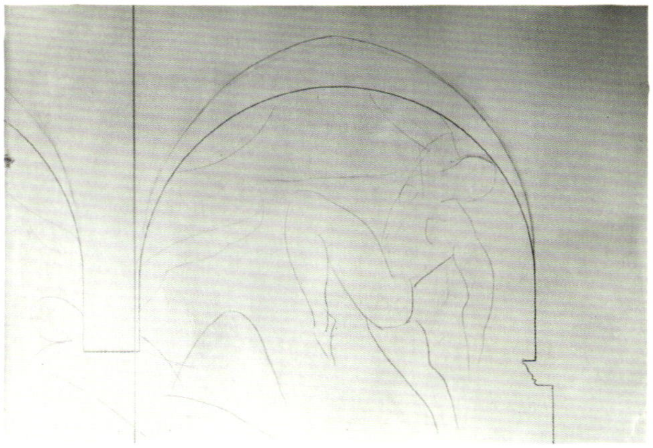

Fig. 15 Photograph of *Unfinished Dance Mural*, 1931
The Barnes Foundation Archives, Merion

versions were systematically documented over the course of two years.[20] The photographs hanging behind Matisse's head in Schall's studio shot were taken later, on 8 March 1932, and depict the other two lunettes of its tripartite composition.[21] We know that these references did not share a wall with the studies for *Rouge et Noir* purely by coincidence, nor did they serve merely as a general cue for the artist. Rather, the relationship between their forms and those of *Two Dancers*, 1937–8 (no. 6), the cut-out that appears in the lower centre of Schall's frame, confirms the extent to which these photographs constituted real compositional tools. Having myriad stages of the mural's progress to choose from, Matisse favoured this one, in which the tumbling figure is tucked into a ball, nose drawn to left knee. Except for its steadying right arm, which is lost in the transposition, the figure lends its shape almost exactly to the tumbler of *Two Dancers*. Matisse also adopts the left-most figure in these Barnes photographs as a model for the black dancer in the ballet design, if less directly. This transformation, from arcing profile to flat frontality, occurs through the same operation noted previously: once the interior line that locates one leg in front of the other is lost, a dynamic back view becomes a compressed anterior one. Even the architecture of *Two Dancers* seems beholden to the Barnes: a vertical strip of black-gouached paper intersects its tumbler's right leg just where the indication of a lunette crosses that of its predecessor.

In extracting these two figures from an intermediary stage of his mural design and rearticulating them in a study for his curtain design five years later, Matisse suppressed the hard-won labour of their piecemeal making in the fluid contours of discrete shapes cut from single sheets. These well-defined silhouettes were now ripe for further replication, and Matisse next split the standing and tumbling figures into two separate compositions. These nascent cut-outs would eventually become maquettes for the first two plates, *The Clown* (no. 18) and *The Toboggan* (no. 39), he executed for the seminal illustrated book *Jazz*. The publisher Tériade, for whom Matisse had already designed two covers of the review *Verve*,[22] had been pressing Matisse to do an album of cut-outs since August 1940.[23] But it wasn't until 1943 when Matisse, Lydia recalled, 'brought me the two unfinished compositions, drawn from elements leftover in his boxes from his work for the ballet (which – perfected – thereafter became *The Clown* and *The Toboggan* of *Jazz*). The project of an album reproducing 20 cut-outs, composed by H.M. specifically to the dimensions of the volume and reproduced in facsimile, was born there.'[24] Repurposing these leftovers required that they be adapted to fit the new book's design, for 'the two already-existing subjects weren't in the right format; one had to be reduced, the other mechanically enlarged.'[25]

In 1938, however, these elements were still meditations on the themes and forms of *Rouge et Noir*. For *The Clown* Matisse would ultimately flip

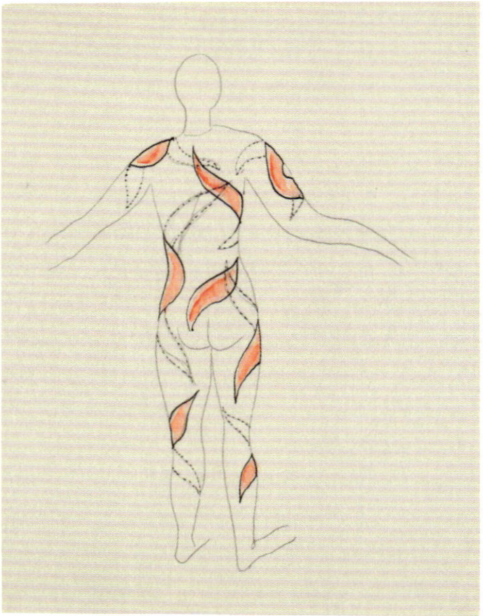

Fig. 16 Sketch for a costume
for the ballet *Rouge et Noir*, 1938

the black figure from *Two Dancers* – an operation facilitated by working with cut forms. And for *The Toboggan* he would rotate the now blue tumbler anticlockwise, just enough to invoke the horizontality of a sledging body. Further, the red motifs that adorn the figure in *The Clown* correspond closely to the forms winding around the ballet's costumes in both Matisse's preparatory drawings (fig. 16) and in the finished versions, which the artist painted directly onto the dancers' unitards.[26] However, unlike the 'large algae-like forms hugging the body',[27] as Lydia described the *Rouge et Noir* designs, the flashes of red in *The Clown* are sharp instead of sinuous, more fire than flora. In fact, their jagged quality seems to telegraph the very act of cutting that created them. Matisse figures forth his new method in another element of the composition as well: a vertical black ribbon results from making a single cut in a sheet of yellow, and simply pulling apart the two sides. He would later repeat this move in *The Wave*, c. 1952 (no. 122), isolating this elemental expression of the cut-out technique.

A gesture such as this – gently undulating, gliding – makes clear why Matisse likened the experience of cutting to the feeling of flying. 'You have no idea how, during the cutout paper period,' he recalled, 'the sensation of flight which emanated from me helped me better to adjust my hand when it used the scissors. It's rather difficult to explain. It's a kind of linear and graphic equivalence to the sensation of flight.'[28] It should therefore come as no surprise that the next iteration of our splayed, standing figure came in the guise of Icarus, that mythological aviator. The white form in a freestanding cut-out (no. 17) and his black double in another maquette for *Jazz* (no. 27) mirror each other, exploiting once again the cut-outs' propensity for reversal. Against a blue ground that stands for sky, the jagged motifs here become stars, demonstrating how Matisse's relatively constant repertory of cut forms adopts a multitude of significations, subject to context. Ultimately, this figure is once again reunited with its tumbling partner, in Matisse's design for the cover of *Verve*, vol. IV, no. 13, 1945. Both an initial multi-hued version (no. 15) and the monochromatic variation that would eventually be used evenly scatter the stars, interspersing them with the letters of the review's title, such that they once again become abstract ornament.[29]

Concurrent, then, with the development and propagation of these two figures – from the Barnes commission to ballet and book design – was

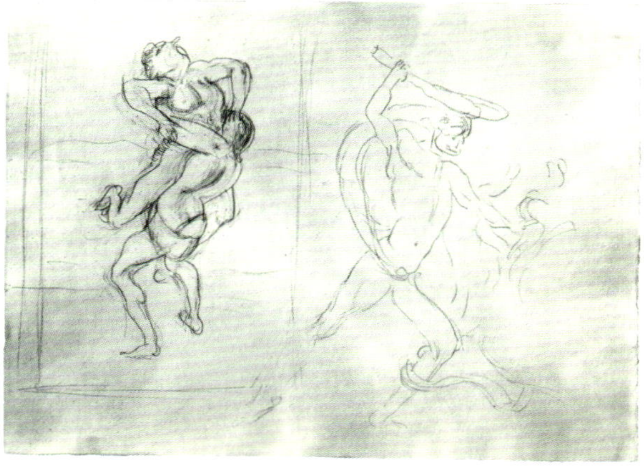

Fig. 17 Study after Antonio Pollaiuolo's *Hercules and Antaeus*, 1935. Pencil on paper, 28.7 × 38.5 (11⅓ × 15¼)

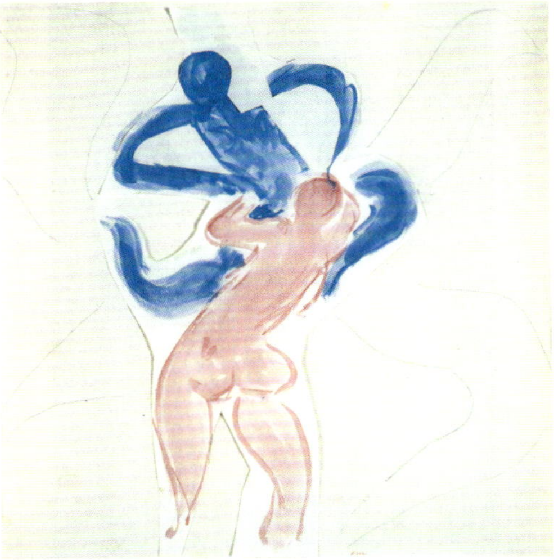

Fig. 18 Study for the ballet *Rouge et Noir* (after Antonio Pollaiuolo's *Hercules and Antaeus*), 1938. Gouache on paper, cut and pasted, mounted on board, 39 × 39 (15⅓ × 15⅓). Private collection

Matisse's gradual embrace of the cut-out method as an independent end, rather than merely a means. Where he once actively concealed the technique, he now, with *Jazz*, began to favour the pinned or pasted maquette to the finished, printed state (see pp. 126–9). Returning to Schall's Nice photograph, we can locate a parallel story about the medium's evolution towards autonomy in the other two works visible on the wall: a pencil study after the Italian Renaissance artist Antonio Pollaiuolo, faintly discernible in the centre, and a gouached paper cut-out maquette for the ballet's curtain design at the photograph's far left.

The drawing at the photograph's centre (fig. 17), for which Matisse copied Pollaiuolo's compositions of Hercules wrestling the giant Antaeus (left) and slaying the Hydra (right), could hardly be more traditional in both subject and technique.[30] Regardless, it was the composition of this 1935 study that Matisse appropriated three years later for the curtain design of *Rouge et Noir* and that played a key role in his development of a new medium. The grappling figures on the left side of the diptych perfectly communicated the ballet's theme – man's struggle with his destiny – and Matisse isolated the interlocked pair in a subsequent work whose awkwardly intermediate character makes it all the more noteworthy. Though the medium used in Study for the Ballet *Rouge et Noir* (after Antonio Pollaiuolo's *Hercules and Antaeus*; (fig. 18) bears the same 'gouache on paper, cut and pasted' designation as its further-developed successors, drawing and cutting are not one and the same here, as they would later, famously, be. Rather, Matisse appears to have first painted the blue-and-pink figures in gouache and then cut around them, pasting the overall shape on a new ground. If this manoeuvre seems to be simply about relocating the figures, another cut-and-pasted element in this work introduces a more radical strategy. Matisse appended a scrap of white paper as a kind of corrective patch, using it to redefine the area around the blue figure's head. It's the same approach of modelling through paper that he learned while composing the Barnes mural, applied on a more intimate scale.

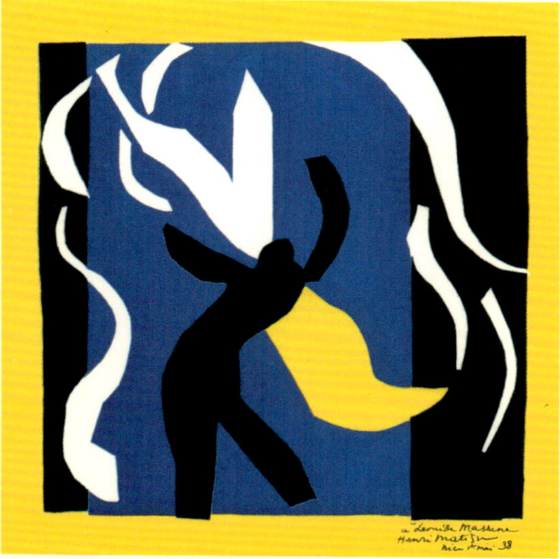

Fig. 19 Maquette for final curtain design for the ballet *Rouge et Noir*, 1 May 1938. Lithographic reproduction of the lost original cut-out, 61 × 61 (24 × 24) Private collection

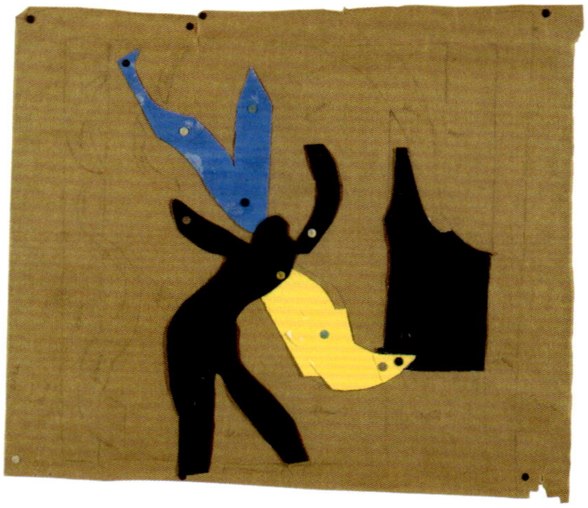

Fig. 20 *Dancer*. Project for the curtain for the ballet *Rouge et Noir*, 1937. Gouache on paper, cut and pasted, pinned on tracing paper, and pencil, mounted on canvas, 58.5 × 69.8 (23⅛ × 27½) Centre Pompidou, Paris. Musée national d'art moderne / Centre de création industrielle

From this transitional work it's easy to see how Matisse made the next step to *Small Dancer on Red Ground* (no. 4), in which the pink figure is now built up from six layered bits of rose-coloured paper.[31] As with the Barnes mural's paper stages, it is, paradoxically, through this three-dimensional construction that the figure is compressed: visual depth and actual flatness are replaced with actual depth and visual flatness. *Dancer* (no. 5), in which the bold red of *Small Dancer*'s background relocates to the foreground, would seem to be the next step in the sequence. Matisse once again uses patches of paper to refine the figure's contour, accentuating the curve of the dancer's hips and reshaping the arch of his back. In this more complete composition, perpendicular bars, similar to those in *Two Dancers*, locate the figure within the architecture of a stage.

The effort evident in this succession of figures shows the extent to which, especially in this preliminary phase of the cut-paper medium, Matisse did not simply carve a perfect contour from a coloured sheet, but arrived at his forms through protracted material experimentation. This sequence of dancers led him to the final design for his *Rouge et Noir* curtain, for which the glued maquette is presumably lost, but whose composition can nonetheless be gleaned from a preliminary state at the left of Schall's photograph, as well as from a lithographic translation (fig. 19) and a related cut-out study, still tacked and bearing colour notes in Lydia's

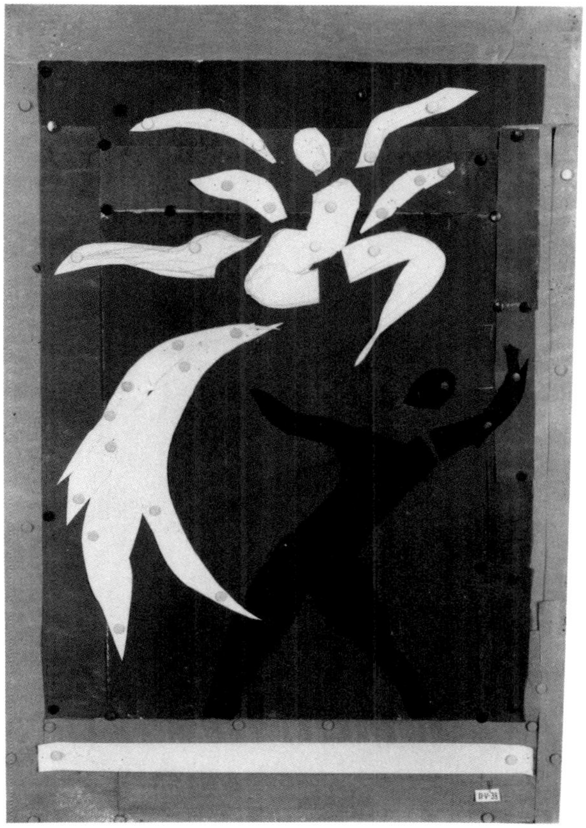

Fig. 21 Photograph of *Two Dancers* (see no. 7) in progress, 11 May 1938

hand (fig. 20). An inscription to Massine, visible on the lithograph, reveals that the definitive design was finished on 1 May 1938, and a note in Matisse's diary tells us that it was on 3 May that he 'glued the maquette for the curtain'.[32]

Though finished with his ballet design, Matisse continued to labour over a closely related composition, *Two Dancers* (no. 7), for several months longer. A photograph dated 11 May 1938 (fig. 21) shows this cut-out still in progress, and Lydia remembered that the 'panel, reworked on several occasions after that, not only at place Charles-Félix but also at the Régina, was therefore finished, at the earliest, in the second half of 1938'.[33] Consequently, Lydia explained, it is something that 'came out of Matisse's work for the ballet as regards its subject, but is already an independent work that was labored over for its own benefit and for a long time, like an easel picture' and that, she concluded, in a phrase that requires no translation, constituted a '"gouache découpée" avant la lettre'.[34]

Indeed, Lydia consistently emphasised the distinction between Matisse's use of cut paper as an expedient for realising a commissioned work in another medium, and his eventual embrace of the medium as an independent practice. Of the use of cut paper in the Barnes mural, 'it was simply a material for implementation', she stressed.[35] When Matisse employed cut paper as a compositional aid for the 1935 painting *Large Reclining Nude*, Lydia clarified: 'It's not a cut-out, it's a system to assist with technique.'[36] Of *Still Life with Shell* (no. 8), a 1940 work Matisse composed with cut paper and string to help him resolve the composition of a related painting (no. 9), the disavowal became downright Magrittean: 'Ceci n'est pas une "gouache découpée".'[37] The 1943–4 cut-outs for *Jazz* were still 'avant' according to Lydia: 'For me it is not yet a cut-out ... he was imagining subjects, translating them into colour, illustrating his image, his ideas.'[38] But it was 'this work', she allowed, 'that gave him the idea that you could draw expression from assembled gouached papers' and that led to the creation, around 1945, of very simple cut-out compositions, which 'he spent a lot of time looking at' (see nos. 45–8).[39] 'Finally,' Lydia recounted, 'he made a cut-out, "The Lyre", a small thing, blue on white, and said "it's my first cut-out", that is to say, a well-thought-out work, which he succeeded in investing with feeling. That was the start.'[40]

Certainly, the lyrical simplicity of *The Lyre*, 1946 (no. 49 and p. 37, as first hatched on the wall), marks an important turning point in the cut-outs' coming of age. And the testimony of Lydia, as Matisse's closest collaborator in the development of the technique, offers invaluable insight into the way he must have perceived this gestational period. If his reluctance to share the nascent medium with Dr Barnes is any indication, we know that a considerable level of ambivalence characterised the artist's attitude to his still-preparatory practice. But to take at face value, for example, Lydia's assertion that 'the decor for the ballet *Strange Farandole* does not have a relationship with the "gouaches découpées" in Matisse's oeuvre'[41] is to discount the critical lessons – both formal and material – learned *avant la lettre*. The research conducted in these early works, cumulatively amassed from one project to the next, was as imperative to Matisse's development of the cut-outs as it is to our understanding of them. The artist himself recognised that the origin of this radical new form preceded even his awareness of it: 'They were a long time in the making, developing in secret.'[42]

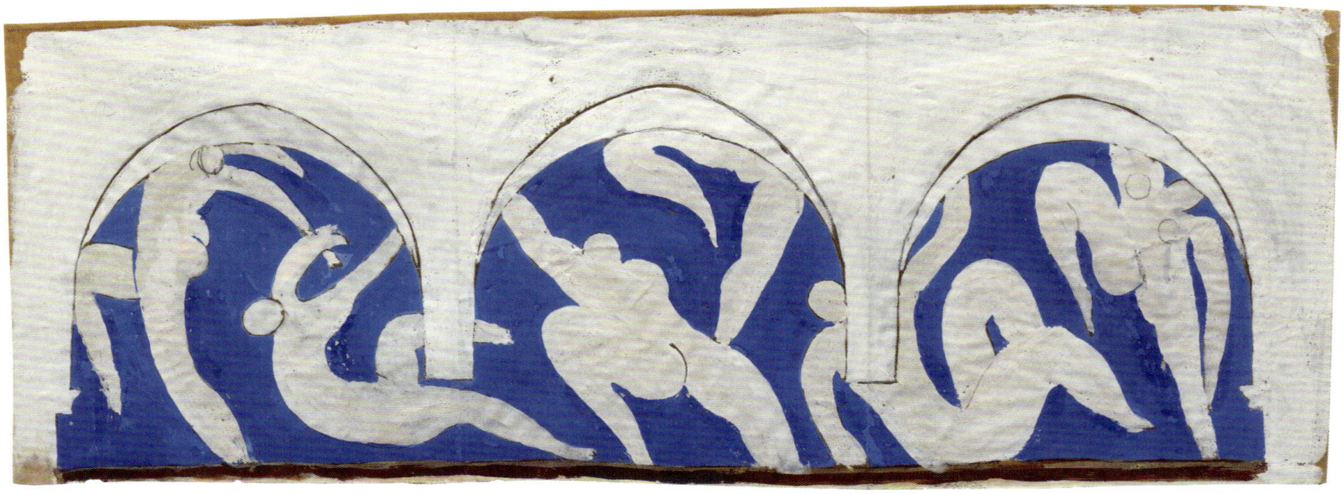

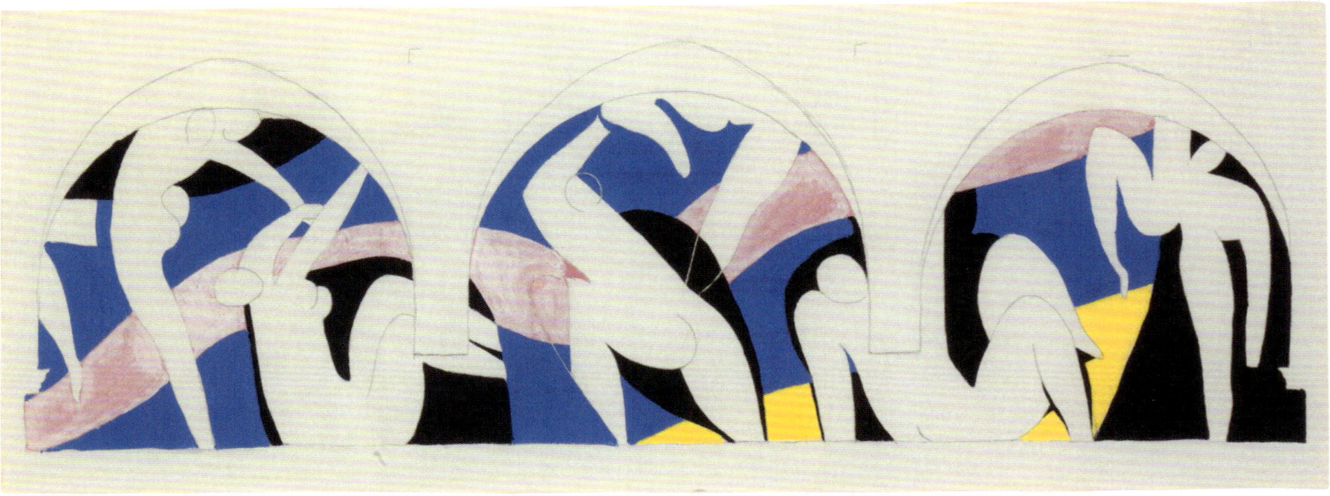

1. *The Dance* 1931
Study for the Barnes mural (Paris version; recto and verso)
Gouache and pencil on paper (recto); pencil and ink on paper (verso), 14 × 40 (5½ × 15¾)

2. *The Dance* 1931–3
Study for the Barnes mural (Paris version)
Gouache and pencil on paper, 27.9 × 75.9 (11 × 29⅞)

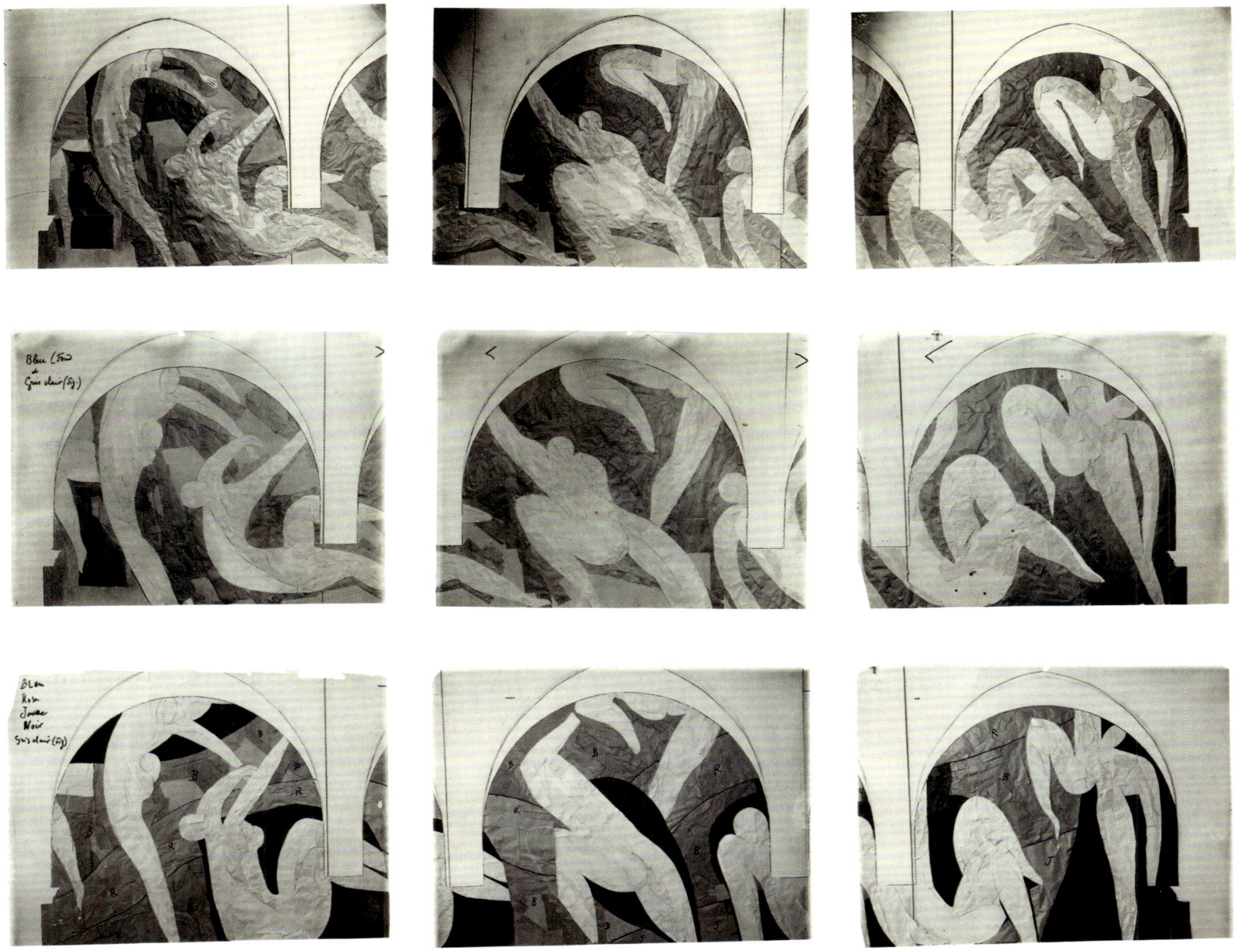

3. Unknown photographer
Photographs of the Barnes mural (Paris version) in progress 1931–3
Gelatin silver prints, dimensions variable

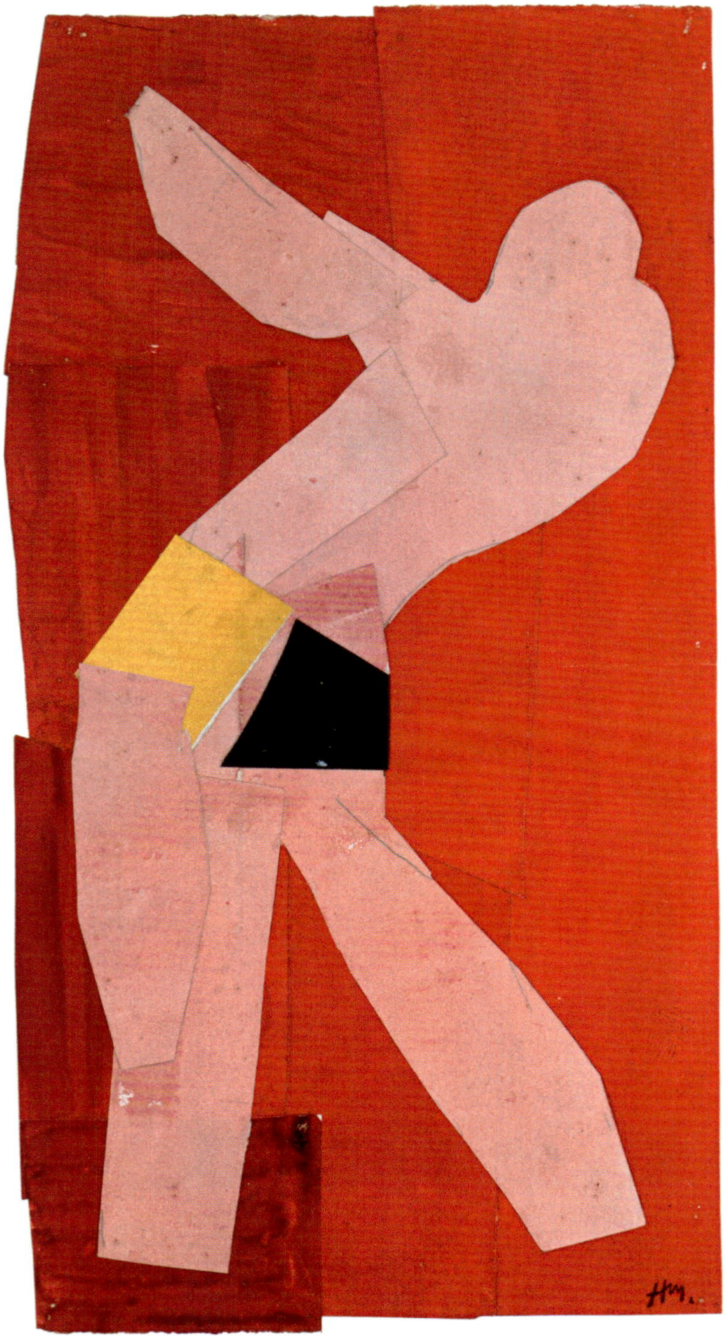

4. *Small Dancer on Red Background* 1937–8
Gouache on paper, cut and pasted
59.7 × 46.4 (23½ × 18¼)

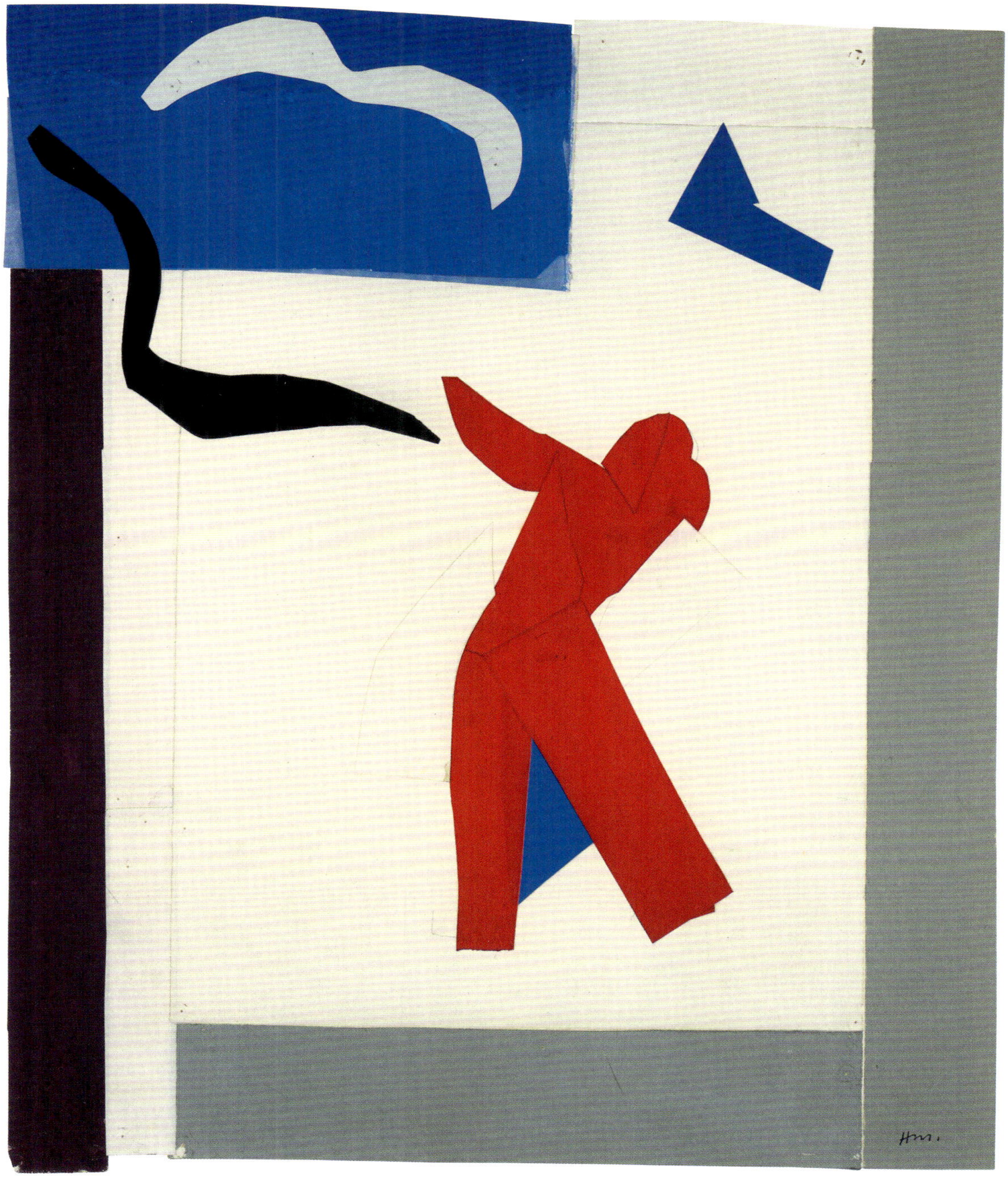

5. *Dancer* 1937–8
Gouache and pencil on paper, cut and pasted
74.9 × 62.2 (29½ × 24⅜)

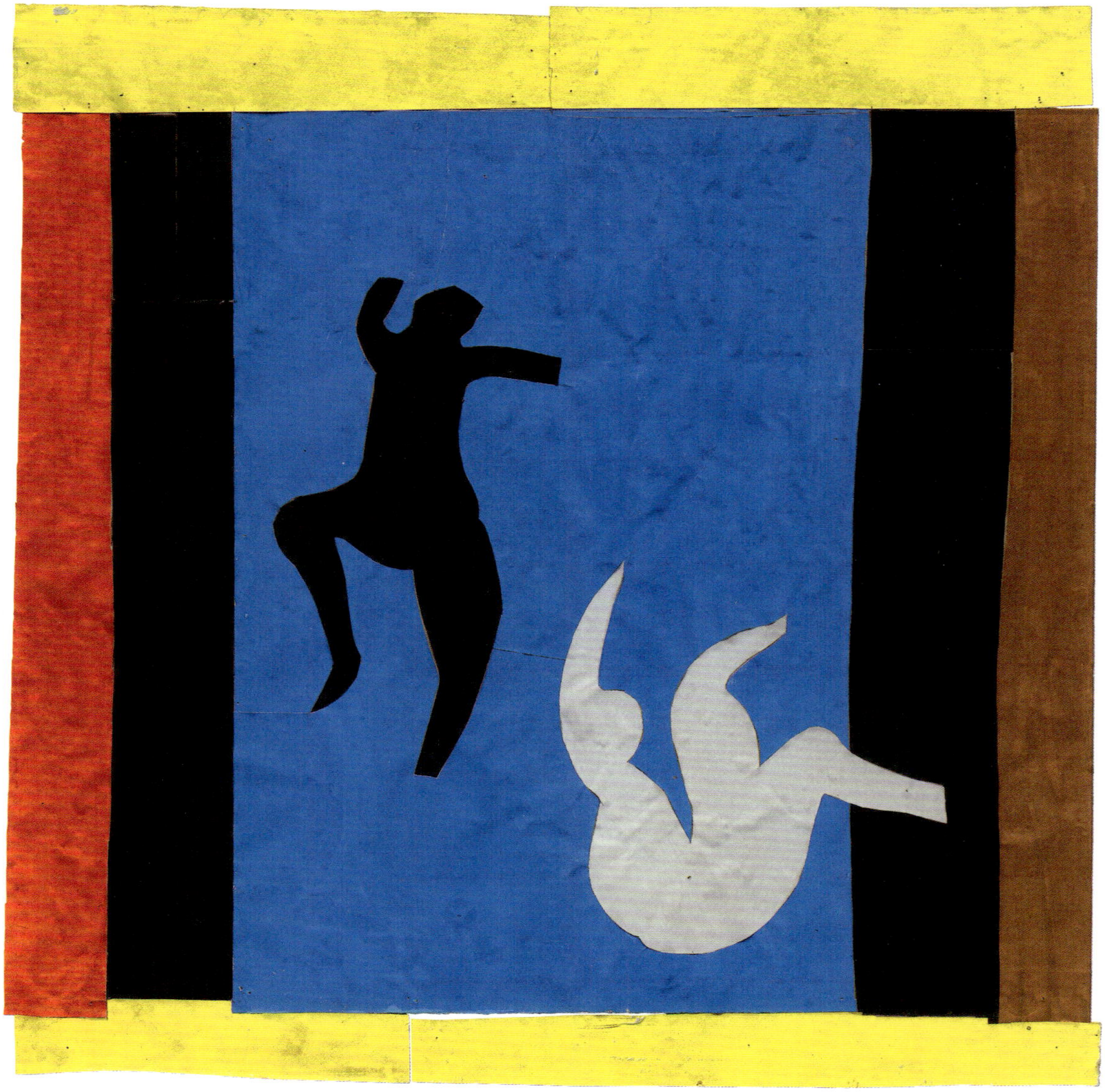

6. *Two Dancers* 1937–8
Stage curtain design for the ballet *Rouge et Noir*
Gouache on paper, cut and pasted, mounted on board
63 × 64.5 (24⅞ × 25⅜)

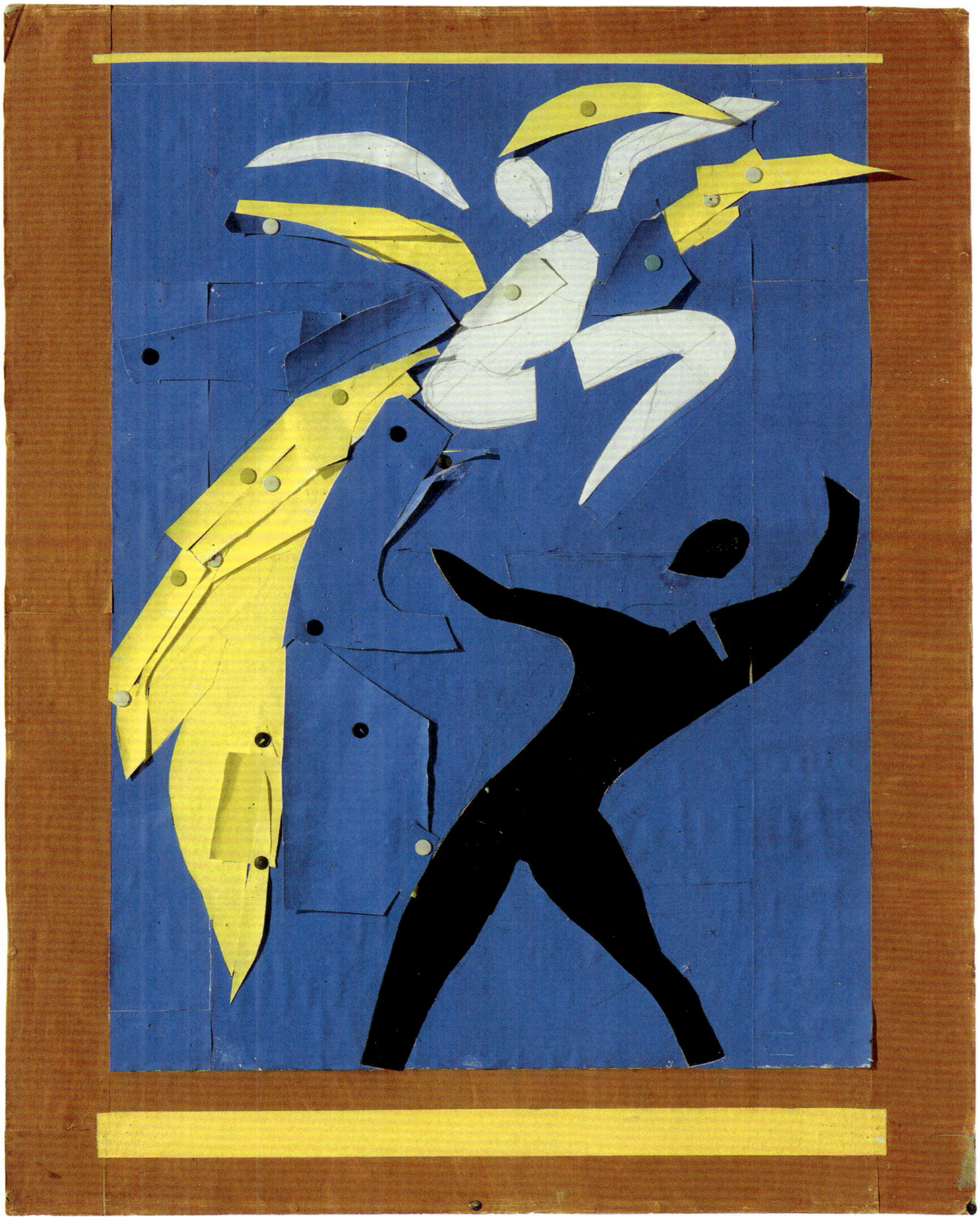

7. *Two Dancers* 1937–8
Stage curtain design for the ballet *Rouge et Noir*
Gouache on paper, cut and pasted, notebook papers, pencil and drawing pins (thumb tacks)
80.2 × 64.5 (31⅝ × 25⅜)

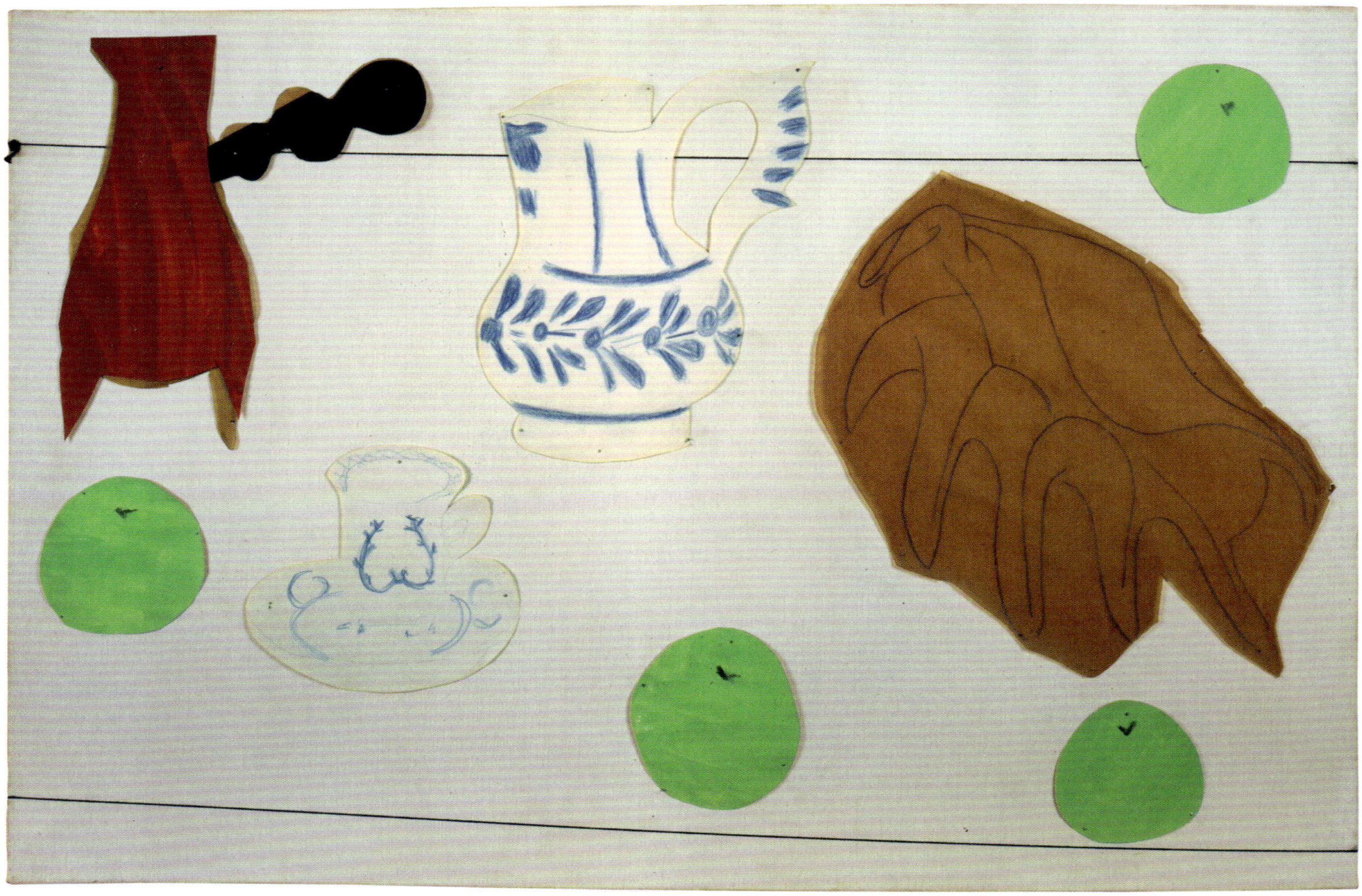

8. *Still Life with Shell* 1940
Gouache, coloured pencil and charcoal on cut paper, and string, pinned to canvas, 83.5 × 115 (32⅞ × 45¼)

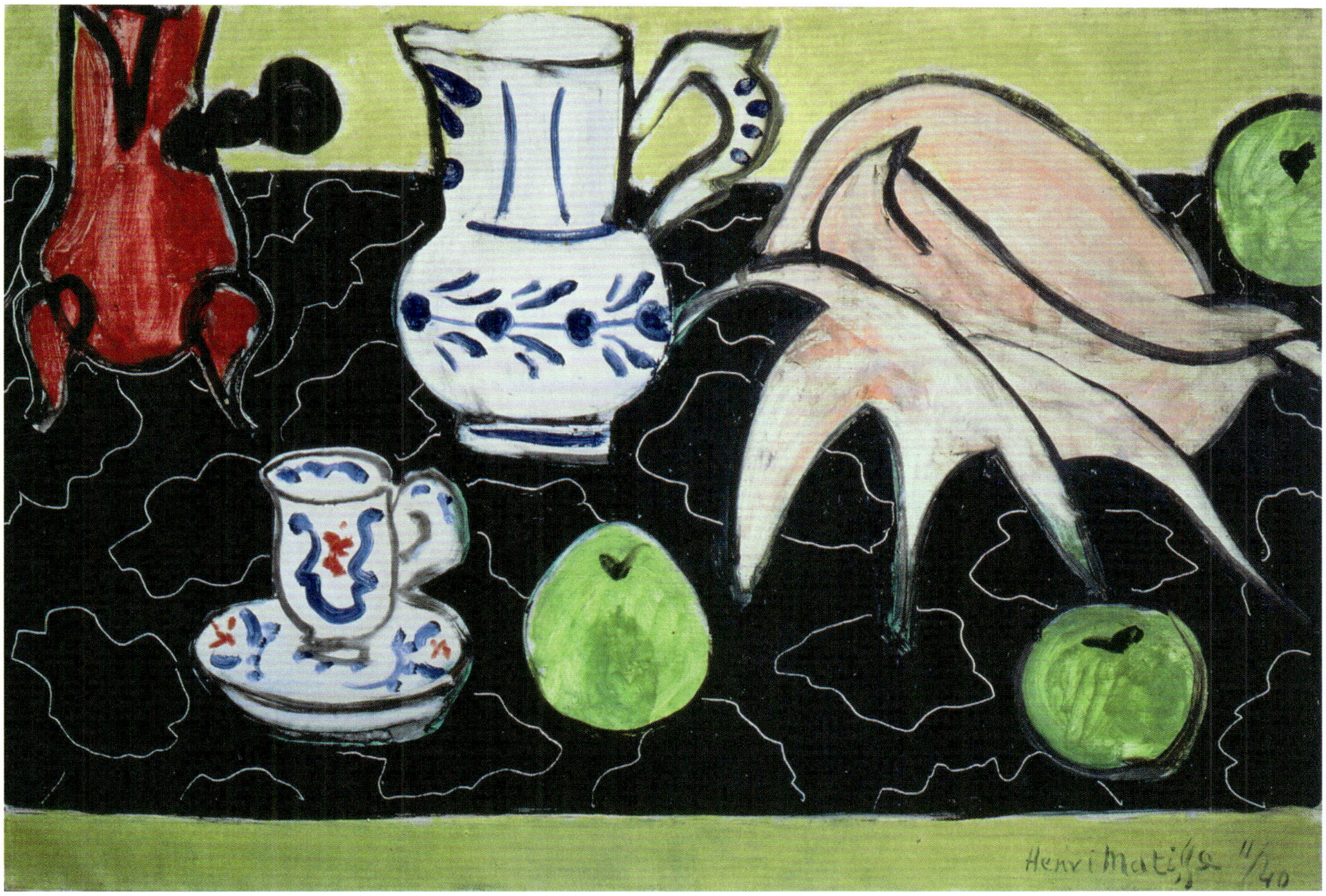

9. *Still Life with Shell* 1940
Oil on canvas, 54 × 81 (21¼ × 31⅞)

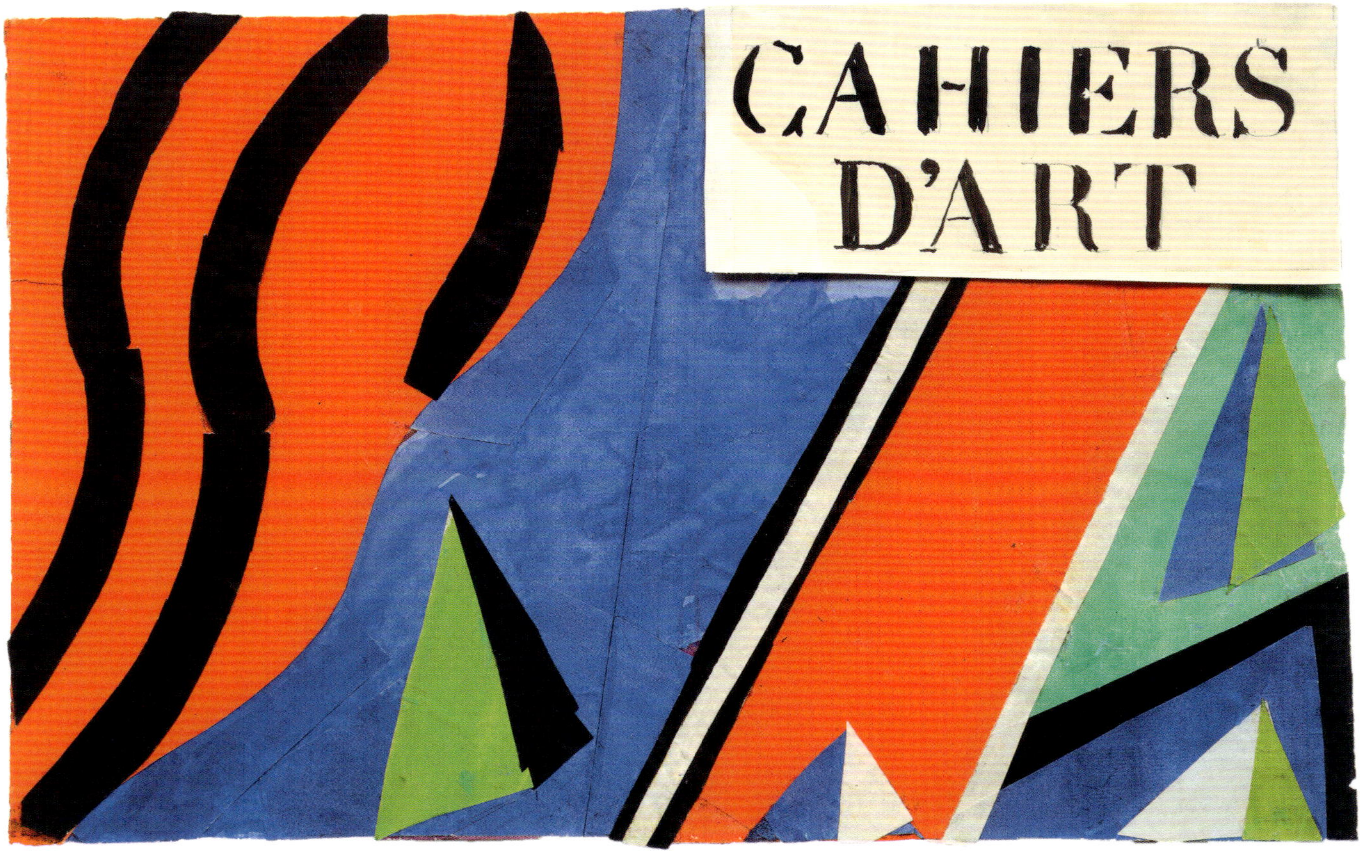

10. Cover maquette for the journal
Cahiers d'Art, nos. 3–5 (1936) 1936
Gouache on paper, cut and pasted
32.8 × 54 (12⅞ × 21¼)

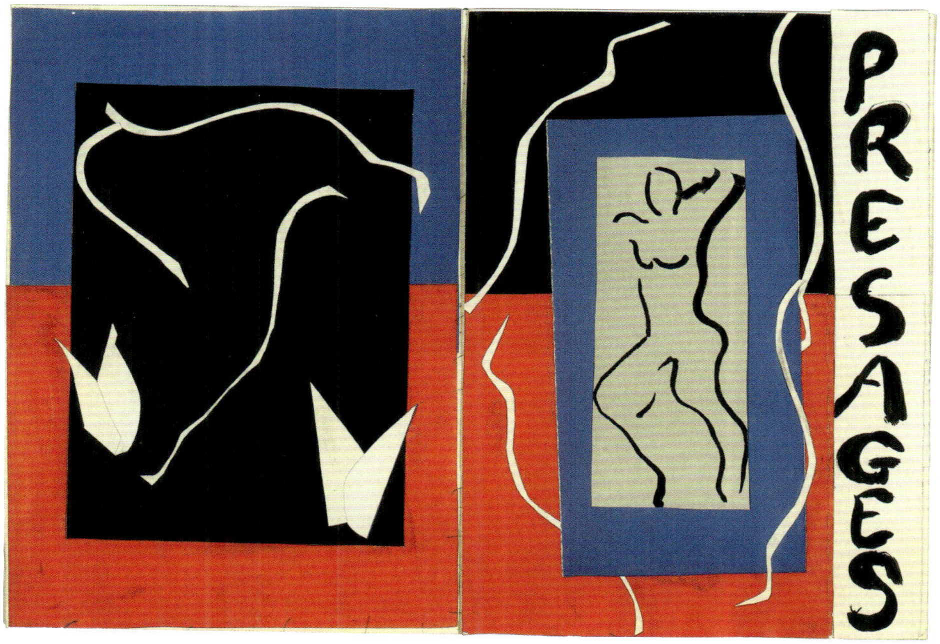

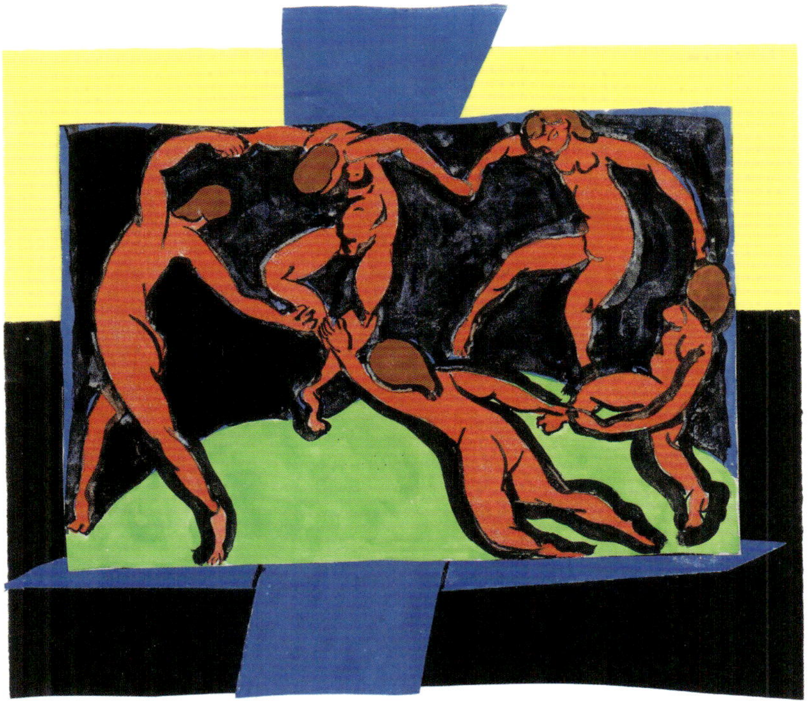

11. *Présages*, cover maquette for the journal *Verve*, vol.I, no.1 (1937) 1937
Gouache on paper, cut and pasted, and ink, 36.5 × 55.5 (14⅜ × 21⅞)

12. *The Dance* 1938
Maquette for a lithographic reproduction for the journal *Verve*, vol.I, no.4, 1938
Gouache on paper, cut and pasted, and ink
48.5 × 61.5 (19⅛ × 24¼)

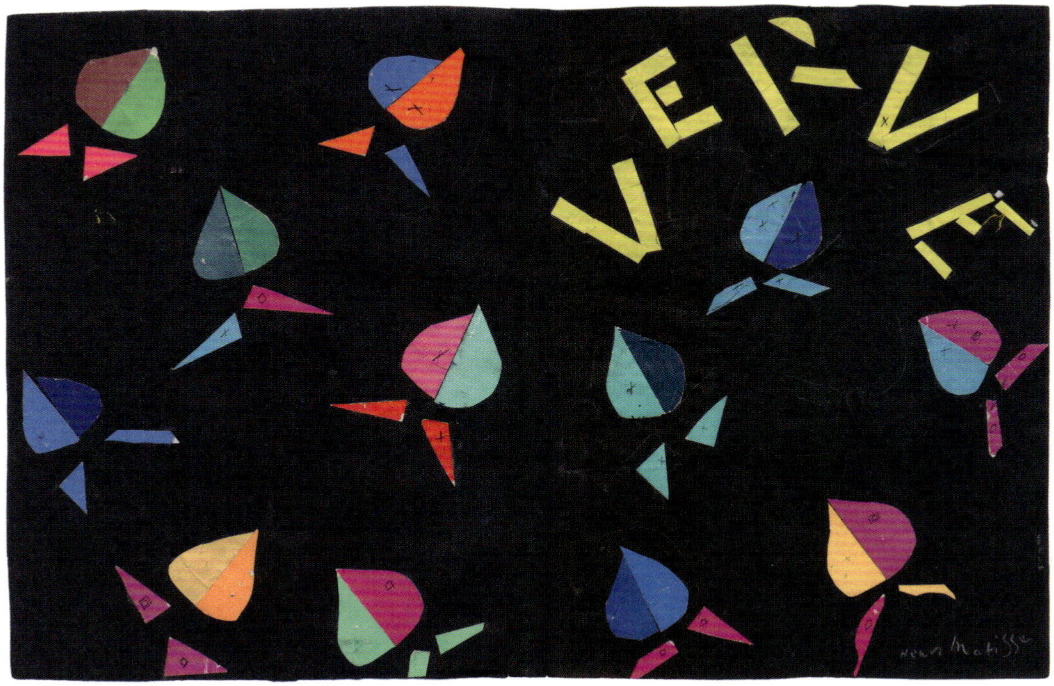

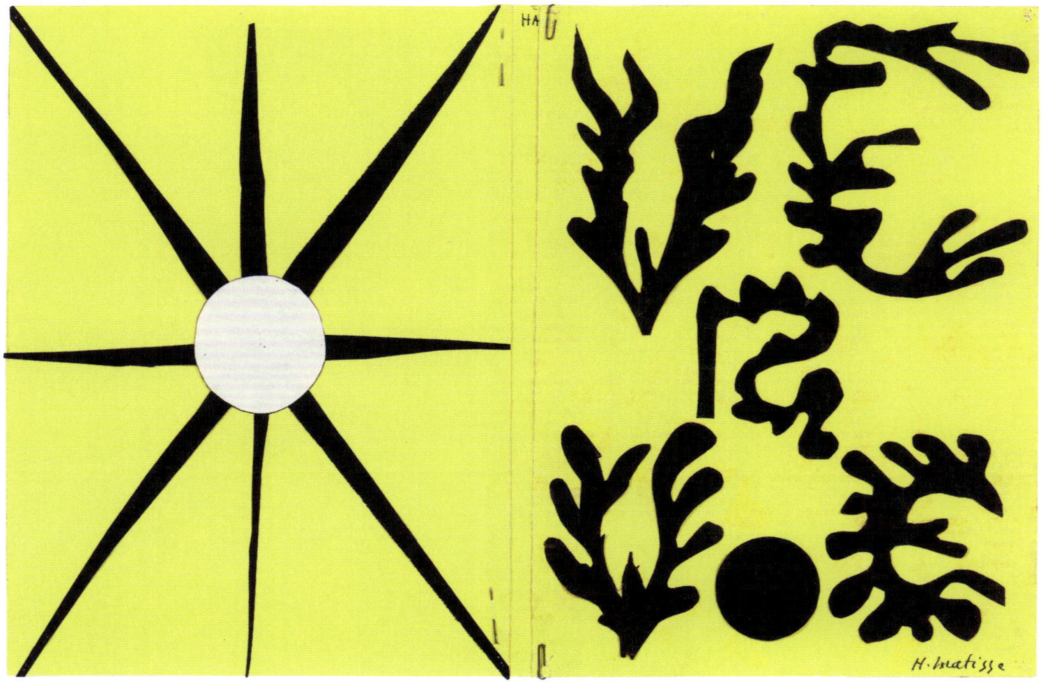

13. *Symphonie chromatique*, cover maquette for the journal *Verve*, vol. II, no. 8 (1940) 1939
Coloured papers, cut and pasted
35.2 × 55.3 (13⅞ × 21¾)

14. Cover maquette for the journal *Verve*, vol. VI, nos. 21–2 (1948) 1948
Gouache on paper, cut and pasted
36 × 54 (14⅛ × 21¼)

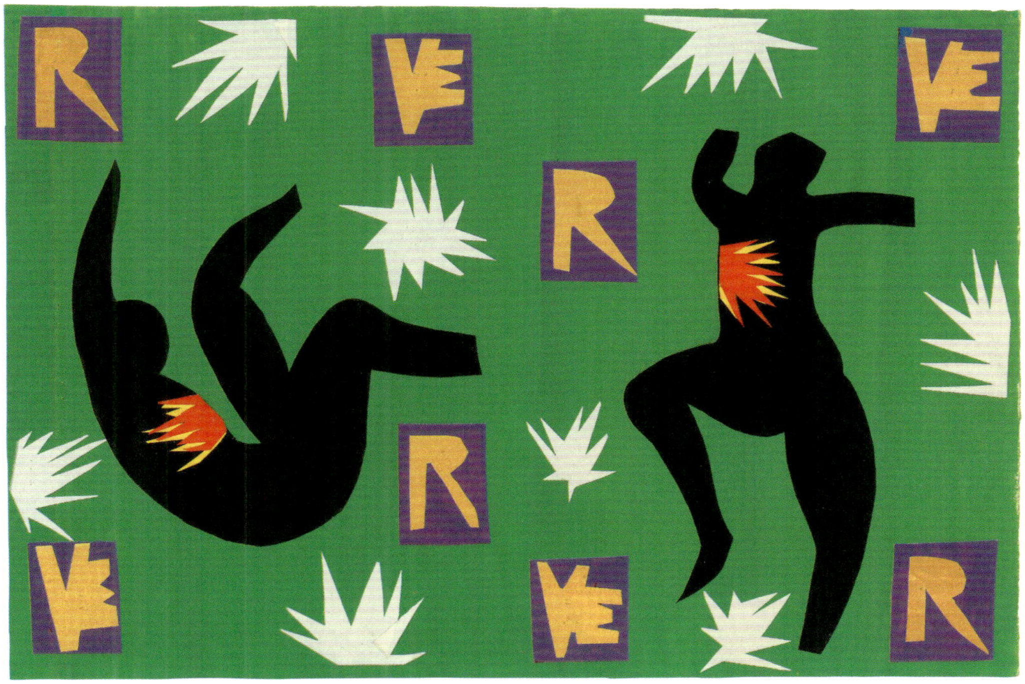

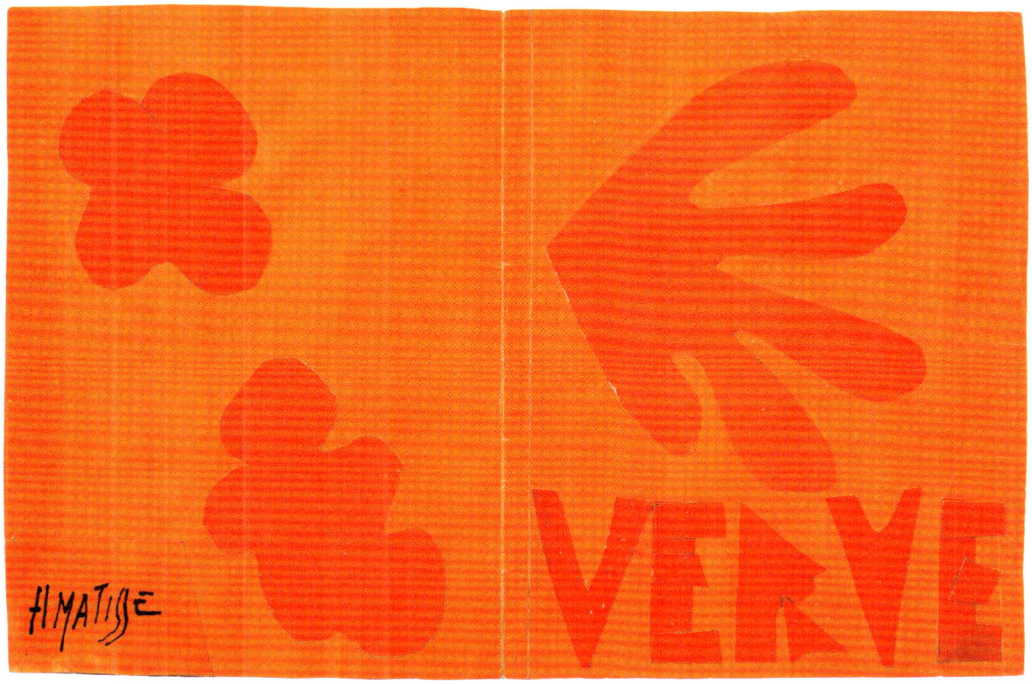

15. Cover maquette for the journal *Verve*, vol. IV, no. 13 (1945) 1943
Gouache on paper, cut and pasted, mounted on canvas, 38.1 × 56.8 (15 × 22⅜)

16. Cover maquette for the journal *Verve*, vol. IX, nos. 35–6 (1958) c. 1954
Gouache on paper, cut and pasted
35.9 × 54.9 (14⅛ × 21⅝)

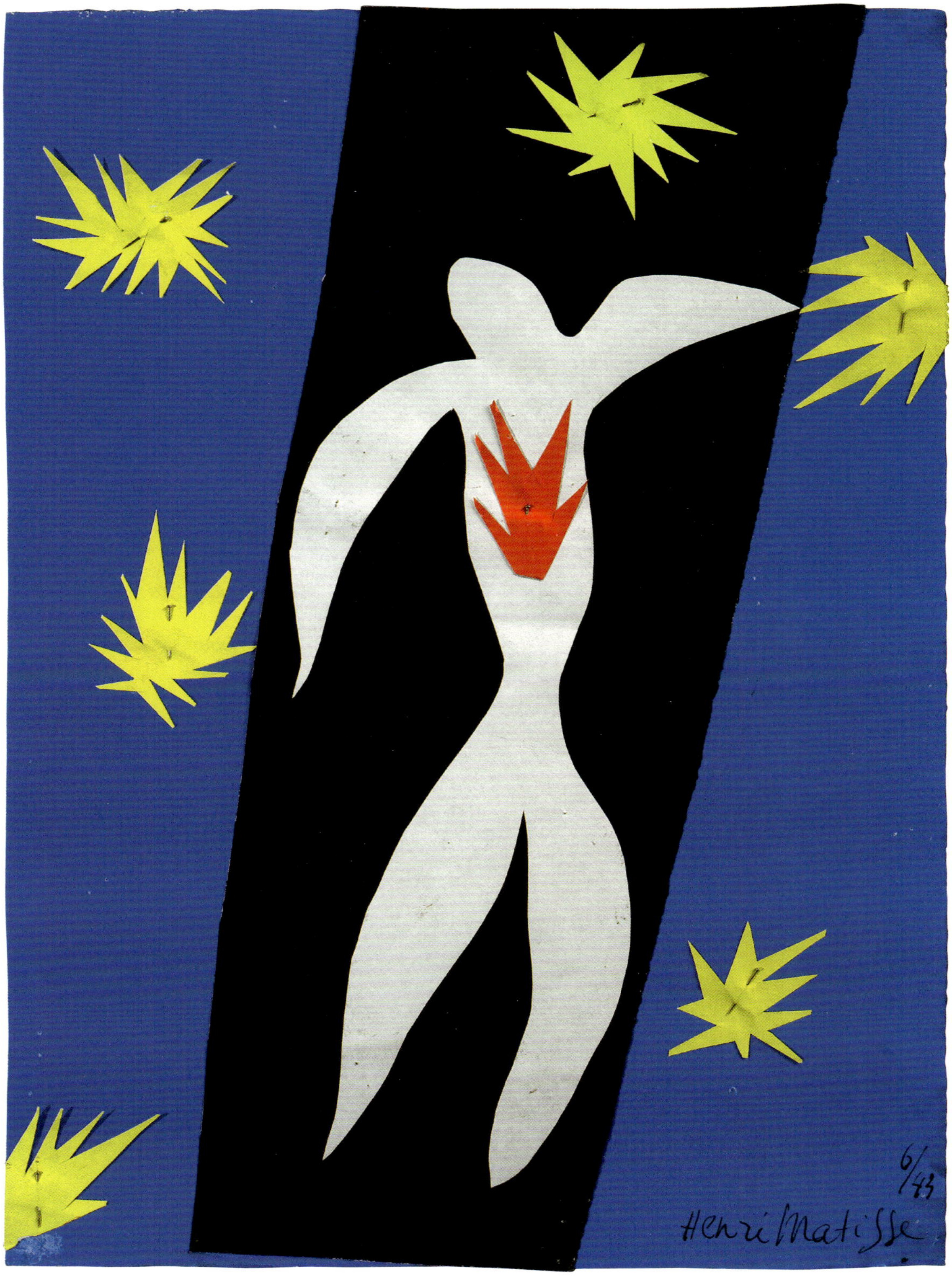

17. *The Fall of Icarus* 1943
Gouache on paper, cut and pasted, and pins
35 × 27 (13¾ × 10⅝)

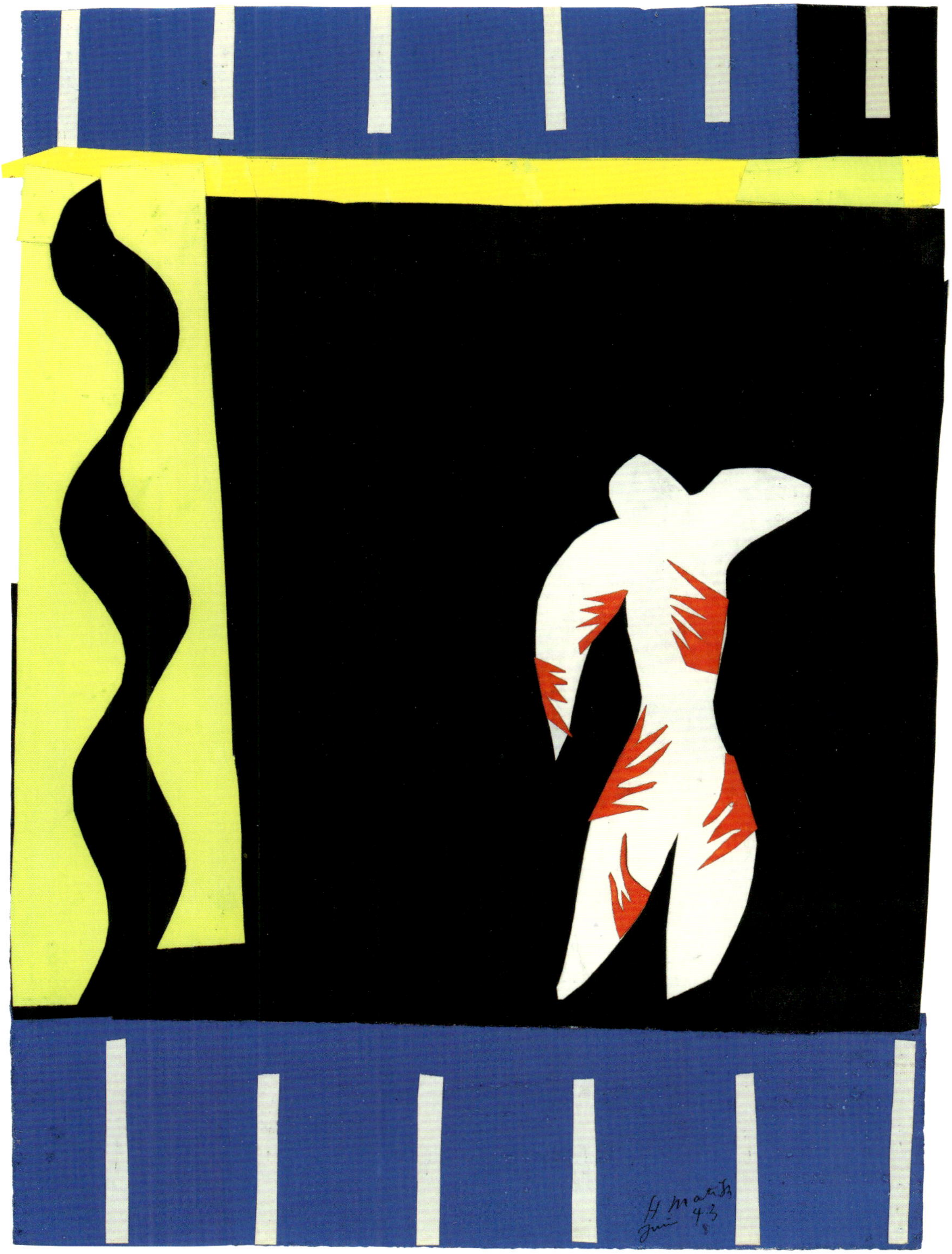

18. *The Clown* (*Le Clown*) 1943
Maquette for plate I from the illustrated book *Jazz* (1947)
Gouache on paper, cut and pasted, mounted on canvas
67.2 × 50.7 (26½ × 20)

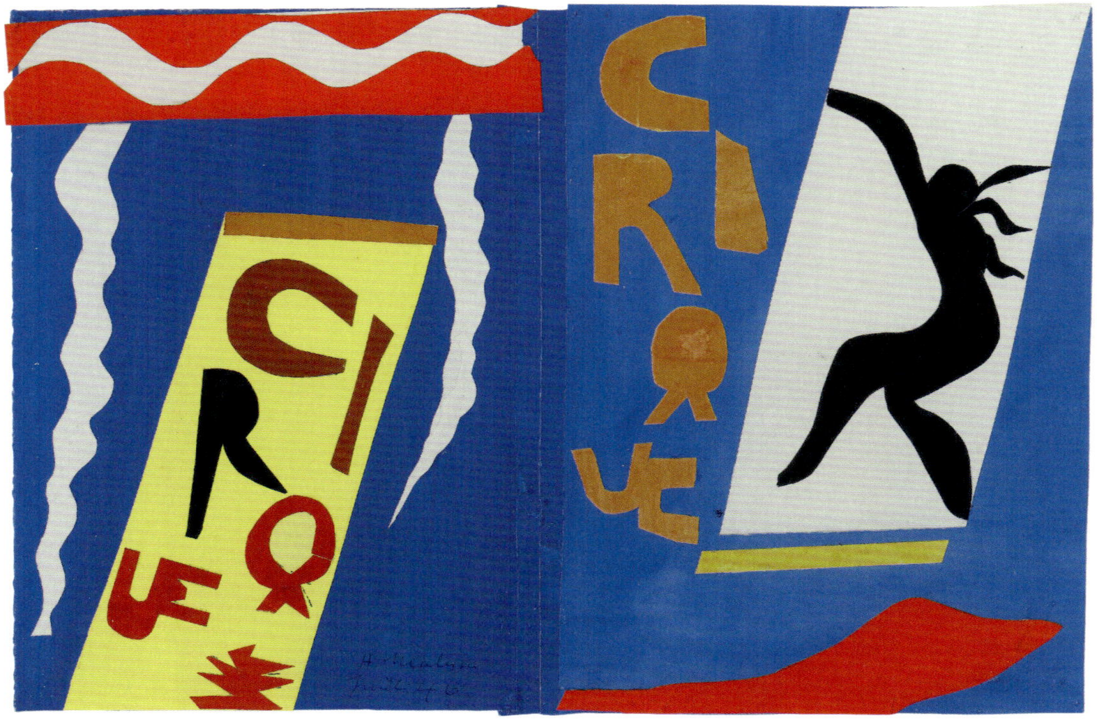

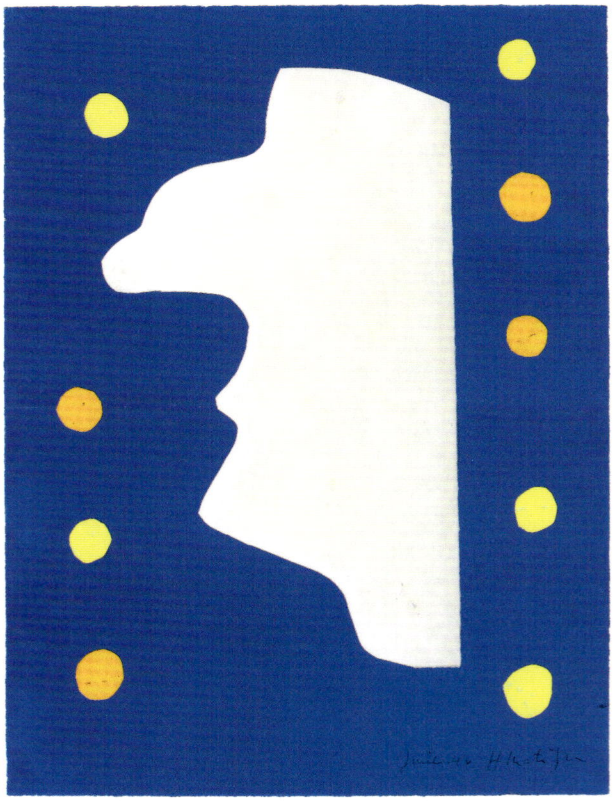

19. *The Circus* 1943
Maquette for plate II from the illustrated book *Jazz* (1947)
Gouache on paper, cut and pasted, mounted on canvas
45.2 × 67.1 (17¾ × 26⅜)

20. *Monsieur Loyal* 1943
Maquette for plate III from the illustrated book *Jazz* (1947)
Gouache on paper, cut and pasted, mounted on canvas
54.7 × 42.7 (21½ × 16¾)

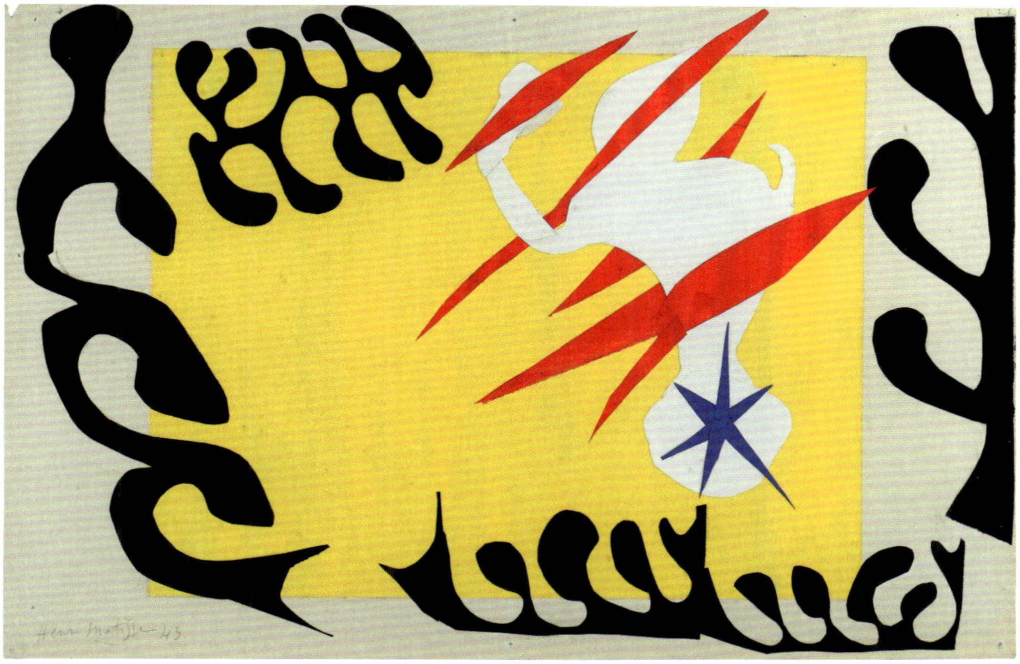

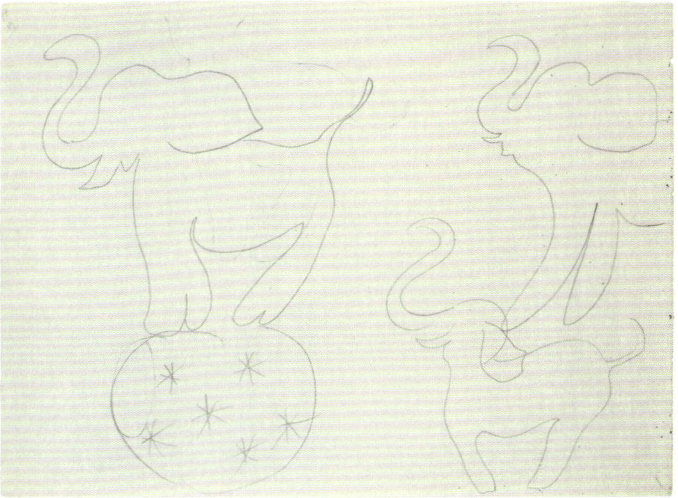

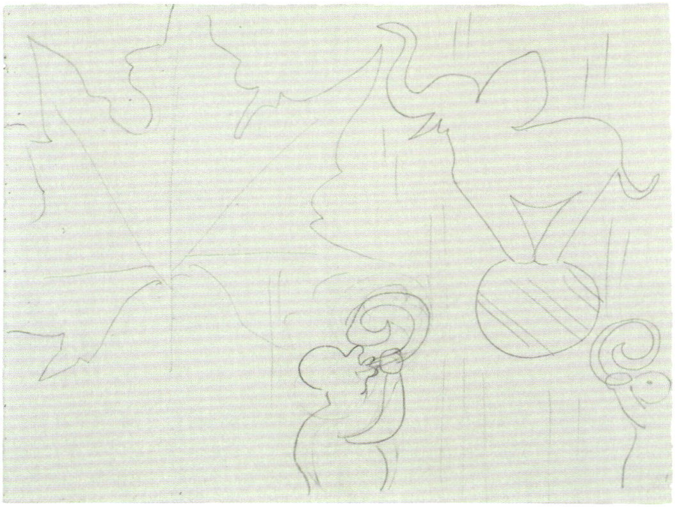

22. *Circus Scene* 1943
Drawing for the illustrated book *Jazz* (1947)
Pencil on paper, 27.9 × 38.1 (11 × 15)

21. *The Nightmare of the White Elephant* 1943
Maquette for plate IV from the illustrated book *Jazz* (1947)
Gouache on paper, cut and pasted, mounted on canvas
43.9 × 66.7 (17¼ × 26¼)

23. *Circus Scene* 1943
Drawing for the illustrated book *Jazz* (1947)
Pencil on paper, 28.3 × 38.4 (11⅛ × 15⅛)

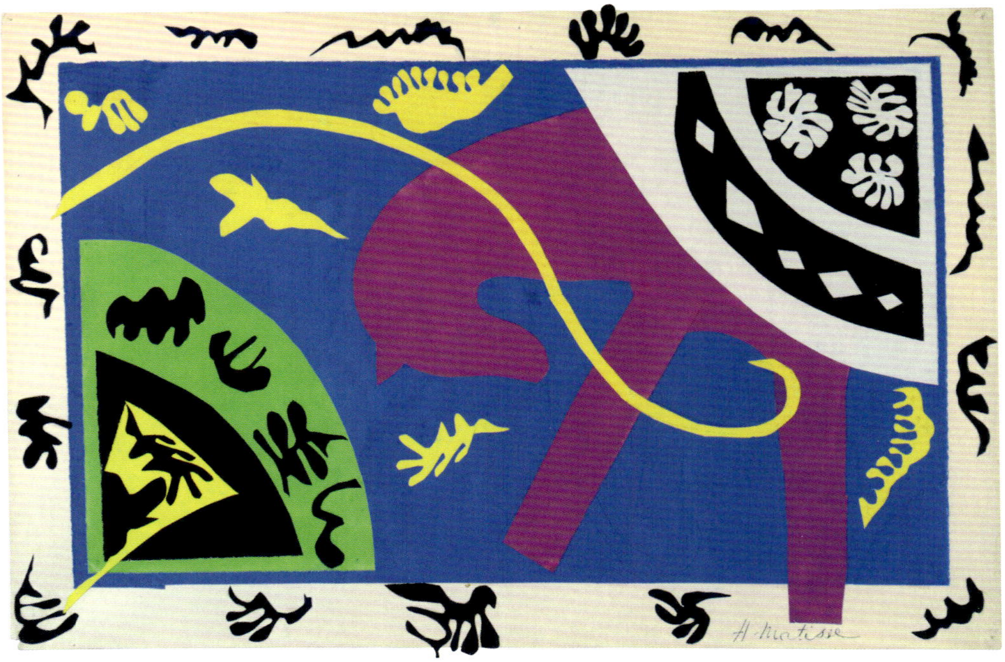

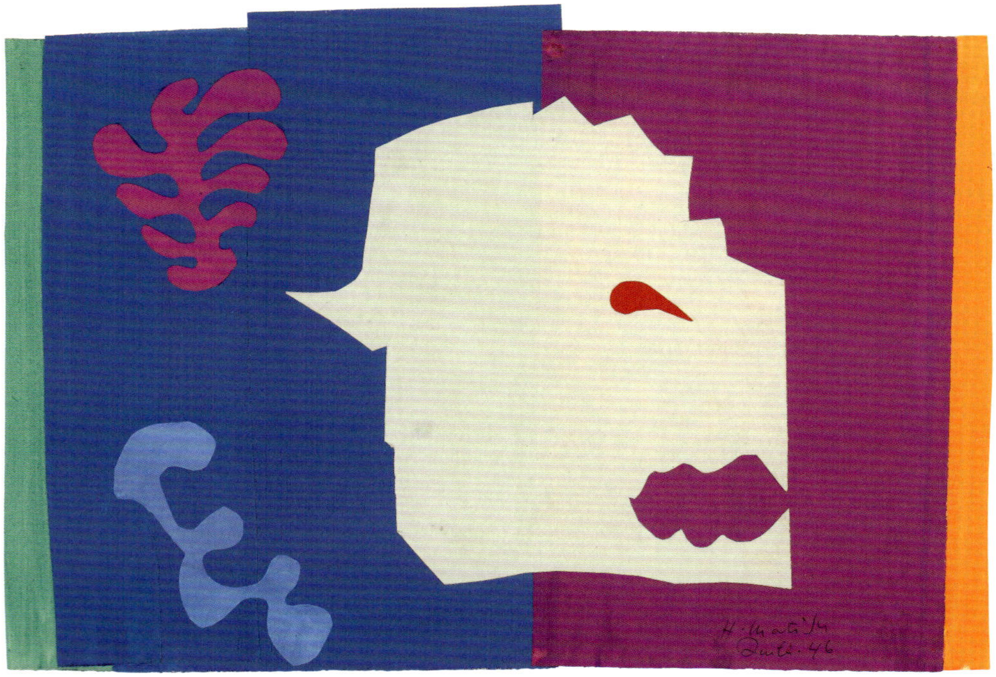

24. *The Horse, the Rider and the Clown* 1943
Maquette for plate V from the illustrated book *Jazz* (1947)
Gouache on paper, cut and pasted, mounted on canvas
42.5 × 65.6 (16¾ × 25⅞)

25. *The Wolf* 1944
Maquette for plate VI from the illustrated book *Jazz* (1947)
Gouache on paper, cut and pasted, mounted on canvas
45 × 67.1 (17¾ × 26⅜)

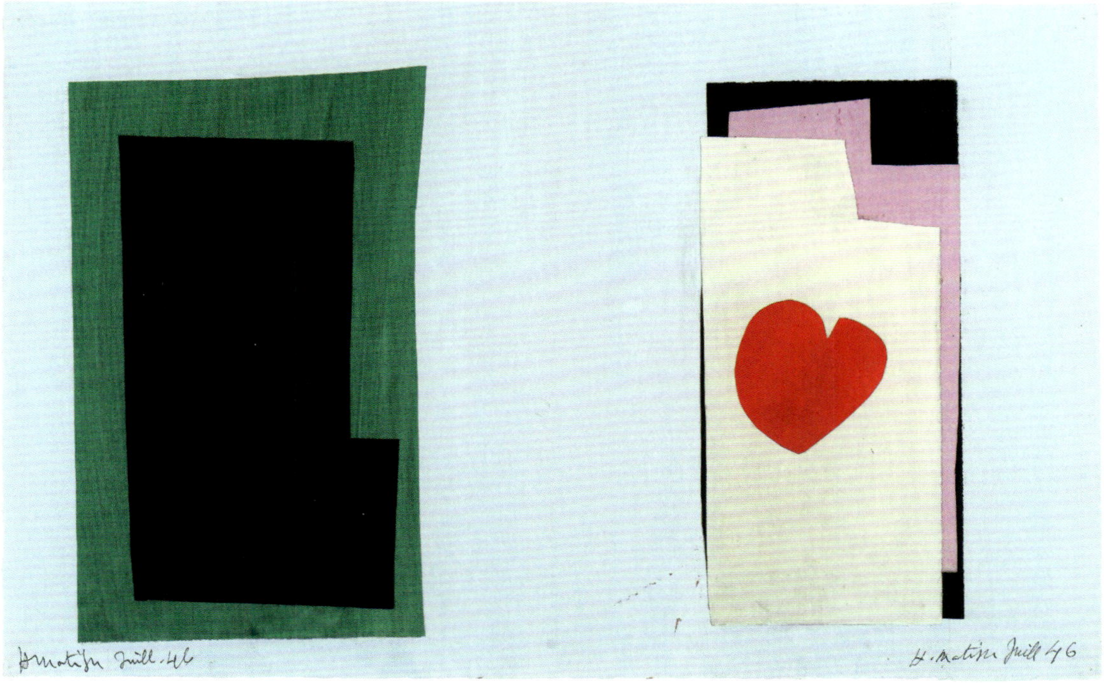

26. *The Heart* 1943
Maquette for plate VII from the illustrated book *Jazz* (1947)
Gouache on paper, cut and pasted, mounted on canvas
44.5 × 67.3 (17½ × 26½)

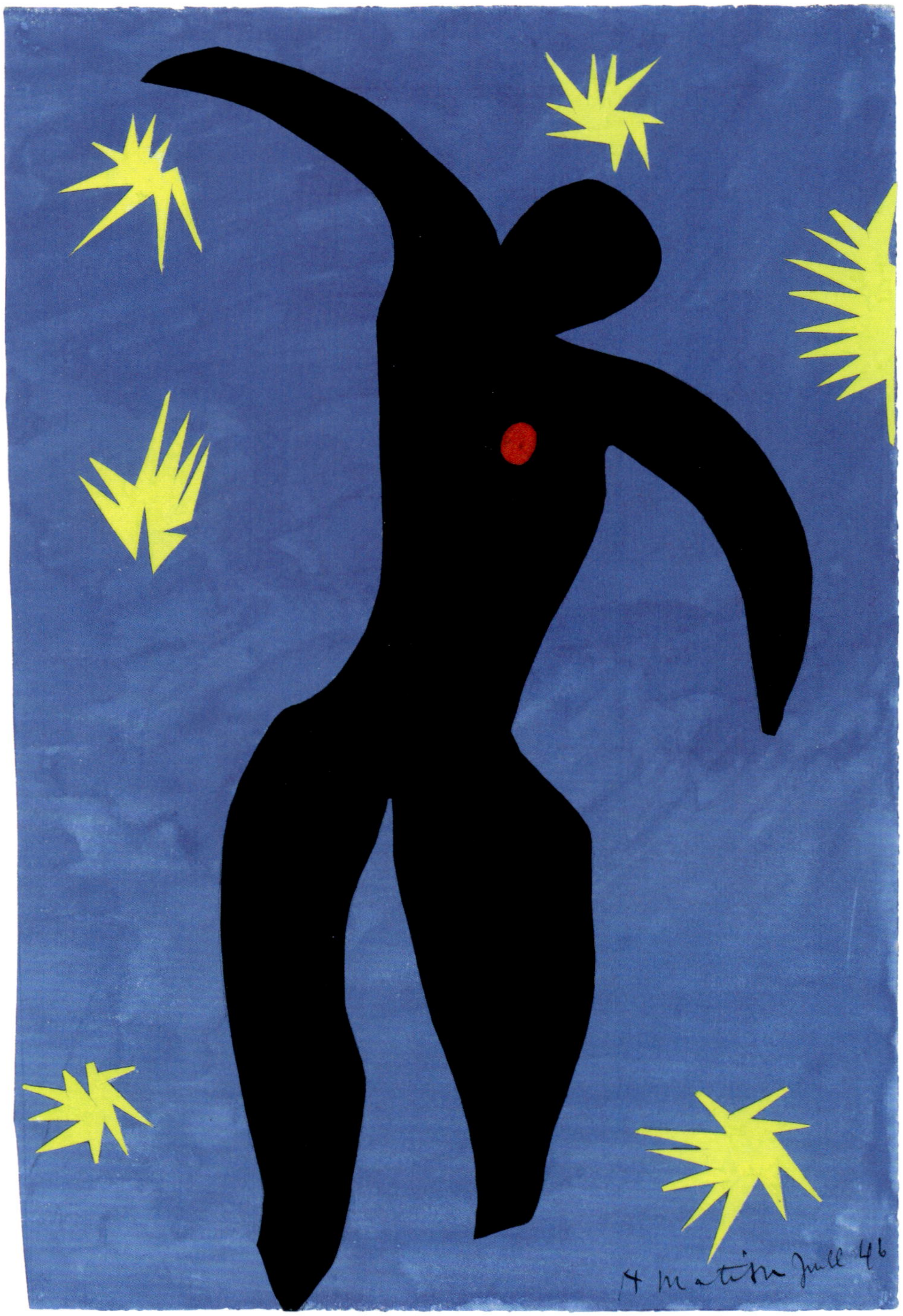

27. *Icarus* 1943(?)–4
Maquette for plate VIII from the illustrated book *Jazz* (1947)
Gouache on paper, cut and pasted, mounted on canvas
43.4 × 34.1 (17⅛ × 13⅜)

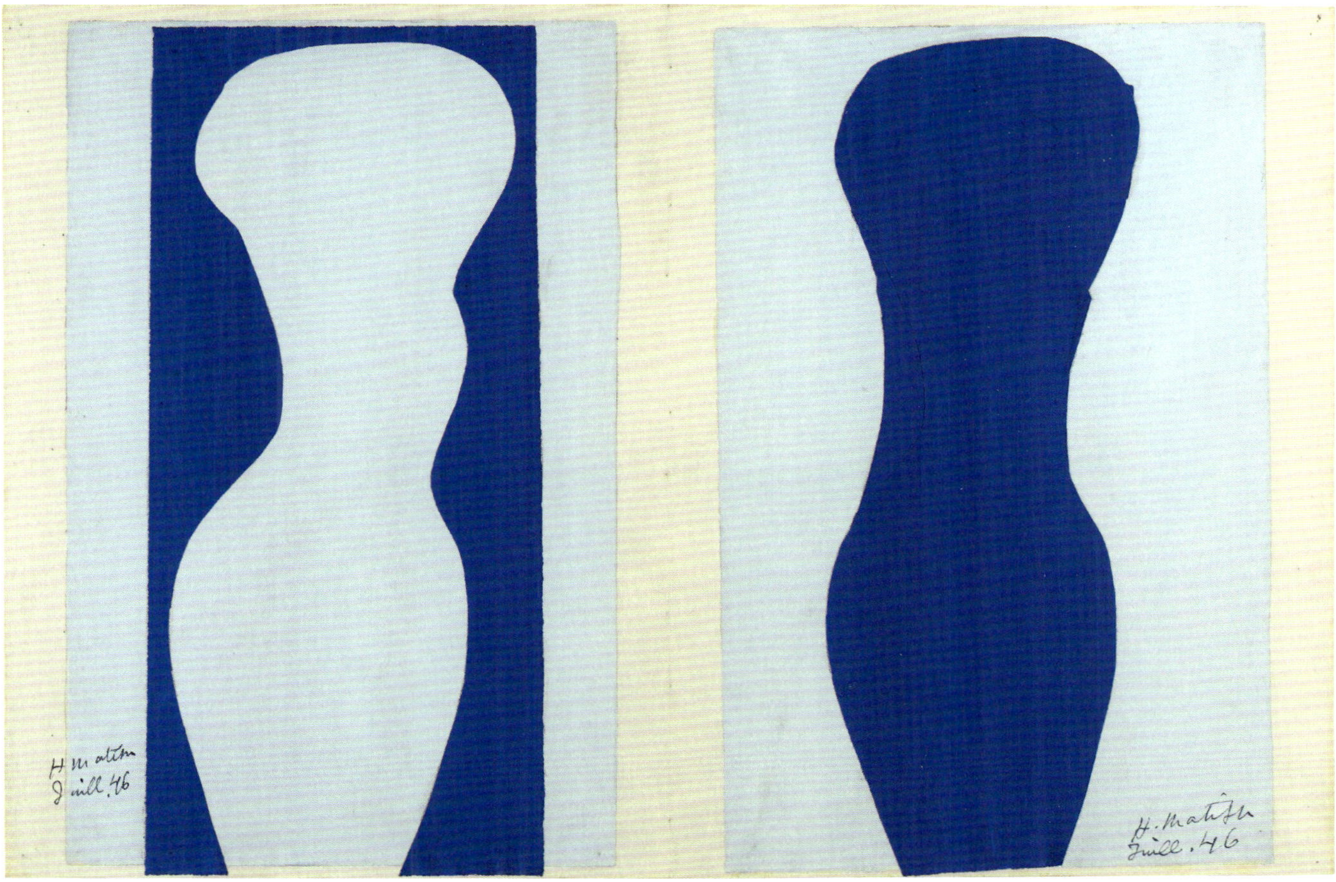

28. *Forms* 1944
Maquette for plate IX from the illustrated book *Jazz* (1947)
Gouache on paper, cut and pasted, mounted on canvas
44.3 × 67.1 (17½ × 26⅜)

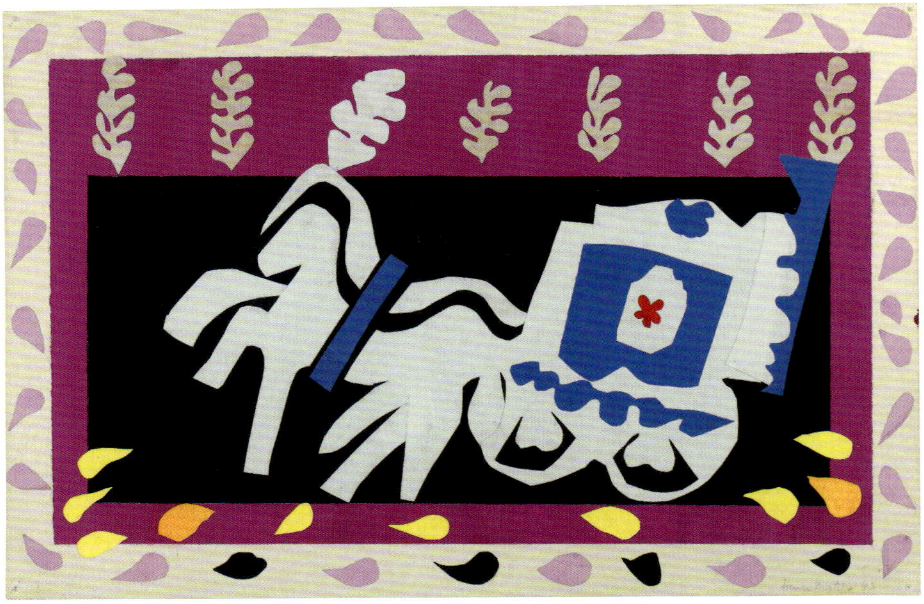

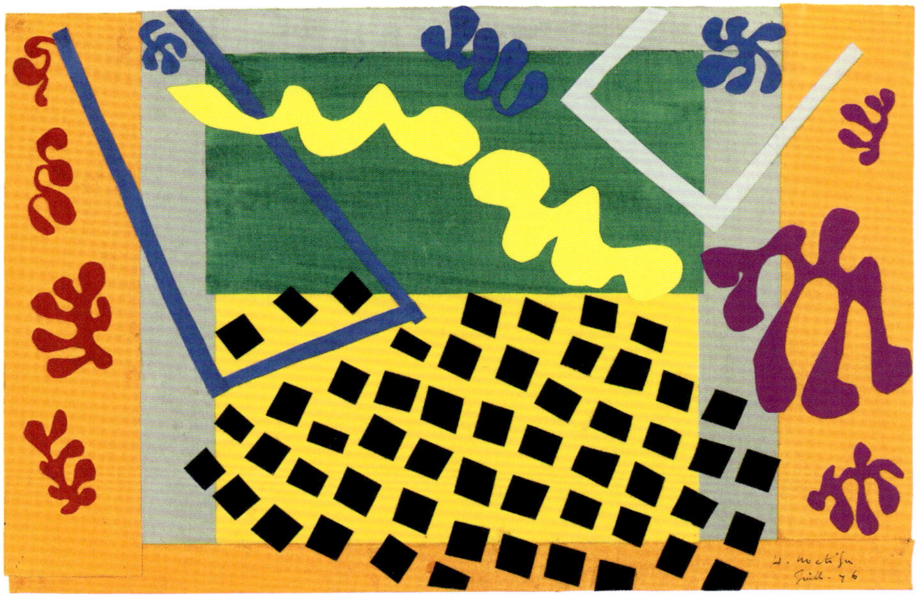

29. *Pierrot's Funeral* 1943–4(?)
Maquette for plate X from the illustrated book *Jazz* (1947)
Gouache on paper, cut and pasted, mounted on canvas
44.5 × 66 (17½ × 26)

30. *The Codomas* 1943
Maquette for plate XI from the illustrated book *Jazz* (1947)
Gouache on paper, cut and pasted, mounted on canvas
43.5 × 67.1 (17⅛ × 26⅜)

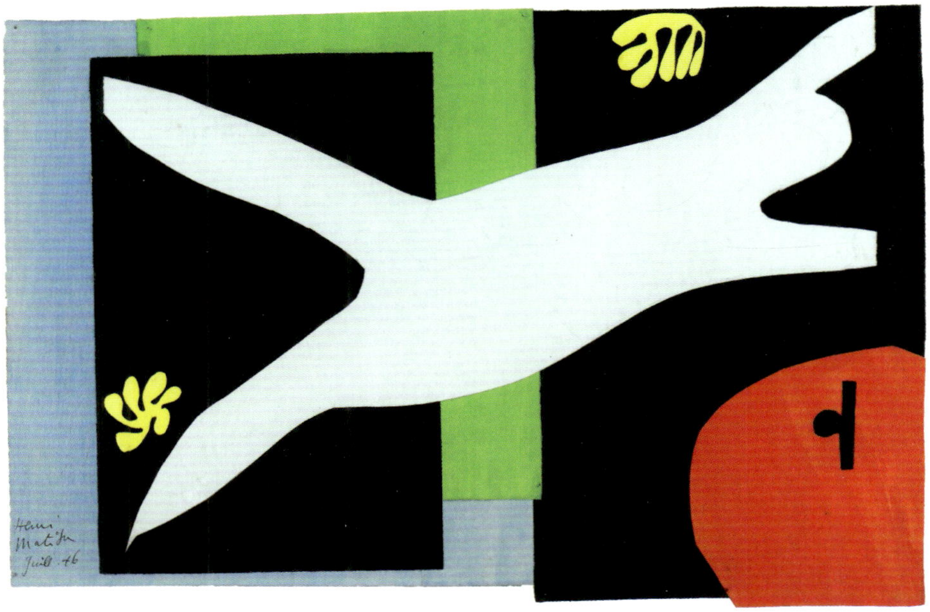

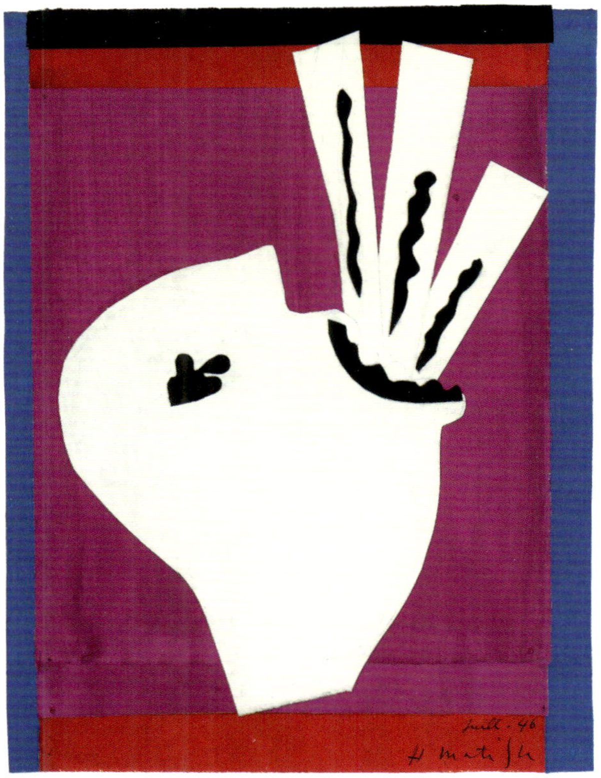

31. *The Swimmer in the Tank* 1944
Maquette for plate XII from the illustrated book *Jazz* (1947)
Gouache on paper, cut and pasted, mounted on canvas
44.2 × 66 (17⅜ × 26)

32. *The Sword Swallower* 1943
Maquette for plate XIII from the illustrated book *Jazz* (1947)
Gouache on paper, cut and pasted, mounted on canvas
43.3 × 34.3 (17 × 13½)

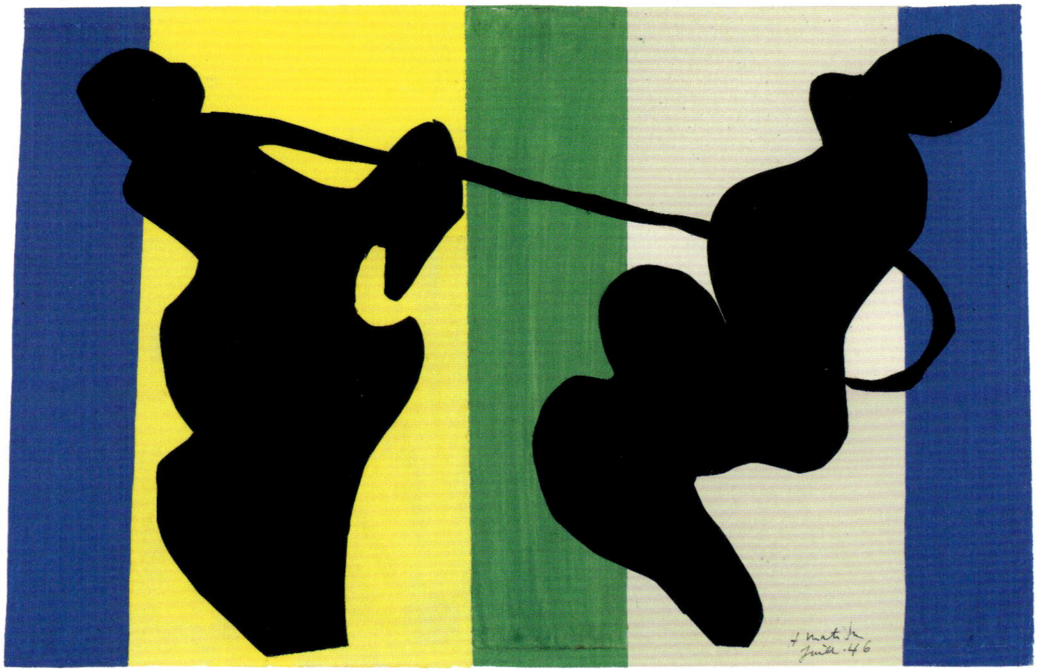

33. *The Cowboy* 1943
Maquette for plate XIV from the illustrated book *Jazz* (1947)
Gouache on paper, cut and pasted, mounted on canvas
43 × 68 (16⅞ × 26¾)

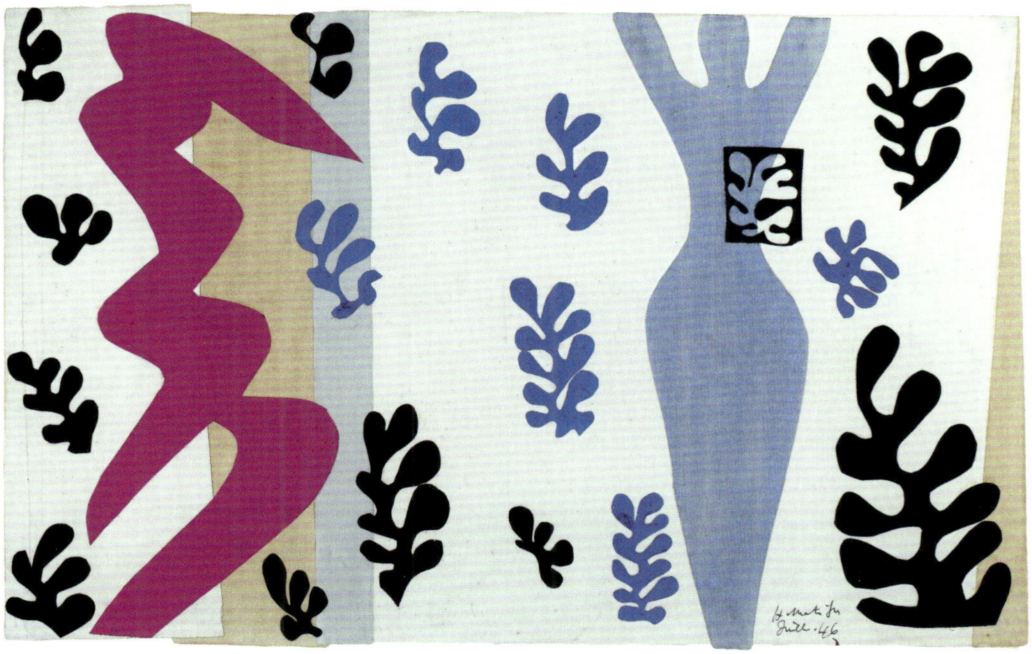

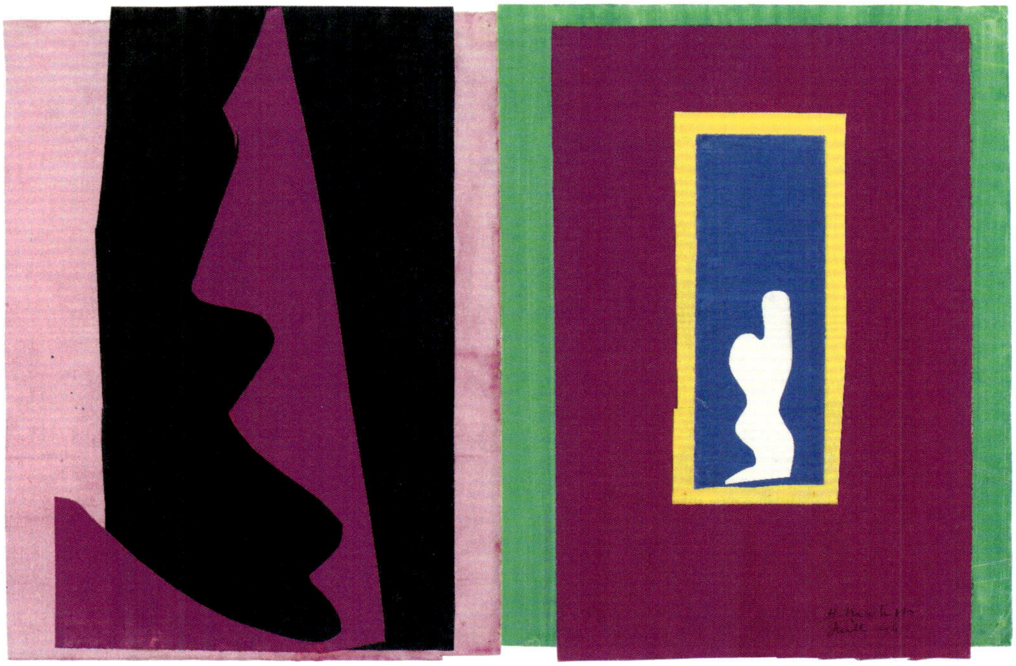

34. *The Knife Thrower* 1943–4
Maquette for plate XV from the illustrated book *Jazz* (1947)
Gouache on paper, cut and pasted, mounted on canvas
43.3 × 67.5 (17 × 26⅝)

35. *Destiny* 1944
Maquette for plate XVI from the illustrated book *Jazz* (1947)
Gouache on paper, cut and pasted, mounted on canvas
44.6 × 67.1 (17½ × 26⅜)

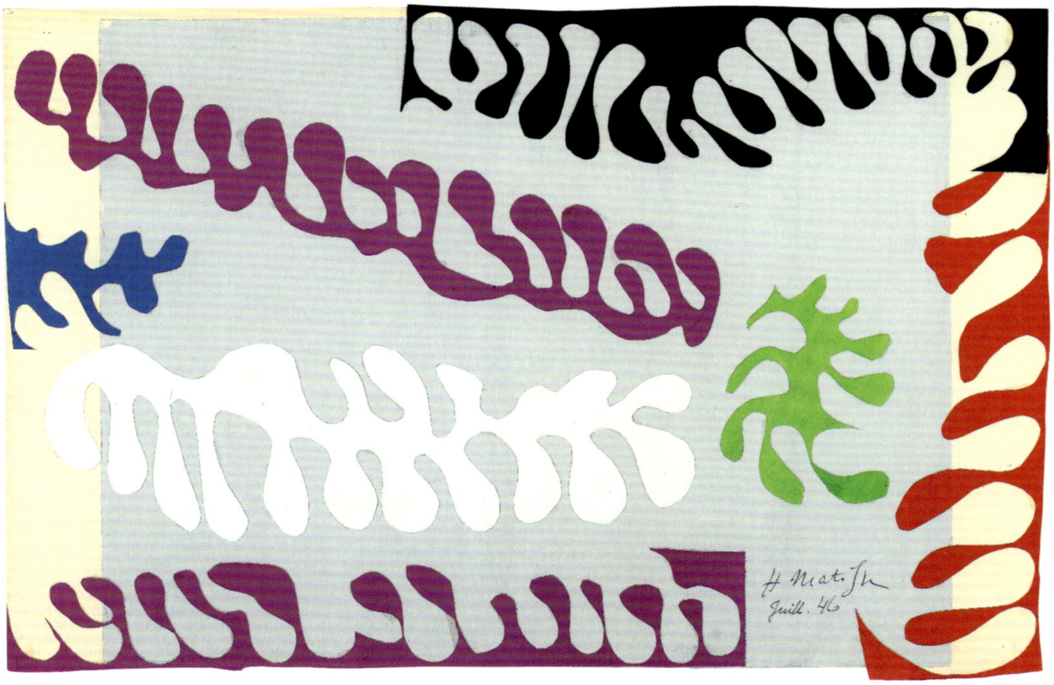

36. *The Lagoon* 1944
Maquette for plate XVII from the illustrated book *Jazz* (1947)
Gouache on paper, cut and pasted, mounted on canvas
44 × 66.3 ($17\frac{3}{8} \times 26\frac{1}{8}$)

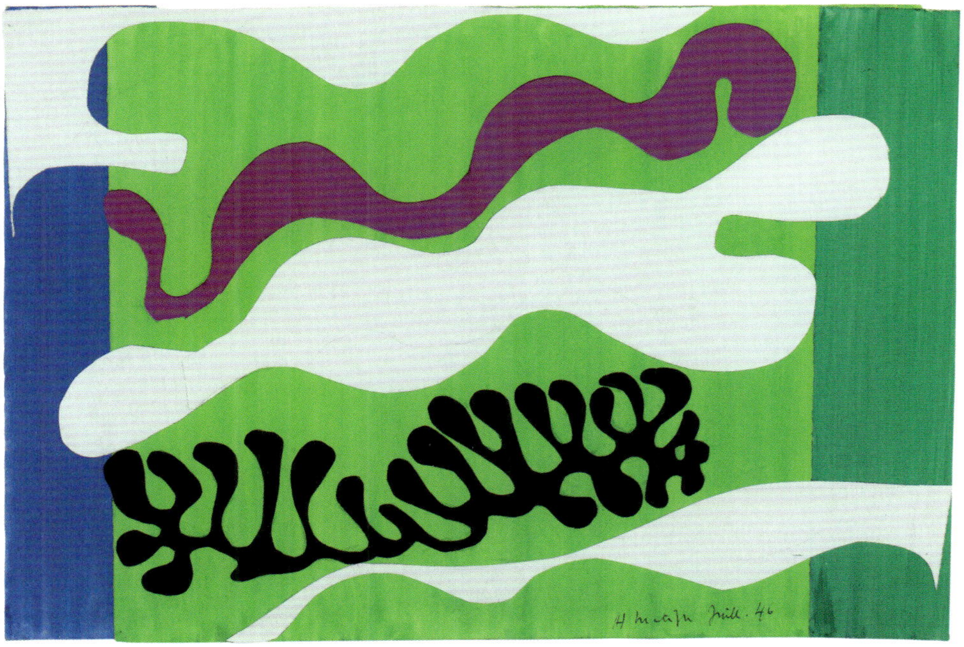

37. *The Lagoon* 1944
Maquette for plate XVIII from the illustrated book *Jazz* (1947)
Gouache on paper, cut and pasted, mounted on canvas
43.6 × 67.1 (17⅛ × 26⅜)

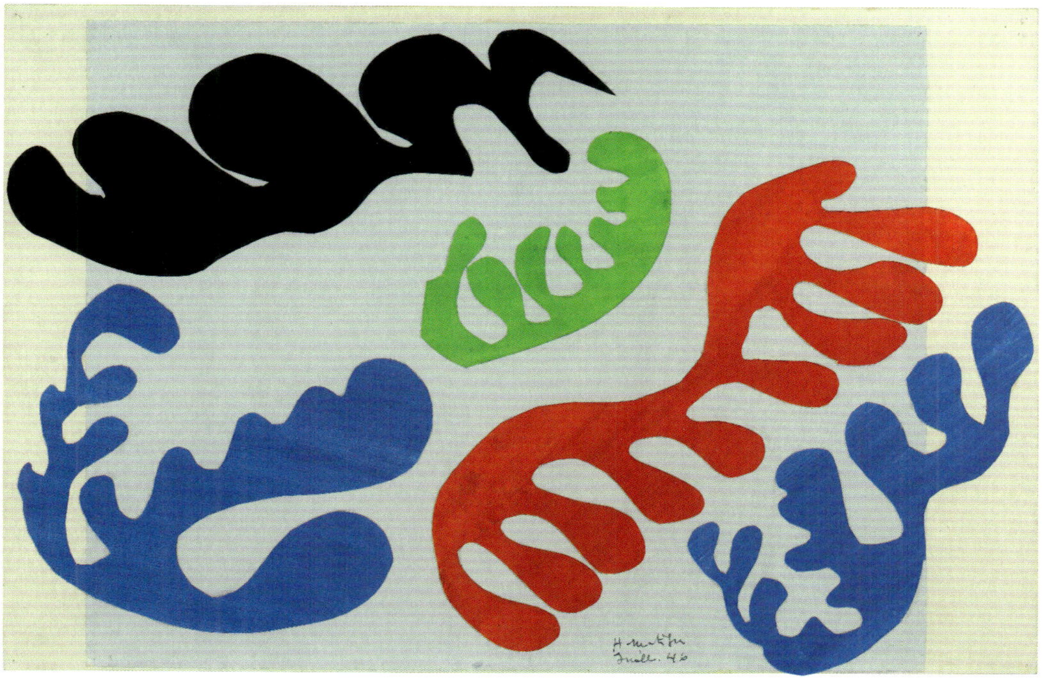

38. *The Lagoon* 1944
Maquette for plate XIX from the illustrated book *Jazz* (1947)
Gouache on paper, cut and pasted, mounted on canvas
44 × 67.1 (17⅜ × 26⅜)

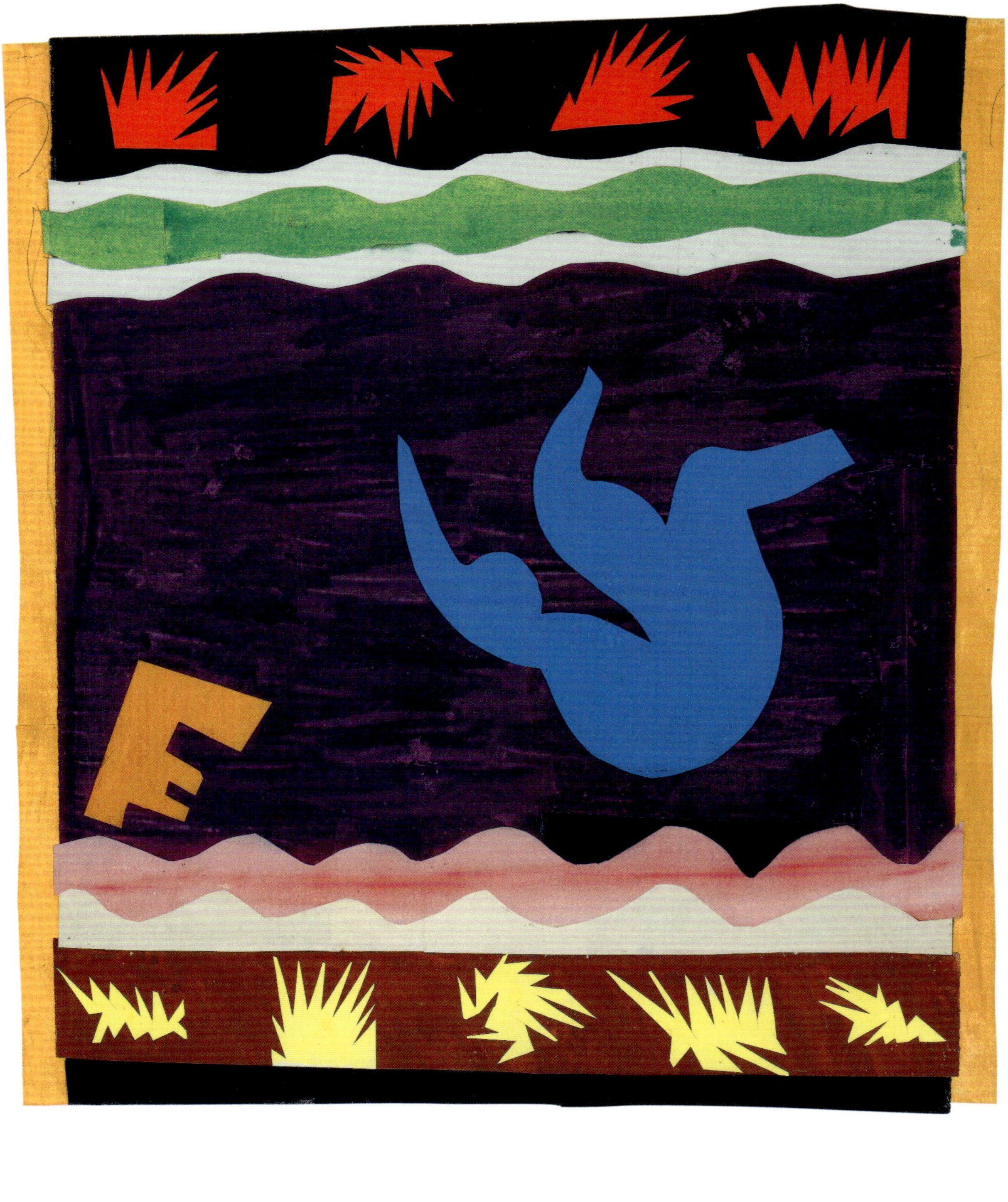

39. *The Toboggan* 1943
Maquette for plate XX from the illustrated book *Jazz* (1947)
Gouache on paper, cut and pasted, mounted on canvas
63.2 × 53.3 (24⅞ × 21)

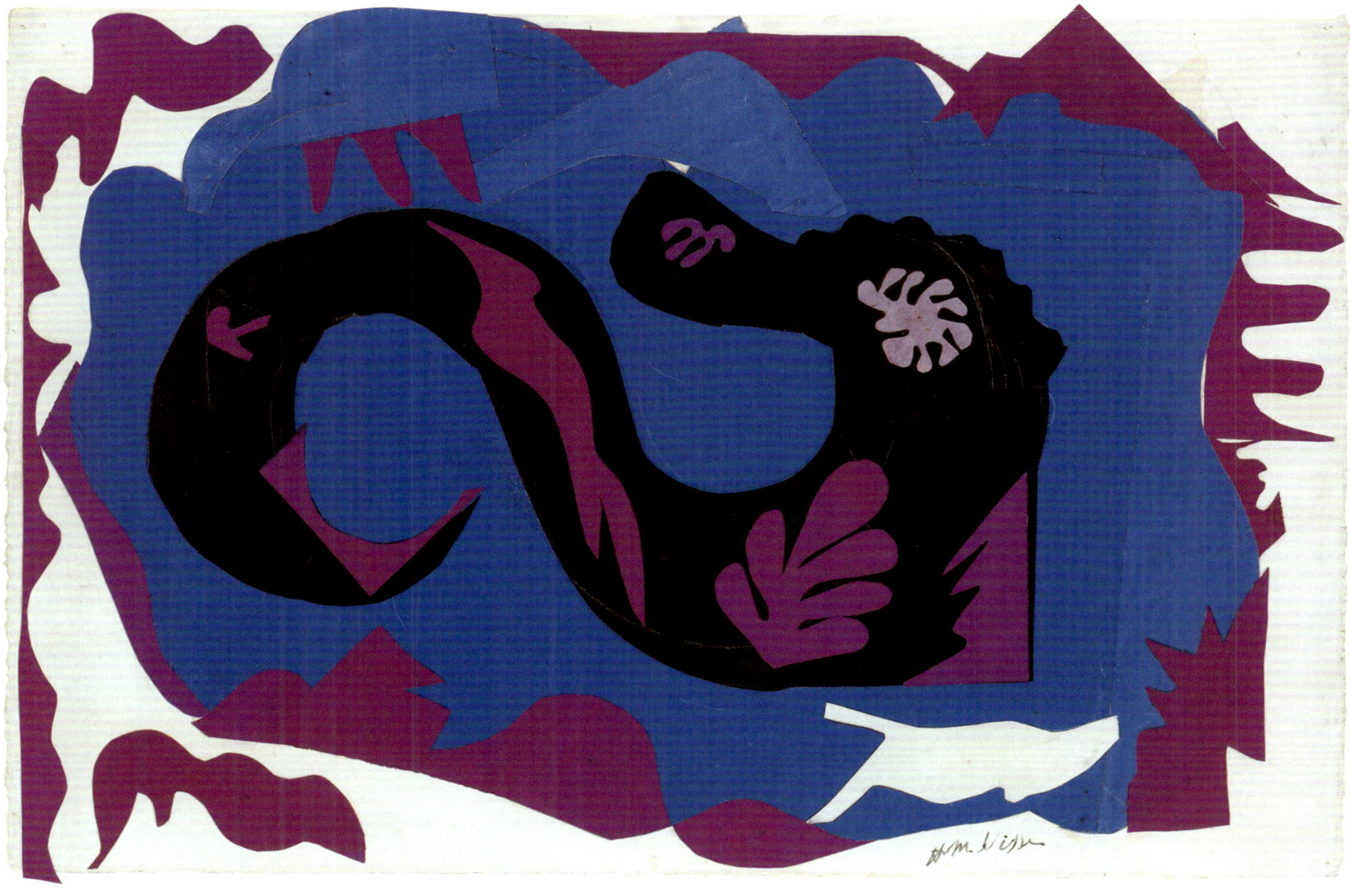

40. *The Dragon* 1943–4
Gouache on paper, cut and pasted, 42.5 × 65.5 (16¾ × 25¾)

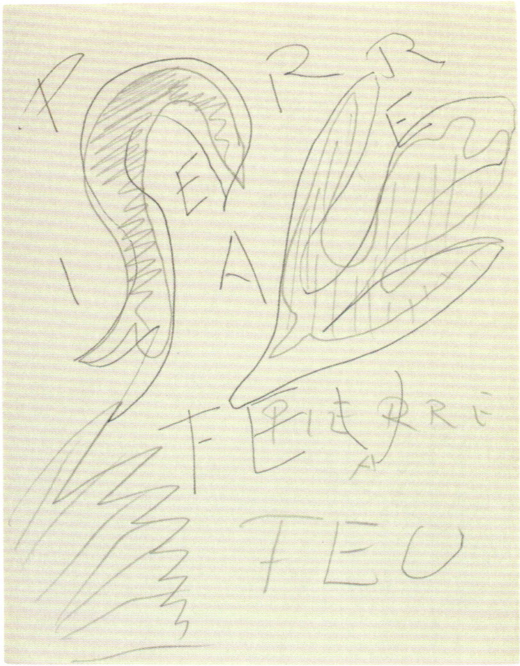

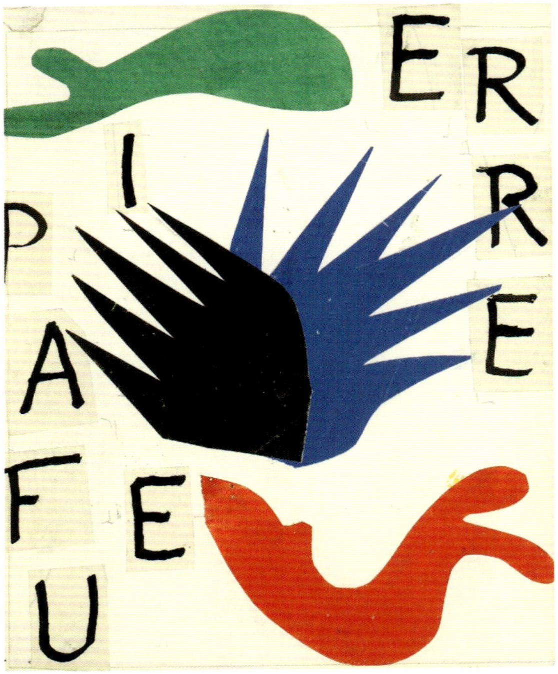

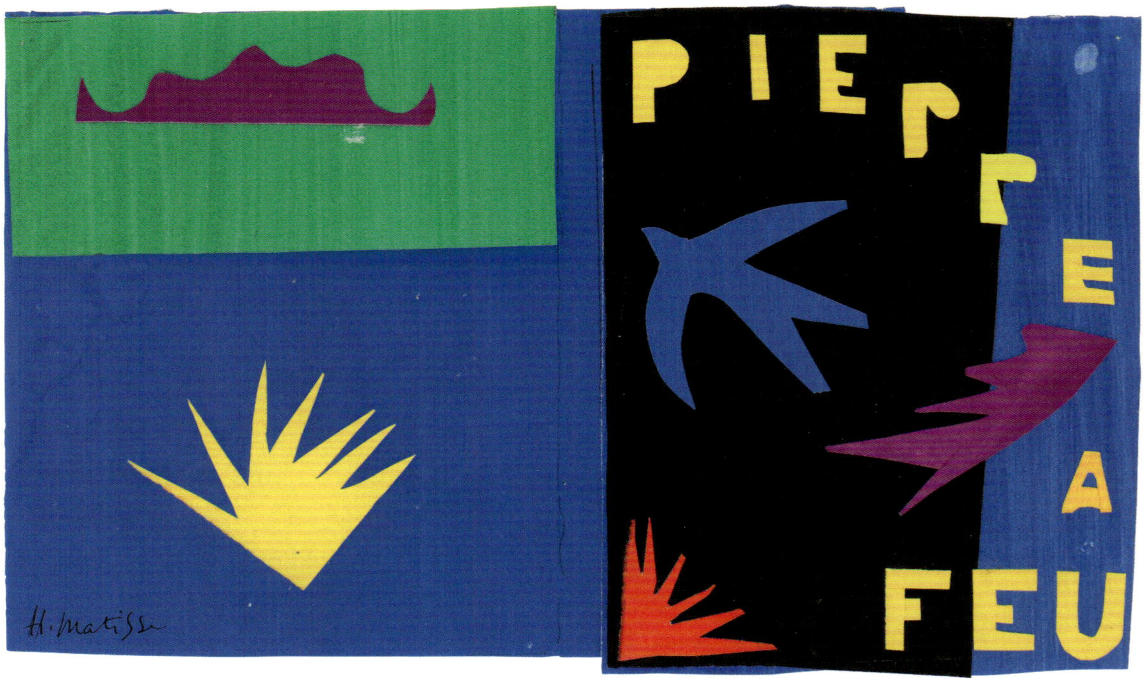

41. Drawing for *Pierre à feu* 1945
Pencil on paper, 27 × 21.1 (10⅝ × 8¼)

42. *Pierre à feu*, cover maquette for the book *Les Miroirs profonds* (1947) 1945
Gouache on paper, cut and pasted, and ink
25 × 41 (9⅞ × 16⅛)

43. *Pierre à feu*, unrealised cover maquette for the book *Les Miroirs profonds* (1947) 1945
Gouache on paper, cut and pasted, and pencil
24.8 × 42.5 (9¾ × 16¾)

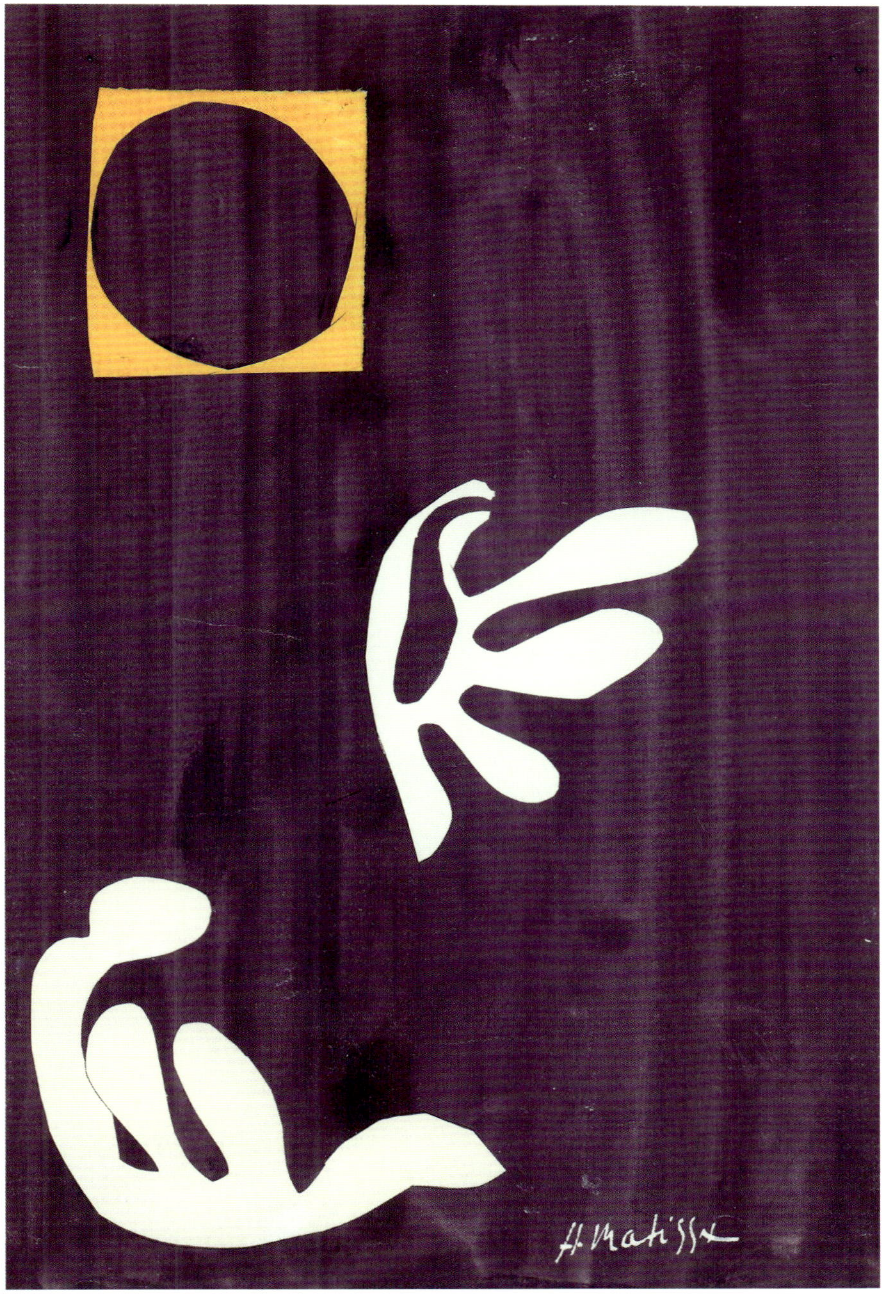

44. *Composition (Tahitian Harmony)* 1945–6
Gouache on paper, cut and pasted
56.5 × 36.5 (22¼ × 14⅜)

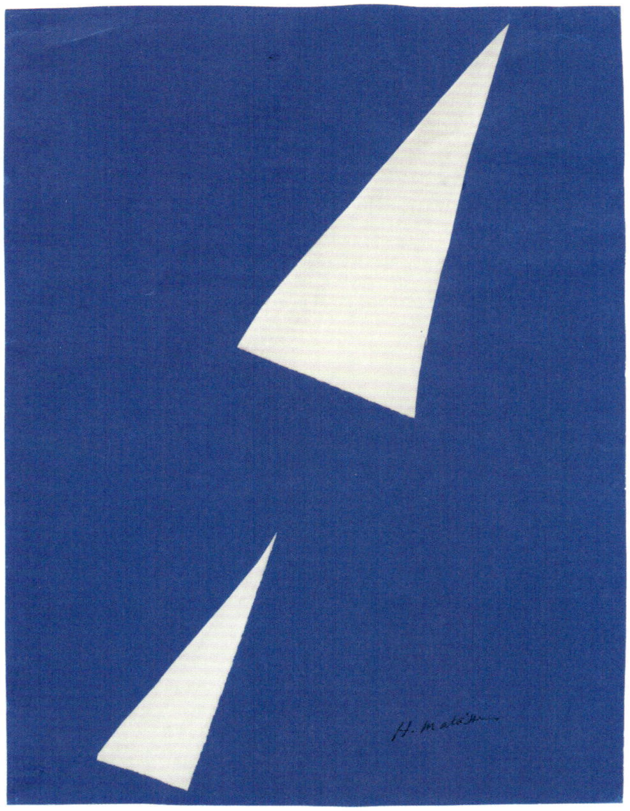

45. *The Sails* 1945–6
Gouache on paper, cut and pasted
52.7 × 40.4 (20¾ × 15⅞)

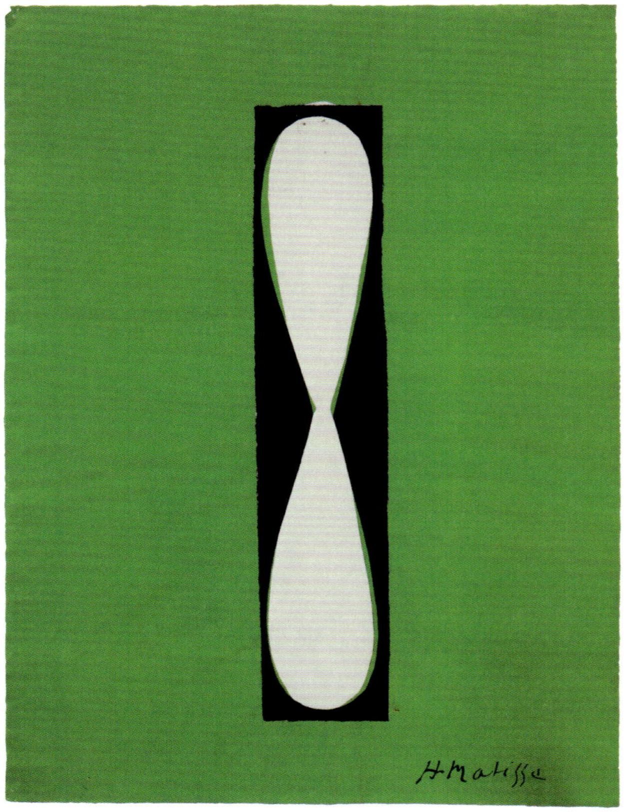

46. *The Propeller* 1945
Gouache on paper, cut and pasted, and ink
52.5 × 40.5 (20⅝ × 16)

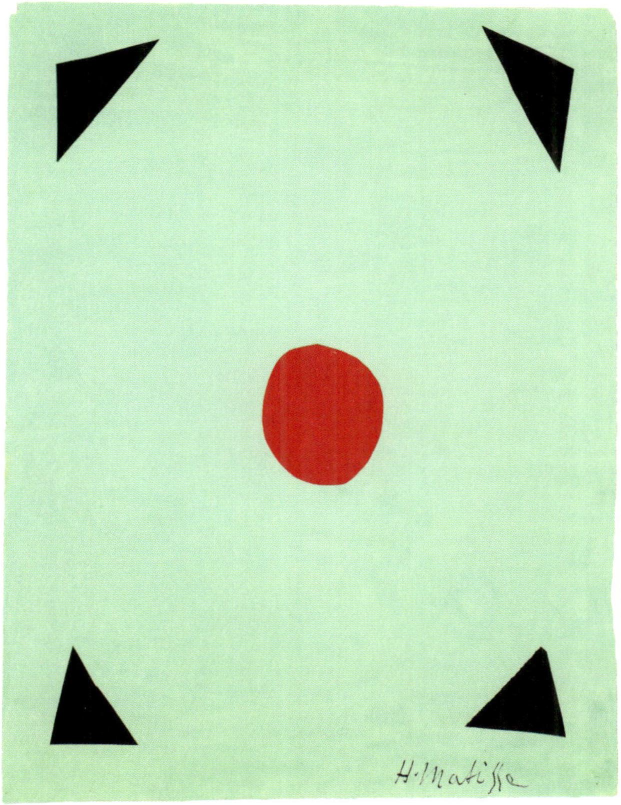

47. *Composition (Red Circle with Four Black Triangles on Green Background)* 1945–6
Gouache on paper, cut and pasted
52.5 × 40.5 (20⅝ × 16)

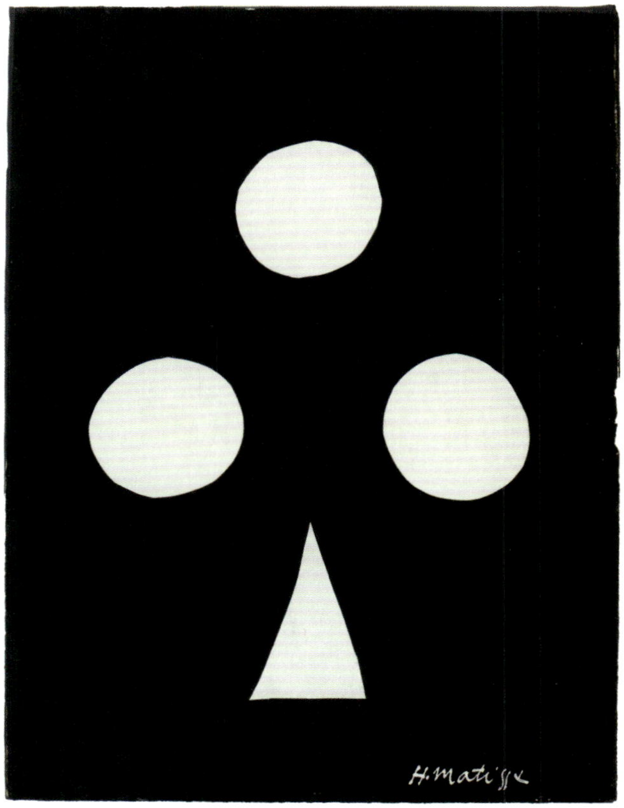

48. *Ace of Clubs* 1945–6
Gouache on paper, cut and pasted
53.7 × 41.4 (21⅛ × 16¼)

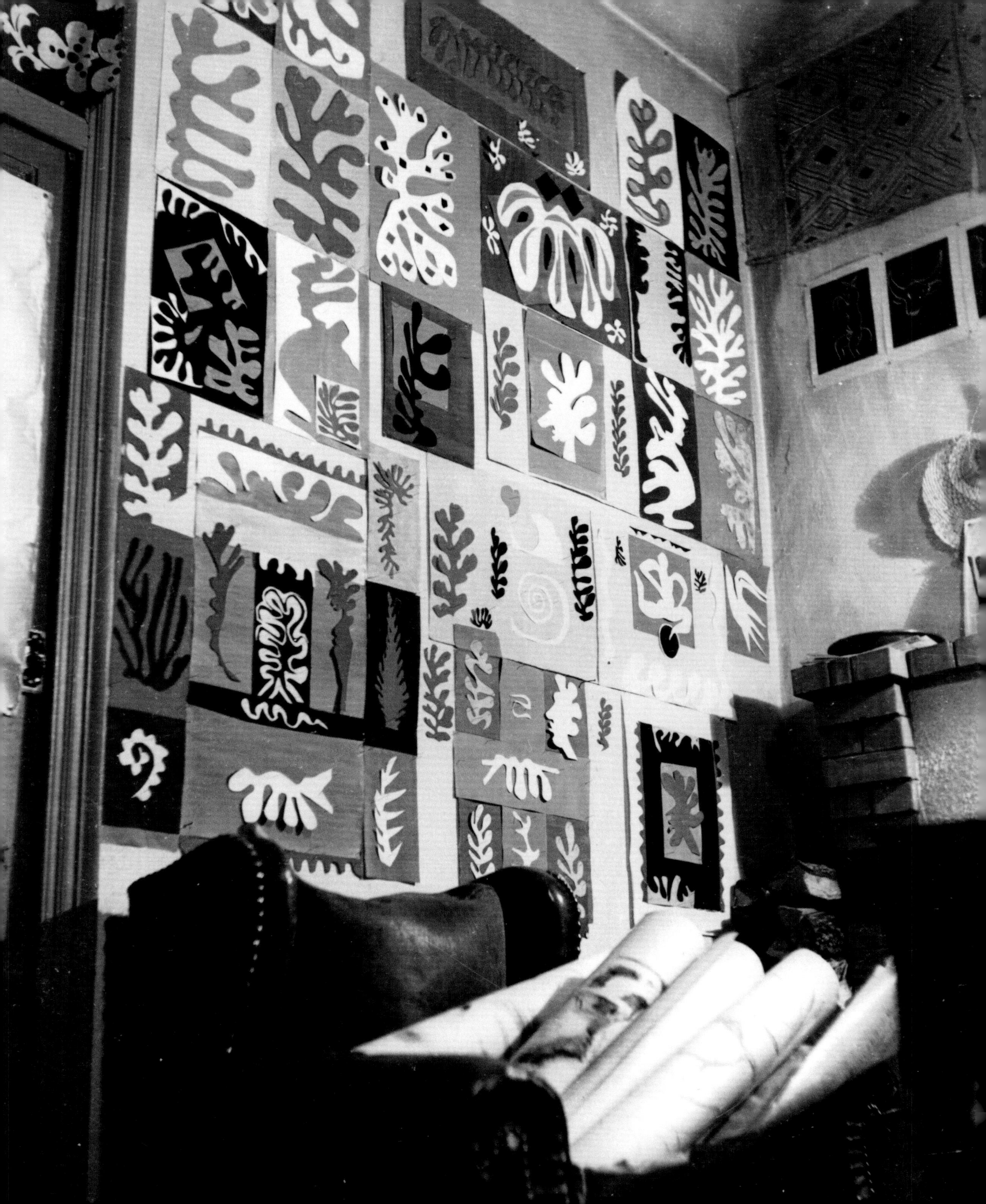

GAME and ENDGAME

Samantha Friedman

Sometime between April 1947, when Matisse returned from a winter in Paris to his Villa le Rêve in Vence, and 5 April the following year, when he declared that he had 'perfected his wall of découpages', the view from his bed appeared as it does in this photograph (fig. 22).[1] The elements of what would soon become fifteen discrete works of art appear here as a continuous forest of forms.[2] Intricately cut, organic shapes clamber across a ground of rectangles, stacked on top of each other like the bricks in the fireplace on the adjoining wall. A few cut forms trespass the horizontal boundaries where sheets of paper meet, making it impossible to tell where one motif ends and another begins. Throughout, the presence of shadows attests to the arrangement's dimensionality, as flaps of paper lift away from the two-dimensional plane. A close look reveals hundreds of pins fixing the shapes to the wall, but Matisse's intricate cuts produced too many tendrils for all of them to be secured.

A little more than one year later, another photograph was taken of many of these same works (fig. 23). This installation shot from *Henri Matisse, Oeuvres Récentes, 1947–1948*, an exhibition at the Musée national d'art moderne, Paris, on view from June to September 1949, shows twelve of the works visible in the photograph of the Vence wall, as well as eight others that appear in additional studio photographs. While they are still stacked four-high, covering the wall in a salon-style configuration, the works are now clearly delimited individual entities, each bounded on four sides by a frame. The pins have been removed in favour of more permanent mounting, the fugitive appendages have been tamed and their attendant shadows have all but vanished.

What happened in the relatively short period between when these two photographs were taken? And how do we account for this dramatic change, in which environment has become object and contingency has given over to permanence? What becomes clear from Matisse's correspondence during this period, and from the visual testimony of his ever-shifting studio walls, is the extent to which the artist himself was undecided about the ultimate form these works would take at the time he was making them. His plans progressed as the forms themselves did – developing organically, embracing ambiguity and unfolding gradually over time.

A close look at the first photograph reveals one work that already appears framed: at the far right of the shot a small leaf rests on top of the fireplace, leaning against what appears to be a straw hat. If this image were in colour (indeed, we must remember that what appears here in black and white was a carefully orchestrated riot of colour), we would see that it is a black leaf on a blue ground (no. 69). Why is this one motif set apart from its compatriots, isolated in advance of them as a distinct composition? The answer requires a brief flashback, but one that usefully demonstrates the role of contingency in the evolution of Matisse's cut-outs.

Like many of Matisse's earliest cut-out experiments – his designs for ballet curtains and his covers for the periodical *Verve* – *Leaf Motif* was a maquette to be realised in another medium. Its shape can be seen repeating radially on a square

Opposite: Fig. 22 Villa le Rêve, Vence, c. 1948

scarf, produced to raise money for the charity organisation Le Bol d'Air (fig. 24). By the time this photograph was taken, the scarf would have already been silkscreened, the cut-out returned to its creator. With a purpose more applied than exploratory, then, this motif had a distinct status, a different lifespan to its counterparts. While they flower progressively on their vertical field, it has already been plucked and preserved.

Directly preceding his work on the wall of the Villa le Rêve, Matisse had completed another decorative commission, with the textile manufacturer Zika Ascher. They began by issuing two scarves, in which the stencil-like remainders of cut-out leaf motifs were silkscreened on the squares' corners (nos. 50–1), much like the Bol d'Air design. The collaboration would expand to include a pair of wall-size panels, *Oceania, the Sea* and *Oceania, the Sky*, whose white forms, printed on beige linen, crystallised Matisse's memories from a 1930 trip to Tahiti.[3] But the cut-outs on which these silkscreens were based (nos. 52–3) were not initially made to serve as maquettes. When Matisse started to pin unpainted forms cut from ordinary white paper on the walls of his Paris apartment (see p. 32), he did not yet have this – or really any – final product in mind. His studio assistant and secretary Lydia Delectorskaya recalled:

> During his stay in Paris during the summer of 1946 Matisse had cut out a swallow from a sheet of writing paper and, as it distressed him to tear up this beautiful shape and throw it away, he said, he put it up on this wall, also using it to cover up a stain the sight of which disturbed him. Over the following weeks other shapes were cut out and put up on the same wall.[4]

According to the photographer Brassaï, who visited the apartment at 132 Boulevard Montparnasse while these works were in progress (see p. 33), Matisse saw the exercise as both provisional and indeterminate: 'I am cutting out all these elements and putting them up on the walls temporarily … I don't know yet what I'll come up with. Perhaps panels, wall hangings.'[5] It was not until Ascher came to the apartment, and saw the nearly finished compositions (see p. 34), that Matisse proposed them as designs for decorations.[6]

If the *Oceania* panels evolved organically, the impulse to create a work with the character of a mural was neither an exceptional whim for this artist nor an isolated phenomenon art-historically. In 1942 Matisse expressed to the writer Louis Aragon that he had 'an unconscious belief in a future life … some paradise where I shall paint frescoes'.[7] Meanwhile, the exhibition *La Tapisserie Française du Moyen Age à nos Jours*, which took place at the Musée d'Art Moderne in Paris in summer 1946, both signalled and furthered modern artists' embrace of the French tradition of decoration scaled to the wall. The trend was also not exclusive to European art. In the 1948 *Partisan Review* article, 'The Situation at the Moment', critic Clement Greenberg sensed in the contemporary state of American abstraction 'a persistent urge, as persistent as it is unconscious, to go beyond the cabinet picture which is destined to occupy only a spot on the wall, to a kind of picture that, without actually becoming identified with the wall like a mural, would spread over it and acknowledge its physical reality'.[8] Matisse was therefore not the only artist wanting to transcend a spot on the wall, and the spread of *Oceania* across his Paris apartment represented a crucial precedent for his provisional mural in Vence.[9]

'The walls of my room are full of découpages,' Matisse wrote to his friend, the writer André Rouveyre, on 22 February 1948 – within the window of time when the Vence wall photograph would have been taken.[10] He went on to express his uncertainty about the fate of these creations to his frequent correspondent, confiding: 'I do not yet know what I will do with these new découpages, certainly not a *Jazz*.'[11] This conviction of what the motifs would *not* become – namely, printed book illustrations – came in the context of a larger epistolary exchange with Rouveyre about the ways in which *Jazz* ultimately disappointed. Their in-depth discussion of the faults of that book's stencil-printed *pochoir* plates coincided with the unfolding of the cut-outs on Matisse's walls, undoubtedly influencing the artist's intentions for them.

With *Jazz* on view for the first time at Galerie Pierre Berès, Paris, in December 1947, Matisse solicited the opinion of his friend, who had seen the cut-out maquettes for this project (nos. 18–21, 24–39) in development two years earlier: 'If you can stop by there, your impression will interest me.'[12] Rouveyre's decidedly negative reaction came a week later: 'It is dry and cold. Just exactly the opposite of that which is your genius … One has the impression of being before, you know, those boxes which, in the manner

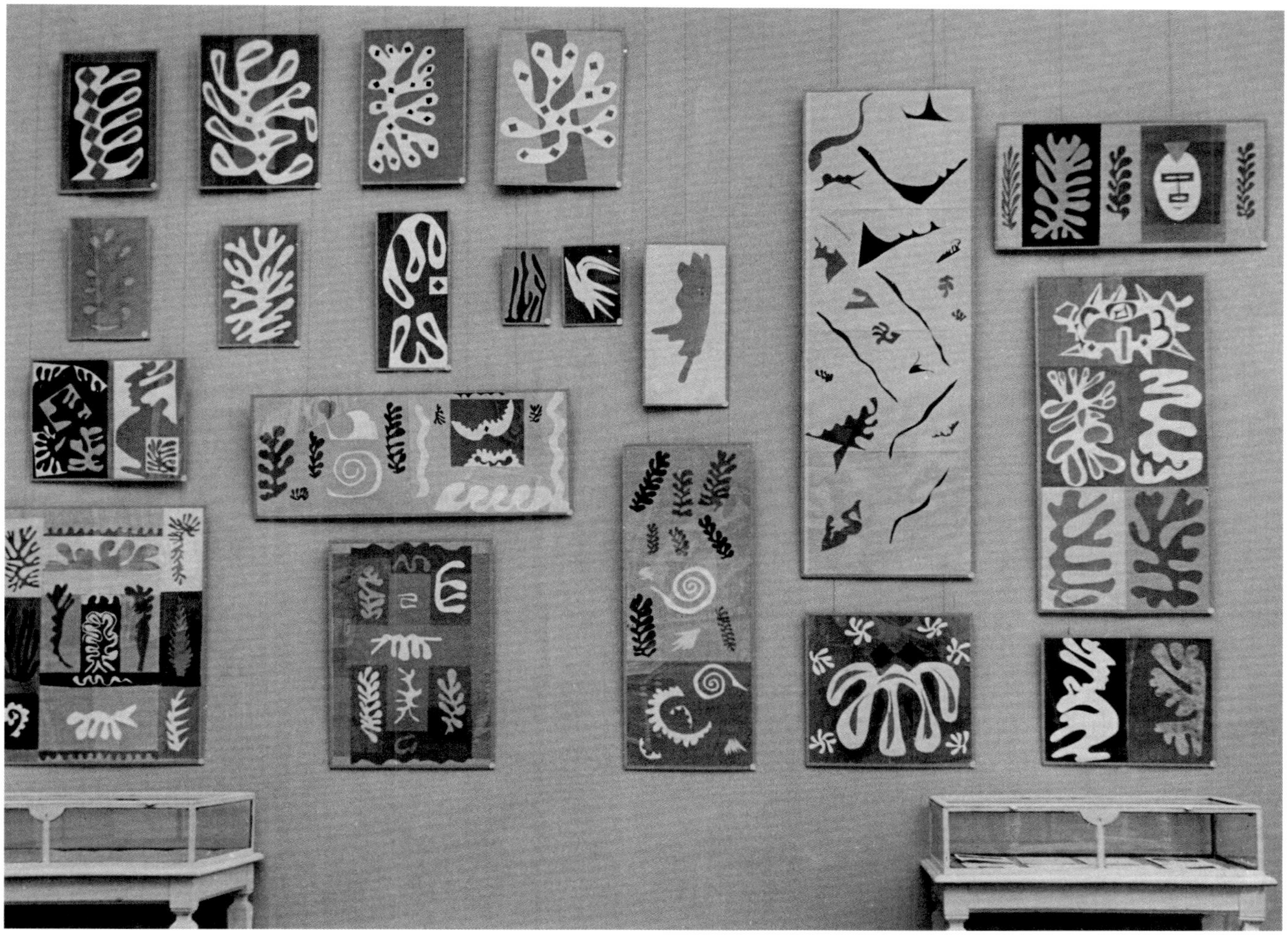

Fig. 23 *Henri Matisse: Oeuvres Récentes, 1947–48*, Musée National d'Art Moderne, Paris, June – September 1949

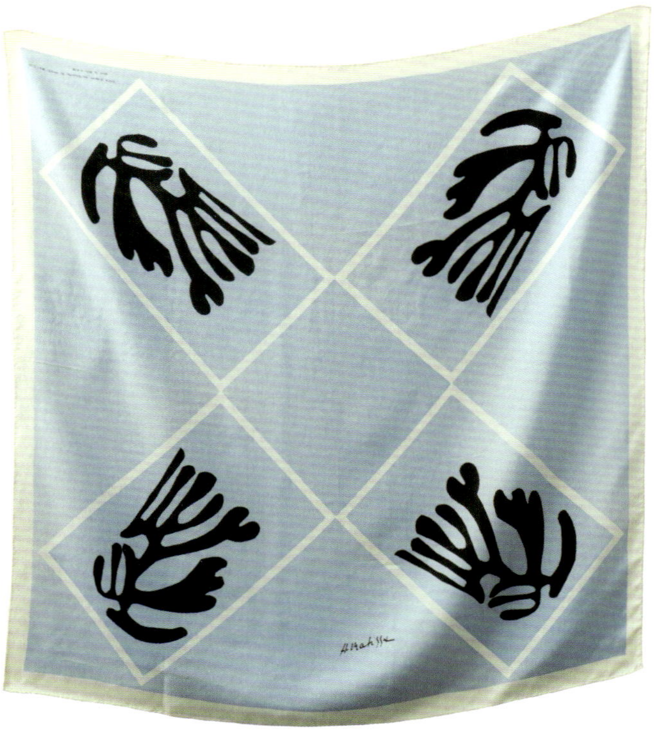

Fig.24 Scarf for *Le Bol d'Air* c. 1948, printed silk, 88 × 86 (34⅝ × 33⅞). Collection Musée Matisse Le Cateau-Cambrésis

of toys, are plaques of wood covered in coloured scenes and cut into pieces that one must scramble and put back together in the right order.'[13] Despite the fact that he tempered this report with warmth ('Your plates very well presented ... I looked at them again with affectionate emotion') and humility ('Say that I'm foolish and that I don't understand anything ... that you have the right to amuse yourself, to cut as you please'), Rouveyre nonetheless wrote to Matisse again several days later, 'intimately chagrined at having written with such extreme liberty on the subject of your *Jazz*'.[14] This time, he offered a more specific assessment, citing the loss of materiality that occurred with the translation to a different medium: 'It's the *material* that's no longer there. When you fix your paper cut-outs it reflects your flame, it's truly a paper cut-out by you. The work of a magician ... From the moment when your work passes through intermediaries the fire is lost along the way.'[15]

Rather than being offended by Rouveyre's critique of *Jazz*, Matisse thanked his friend for his honesty and replied that he was '*absolutely of the same opinion* ... It is absolutely *a failure*.'[16] He compared the finished *pochoir* plates to the cut-outs' lively existence in his studio, speculating as to 'why these cut-outs when I make them, that I see them on the wall are sympathetic to me and without the character of a puzzle that I find in them in Jazz. I think that what absolutely ruins them is the transposition, which removes their sensitivity.'[17] Nonetheless, he assured Rouveyre that he was 'not at all discouraged' and was 'busy this afternoon making new combinations of colours with the paper cut-out system'.[18] Adding that his present work was benefiting from the lessons learned with *Jazz*, he declared: 'I know that these things must stay as they are, originals – very simply, gouaches.'[19]

So the cut-outs affixed to Matisse's walls would not become a *Jazz*, but what Rouveyre marvelled at was not only the works' original medium – as opposed to their translation to *pochoir* – but the 'precarious, fragile existence'[20] particular to their life in the artist's studio. Aware now that Matisse appreciated, even shared his judgment, Rouveyre went on to even more freely extol the cut-outs' virgin state:

> You are right, I think, and it's also my opinion, these paper cut-outs have a very pure existence when they escape from your hands, from your scissors. Their papery material, with subtle plays of light on their flexibility, the very physicality of this flexibility, all of this contributes to making

something miraculous that loses its essence when laid out flat. But it retains its essence when stuck up on the wall with pins by Lydia. For doing that preserves the vitality of the paper I mentioned, by subjecting it to constant changes. Wanting to dryly flatten is to imagine wanting to stretch flat the surface of a beautiful girl's skin, like drying the skin of a rabbit. You understand me of course![21]

Rouveyre draws a clear distinction between the cut-outs' supple material life and the possibility of their dry, taxidermic death. But what exactly did Matisse mean when he told his friend that the works developing on his wall would remain 'originals'? Simply that he would not transpose them into another medium, such as an illustrated book, or that he would also, somehow, attempt to preserve this essential flexibility, this capacity for change?

In this correspondence between Matisse and Rouveyre the metaphor of a puzzle emerges as something to be avoided in the character of the cut-outs.[22] That *Jazz* reminds Rouveyre of a wooden toy to be scrambled and reassembled is part of his critique, and Matisse adopts the comparison, noting that his wall-bound cut-outs happily manage to avoid this jigsaw effect. Their exchange also prompts another analogy in which Matisse distinguishes the cut-out practice as a *system*, rather than simply a medium. Defined in the dictionary as 'a regularly interacting or interdependent group of items forming a unified whole', the notion of a system suggests that Matisse was considering the wall not only as a collection of individual parts but as an overall entity, an entirety.[23]

Ultimately, it is yet another metaphor – one that Matisse himself invoked several times during the period of his work with cut paper – that may best elucidate how he regarded the ever-shifting elements on his wall. In 1935, soon after he had employed an early version of the 'paper cut-out system' in designing the Barnes mural, Matisse likened a pair of paintings with different palettes to 'two aspects of a chessboard in the course of a game of chess. The appearance of the board is continually changing in the course of play, but the intentions of the players who move the pawns remain constant.'[24] A decade later he drew a comparison to a related game when reflecting back on the method employed for the Merion project, recalling: 'I worked on this for three years, constantly moving around 11 flat tinted shapes, a bit like the way one moves around the pieces during a game of checkers (I [should] add that these shapes were pieces of coloured paper) until I found an arrangement that satisfied me completely.'[25] And in 1951, as his cut-outs were on the verge of growing into room-sized, decorative murals, he reflected on 'why I have never tried to play chess, although it was suggested to me by friends who thought they knew me well. I told them: "I can't play with signs that never change. This Bishop this King, this Queen, this Castle, mean nothing to me. But', he continued, imagining a scenario in which the game might suit him, 'if you were to put little figures that look like so-and-so or such a one, people whose life we know, then I could play; but still inventing a meaning for each Pawn in the course of each game."'[26]

It was according to these new rules, then – in which the signs for and the meanings of the pieces can change throughout the course of a game – that Matisse played chess on his wall in Vence. Against a gridded board of coloured sheets, he moved plentiful pawns in the form of varied leaves, rarer silhouette shapes that we might think of as rooks, bishops or knights, and unique instances of a bird or a shark, his version of a queen or a king. Thanks to a second photograph, taken slightly later but in the same year-long window (p. 38), we can study the progression of the master's moves. And with our foreknowledge of the endgame, when the pieces have left the board as autonomous works, we can observe how these fluid signs shift towards their ultimate significations.

The left side of the wall's composition changes very little from the earlier photograph to the later one. A vertical stack of three recognisable works – from top to bottom, *Panel with Mask* (no. 56), *Composition, Black and Red* (no. 64), and *Amphitrite* (no. 55) – is already established in the earlier shot. The only detectable change is the replacement of the form in *Amphitrite*'s top-left corner from a lighter-coloured broader-branched species of flora to the deep-green specimen with spindlier offshoots that remains in the final work. Though the overall structure of the wall's lower-right quadrant remains relatively stable as well – with the works we will come to recognise as, clockwise from top, *The Bird and the Shark*,[27] *Bird*,[28] *Flowering Tree (Mural Scroll)* (no. 61) and *Composition with Red Cross* (no. 54) – significant changes occur within these individual compositions. From the first photograph to the second, for example, the motif featured in the right half of *The Bird and*

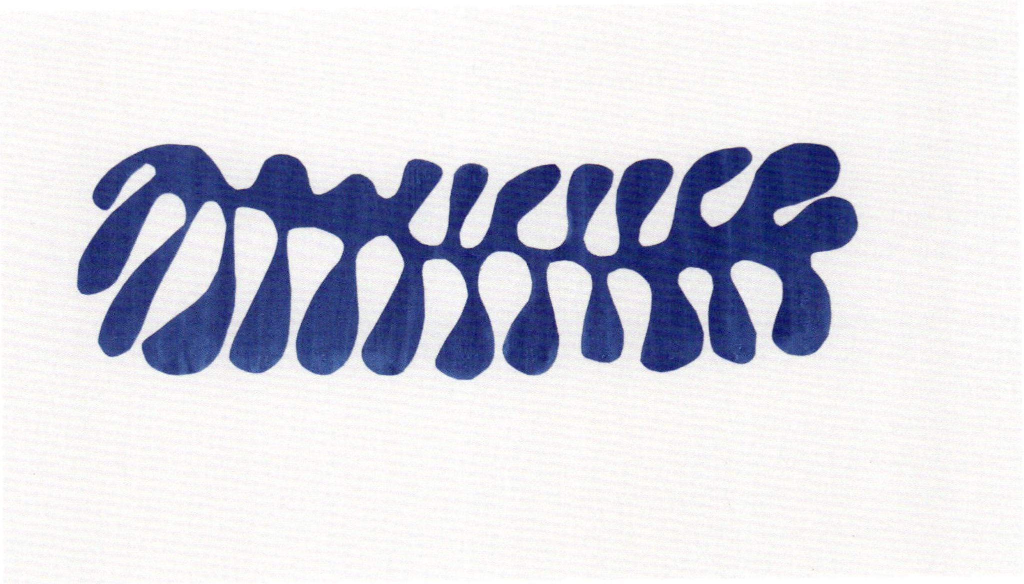

Fig. 25 Unused gouache element, no. 487, Musée Matisse, Nice. Gift of the Matisse family

the Shark changes from a human figure, balancing on a ball like the elephant in *Jazz,* to a sign for a bird in flight. Thin, vertical leaves are appe nded to either side of *Composition with Red Cross,* though they will later shift again, to flank the central panel of *Flowering Tree (Mural Scroll),* the next motif to the right. *Composition with Red Cross* will also subsequently lose the silhouette shape in its top-right corner, seen in both of these photographs, in favour of the abstracted medusa we see today.

Matisse shuffles his chessmen most actively in the remaining area, at the wall's upper right. One piece, *White Alga on a Red and Green Background* (no. 59),[29] captures another, a long, horizontal motif at the top of the wall, kicking it off the board and taking over its position (top row, second from the left). Once that man moves up, *Two Masks (The Tomato)* (no. 62) is free to slide leftwards into the vacated square. Though similar in composition to the four-part base of *Panel with Mask,* which is ultimately kept intact, the quartet at the wall's upper-right corner is broken up into individual works: from the first photograph to the second, *Black and Violet Arabesques on an Orange Background* (no. 68) leaves the wall entirely; *Snow Tree*[30] shifts left to occupy that work's former position (second row down, third from right); *Blue Algae on Red Background*[31] makes a diagonal cross into *that* work's previous spot (second row down, far right); and the green leaf on a black ground at extreme upper right moves down and to the left to replace *Negro Boxer* (no. 63), which leaves the wall. Here this green leaf joins an arrangement that will eventually become *The Eskimo* (no. 57), once its head in profile is eventually swapped out for a front-facing mask.

What happens to those motifs that Matisse removes from the state of play? Some, like the long, horizontal form that disappears from one image to the next, are simply set aside (fig. 25).[32] Others, such as the bold black, red and green *Negro Boxer,* leave this chessboard only to join another. Appearing in the first photograph but not in the second, *Negro Boxer* resurfaces on another of Villa le Rêve's walls (p. 39). In this sparser, more heterogeneous arrangement *Negro Boxer* is comparatively self-sufficient, sharing merely the plumb line of an architectural seam with two leaves from *Composition (The Velvets)* (no. 65). Nonetheless, the fact that Matisse incorporated it into an active new configuration suggests the extent to which he continued to conceive of the cut-outs as interdependent parts of a working system. The visual presence of *Negro Boxer* within this new arrangement would surely affect, however subtly, the fate of motifs still in play, such as the vertically stacked components that are soon to become *Composition Green Background* (no. 66) but continue to appear here side by side.

Returning to the first photograph, we know that Matisse at least considered the possibility of treating the tightly clustered contents of this wall as a single work. After the declaration to his son Pierre that he had 'perfected his wall of cut-outs', he reported that 'a shipowner who is making a luxury boat called "The Spirit of France" destined for the Orient as far as Japan proposed to buy it from me to put it in his boat in a serious frame and under glass – I said that I would think about it.'[33] Interestingly, the artist's main concern was more conservation-minded than conceptual, citing a 'large obstacle: in this country of excessive humidity all of my gouaches would get moldy'.[34] Though he rejected the offer, perhaps the proposition impelled him towards a decision about the works' future, for he concluded: 'I would rather keep them, or better, frame them as motifs.'[35]

In the end, of course, that's just what he opted to do. On 13 October 1948 Matisse wrote to his son Pierre: 'The works for an exhibition are all gathered and placed in a corner.'[36] In addition to the thirteen paintings and twenty-two drawings enumerated, he lists 'the paper cut-outs, 22 motifs (rather fragile)'.[37] The next time we see the motifs, they're on view at Pierre Matisse's New York Gallery in February 1949 in yet another arrangement, no longer 'pricked to the wall with pins', but hung from a horizontal picture rail (fig. 26). Not having been transposed to another medium, as *Jazz* was, these cut-outs retain, even today, material reminders of their former existence on the studio wall: the lifting of a leaf, countless telltale pinholes. And if these early products of a new system of working did not ultimately retain their original status as a kind of installation art, such environmental conditions would become a lasting concern in the cut-outs' next chapters.

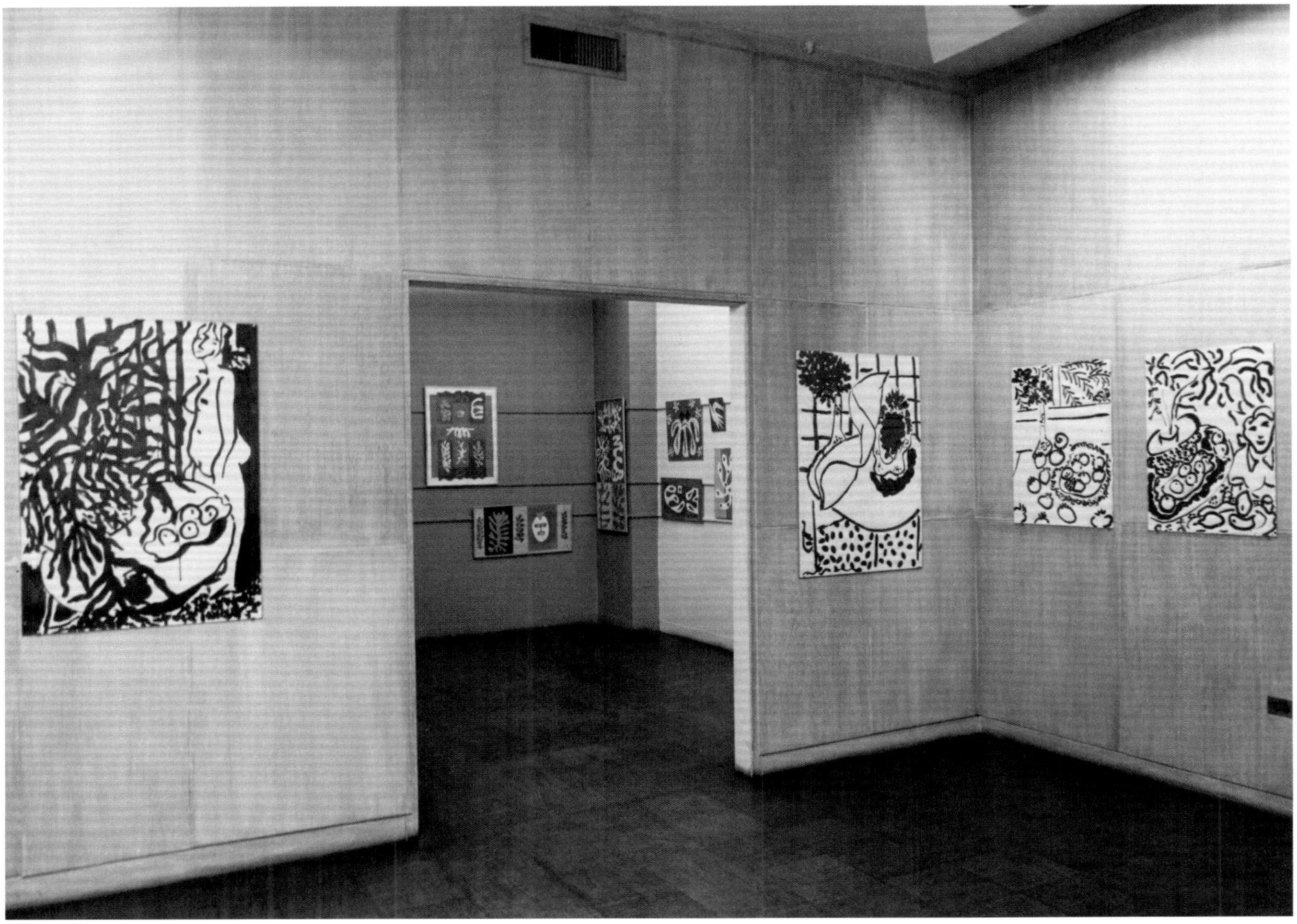

Fig. 26 *Henri Matisse: Paintings, Papiers Découpés, Drawings 1945–1948*, Pierre Matisse Gallery, New York, 1–28 February 1949

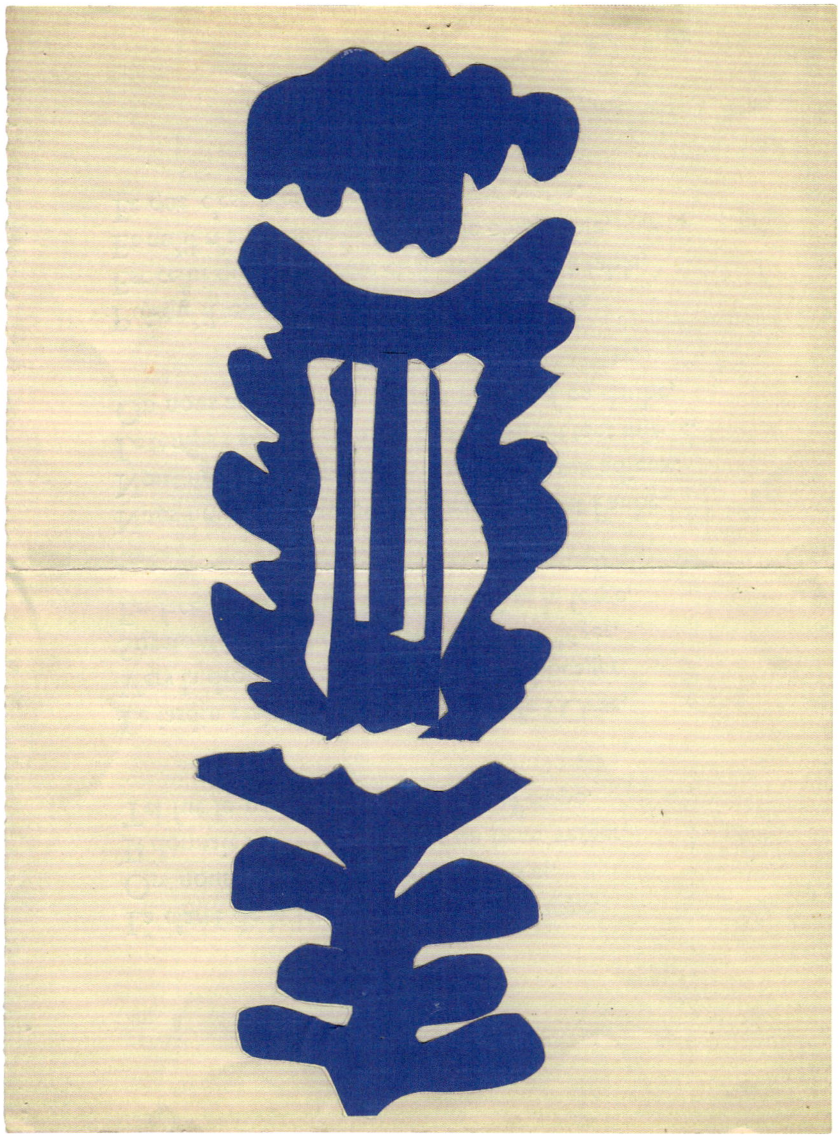

49. *The Lyre* 1946
Gouache on paper, cut and pasted
31.6 × 23.3 (12½ × 9⅛)

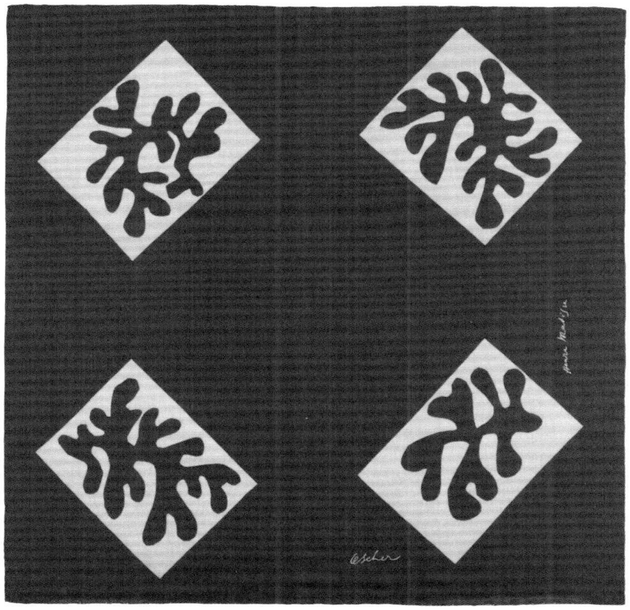

50. *Ascher Square A* 1947
Printed blue silk, 91.44 × 91.44 (36 × 36)

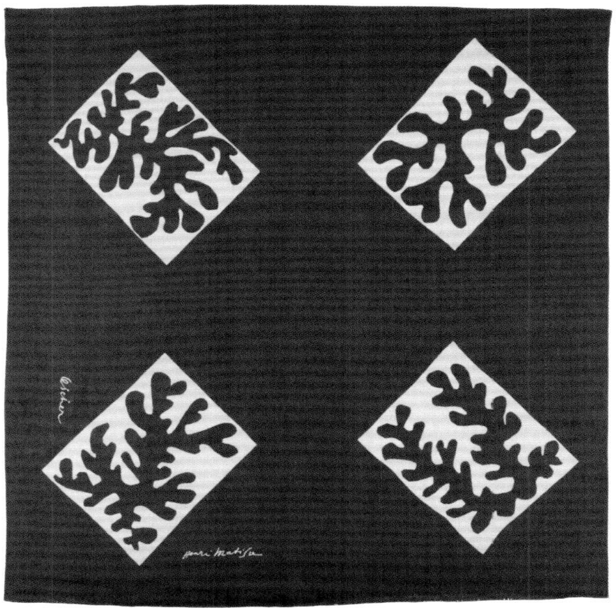

51. *Ascher Square B* 1947
Printed grey silk, 91.44 × 91.44 (36 × 36)

52. *Oceania, the Sky* summer 1946
(realised as silkscreen 1946)
Gouache on paper, cut and pasted, on paper,
mounted on canvas, 178.3 × 369.7 (70⅛ × 145½)

53. *Oceania, the Sea* summer 1946
(realised as silkscreen 1946)
Gouache on paper, cut and pasted, on paper,
mounted on canvas, 178.5 × 392.8 (70¼ × 154⅝)

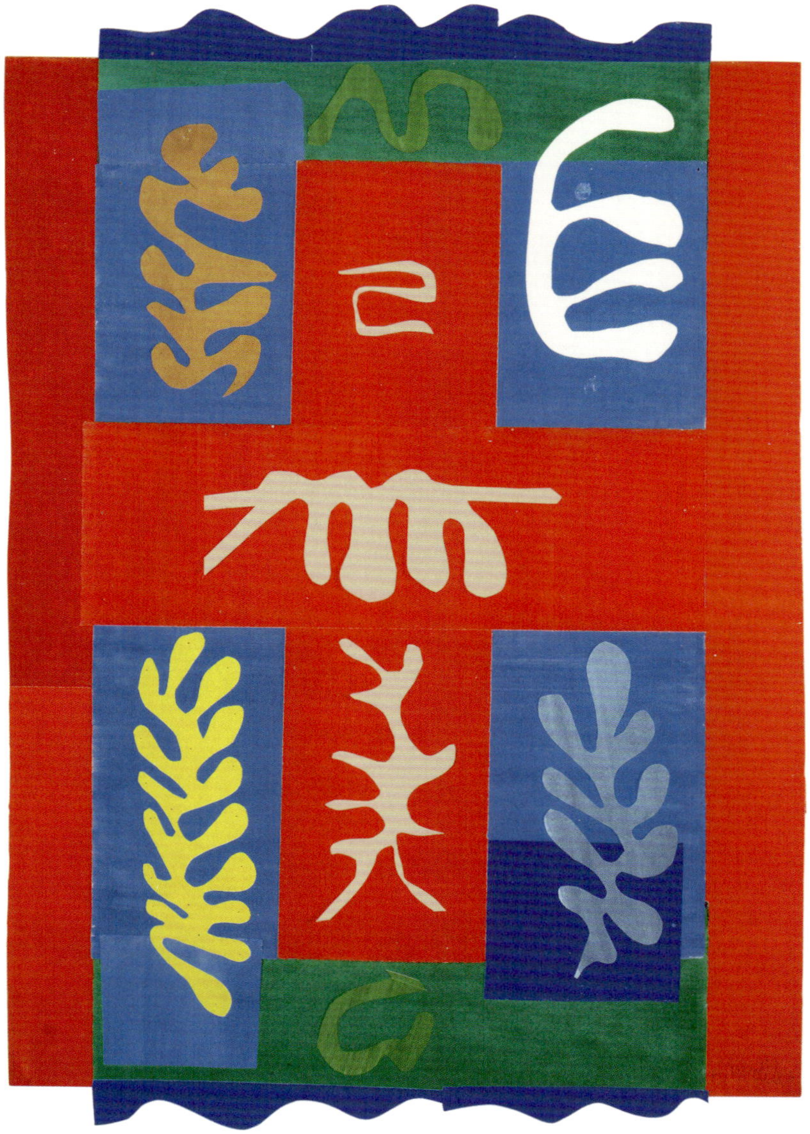

54. *Composition with Red Cross* 1947
Gouache on paper, cut and pasted
74.1 × 52.4 (29⅛ × 20⅝)

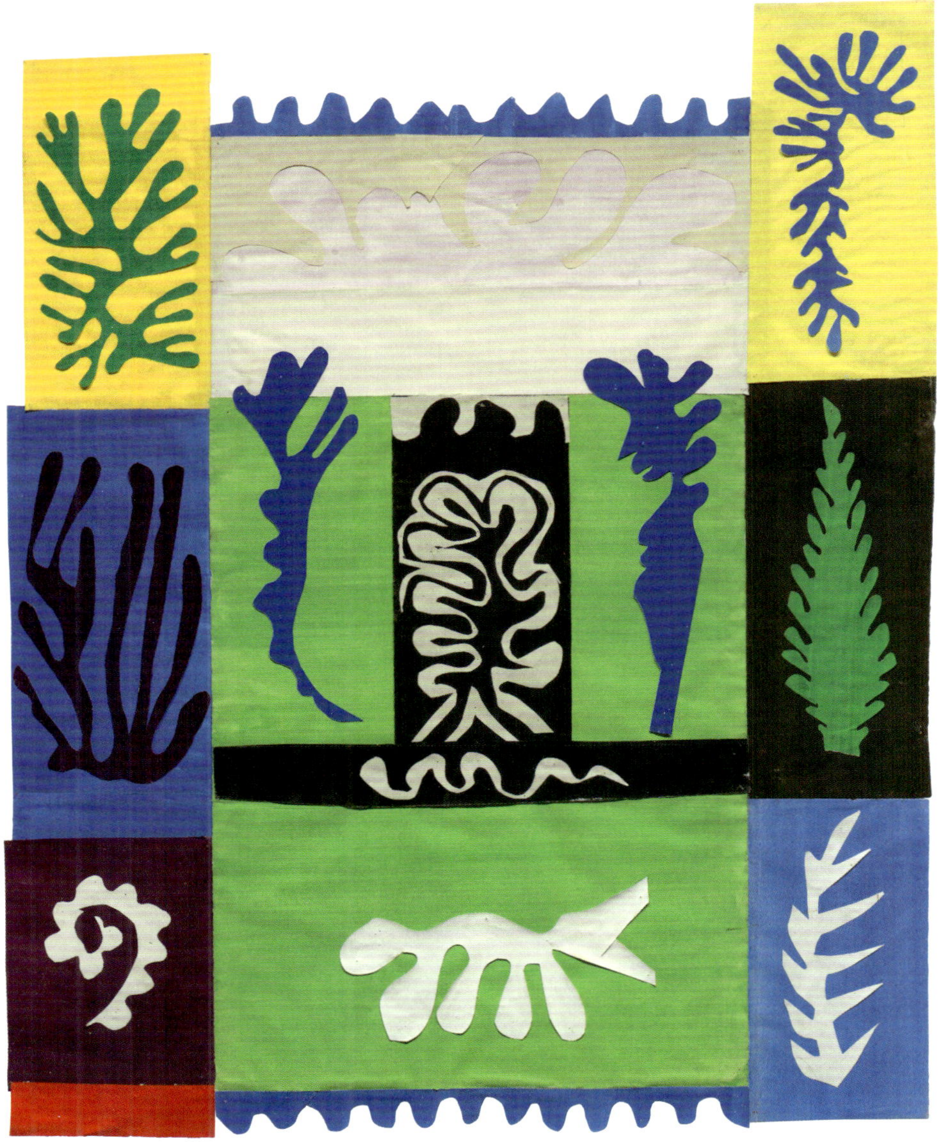

55. *Amphitrite* 1947
Gouache on paper, cut and pasted
85.5 × 70 (33⅝ × 27½)

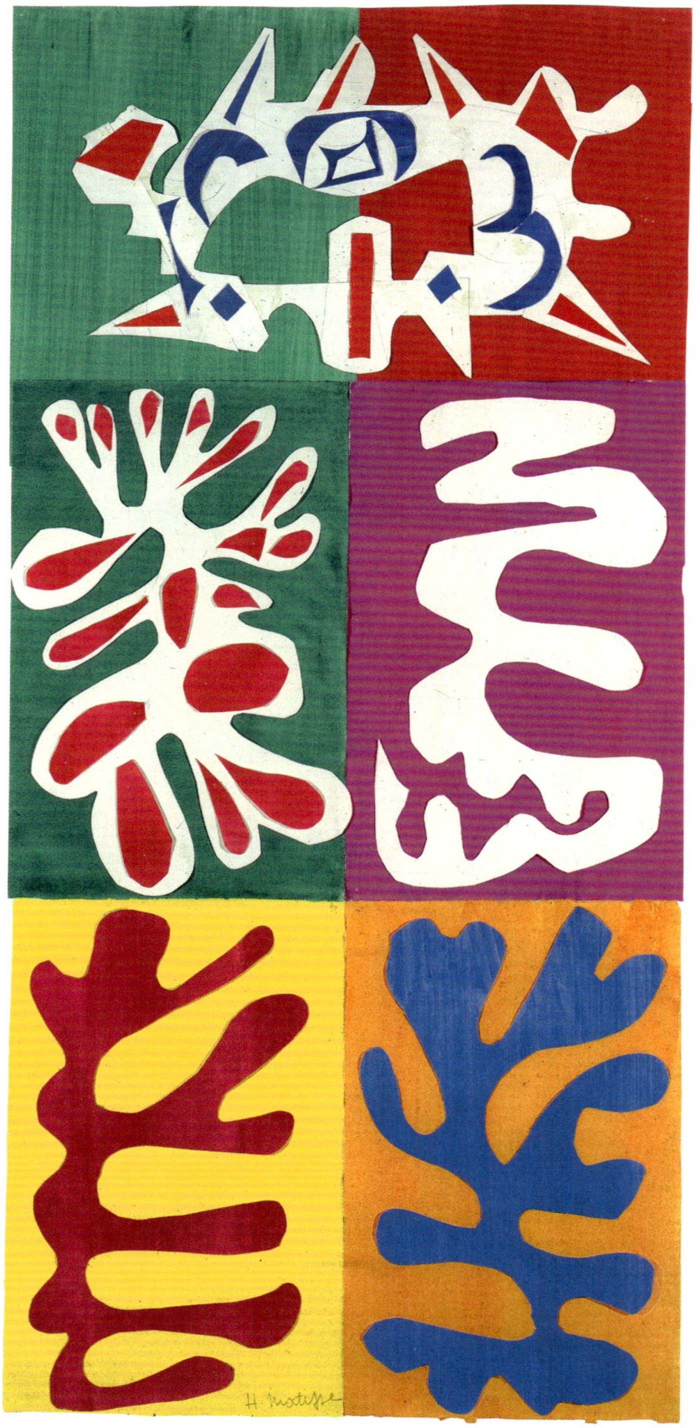

56. *Panel with Mask* 1947
Gouache on paper, cut and pasted
110 × 53 (43¾ × 20⅞)

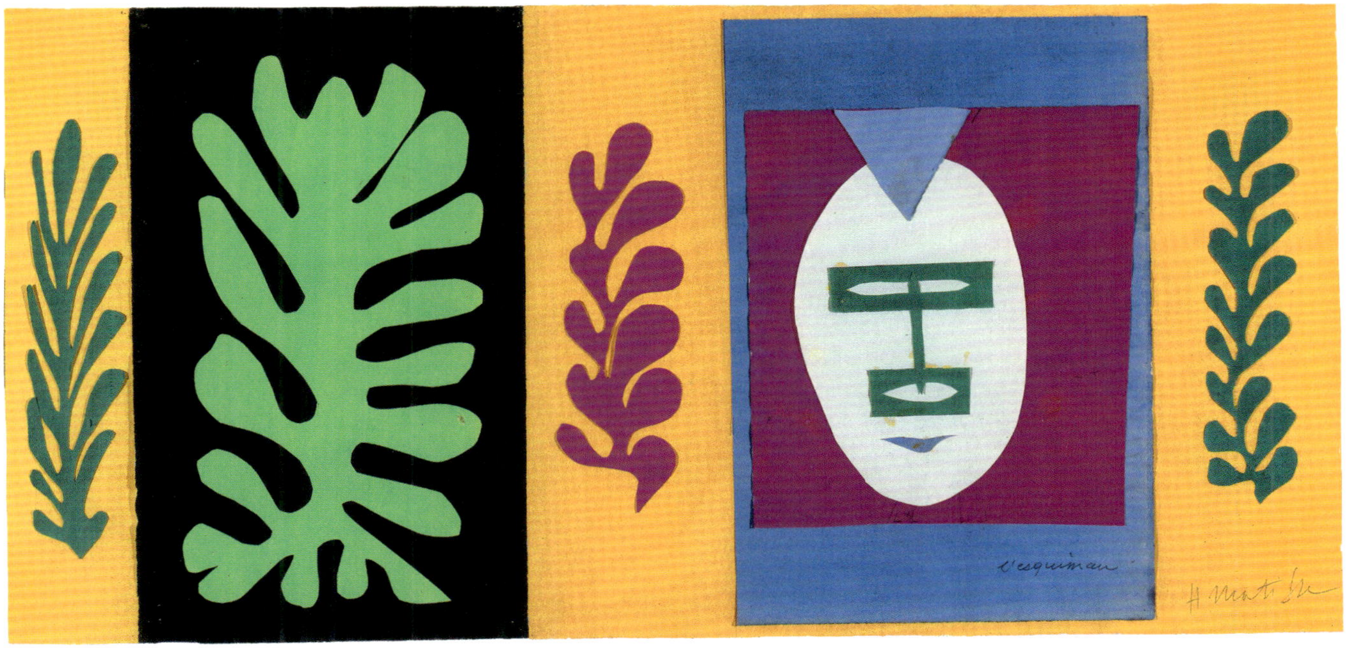

57. *The Eskimo* 1947
Gouache on paper, cut and pasted
40.5 × 86 (16 × 33⅞)

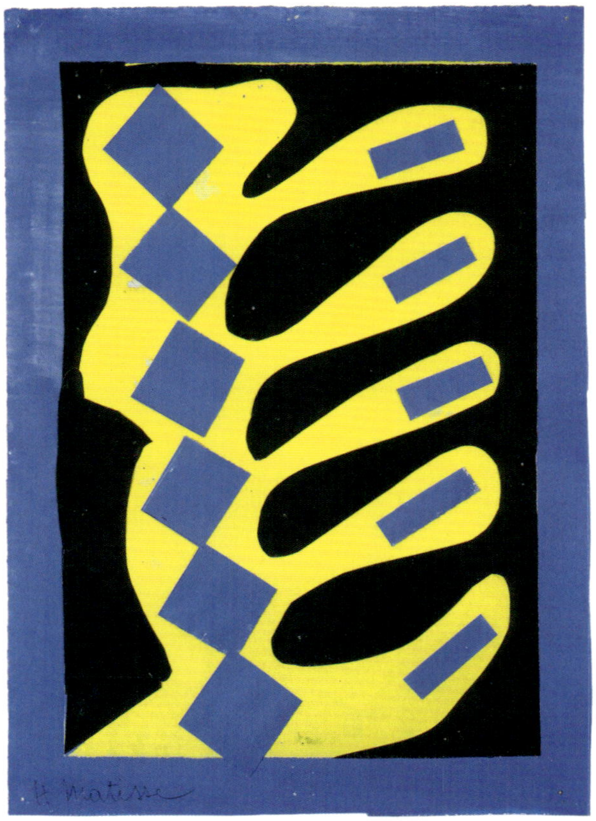

58. *Composition, Yellow, Blue and Black* 1947
Gouache on paper, cut and pasted
47 × 34 (18½ × 13⅜)

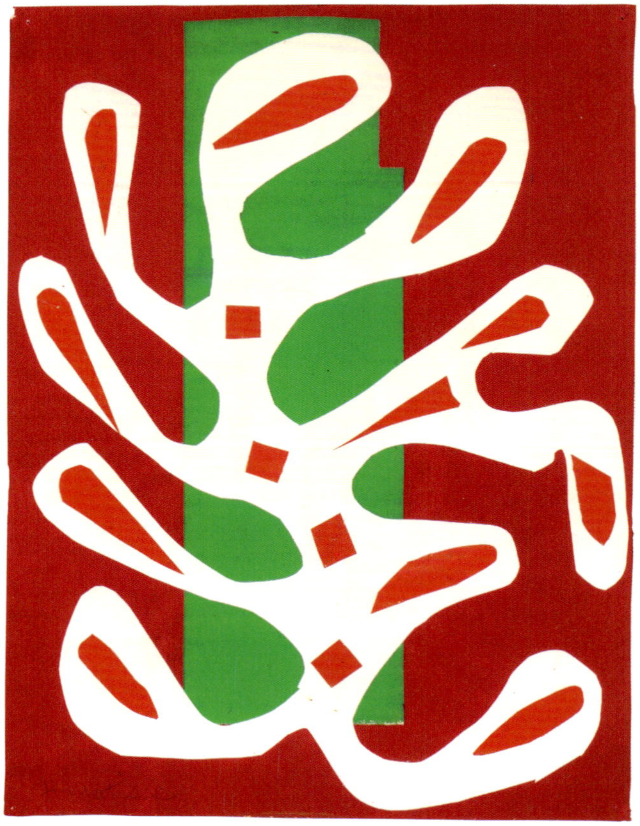

59. *White Alga on Red and Green Background* 1947
Gouache on paper, cut and pasted
52.5 × 40.5 (20¾ × 16)

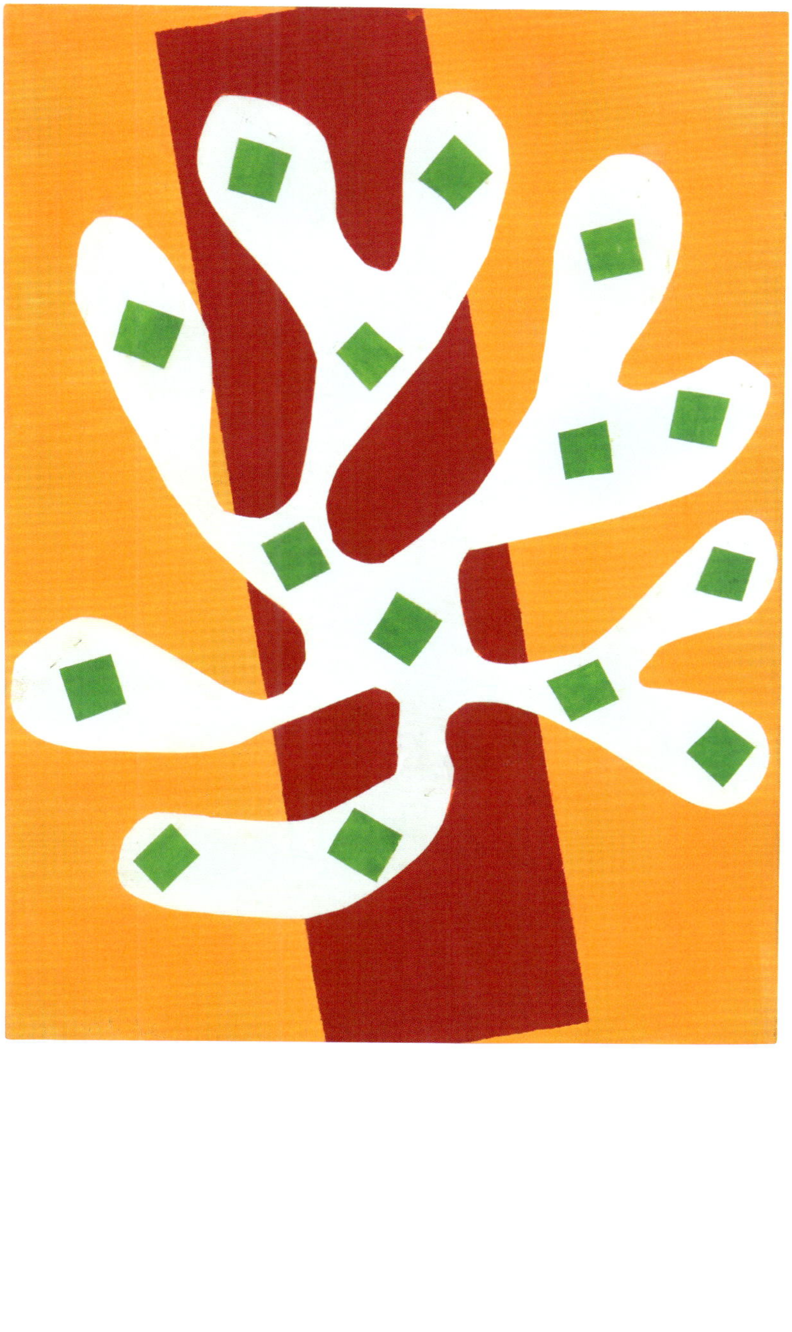

60. *White Alga on Orange and Red Background* 1947
Gouache on paper, cut and pasted
52.5 × 40.5 (20⅝ × 16)

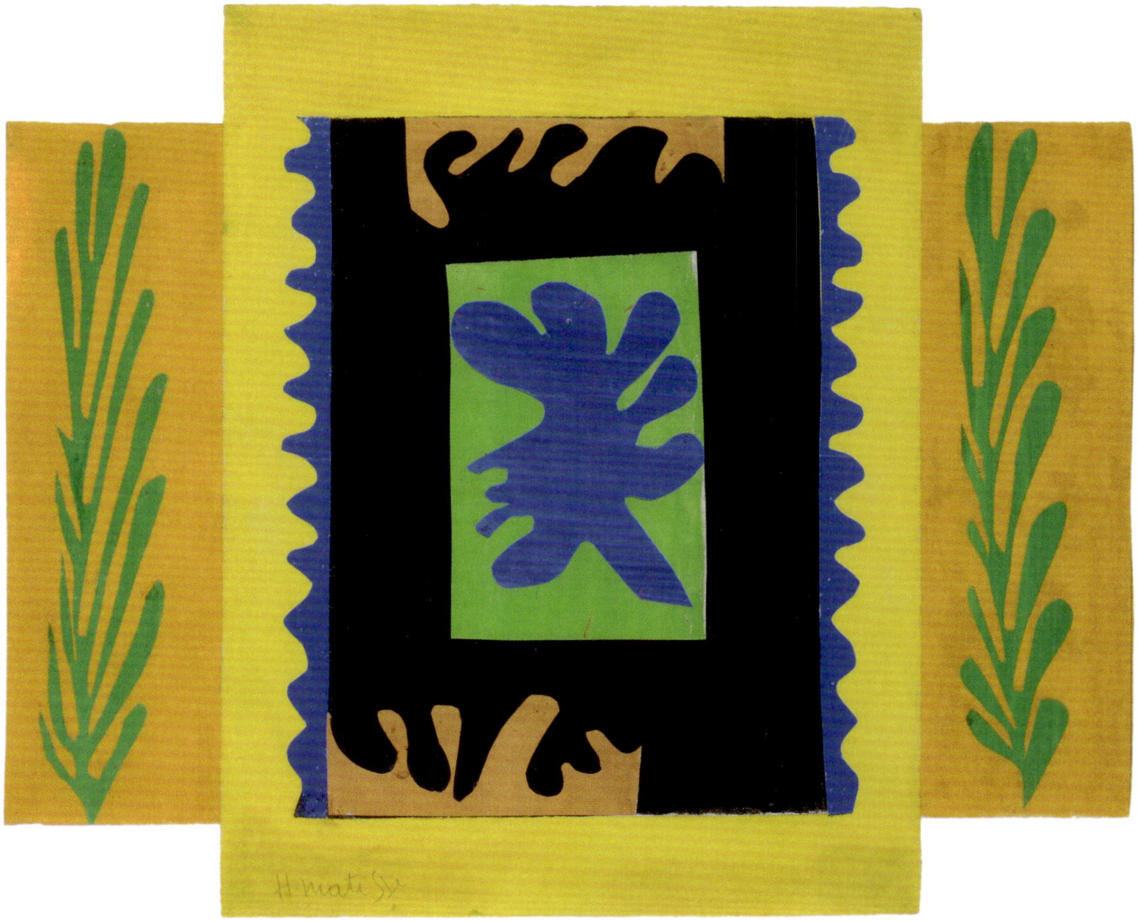

61. *Flowering Tree (Mural Scroll)* 1948
Maquette for silkscreen (realised 1949)
Gouache on paper, cut and pasted
51.2 × 63.7 (20⅛ × 25⅛)

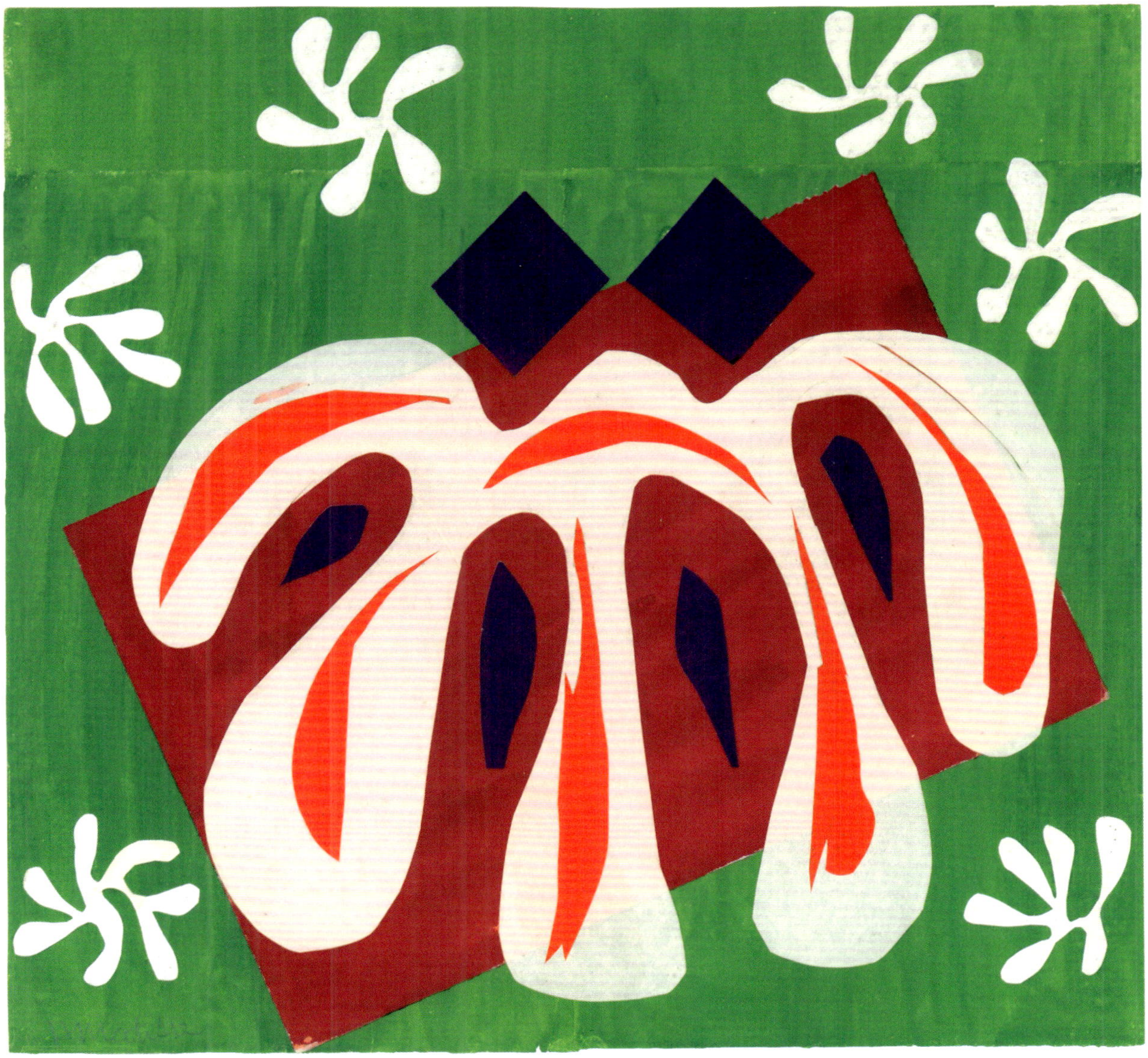

62. *Two Masks (The Tomato)* 1947
Gouache on paper, cut and pasted
47.7 × 51.8 (18¾ × 20⅜)

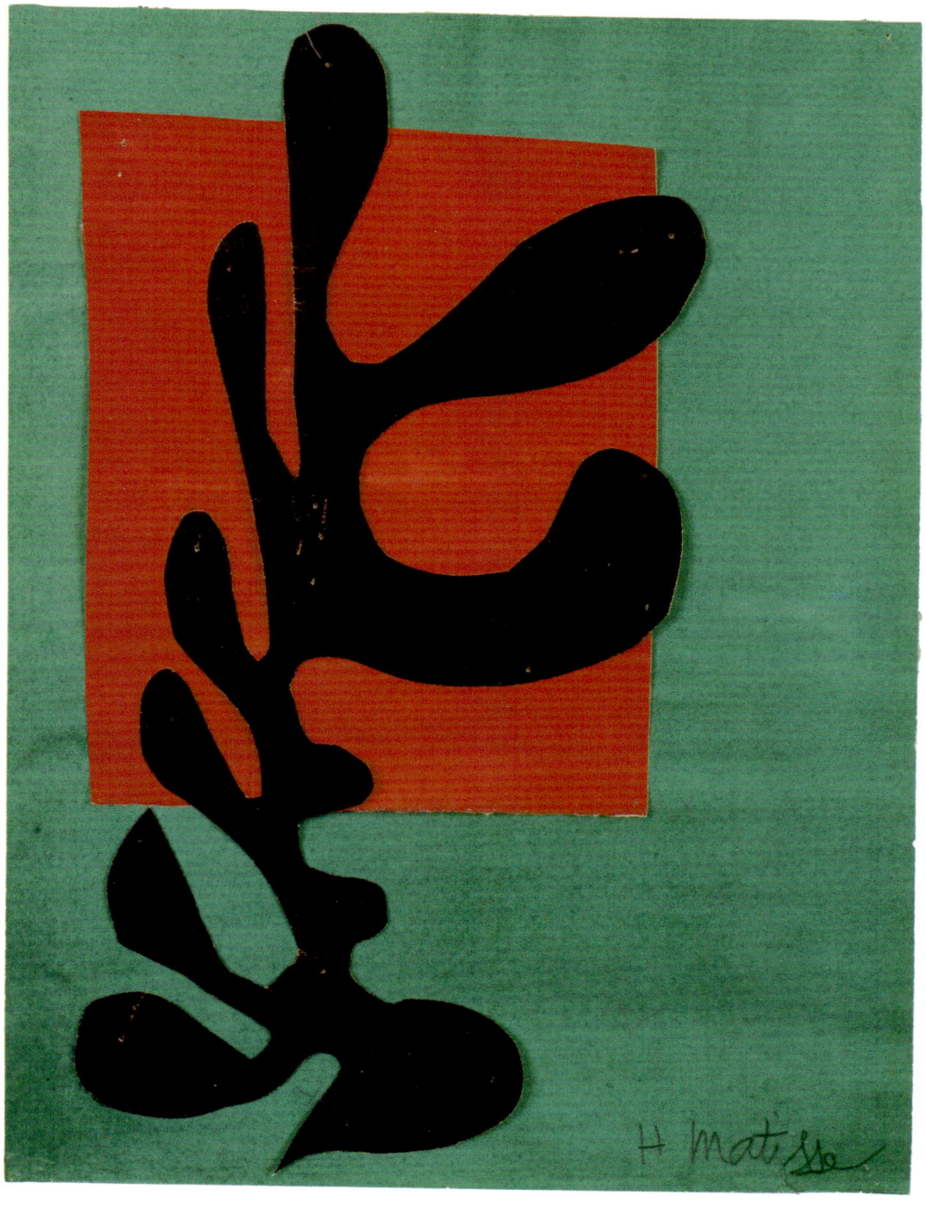

63. *Negro Boxer* 1947
Gouache on paper, cut and pasted
32 × 25.5 (12⅝ × 10)

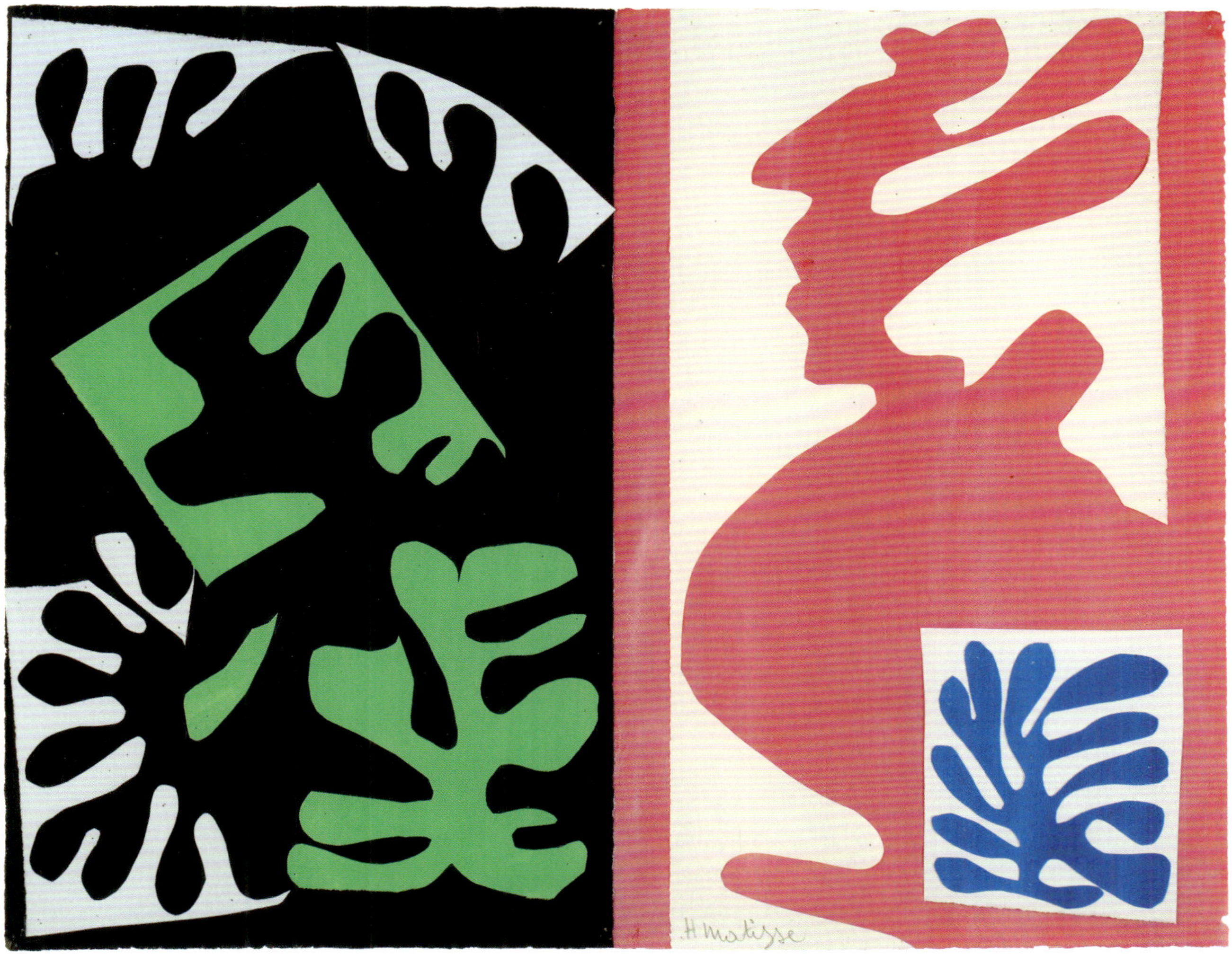

64. *Composition, Black and Red* 1947
Gouache on paper, cut and pasted
40.6 × 52.7 (16 × 20¾)

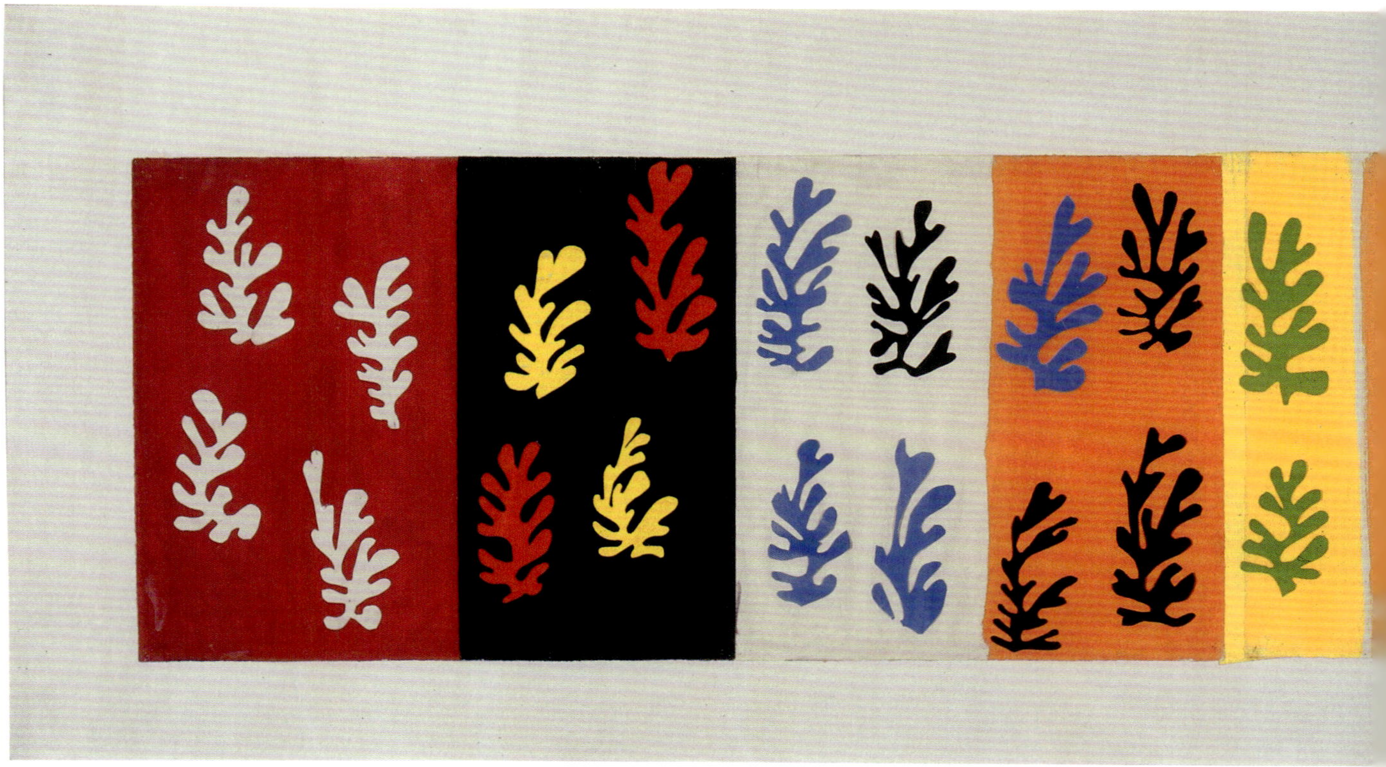

65. *Composition (The Velvets)* 1947
Gouache on paper, cut and pasted
51.5 × 217.5 (20¼ × 85⅝)

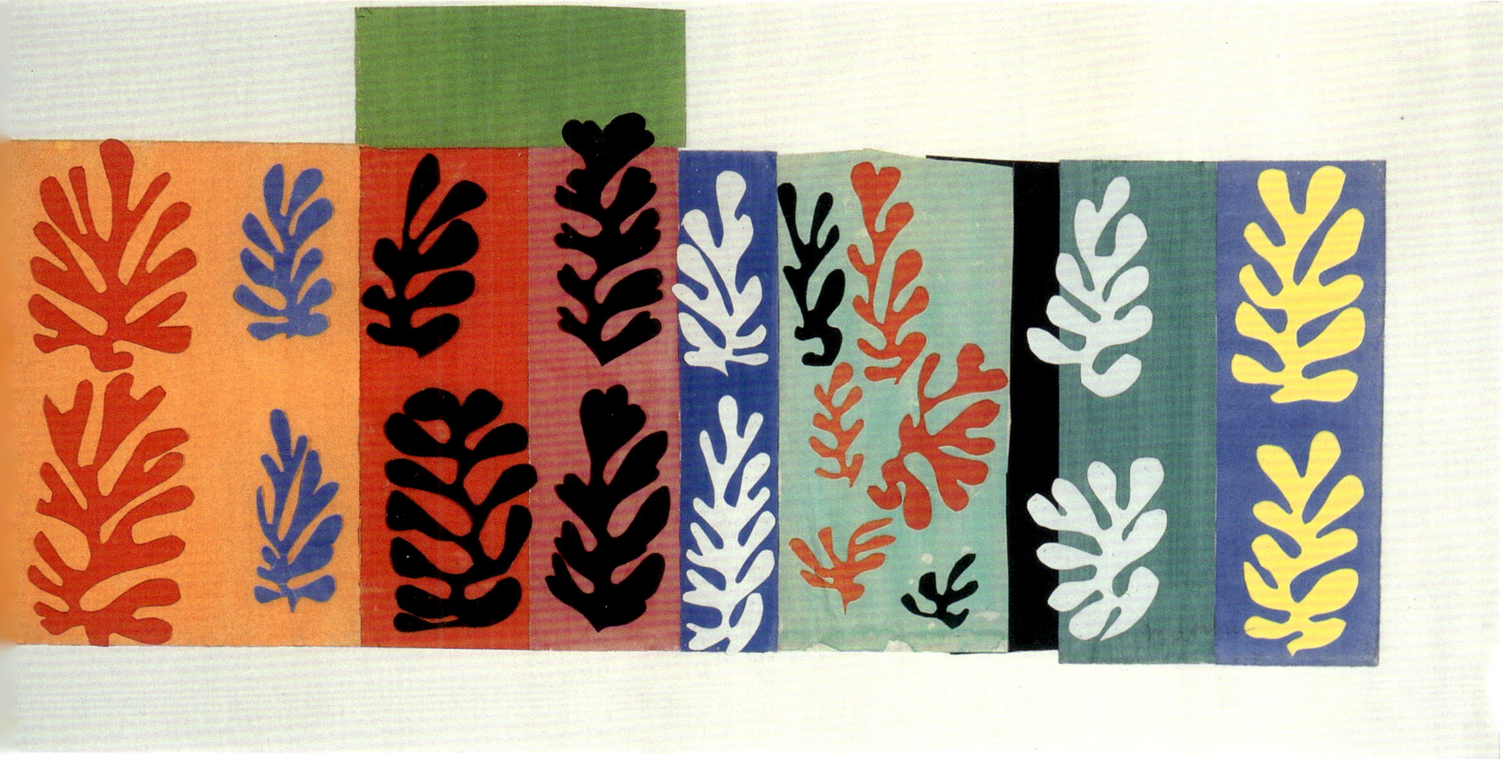

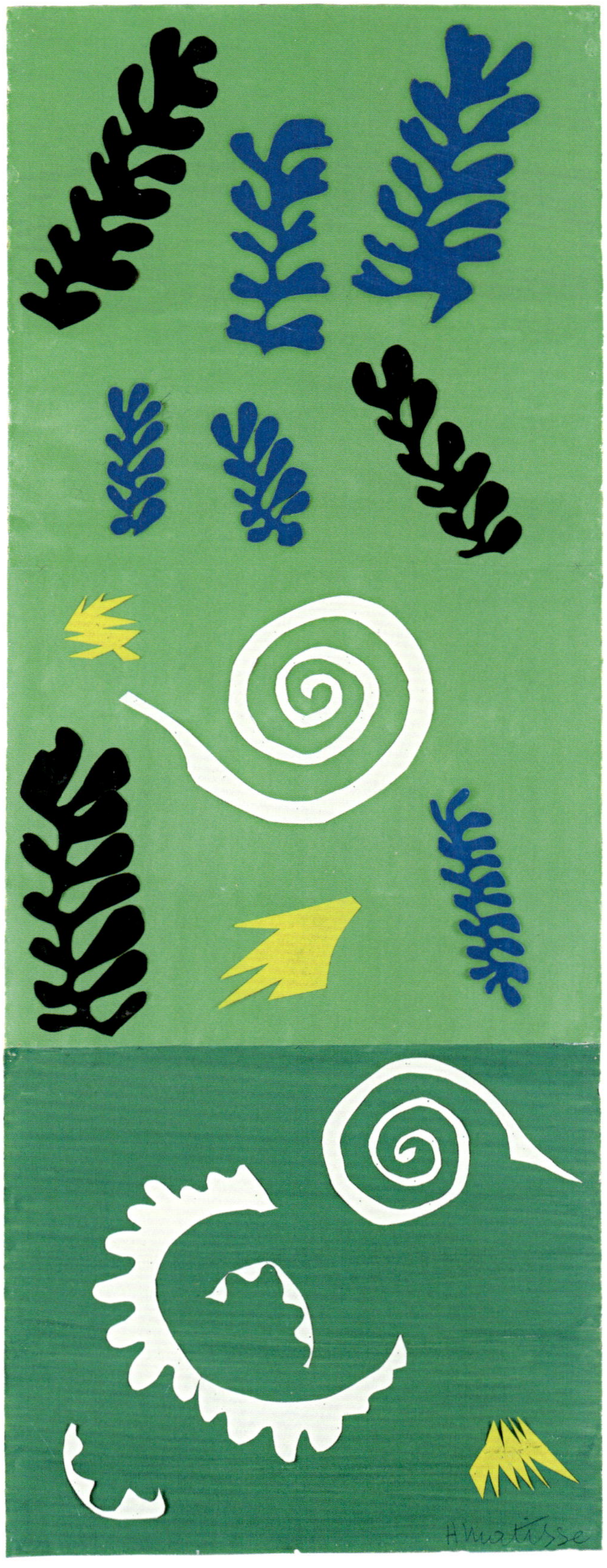

66. *Composition Green Background* 1947
Gouache on paper, cut and pasted, and pencil
104.1 × 40.3 (41 × 15⅞)

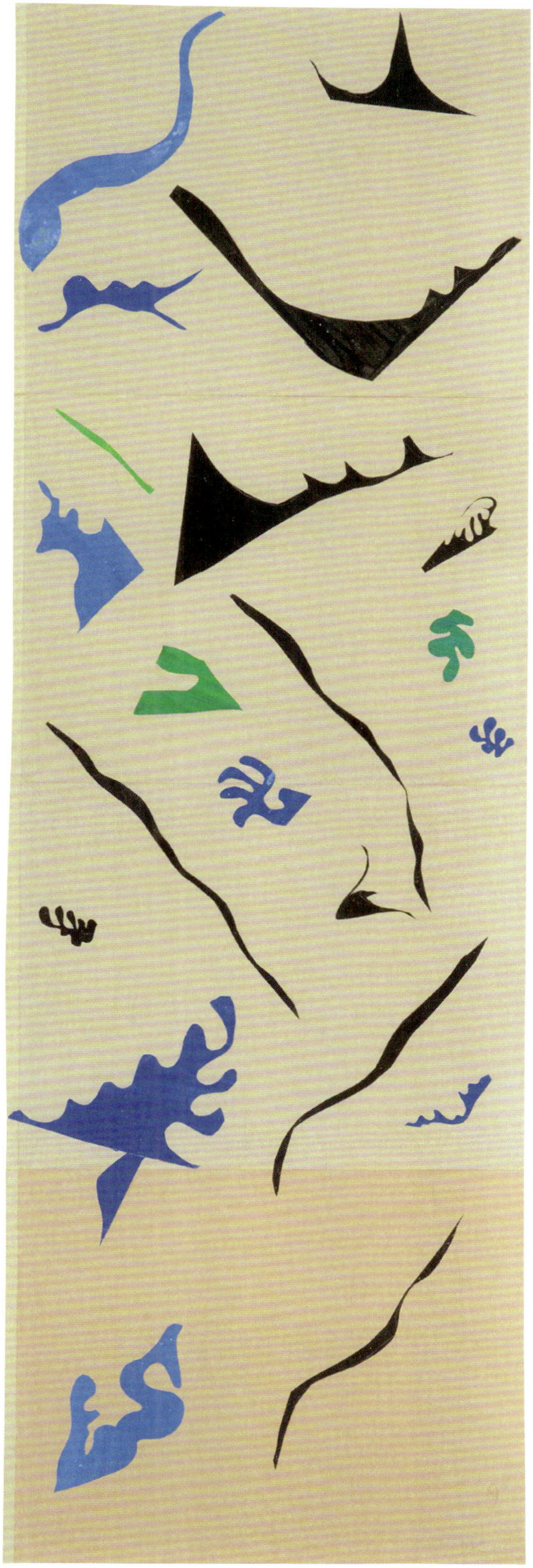

67. *Screen Panel, Beige Background* 1947
Gouache on paper, cut and pasted
162 × 53.5 (63¾ × 21)

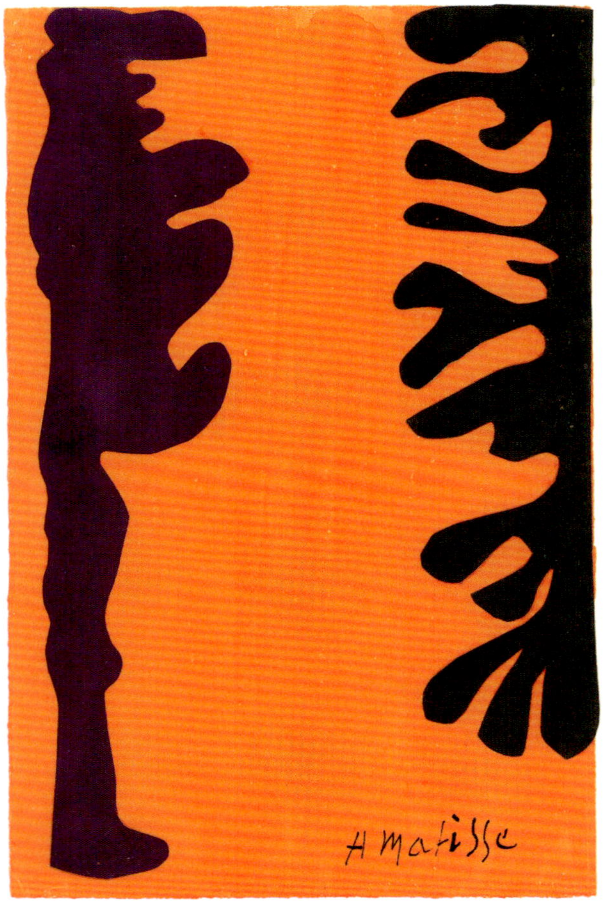

68. *Black and Violet Arabesques on Orange Background* 1947
Gouache on paper, cut and pasted
40 × 26.5 (15¾ × 10⅜)

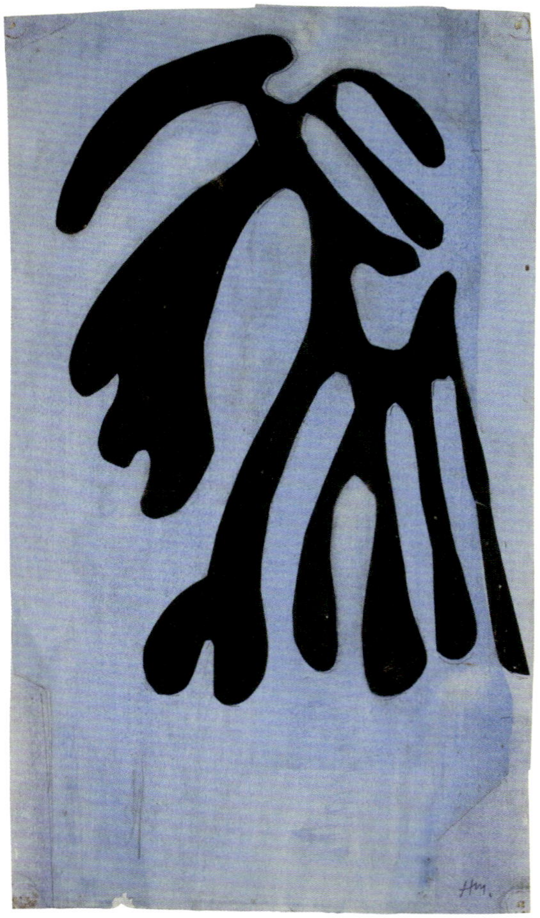

69. *Leaf Motif* c.1948
Maquette for scarf (realised c.1948)
Gouache on paper, cut and pasted, and ink
34 × 19.5 (13⅜ × 7⅝)

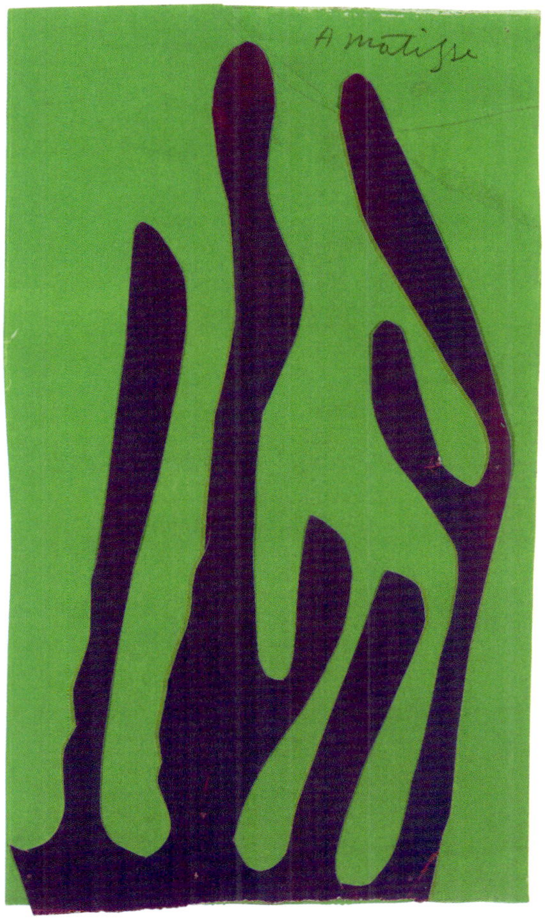

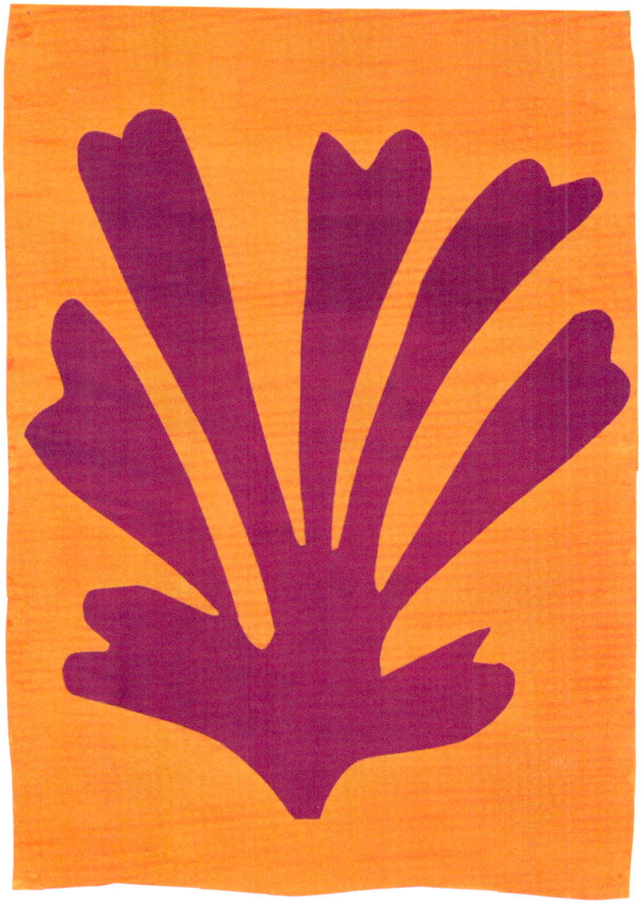

70. *Alga on Green Background* 1947
Gouache on paper, cut and pasted
24.8 × 14.6 (9¾ × 5¾)

71. *Palmette* c. 1947
Gouache on paper, cut and pasted
71.1 × 53.3 (28 × 21)

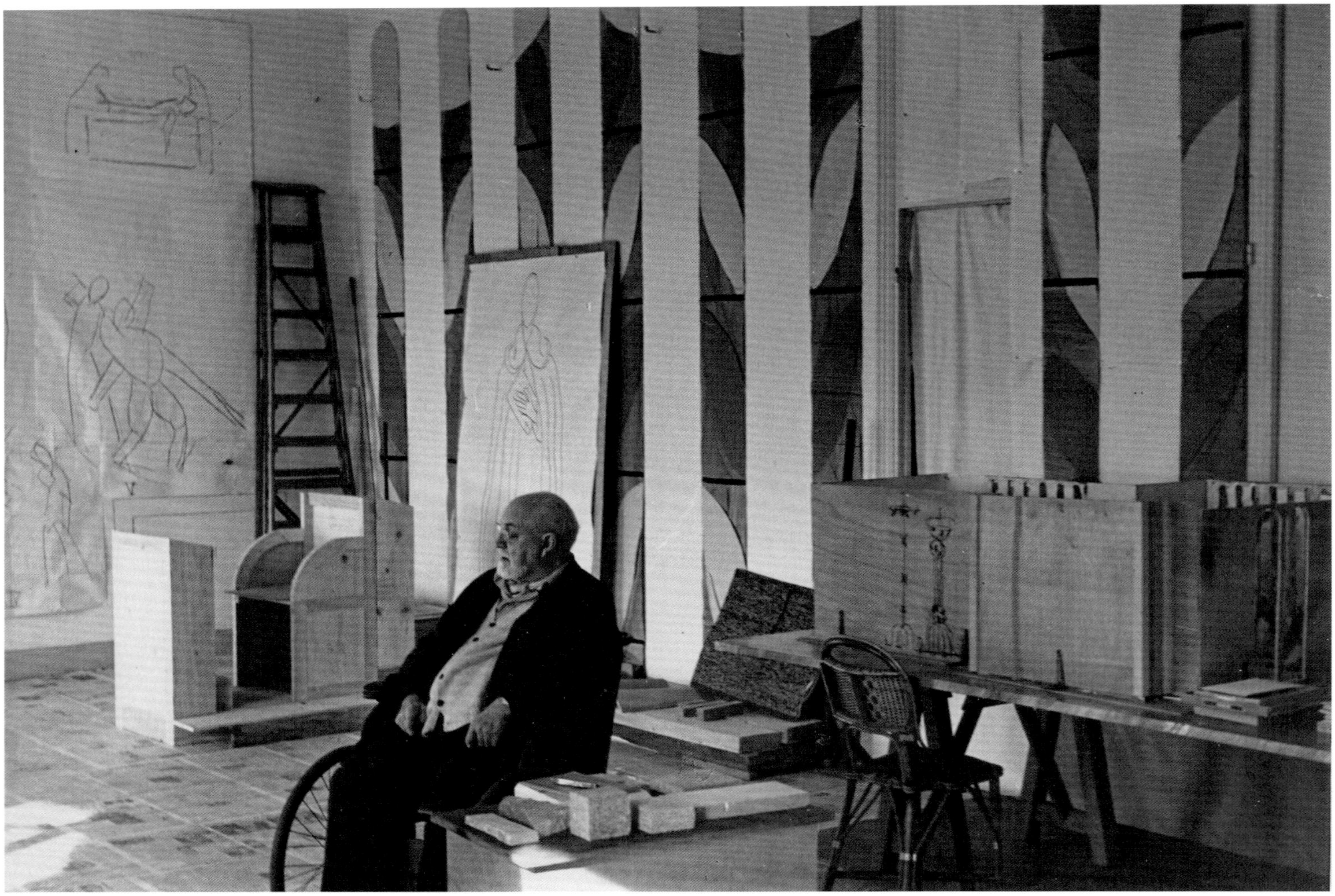

Fig. 27 Felix Man, Matisse at the Hôtel Régina, Nice, c. 1950

CHAPEL FACTORY

Flavia Frigeri

On 7 May 1949 Henri Matisse wrote to the art-minded Dominican priest Father Marie-Alain Couturier describing his progress on the decorative scheme for the Dominican Chapel of the Rosary in Vence (Chapelle du Rosaire de Vence): 'I'm in my studio opposite the narrow windows. I have the Stations of the Cross to my left – and to my right the large panel of the Holy Virgin, and I can glimpse the large double windows through the open door. I'm virtually in the chapel.'[1] An almost direct illustration of Matisse's sense of the conflation of chapel and studio can be seen in Felix Man's portrayal of the artist in his studio at the Hôtel Régina in Cimiez on the outskirts of Nice (fig. 27). One of three studios used by Matisse – the others being located in Paris and Vence – the one at the Régina offered a working space approximating the actual size of the chapel itself, a factor that favoured this studio for the project over the others. The big room in which Man photographs Matisse came to be known as 'the factory', where a large-scale decorative scheme was put into production.[2] And precisely this factory of sorts was witness to the many trials and errors that went into the making of the chapel – a narrative that can be traced through the copious photographic records left behind by those who ventured into Matisse's factory.

Man's photograph, for instance, captures Matisse's full immersion in the construction of the chapel's environment. A ladder is propped against one of the many preparatory drawings for the large ceramic panel of the *Stations of the Cross*, and out of sight, but confirmed by Matisse's words, is an equally large preparatory drawing depicting the *Virgin and Child*. The wall adjacent to the *Stations* accommodates a sketch of *St Dominic*, which in turn rests against the cut-out maquettes for the narrow stained-glass windows of the chapel's nave. Completing the scene are a series of props including one of many scaled models of the chapel and a pew for the nuns' stalls. The overall effect is of a work in progress in which different components are not treated individually but conceived as a cohesive whole. It was this opportunity to construct a full environment that first appealed to Matisse.

The story of the Vence chapel, widely regarded as the crowning achievement of Matisse's career, is best told in Couturier's 'Church full of joy', a feature published in *Vogue* in December 1951.

> About ten years ago, when Matisse was very ill, he was nursed by a young woman whose intelligence and kindness were, he said, extreme. A few years later, a letter from her announced that she was entering a convent. A short time passed. Then one day some Dominican nursing sisters settled in Vence, and among them was the one who was henceforth to be 'Sister Jacques.' She had only to cross the Saint-Jeannet road and a field of wild grass to reach the modest villa under the olive trees from which Matisse, confined to his bed, often called on her care.
>
> The sisters were planning to build their chapel, and Sister Jacques did a little water-colour painting. 'Since this Monsieur Matisse was a painter,' why shouldn't they ask his advice? One morning, Sister Jacques showed him a little sketch which she had made for a window. Matisse gave his advice. Several days later, he decided to design this window himself ... then all the windows and, finally, the entire chapel.
>
> For, in the meantime, there had come to Vence, to cure a bad pleurisy, a young Dominican novice, who, for his part, knew very well who this Monsieur Matisse was. And it was he who, seeing what the intuition and the severity of a Matisse

might bring to anaemic Christian art, proposed Matisse do the sisters' chapel himself.[3]

Notwithstanding the fairytale-like overtones, Couturier's story identifies the primary elements of this undertaking. Firstly, he introduces some of the chapel's main players: Sister Jacques, the project's catalyst, and Brother Rayssiguier, the young Dominican novice whose support was vital to the chapel's realisation. Secondly, he stresses the importance of revitalising 'anaemic Christian art' by turning to contemporary masters, an endeavour that Couturier had most notably spearheaded at Notre-Dame de Toute Grâce, a church on the plateau of Assy, where the decorative scheme counted among its contributors Fernand Léger, Germaine Richier, Georges Braque, Marc Chagall as well as Matisse himself.[4] Passionate about rescuing the Church from the dreariness of banal craftsmanship and ready to seize the opportunities offered by the Church's desire to reposition itself in the aftermath of the Second World War, Couturier found the answer to his plea in the work of contemporary artists like Léger, who notably contributed the lavish mosaic depicting the Litany of the Blessed Virgin Mary on the façade of the church in Assy.[5] In his words:

> The day when Dufy, Segonzac, Picasso, Derain, Matisse, Bonnard will be commissioned for Saint-Sulpice, for Notre-Dame or for the Faubourg Saint-Honoré, the day when Perret, Le Corbusier, Mallet-Stevens will have to build in the cardinal's construction sites as many churches as Mr. Barbier or Mr. So-and-so, most of our task will be completed. It may not be enough in our opinion, to guarantee Christian art's revival (nor are we certain that the artworks produced by those renowned hands are all very religious) but one essential element will be restored: the Church will recover the sense of grandeur in this field, the habit of engaging with the greatest, the true masters rather than more or less mediocre specialists.[6]

While certainly aware of Couturier's vision, Matisse saw the Vence chapel as a personal challenge rather than a stepping stone in the priest's quest for a more progressive Church. Looking back on this undertaking, Matisse stated: 'This is not a work that I chose, but rather a work for which I was chosen by fate, towards the end of the course that I am still continuing according to my researches; the chapel has allowed me the possibility of realizing them by uniting them.'[7] It was colour and drawing that he endeavoured to unify: 'In the chapel there will be one side based on my studies in cut paper, that of the luminous and coloured stained-glass windows, opposed to the other side decorated in black and white.'[8] Matisse harnessed the full potential of colour and line for the decorative scheme, which included stained-glass windows, monumental ceramic representations of the *Stations of the Cross* and the *Virgin and Child*, liturgical garments and furniture (fig. 28, 30). While Matisse devoted his full attention to the chapel's decoration, Brother Rayssiguier with the assistance of architect Auguste Perret was in charge of the architectural design.

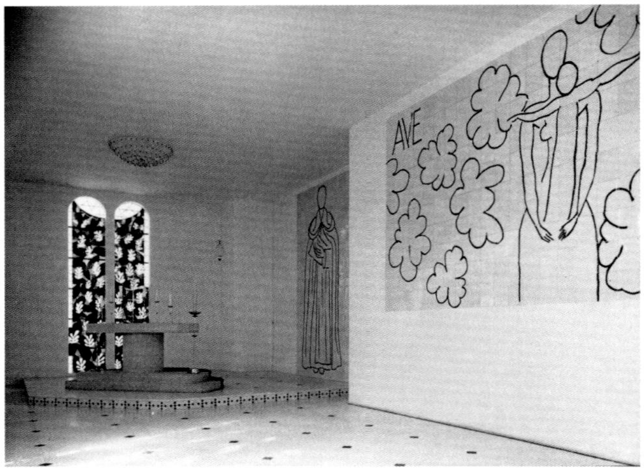

Fig. 28 Hélène Adant, Chapel of the Rosary, Vence, c. 1951

The first encounter between Rayssiguier and Matisse took place on 4 December 1947 at Matisse's Villa le Rêve in Vence. Showing the young novice images from *Jazz*, Matisse explained: 'These are stained-glass window colors. I cut out these gouache sheets the way you cut glass: only here they're organized to reflect light, whereas in a stained-glass window they have to be arranged differently because light shines through them.'[9] And it was exactly this fluid notion of the cut-outs as a stand-in for stained glass, and vice versa, that most appealed to Matisse from the project's outset. Rayssiguier, on the other hand, came out of this first meeting feeling that he was not giving Matisse 'a subject, but an opportunity to work with colour', although he had offered an appropriate subject, as he went on to say: 'I read him the Heavenly Jerusalem for the two big windows.' This passage from the Book of Revelation in the Bible, describing the divine re-creation of the city of Jerusalem, would inspire Matisse's first design for the big double windows behind the altar.[10]

Taking his cue from the Bible's description of a heavenly city glittering 'like some precious jewel of crystal-clear diamond', Matisse created *Celestial Jerusalem* (no. 75). The effect was a dazzling array of interlocking geometrical shapes stripped of any natural or figurative reference, although the cut-out sheets were reminiscent of the holy city's precious foundation stones. A preliminary design for the flanking windows, the cut-out maquette *The Bees*, (no. 74) like *Celestial Jerusalem*, relies on a heavily abstracted approach to religious themes. In this instance Matisse took as a starting point a nun's bee-like headdress and combined it with the long-standing presence in religious narratives of the beehive as a symbol for a 'pious and unified community'.[11] The result, however, evinces none of these religious qualities and instead conjures up a chequerboard-like fan of miniscule tesserae, intended to vibrate in the light of southern France.

Happy with *Celestial Jerusalem*'s 'coloured equilibrium', Matisse 'transferred [it] onto the wall of [his] studio in Paris', where he travelled from Vence in June 1948.[12] Alfred H. Barr, Jr, who paid him a visit the following month, reported that Matisse treated the walls of his bedroom as rough equivalents of the chapel's spatial set-up, with two walls covered in ink drawings standing in for the ceramic panels, and 'one wall covered with dozens of small, brightly coloured scissors-and-paste compositions' acting as placeholders for the stained-glass windows.[13] Barr's account highlights the artist's immersive working method and his deep-seated interest in living, sleeping and experiencing at first hand the spatial environment he envisaged for the chapel.

Matisse shared his plans for the chapel with another visitor over the summer, friend and fellow artist Pablo Picasso. However, unlike Barr, Picasso was outraged by Matisse's commitment to a religious project of this extent: 'Why don't you do a covered market instead? You could paint fruit, vegetables.'[14] Matisse later confided to Couturier: 'I don't give a damn about fruit and vegetables: my greens are greener than my pears and my oranges more orange than pumpkins. What would be the point? He was furious.'[15] Picasso's reaction was not dictated so much by the project itself as by the implication that Matisse had become a believer. Significantly, Picasso also embarked on a project similar in scale to Matisse's but under a very different premise. In fact, in 1952 he went on to create two frescoes for a deconsecrated chapel in Vallauris. Dealing respectively with the themes of war and peace, Picasso's murals could be read as a direct response to the religiously driven project in Vence. Similarly, Louis Aragon snappily commented at the sight of the chapel's model in Matisse's studio: 'Very pretty – very gay – in fact when we take over we'll turn it into a dance hall.'[16] As members of the Communist party, Picasso looked at the Catholic Church's attempt to improve its image through the co-option of avant-garde artists with suspicion, while Aragon, who campaigned for a socialist realist art, was also sceptical of this regeneration of sacred art.[17]

Although Matisse never made his political or religious inclinations public, his prominent involvement in the chapel forced him to the forefront of this regeneration. Arguably, it is the very absence of a clear stance on his part that fuelled these criticisms. Many, like Picasso, have in fact speculated, both during the chapel's making and in its aftermath, whether Matisse's embrace of this project was marked by a new-found religious commitment, and to some extent Matisse's confidential rebuttal of Picasso to Couturier seems to contain the answer to this question. However, in the same way that nature could

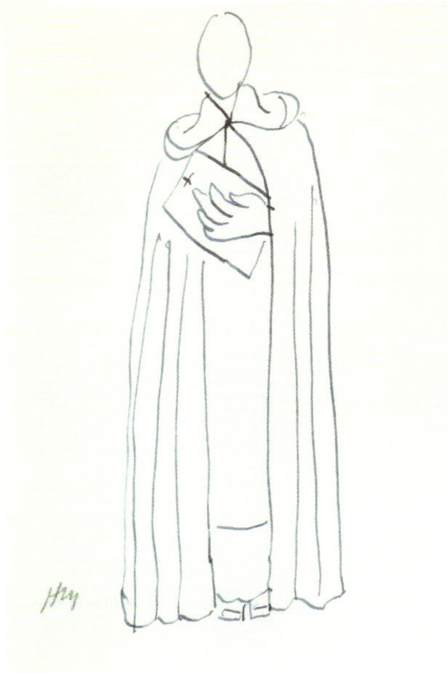

Fig. 29 Study for *St Dominic* 1949
Ink on paper, 22.1 × 14.8 (8⅝ × 5⅞)
Private collection

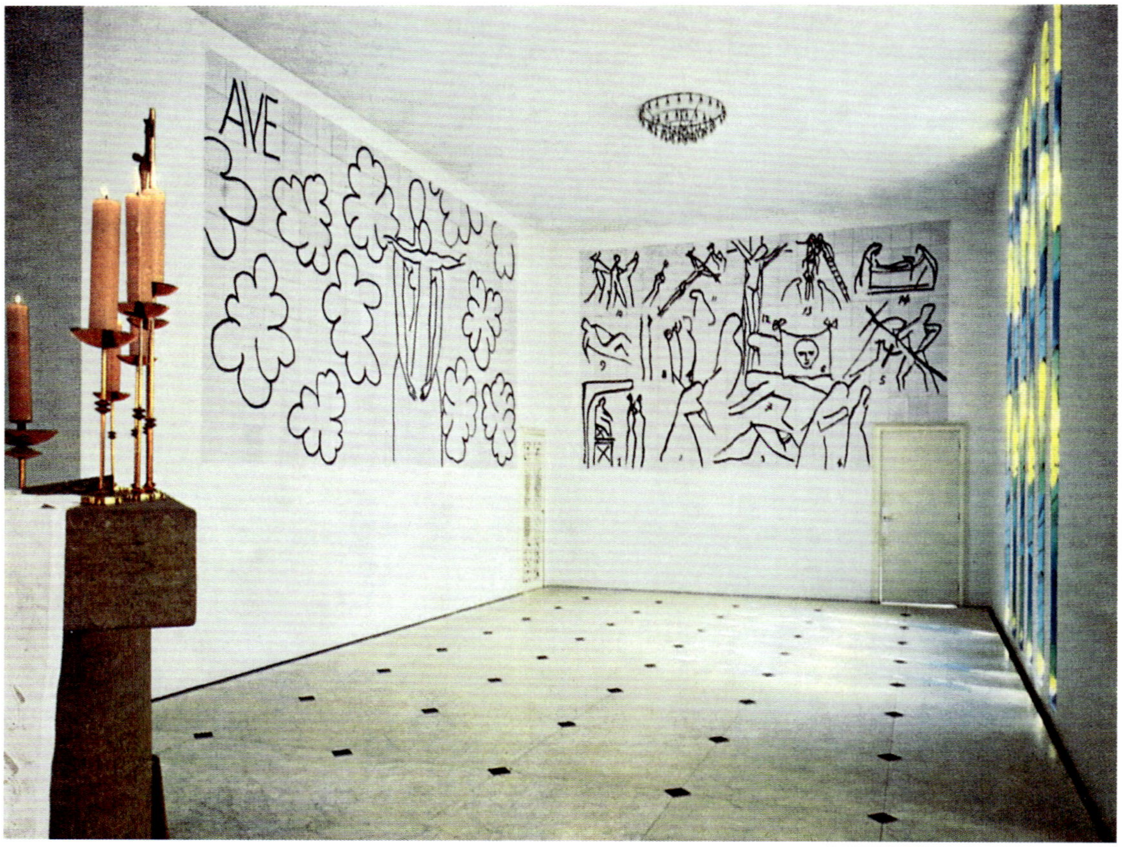

Fig. 30 Hélène Adant, Chapel of the Rosary, Vence, c. 1951

not stand in the way of his colouristic achievements, so religion had to undergo an aesthetic review in order to comply with his artistic project. It would appear to be the idea of a complete environment, rather than religion, that had led him to the chapel.

Certainly, one aspect of Matisse's artistic devotion to the chapel is his almost concurrent abandonment of painting. Increasingly fatigued and with diminishing eyesight, he could no longer sustain the long hours required by easel painting, and in 1948, with the completion of the 'Interiors of Vence' series, Matisse bade farewell to painting.[18] Again it is a photograph of Matisse sitting comfortably in his studio – this time in Vence – that offers us some insight into this transitional body of works (p. 42). A scale model for the chapel, a smaller painting of *Pink Nude, Red Interior* (1947), a string of drawings and the many objects scattered around the room are all indications of the artist's varied production, but it is the newly completed *Plum Blossoms, Ochre Background* (1948) and *Interior with Egyptian Curtain* (1948), paraded on the wall behind him, that occupy the spotlight.

The two paintings exemplify two distinct takes on the interior, one with a figure and one without. In the case of *Plum Blossoms, Ochre Background* and its pendant painting *Plum Blossoms, Green Background*, the contrast between the flattened table top and the wallpaper in the background is heightened by the faceless figure sitting in between. In both of these paintings – as is true of the series as a whole – perspectival space is suppressed and bright colours take the lead. It is, however, the seamless combination of objects and natural motifs that most poignantly characterises this body of work. In *Interior with Egyptian Curtain*, for instance, the palm tree outside the window bursts into the indoor space, refuting any spatial distance and bringing the elaborate design of the curtain onto the same plane as the tree. Indoor and outdoor are merged in a move that foreshadows their integration in the chapel's stained-glass windows through the use of natural motifs. In fact, in the black leaves on the green wallpaper in *Plum Blossoms, Green Background* and in the lush palm leaves of *Interior with Egyptian Curtain* and *Red Interior, Still Life on a Blue Table* (1947) (no. 73) one can trace the fine line connecting this farewell to painting with the blossoming of paper cut-outs.

Matisse made this connection explicit in the 1948 issue of the journal *Verve* (no. 14) devoted to his most recent production. The Vence paintings and a selection of drawings represented the artist's most current work. The cover, designed with the aid of cut-out shapes, brought that medium into consideration. The treatment of the lettering in particular – a combination of black swirling vegetable forms – drew a subtle connection between the paintings' multifaceted natural motifs and the front cover's floating shapes. The back cover, however, with its starker lines showed a shift in register, which arguably mirrored the transition from the controlled geometrical patterns of *Celestial Jerusalem* to the fluid natural forms of *Pale Blue Window* (no. 77).

By the time Matisse returned to Vence in October 1948, Perret had uncovered a mistake in Rayssiguier's initial designs for the chapel, forcing the artist to rethink his own plans for the stained-glass windows. In a letter to Couturier from 14 November 1948 he spelled out the positive impact of this mishap:

> The main news is the window [*Celestial Jerusalem*] I worked on during my holidays in Paris is unusable. I like it in itself, but it won't work in relation to the chapel. The rather problematic architecture ... hindered me from seeing my windows as an ensemble and I went astray ... When I got back to my house in Vence, after the journey in Paris, I hurried to have a look at it [the model] – and found the position of the windows, their proportions, and the few colors I had set down composed a much more satisfying ensemble than the Paris one – I knew in that instant I would start over again.[19]

The product of this shift is *Pale Blue Window*, an ensemble of two large windows for the altar, flanked by a row of narrow windows for the aisle. Drawing on the beloved algae motif, Matisse was able to unite the main windows with the flanking ones. The algae in their varying colours and relationships acted as the windows' main subject and also as a conduit for this seamless sense of continuity between the two parts. Such an approach was distinct from the one initially adopted with *Celestial Jerusalem* and *The Bees*, which, though seen as part of the same decorative scheme, had been treated independently. With *Pale Blue Window* this disconnection was rectified and the main components carefully attuned.

The photographer Clifford Coffin, who visited Matisse's Vence studio in late 1948, was a witness to the stained-glass maquettes' change in stylistic and thematic gears. Coffin's photograph draws us into the chapel's worksite, where sketches for the ceramic decorations were pinned to the wall, surrounded by cut-out maquettes for the stained-glass windows (p. 43). The Interiors of Vence paintings, which had dominated the space earlier in the year, have vanished. An empty easel confined to the corner of the room stands as a testament to the artist's leave-taking from painting. The changeover in the room's layout reflects the shifting focus from painting to cut-outs, from a depiction of space to the creation of spatial environment.

What Coffin's image captures best, though, is the artist's working method. In particular, he shows how the walls of Matisse's studio accommodated the project's changing nature. *The Bees*, which by this stage had been discarded, is sitting amid sketches for the ceramic panels and in proximity with the new set of flanking windows. From his bed placed at the opposite end of the room Matisse was able to commandeer both compositions and measure the

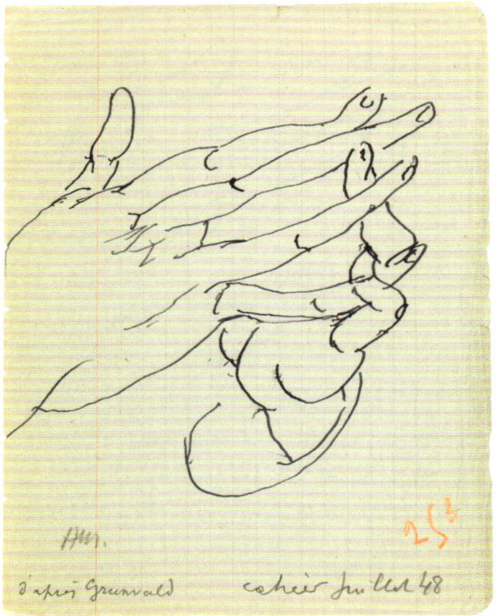

Fig. 31 Study for the hands of *St Dominic* 1948
Ink on paper, 21.5 × 17 (8½ × 6⅔)
Private collection

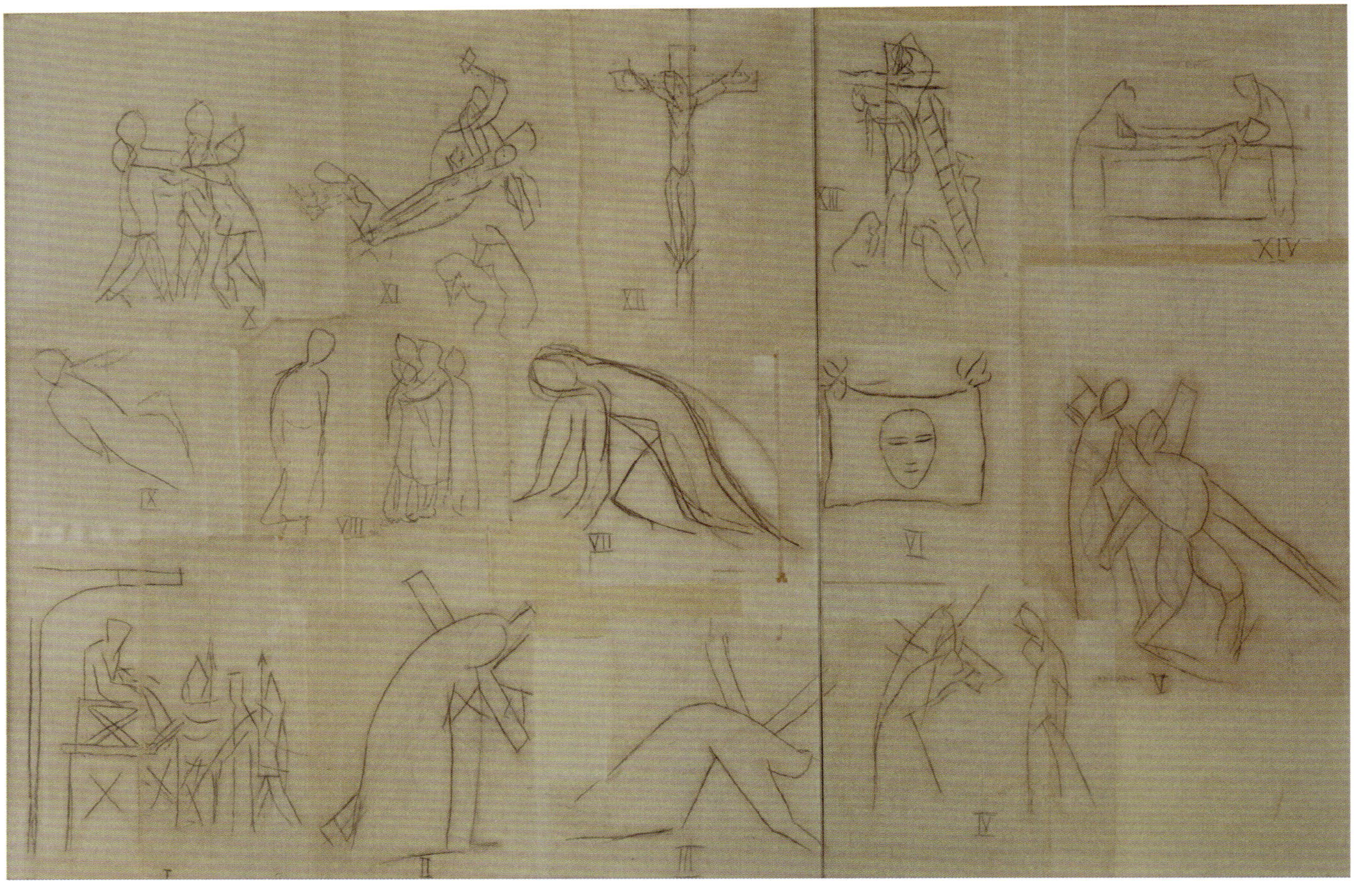

Fig. 32 *Stations of the Cross*, full-scale sketch for the Chapel of the Rosary, Vence 1951. Charcoal on paper, 329 × 503 (129½ × 198)
Skissernas Museum – Museum of Artistic Process and Public Art, Lund, Sweden

effects of his swirling algae against the geometrical chequerboard of *The Bees*. In a pendant photograph – also by Coffin – we see Matisse sitting in bed, hard at work on the algae (p. 45).[20] Scattered around are the products of his labour, an array of multi-coloured seaweed shapes waiting to be pinned onto the thin columns covered in brown packing paper, reflected in the mirror. The algae are here charged with a stable yet constant descending rhythm that is at once calm and engaging. Matisse feared the composition was 'too exalted, not peaceful enough', yet he concurred with Rayssiguier that the overall effect is 'more stable than the Paris maquette [*Celestial Jerusalem*]' and that 'the dynamism helps unify it'.[21] Stability is thus coupled with dynamism. The lush vegetation sitting outside Matisse's window in the Interiors of Vence paintings is here drawn into the window itself, and the effect is a fantastical coloured lens through which the world can be contemplated.

Coffin's photographs reveal that Matisse was also working on studies for the ceramic panels of *St Dominic* and the *Stations of the Cross*. Having established from the outset that St Dominic would be a tall, narrow and meditative figure, but also one that would instigate a devotional attitude, Matisse asked Father Couturier – who encompassed all of these traits – to model for him in the summer of 1948 (fig. 29).[22] Matisse's representation of St Dominic went through numerous stages, starting with detailed studies of the vestments and pose, but gradually refined them so as to eradicate all superfluous traits (fig. 31). The end result is a stark depiction of the saint: all facial features have been removed and only the saintly props are left to carry the message.

Contrasting with this meditative stability are the studies for the *Stations of the Cross* (fig. 32), the dramatic frenzy of which proved to be the most trying of the three ceramic decorations. Challenged by having to integrate all fourteen Stations in one panel, Matisse started out by studying each Station individually and affixing the sketches to the wall beside his bed (as reflected in the mirror in Coffin's photograph) (no. 79). By tackling each scene separately, Matisse was able to come to grips with their iconography, a subject with which he was not familiar and for which he often called on Brother Rayssiguier's support. Additional guidance came from the work of Renaissance and Baroque masters such as Dürer, Mantegna and Rubens. First studying their interpretations of religious scenes – Rubens's *Descent from the Cross*, for example – Matisse then eradicated all excess detail from the Stations. The end result was a handful of 'rough, very rough' drawings telling the story in crude terms.[23] Aware that such a treatment would 'dismay most people who see it', Matisse nonetheless pursued this approach in the hope of making what he described as the Passion's 'odor of drama' visible.[24] While in the final version the biblical order was maintained by identifying each scene with a number, the narrative itself circled around the central Crucifixion. Couturier poignantly evoked the effect: 'I see it as a page covered in gestures which resemble the altered, scarcely legible letters which are written in haste under the influence of too great an emotion ... What other kind of writing would be appropriate when speaking of the Passion? These violent signs suffice me: they tell me the essential story. Why should I need anything else?'[25]

One of the final studies for *Stations of Cross* can be seen in Hélène Adant's photograph of Matisse's studio at the Hôtel Régina in Cimiez on the outskirts of Nice, where the artist relocated at the beginning of 1949 (p. 52). Adant's photograph offers us an insight into the studio's layout, showing the *Stations of the Cross* on the end wall, a large drawing of *St Dominic* on the left, and the third and final set of cut-out

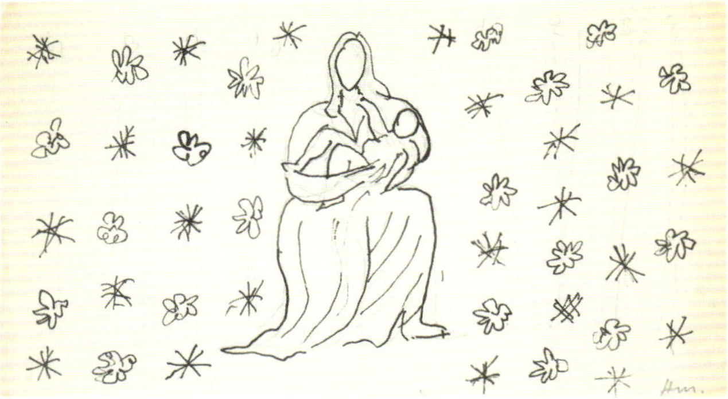

Fig. 33 Study for *Virgin and Child* 1949. Ink and pencil on paper, 16.5 × 30.2 (6½ × 11⅞). Private collection

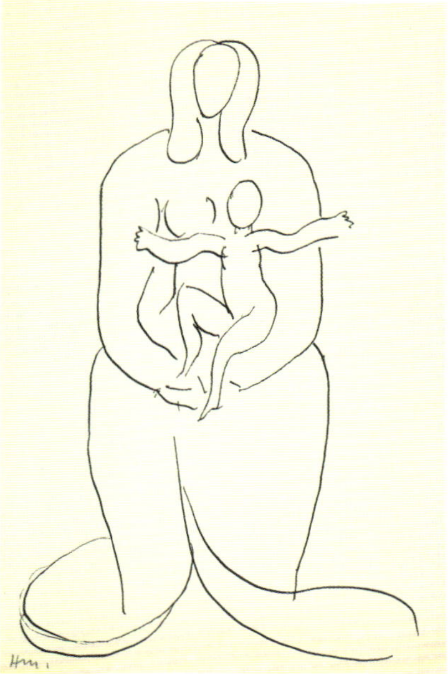

Fig. 34 Study for *Virgin and Child* 1949
Ink on paper, 16.8 × 25.1 (6⅝ × 9⅞)
Private collection

maquettes for the nave windows on the right. Clustered in the centre are Matisse's 'tools': a scale model of the chapel, his wheelchair and a chair propped on top of a wooden altar-like structure, from which he conducted the chapel's waltz with his bamboo wand.[26] Finally, adding to the factory-like feel is a sea of newspaper sheets covering the floor tiles.

Having rehearsed his biblical scenes endlessly to the point that he could draw them blindfold, Matisse proudly reported on 7 April 1949: 'The day before yesterday I mapped out the Stations of the Cross using a charcoal stick on the end of a bamboo pole. I'm satisfied with it because it flowed out in a single spurt between 10 o'clock and noon – and it shows.'[27] As Matisse's words reveal, the spontaneity of the drawing was crucial to its success, yet the automatism could only be achieved through extensive practice. This was especially relevant in relation to the ceramic tiles, which were the final stage of the process and also had to be decorated in a single spurt.[28]

A photograph by Lucien Hervé captures Matisse at work on a study for the large panel of the *Virgin and Child* (p. 54). Sitting on a chair in the corner of his 'factory' studio, the artist sketches on sheets tacked to the wall with his bamboo wand. To his left the maquettes for the stained-glass windows in the nave, already visible in Adant's shot of the studio, act as a connecting device between the *Stations of the Cross* and the *Virgin and Child* (no. 76). Conceived as related decorations, they were nonetheless infused with very different spirits, and placing them opposite each other certainly helped achieve this differentiation. The *Stations of the Cross* were 'tempestuous', a tragic composition that expressed the artist's own sense of pathos, while the *Virgin and Child* was endowed with a 'character of tranquil contemplation'.[29] The difference is evinced by the stylistic treatment of the two subjects. The raggedness of the *Stations* was replaced by a clean and continuous line in the *Virgin and Child*. However, like the *Stations*, the *Virgin* also went through innumerable gradual stages of reduction to reveal its core elements (fig. 33–4). The flowers originally decorated with palm-like petals – very similar to the black leaves in *Plum Blossoms, Green Background* – are reduced to a faint outline in the final composition, making the solid and maternal Virgin holding the 'squirming, twisting' Child the sole focus of the scene.[30]

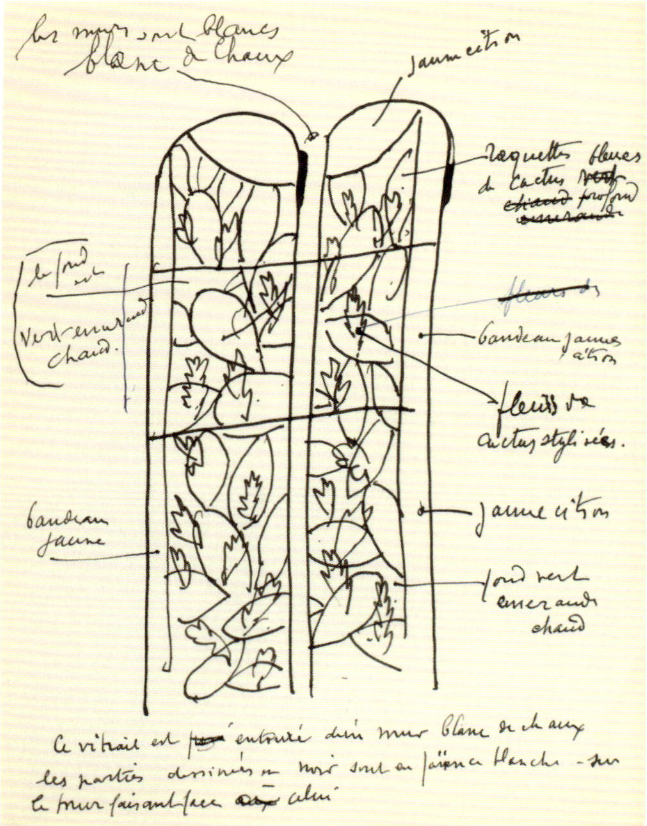

Fig. 35 Study for *The Tree of Life* c. 1949
Ink on paper, 27 × 21 (10⅝ × 8¼). Private collection

The figurative references of the ceramic panels are grounded in a biblical tradition, while the stained-glass windows' natural shapes are drawn directly from the artist's imagination. The spatial integration of these two very different registers required fine-tuning, and the presence in the 'factory' studio of the black and white drawings alongside the colourful cut-outs points to the artist's desire to seek a balance between the two.

The photographs by Adant and Hervé record a further shift in designs for the nave windows. Moving away from the algae motif of *Pale Blue Window*, this third and final set, known as *The Tree of Life* (pp. 48–9), relied on a simplified pattern of cascading cactus leaves. It dispensed with the kinaestheticism of *The Bees* and also the effervescent feeling of the second set to create a balanced and distilled distribution of forces.

After mistakenly omitting from his cut-out maquette the horizontal rods needed to support the glass in the *Pale Blue Window*, Matisse was forced to start all over again and resolved in early February 1949 to make a new design for the stained-glass windows (fig. 35). While rising to this new challenge, he did not lose sight of his earlier designs and reminisced about their value: 'This first maquette is like a rough gem; the new one [discarded because of the rods] is the same gem cut and polished.'[31] *The Tree of Life*'s structure is in fact drawn directly from *Celestial Jerusalem*'s block-like geometrical rhythm, though reduced to a green surface, with touches of yellow on its sides (p. 47). Enriching this surface are the yellow algae, reminiscent of the second version, and interspersed among them are blue cactus leaves, a trait unique to the third scheme. Ultimately, the unity of this composition is generated by the careful interweaving of these three colours: 'The yellow is the foreground, reality, and the blue and green are the space.'[32]

Satisfied with this final design, Matisse was now confronted with the challenge of having to translate it into glass, for which he would rely on the expertise of glass-maker Paul Bony, based in Paris. The biggest challenge in translating paper to glass proved to be the yellow sections:

> Here is the situation concerning the stained-glass window. We have the blue and the green. Things aren't as simple for the buttercup yellow: the first experiments at backing it with frosted white weren't successful: the frosting kills the brilliance

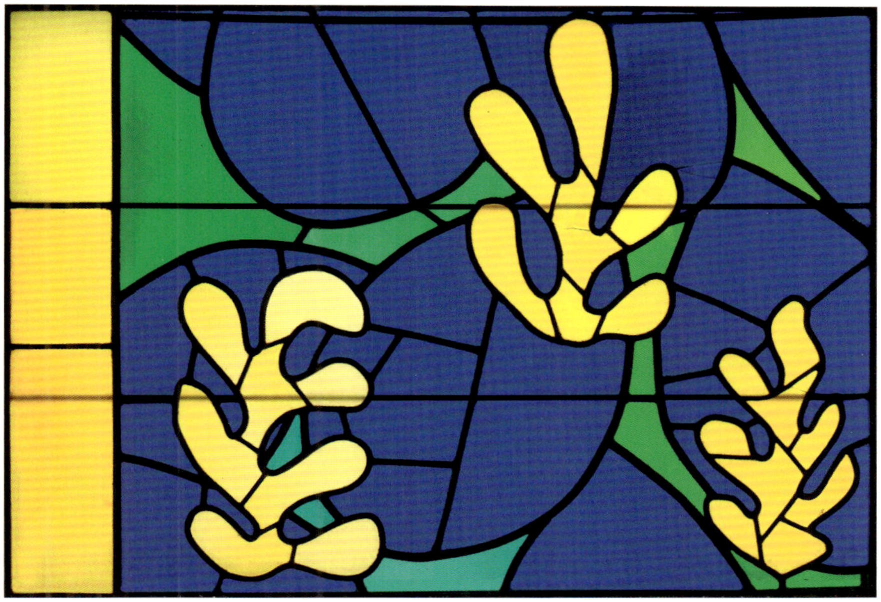

Fig. 36 Study for the stained-glass window *The Tree of Life* (*L'Arbre de vie*) 1950
Frosted coloured glass, set with lead, 62.3 × 85 × 2 (24½ × 33½ × ¾)
Produced in collaboration with Paul Bony (French, 1911–82). Musée Matisse, Nice
Bequest of Madame Henri Matisse, 1960

> of the yellow and the result is a yellow gray. We're now trying another solution: frosting the sheet of yellow itself. We'll have the result the day after tomorrow.[33]

There would be several more exchanges before the right yellow could be identified (fig. 36). One of the primary issues was that each colour should not only produce a different effect in compositional terms, as described above, but also establish a unique relationship with the exterior. The association between interior and exterior, which had been at the heart of his Vence paintings, was again a primary concern for Matisse, who here worked it into the physical structure of the works. He went, in fact, from the representation of the windows to their actual making in an almost seamless transition, with the cut-outs mediating the process.

On 12 December 1949 Monsignor Remond, Bishop of Nice, laid the chapel's cornerstone marking the beginning of construction work in a ceremony attended by Matisse, among others. By that point, though, Matisse felt that the project had entered a new phase, one in which his direct involvement was no longer necessary. Surveying the construction site the following summer, he found it 'coming along nicely' and concluded by stating: 'It's not surprising, considering how long I've been sleeping in it.'[34] Having spent almost two years living in the chapel factory set up in his studio, Matisse felt his devotion to the project had been fulfilled long before its existence as a fully fledged sanctuary. The endless and trying exercises Matisse had undertaken in devising the chapel's decorative scheme had virtually turned the studio into the chapel, erasing the traditional separation between studio and final environment.

As Matisse slowly distanced himself from the chapel, he was able to take up a new project. This consisted of a series of large-scale cut-outs compositionally aligned with painting, through which he conflated the narrative properties of painting with the formal qualities offered by the cut-outs. *The Thousand and One Nights* (no. 86), a horizontal scroll inspired by the legendary stories, is exemplary of this body of work. Narrated by the heroine Scheherazade to avoid death at the hands of the Persian king, each tale is interrupted just before dawn: 'She saw the light of day / She fell discreetly silent [Elle vit paraître le matin / Elle se tut discrètement]'. With these words spelled (without accents) across the upper-right corner of the cut-out, Matisse draws us into Scheherazade's universe. He avoided a literal representation of the heroine's tales, interpreting the atmosphere of her fiction by drawing on his repertoire of fantastical motifs. Organised in five sections, each dominated by a distinct design, the composition is to be read like a scroll from left to right. In the first panel a sensuous lantern, from which darkness spills out, metaphorically draws us into Scheherazade's storytelling. A fragmented stylised blue figure, possibly a representation of the narrator herself, stretches across the second panel, while the third panel combines different motifs – including algae – in a starry night of sorts. The fourth panel again features a lantern, but this time it announces the approach of dawn, followed by the rise of the sun in the fifth and final panel. Completing the scene are hearts and algae sprinkled around the outer edges of the work. The significance of this composition lies primarily in Matisse's attempt to reconcile narrative with his cut-outs' vocabulary.

Again it is a photograph of the artist's studio that offers us some insight into the making of this work. On 15 April 1950 Walter Carone visited Matisse at the Hôtel Régina, where he took some pictures of the artist for publication in *Paris Match* of 6 May 1950 (pp. 50–1). The wall beside Matisse's bed is covered in portions of what will become *The Thousand One Nights* and *The Beasts of the Sea*, another composition with fantastical overtones. The two works are at this stage incomplete, and elements of each merge seamlessly on the studio wall. Interspersed among the upper half of *The Beasts of the Sea* are the two lanterns, the fragmented nude and the rising sun from *The Thousand One Nights*. Also among them are compositions that later became independent such as *The Japanese Mask* (no. 88), *Composition, Blue Background* and *Vegetal Elements*, presumably a left-over from the Vence studio wall of 1949. The equal distribution of these disparate elements on Matisse's studio wall suggests that they were first conceived as individual motifs and only at a later stage were some of them incorporated into a narrative scheme.

On 19 June Rayssiguier visited Matisse's studio at the Régina and noted that in place of the chapel a new set of works had appeared. Pinned to the wall beside the fireplace was a strange creature that reminded Rayssiguier of a dragonfly and Delectorskaya of a rococo chair with a flowerpot on top of it; while both interpretations were valid, neither was completely accurate, as the large inscrutable cut-out featured a *Creole Dancer* (no. 85).[35] Designed in one day, with the help of Paule Martin, one of Matisse's studio assistants, using scraps of paper that were to hand, the majestic dancer instantaneously sprang to life on Matisse's walls. It was partially based on life studies of Christiane, a young dancer from the Nice opera, who had been summoned to dance in the hall of Matisse's studio at the Régina, but the composition was also, according to Aragon, inspired by American dancer and choreographer Katherine Dunham, whom Matisse had previously seen perform.[36]

The vivacity of *Creole Dancer* stems from the contrast between the rigid, colour block sheets and the dancer's explosive movements. With folded legs ready to spring to a plié, *Creole Dancer* is virtually leaping out of the work and into the viewer's space – an effect enhanced by the tight wove of gouache sheets forming the backdrop to the dancer's movements. Supposedly drawn from Matisse's reservoir of gouache sheets, this geometrical configuration is reminiscent of *Pale Blue Window*'s compositional structure with a vegetal motif overlaid on top of a geometrical pattern. The exuberant effect of *Creole Dancer* moved Matisse's son Pierre to offer to buy it immediately. Unwilling to part with a work of such 'exceptional quality', Matisse declined, as *Creole Dancer* represented the ultimate summation of painting's qualities translated into cut-out terms.[37]

An additional reason for not wanting to part with *Creole Dancer* can be found in the parallel loss of its associated work *Zulma* (no. 84), sold shortly after its making to the Statens Museum in Copenhagen. *Zulma* was exhibited at the Salon de Mai (9–31 May 1950), where it was hailed as one of Matisse's most outstanding and innovative masterpieces. Couturier, who was present at the opening, reported to Matisse on 24 May 1950:

> I trust you saw in the papers what success your painting at the Salon de Mai is having. Everybody is saying, 'It's the youngest and most innovative work there,' and it's true, compared to it everything else looks wilted and laborious. But, it seems to me, it also has all the greatness, and notwithstanding its joyful, brilliance, gravity of life.[38]

And in a similar vein Tériade remarked:

> What a surprise, what a dazzling picture your nude is at this youthful May Salon of which you are the youngest exhibitor! And how healthy it is! I would really have liked you to see your entry hanging

among the others. It radiates good health. That's the word that comes to mind amidst all these tormented paintings, of equivocal audacity and sad and shaky faith. One can breathe in front of your colourful construction and believe that all is not yet lost. But what a joke ... for the young exhibitors! Thanks for the splendid lessons.[39]

Given the audacity of Matisse's composition in the face of the gestural and tormented Art Informel at the Salon, Paule Martin's recollections of the making of *Zulma* are remarkable for their description of its spontaneity:

> The year was 1950. Matisse and I were in the winter bedroom. The master, in his wheelchair, was cheery and relaxed. He started by cutting the central blue figure, her breasts integral to her form; then he had me slide green and yellow sheets behind the figure. The undulating orange streak down the front came later, like the brush and ink strokes defining the pubis and the legs. At the end of the first day, we left it there.
>
> Matisse must have studied the work during the night, because, when I arrived the next morning, he made me add the table and the purple decoration on top, then the orange-brown parquet. Finally came the blue and sienna vase with its bouquet outlined in soft lead pencil. We had finished in two days.[40]

Paule Martin's words confirm the immediacy of Matisse's process already seen in *Creole Dancer*. The structure of the two works, though, is very different: unlike the *Creole Dancer*, which was made from found pieces, each section of *Zulma* was carefully crafted, starting with the imposing blue body and moving outwards to include still-life elements. Vegetal motifs, which up to this point had been the main protagonists of Matisse's cut-outs, are relegated here to a secondary role, leaving the spotlight to the naked figure. Balancing between the two chairs, *Zulma* is the main subject of this painting-like cut-out yet, unlike *Creole Dancer*, is grounded in a clearly defined spatial environment. Perspective, which had noticeably been absent from previous cut-out compositions, is here introduced in a way that aligns this work with his Interiors of Vence paintings. Incorporating the same principles of skewed viewpoint integrated with elements drawn from his studio, *Zulma* shows a distinct similarity to *Pink Nude, Red Interior*, a small painting from 1947 depicting a standing nude in a precarious equilibrium between two chairs. Made at the time of the Interiors of Vence, *Pink Nude, Red Interior* featured in the photograph of Matisse sitting among these works in Vence. It is hung above the mirror, slightly removed from the heart of the group, yet its presence suggests a connection, also explicitly confirmed by its prominent position in the studio. The resemblance between *Zulma* and *Pink Nude, Red Interior* indicates that Matisse was not only reinvigorating painting through cut-outs but also using the technique as a way to revisit earlier compositions on a much larger scale. The inclusion of *Zulma* at the Salon de Mai demonstrated Matisse's perception of the cut-outs as works in their own right and not simply preparatory maquettes to be transferred into a different medium.

Having established a public recognition for his cut-out works, Matisse went on to add one last aspect to his chapel mosaic: the chasubles (nos. 80–3). Considered an integral part of the chapel's decorative scheme, the priest's robes were instrumental, as emphasised by Cowart, in bridging 'the gap between the chapel as a structure and the chapel as a setting for the performance of cultic rites'.[41] The chasubles were thus a pivotal component of Matisse's all-encompassing vision and are still a prominent feature of the ritual taking place every Sunday to this day. Hailed by Picasso as the most astounding aspect of Matisse's scheme, they combine the chapel's dazzling array of forms and colours with movement. As garments worn by the priest officiating mass, they tie together all the elements of the chapel. They offer a coloured animation that sways between the brilliance of the stained-glass windows and the starkness of the black and white ceramic panels, significantly the final element of the great scheme conceived by Matisse. From that point onwards the chapel would no longer exist as a private work in progress in his studio, but would become the site of public reverence and prayer.

Too ill to attend the consecration ceremony on 25 June 1951, Matisse sent a written statement in which he declared: 'This work is the outcome of four years of exclusive and concentrated work, and it is the result of all my active life. Despite all its imperfections I consider it as my masterpiece.'[42] Today only the chapel survives, but the 'factory' nevertheless represents a fundamental stepping stone in the evolution of Matisse's cut-out oeuvre.

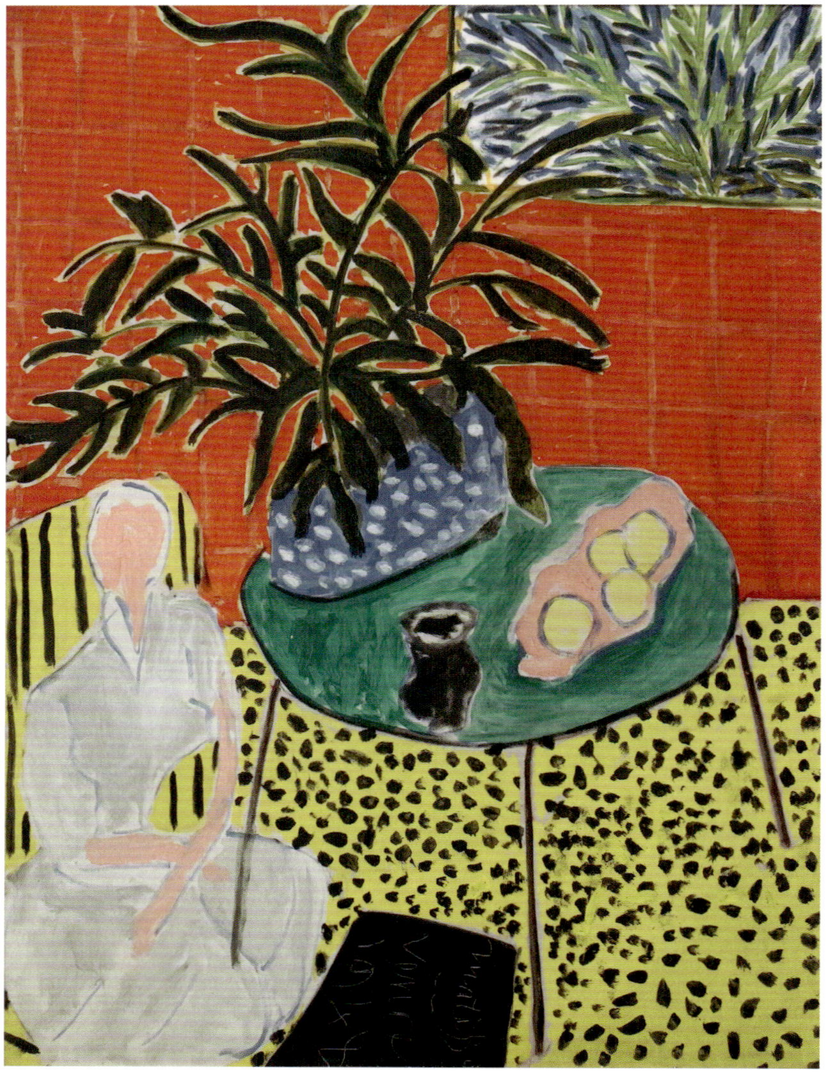

72. *Interior with Black Fern* 1948
Oil on canvas, 116.5 × 89.5 (45⅞ × 35¼)

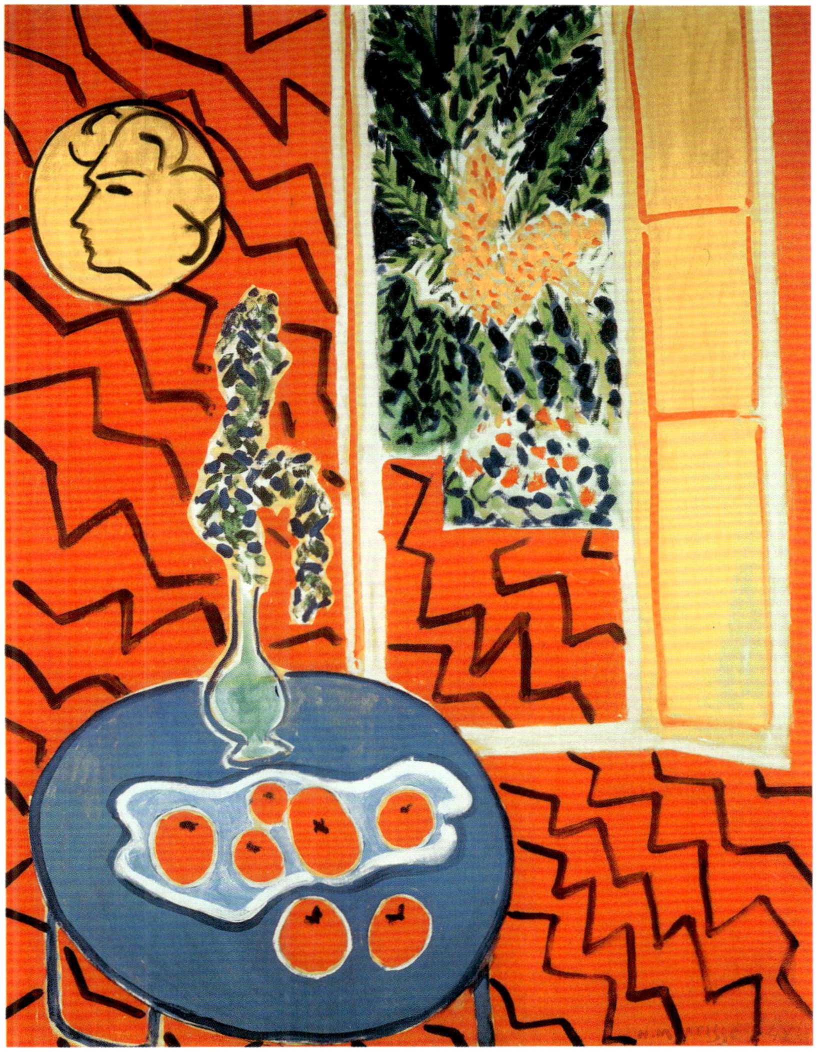

73. *Red Interior: Still Life on a Blue Table* 1947
Oil on canvas, 116 × 89 (45⅝ × 35)

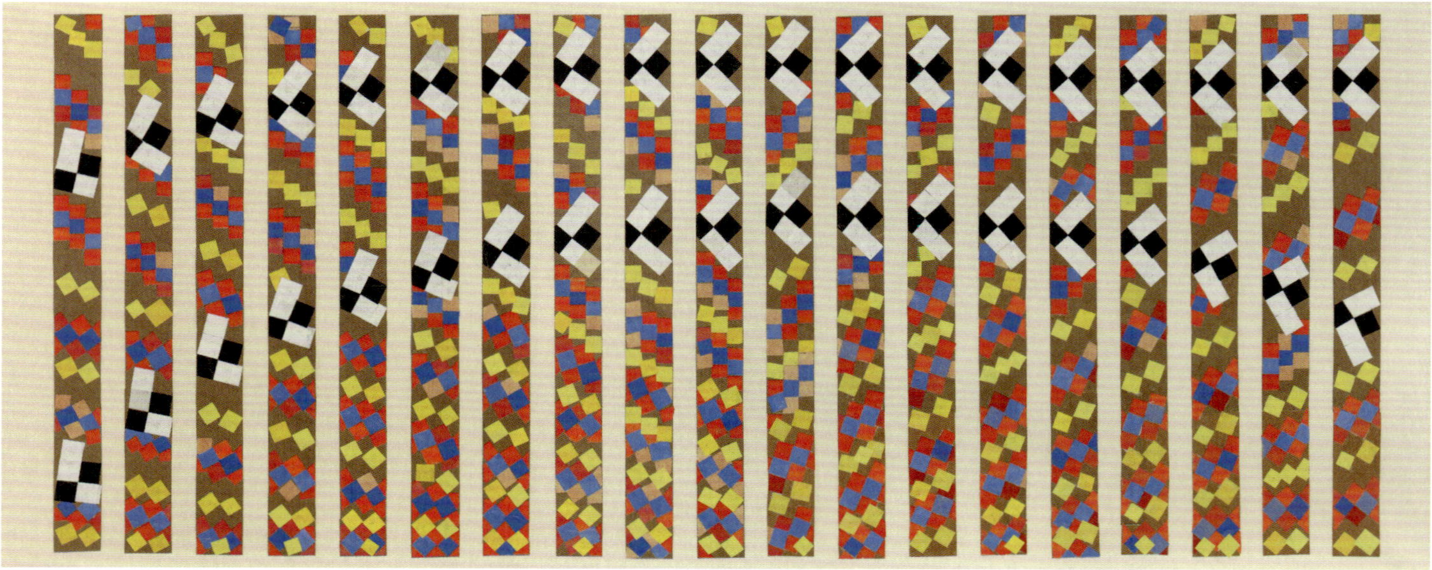

74. *The Bees* summer 1948
Preliminary maquette for the side windows of the Chapel of the Rosary, Vence (realised 1955 for H. Matisse primary school, Le Cateau-Cambrésis)
Gouache on paper, cut and pasted, mounted on canvas, 101 × 241 (39¾ × 94⅞)

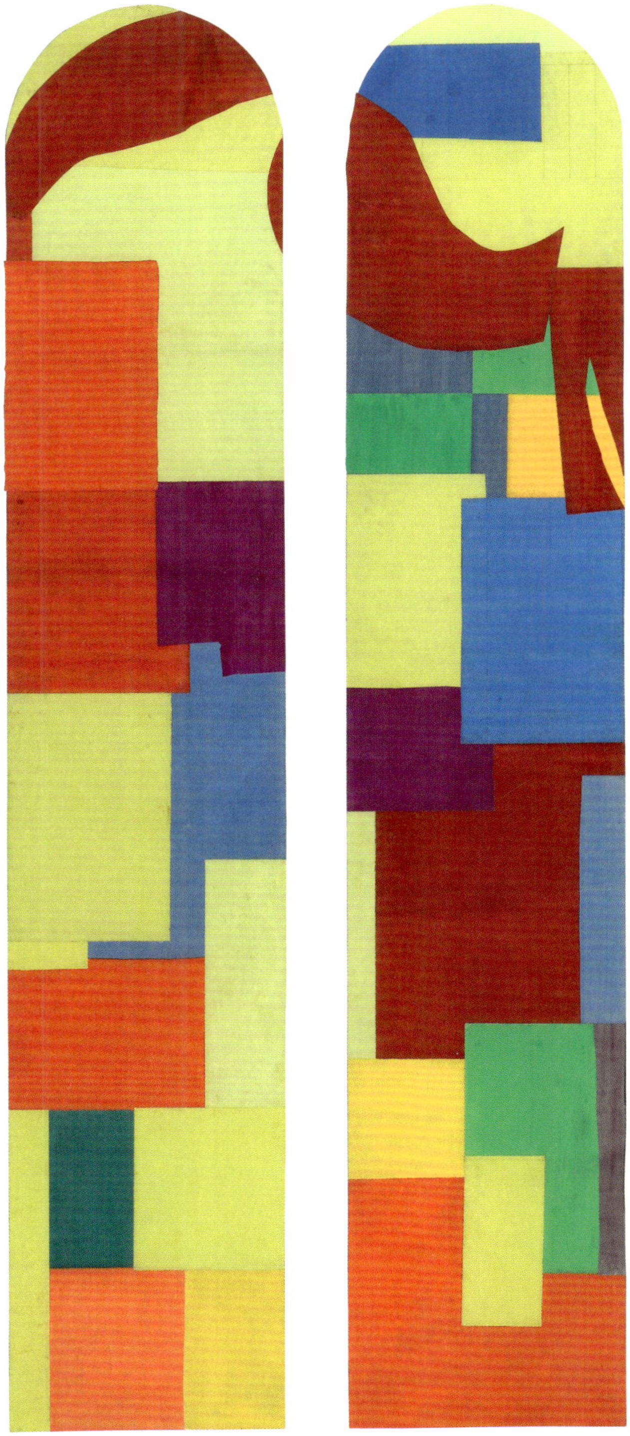

75. *Celestial Jerusalem* early 1948
First maquette for the apse window
of the Chapel of the Rosary, Vence
Gouache on paper, cut and pasted, on paper,
mounted on canvas, 265.5 × 130 (104½ × 51⅛)

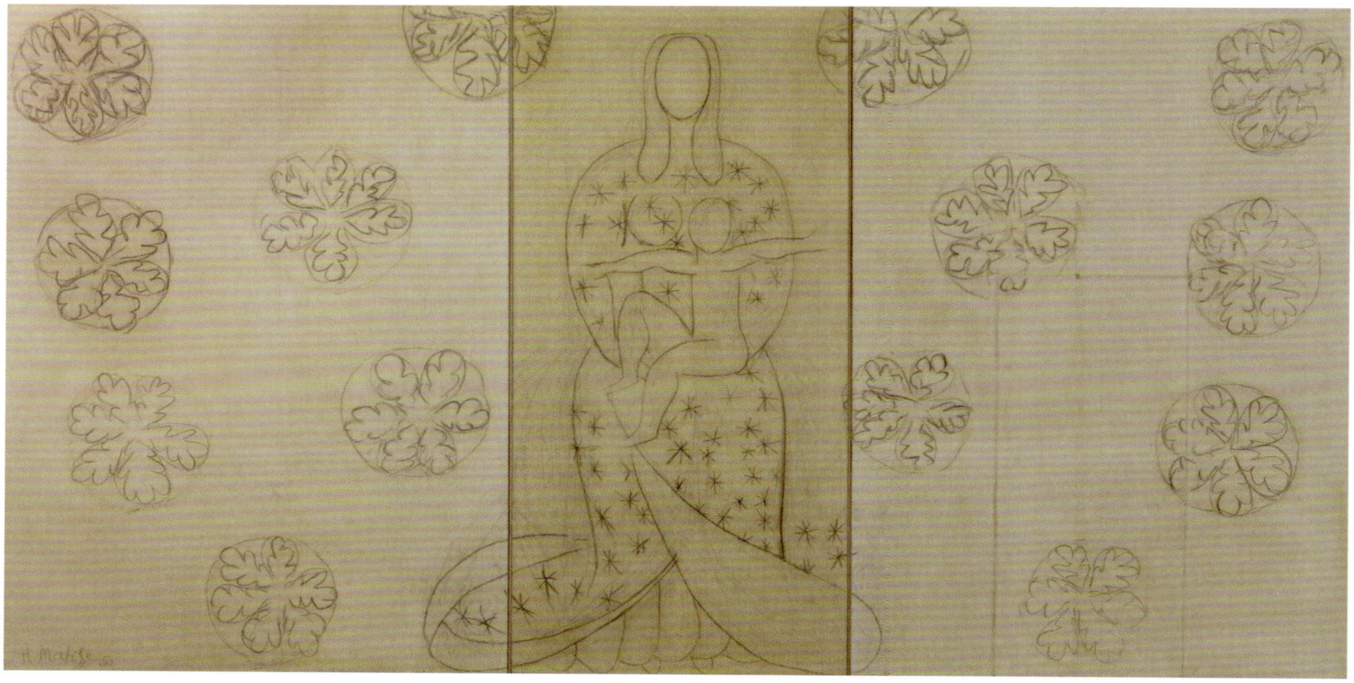

76. *The Virgin and Child* c. 1950
Charcoal on paper, 330 × 610 (130 × 240¼)

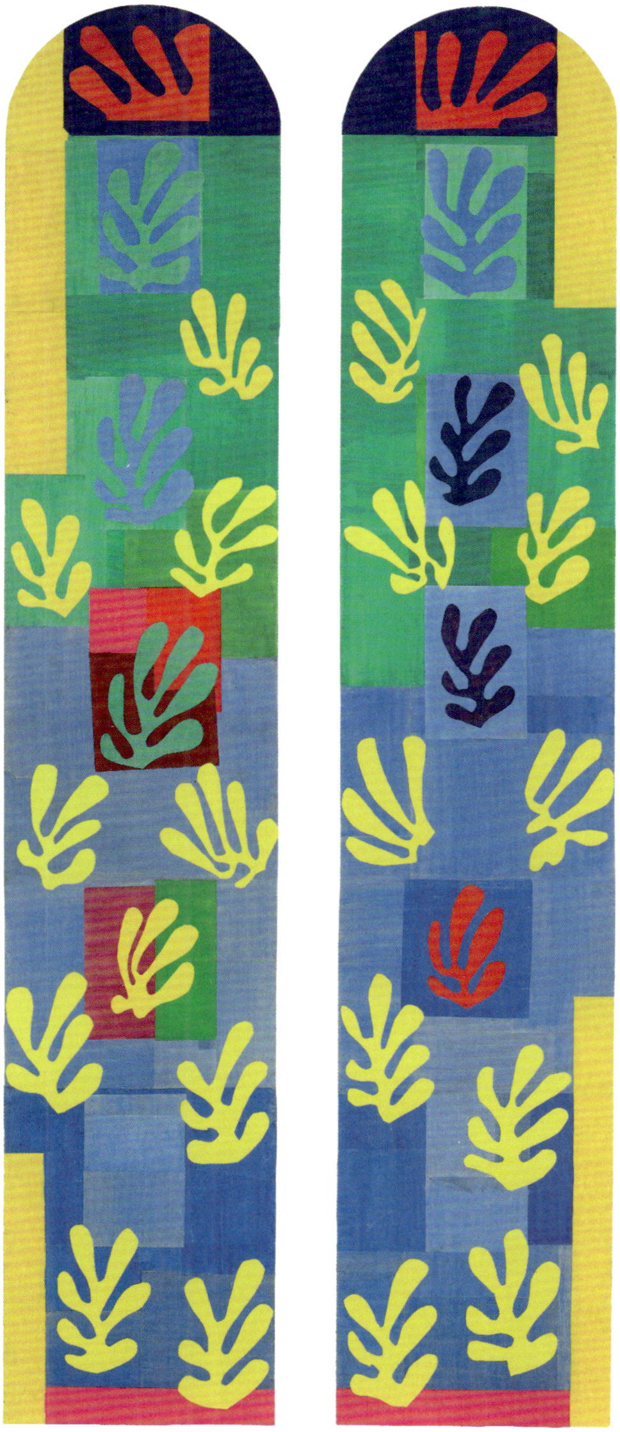

77. *Pale Blue Window*
November 1948 – January 1949
Second maquette for the apse window for
the Chapel of the Rosary, Vence
Two-part panel: gouache on paper, cut and
pasted, on kraft paper, mounted on canvas
509.8 × 252.3 (200¾ × 99 ⅜)

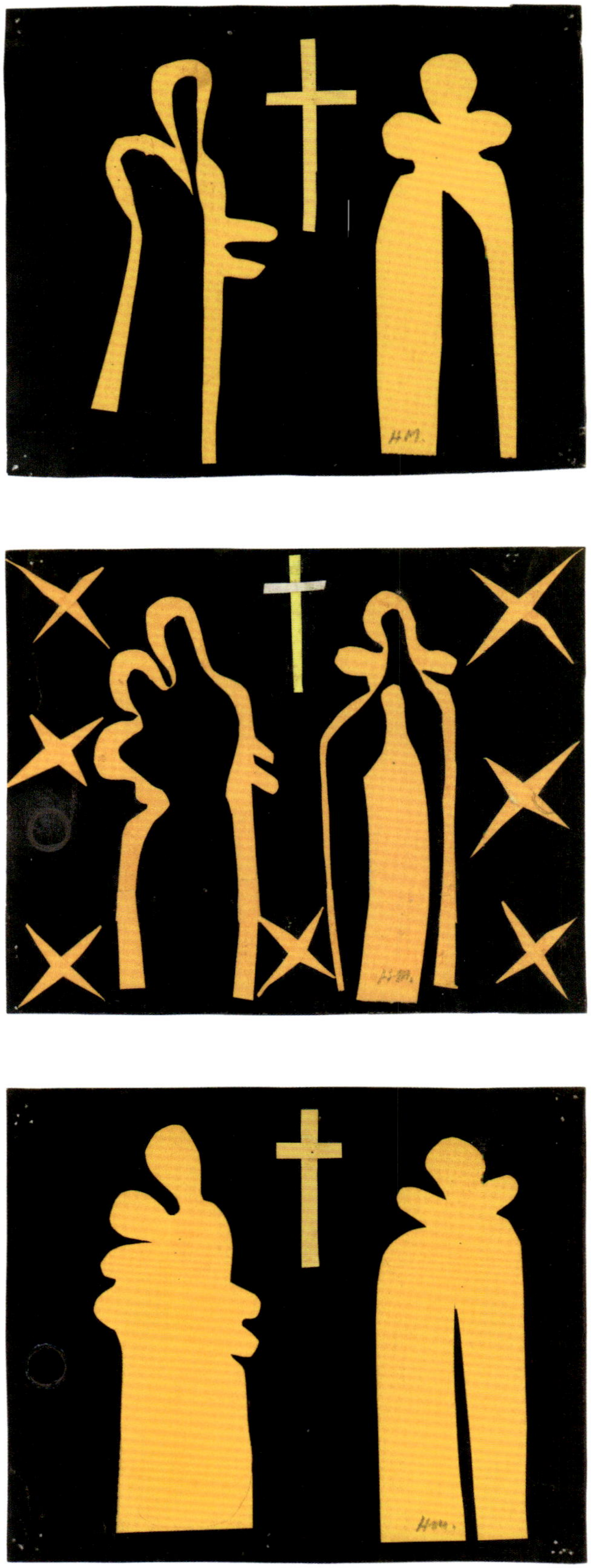

78. Maquettes for the tabernacle of
the Chapel of the Rosary, Vence c.1949
(related design realised 1951)
Gouache on paper, cut and pasted

a: 20.3 × 24.8 (8 × 9¾)
b: 19.7 × 24.8 (7¾ × 9¾)
c: 20.3 × 25.4 (8 × 10)

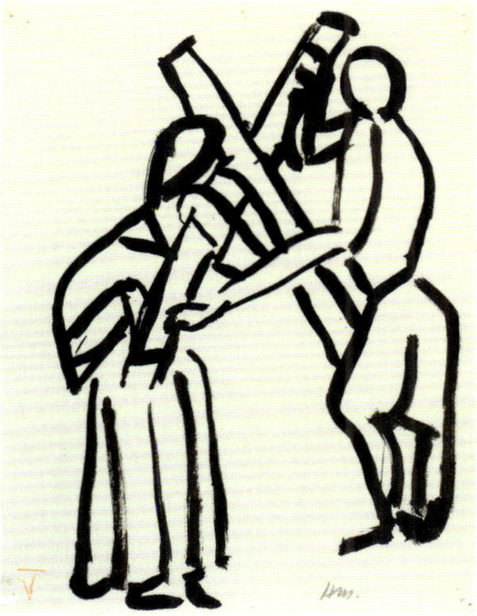

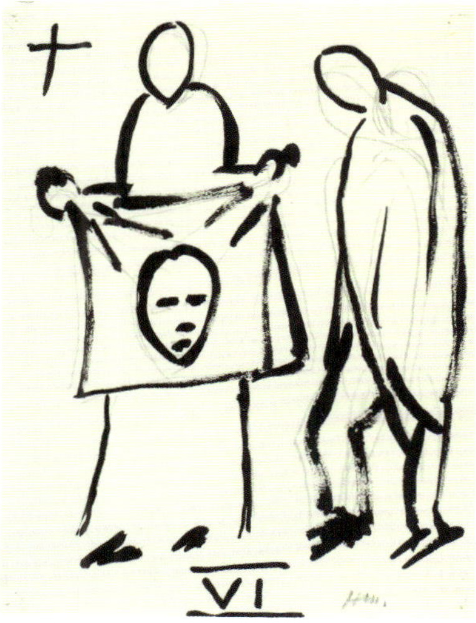

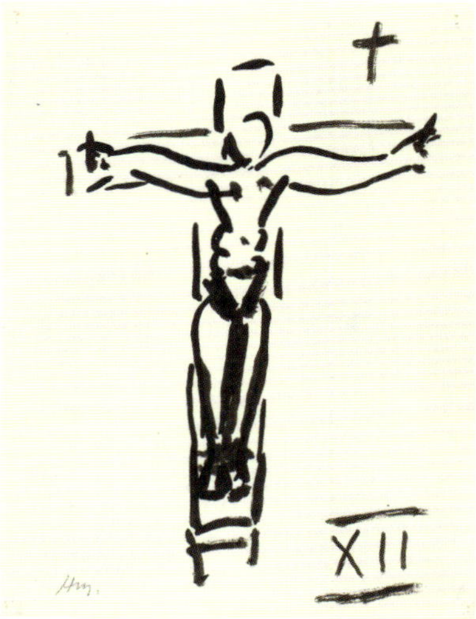

79a. *Simon of Cyrene Helps Jesus to Carry the Cross* 1949
Study for the Fifth Station of the Cross
Ink on paper, 26.7 × 20.3 (10½ × 8)

79b. *Veronica Wipes the Face of Jesus* 1949
Study for the Sixth Station of the Cross
Ink on paper, 26.3 × 20.3 (10⅜ × 8)

79c. *Christ on the Cross* 1949
Study for the Twelfth Station of the Cross
Ink on paper, 26.7 × 20.3 (10½ × 8)

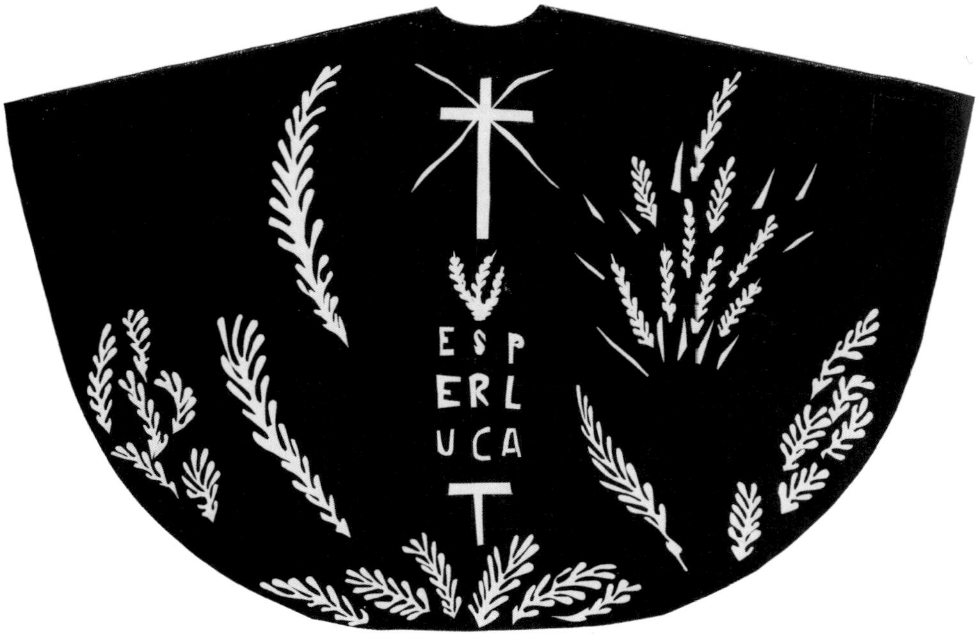

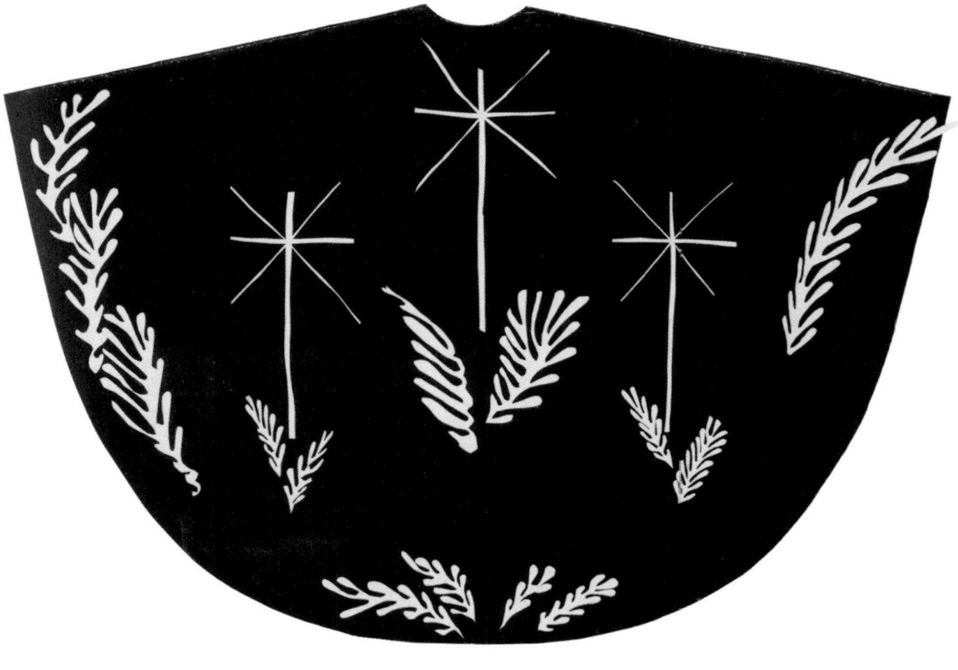

80. Maquette for *Black Chasuble* (front: *'Esperlucat'*) 1950–2
Gouache on paper, cut and pasted, mounted on canvas
125.6 × 197.6 (49½ × 77¾)

81. Maquette for *Black Chasuble* (back) 1950–2
Gouache on paper, cut and pasted, mounted on canvas
132 × 197 (52 × 77⅝)

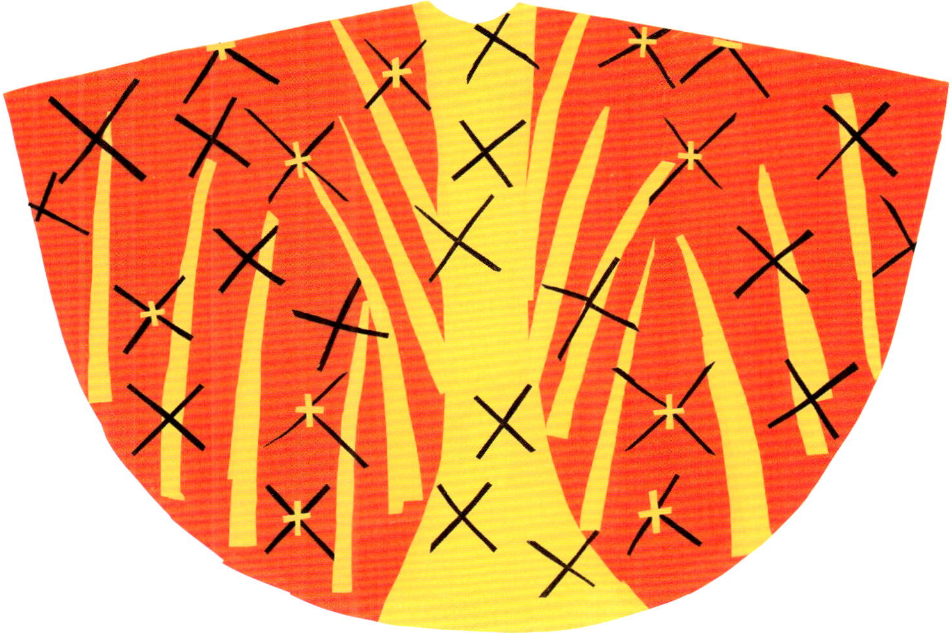

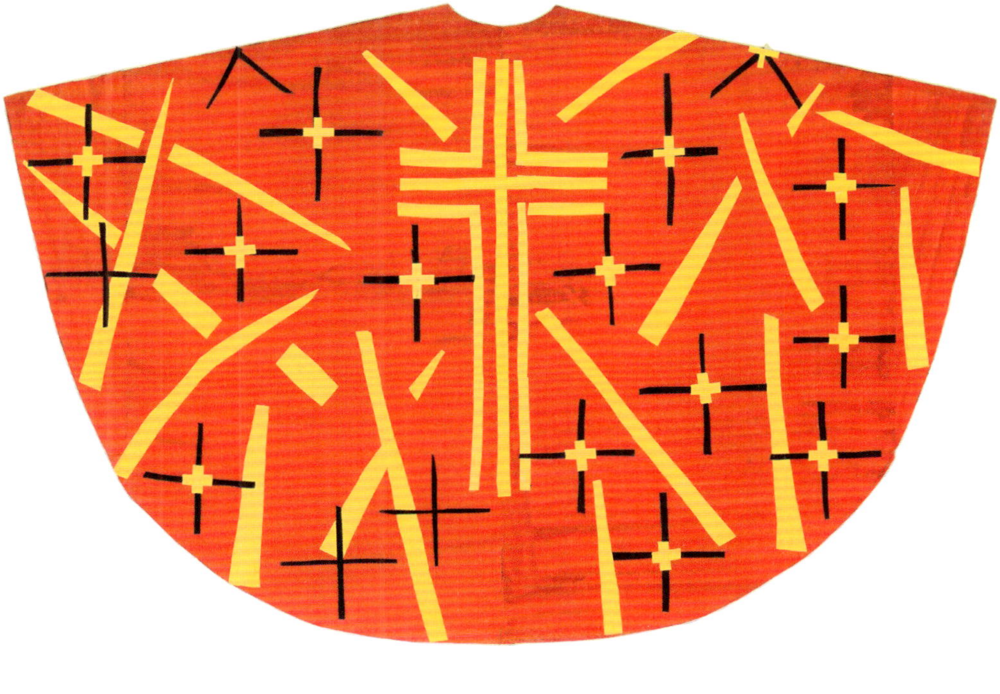

82. Maquette for *Red Chasuble* (front) late 1950–2
(realised 1952)
Gouache on paper, cut and pasted, 133.4 × 198.4 (52½ × 78⅛)

83. Maquette for *Red Chasuble* (back) late 1950–2
(realised 1952)
Gouache on paper, cut and pasted, 128.2 × 199.4 (50½ × 78½)

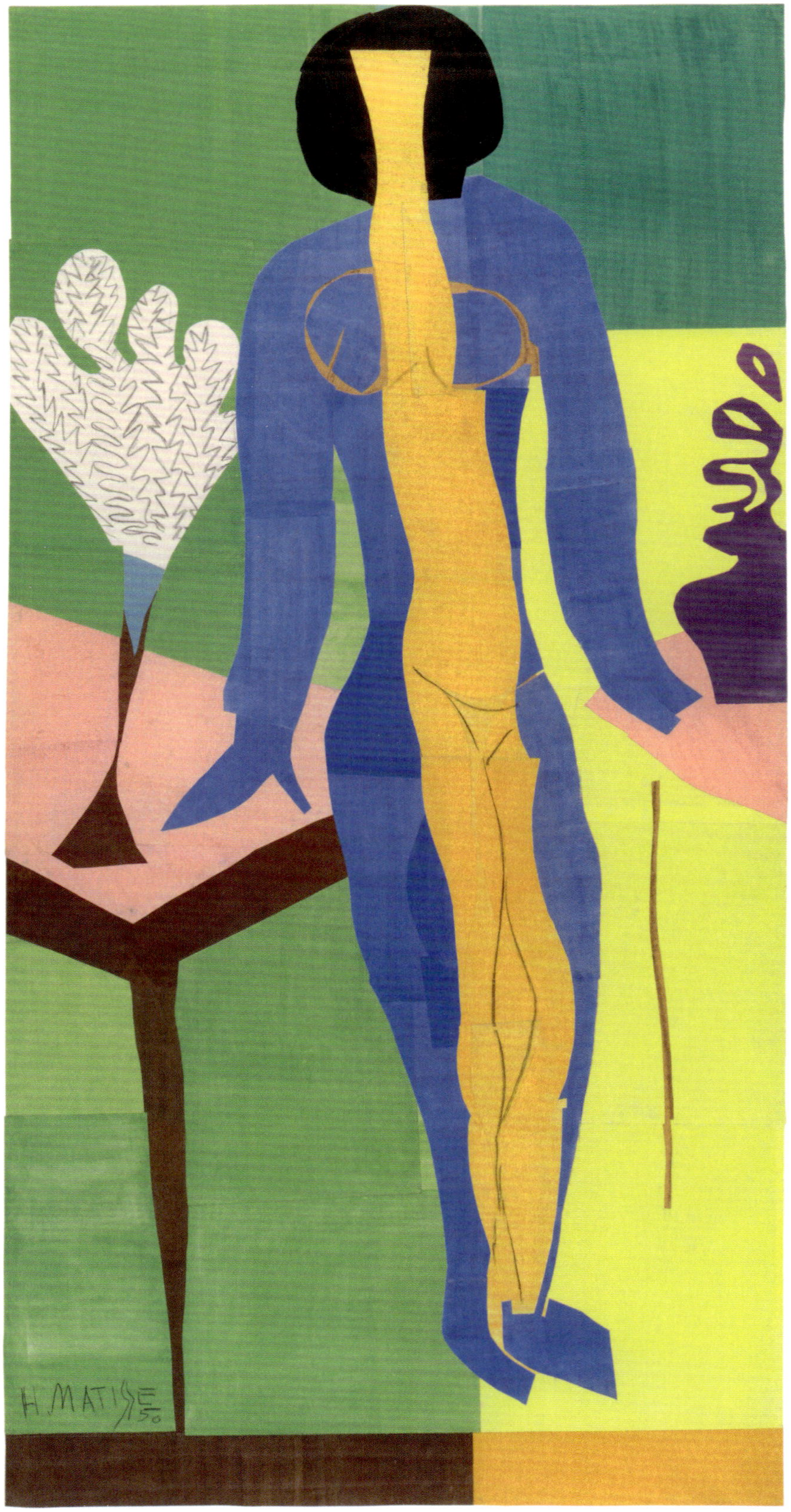

84. *Zulma* early 1950
Gouache on paper, cut and pasted
238 × 133 (93¾ × 52⅜)

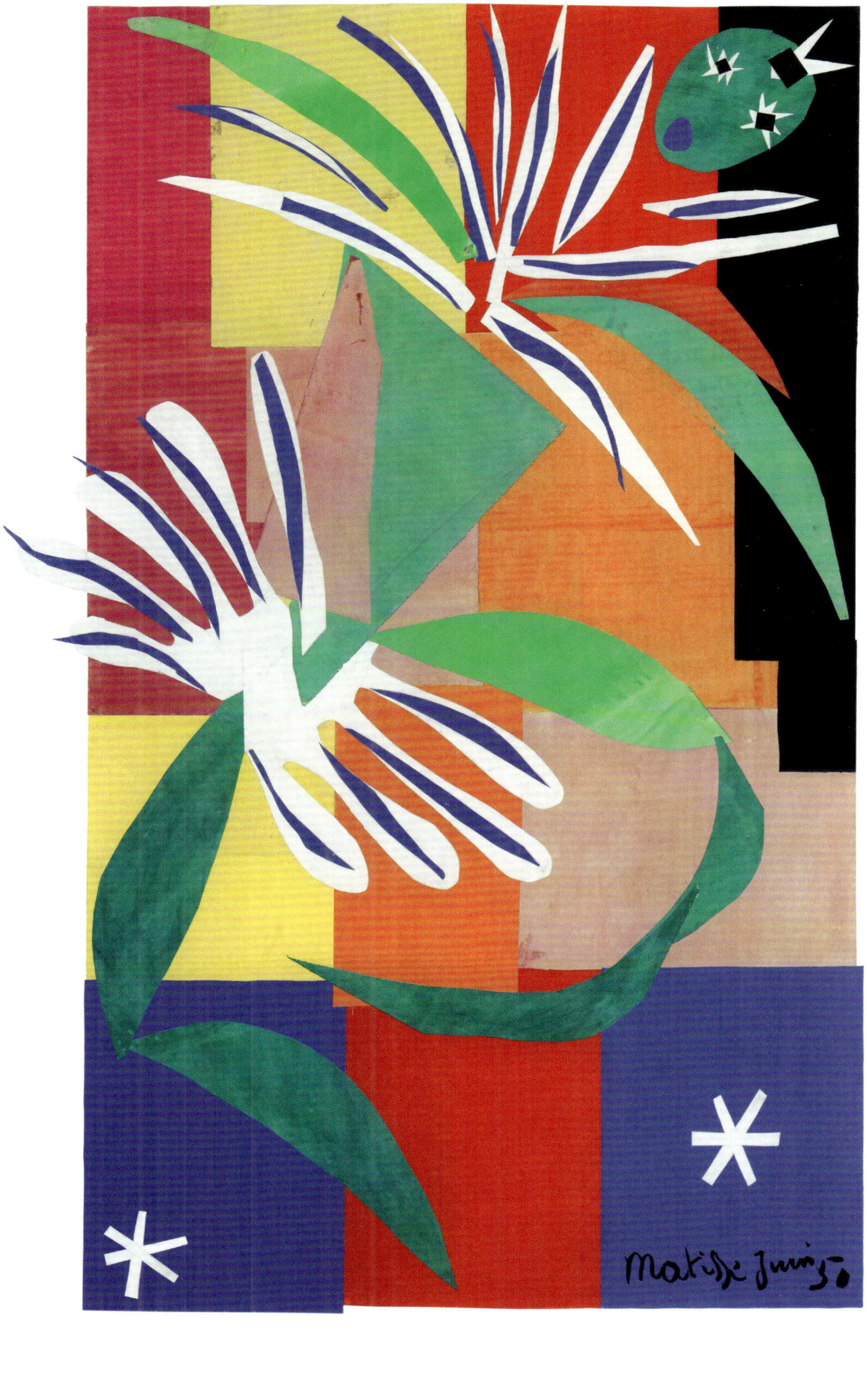

85. *Creole Dancer* June 1950
Gouache on paper, cut and pasted, on paper,
mounted on canvas, 205.1 × 120 (80¾ × 47¼)

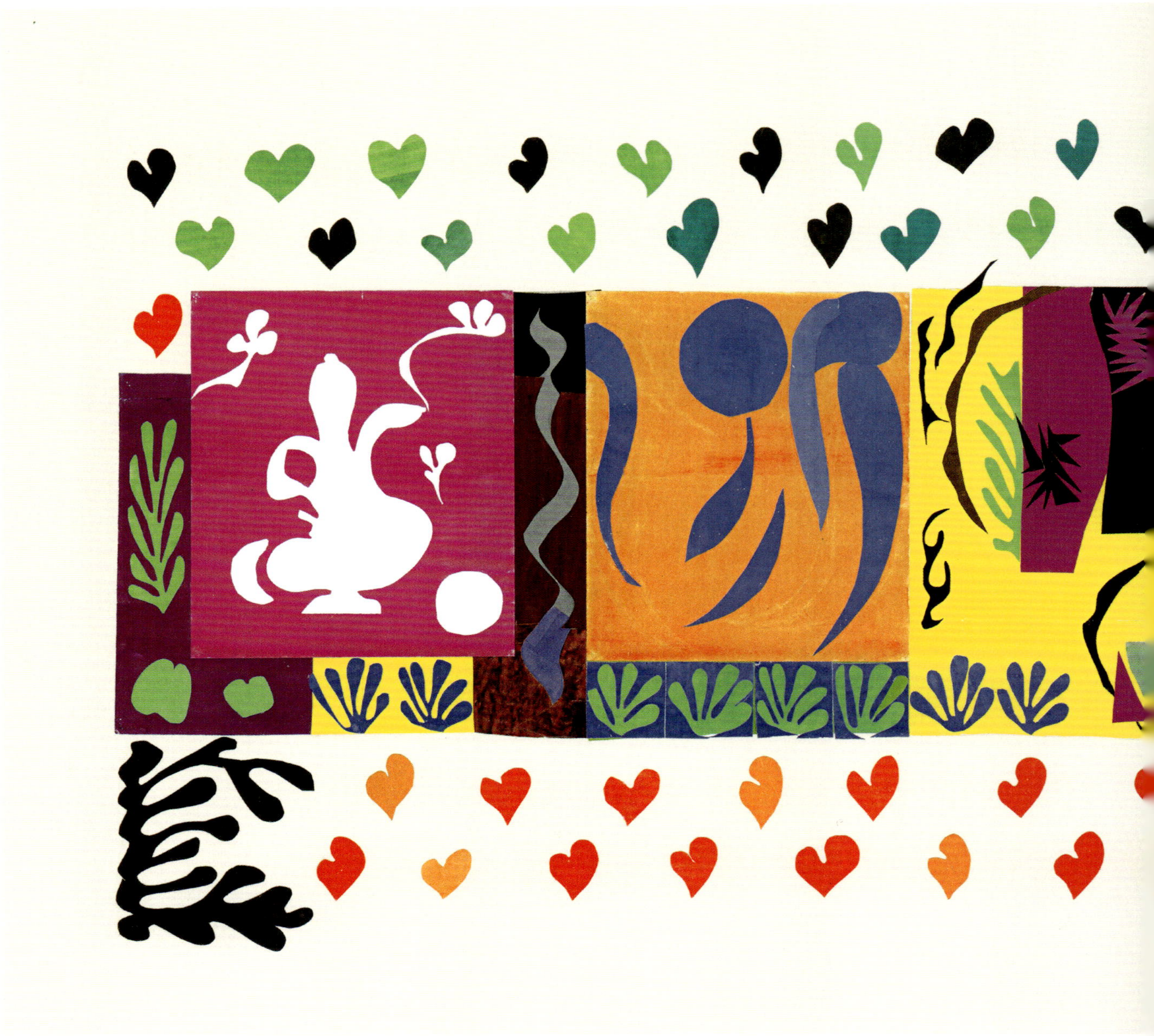

86. *The Thousand and One Nights* June 1950
Gouache on paper, cut and pasted, 139 × 374 (54¾ × 147¼)

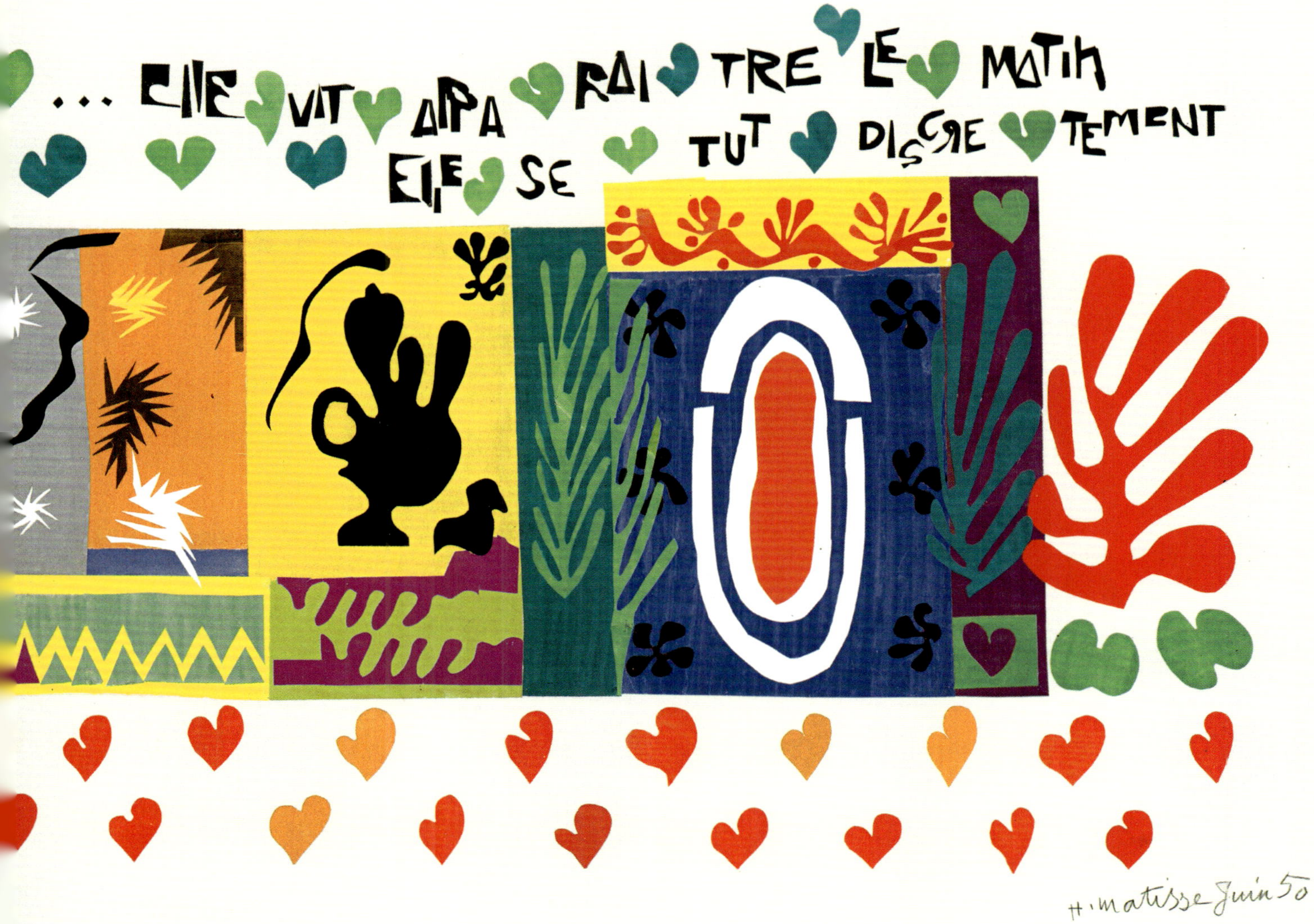
... ELLE VIT APPA RAI TRE LE MATIN
ELLE SE TUT DISCRE TEMENT
H. Matisse Juin 50

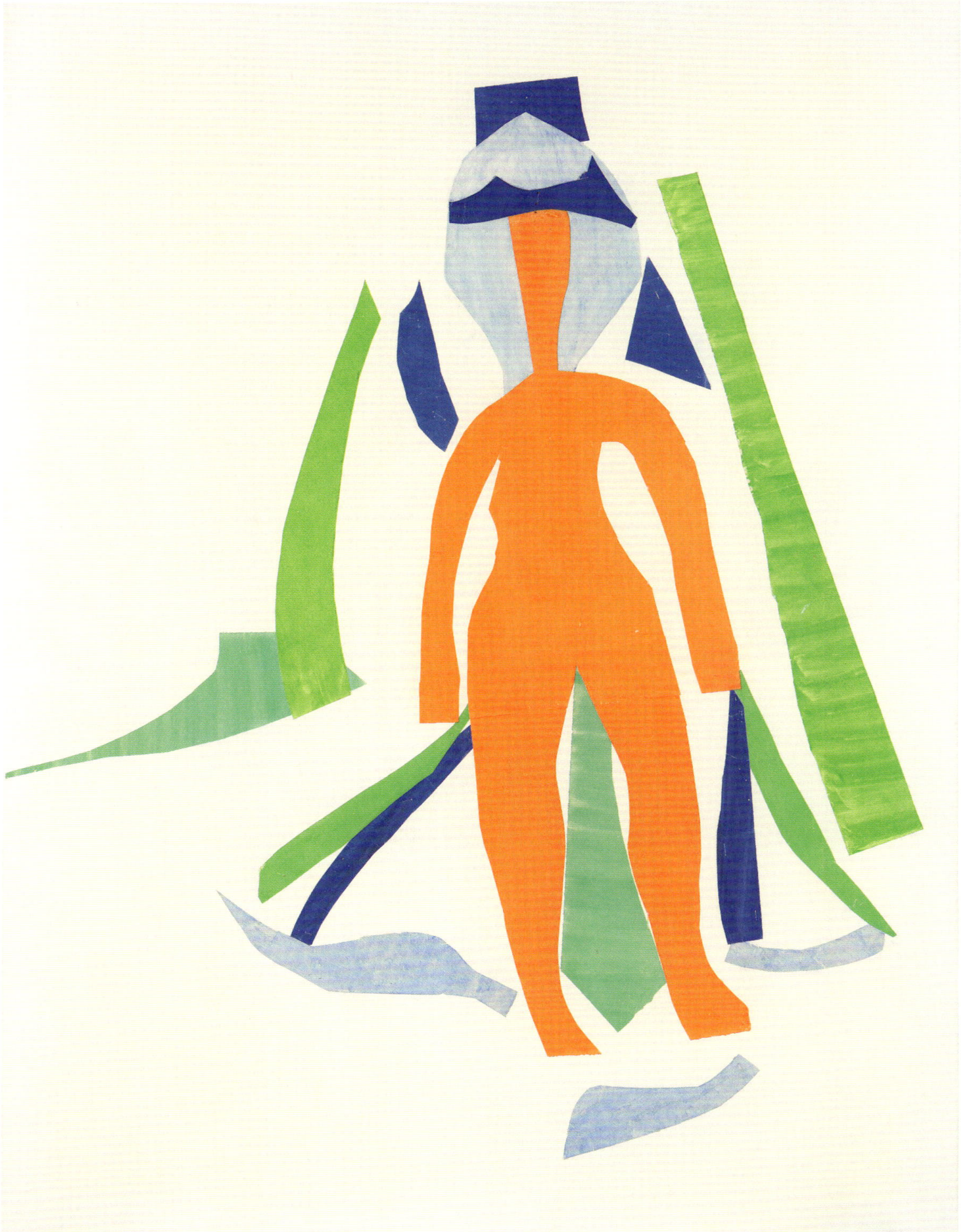

87. *Little Girl* c.1952
Gouache on paper, cut and pasted
152.4 × 117.5 (60 × 46¼)

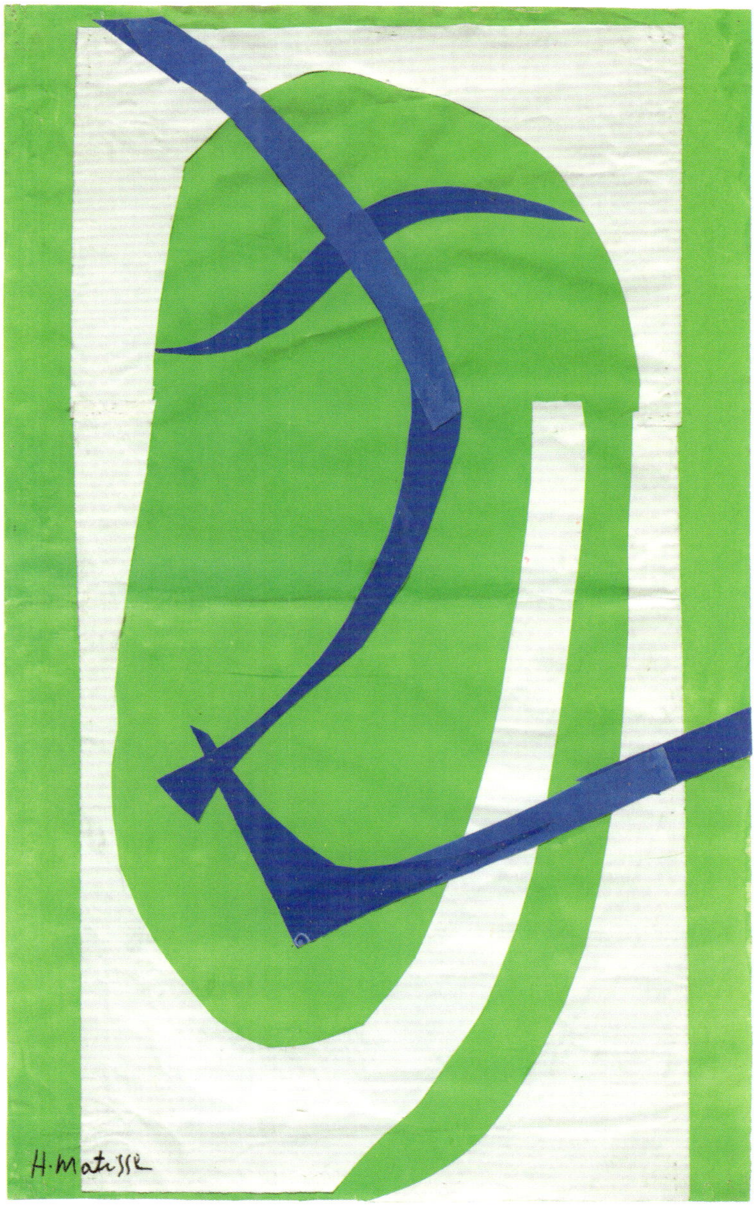

88. *The Japanese Mask* early 1950
Gouache on paper, cut and pasted
79.5 × 49.5 (31¼ × 19½)

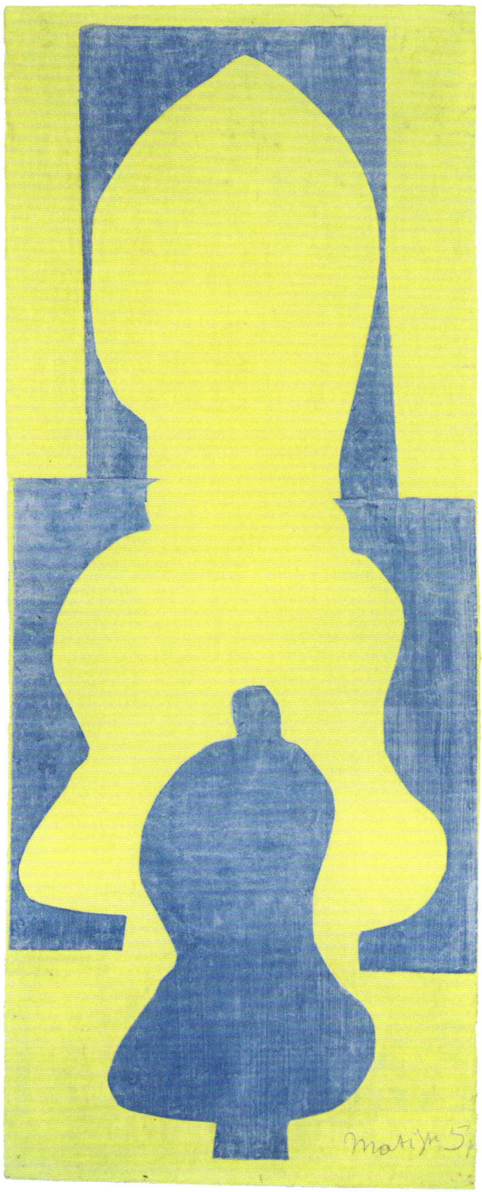

89. *The Bell* 1951
Gouache on paper, cut and pasted, and watercolour, mounted on canvas, 122 × 48.5 (48 × 19⅛)

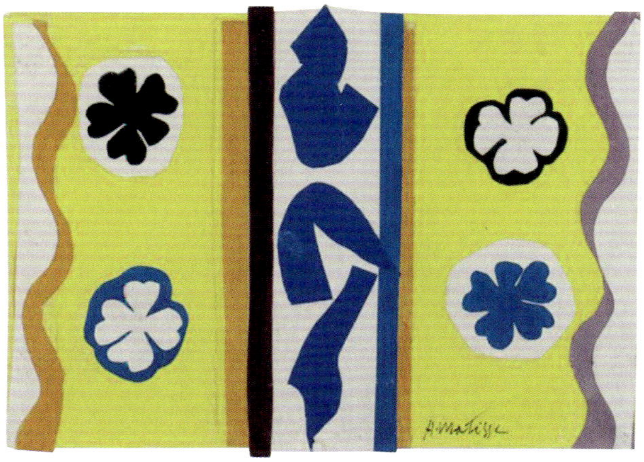

90. *The Four Rosettes with Blue Motifs* 1949–50
Gouache on paper, cut and pasted, 38 × 54 (15 × 21¼)

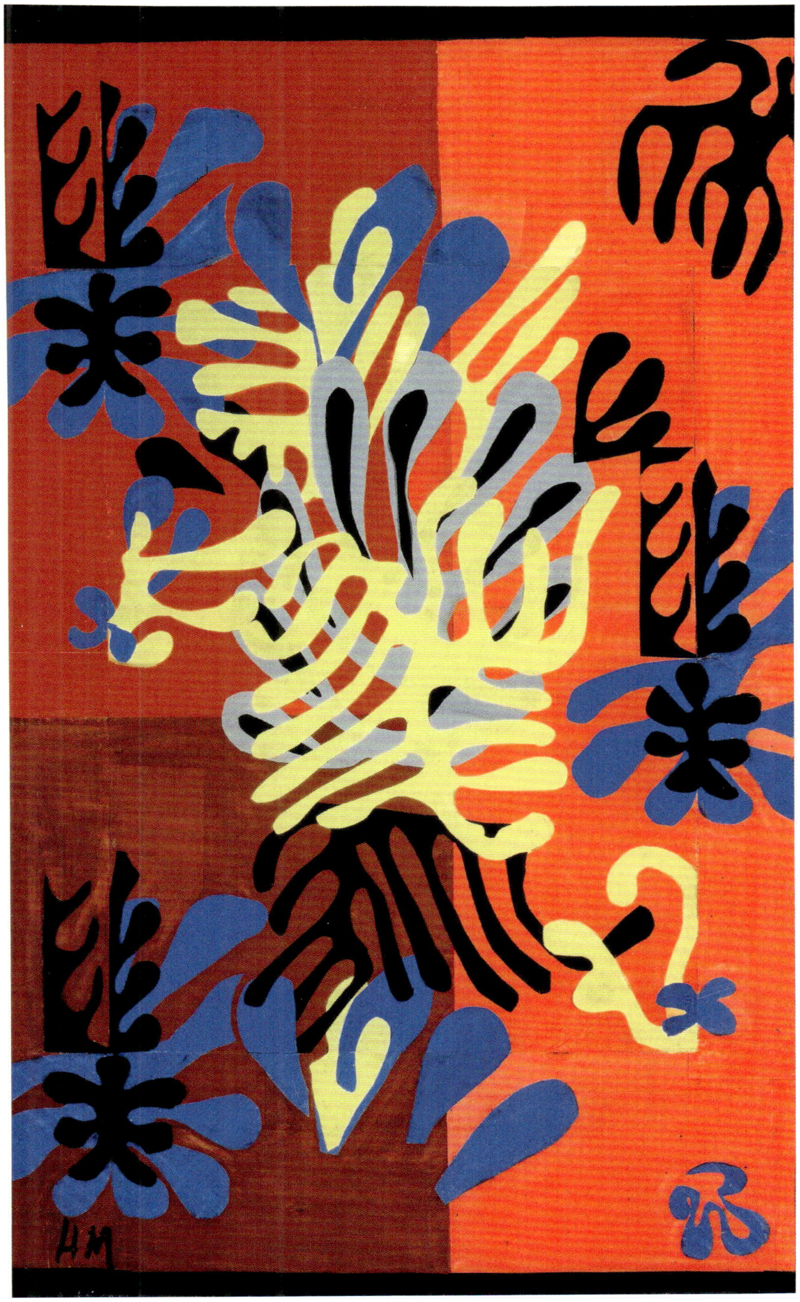

91. *Mimosa* 1949–51
Maquette for rug (realised 1951)
Gouache on paper, cut and pasted, mounted on canvas
148 × 98 (58¼ × 38⅝)

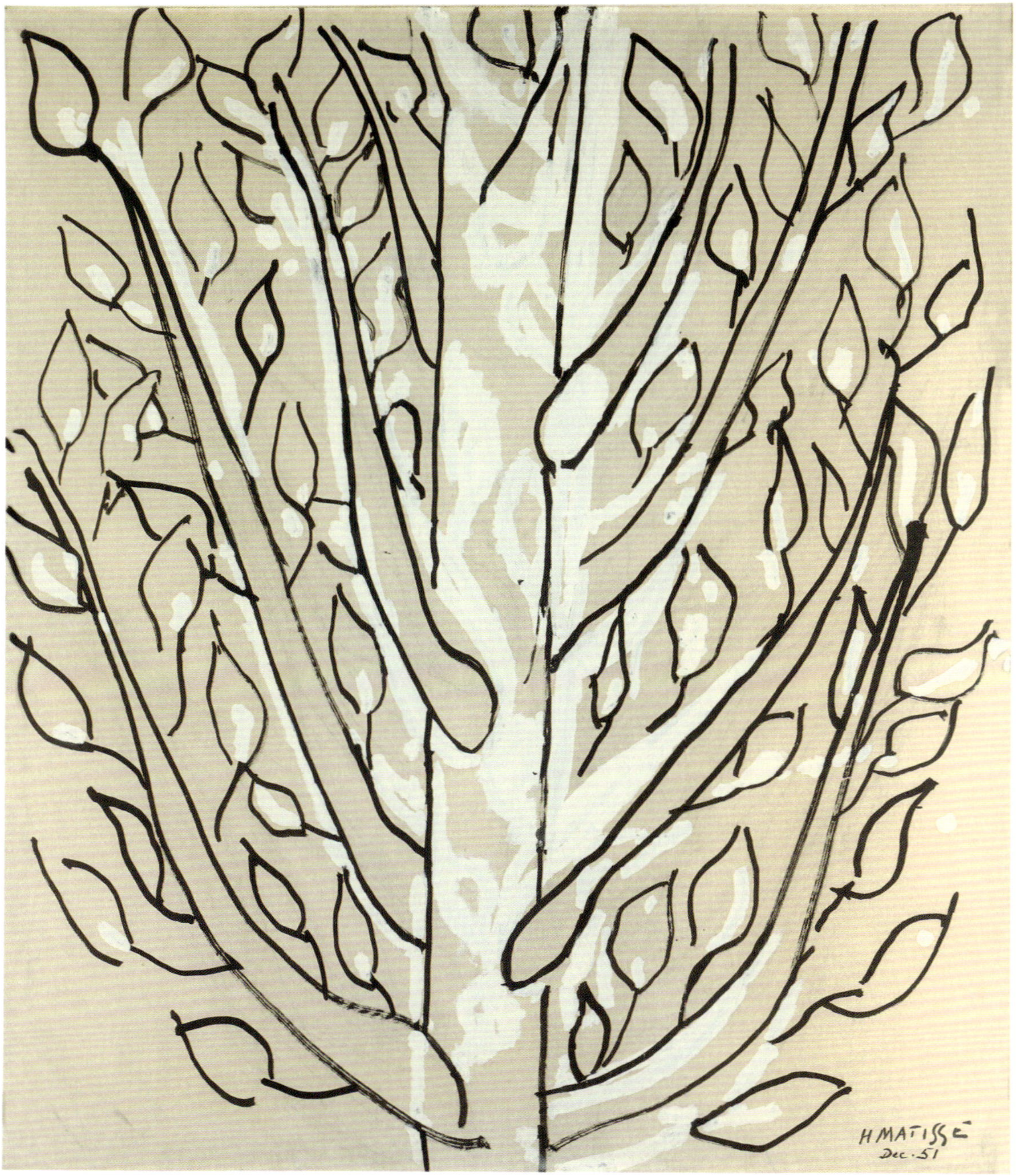

92. *Tree* December 1951
Ink, gouache, and charcoal on paper,
mounted on canvas, 177.8 × 152.4 (70 × 60)

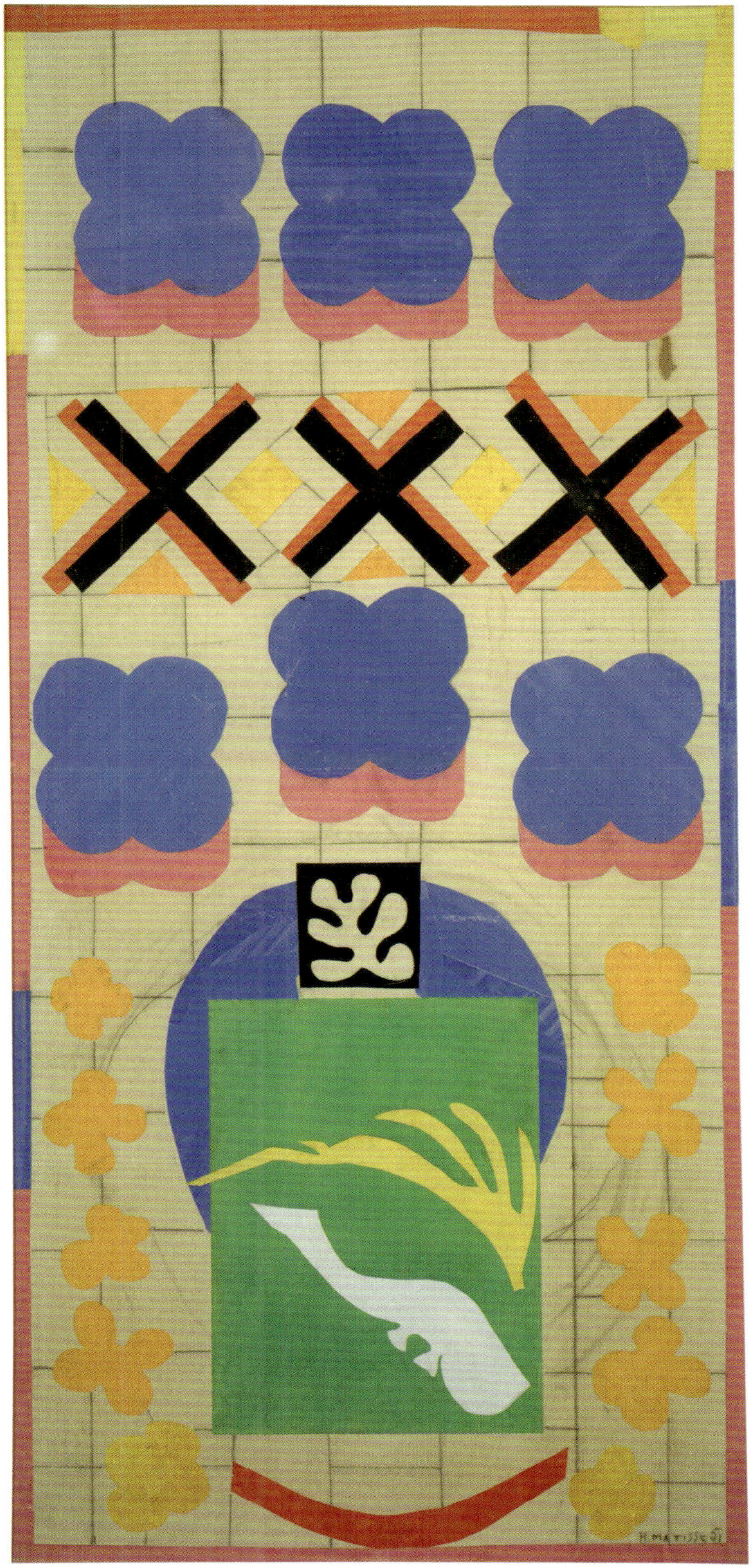

93. *Chinese Fish* 1951
Maquette for stained-glass window (realised 1951)
Gouache on paper, cut and pasted, and
charcoal on white paper, mounted on canvas
189.9 × 90.2 (74¾ × 35½)

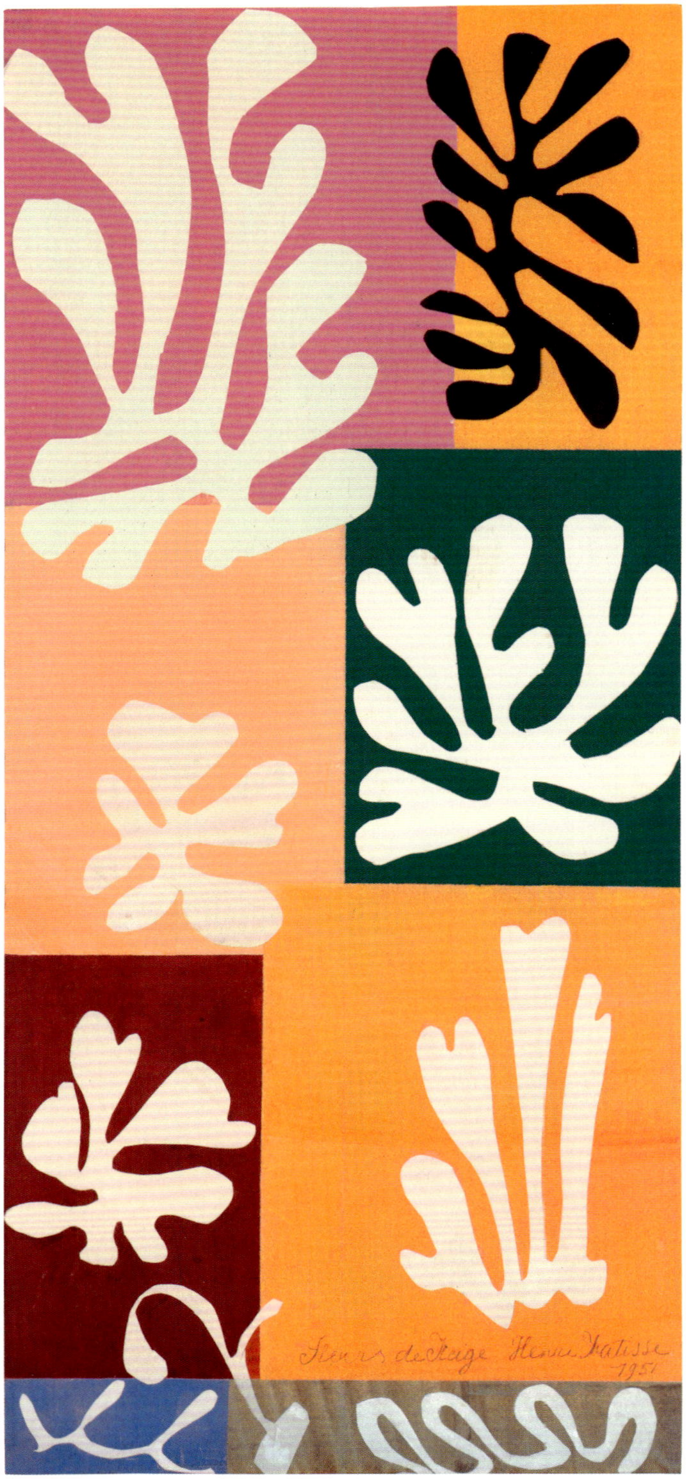

94. *Snow Flowers* 1951
Gouache on paper, cut and pasted, on paper, mounted on canvas, 174 × 80.6 (68 ½ × 31 ¾)

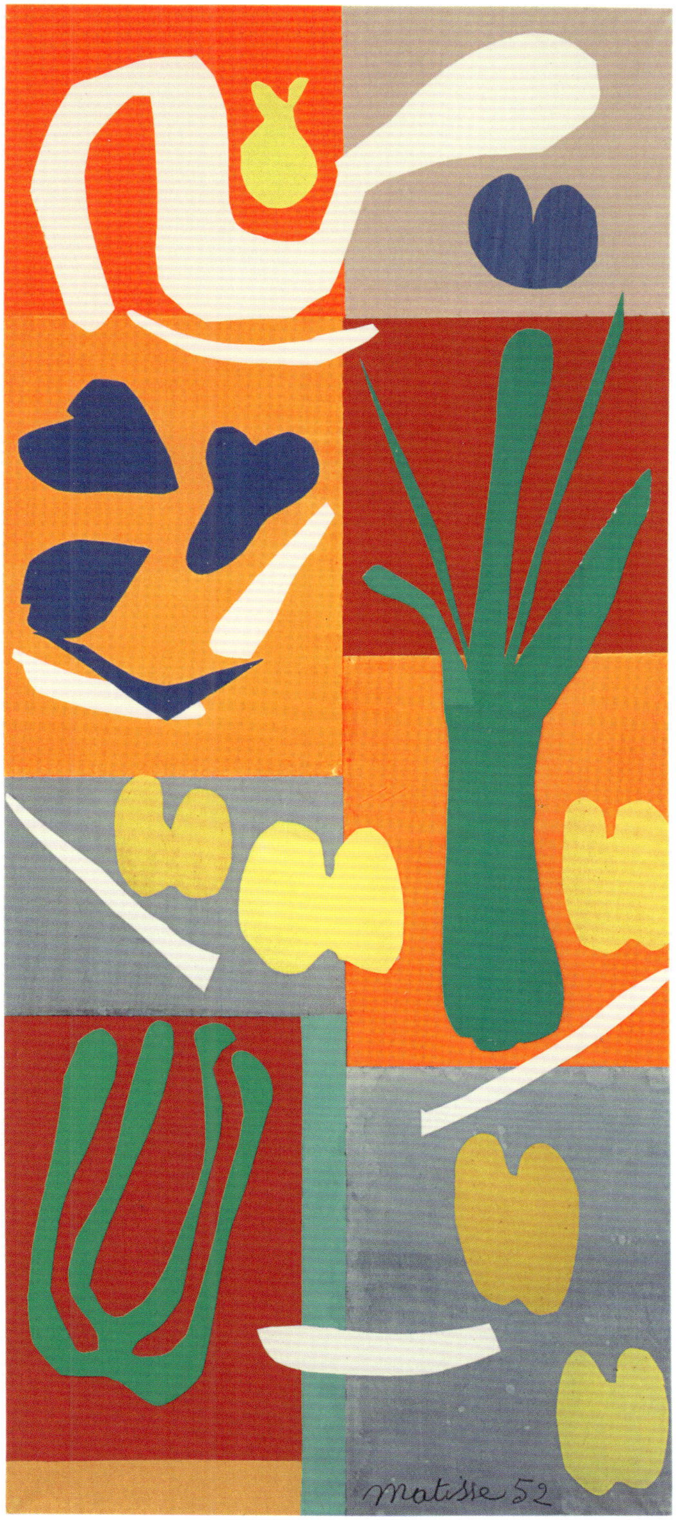

95. *Vegetables* c.1951
Gouache on paper, cut and pasted
175 × 81 (68⅞ × 31⅞)

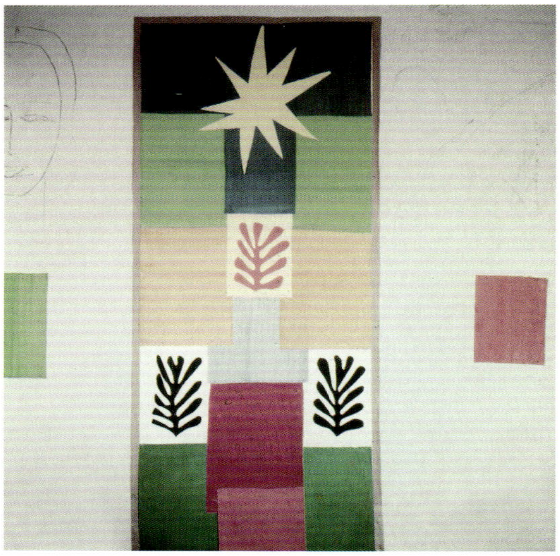

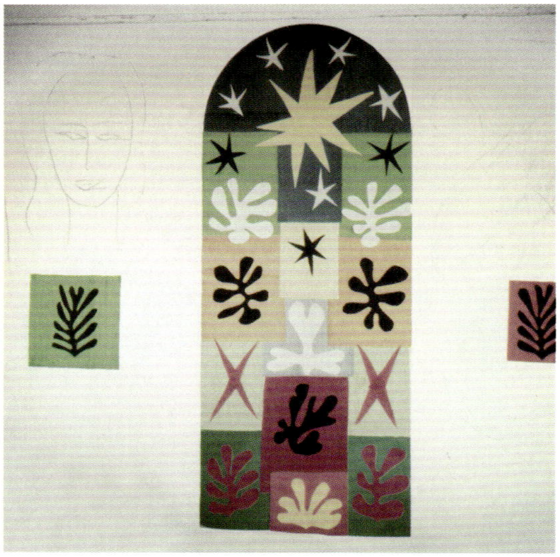

Fig. 37 Two states of *Christmas Eve* with *Black Leaf on Green Background* and *Black Leaf on Red Background*, Hôtel Régina, Nice, c. 1952

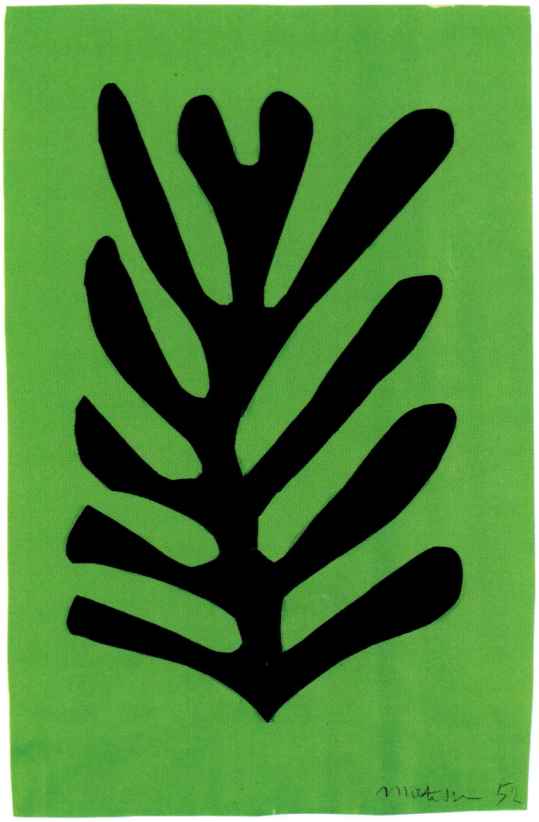

96. *Black Leaf on Green Background* 1952
Gouache on paper, cut and pasted
60 × 39 (23⅝ × 15⅜)

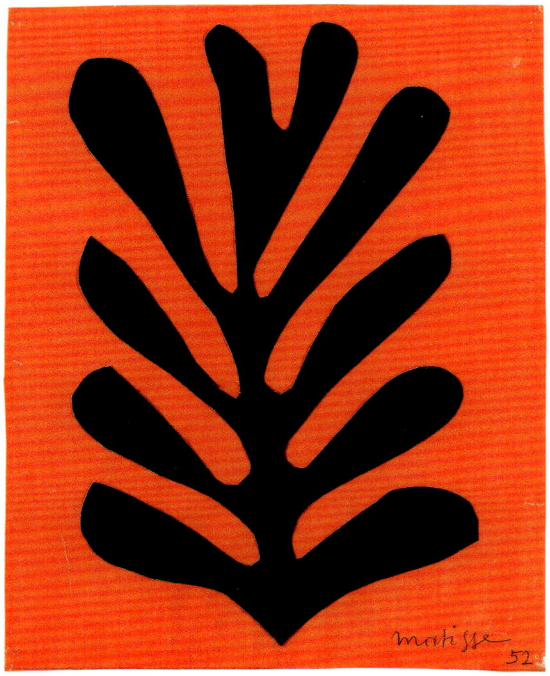

97. *Black Leaf on Red Background* 1952
Gouache on paper, cut and pasted
50 × 40 (19¾ × 15¾)

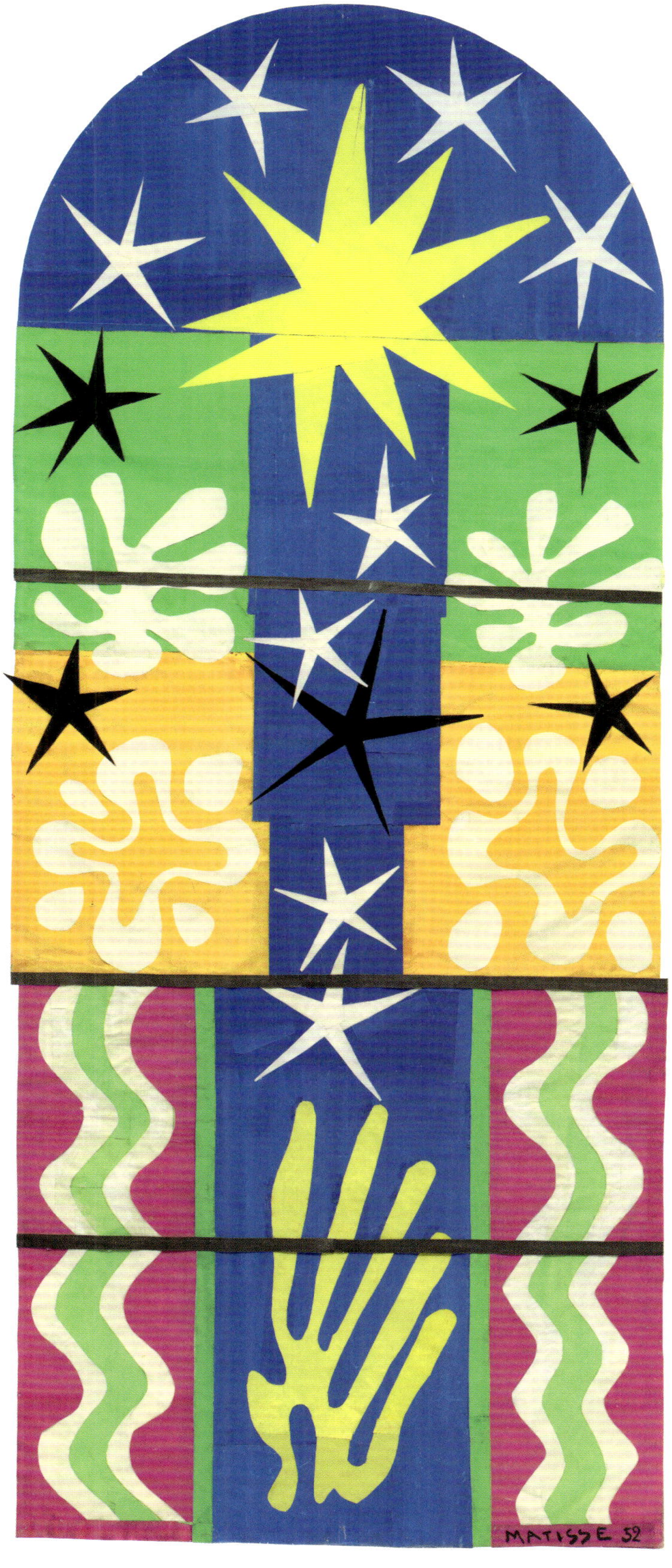

98. *Christmas Eve* 1952
Maquette for stained-glass window (realised 1952)
Gouache on paper, cut and pasted, mounted
on board, 322.8 × 135.9 (127 × 53½)

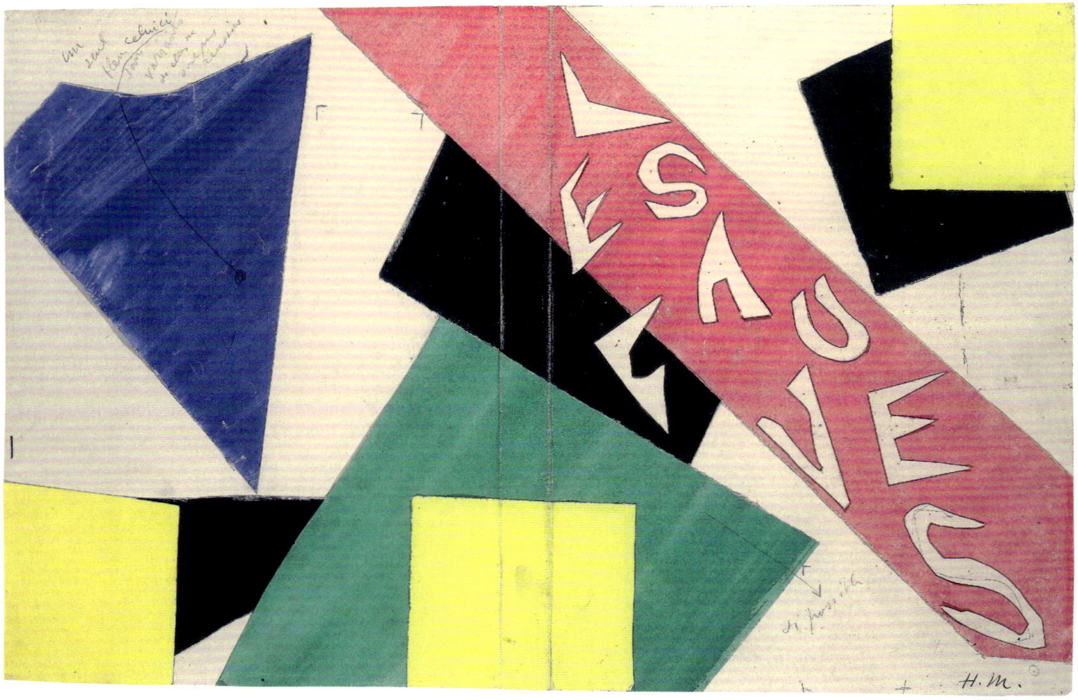

99. Cover maquette for the book *Les Fauves*
by Georges Duthuit (1949) 1949
Gouache on paper, cut and pasted
32.3 × 50.8 (12¾ × 20)

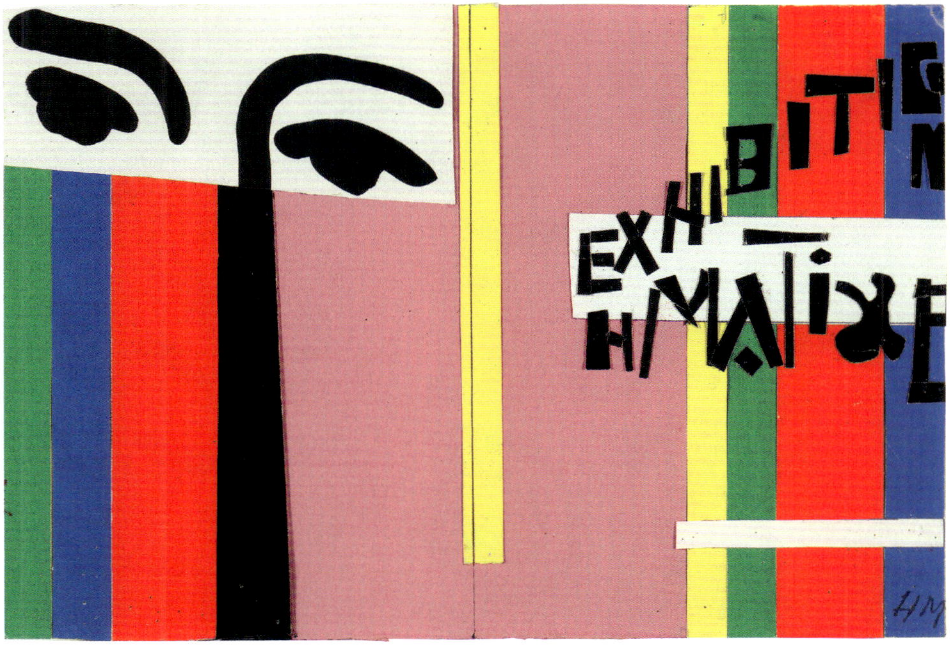

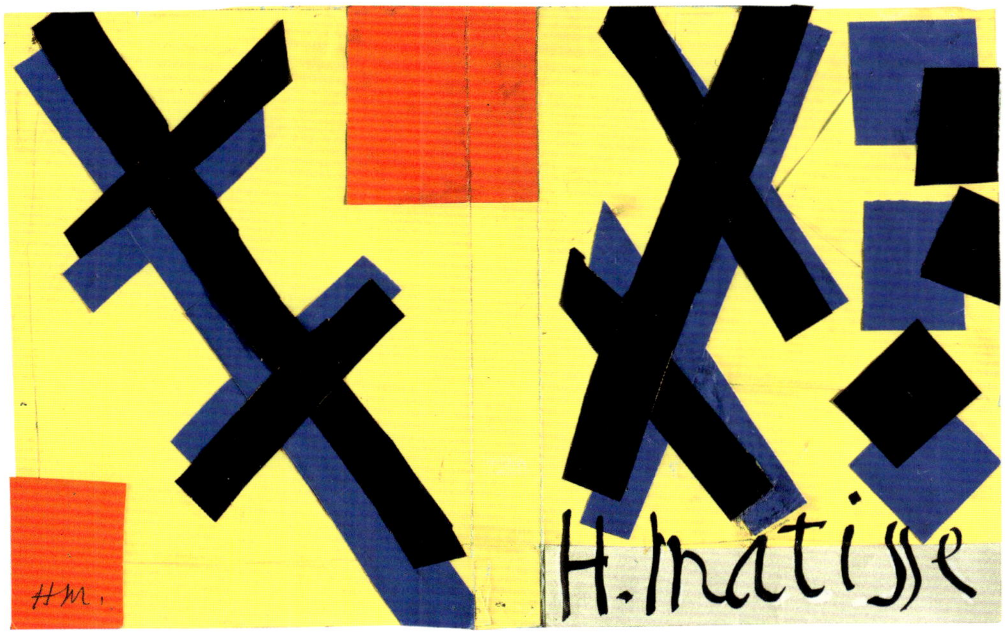

100. Cover maquette for the exhibition catalogue *Henri Matisse* (1951) 1951
Gouache on paper, cut and pasted
27 × 40 (10⅝ × 15¾)

101. Cover maquette for the book *Matisse: His Art and his Public* by Alfred H. Barr, Jr (1951) 1951
Gouache on paper, cut and pasted
27 × 42.9 (10⅝ × 16⅞)

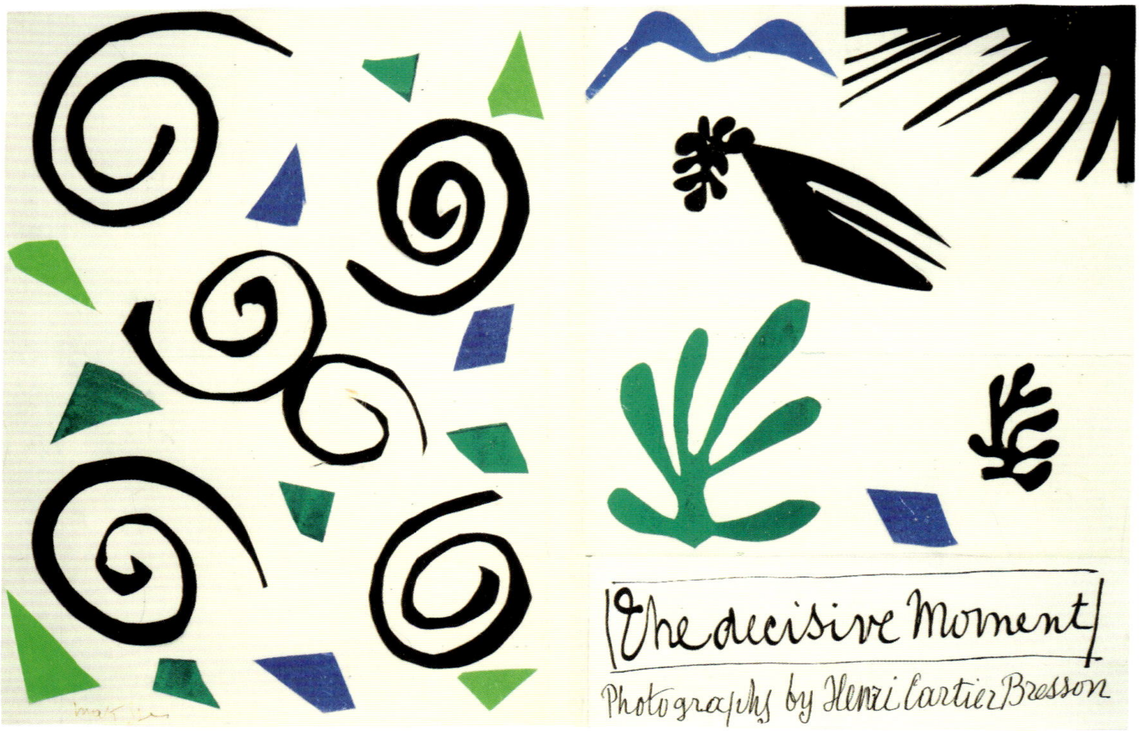

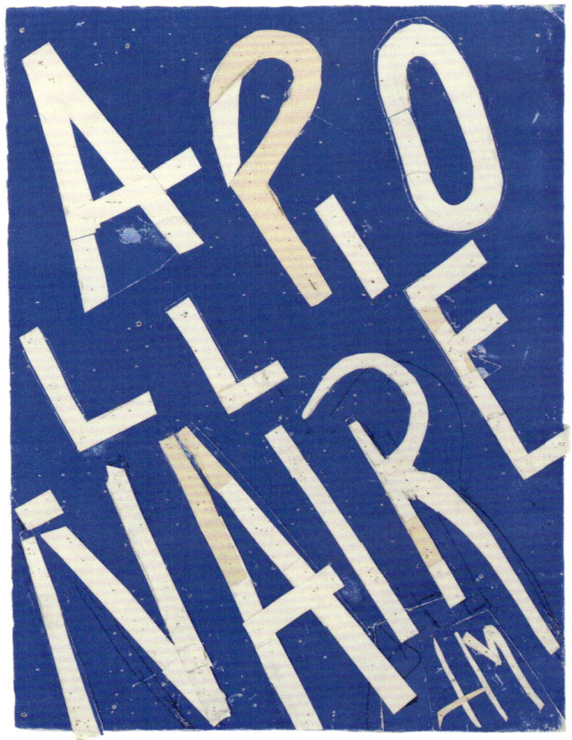

102. Cover maquette for the book *The Decisive Moment* by Henri Cartier-Bresson (1952) 1952
Gouache on paper, cut and pasted, and ink
36 × 57 (14⅛ × 22½)

103. Cover maquette for the book *Apollinaire* by André Rouveyre (1952) 1951–2
Gouache on paper, cut and pasted
32.7 × 25.4 (12⅞ × 10)

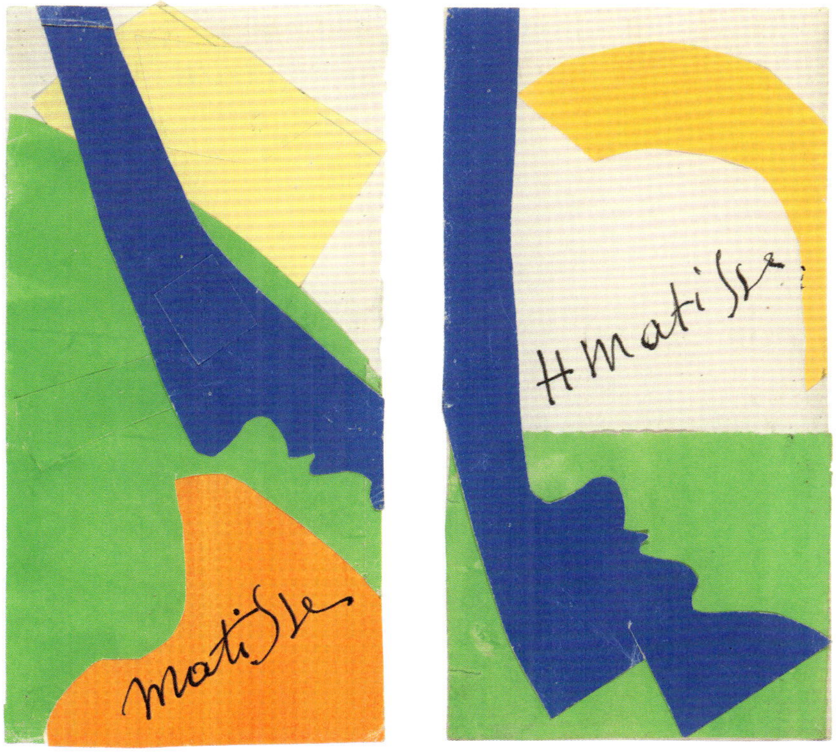

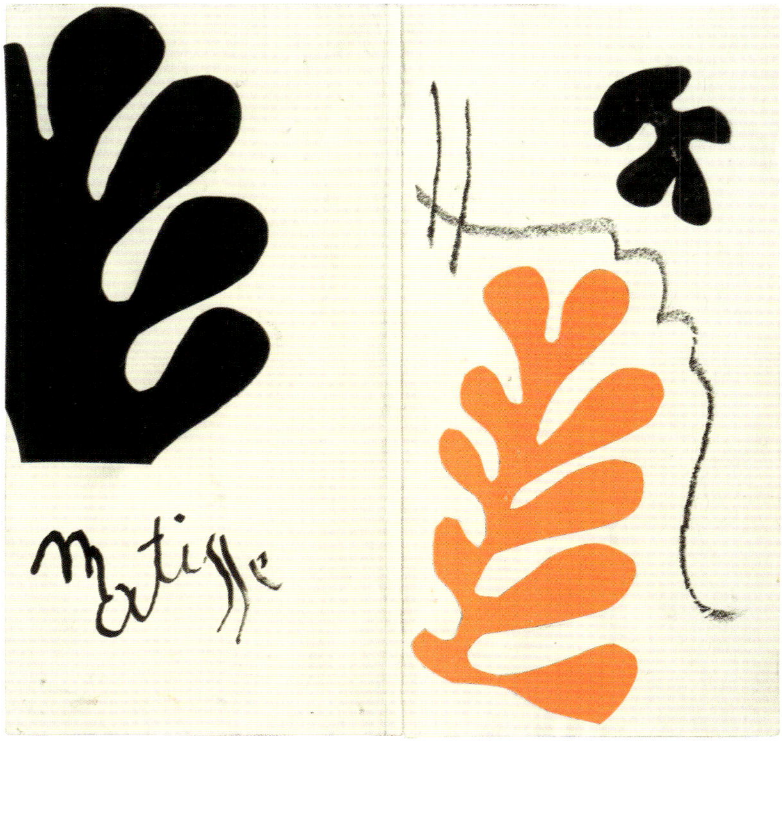

104. Cover maquette for the exhibition catalogue
Henri Matisse: papiers découpés (1953) 1952
Gouache on paper, cut and pasted, 23.2 × 12.2 (9⅛ × 4¾)

105. Cover maquette for the exhibition catalogue
Henri Matisse: Lithographies Rares (1954) c. 1954
Gouache on paper, cut and pasted, 22.1 × 23.6 (8¾ × 9¼)

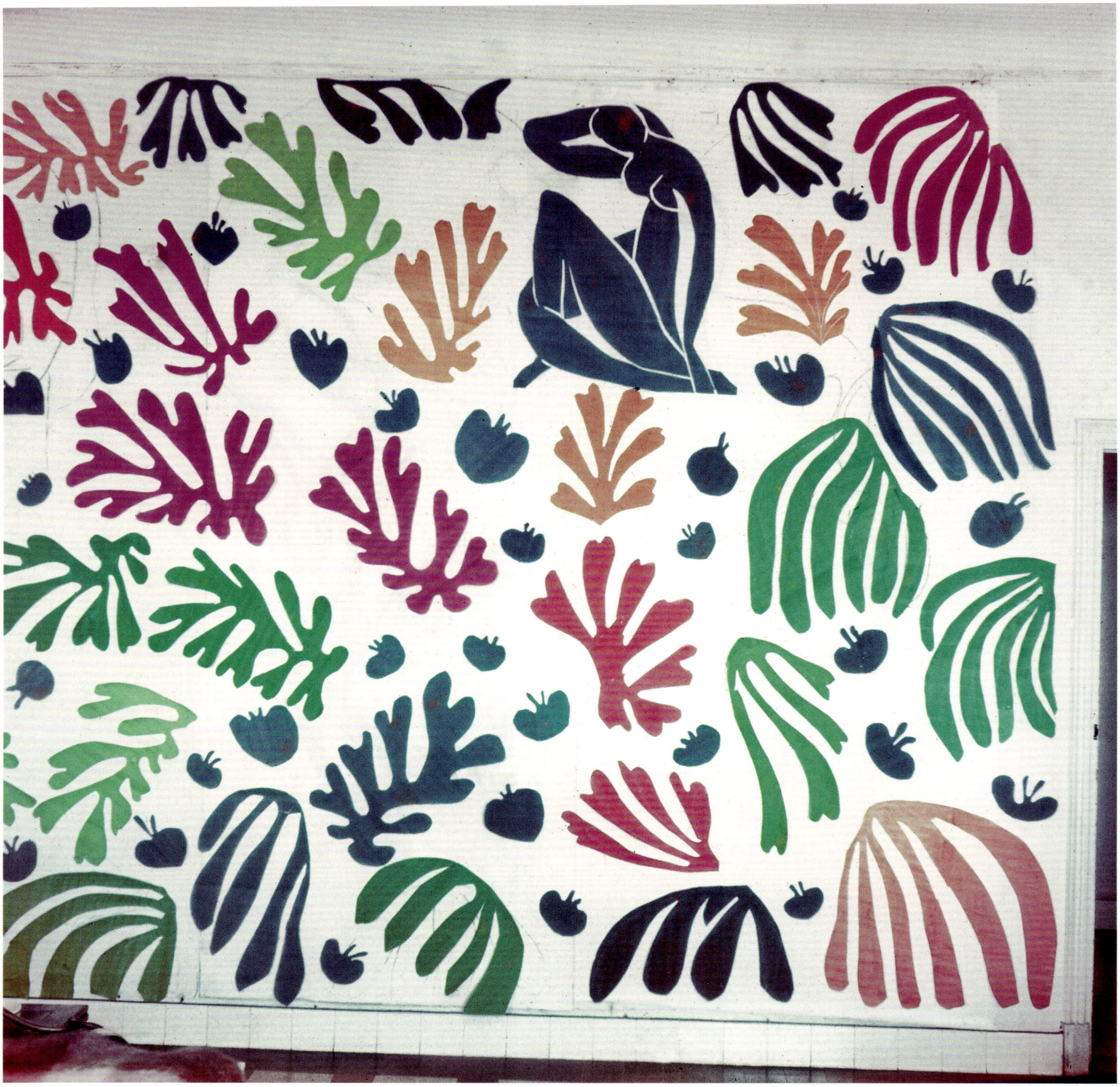

Fig. 38 Lydia Delectorskaya, *The Parakeet and the Mermaid* in progress with *Blue Nude II* inserted, 1952

BODIES and WAVES

Jodi Hauptman

In July 1952 Henri Matisse inserted a *Blue Nude* into his large wall composition *The Parakeet and the Mermaid* (fig. 38). Moving aside pomegranates and leaves, he made a small clearing in his garden, as he then called it, to provide enough room for a single form meant to balance the large ultramarine bird already set on the opposite wall. This *Blue Nude* – known today as number II – was one of a group of cut blue forms Matisse tried in that location. Photographs and accounts of studio assistants and visitors reveal that, in addition to this and the other three *Blue Nudes*, Matisse sampled *Snail*, *Standing Blue Nude* (no. 114), *Venus* (no. 115) and an element of what would become *Women and Monkeys* (no. 120) (for each he would adjust the position of the fruit and foliage to make a comfortable spot) until settling on the abstracted arched mermaid seen in the final version (nos. 118–19).[1] This compositional card game was of crucial significance to Matisse's efforts and ambitions of that moment, as it allowed him to think through the relationship and role of the figure to a decorative composition and to the wall. But before embarking on such combinations and re-combinations, Matisse took great pains in making his *Blue Nudes*. It would seem that the intense effort to create a lone figure out of cut paper – the precise focus on the female body, its easel scale, its assembly from bits, its single colour – would mark a retreat from his aspirations for and progress on mural-size works already in process. However, what Matisse learnt from the *Blue Nudes* fuelled his most significant achievement, that of the cut-outs' expansion into a full-scale environment: a complete rethinking of pictorial space.

The year 1952 was an extraordinarily productive one for Matisse.[2] The production-line process of making the cut-outs was already well established: assistants managed the painting and drying of sheets of paper and then, outfitted with pincushions on their wrists and hammers slung around their necks, moved and fastened paper at Matisse's direction. The year began with the commission for a stained glass on the theme of Christmas for the Time Life Company in New York (no. 98). And late winter and early spring were devoted to the epic *The Sorrow of the King*, one of Matisse's most painterly compositions – and the largest cut-out to date (p. 57). With that work complete, the leaves and fruit that would become *The Parakeet and the Mermaid* began to appear on his studio walls. Matisse added to, moved around and considered various foliate compositions throughout the summer. It was in this context, and in the wake of the figural concerns of *Sorrow of the King*, that Matisse began his first *Blue Nude* (which became known as number IV, no. 107).

The process was arduous. Matisse laboured for a number of weeks, relentlessly revising. His studio assistant at the time, Paule Martin, pushed by Matisse to work with equal rigour, describes the tense conditions:

> Whereas subsequent forms were cut in a single movement, the first figure demanded such patience and attention on Matisse's part, but also from me, that it exhausted me and I was on the brink of collapse. He made me pin tiny squares of paper to enhance the curvature of the thigh or some other part of the body, then remove parts

of the figure to remove colour strips, then set it back in place as my febrile fingers fumbled with the pins.[3]

These enhancements and removals along with markings in chalk can be seen in a series of black and white photographs made by Lydia Delectorskaya to document each stage, reminding the artist where he was and where he had been in order for him to decide where to go next (no. 106). These pictures offer unique insights into Matisse's process and thinking. He constructed the figure from many small pieces of painted paper; the shapes and sizes of these bits do not appear to have a precise compositional function, though their layering and the resultant gradations of texture and dimension could be a kind of modelling in relief, undulations or imperfections in the flesh.

The overall silhouette is simplified, lacking individual defining features; Matisse seems most concerned with determining the outer contour of the body and the positions of the anatomical parts. Looking sequentially, from one photograph to the next, significant changes are evident – such as shifts in the position of the right arm or a sharper incline in the bend of the left leg – along with less bold alterations: the splitting of the hoofed hand, the flexing of the left foot, the shaping of the head into an oval and its progressive diminution. Even with the photographs as a record, Matisse still traced

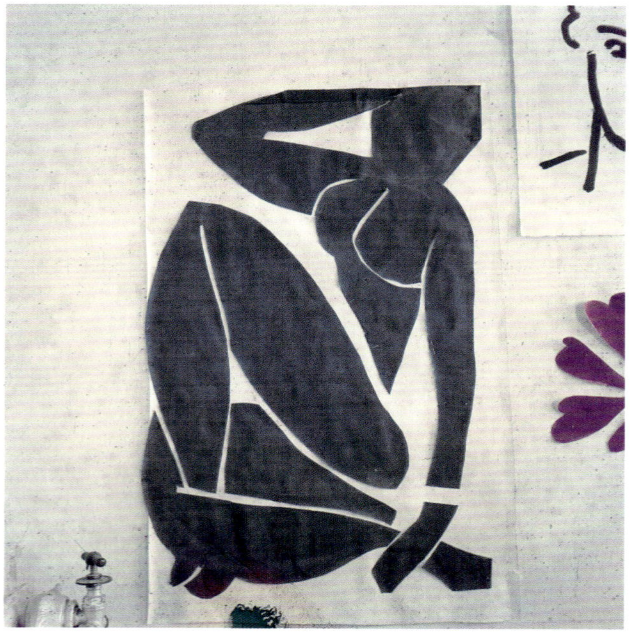

Fig. 39 *Blue Nude III* on the wall of Hôtel Régina

elements before he moved them, leaving a network of smudged charcoal lines on the white support, an index of his labour.

In the course of his work Matisse developed a technique of aeration – cutting and opening up the figure to let in air, light and space. The nude's earliest documented state is bulky and closed, akin to the solid and rounded forms of *The Sorrow of the King*'s guitarist and drummer (p. 57). Though each figure is constructed from a patchwork of sheets, the overall effect in that work is of bodies swathed in colour: the guitarist, a black eggplant with yellow ornaments, and the drummer, a pear in two tones of green. In the case of the *Blue Nude's* first stage, the silhouette is equally solid. The rhomboid head is directly attached to the body, with no neck, while the hefty bottom and thigh (the inverse position of the drummer's bottom) anchors her to the ground. The only break from the density is in the outsized arm that, swinging up and around in an arc, is fully detached from the figure's shoulder, making only slight contact at the knee. Chalk lines on the blue paper indicate possible alterations, thinning out the breast and opening up the spaces around the legs. The next photograph in the sequence confirms these changes. In fact, from photograph to photograph, from stage to stage, Matisse progressively cuts away at the body until the waist is no more than a point, the far smaller head is completely disengaged from the body, and the thighs, though still substantial, are much slimmer. To open up the form – to aerate it – Matisse cuts a small gully in the blue, revealing the white ground. These slits or slices – which mimic the scissors' own course as they slide through the sheet – are made at locations where the body bends in on itself (breast against breast, calf against thigh, calf against ankle), creating a sense of dimension.

This method of aeration is put to even better effect in three subsequent *Blue Nudes*. Before he was finished with the first *Blue Nude*, Matisse temporarily set it aside, perhaps frustrated with his progress. 'The other *Blue Nude* cut-outs came as explosions of inspiration during the same weeks,' Lydia explains. The first *Blue Nude* thus became known as number IV as it was taken up again later and finished last, while the other three became known in cutting order as numbers I, II and III. These three, Lydia tells us, were cut 'with mastery. Each on a different day, they had been cut in one line/stroke, with one stroke of the scissor, in 10 minutes or 15 at the maximum' (nos. 109–11, pp. 58–9).[4] Concurring with this description of Matisse's ease, Louis Aragon – a visitor to Matisse's studio – makes the following plea to his reader, 'May I ask you to follow Matisse's hand as he cuts out the blue women? Imagine the first slash being made, the scissors turning, moving upward, drawing upside down, starting off again: we can see thus how these gouaches were cut in great pieces with an unbroken line ... One cannot but emphasise the prodigious mental discipline involved as Matisse swings his scissors round and all the time, against all probability, never loses sight of the anatomical development of his drawing.'[5]

Before cutting, Matisse used pencil to ruminate on an alternative pose, belying the myth that his cutting was always absolutely spontaneous.[6] A sketchbook from this time (now dispersed) begins with a single drawing depicting a figure in the position of *Blue Nude IV*.[7] More than twenty other drawings in the book represent the seated nude in a slightly different pose: legs remain intertwined, but the right arm is no longer curved downwards; instead, it bends at the elbow so that the hand can reach back behind the head. Drawing this pose again and again in standard grey and coloured pencil – sometimes even using two colours on one sheet – Matisse learnt the linear construction of the nude, its threaded and knotted body, fostering his ability to cut numbers I, II and III quickly and easily, 'with mastery' (no. 108). Although the drawings display the way one limb overlaps another, creating a kind of dimensionality, they do not address density or mass. This is the very challenge Matisse tackles when he picks up his scissors and begins to cut. In each nude and for each cut Matisse uses a single blue sheet. He slices open the blue ('cutting directly into colour', as he would say), then slides apart the two halves that are left in the blade's wake, creating a small separation – a trough or gully – that, even in its simplicity, defines the body's shape (fig. 39). That white trough, Matisse recognised, creates a sense of dimension while remaining true to the flatness of the paper. The slight gaps of white between the blue hint to the viewer that these pieces were once attached, that they would fit back together like a puzzle. Matisse also removes small pieces of blue to define the crook of an elbow or a triangular gap between thigh and calf, but, overall, the sculpting is executed in such a way that the viewer can imagine reassembling the sheet, as if a marble bust could be returned to its block. The artist emphasises each nude's origin in flat, pliable paper.

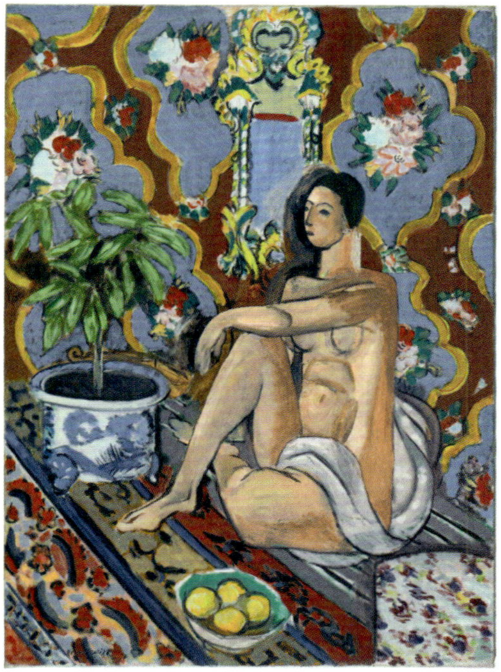

Fig. 40 *Decorative Figure on an Ornamental Ground*, late 1925 – spring 1926. Oil on canvas, 129.9 × 98.1 (51⅛ × 35⅝). Centre Pompidou, Paris. Musée national d'art moderne / Centre de création industrielle

Matisse's approach in all four of the nudes – constructing from bits, creating dimension out of flatness, aerating planes of colour – and his consideration of them as part of a decorative scheme was not new in his practice. His efforts must be seen in the light of a career representing the female body. The *Blue Nudes* might be productively compared, for example, to his infamous *Blue Nude (Memory of Biskra)* of 1907, a work that foregrounds its own painterly process; to *Aurora*, 1906–7, a sculpted reclining nude with arm similarly raised, which Matisse often depicts in his paintings; or to *Decorative Figure on an Ornamental Ground*, 1925–6 (fig. 40), which explores the relationship between figure and decoration, nude and background. In terms of his method of construction, comparable small shapes of cut paper were utilised in composing the dancers for the Barnes mural, a technique that allowed Matisse to alter and enhance bodies on a vast scale (fig. 12), as well as in working through the numerous corporeal states of the *Pink Nude*, 1935.[8] In both of these cases, paper resulted in a further flattening of the figure, as opposed to its use in the *Blue Nudes*, which sought to balance flatness and depth. On this front, the *Blue Nudes* can also be seen

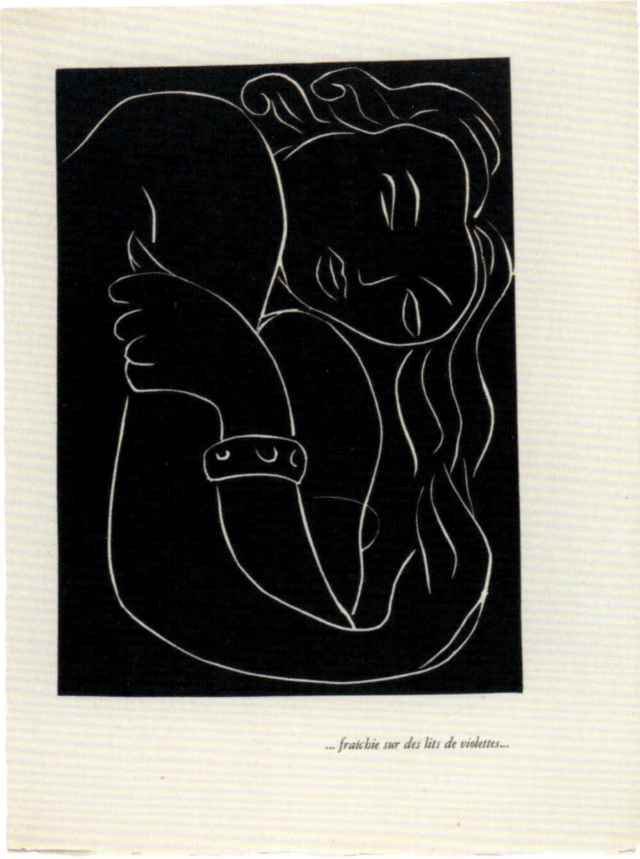

Fig. 41 '... freshened on beds of violets ...', plate from Henry de Montherlant, *Pasiphaé*, 1943–4. Linoleum cut, composition: 24.5 × 18 (9⅝ × 7⅛). The Museum of Modern Art, New York
The Louise E. Stern Collection, 1964

in the context of Matisse's sculptural practice. Calling them a 'new order of sculpture', William Tucker argues: 'They [the *Blue Nudes*] follow from *The Back* reliefs in their acceptance of the condition of flatness as a basis for creating an illusion of volume that has no dependence on deep perspective.'[9] The cutting away seen in sculptures like *The Back* is also a key element in Matisse's printmaking, put to great dramatic effect in his linocuts. In *Pasiphaé*, for example, white lines – where Matisse had carved into the linoleum block and were therefore un-inked – slice through the prints' deep blackness (fig. 41). As is true for the troughs in the *Blue Nudes*, these also confer shape, depth and a sense of luminosity to bodies, manes of hair, stars and animals. The *Blue Nudes* encouraged Matisse to think about how those troughs, those gullies, that white space may be put to even grander use.[10]

At about the same time as he was working on the *Blue Nudes*, Matisse embarked on the representation of another figure – this time a dancer – for which white space is deployed in a broader and bolder way. He began in about March 1952 to compile the shapes of *La Négresse*, an evocation of Josephine Baker, an extraordinarily popular performer in Paris in the 1920s and 1930s and a complicated figure because of the 'stereotyped images she embodied, both spectacular Primitive and fashionable French star'.[11] Matisse continued to rearrange the composition through the beginning of January 1953. An assembly of forms with no actual body, *La Négresse* is fully aerated, completely devoid of corporeal mass. In building her – and it does seem like an act of construction, part by part, as opposed to the act of carving we have seen in the *Blue Nudes* – Matisse engaged in a form of semiotic play: each form takes its meaning from the function it has been assigned. A crescent-shaped segment is at once the wings of a bird in flight and the dancer's shoulders, thighs, calves, upper arms and lower arms. An ovoid is used for both head and belly, while the upper torso, in the shape of a small stool or table, represents dangling breasts. Baker's trademark banana skirt – a sign for her sexualised and exotic presence on stage – is made from one of Matisse's vegetal forms.[12] Studio photographs indicate that Matisse tried a variety of different motifs as background (pp. 74–7). André Verdet, who visited the studio during *La Négresse*'s making, describes the importance of negative space in composing this work: 'The connections are delicate, concentrated and simplified in the extreme. There are rapid voids between certain body parts. Through these voids, air glides, augmenting thus the sensation of movement within the ensemble. Void between the bust and belly, void between the belly and legs.'[13] This void – the air Matisse has directed into the composition – continues into three-dimensional space; the dancer's feet literally step off the wall into the space of the viewer. Verdet also highlights the work's dynamism and implied motion, alluding to Baker's personification, as she herself would tell it, as 'the savage on the stage'; he says: 'The belly isolated as such is a marvelous balloon where the spirit of the dance vibrates.'[14] We can only speculate on why Matisse would have turned to void and extreme openness to depict an abstracted Baker. The notion of the exotic and primitive as elusive – and therefore barely representable, only available via a series of signs – may have been a trope to which Matisse subscribed.

With the four *Blue Nudes* complete and with the use of the void as a compositional element and aeration as a fully established technique, Matisse began work that summer on *The Swimming Pool*, a frieze of spirited swimmers, divers and splashers, along with aquatic beasts, created for the dining room in his apartment at the Hôtel Régina in Nice (no. 121). Remaining focused on using cut paper to represent the female body and continuing to limit his palette to blue and white, Matisse channelled lessons learnt from the *Blue Nudes* into this more elaborate effort, deploying his ideas on an environmental scale. Matisse had already been using the walls of his studio to compose and consider his work in cut paper: installing, editing, shifting and altering assemblies of forms. From smaller works clustered on architectural surfaces to form patchwork wholes, each element subject to continual editing, Matisse's ambitions grew, provoking him to stretch larger compositions across his studio walls, extending them into corners, from floor to ceiling, and exploiting the compositional, structural and decorative possibilities of the wall as a surface without a frame. The Vence chapel gave Matisse the opportunity to think holistically. The environmental reach of that project ranged from the luminous effects of stained glass and the contrasting whiteness of the tiles to the way the colours of the garments worn by the priests as they moved through the chapel's interior would impact on the visual and physical experience of worshippers. The influence of this project was immeasurable, fuelling Matisse's desire to go bigger with cut paper; however, there is an important distinction between his approach in the chapel and that in *The Swimming Pool*. At Vence Matisse uses the cut-outs to design elements for a space; in *The Swimming Pool* the cut-outs determine and define the space itself.

With the *Blue Nudes*, *The Parakeet and the Mermaid* and the Vence chapel in mind, Matisse was fully primed to embark on *The Swimming Pool*, the first and only instance of a truly self-contained site-specific cut-out.[15] One of Matisse's great achievements in cut paper, *The Swimming Pool* is the culmination of his work up to that point: a summary and a re-energisation of long-practised strategies, and an epic demonstration of the cut-out's pictorial and environmental potential. *The Swimming Pool* combines a radical simplification of form; the dynamism of the arabesque; the optical rhythm of sparring positives and negatives; the spatial ambiguities created by an uncertain viewing position; the potentiality of white, blankness and void; and the possibilities of infinitely expanding space – all in a single composition.

Lydia explains how Matisse came to this subject:

> One morning he announced that he wanted to see divers. We called up the usual rental car and he was off to Palm Beach at Cannes. We arrived there just at midday. Blazing sun! And not a swimmer at the pool! HM laughed and, having taken scarcely a few steps along the pool (of modest dimensions), he gasped to me: 'Let's leave quickly: with this sun, I will get sick.' Once returned to the house, he said: 'I will make myself my own pool.' And he had me place on the walls all around the room where he lived a band of white paper 70 cm wide at the height he indicated.[16]

This band of white paper, positioned with its bottom at the level of the top of Matisse's head so it would function as a decorative frieze, was pinned by Lydia onto the room's walls, which themselves were covered with tan fabric, a popular wall covering of the time (pp. 63–5). The paper ringed the room, only breaking for the large square-mullioned window at one end and the glass entrance doors at the other. The floor was tiled in a chequerboard pattern, and there was a large ornate mantelpiece on one side. Photographs taken before and after *The Swimming Pool*'s installation indicate that the room served as both studio and lounge: works by Matisse are hung around the room and the furniture is adorned with knick-knacks from a lifetime of collecting (pp. 62, 66).

Lydia goes on to describe the process:

> Next, over the course of the following weeks, sometimes during the day and other times having me called in the middle of the night; he placed there one after another human forms – divers or swimmers – but not in successive locations, tossing/plunging them here and there. Most of the bodies were born spontaneously, as though, before asking for blue paper and scissors, he had meditated for a long while on the silhouette to create and its placement.[17]

The Swimming Pool swirls – or really swims – around the viewer, generating a feeling of centre-less circulation and immersion that Matisse hoped to evoke: 'I have always adored the sea and now that I can no longer go for a swim, I have surrounded myself with it.'[18] The white band fosters the work's horizontal energy and sense of limitless flow, while also delimiting the pool's boundaries. As we enter the room, where are we? The frieze is above us – and Matisse probably composed it seated – so are we at the bottom of the pool looking up? Above the pool looking down? Treading water alongside the swimmers, watching as their bodies cross in and out of the water?

This uncertainty regarding where we are is only one of many oscillations, permutations and slippages around which *The Swimming Pool* is organised. These optical, physical and representational tensions give the work a dynamism and vigour (even, in the words of one writer, a sense of 'exhilaration'[19]) inhibiting any possibility of visual rest: blue and white, positive and negative, figure and ground, limitation and expansion, inside and outside, up and down, air and water, animal and human, parts and wholes, forms and their inverses. These oppositions – whether chromatic (blue vs. white), compositional (figure vs. ground), spatial (inside vs. outside) or narratival (animal vs. human) – both butt up against each other and slide together, demonstrating a slippery fluidity of form. Slipping and sliding are liquid metaphors and are thus perfectly suited to Matisse's subject, whose pool water dissembles and dematerializes, causing the clear contours of bodies to enlarge or stretch as if in a funhouse mirror or to dissolve entirely. It is always summer at this pool, and, like water, sunshine has a similar mutative effect, bleaching out colour and splintering across watery surfaces. Such transformations and transmutations are also endemic to the practice of cutting, which itself always creates two forms with every slice, an interchangeable positive and negative. One of the *Pool*'s strengths is its play with positive and negative: the slippage, alternation and oscillation of seeing a figure from one perspective and ground from another, air from one perspective and water from another, body from one perspective and liquid from another, and so on. The natural deforming and reforming of cutting made Matisse uniquely able to see the possibilities and potential of such visual reversals.

Such fluctuation is especially powerful in the constant and dynamic back and forth between white and blue. Though Matisse's scissors only ever make contact with the blue paper, he also harnesses, via composition and juxtaposition, the physical, sculptural and illuminative power of white. In constructing the *Pool*'s bodies and spaces, Matisse enlarges the white troughs that are cut to define dimension in the *Blue Nudes*, lengthening and widening them until they have their own physical presence. Stretching out the forms horizontally (following the band of white paper's cue), Matisse fully aerates the composition. In the figure immediately to the left of the door, for example, the arched swimmer is cut from two sheets of blue paper, but the white billowing shape carved out

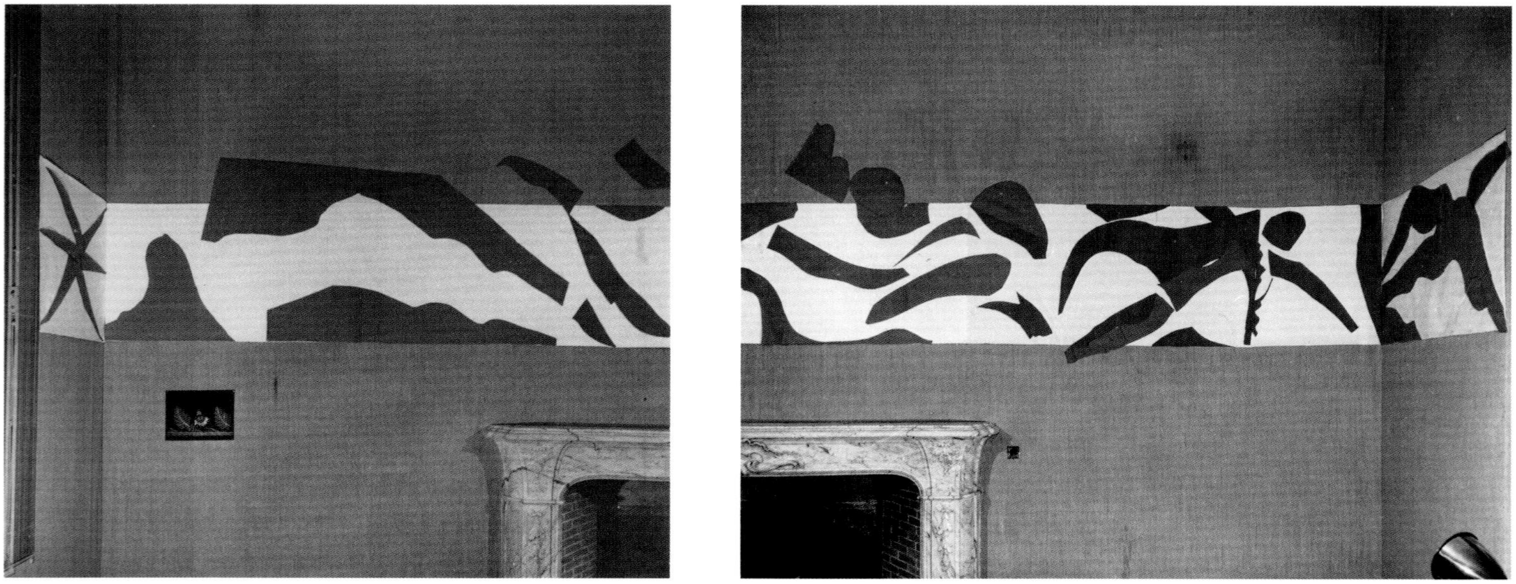

Fig. 42 *The Swimming Pool* on the walls of Hôtel Régina

below her pushes forward as positive and material (p. 64). Similarly, the freestyle swimmer on the right side of the room is easy to identify by her round head and outstretched arm (which interestingly looks like a leaping fish), but her body is more difficult to pinpoint (p. 65). Is it the white space between the two blue horizontal squiggles? Is it wholly submerged underneath the white water? Are the squiggles the wake from her forward-moving path? For the work's longest and most grandly sculptural body Matisse slices open a large blue sheet and slides the halves apart to create part of the female silhouette from the space in between (fig. 42, left). A jumble of cut forms on the left wall is the pool's most ambiguous section. Here, blue and white are equally dispersed, turning liquid into shards and back again, and representing water as an up-and-down, in-and-out flow (fig. 42, right).

A group of sketches in Matisse's diary, newly published here, offers a key to the pool's abstraction and dynamism – and ambitions. On a sheet in the diary dated 20 July, Matisse depicts a diving figure, head down, arms stretched and tight against the head, legs pushing off the ground (fig. 43). In four similar drawings Matisse concentrates on the arc formed when the spine curves over to dive, but he also addresses the body's limbs and breasts, reducing the female form to these features. Such reduction and simplification, the body condensed to arch, breast and behind – what Matisse describes as 'a form filtered to its essentials'[20] – are seen in other works made that summer, including the great *Acrobats*, which like *Blue Nude IV* demanded multiple revisions and related large- and small-scale ink drawings (no. 112, fig. 45).[21] In back-bends that match arm to leg, bulging head to buttock, these contortionists echo the *Pool*'s vaguely corporeal figures, which, similarly, are all arched spine, breasts and mermaid tail limbs.

In a second set of drawings rendered over a double page, Matisse makes a visual rhyme between body and wave (fig. 44). He explores two different curves – a reverse 'c' and an 's' – in relation to the female body. A languid swimmer moves horizontally across the left-hand page, one arm reaching out of the water, the other stroking forward; the entire body is a serpentine line. Matisse practises in ink the reverse 'c' of the arm as it lifts, transforming it into a wave – which also can be read as an ornamental leaf. In another sketch the curve of the body mutates into a wave moving in the

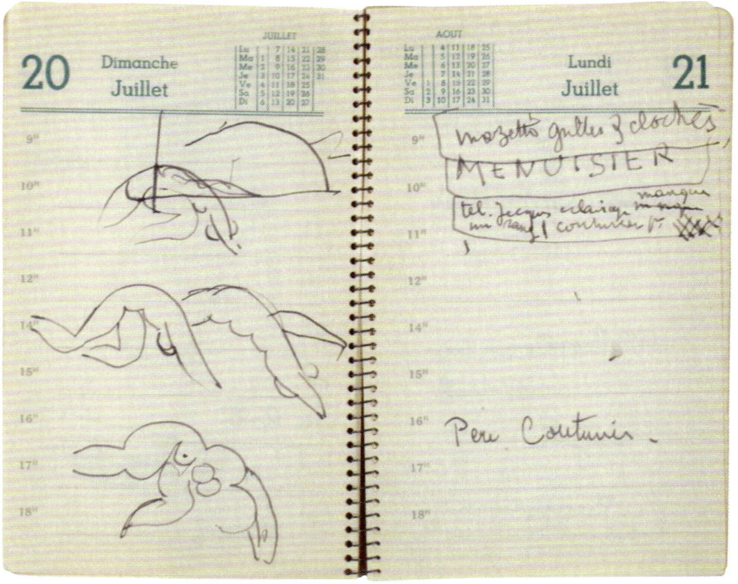

Fig. 43 Page from Matisse's diary, open at Sunday 20 July and Monday 21 July

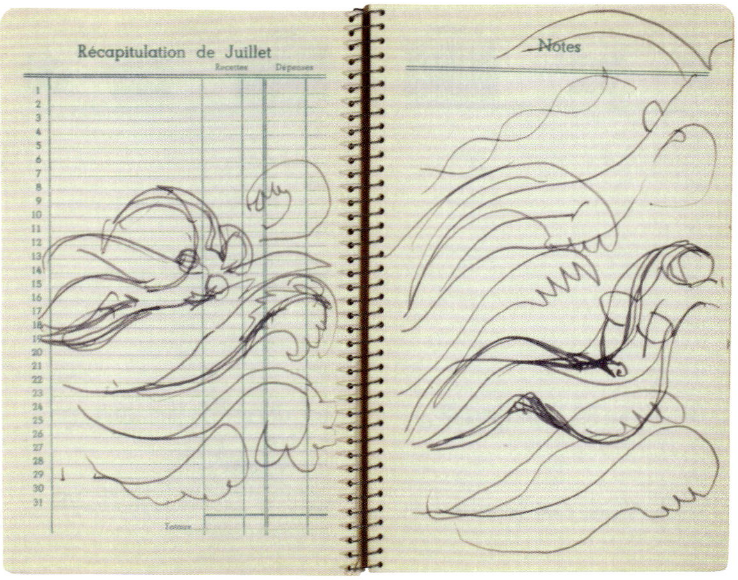

Fig. 44 Page from Matisse's diary, open at 'Summary of July' and 'Notes'

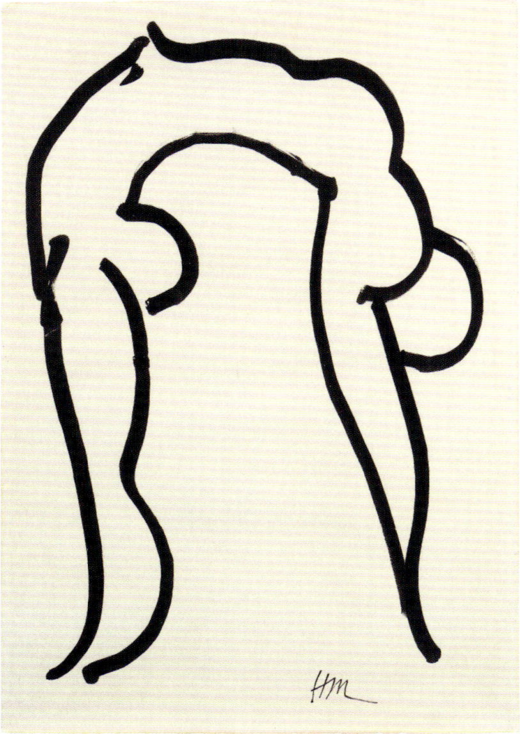

Fig. 45 *Acrobat*, 1952. Ink on paper, 105.5 × 74.5 (41½ × 29⅜). Private collection

opposite direction, this time rolling up and curving forward, poised before crashing onto shore. Matisse embellishes the multiple s-curves on the sheet, either with rounded or spiky petals, connecting them with border ornaments found in architecture or textiles. In another instance, he has the curve swing around until it closes, transforming it into a wing. On the opposite page a figure lolls lazily in the water and the s-shape of her body, legs out, bottom down, left arm stretched, is also drawn in multiple configurations: curve, wave, wing.

In each, the forward tilt of the diver, the arched back and arm of the swimmer, and the undulating curve of the lounger are abstracted in a set of repeated strokes, creating watery waves, the serpentine shape of the arabesque. The arabesque, we know from art historian Roger Benjamin, is a key pictorial strategy for Matisse, which he borrowed from Islamic art (though, as Matisse probably knew and Benjamin recounts, it can be documented from classical antiquity and throughout western representation) and deployed from almost the very beginning of his career to create 'an abstract plastic and pictorial energy'.[22] A consistent visual rhythm in Matisse's work, the arabesque is also responsible for the pool's energy, dynamism and force. Almost all of the bodies – whether human or fish – are arched. Threading one to another produces a sine curve. This curve, echoing the diary's s-shapes and waves, the serpentine line of the drawn bodies – an arabesque – presents a perfect meeting of compositional force and subject. This up and down curve, this wave, drives the figures around the dining room/pool, propels the swimmers through the water without stopping, giving the work a sense of endless circulation and limitless expansion. The arabesque is the perfect sign for water, which itself moves in undulating, sinuous curves, pushed by breezes or bodies.

Most striking among these sketches related to *The Swimming Pool* is an intertwining sine curve or double helix that appears in the upper left of the right-hand spread. Though Matisse only renders three hills and three valleys for each, the curve nonetheless alludes to infinity, continuation, perpetuation. This curve is an emblem for the *Pool*, a symbolic shorthand for the project, linking the arabesque line to infinite expansion. Matisse had long believed that the arabesque required containment in order to function dynamically, arguing to Verdet: 'The arabesque is effective only when contained by the four sides of the picture. With this support, it has strength.'[23] Working primarily in the realm of the easel picture, Matisse was perhaps resigned to 'amplification that happened in the imagination'.[24] However, the cut-outs and specifically their visual play on the studio walls allowed Matisse to imagine a curve infinitely expanding without any frame. Matisse articulated the arabesque's role and its formation on the wall as he saw it in *The Parakeet and the Mermaid*. 'Look at this large composition: the foliage, fruits, scissors: a garden,' Matisse exclaims. 'The intermediary white is determined by the arabesque of the colored cut-paper that gives this ambient white a rare and intangible quality. This quality is that of contrast. Each particular group of colors has in itself a particular atmosphere. It is what I call the expressive ambiance.'[25]

In *The Swimming Pool* the arabesque is not only found in between cut shapes (though we certainly see its curve there), it is the very compositional dynamic of this ever-circulating work. The arabesque is a force propelling a continuous circular movement without centre and without end, up and down, up and down, up and down, into infinity, finally fulfilling Matisse's aspiration to create 'space [that] extends as far as my imagination', to 'give the impression of vastness in a limited space'.[26] As far back as *Le Bonheur de Vivre*, 1906, Yve-Alain Bois eloquently tells us, Matisse's work displayed a 'system' of circulation, tension and expansion that introduced 'a sense of dynamism' into the picture.[27] The arabesque and its generation of limitless space, the lack of focus and 'all-over visual effect' at work in the *Pool* have deep roots in Matisse's practice, and are part and parcel of the artist's engagement with decoration, especially that of Islamic art, including textiles and calligraphy. *The Swimming Pool* and the cut-outs more generally should be seen as part of Matisse's efforts to, as Rémi Labrusse has written, 'make a radically decorative, almost iconoclastic impact', 'as a means of turning the Western visual tradition against itself'.[28] But this 'stroboscopic pulsation', the 'nothingness and plenitude' of all-over decoration in paintings like *Harmony in Red*, 1908, or *Dance (I)*, 1909, is given new life in the cut-outs and new possibilities because of their relationship to the studio wall.[29]

We should not discount the importance of his subject. For Matisse the experience under water offered another way to envisage expansion. In a conversation with Louis Aragon, Matisse associated his aspiration to move beyond the limitations of frames and walls with the sensation of being under water. Explaining to the writer that he often wondered about how an artist might escape from the traditional confines of the picture space – one that was 'sufficient for painters in the past' but not for him – Matisse imagined a 'cosmic space in which I was as unconscious of any walls as a fish in the sea'.[30] Matisse's earliest attempt at engaging the wall – his *Oceania, the Sky* and *Oceania, the Sea*, with their expanse of white plant and sea life, which originally covered the surfaces of his Boulevard Montparnasse studio (no. 52–3, pp. 32–5) – also represented water, in this case from his memories of a trip to Tahiti in 1930. In recalling Tahiti, he often described its special light, but he also, on occasion, evoked its lagoons. Experiences of swimming there no doubt coloured his subsequent depictions of water and its metamorphic effects. In one telling moment Matisse describes swimming in the lagoon: 'I would plunge my head into the water, transparent against the absinthe bottom of the "lagoon", eyes wide open … and then suddenly I would lift my head out of the water and stare at the luminous whole.'[31] In the *Pool*, Matisse used paper to capture the sense of being under water as well as the undulations of the current, the wake formed as fluid passes over bodies, the crystallization of liquid as it splashes.

Paper's pliability reflects the fluidity of water. In this way *The Swimming Pool* presents a perfect melding of subject and means: cutting through paper is shown to be equivalent to swimming through water. Matisse had once compared cutting to flying: 'You cannot imagine to what point, in this period of cut-out pieces of paper, the sensation of flight which springs loose in me helps me better to adjust my hand when it steers the path of my scissors. It's pretty hard to explain. I'd say it's a sort of linear, graphic equivalence of the feeling of flight.'[32] The *Pool* argues for a different analogy, demonstrating that the sensation of swimming is like 'steering the path of scissors', where cutting is a graphic equivalent to stroking through water: its purposeful course, its buoyancy, the way it leaves a wake in its path, and its arabesque line.

Given *The Swimming Pool*'s pictorial and metaphorical chain of body–arc–arabesque–wave, we might look more closely at what seems to be the simplest of cut-outs, a blue and white work called *The Wave* (no. 122). An echo of the sinuous swimmer–wave–sine curve in Matisse's diary, *The Wave* is the apotheosis of this moment in Matisse's production and an emblem of his cut-out practice as a whole. Made by cutting a sine curve or arabesque into a rectangular blue sheet, dividing it in half and sliding the two resulting sides apart to reveal the white that is not so much below it but equivalent to it, the work's simple power derives from the tension Matisse creates between blue and white, positive and negative, flatness and depth. Though it is small, it refers to limitlessness, the infinite expansion to which Matisse had always aspired. This expansion seems to be lateral, but it should be noted that Matisse tried out *The Wave* in a vertical orientation (p. 78), a paper equivalent to Brancusi's wooden *Endless Column*. As an abstraction of water and body and as a perfect reflection of the arabesque or serpentine line, *The Wave* demonstrates with absolute directness the cut-out's economy of means. Its subject coincides perfectly with its material conditions: the endlessly rolling fluid repetition of waves. In its representation of infinity, as a sign for expansion, it also stands for potentiality; for Matisse in 1952 possibility and promise – the inestimable lexicon of cut form – proliferated unbounded across his studio walls.

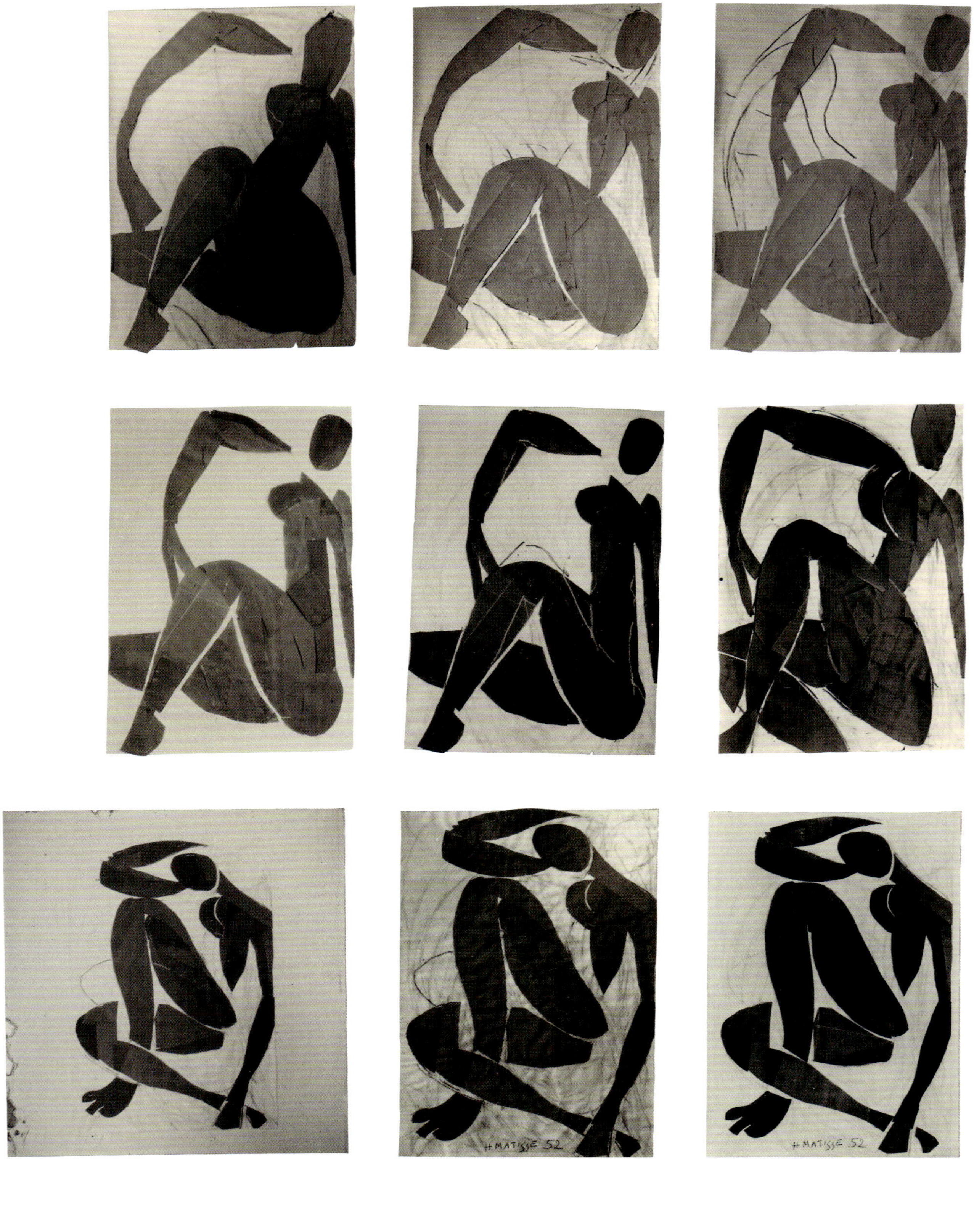

106. Nine states of *Blue Nude IV*, Hôtel Régina, Nice, 1952

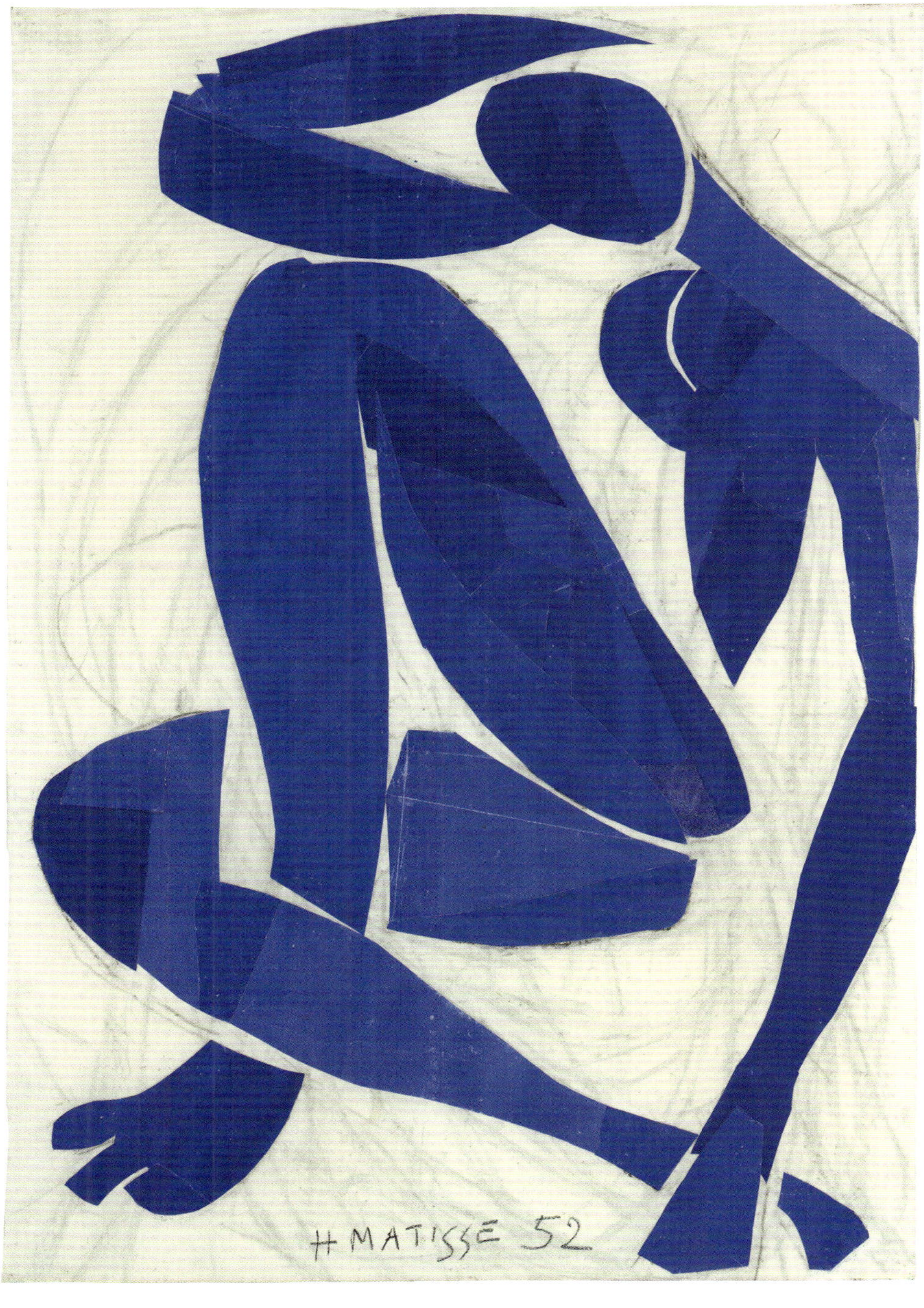

107. *Blue Nude IV* spring 1952
Gouache on paper, cut and pasted, and
charcoal on white paper, mounted on canvas
102.9 × 76.8 (40½ × 30¼)

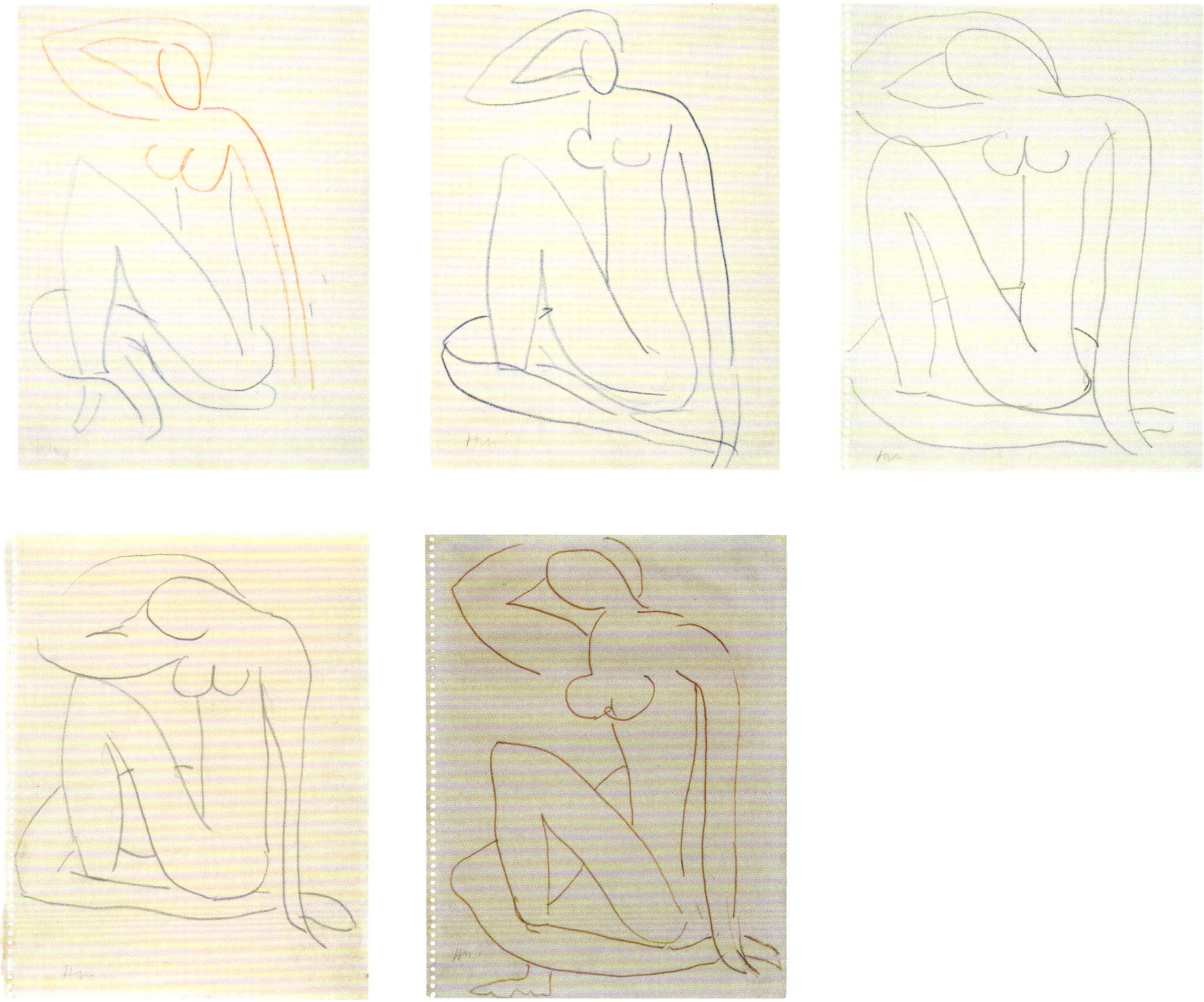

108a–e. All: Untitled (study for *Blue Nude*) c.1952
Pencil and ink on paper, 27 × 21 (10⅝ × 8¼)

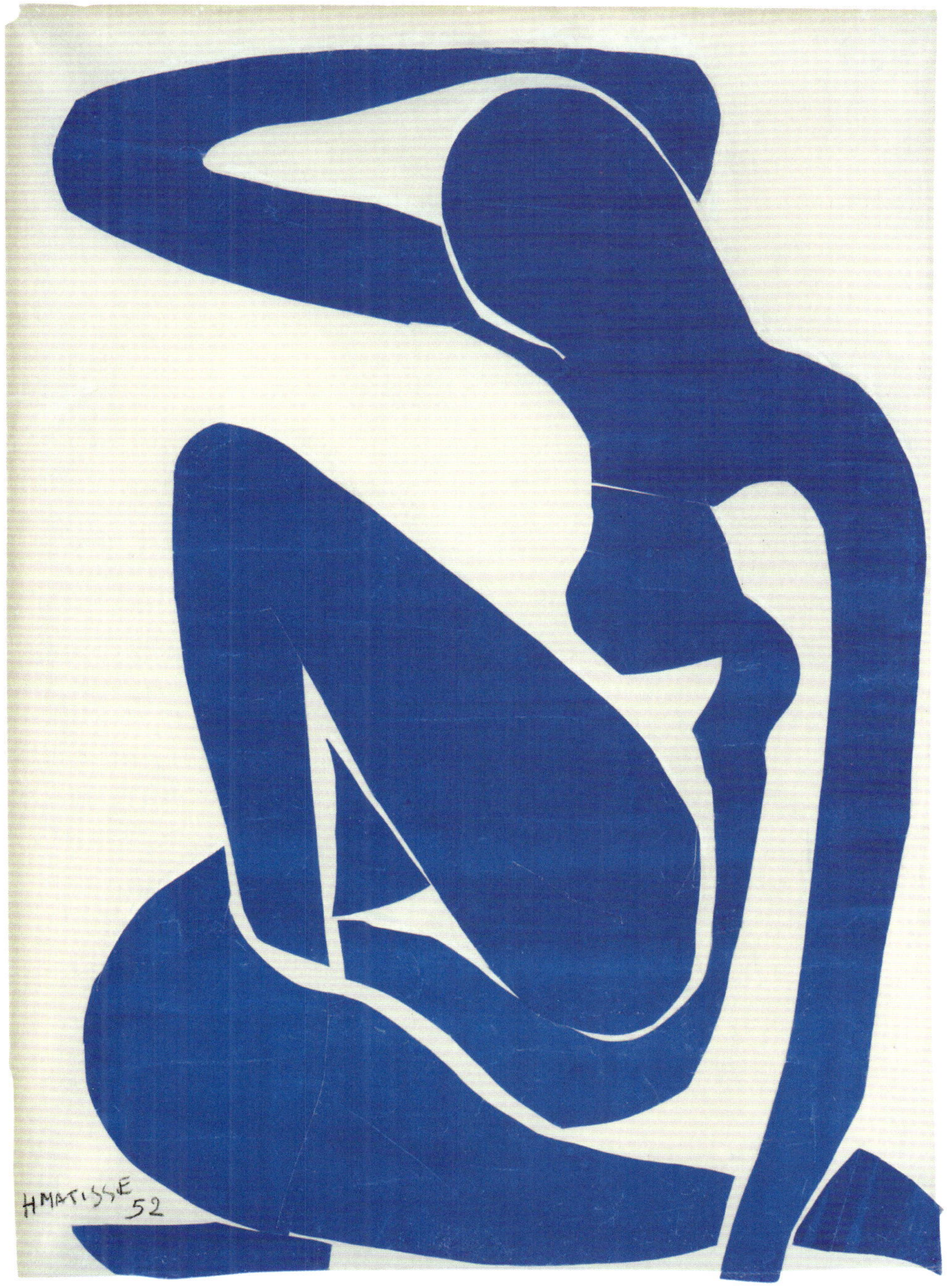

109. *Blue Nude I* spring 1952
Gouache on paper, cut and pasted, mounted
on canvas, 106 × 78 (41¾ × 30¾)

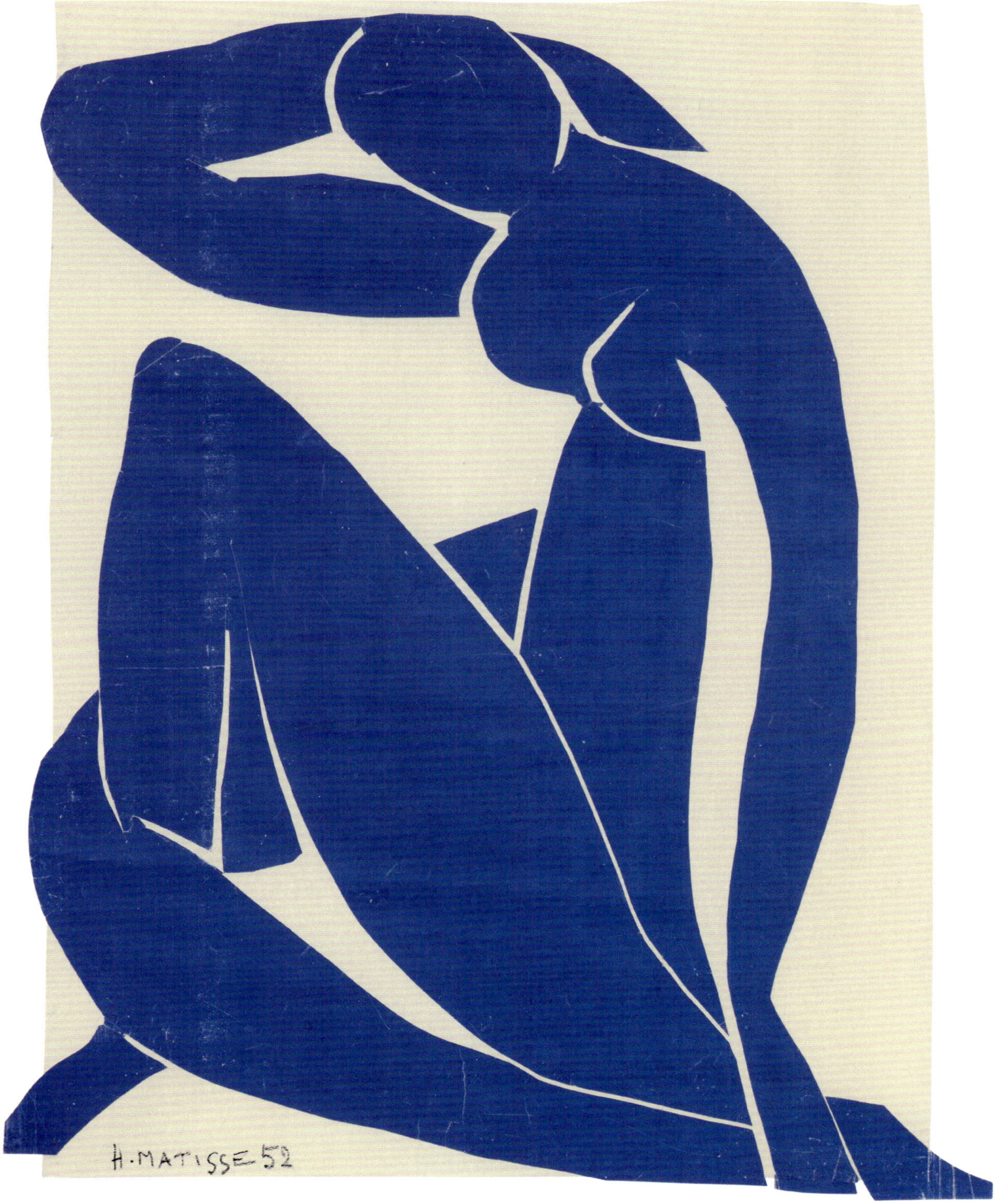

110. *Blue Nude II* spring 1952
Gouache on paper, cut and pasted, on white paper,
mounted on canvas, 116.2 × 88.9 (45¾ × 35)

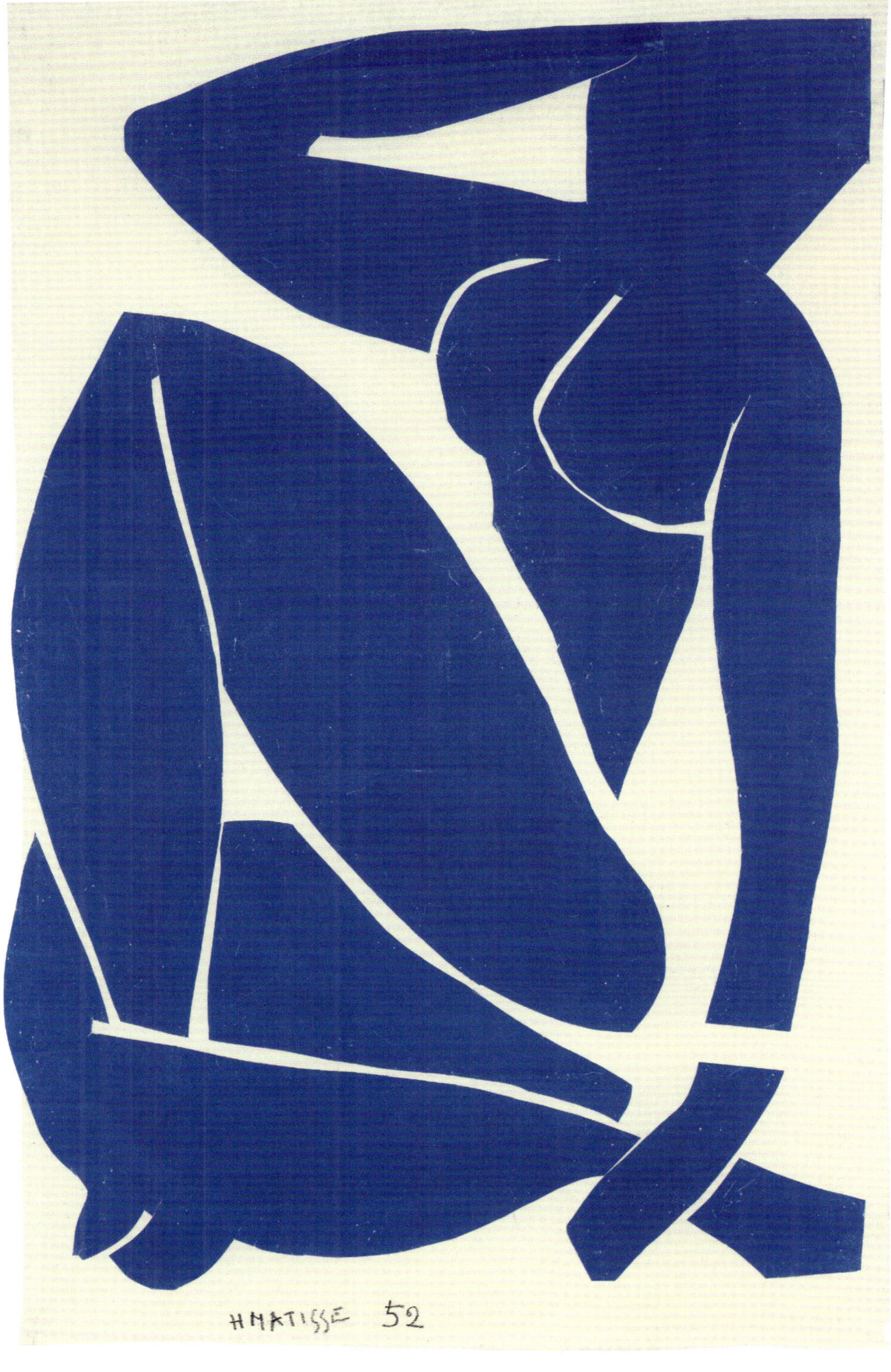

111. *Blue Nude III* spring 1952
Gouache on paper, cut and pasted, on white paper,
mounted on canvas, 112 × 73.5 (44⅛ × 29)

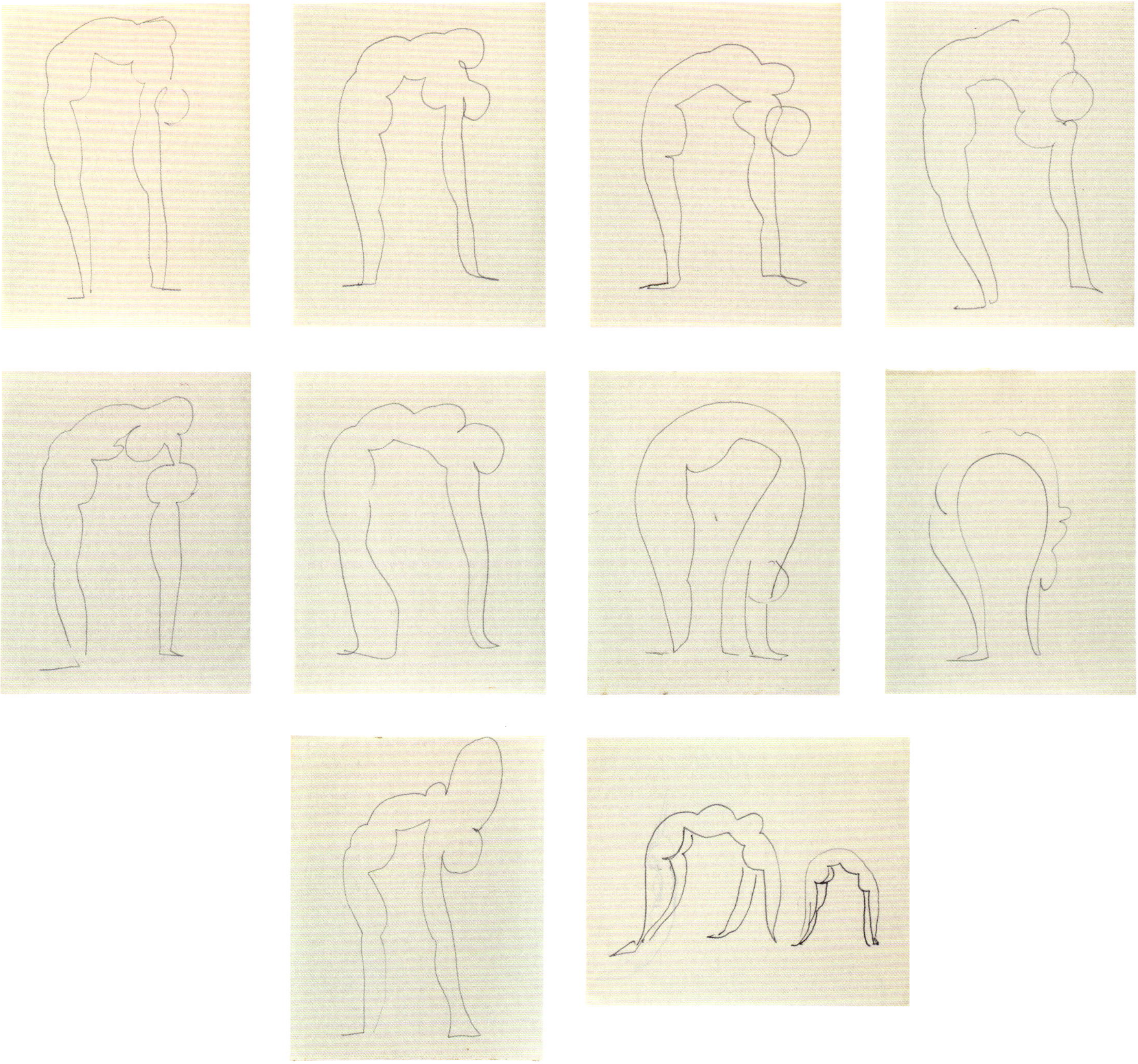

112. Ten drawings of *Acrobats* c. 1952
Ink on paper, each (vertical or horizontal)
27 × 21 (8¼ × 10⅝)

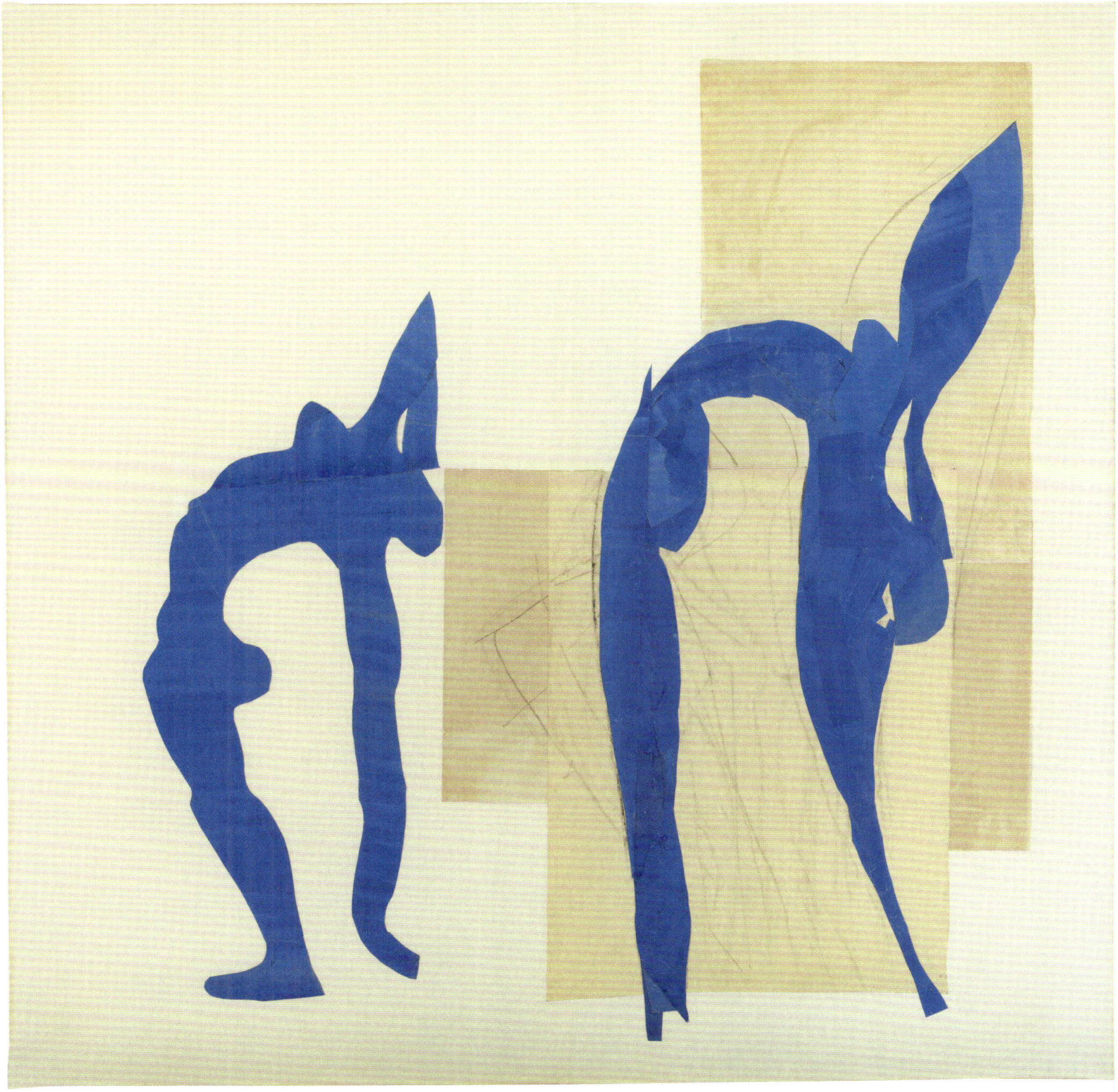

113. *Acrobats* spring – summer 1952
Gouache on paper, cut and pasted, and
charcoal on white paper, mounted on canvas
213 × 208.3 (83⅞ × 82)

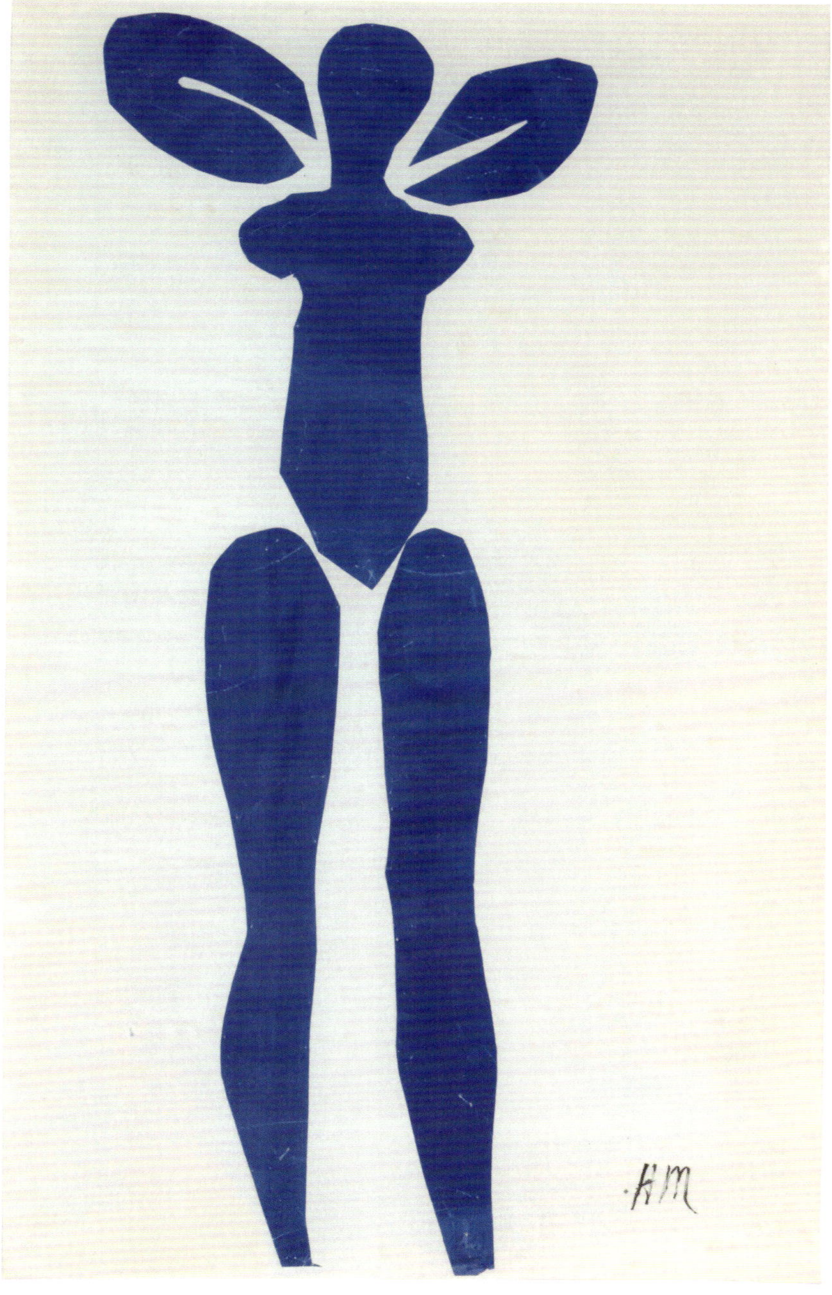

114. *Standing Blue Nude* 1952
Gouache on paper, cut and pasted
112.7 × 73.7 (44⅜ × 29)

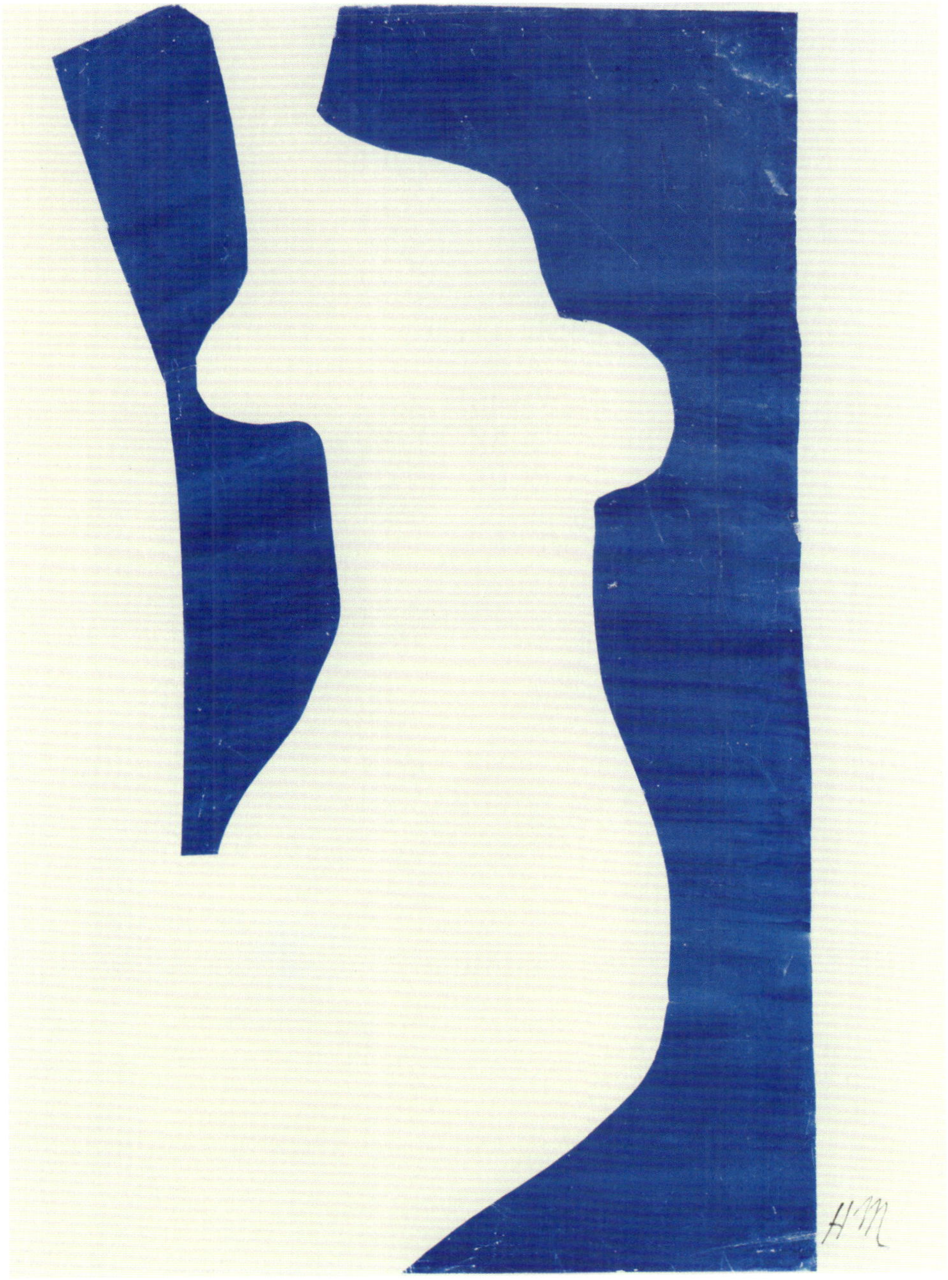

115. *Venus* 1952
Gouache on paper, cut and pasted,
on white paper, mounted on paper panel
101.2 × 76.5 (39⅞ × 30⅛)

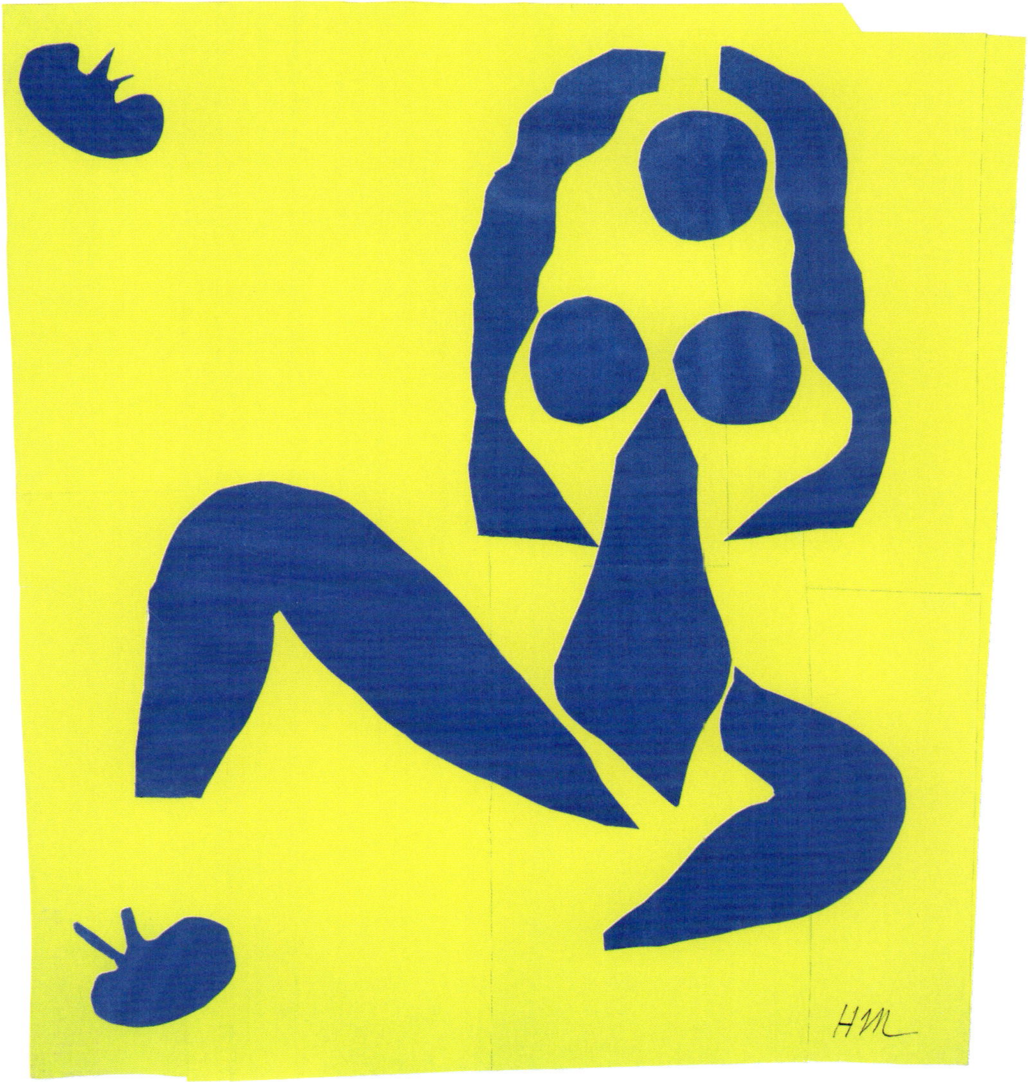

116. *Blue Nude, the Frog* 1952
Gouache on paper, cut and pasted,
mounted on canvas, 141 × 134 (55½ × 52¾)

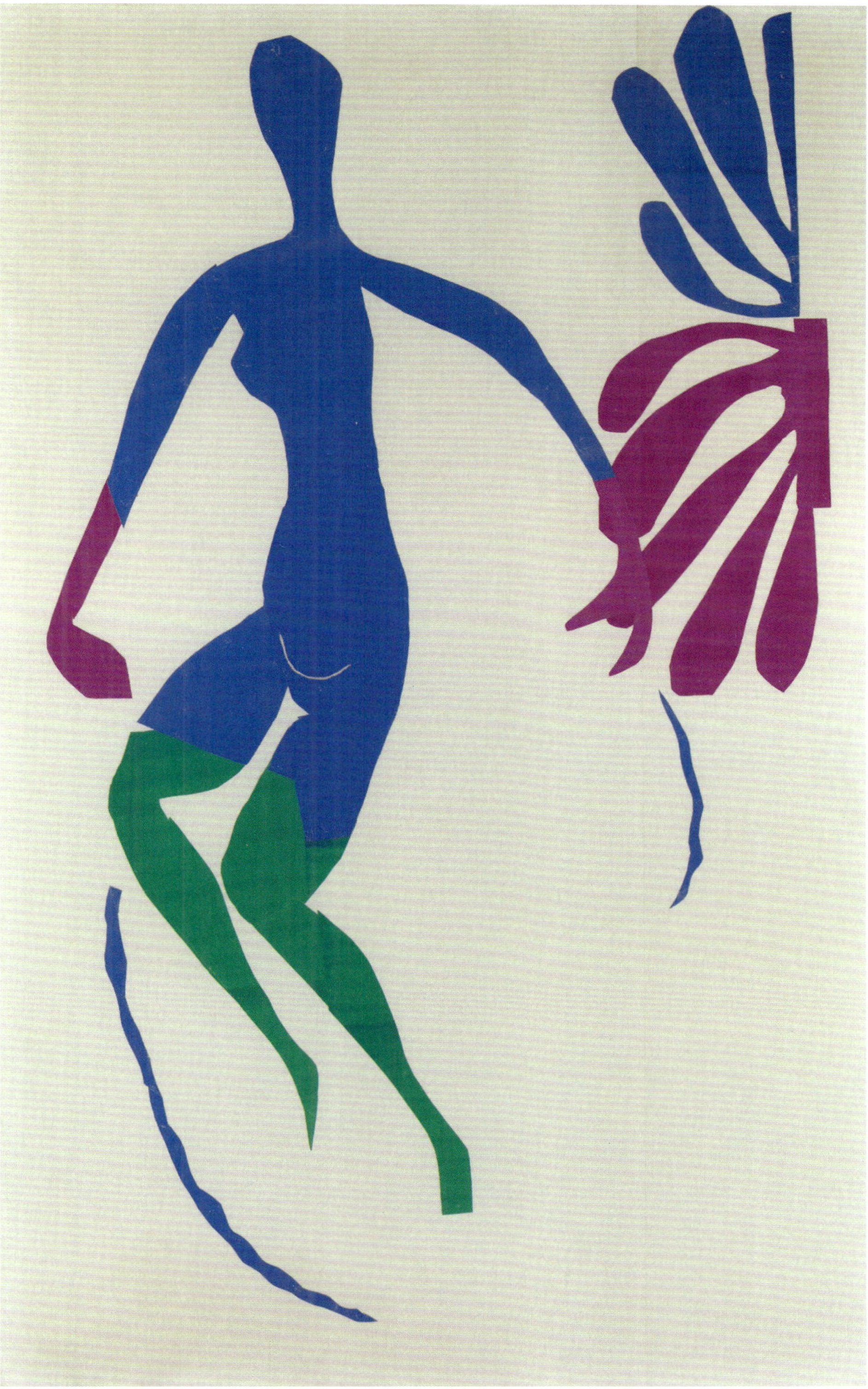

117. *Blue Nude with Green Stockings* 1952
Gouache on paper, cut and pasted
260 × 168 (102⅜ × 66⅛)

118. *The Parakeet and the Mermaid* 1952
Gouache on paper, cut and pasted, and charcoal on white paper, 337 × 768.5 (132⅝ × 302½)

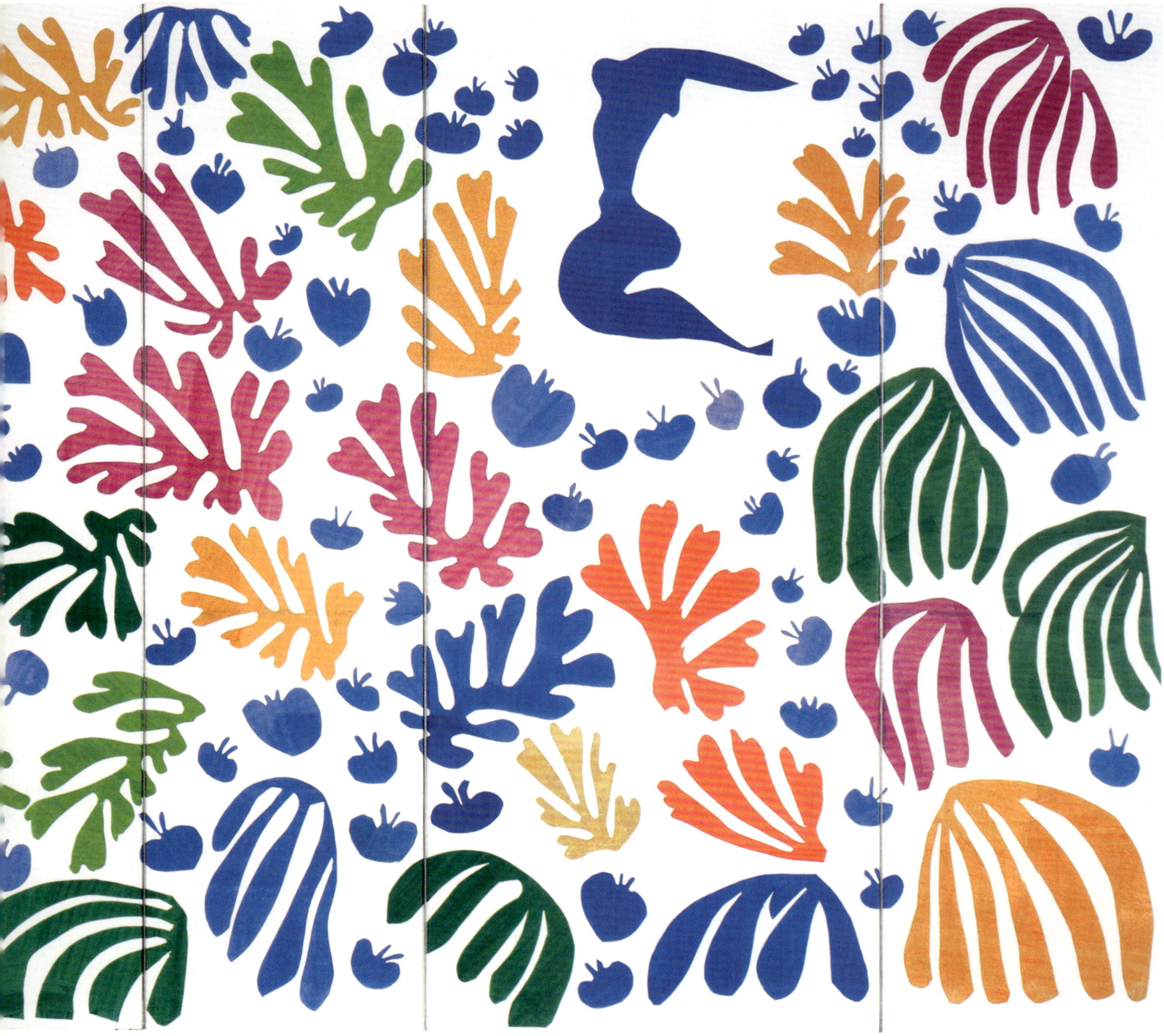

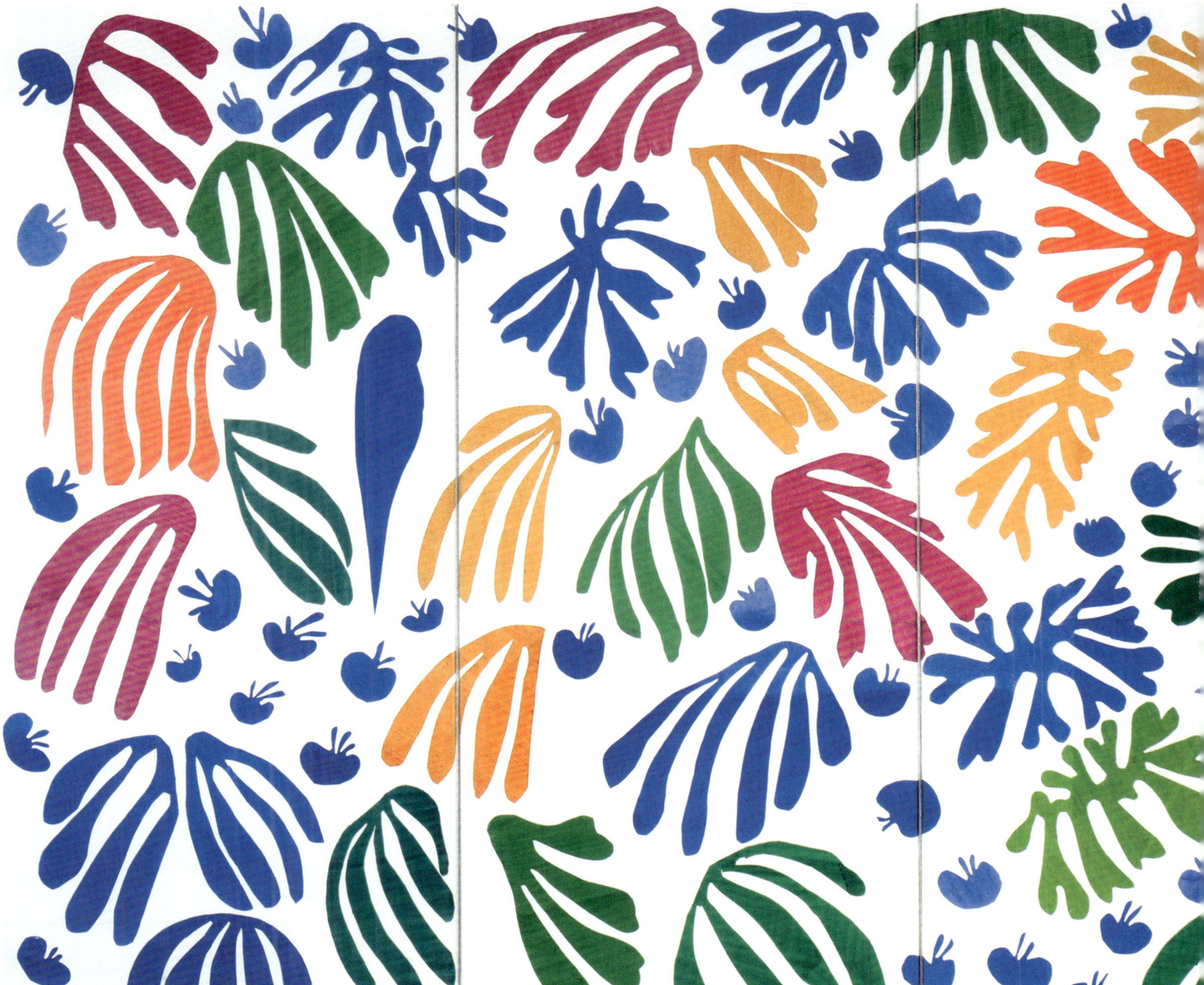

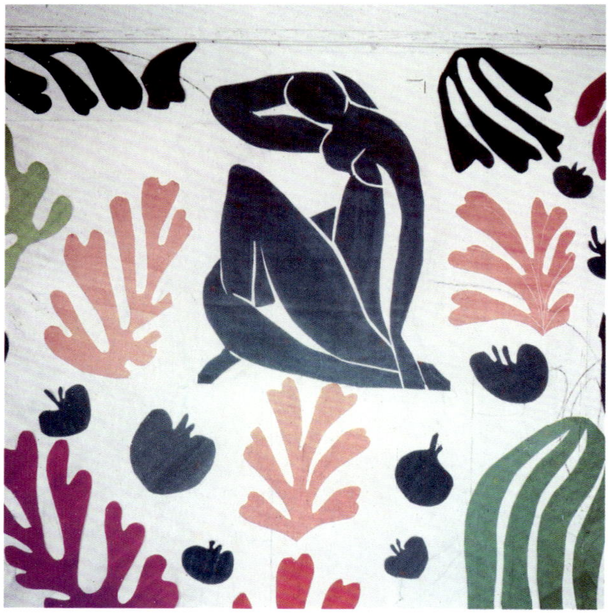
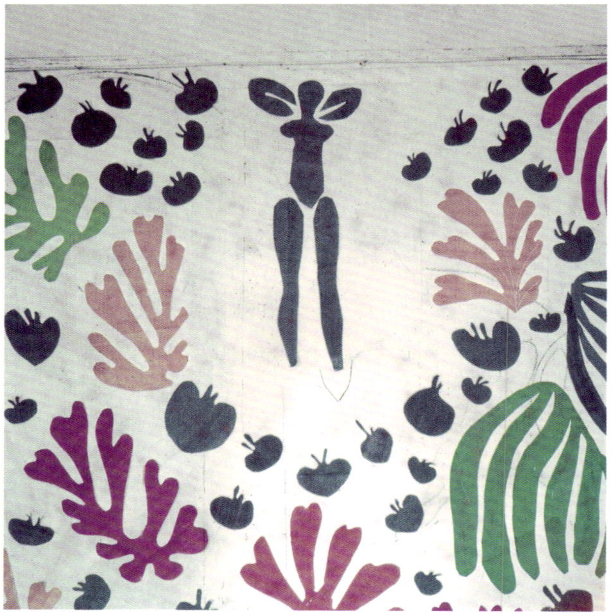

119. Four states of *The Parakeet and the Mermaid* (details) showing insertions of *Blue Nude II*, *Standing Blue Nude* and *Venus*, as well as the final state, Hôtel Régina, Nice, 1952

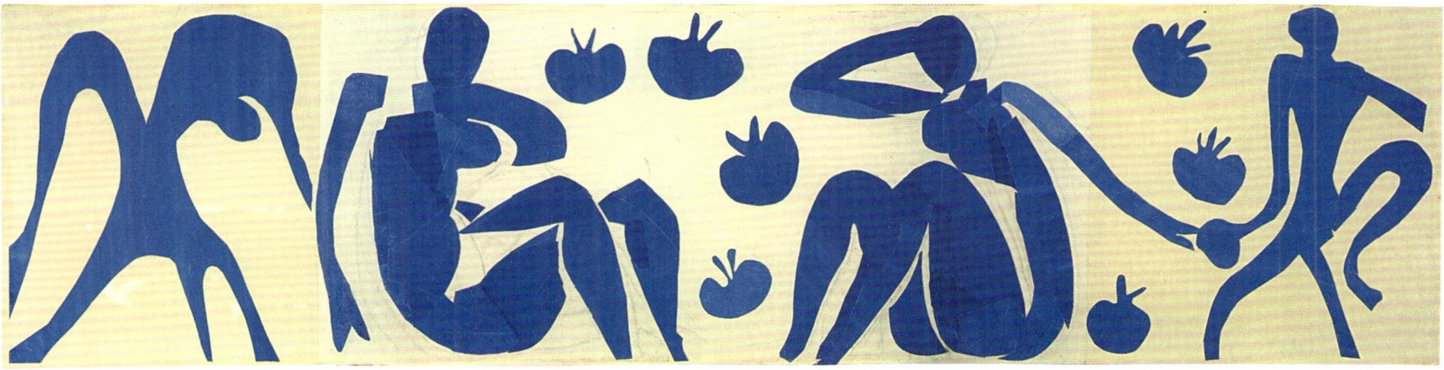

120. *Women and Monkeys* 1952
Gouache on paper, cut and pasted, and charcoal on white paper, 71.7 × 286.2 (28¼ × 112⅝)

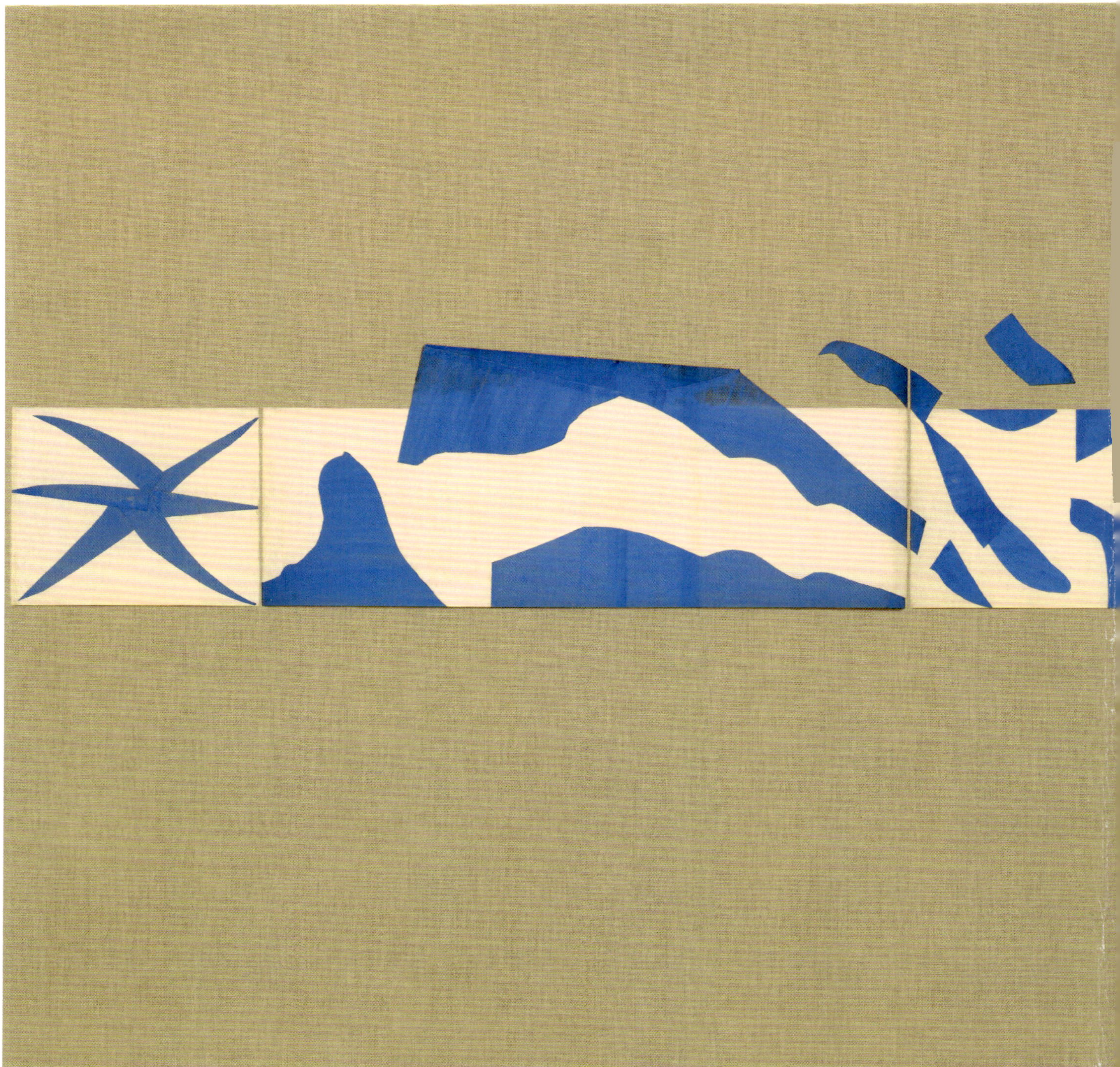

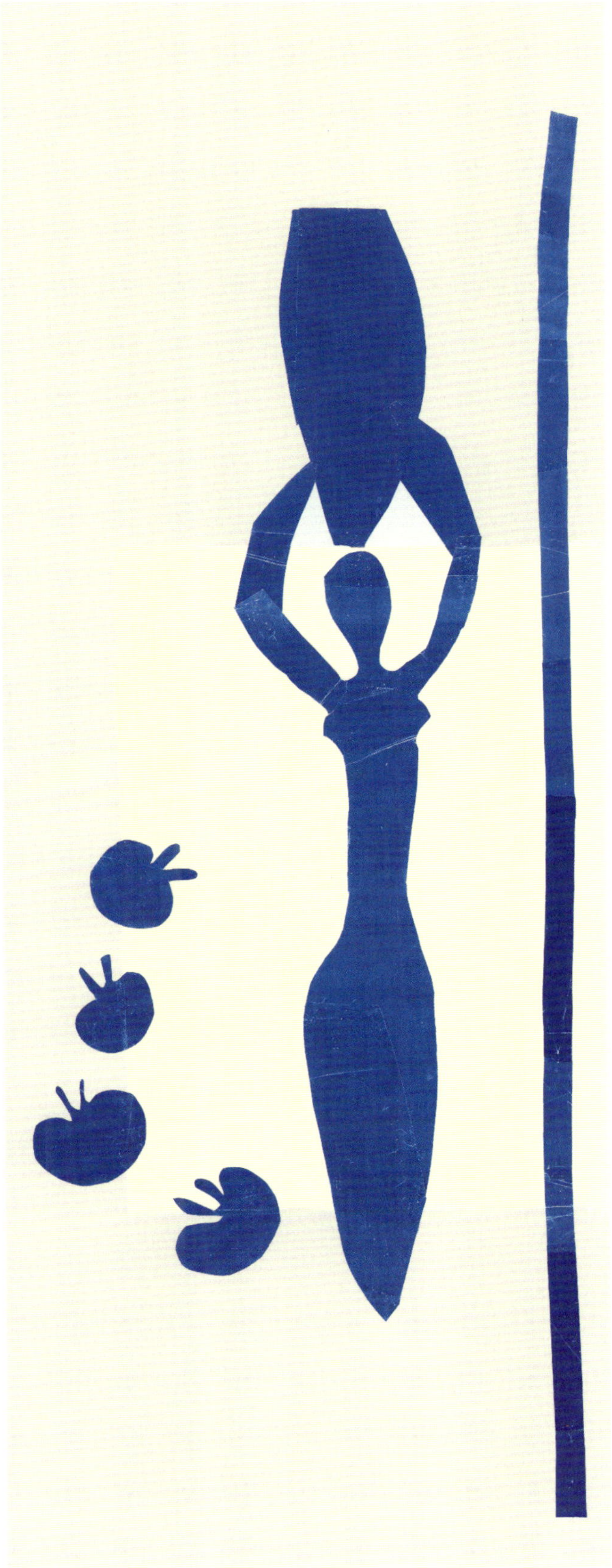

123. *Woman with Amphora and Pomegranates* 1953
Gouache on paper, cut and pasted, mounted on canvas
243.8 × 96.2 (95⅞ × 37⅞)

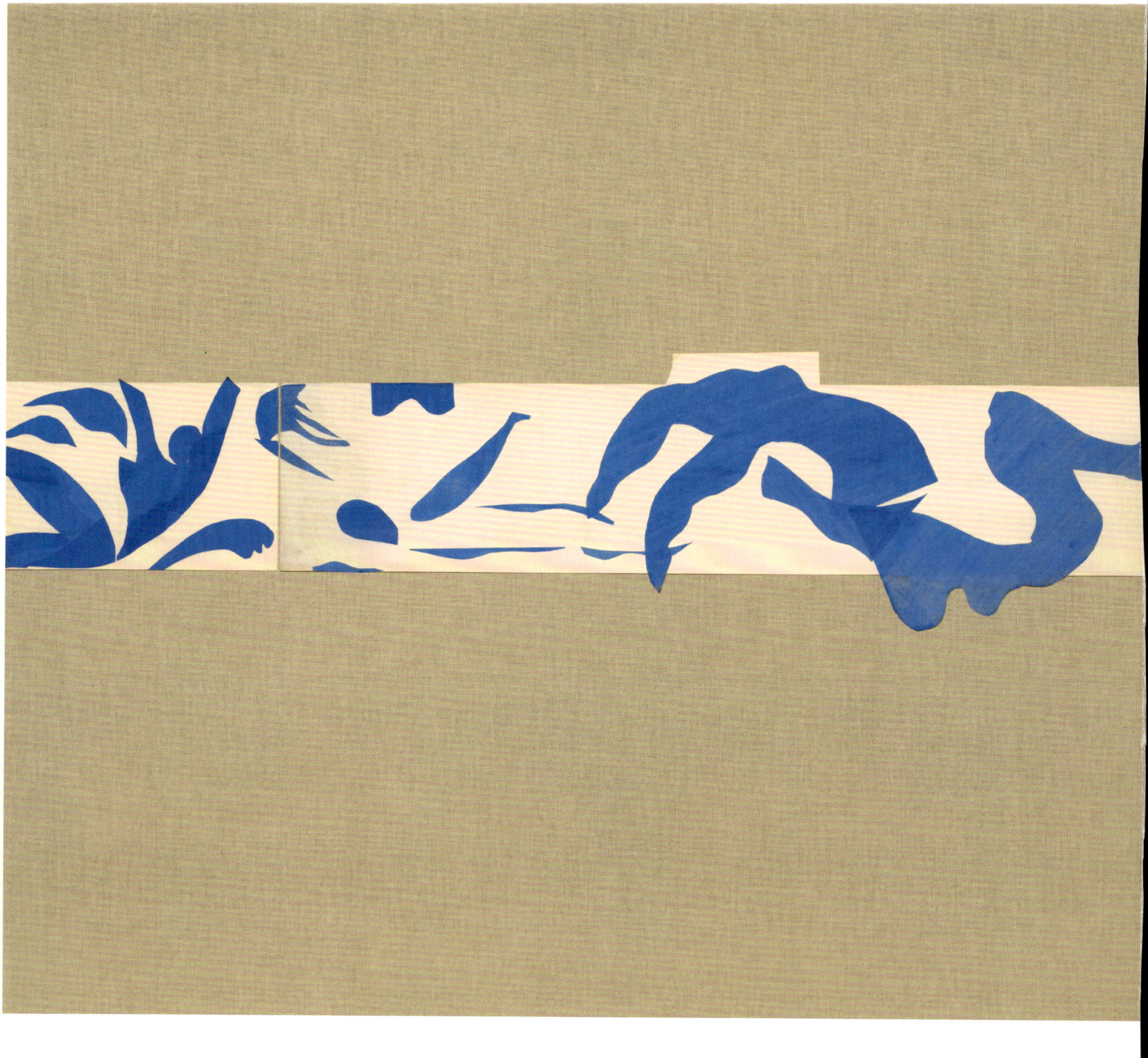

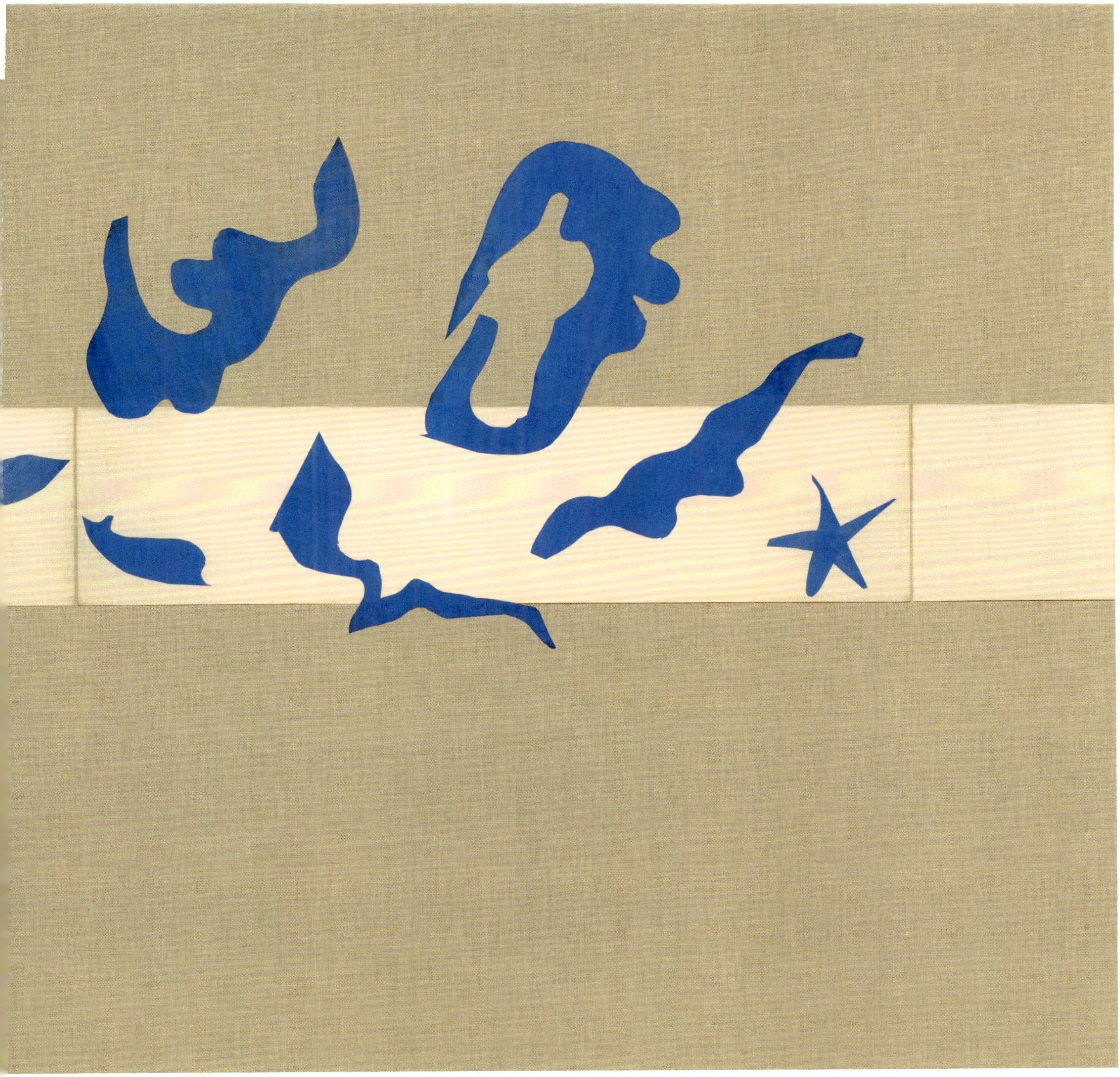

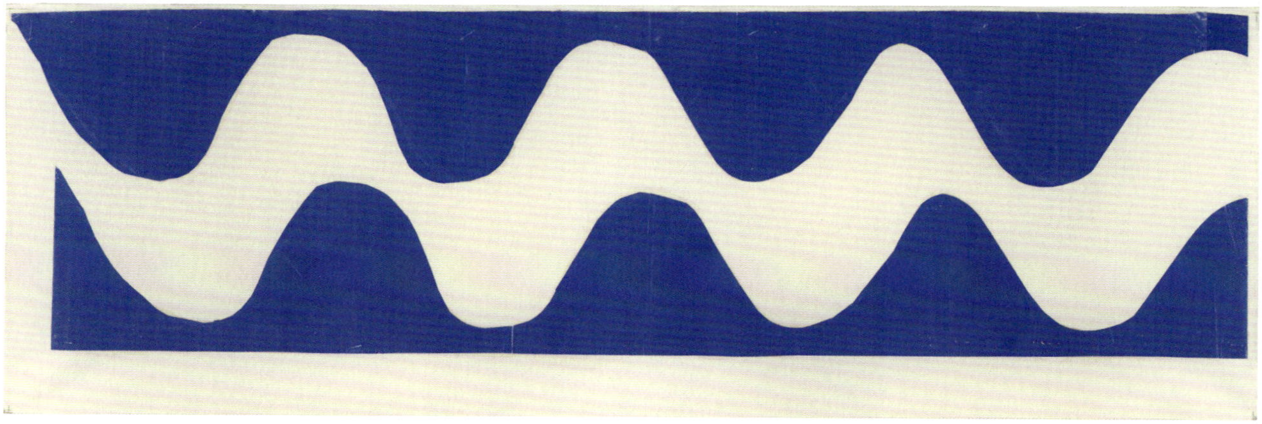

122. *The Wave* c. 1952
Gouache on paper, cut and pasted
51.1 × 158.4 (20⅛ × 62⅜)

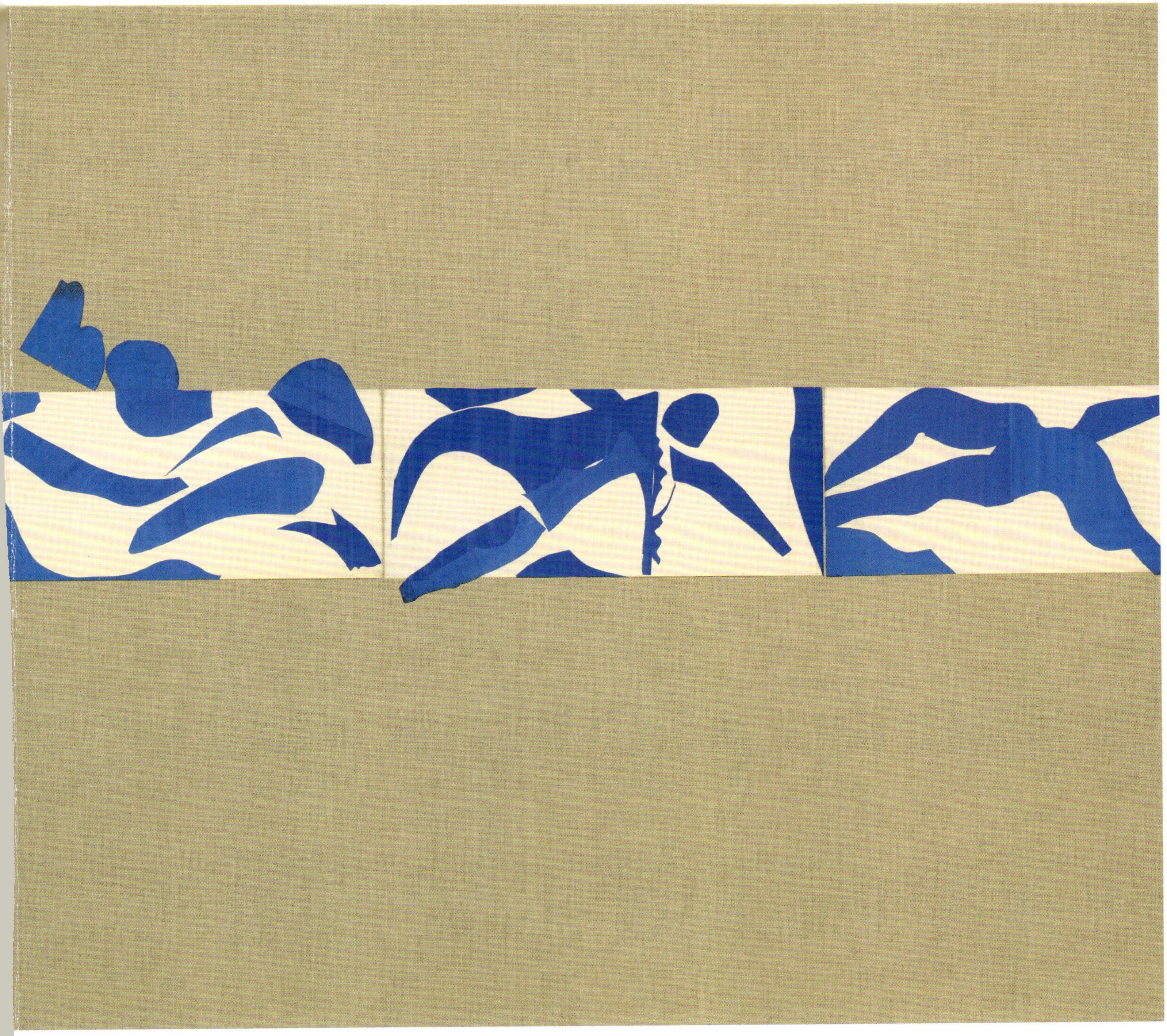

121. *The Swimming Pool* late summer 1952
Maquette for ceramic (realised 1999 and 2005)
Gouache on paper, cut and pasted, on painted paper,
overall 185.4 × 1643.3 (73 × 647)
Installed as nine panels in two parts on burlap-covered walls
345.4 (136) high. Frieze installed at a height of 165 (65)

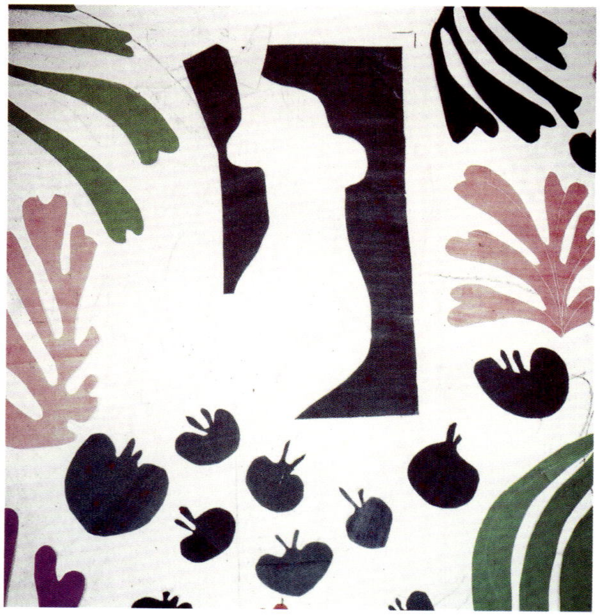

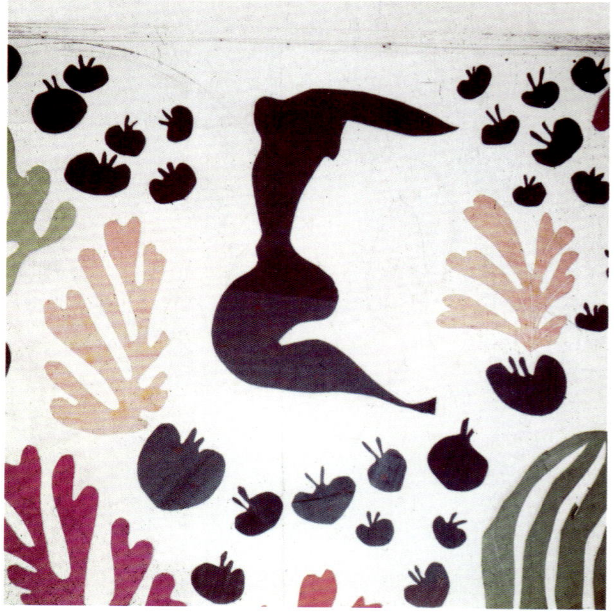

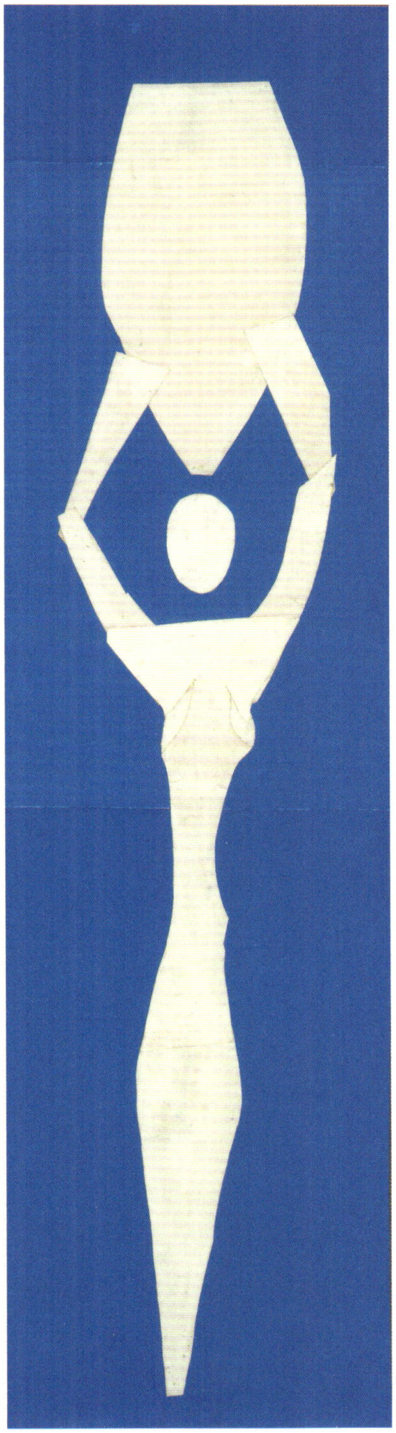

124. *Woman with Amphora* 1953
Gouache on paper, cut and pasted, mounted on canvas, 168.5 × 48 (66⅜ × 18⅞)

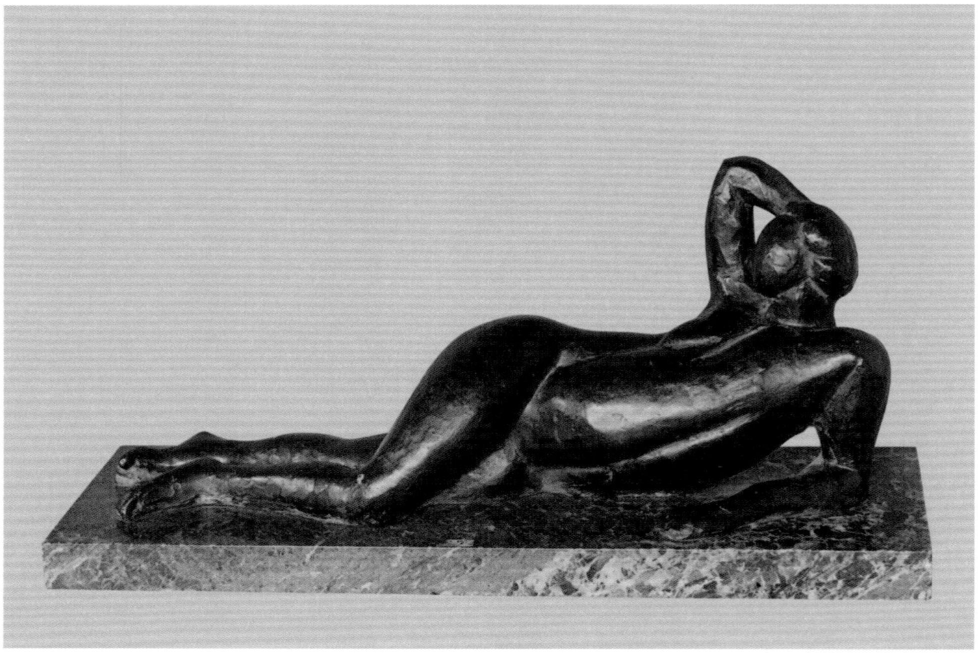

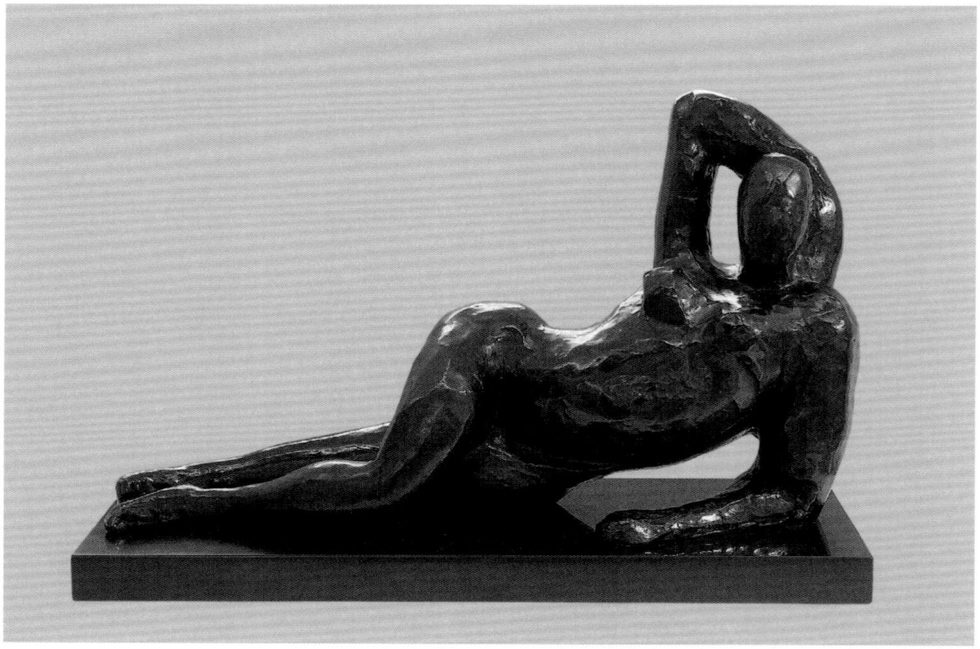

125. *Reclining Nude II* 1927
Bronze, 28.3 × 49.5 × 14.9
(11⅛ × 19½ × 5⅞)

126. *Reclining Nude III* 1929
Bronze, 18.7 × 46.5 × 15.1 (7⅜ × 18⅜ × 6)

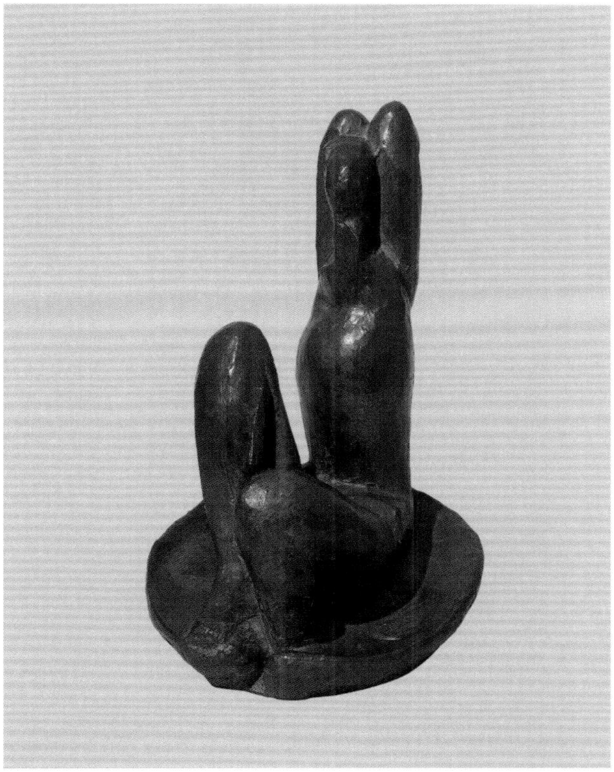

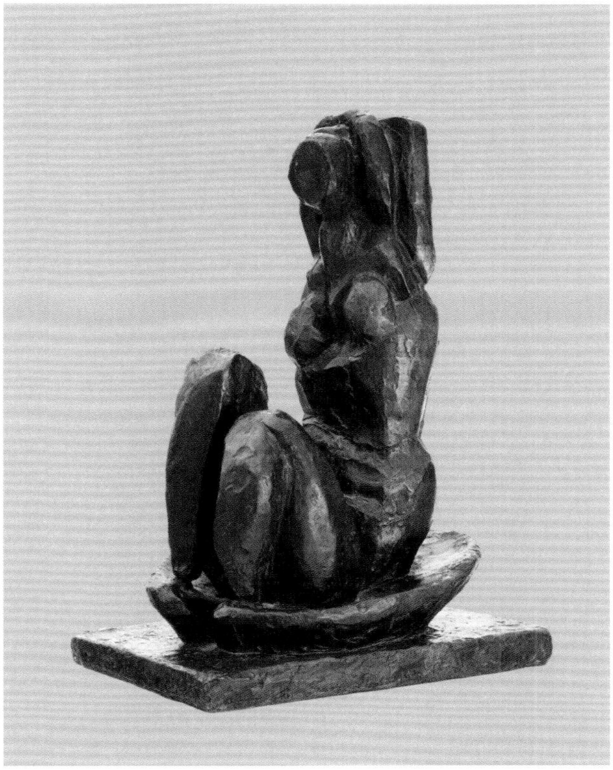

127. *Venus in a Shell I* 1930
Bronze, 31.1 × 18.2 × 20.2 (12¼ × 7⅛ × 8)

128. *Venus in a Shell II* 1932
Bronze, 32.4 × 20.3 × 23.2 (12¾ × 8 × 9⅛)

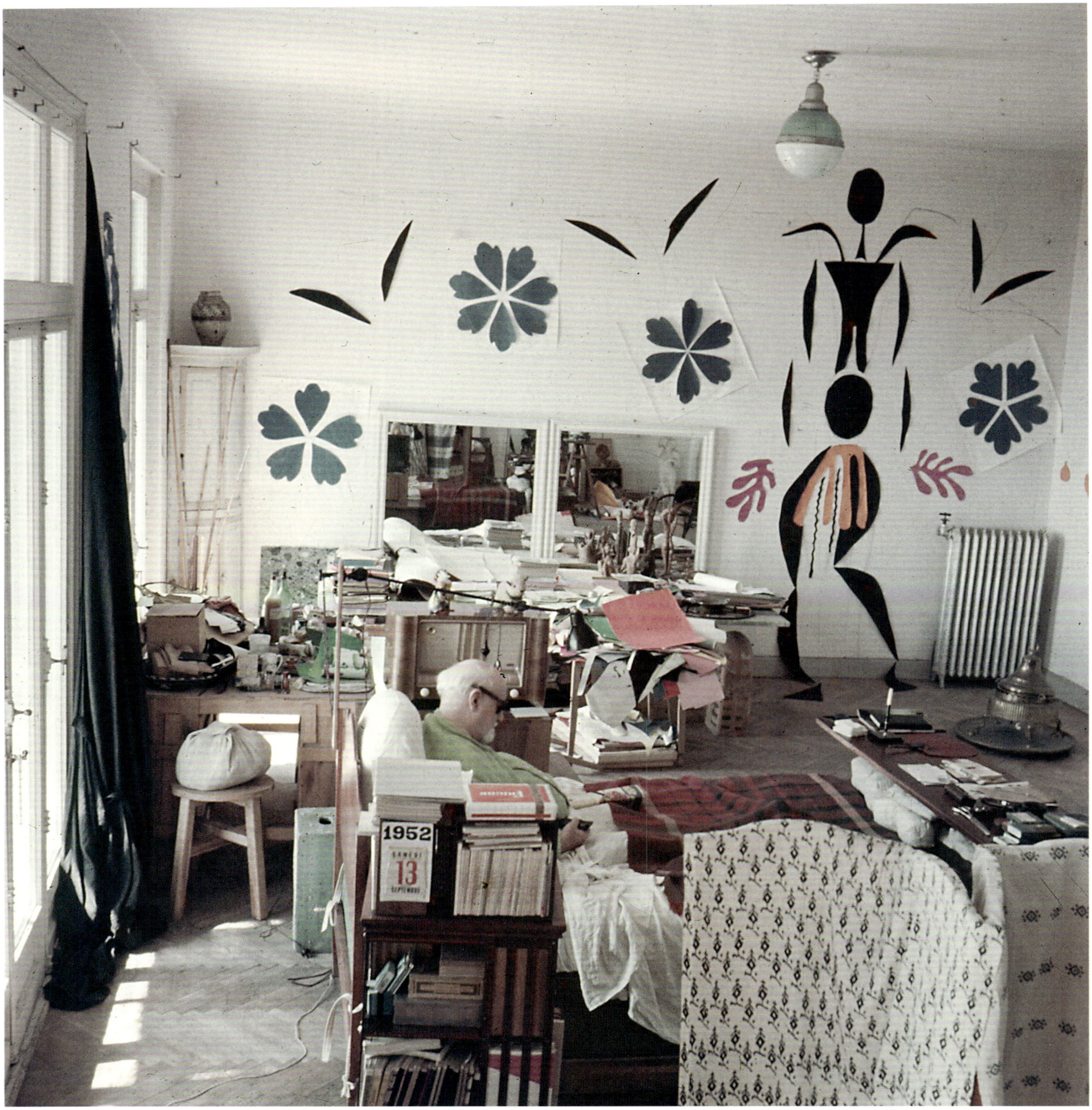

Fig. 46 Hélène Adant, Matisse at Hôtel Régina, Nice, c.1952

CHROMATIC COMPOSITION

Nicholas Cullinan

Saturday, 13 September 1952: Matisse is sitting propped up in bed (fig. 46). The magazine rolled up on his lap, at which he appears to gaze, suggests that he is reading. But his drooped head implies that he is perhaps sleeping or just lost in thought, and the dark glasses that he wears to protect his sight from the highly keyed colours of the sheets of *gouaches découpées*, which occupy all his days and much of his nights, here shield his eyes from us, making his true state of repose inscrutable. He certainly looks tired. And well might he be, for the signs of his incessant work are all around him. On the wall behind is pinned an intermediate version of *La Négresse* from 1952–3, now in the National Gallery of Art, Washington. The Amazonian female form – schematically modelled on that of the dancer Josephine Baker and another reference to African-American music and culture articulated in the cut-outs after *Jazz* and *Creole Dancer* (nos. 18–21, 24–39, 85) – towers over its maker in his bedroom-cum-studio in the Hôtel Régina, Cimiez, Nice. The feet of this athletic figure – the very opposite of the fatigued old man who has made it – actually drape on to the floor, while her head reaches almost to the ceiling. The composition radiates out from her form and fills the wall: pencil marks are scattered around and the blue rosettes are backed by the sheets of the white Canson paper Matisse used to mount his cut-outs.

Hardly visible, another lithe female form – a version of what appears to be *Blue Nude IV* also of 1952 (no. 107) – is tacked to the wall on the left between the two French windows, through which the light streams in, now that the blackout curtains are drawn apart, and beyond which, out of our view, lies the bay of Nice. On the table next to *La Négresse* are strewn offcuts from the cut-outs and painted sheets of pink, green and black yet to be tackled by Matisse's scissors, while in the two mirrors behind this cluttered surface a *mise en abyme* view of the studio unfolds, revealing Matisse's plaster cast of Michelangelo's *Dying Slave*. In the corner of the room, next to the window, are a group of bamboo poles of varying lengths, presumably the ones Matisse used to draw on the walls with charcoal, whose marks appear in several compositions around this time, including *La Négresse*.[1] We can tell the exact date that this photograph of Matisse's studio was taken from the calendar on the *tournante bibliothèque* – the rotating bookcase besides Matisse's bed – in which he kept the pins he used to fix his cut-outs to the wall, and which appears in so many of the photographs of his studio from this time.[2]

But the moment in the studio captured in this snapshot is transitory, and *La Négresse* will take on a different form from the one glimpsed here, once it is unencumbered by such domestic constraints as the radiator to the lower right-hand side of it and the mirrors and corner cabinet that hem it in, obstructing it from filling the entire wall on which it sits. Eventually, the blue foliates will be replaced by multicoloured quatrefoils, dispersed over a greater surface area and quite possibly having migrated from the wall opposite, where Matisse was working simultaneously on *Large Decoration with Masks* of 1953 (no. 131).[3] Equally, these blue rosettes will become the central panel of *Large Decoration with Masks*, complete with their white backing paper. Part of the appeal of the cut-outs for Matisse, it seemed, in addition to the greater ease it afforded him in reaching the final, resolved state of a given work, was their ability to be continually reconfigured, rearranged and have multiple possible states – all of which were captured in photographs such as this one.[4] Perhaps never before had Matisse, or any other

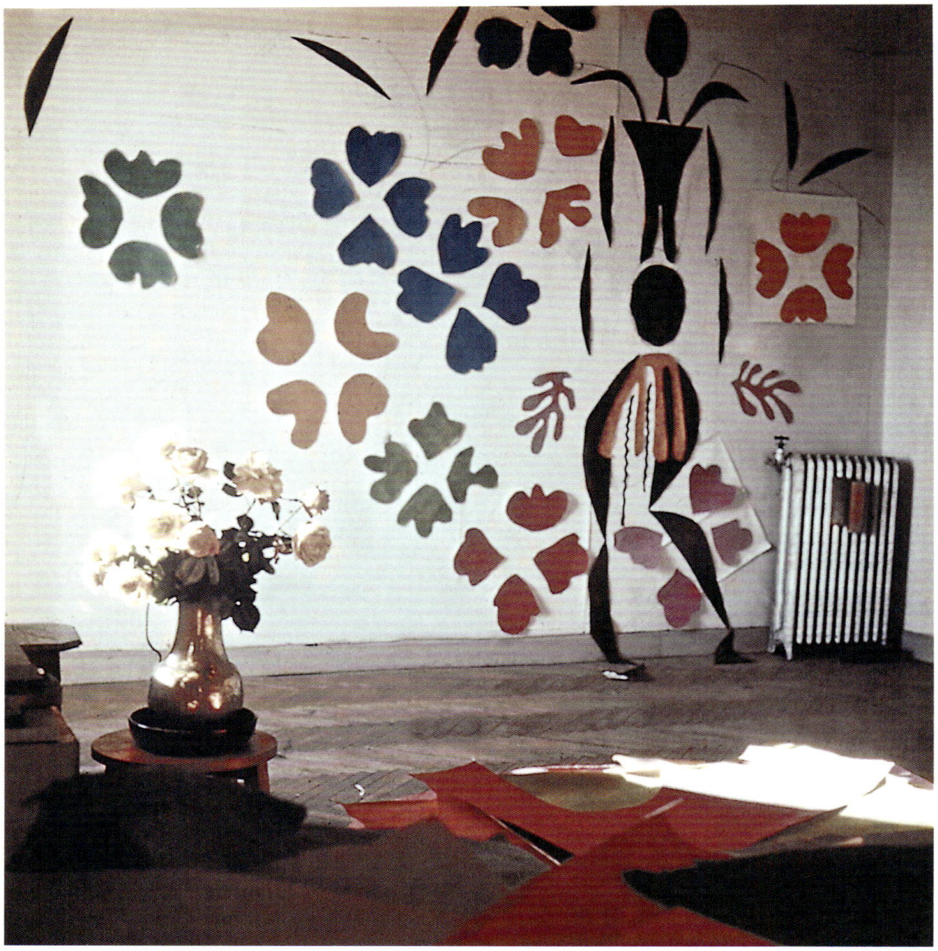

Fig. 47 Lydia Delectorskaya, Hôtel Régina, Nice, c. 1952

artist for that matter, made works that could be so perpetually altered and transformed.

While Matisse was arranging *La Négresse*, which took shape over many months in his studio during 1952–3, he was also working on several other compositions in different rooms and spread across various walls of the apartment in the Régina, as was his habit during this particularly productive period in his work. In trying to reconstruct the chronology of activity in Matisse's studio during this time, it quickly becomes apparent that it is impossible to separate out discussions of individual works chronologically, for they were often produced concurrently rather than consecutively (especially when it came to larger and more complicated compositions), with elements migrating from one arrangement to another, or at least informing the other.[5] This is especially true of the period from 1952 to 1953, which was defined by its remarkable activity and creative invention. As the photographs of the studio from this time demonstrate, there hardly seems to have been enough wall space to accommodate Matisse's flow of ideas and furious pace of work.

Around April 1952 a photograph documents an early version of *La Négresse* in the studio, showing it pinned up on the wall next to the radiator with a preliminary state of *Blue Nude IV* on a picture easel reflected in a mirror across from it (p. 74). Although *La Négresse* was modelled on Josephine Baker, its intense physicality may in part have been inspired by the memory of the dancer Yvette Chauviré, who, as reported by Matisse's assistant Jacqueline Duhême, had come to dance for Matisse in the studio in Villa le Rêve in Vence some years before.[6] According to Louis Aragon, the subject of Matisse's cut-out *Creole Dancer* from 1950 (no. 85) was the dancer Katherine Dunham, whom Matisse had also seen perform.[7] In making *La Négresse* in homage to Baker, Matisse was not only continuing his interest in depictions of jazz music and dancing, articulated in previous cut-outs, as already noted, but he may also have been fashioning a coda to the works of two other contemporaries who had made works inspired by Baker – Alexander Calder's wire sculpture, *Aztec Josephine Baker*, c.1929 (now, like Matisse's cut-out, also in the National Gallery of Art in Washington), and the strikingly similar collage, *Josephine Baker*, 1915 (now in the Centre Pompidou, Paris), by Matisse's friend Henri Laurens.[8]

Matisse's *La Négresse* is a human form stripped to often jarringly simplified anatomical signs, such as legs and arms, head and torso, which play off the tension between the circular and the angular to conjure a physique as voluptuous as it is sleek and powerful. Two black ovoids form her head and belly, accompanied by an attenuated torso and arms, and markedly more muscular thighs and legs, and ending in triangular, wedge-like feet. In place of hands she has rose pink vegetal forms, which convey more movement than perhaps mere signs for fingers could, and her figure is completed by the addition of an orange and black grass skirt, whose undulating silhouette seems to imbue it with motion (fig. 47). In a photograph of the studio we see Matisse's sculpture, *Reclining Nude I* from 1906–7 (p. 74), directly in front of *La Négresse*.[9] Why bring out this work from five decades earlier and place it temporarily in front of a work in progress, unless Matisse hoped to impart something of its sculptural mass to the flat outline of the paper silhouette of *La Négresse* and to compare the handling of volumetric form in these two works from different periods and in different media? Nothing in Matisse's studio was arranged by accident, as is demonstrated by Hélène Adant's numerous documentary photographs and artfully orchestrated 'still lives' of objects and props used in his paintings, which essentially elevate Matisse's studio to an art form in itself.[10]

In April and May 1952 André Verdet conducted a series of revealing interviews with Matisse at the Régina in Cimiez, and a photograph of a very early state of *La Négresse* appears in the resulting book *Prestiges de Matisse*, which was published later that same year.[11] Matisse designed the cover, which consists of a series of blue quatrefoils on a white background, a schema that perhaps provided the prototype for the subsequent tessellated compositions of *Large Decoration with Masks* and Large *Decoration with Fruits* of 1953.[12] The photograph of *La Négresse* reproduced in Verdet's book shows the work in progress with just the human form surrounded by a few charcoal lines on the wall and the three black 'bird' shapes that surround it. This photograph also shows Matisse's plaster *Nu de dos IV* of 1930 reflected in the mirror on the opposite wall and, intriguingly, a potted palm placed on the floor in front of *La Négresse*, suggesting that perhaps the lolling black forms that surround the dancer are not birds but, rather, palms.[13]

Around the same time as working on *La Négresse*, Matisse was beginning to produce two cut-outs on the theme of a snail, which would bring him perhaps as close to abstraction as he would ever reach, albeit an 'abstraction rooted in reality', as Matisse carefully phrased it.[14] Although Matisse acknowledged that he had gained 'greater completeness and abstraction' in the cut-outs, 'a form filtered to its essentials', he always maintained an ambivalent and sometimes sceptical attitude to abstraction, made manifest through the cut-outs themselves and the words he used to characterise them to his interlocutors.[15] 'A purified sign for a shell' was how Matisse described to André Verdet in similarly careful terms – balanced between abstraction and figuration – his first variation on the theme of a snail's shell executed in 1952 (p.63).[16] Reproduced in Verdet's book as a small *gouache découpée*, it adopts an arabesque form that seeks to distil and stylise the shape of a

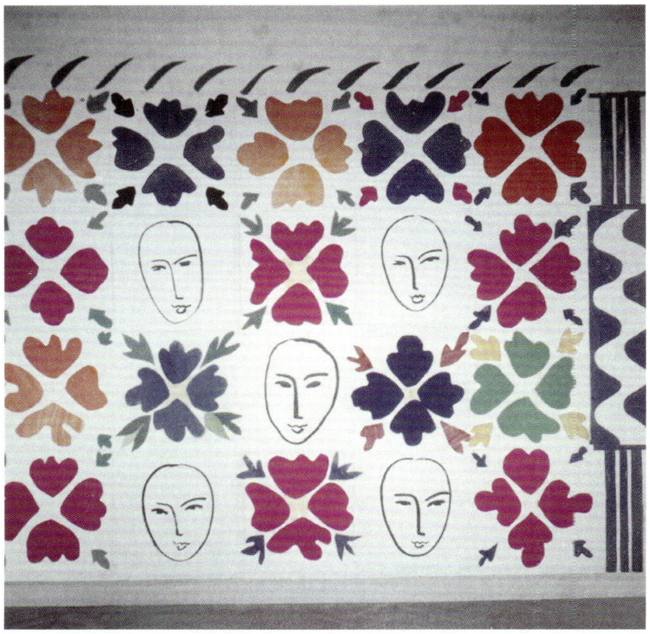

Fig. 48 State of *Large Decoration with Masks* with *The Wave*, Hôtel Régina, Nice, 1952–3

shell and appeared with the title, apparently given by Matisse, *Panneau abstrait sur racine de réalité (Abstract Panel Rooted in Reality)*.[17] Matisse's words show this first work also anticipated his later version of *Acanthuses* of 1953 (no. 135):

> The decision of the line comes from the artist's profound conviction. That paper cut-out, the kind of volute acanthus that you see on the wall up there, is a stylized snail. First of all I drew the snail from nature, holding it between two fingers; drew and redrew. I became aware of an unfolding, I formed in my mind a purified sign for a shell. Then I took my scissors. It was necessary that the end be alive right in the beginning.[18]

As Matisse also related to Verdet, this first *Snail* was originally intended to become part of a composition called *Le Jardin* (perhaps *The Parakeet and the Mermaid,* no. 118):

> But the musical movement of the whole ensemble was broken. So I removed the snail; I have put it aside while awaiting another place for it.[19]

Exiled from the composition of *Le Jardin*, *The Snail* never really found an alternative home; instead, it existed on its own. It also prefigured one of Matisse's boldest compositions employing the cut-out medium.

In the case of the second, larger version of *The Snail* 1953 (no. 129), a series of photographs show it in almost final form on the wall, next to the poster *Affiches d'Expositions Réalisées Depuis 25 Ans Par l'Imprimerie Mourlot* ... of 1952, which is arguably the most abstract work Matisse ever attempted and whose forms and colour palette perhaps influenced the more ambitious second version of *The Snail*. Not only is *The Snail* one of the most abstract works Matisse ever made,[20] but rather than cutting into the coloured sheets of paper that had been painted with gouache, Matisse now tore and ripped into them directly, as if the size and sheer excitement of producing this large-scale work demanded it.[21] The concentric composition is formed by coloured sheets, which radiate out from the centre in contrasting colours of red and green, orange and blue, and yellow and mauve, echoing the spiral pattern of a snail's shell.[22]

Lydia Delectorskaya described the making of *The Snail* in a letter to Ronald Alley at the Tate Gallery on 30 March 1976. Among the many details of the impetus and process behind the work, Lydia commented:

> Its title 'The Snail' comes from the form made up of a succession of patches of colour: they curl round like the shell of a snail. The spiral form of a snail's shell echoes the direction of universal movement. The composition so named is therefore not at all abstract. But if you want to treat it as 'abstract', you can give it the alternative title also chosen by H. Matisse: 'La Composition Chromatique' [Chromatic Composition].[23]

However, Lydia's unequivocal assertion in this letter that 'there were no preparatory drawings for this work by H. Matisse' is complicated not just by Matisse's comments to Verdet but also by a letter from Maurice Lefebvre-Foinet to Alley of 19 February 1976, which added:

> Mme Duthuit [Matisse's daughter] told the compiler that her father made many drawings of snails at this time and the idea for the *papier découpé* grew out of these. Shortly afterwards he designed a stained-glass window for the proposed mausoleum of Albert D. Lasker ('Ivy in Flower') and also designed an ironwork grill doorway to the mausoleum based on drawings of snails, which however was never executed.[24]

This is supported by a photograph of the studio from around this time, which shows Matisse sitting up in bed with an early stage of *Ivy in Flower* (no. 134) next to a drawing of several snails – probably early treatments for the door he was designing for the Lasker monument, which we shall explore in more detail later (fig.2).

A colour photograph of Matisse's studio taken by Lydia Delectorskaya is particularly interesting for our consideration of the way in which works were created together in Matisse's studio at this time. It shows that *The Snail* was originally (or at least momentarily) one panel in a larger composition, forming the left-hand side of a triptych made up of *Memory of Oceania* (no. 130) on the right and *Large Decoration with Masks* in the middle, so these works were made in tandem with each other and presumably used some of the same coloured sheets and elements (p. 83).[25] This photograph also shows *Creole Dancer* laid flat in front of this tableau

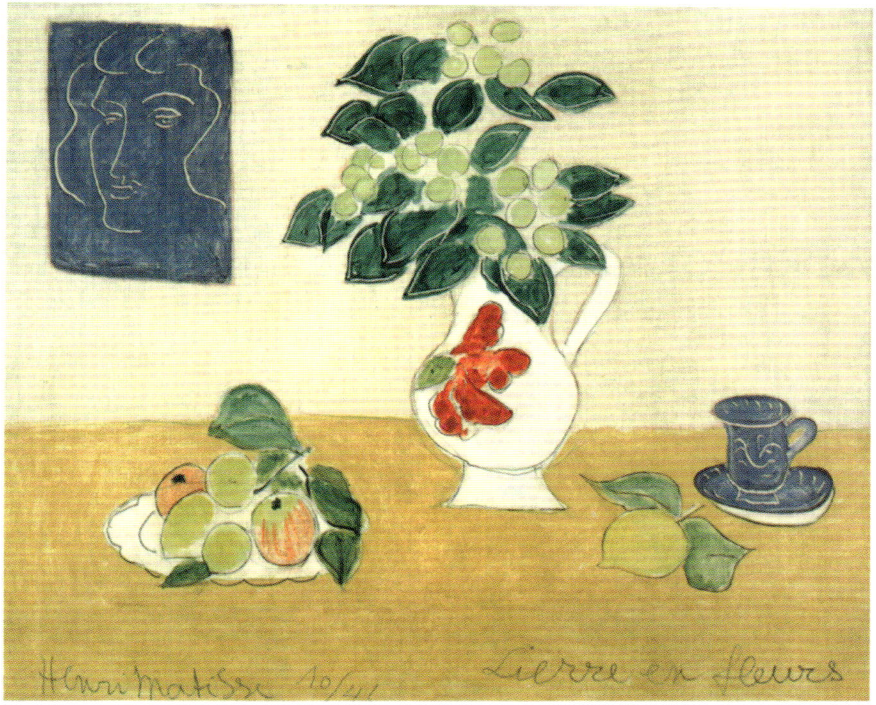

Fig. 49 *Ivy in Flower (Lierre en fleurs)*. Oil on canvas, 72.4 × 92.7 (28½ × 36½)
Private collection

and probably finished, given that its signed date of completion is 'Juin 50' (June 1950) and that it had already been exhibited in *Henri Matisse: chapelle, peintures, dessins, sculptures* at the Maison de la Pensée Française in Paris, running from 5 July to 24 September 1950. The presence of *Creole Dancer* once more in Matisse's studio c.1952–3, while he was also working intermittently on *La Négresse*, perhaps suggests that this earlier cut-out on the subject of dance may have proved useful to Matisse in constructing the larger and later work on this theme.[26]

Begun during the summer of 1952 and completed early in 1953, *Memory of Oceania*, as the title makes clear, was Matisse's way of evoking places from his past to which he knew he could no longer return, as well as aspects of the world that lay outside his studio windows and were now beyond his reach: swimming in the sea, walking in a garden and, in this particular case, his visit to Tahiti in 1930, where he spent three months when aged sixty. In this sense, the title of the work recalls Sigmund Freud's formulation of the 'oceanic feeling' as one that returns us to earlier experiences.[27] Matisse was also drawing a line between past and present, recalling the scope of the world that used to be available to him compared to the more physically restricted life that he now lived. But this circumscription is merely physical, and as this work makes clear, Matisse's imagination, sparked by memory, shines brightly, the only sense of wistfulness lying in the title of the work. If *The Snail* and *Memory of Oceania* made at the same time mark the change to the more abstract, late cut-outs, then Matisse's aforementioned comments about *The Snail* being made 'from life', and the prominence given to memory and nostalgia in *Memory of Oceania*, flag up the sources of Matisse's inspiration at this period as ranging from memories past to observations present.[28]

For Gauguin, Tahiti had a transformative effect on his sense of light and use of colour. For Matisse, oddly, it had an effect on line. His numerous photographs of this trip focus on the jagged, serrated edges of palm leaves silhouetted against a blanched sky; these contrasts are only heightened further by the black and white gelatin print of the photograph. Equally, in Matisse's sketchbook of elegantly sparse, pen-and-ink line drawings of the South Sea island, forms are reduced to impatient, curlicue black markings set against the bare cream background provided by the paper. This approach is found episodically in his etchings for Stéphane Mallarmé's *Poésies* in 1932 and in both versions of the painting *Window in Tahiti* of 1935–6, so it is entirely fitting that some of Matisse's earliest cut-outs, such as the diptychs of *Polynesia, the Sky* and *Polynesia, the Sea*, produced in 1946 as paper maquettes for tapestries, also largely forgo colour to focus instead on silhouette. Oceanic lagoons would go on to influence some of the plates in *Jazz*, culminating with the fusion of line and colour in *Memory of Oceania*, so the memory of this trip cast a shadow over the entire period in which Matisse worked on his cut-outs.

A photograph of Matisse's studio taken by Hélène Adant in 1952 shows three of the *Blue Nudes* pinned on the wall, with the paintings *Window in Tahiti* of 1935 and *Window in Tahiti II* of 1936 propped up below them (p. 58). The fact that Matisse retrieved both versions of the latter subject, themselves reminiscences of his three-month sojourn in Tahiti six years earlier in 1930, suggest that he was reshaping their compositions, motifs and memories into the paired-down and more geometrical aesthetic of the paper cut-outs, as in *Memory of Oceania* begun that summer in 1952, and that he was also thinking back to his own photographs, earlier paintings and 1946 cut-outs on this South Seas theme. Matisse had of course already revisited the South Pacific, courtesy of the cut-out technique, in some of his earliest works in this medium. *Still Life with Shell* of 1940 (no. 8), one of the earliest works to employ cut-outs, included a shell, rendered in cut paper and drawing, that Matisse had brought back from Tahiti in 1930 – a studio prop that he deployed often. In other attempts to decipher the iconography presumably present in *Memory of Oceania* and search for figuration among the flat signs, it has been suggested that the composition is based on a photograph that Matisse took of a schooner from his window in Tahiti in 1930.[29] Lydia Delectorskaya, on the other hand, relates *Memory of Oceania* to drawing.[30] Either way, unlike *The Snail*, which is 'drawn from life', *Memory of Oceania* is mediated through memory at several removes. The curtain, window, tropical vegetation, boat and mast seen in both paintings of *Window in Tahiti* are all transposed to the abstracted, flat, geometrical planes of pure colour in *Memory of Oceania*.

Matisse's use of gouache to render the large, solid areas of colour in these two paintings also foreshadows the medium, technique and aesthetic of the cut-outs. The black and white photograph that served as the basis for the composition, and presumably reverberated in later returns to this theme and memory, was taken from the window of his hotel overlooking the port of Papeete; in the foreground it shows thick tree foliage, which is silhouetted against the light of the sea and landscape beyond, and through which the body and mast of a boat moored in the harbour are just visible. Louis Aragon, however, noted that the view through the window in *Memory of Oceania* is not based on Tahiti, but Nice.[31] This act of substitution, of something local and mundane transformed into something exotic and wonderful, was also apparently enacted for other cut-outs dealing with Matisse's (idealised) memories of the South Pacific. Jacqueline Duhême recalled of the making of Matisse's 1946 *Oceania* and *Polynesia* panels that, when 'he was starting work on a tapestry of printed textiles with birds ... we would go to the exit of the municipal sewers in Nice', where he would sketch the seagulls hovering over the sea (see p. 256).[32]

In autumn 1952 Pierre Matisse began to negotiate with Sidney Brody and his wife on behalf of his father for a large-scale ceramic commission, to be situated in the open-air patio of their house in Los Angeles.[33] Eyewitness testimony, either in terms of written accounts or photographs of the studio that can be dated, helps us to reconstruct certain moments precisely. In September 1952, for example, Alfred H. Barr, Jr and his wife visited Matisse at Cimiez and saw *The Snail* and *Memory of Oceania* under way, which were presumably both begun that summer while Matisse was working on *The Swimming Pool* in the evenings (both of the former works are dated 1953, which is when their forms were set). On 28 September 1952 the photographer Tetsuo Abe took a series of colour photographs of the Hôtel Régina, which documented several of Matisse's cut-outs in progress. In one we see just the right-hand section of *The Parakeet and the Mermaid* still pinned to the wall, while the rest of the composition has already been traced and transferred; next to it are a drawing of St Dominic for the Vence chapel and a series of coloured squares and rectangles of gouached paper pinned to the wall and presumably ready for use in another work, together with a couple of shapes already cut into foliate patterns (p. 69). Another photograph from the same day documents *The Bell* (no. 89), *Venus* (no. 115), and *Flowing Hair*, which are pinned

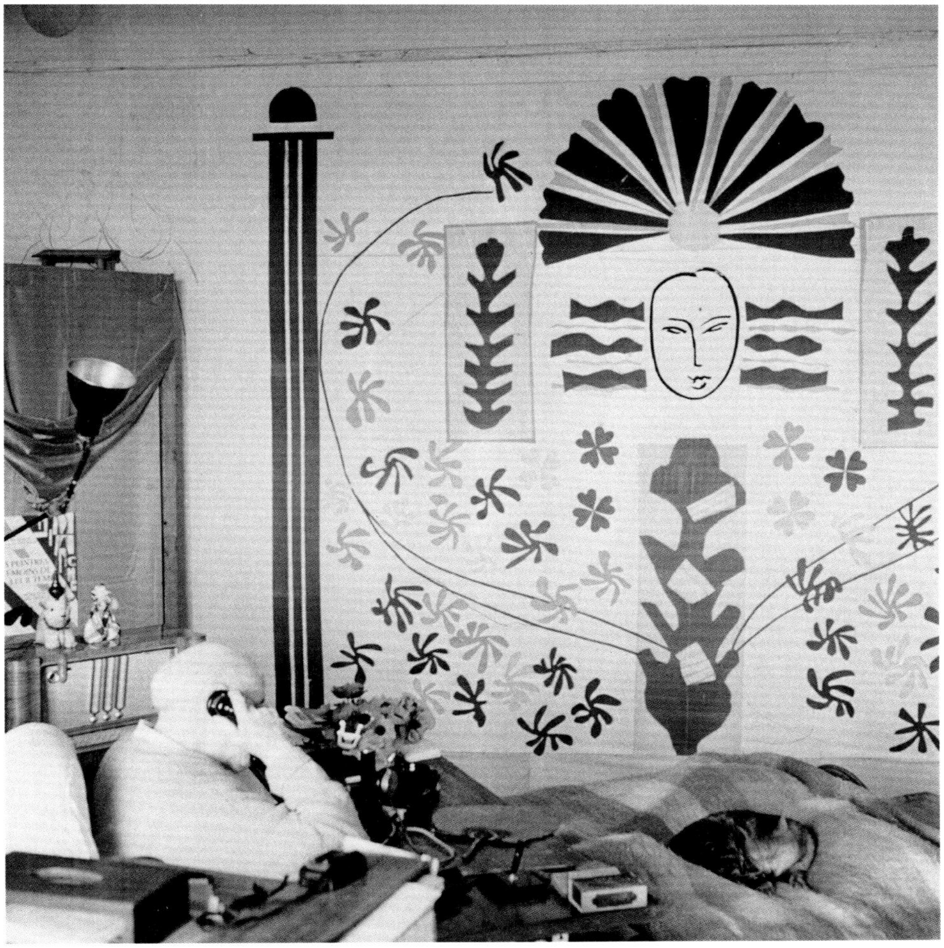

Fig. 50 Hélène Adant, Matisse at the Hôtel Régina, Nice c. 1953

up on the wall next to the painting *Sleeping Nymph and Faun Playing the Flute*, begun in 1935 (p. 81). Photographs of *Large Decoration with Masks* in progress reveal that the work was constructed across the wall from right to left and also that Matisse paired the composition down from its early state, choosing to reshuffle the colour combinations of the quatrefoil patterns and subtract some of the details, such as the 'head' at the centre of each of the four 'petals' (a detail that the photographs show was added after the quatrefoils and that Matisse must have decided was an unnecessary embellishment) as well as some extra 'leaves' of foliage surrounding the quatrefoil motif (pp. 78–80, 82).

These photographs document the meticulous and painstaking process of building up, reconfiguring and editing the compositions over the weeks and months that they took shape in Matisse's studio, with *La Négresse* also captured still in progress.[34] The tessellated pattern of *Large Decoration with Masks*, with its schema of multicoloured quatrefoils intended as a ceramic decoration, recalls the mosaic tilework of the Alhambra in Granada. Matisse visited this Moorish palace while spending some months in the south of Spain, in both Cordoba and Seville, in late 1910 and early 1911, just after he visited a major exhibition of Islamic art in Munich and just a year before he made his first trip to Morocco, arriving in Tangiers in 1912. During this time Matisse apparently even acquired tiles from the Alhambra.[35]

Matisse must have embarked on the Brody commissions almost immediately, judging by the photographs of it already well under way in the studio that September.[36] The speculative nature of *Large Decoration with Masks* – begun without Matisse having the measurements of the space that the piece was to occupy in the Brodys' home, nor with a contract – echoes some of the mishaps around the Barnes *Dance*, which would also result in no fewer than three versions being produced (fig.12). A letter from Pierre Matisse to his father from 8 October 1952 outlined a little of what the Brodys wanted from this outdoor ceramic work and included a sketch of the proposed place for it and the height of the space allocated, though not the width, which had yet to be determined.[37] But Matisse had already begun work on *Large Decoration with Masks*, which would prove far too wide for the available space. On 12 October 1952 Matisse wrote to Pierre that Picasso had visited him and admired the maquette for the Brody commission (presumably *Large Decoration with Masks*), remarking of his friend and rival: 'He never says anything, as a rule. But on this occasion he said spontaneously that it was "very beautiful. Only Matisse can make something like that."'[38] By 2 November 1952 Matisse wrote to his son triumphantly: 'It's a complete success ... I think it will be my last work in this genre. I have given it all my strength, and I shall not try to do anything better. As you know, I only ever made *one* theatre decor, *one* chapel ... and now this *one* ceramic.'[39] On 12 November Matisse continued

> My anxieties fade away when I am taken to see the maquette for the ceramic panel. It's so clear and strong. The combination of the masks and the flowers is something that has never been done before. It is such a consolation for me to have achieved this at the end of my life. As I already told you, both Picasso and Jacques Prevert liked it very much. So did the General of the Dominicans, who saw it the day before yesterday, and Father Couturier, who came today. I felt that they really admired it.[40]

But the Brodys turned down this work, a rejection that must have been all the more painful to Matisse, given how satisfied he was with it.

Large Decoration with Fruits of 1953 was Matisse's second attempt to meet the requirements of the Brodys after the first had been declined, demonstrating the unbridled enthusiasm and energy Matisse displayed during this time. Like *Large Decoration with Masks*, this work would also prove to be too large for the Brodys and would be rejected. Matisse originally employed three of the same line drawings of masks or faces that he used in *Large Decoration with Masks*, before replacing these with the oranges, some of which then most probably spilled over into the brush and ink drawing *Nude with Oranges* of 1953. Matisse seemed to have learned the lessons of *Large Decoration with Masks* and of having a more stripped-down composition. However, after *Decoration Fruits*, too, was rejected by the Brodys, Matisse began his third successive composition for them, *Apollo*, of 1953 (fig. 50).[41] In mid-May 1953 the Brodys visited Matisse in Nice, where they saw the finished version of *Apollo*. On 18 May 1953 Matisse wrote to his son:

> The two California giants, Mr. and Mrs. Brody, came to see me. Their first visit was very discouraging. They seemed to be completely unresponsive, looked at nothing when they walked around the apartment and were in no way stirred or enthused when they came to the maquette for their ceramic ... The next time they came, they confirmed that my maquette was much too large for their wall. I told them that it was theirs, if they wanted it. But if they didn't want it, that was of no importance, because I would keep it for myself.[42]

The Sheaf from 1953 (no. 136) was Matisse's fourth and final attempt to produce a maquette for a ceramic mural decoration for the Brodys' patio in Los Angeles, and, following their visit to Matisse in Nice in May 1953, this was accepted. If Matisse's letter to his son on 18 May 1953 initially expresses disappointment with the Brodys' visit to his studio in the Hôtel Régina and their rejection of *Apollo*, the same letter also relates that an agreement had been reached about what they were seeking in this commission, after seeing samples of ceramic that had just been delivered to Matisse, and that they were hoping for, as Matisse put it to his son, 'a vivid scatter of color on a white background'.[43] Matisse must have begun work on *The Sheaf* shortly afterwards. Its vegetal forms and colour palette clearly follow on from *The Parakeet and the Mermaid* (no. 118) from the year before (one wonders if they might even be remnants). A series of four colour photographs document its development and reveal that a centrifugal composition radiated out from the bottom and centre, gradually extending out in all directions towards the black line on the wall that demarcates its limits.

The Brody commission, which resulted in one successful design and three rejected ones, must have exhilarated and infuriated Matisse in equal measure. Not all of the commissions that Pierre Matisse secured for his father during this time resulted in even one of the designs being accepted. In the case of *Ivy in Flower* (no. 134) – the commission for the design of a stained-glass window in the mausoleum of Albert Lasker at Sleepy Hollow, New York – Matisse worked on a design he was very pleased with for several months, only to have it rejected. Lasker owned nine paintings by Matisse and was the father of Mrs Frances Brody, who commissioned Matisse for the ceramic tile decoration in Los Angeles around this time. Mr and Mrs Lasker had visited Matisse in Nice in 1949, while in April 1952, only the month prior to his death, Mr Lasker had been pleased to receive a letter from Matisse decorated with red and blue flowers. A letter from Pierre Matisse to Mary Lasker on 5 December 1952 accepted the commission. Lasker owned Matisse's painting of the same name from 1941, the first work he produced after his gruelling operation for intestinal cancer (fig. 49). This painting shows that Matisse essentially based the later cut-out version on a detail of the ivy in flower in a vase and the formal contrast between the berries and the leaves in the earlier painting. Matisse began the cut-out composition in November 1952 and it was finished in April 1953. *Ivy in Flower* continues the central motif of a window with foliage visible beyond it, as seen in the Vence interior paintings of c.1947–8 and the stained-glass window designs for the Vence chapel.[44]

On 31 March 1954 Alfred H. Barr, Jr wrote to Matisse to ask him to consider designing a stained-glass window for the Union Church in Tarrytown, New York, in memory of Abby Aldrich Rockefeller.[45] It was to be Matisse's last commission. An undated letter from René d'Harnoncourt to Barr after the former's visit to Matisse in Nice, received by the latter on 6 July 1954, gives a vivid glimpse into Matisse's studio and health that final summer:

> Matisse in spite of his condition (he seems almost paralyzed, speaks with a low voice but shows by his questions that he is really listening) has started yesterday on the window. The start was handsome but not yet exciting. He will go ahead with it but cannot promise to finish nor can he give a date by which he hopes to have it ready. He is leaving today for the country and will take it with him but there is a question if he wants or can work in the country.[46]

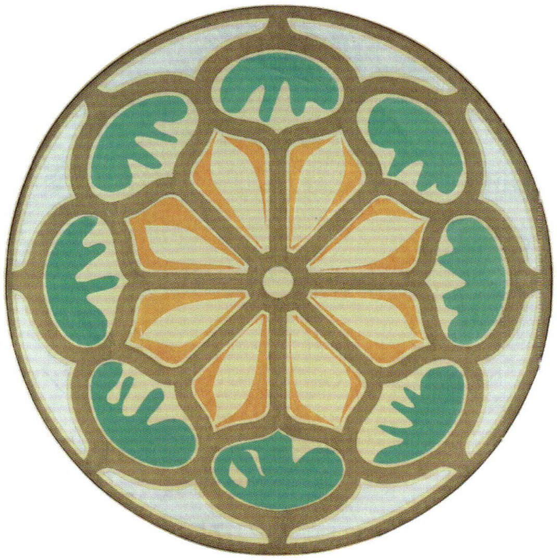

Fig. 51 *The Rose Window (La Rosace)*, maquette for the stained-glass window in the Union Church, Pocantico Hills, Tarrytown, New York 1954. Gouache on paper, cut and pasted, and pencil, 109 × 109.4 (42⅞ × 43⅛). Private collection

On 23 August 1954 Matisse wrote to Barr from the Régina to inform him of his progress on *The Rose Window* (fig. 51). His letter emphasises the way in which he lived with his works and benefited from sustained observation of them, including an architectural blueprint of the window, which Barr sent him as an aid to the composition: 'I have installed the latter on the wall of my studio and have lived daily in sympathy with them.'[47] But Matisse's increasing exhaustion was also showing: 'Being fatigued at the beginning of the summer, I have spent some weeks in rest before giving you this news that I felt my spirit caught by this project.'[48]

During the spring and summer of 1954 Alberto Giacometti drew Matisse's portrait. As Hilary Spurling recounts, Giacometti 'told Françoise Gilot that what moved him most at these encounters was to see "a great artist still so absorbed in trying to create when death was at his doorstep … when there was no longer time"'.[49] With *The Rose Window*, Matisse's work, like his life, had come full circle. The increasing escalation of scale and ambition, combined with an ever-quickening pace of production in the final two years of Matisse's life, is remarkable. Each of these works by Matisse was completed in an ever-closer race with death, *against* death, in fact. As Matisse knew all too well, labouring ceaselessly in his studio to make these apparently effortless compositions, creation is hard work, with no time to spare.[50]

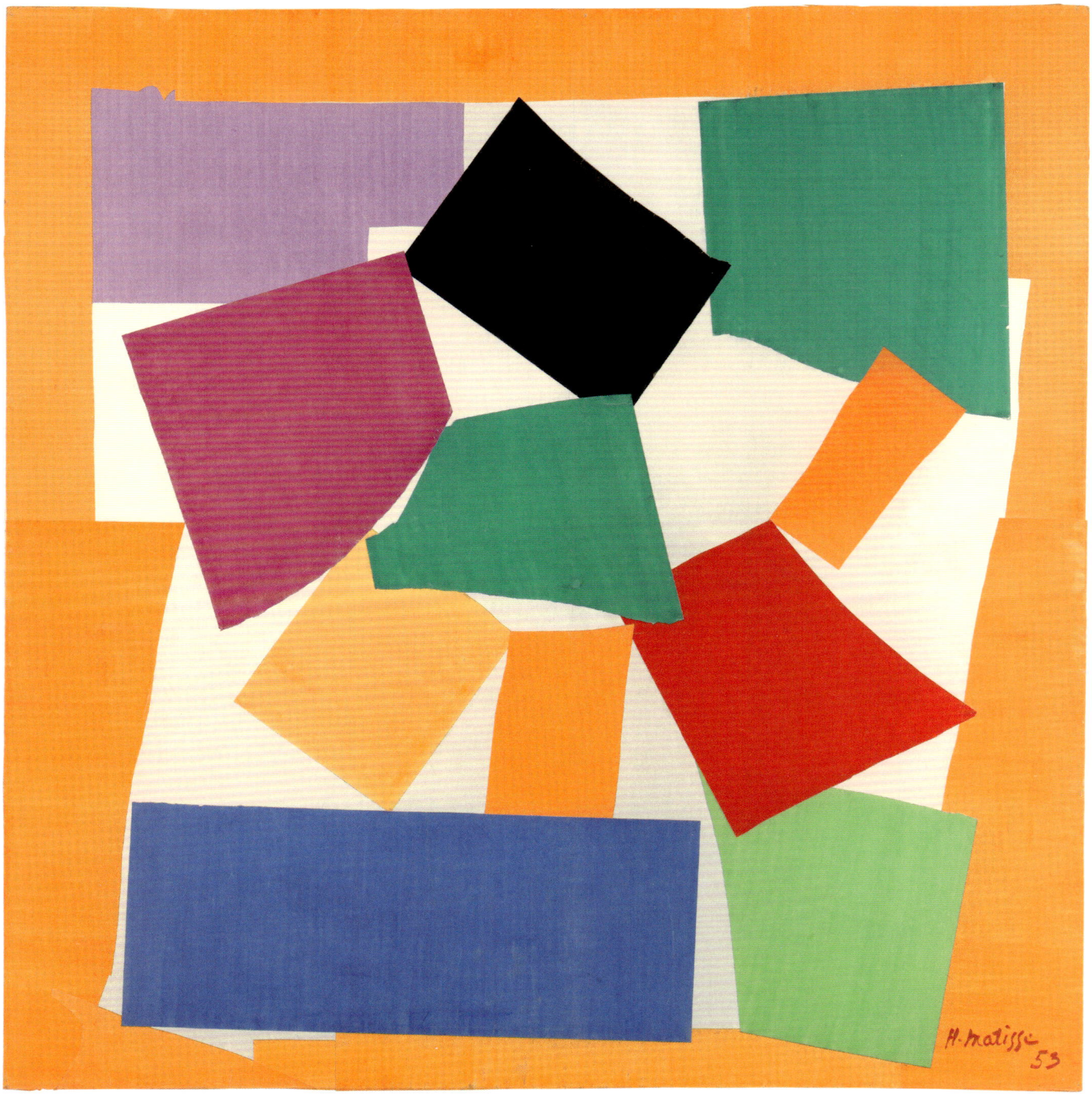

129. *The Snail* 1953
Gouache on paper, cut and pasted, on paper,
mounted on canvas, 286.4 × 287 (112¾ × 113)

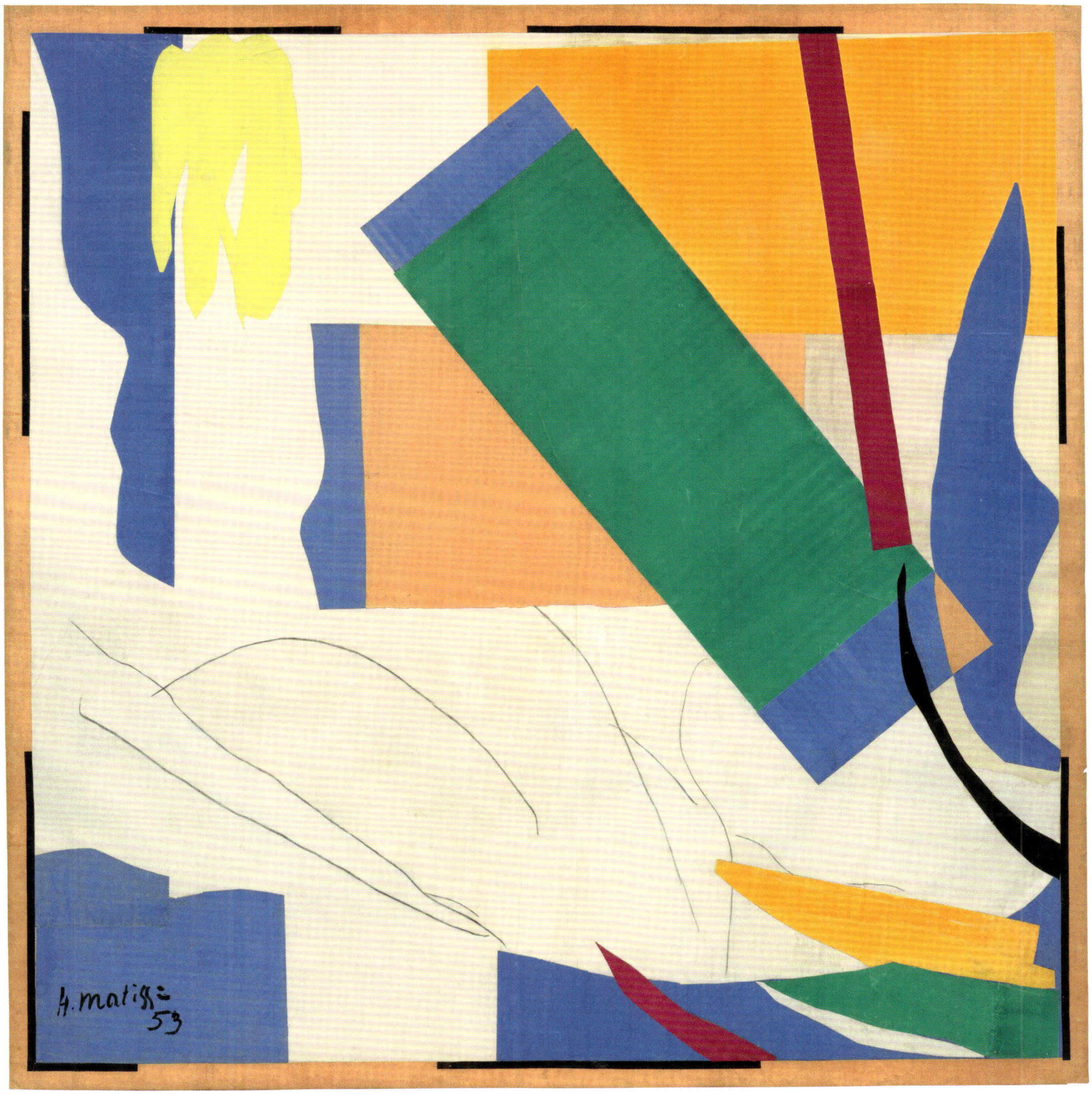

130. *Memory of Oceania* summer 1952 – early 1953
Gouache on paper, cut and pasted, and charcoal on paper, mounted on canvas, 284.4 × 286.4 (112 × 112⅞)

131. *Large Decoration with Masks* 1953
Preliminary maquette for ceramic
Gouache on paper, cut and pasted, and
ink on white paper, mounted on canvas
353.6 × 996.4 (139¼ × 392¼)

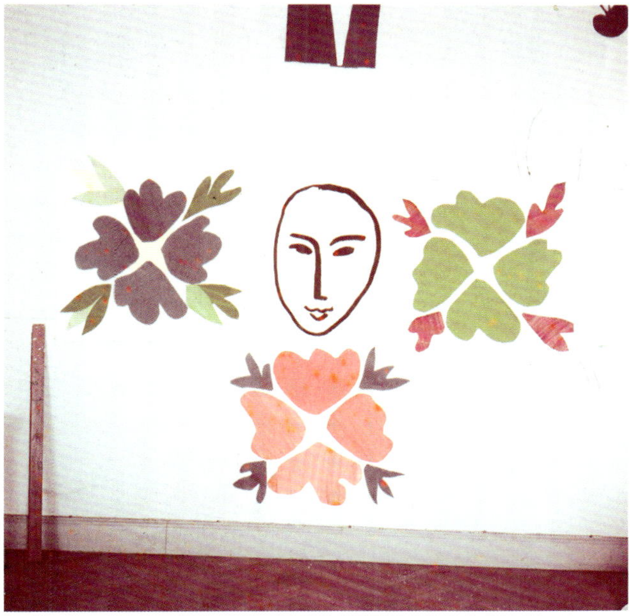

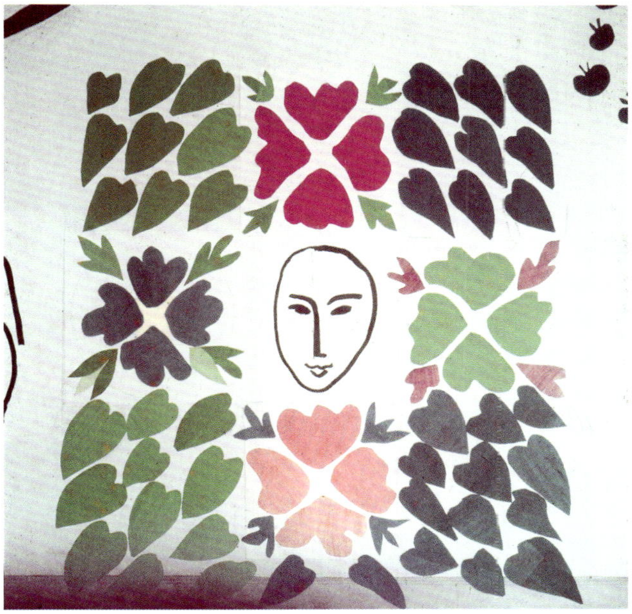

132. Four states of *Large Decoration with Masks*, Hôtel Régina, Nice, 1953

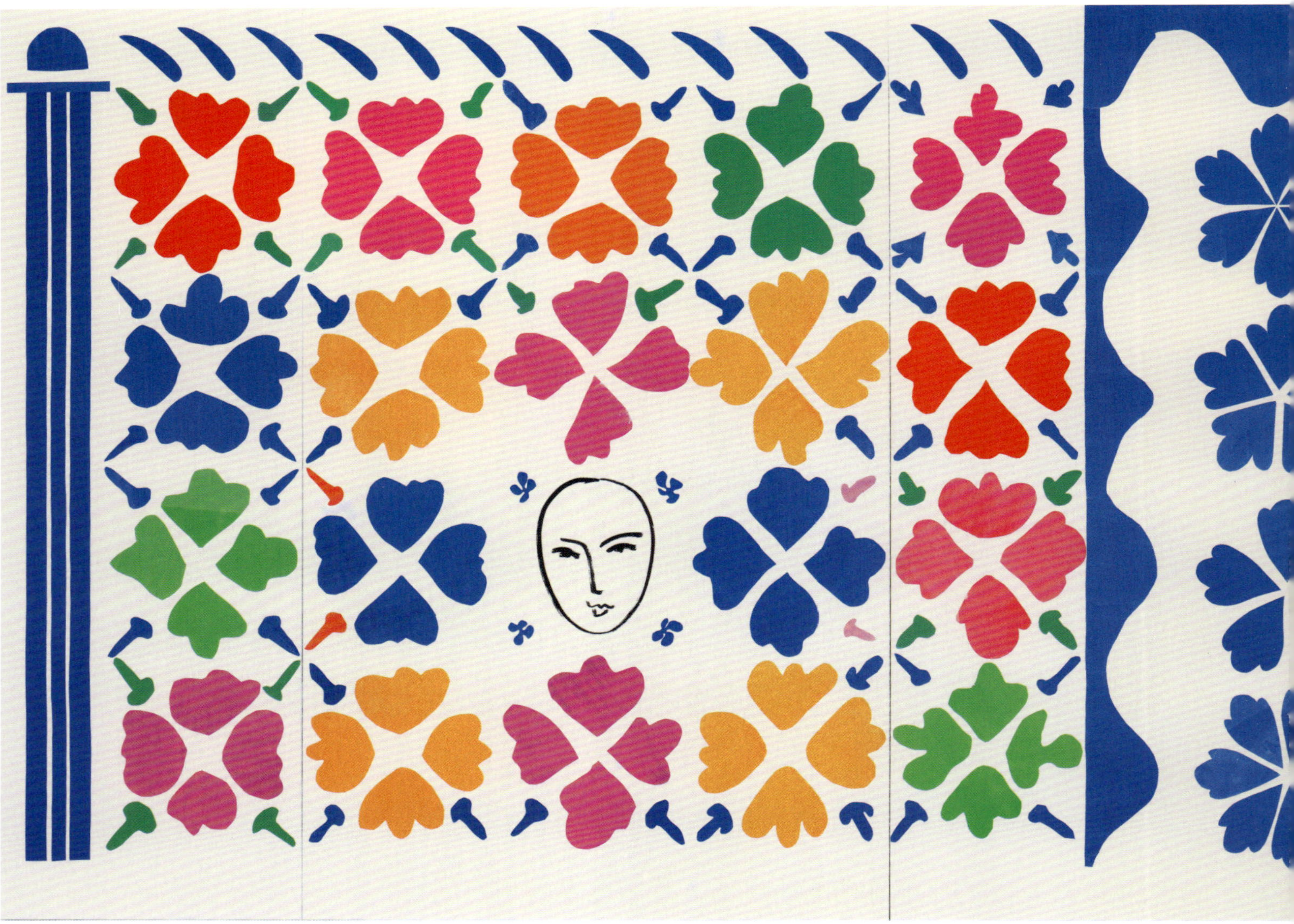

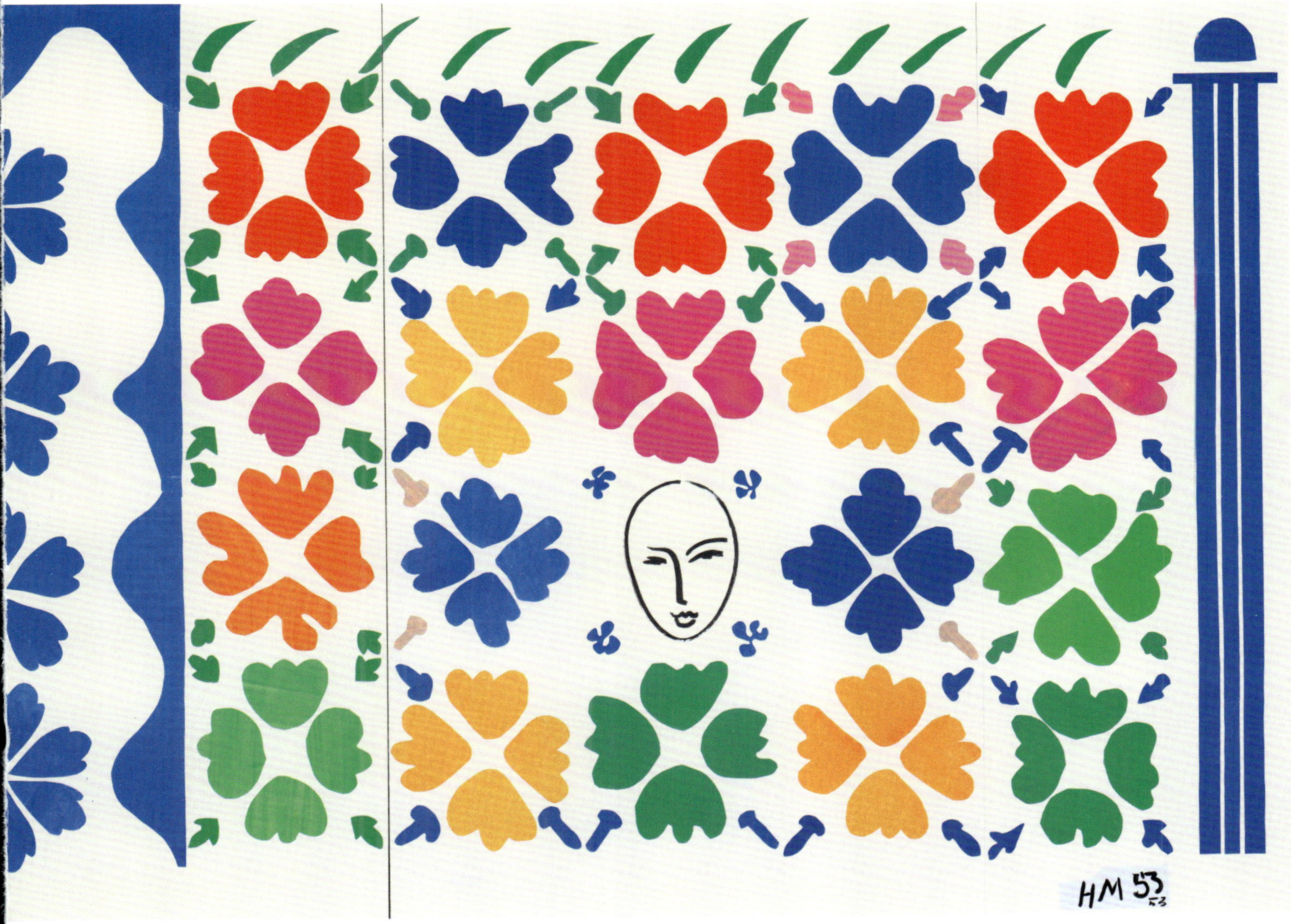
HM 53

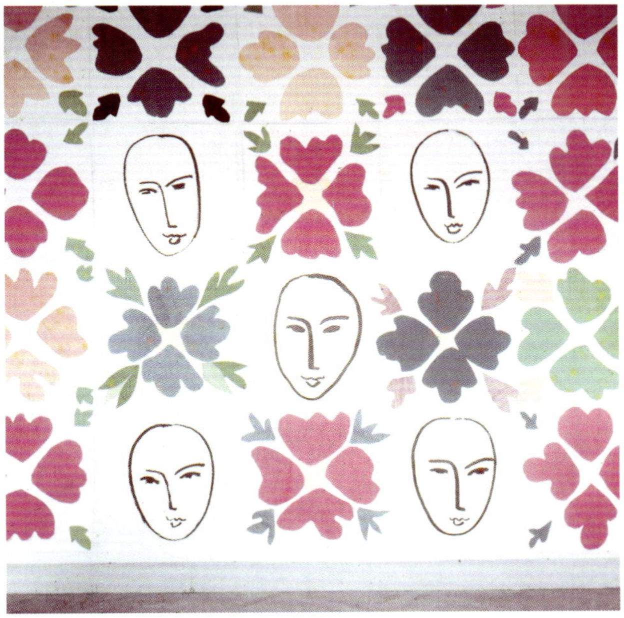

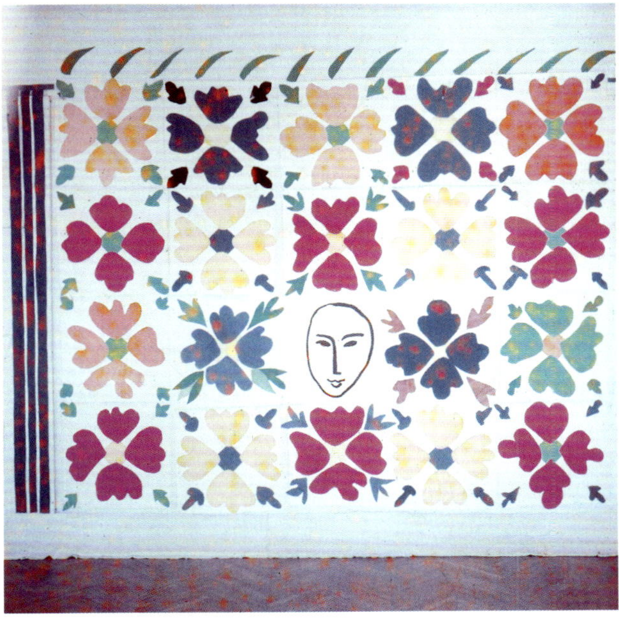

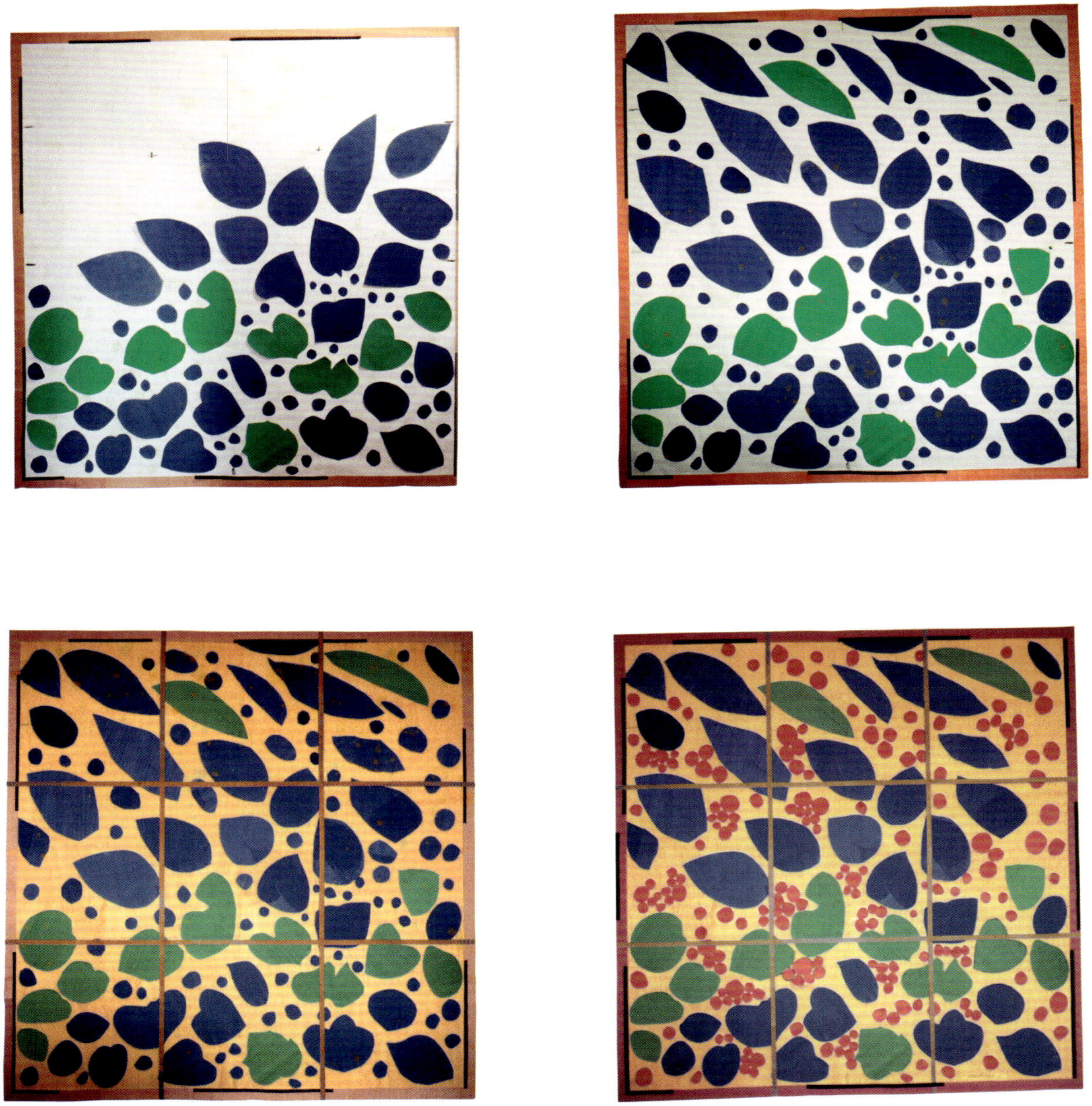

133. Four states of *Ivy in Flower*, Hôtel Régina, Nice, 1953

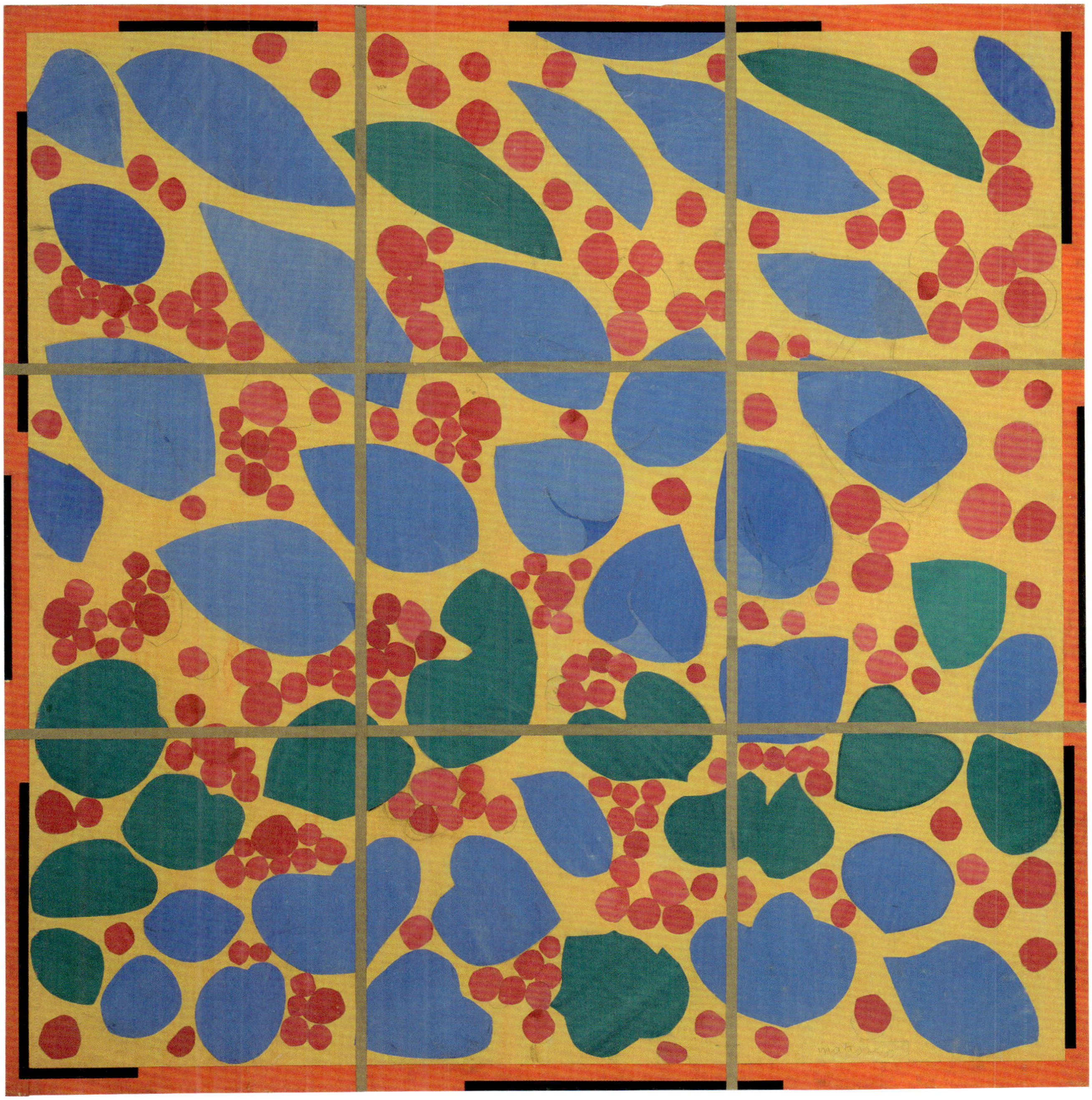

134. *Ivy in Flower* 1953
Maquette for stained-glass window (realised 1956)
Gouache on paper, cut and pasted, and pencil
on coloured paper, 284.2 × 286.1 (111⅞ × 112⅝)

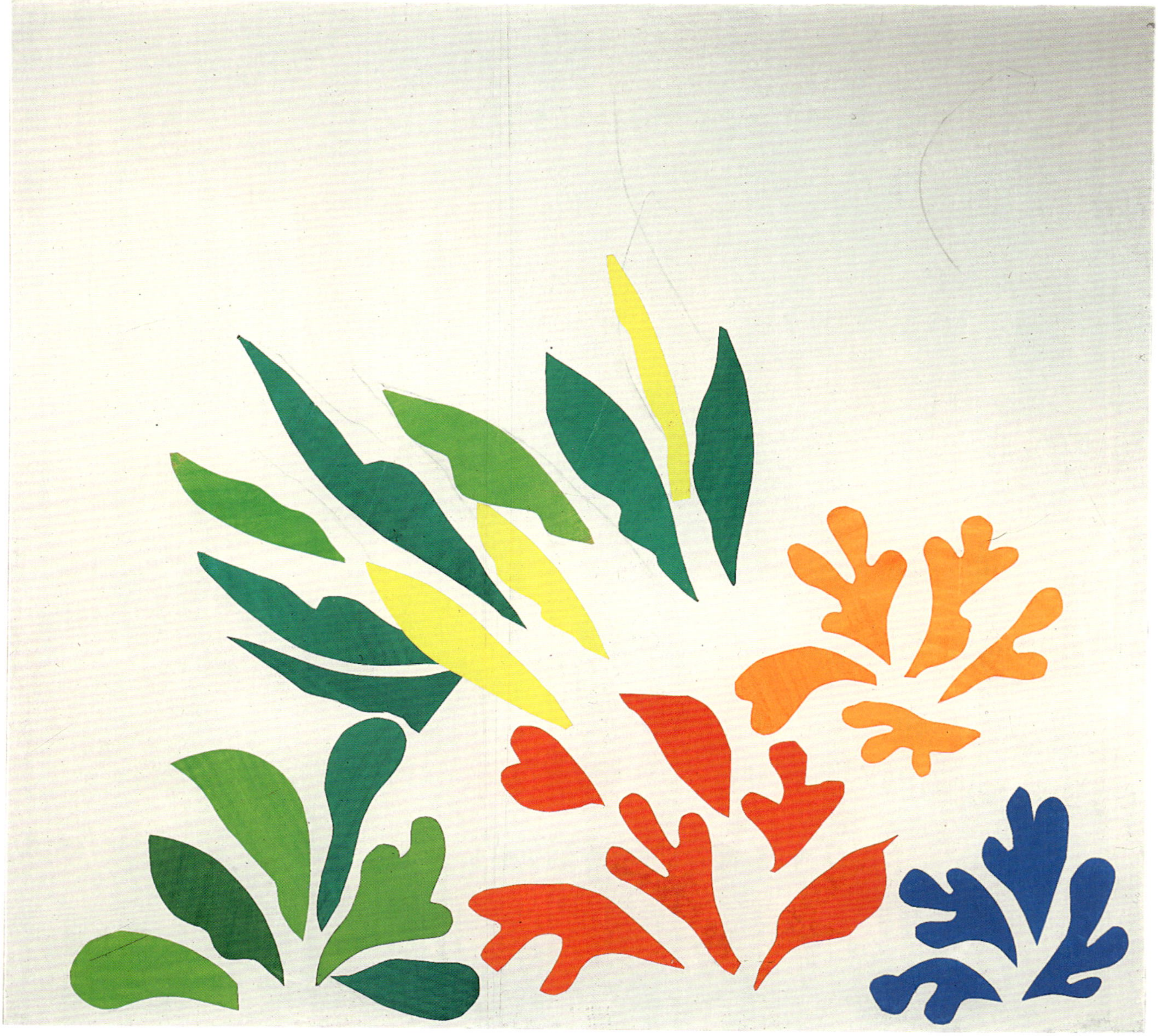

135. *Acanthuses* 1953
Maquette for ceramic (realised 1953)
Gouache on paper, cut and pasted, and charcoal
on white painted paper, mounted on canvas
311.7 × 351.8 (122¾ × 138½)

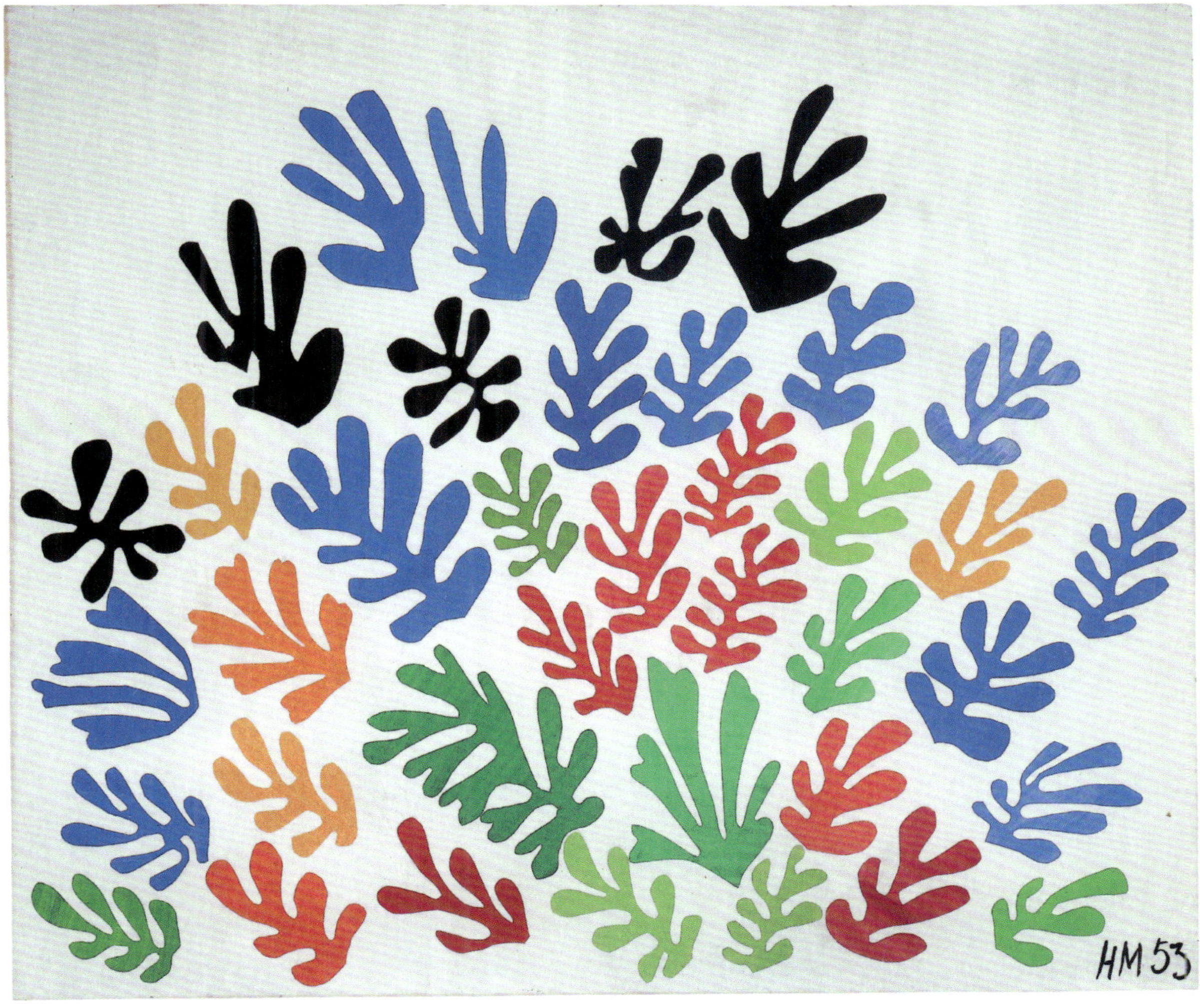

136. *The Sheaf* 1953
Maquette for ceramic (realised 1953)
Gouache on paper, cut and pasted, on paper,
mounted on canvas, 294 × 350 (115¾ × 137¾)

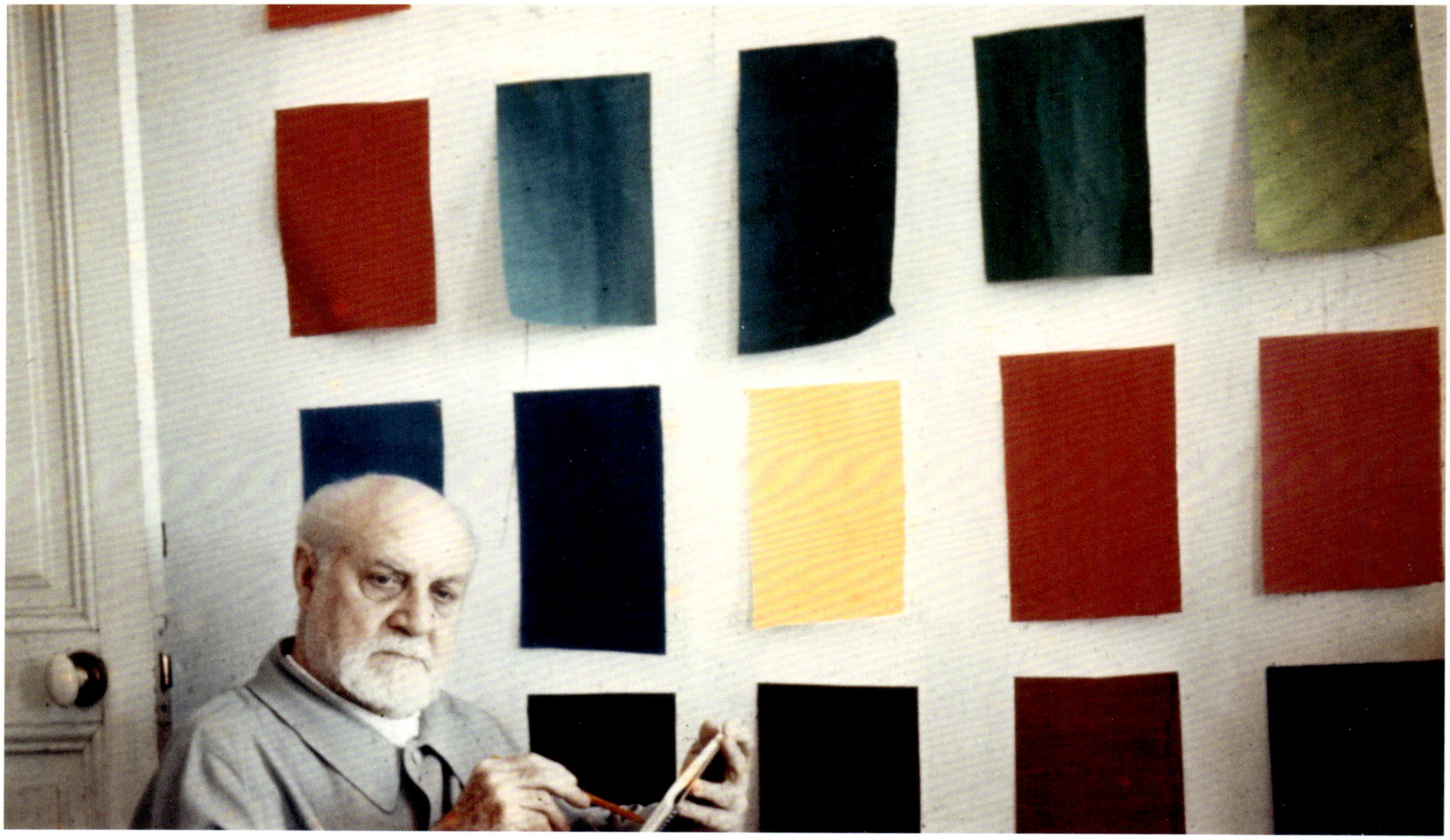

Fig. 52 Matisse in front of gouache-painted papers

MATERIALS and TECHNIQUES

Karl Buchberg, Markus Gross and Stephan Lohrengel

During the last decade of his life Henri Matisse deployed two simple materials – white paper and gouache – to create works of wide-ranging size and complexity. An unorthodox artist's implement, a pair of scissors, was the tool Matisse used to transform paint and paper into a world of plants, animals, figures and symbols.

The artistic importance of these late works is widely recognised. However, there is an almost complete absence of systematic technical investigation into the cut-outs. The only detailed study of materials, techniques, studio practices, conservation and long-term preservation of these works was published in 1977 by Antoinette King, then Paper Conservator at The Museum of Modern Art, New York.[1] Information gained from conservation carried out on *The Parakeet and the Mermaid* (no. 118) and other works has also been published.[2] The present essay seeks to fill that gap by presenting findings from investigations conducted at Fondation Beyeler, Riehen/Basel,[3] and The Museum of Modern Art, New York.[4]

The cut-outs were created in distinct phases. The raw materials – paper and gouache – were purchased, and the two materials combined: studio assistants painted sheets of paper with gouache. Matisse then cut shapes from these painted papers and arranged them into compositions. For smaller compositions the artist worked directly on a board using pins. The larger compositions were arranged on the walls of the studio by assistants, as Matisse directed. Subsequently, cut-outs were mounted permanently, either in the studio or in Paris by professional mounters.

The preparation of materials in the studio

Paper

During the early period of the cut-outs Matisse would use a variety of papers: most often papers painted with gouache in his studio but also white writing papers, printers' coloured papers that had been sent to him by the publisher Tériade, and blue wrapping paper.[5] For the vast majority of the cut-out oeuvre, however, Matisse chose papers, as for his drawings, that were standard French artists' papers made by Arches, Barjon Moirans, and Canson & Montgolfier.[6] It is not possible to demonstrate any preference for one make or another. It seems fair to assume that he purchased readily obtainable artists' papers.[7]

Paper from the manufacturer Arches is found mainly in works made between 1943 and 1948. A single sheet measured 40.5 × 52.5 cm. This wove paper, without laid lines, was made sheet by sheet on a cylinder mould, which gave it its distinctive surface texture and visible deckle edge on all sides. The watermark, in horizontal capitals, is in the lower right corner (fig. 53). Very occasionally, Matisse used other papers made by Arches, such as 'MBM MADE IN FRANCE INGRES D'ARCHES' with laid lines, as in *Vegetal Elements*[8] and *The Sheaf* (no. 136).

Papers made by Papeteries F. Barjon in Moirans, Isère, were mainly used for the blue shapes in the *Blue Nude* series of 1952–3. These papers were produced on a Fourdrinier machine. The pressmark takes the form of continuous writing along the edge of the paper, and one side of the paper has a distinct, lozenge-shaped surface texture (fig. 54).

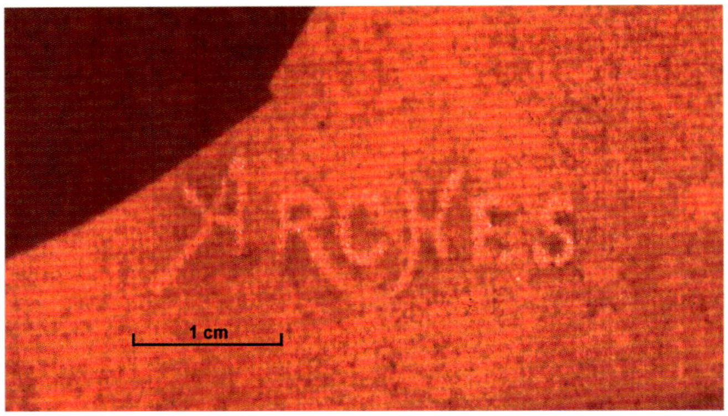

Fig. 53 Arches watermark (detail) in transmitted light, *White Alga on Red and Green Background*

Fig. 54 Barjon Moirans watermark (detail) in raking light, *Blue Nude I*

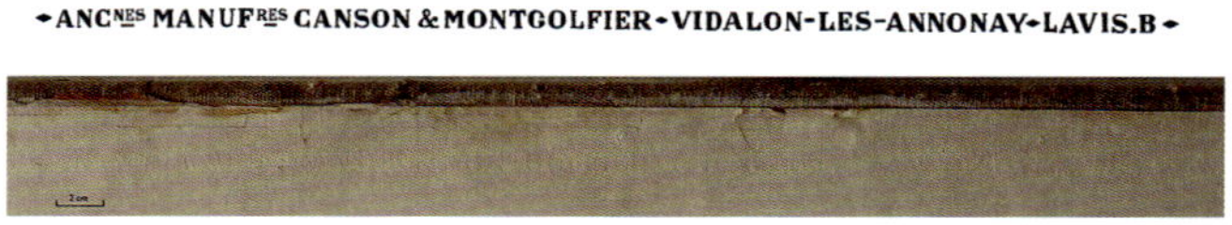

Fig. 55 Canson Lavis B watermark (detail) in raking light (below) transcribed in ink (above), *Acanthuses*

Fig. 56 Pencil drawing on verso of *White Alga on Red and Green Background*

The paper 'Lavis B', made by Canson & Montgolfier in Vidalon, is predominantly found in the late, large-format works, often also as the plain picture ground. This faintly cream-coloured paper was made on a Fourdrinier machine. The pressmark runs forwards along the edge of the paper, and the mould side, unlike the felt side, has slight graining. The papers used in Matisse's studio were taken from a roll that was 150 cm wide. This was either cut into manageable sheets or used as long lengths of paper (fig. 55).

'S.A.V. Velin',[9] made by Canson & Montgolfier, was not used in the studio but was added later when a work was mounted in Paris, for example in *Blue Nude with Green Stockings* (no. 117). Matisse occasionally employed other makes of paper, such as 'Canson & Montgolfier Technique' as the background paper in *Creole Dancer* (no. 85), 'Canson & Montgolfier Ingres' in *Zulma* (no. 84), and 'Paris Teinte Fort' in *Acanthuses* (no. 135).

It is not unusual to find several different papers in one work. In *Acanthuses*, for instance, the picture ground and most of the shapes are made from Lavis B by Canson & Montgolfier. The blue shapes are cut from paper made by Papeteries F. Barjon, and some of the green shapes are cut from Paris Teinte Forte by an unidentified manufacturer.

Discarded drawings and sketches can be found on the unpainted backs of certain shapes. Evidently, if a drawing was not considered to be of sufficient quality to be kept permanently the paper could be reused for other purposes. A pencil drawing of a seated woman appears on the reverse of *White Alga on Red and Green Background* (no. 59, fig. 56), and there are ink sketches on papers in *Blue Nude, the Frog* (no. 116), *Composition (The Velvets)* (no. 65) and *The Sheaf*.

Gouache

The colour on Matisse's cut-outs is produced using gouache – a water-based, opaque, quick-drying, matte paint that consists of pigment, binder and often a white pigment or filler to increase opacity.

Manufacturers of gouache supplied a wide range of hues in each colour, which is seen in period sample charts. Lydia Delectorskaya said: 'The palette of gouache H. Matisse used was very rich, each colour contained 5, 6, or 7 varieties: the red went from madder to vermillion, the orange, from cadmium red to lemon yellow, etc. Each, in addition, could have been more or less diluted, which presented for the artist a very large choice.'[10]

In 2012 the Conservation Department at The Museum of Modern Art was given a set of seventy-nine gouache-painted paper samples for research purposes taken from sheets remaining in the Matisse studios.[11] This 'sample set' has been analysed for both composition and light stability.[12] The cut-outs in the Beyeler Collection have also been analysed.[13] The results indicate that Matisse indeed used many distinct variations within each colour. For example, there are over fifteen varieties of orange, eight turquoises and ten greens. A few colours contain only inorganic pigments: the range of blues consist of only ultramarine, and two of the four browns consist of only iron oxide with silicates. Many contain an inorganic pigment with one or more organic pigments.[14] Colours composed of only organic pigments are also present. A traditional pigment such as vermillion is used alongside organics that would have been first fabricated only in the 1950s. By this time the variety of hues available within each colour would have afforded Matisse a wide choice without having to mix to produce a desired result.

Recent interviews have raised questions about two long-standing and often published truths about the use of colour in Matisse's studio practice. The first is that Matisse used only Linel gouache, produced today by the French firm of Lefranc & Bourgeois, and the second is that colours were always used straight from the tube, never mixed. Jacqueline Duhême, studio assistant from July 1948 to August 1949, says that Matisse also used Sennelier gouache paints.[15] She also remembers mixing colours.

> Yes, sometimes he would use pure colours. And sometimes, he would experiment and say 'Let's put a pinch of purple, a pinch of red.' So I would 'cook' that up for him and try it on a piece of paper and he would say: 'Yes, that's interesting, keep going that way.' The hard work would then be to calculate the right quantity. We would usually obtain a different colour first and he would exclaim (hits on the table): 'No, I want this colour!'[16]

Paule Caen-Martin, studio assistant from February 1949 to 1952, says that Matisse would personally go to Maison Franco, art material suppliers in Nice, to choose and inspect gouache tubes for colour and freshness and that un-mixed Linel gouache was used exclusively.[17] Perhaps the variety of brands and mixing of colours occurred slightly earlier and was then discontinued as studio practice shifted.

Painting the paper

Sheets of paper, often cut from a much larger roll of paper, were painted by studio assistants. There was no apparent preference for one side of the paper as virtually none of the papers used for these works had a noticeable texture.[18] The goal was a sheet coated with intense saturated colour. Claude Duthuit, the artist's grandson, remembers large quantities of gouache being mixed in containers at the beginning of each day in the studio in Nice.[19] Varying quantities of pigment used in the commercial manufacture of each colour meant that the amount of water needed to thin each colour varied. When diluted gouache was applied to dry paper, the moisture would immediately sink into the paper making an even deposition of colour difficult. Multiple layers of paint had to be applied very swiftly, since dried gouache easily softened again if a wet brush was applied to it. The paint application on almost all the papers, therefore, had more or less obvious stroke variations.[20] Paule Caen-Martin remembers: 'I applied a first top coat, top to bottom, then, with the sheet still wet, I'd turn it round and perform the same operation the other way. I liked dense colors but other assistants, before or after me, left more transparency. Hence we intervened on the creation, in our own ways'.[21] Wet paint, at times, ran on the top side of a sheet and along the edges of the underside. One application of paint sometimes crossed another and there are traces where the brush was put down at the edge of the paper. There are occasional instances of the top side of the paper being roughened, of fresh paint being accidentally smeared, or of small bare patches that the brush missed. Finger marks on the edges and patches of smeared paint occurred when still damp papers were moved or fixed in position.[22] Papers were sometimes painted white.[23] In both *Composition Green Background* (no. 66) and *Composition (The Velvets)* shapes that had been painted white were

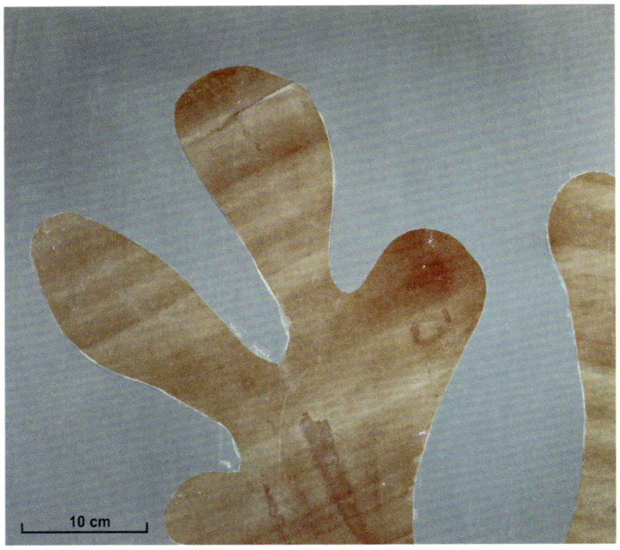

Fig. 57 Gouache on paper – application enhanced when viewed with reflected ultraviolet illumination, *Acanthuses*

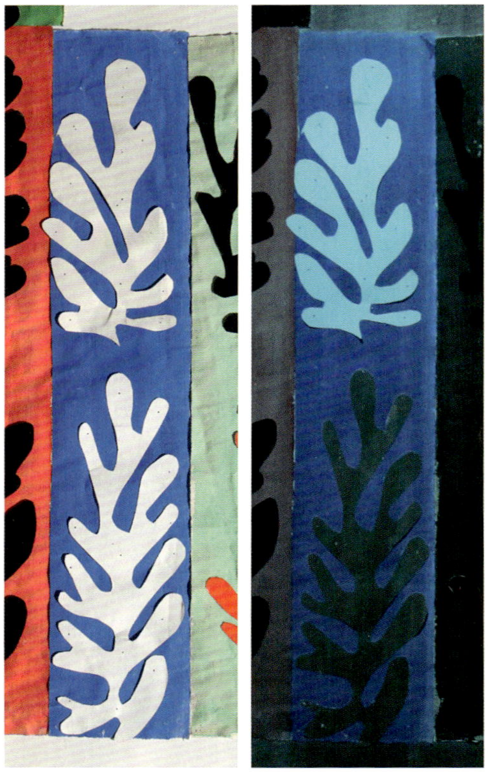

Fig. 58 White painted paper reversed to show unpainted side (top) and white painted paper, painted side up (below) under normal reflected light (left) and reflected ultraviolet light (right), *Composition (The Velvets)*

reversed and used with the unpainted underside as the viewing side. Shape, in these instances, was clearly more important than any intended tonal nuance (fig. 58). Sheets of paper acquired a gentle undulation due to the application of gouache on only one side of the sheet. The still-damp painted papers were either hung on the wall to dry or laid out on tables or on the floor and dried under weights. Dry coloured papers were stored until required for use.

Creating the cut-outs

Cutting

The process of cutting demonstrated Matisse's skill and confidence. A shape had been thought out in advance or evolved as it was being cut.[24] Matisse made numerous preparatory sketches in notebooks for motifs to be used in the cut-outs; however, these drawings were never transferred onto painted paper sheets as guides for cutting. Jacqueline Duhême remembers that the forms of the *Polynesia* tapestries resulted from sketches of birds Matisse made at the water's edge in Nice:

> There you have all these birds, seagulls that would hover and come to eat the sewage that flowed into the sea. This created large movements of seagulls, something he really liked. We would take a cab to go there and he would sketch in his sketchbook. The shapes of his cut-outs were never random. While cutting the papers, he would think of a shape he had seen. It was like drawing but with scissors. At some point, he became so skillful that he did not need to draw the shape: he would cut directly into the paper.[25]

Matisse used a range of tailoring and paper scissors, sometimes with relatively long blades, and held them in his right hand.[26] He would sit either in bed or in a chair holding the painted paper with his left hand and cutting swiftly, even when he was creating a complicated shape. Some shapes are very fine and complex as in *Composition (The Velvets)*; others are large, simple shapes, as in *The Swimming Pool* (no. 121) and *Acanthuses*, which were made from correspondingly large sheets of painted paper.

It is only on close examination that the viewer can see traces of the work process. Particularly in rounded shapes, there are angled edges and multiple small cuts into the shape itself that have arisen from the repeated re-setting of the scissors in order to adjust the direction of the blades (fig. 59). Some cuts are the result of the shape being corrected during the cutting process; this is seen very clearly in *Blue Nude I* (no. 109) in the area of the upper thigh. Occasionally, there is also evidence of paper having been torn.

Securing the composition: pins

Pins, drawing pins (thumb tacks) and thin nails were used as the method of attachment during the creation of the composition of the cut-outs: pin holes remain as visible evidence in most cut-outs.[27] When he was making the early, small-format works, Matisse worked on a board, which allowed him to arrange and pin shapes while sitting in a chair or sitting up in bed (fig. 60).

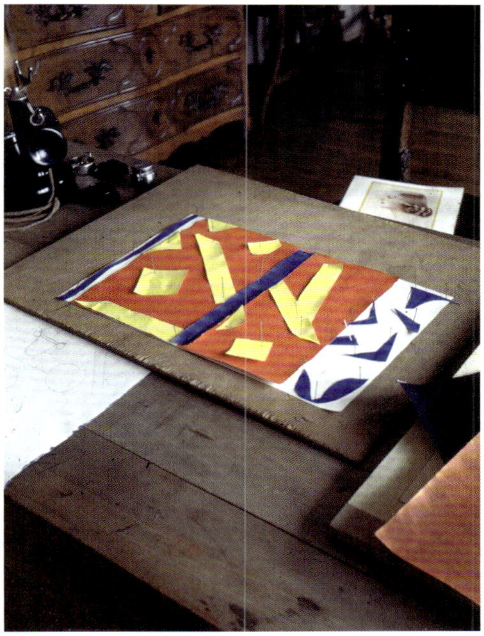

Fig. 60 *Matisse: His Art and His Public* (no.101)
An early state with pins photographed at Matisse's studio, Boulevard Montparnasse, Paris, 1951

In the case of the later, large-format works, Matisse would be far enough away from the wall to have the whole composition in his field of vision and would either give verbal instructions or point with a stick so that an assistant would know exactly where to hold the shape on the wall and how to move it if necessary. Once the position of the shape had been determined, it would be pinned to the wall. This method allowed the composition to be adjusted quickly and easily, since the pins could very simply be inserted into a board or hammered into the wall, and just as simply removed again. The more often the position of a shape was changed, the more pin holes there are, which sheds light on the making of individual works.[28] Countless pins were used in early works, such as *Oceania, the Sky* (no. 52) and *Oceania, the Sea* (no. 53), whereas the large shapes in *Acanthuses* were fixed to the studio wall with just five or six pins. It was less important to attach shapes flat on the wall with numerous pins than it was to determine their position within the composition as a whole.

The Fall of Icarus (no. 17) is one of very few cut-outs that still contains pin attachments. Unused shapes recently donated to the Musée Matisse, Le Cateau-Cambrésis, and Musée Matisse in Nice by the Matisse family show that, prior to being included into a composition, individual shapes were sometimes attached to each other to create a more complex shape by means of fine pins.[29] The pins were inserted into papers in the same way that a tailor pins a hem (fig. 61). In fewer instances a shape would be glued onto a white or coloured paper with dabs of glue and then incorporated into a composition.

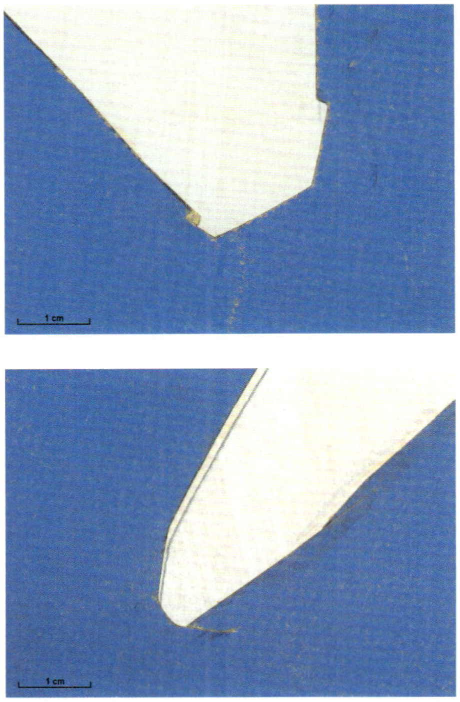

Fig. 59 The cutting process (two details), *Acanthuses*

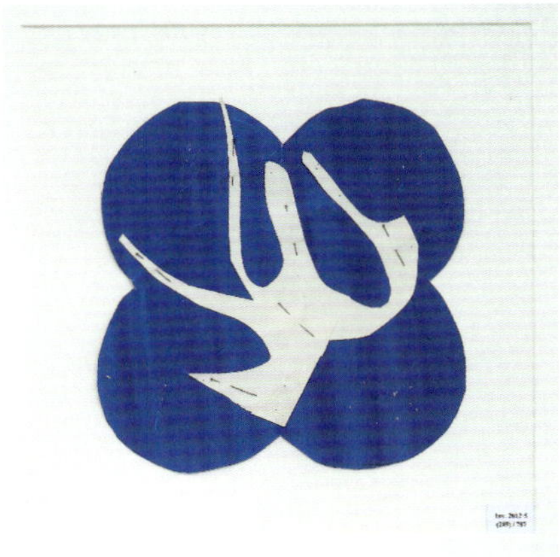

Fig. 61 White element pinned to blue. Inv. 2012–5 (289)/787. Musée Matisse, Le Cateau-Cambrésis. Gift of the Matisse family

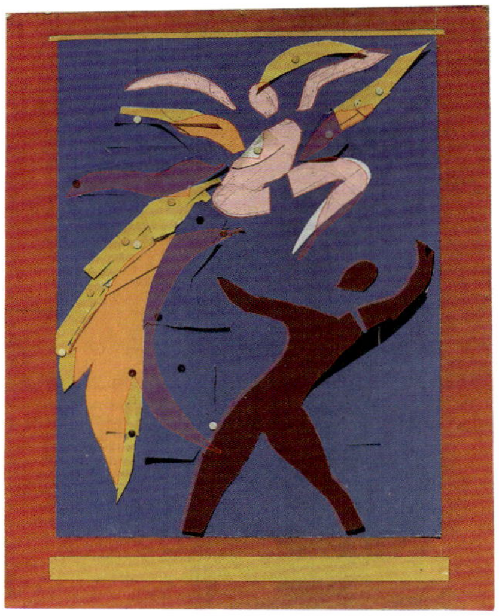

Fig. 62 Original composition (in red) superimposed on finished work, *Two Dancers*

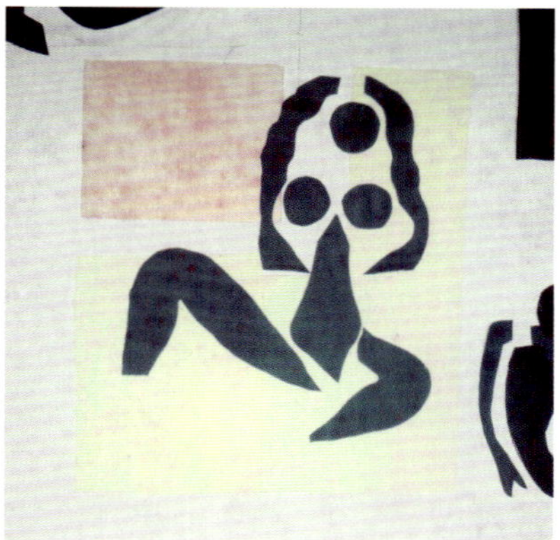

Fig. 63 Intermediate state, *Blue Nude, the Frog*, Hôtel Régina, Nice, c. 1952

The composition process

The act of cutting was inextricably intertwined with the almost playful process of constantly adding new shapes and removing others, of rearranging and re-pinning. While composing *Two Dancers* (no. 7), the basic working process was already emerging. The coloured cut shapes were arranged, pinned and glued on top of a preparatory drawing executed on a sheet of white paper. A photograph from 11 May 1938 shows the work in an early state (see fig. 21).[30] Matisse later altered it, adding shapes cut from both coloured, painted papers and white writing paper, attaching these in place with drawing pins (thumb tacks) in matching colours. The original composition still exists underneath these later additions (fig. 62). The process of composing over a drawing was only once repeated: in 1950 on *Zulma* (no. 84).

Matisse created shapes that were cut from one or more pieces of paper, often within a single work (e.g. *The Swimming Pool*). The final contour was most important to Matisse; the extent of overlap seems to have been of no importance. An image could be created using either a positive or a negative shape, often cut from the same sheet of paper, as can be seen in the left-hand section of *Composition, Black and Red* (no. 64). In *The Wave* (no. 122) one cut created the composition as the two sections were separated.

Photographs of the studio along with evidence in the cut-outs themselves show that the composition of the cut-outs often shifted. An early state of *Composition with Red Cross* (no. 54) can still be seen in a photograph of the studio wall in Vence in 1947 (p. 38). Where there is now a white frond in the upper right, the photograph shows a pale head shape. The residue of two dabs of glue and three pencil lines still mark the position of the head.[31] In the final state of the work two palm-like shapes, to the right and the left, have been replaced by red bands; green and blue bands have also been added above and below. The two palm shapes and the negatives of the orange shape in the upper left were subsequently used in *Flowering Tree (Mural Scroll)* (no. 61). On the photograph the pins attaching the shapes to the wall are clearly visible. The small holes left by the pins are still visible today.

For *The Parakeet and the Mermaid* (no. 118) Matisse searched for a compositional counterbalance to the parrot. During the course of this process he created first *Blue Nude IV* and then *Blue Nude I, II* and *III* (nos. 107, 109–111), some of which he tried out in the position now occupied by the siren. Additionally, many small pencil sketches for this series exist (no. 108). Initially uncertain as to the shape he was aiming for, Matisse drew directly with charcoal on the white support paper and gradually built up *Blue Nude IV* from a total of forty-six blue shapes. Lines partially erased during the compositional process are still visible on the background paper. Matisse was then so sure of the form of the seated female nude that he was able to cut the following three nudes, *Blue Nude I, II, III*, each from a single sheet of paper. Moreover, he cut these three figures in less than an hour.[32]

Matisse developed *Blue Nude, the Frog* in at least three identifiable stages. First he cut the blue shapes of the figure. A photograph has survived showing that he then tried out both red and yellow painted paper as the background (fig. 63). Ultimately he decided on a pure yellow background that is made up of fourteen irregular rectangles, in different sizes, of yellow painted paper. At the third and final stage the two pomegranates were added to the composition. Numerous pin holes in these shapes, which suggest an equally large number of position changes, indicate that they might have been originally used in *The Parakeet and the Mermaid,* which contains identical shapes and underwent numerous compositional changes over time.

When Matisse started to create large-format compositions in 1952, coloured picture grounds were replaced by the white wall of the studio or a white paper background. For these larger works Matisse developed a more economical working method. In the case of *La Négresse,*[33] *Large Decoration with Masks* (no. 131) and *Large Decoration with Fruits,*[34] for instance, the groups of four leaves or petals were first pinned to a piece of square paper, which was then attached to the wall. This method made it possible to swap or adjust the positions of these individual square blocks within the composition. The swapping of positions in this way is particularly evident in the documented four different states of *La Négresse*. When these compositions were mounted, the squares of white paper were removed and the shapes were attached to a single sheet of background paper.

In the case of *Acanthuses* the first step was to nail four sheets of background paper to the wall, which established the work's subsequent dimensions. Matisse then used a piece of charcoal on a long stick to draw lines on this background, as he also did for other works. On the basis of the number of pin holes in each shape, it has been possible to show that the

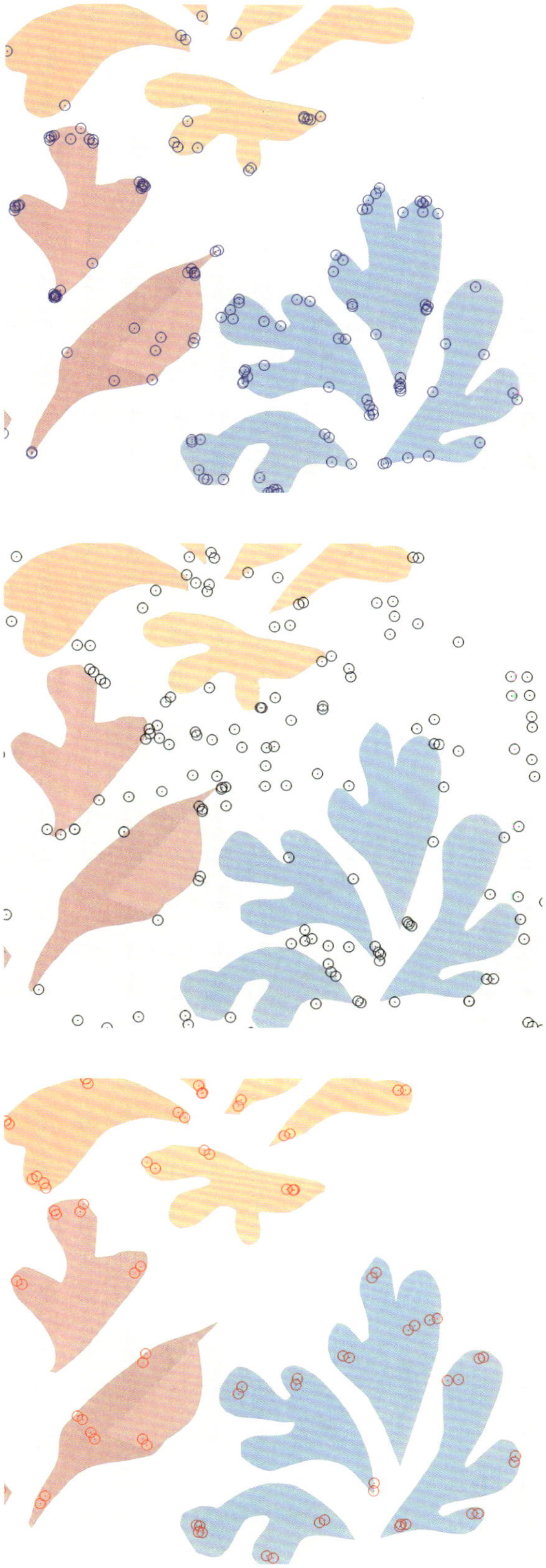

Fig. 64 *Acanthuses*, details of lower right corner. Top: pinholes from composition process (blue), centre: pinholes in background paper from composition process (black) and bottom: pinholes from tracing process (red)

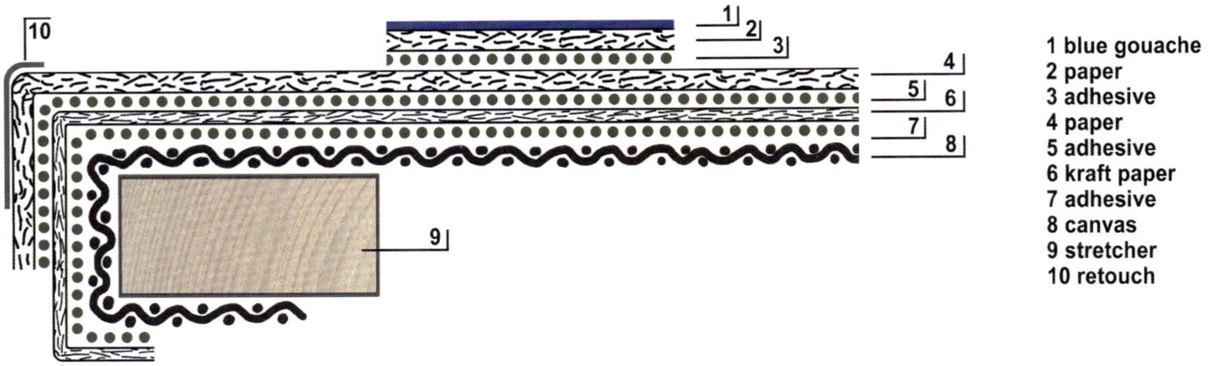

Fig. 65 Layered structure of a mounted cut-out, *Blue Nude I*

composition was built up from the lower right to the upper left (fig. 64). All but one of these shapes were cut from a single piece of paper; the single exception is constructed from three separate red shapes. Shapes sometimes share an identical contoured edge, where Matisse cut a second shape directly after the previous shape from the same sheet of paper.

Ink drawings, charcoal lines and pencil guidelines were included in the cut-outs, each for a distinct purpose. *Large Decoration with Masks*, for instance, contains ink drawings that are compositional elements in their own right on a par with the shapes cut from paper. Charcoal lines in *Memory of Oceania* (no. 130) were drawn by Matisse onto the original white support paper and are integral elements in the overall composition. *Blue Nude IV* (no. 107) retains myriad charcoal lines, which are remnants of Matisse's evolutionary composition process. Partially effaced during this complex procedure, they remain as visual testimony and are important as such. Original, but perhaps less a part of the composition, are the charcoal lines in *Chinese Fish* (no. 93), which are guidelines marking the divisions and eventual lead cames, or leading, for the planned stained-glass window. Pencil lines on support papers and cut-out shapes are an artefact of the mounting process (see next section) and are not from the hand of the artist.

Mounting

While Matisse was surrounded by his cut-outs in Paris, Nice and Vence, they existed in a temporary unmounted state – fragile but also alive with three-dimensionality. The idea that works on paper could remain in such a seemingly impermanent state is one that we now have come to accept and embrace, but was not conceivable at the time of the creation of the cut-outs. From the artist's few direct statements it is clear that he was very concerned about the long-term preservation of his cut-outs. As early as 1943 when Matisse was working on *Jazz* (nos. 18–21, 24–39), he was considering how individual cut shapes and figures could permanently be fixed or glued.[35] As this set of maquettes was to be sent to the publisher Tériade and then used by printers as composition and colour guides for the illustrated book, Matisse could well have been worried that temporary spot-gluing would not be strong enough for this working process.[36] Up until 1950–1 Matisse and his assistants could easily handle the mounting of works, since they were still quite moderate in their dimensions. Having been placed in their final positions, the shapes and papers were either connected by means of pins or drawing pins (thumb tacks), or were partially glued. In *Composition with Red Cross* and *Composition (The Velvets)* shapes were attached to the coloured picture ground by means of small dabs of glue, while strips of paper on the back of the works held the composition together. Small crosses or pencil lines marked the positions of shapes that were initially pinned to each other. Some shapes or picture grounds have numbers on the reverse, in order to prevent any confusion.

In 1949–50 *Panel with Mask* (no. 56) and *Composition, Violet and Blue* were sold by Matisse to the Designmuseum Danmark, Copenhagen: both were only spot-glued and still retain a three-dimensional liveliness.[37] At this stage Matisse was evidently happy to allow partially mounted works to leave the studio. It was only in 1950 that Matisse was faced with the question as to how his increasingly large compositions could be permanently secured. This was necessary when room had to be made on the studio wall for new works or when an individual work was to be exhibited or sold. Lydia Delectorskaya remembered Matisse's concern that the dabs of glue used hitherto would not last and that his compositions would suffer.[38]

Matisse learnt of Lucien Lefebvre-Foinet, Parisian art suppliers and restorers, from Marc Chagall, for whom they had mounted lithographs on canvas.[39] In early 1952 the Lefebvre-Foinet firm adapted a traditional painting relining process to the specific needs of mounting Matisse cut-outs.[40] The one documented comment by Matisse indicates that this technique was a satisfactory answer to his needs.[41] The coloured, painted shapes were glued, in a several-step process, to a fabric support, which was subsequently attached to a stretcher.[42] The characteristic layers arising from this process can be seen in *Blue Nude I*.

Approximately half of all the cut-outs, including almost all the large-format works, were mounted in this way. *Creole Dancer*, which Matisse gifted to the city of Nice in October 1953 and had been one of the first works to be mounted in 1952–3, allowed Matisse to see how well this process functioned. The majority of Matisse's cut-outs were not mounted until after his death. This operation was supervised by Marguerite Duthuit, his daughter, and Lydia Delectorskaya. The work at Lefebvre-Foinet was carried out by Gloria de Herrera until 1959,[43] and after that, until the 1990s, by Lydia Delectorskaya.

The first step in the transfer from Matisse's studio to the Lefebvre-Foinet atelier was to make an accurate tracing of the composition.[44] To make a completely accurate tracing, all protruding pins had to be removed to allow the tracing paper to be placed flat over the cut-out shapes. When there was already a background paper, the shapes were re-pinned in a flat sewing technique or spot-glued to this background. If there was no background paper, as in *La Négresse* and *Blue Nude with Green Stockings*, the pins were replaced with drawing pins (thumb tacks), which were flat. Once the tracing paper was laid over the composition, the outlines of the forms were traced in pencil (fig. 66). In the case of works with shapes made up from a number of pieces or with a large number of similar shapes, as in *The Swimming Pool*, *The Parakeet and the Mermaid* and *Blue Nude, the Frog*, the papers were numbered on the reverse.

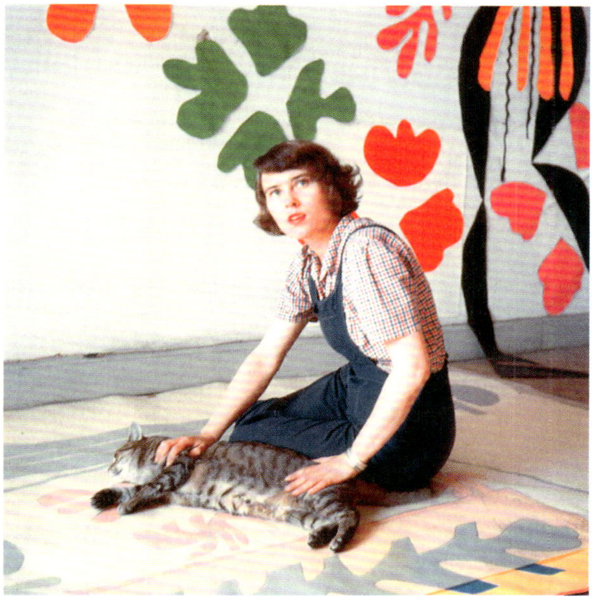

Fig. 66 Studio assistant Annelies Nelck sitting on tracing of *Apollo* on floor of Hôtel Régina, Nice c.1953

A plain weave linen was stretched over a temporary stretcher, which was slightly larger than the work to be mounted and was reinforced in order to deal with dimensional stresses that could arise during the mounting process.[45] In the case of the largest works, the canvas, which came in a width of 310 cm, was not wide enough, which necessitated sewing on an extra strip, as can be seen in *La Négresse* and *Acanthuses*. The raw canvas was tacked to the stretcher and repeatedly moistened to reduce its susceptibility to atmospheric changes. In *Blue Nude I* there are still traces of the use of a temporary stretcher visible at the back.

A reinforcing layer of kraft paper was attached to the canvas. This ensured that the weave of the canvas did not leave an imprint in the background paper and also that the canvas only stretched marginally when the background paper was glued in position. The kraft paper, which came in a width of approximately 120 cm, was glued with the ribbed side towards the fabric. Overlaps can be up to around 20 cm wide, as in *Acanthuses*. In many works the kraft paper is visible in places along the edges and in pin holes.

The adhesive, which appears to have been a classic French relining paste, consisted of rye flour, wheat flour, water, animal glue, linseed oil and Venice turpentine as an emollient.[46] There are no precise recipes, because the ingredients were

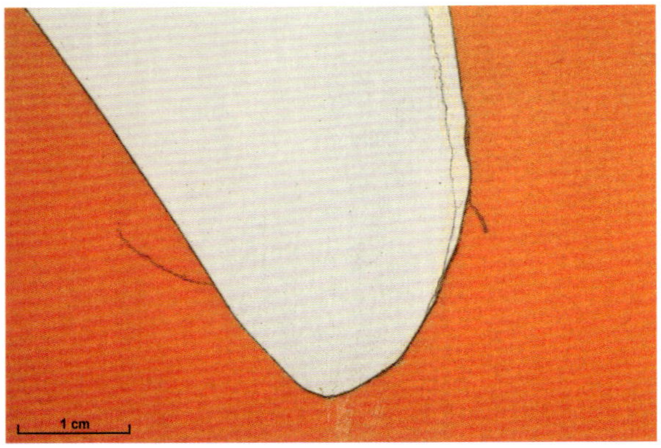

Fig. 67 Detail of pencil tracing lines from the mounting process, *Acanthuses*

adjusted for different uses, so as to create a homogeneous substance that would adhere well. This glue was not used for all the cut-outs that were mounted; the analysis of the adhesive used in *Venus* and *The Swimming Pool* identified cellulose ether.[47] A background paper, usually white, was then attached to the kraft paper. If an existing background paper was big enough, or if the background consisted of coloured papers that reached right to the edge, then these would be glued directly to the kraft paper. In works such as *Acanthuses*, where the background paper still bears charcoal lines drawn by Matisse, or *Memory of Oceania*, where, in addition to charcoal lines, he made a definitive border, no new background paper was used.

If any parts of the composition extended beyond the background paper used in the studio, a larger, new sheet of paper was used in order to create an additional border. Thus the blue shapes and the background papers bearing the artist's signature in *Blue Nude II*, *III* and *IV* were mounted on a new, larger sheet of background paper. The irregular yellow background of *Blue Nude, the Frog* was also glued to a larger sheet of paper.

In cases where the shapes had been attached directly to the studio wall, such as *Blue Nude, Jumping Rope* and *La Négresse*, or where the original background paper showed no evidence of the artist's hand, such as *Large Decoration with Masks*, *Large Decoration with Fruits* and *The Sheaf*, Matisse's compositions were glued to a completely new background paper.

The new papers added in Paris were Lavis B and S.A.V. Velin made by Canson & Montgolfier. The latter was only used at Lefebvre-Foinet and is seen in *Blue Nude, Jumping Rope* and in the left and right sections of *Women and Monkeys* (no. 120). The required lengths of paper were cut from rolls that came in a width of 150 cm. Once the lengths of paper for the background had been moistened, a layer of glue was applied and the paper was glued to the kraft paper, which had also received a coat of glue. Overlaps are between 1.5 cm and 5 cm in width.

The contrast between the white background and the coloured shapes was very important to Matisse.[48] In order to maintain this relationship, background papers were sometimes painted white at the Lefebvre-Foinet atelier. The reasons for this could be either that the Canson paper was not a pure white, or to forestall the effects of possible later discoloration of the paper. The white paint was applied with a broad brush, somewhat irregularly, and could either be a thin wash or a more opaque coat. The brushwork is often visible in incident light and is unmistakable in UV fluorescent lighting. The often irregular discoloration of the paper support is accentuated by the whiteness of this paint layer.[49]

The tracing of the composition made in the Matisse studio ensured that the shapes were mounted in their correct positions in the workshop in Paris. First the shape was inserted between the background paper and the tracing paper, then the tracing paper was peeled back and the outline of the shape was transferred to the background paper as a thin pencil line. The countless pencil lines that are visible in these works are therefore not preparatory drawings for the shapes (fig. 67). Occasionally, the shape is not quite congruent with lines on the paper underneath it. Lines may be seen under the shape, next to it or even on its edges. In places the pencil has slipped when the outline was being drawn and is now visible as a tiny line on the coloured shape. Once the outlines had been drawn on the background paper, the shapes could be coated with glue and fixed precisely in position. Traces of glue are visible on the edges of the shapes; they are rarely seen on the upper sides of the shapes. In some instances the glue has oozed upwards through pin holes, causing the surrounding areas to take on a darker tone due to saturation with glue. The upper arm of *Blue Nude I* was initially glued in the wrong position, and although it was immediately corrected, there are traces of glue and signs of damage on the surface of the paper. Once all the coloured shapes had been glued in position, the temporary stretcher was removed and the work was attached to its final stretcher.

The final dimensions of the cut-outs were determined by Matisse or subsequently in the Paris workshop when they were mounted. The dimensions of *The Snail* and *Memory of Oceania*, for instance, were determined by the motifs. Commissioned works, such as *The Sheaf* (no. 136) and *Ivy in Flower* (no. 134), were created according to the agreed dimensions. The dimensions of works that had been created directly on the studio wall, such as *Blue Nude, Jumping Rope*, were only finally determined when they were mounted; that is to say, the mounters in the Paris workshop took the motifs as their guide and added a border.

Large Decoration with Masks and *Large Decoration with Fruits*, each of which is particularly long, were mounted on five panels, taking into account the existing layout of the composition. *The Parakeet and the Mermaid* was initially divided into sections by Matisse and later subdivided.[50] Some works, such as *Blue Nude I, II, III, IV, Blue Nude, Jumping Rope* and *Women and Monkeys*, still have their original stretchers (fig. 68). However, all the large-format works have been re-stretched several times, mostly having been removed from their stretchers so that they could be transported from one venue to another. In the cases of *The Parakeet and the Mermaid, La Négresse* and *Large Decoration with Masks*, the original stretchers have been replaced at some point. They may have developed weaknesses or shown signs of wear and tear, or it may simply be that in the past the stretchers were not valued as original materials worthy of preservation.

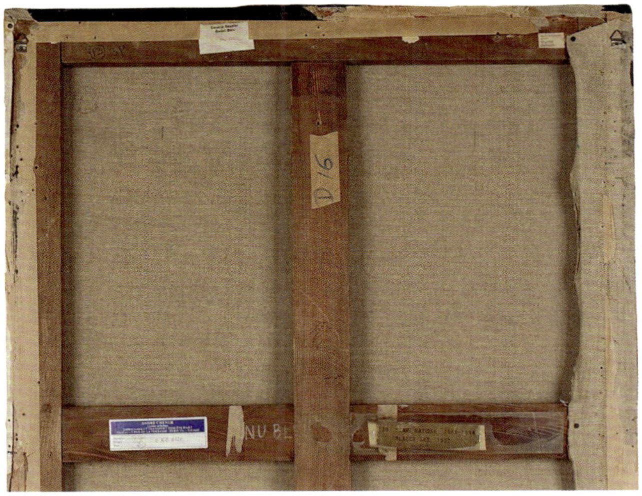

Fig. 68 *Blue Nude I* on original stretcher seen from behind (detail)

Signatures and dates

All the works that were exhibited or sold during Matisse's lifetime, and therefore left his studio, were signed by him and often dated, too. The signatures can be in pencil, charcoal, chalk or ink. In certain large-format works, such as *Large Decoration with Masks, Apollo*[51] and *The Sheaf*, the signature is on a separate piece of paper, which is glued to the background paper like a cut-out shape (fig. 69). The majority of the cut-outs that were still in Matisse's studio when he died, such as *The Swimming Pool* and *Acanthuses*, are not signed.

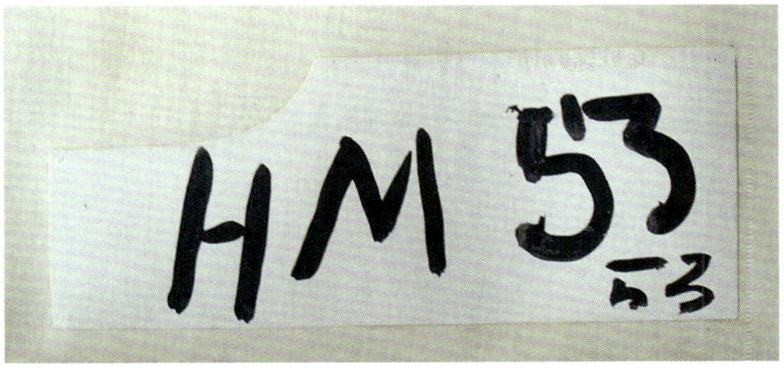

Fig. 69 Signature of *Large Decoration with Masks*, National Gallery of Art, Washington DC

Stability and deterioration

When a viewer stands in front of a Matisse cut-out today, does the work appear as it did when Matisse created it? The answer depends on many factors. Paramount is the colour of the gouache-painted paper shapes. Matisse himself was anxious about the light stability of his works, because he had seen both a violet and a pink gouache fade quickly in his studio.[52] Detailed recommendations from Matisse regarding the lighting for *The Parakeet and the Mermaid* reflect his concern for the work's permanence. In an exchange of letters with Pierre Berès, the original owner of the work, it is clear that the contrast Matisse had created between individual colours and the background paper was an essential component of the work.[53]

Scientists working with conservators have observed various types of colour alterations. Two scientific tools, a spectrophotometer and a microfader, have been used to analyse this.[54] This scientific data is important as colour changes can proceed undetected to the naked eye.

Spectrophotometric data collected from *Blue Nude I* taken at an interval of seven years confirmed colour changes: both decreasing brightness and browning.[55] Microfading data from *Acanthuses* shows that there is a time limit to the colours' light stability.[56] Analysis of the sample set of Matisse papers demonstrates that there is a wide range of light stability within each colour. Matisse often composed an area of colour using multiple small sections of one colour. However, if these small sections were painted with different tube colours, the complexity stemming from subtle colour juxtapositions that appealed to Matisse might over time evolve into different colour relationships. All the blue samples are composed of ultramarine, yet there is a range of sensitivities that points to the conclusion that the application of gouache onto the paper support by studio assistants not only affected the look of the sheet initially but also affects the perceived colour change over time. Areas of thinner application alter differently, due to the increased effect of paper degradation in relation to the effect of colour change. Within the sample set of seventy-nine papers, fourteen are extremely light sensitive; all of these are pink, violet or orange. Thirty-one samples, of all colours, are moderately light stable and thirty-four are stable.[57] Understanding that the gouache colours will alter from exposure to light must signal to the viewer that a colour in a cut-out might, or might not, reflect the colour as originally used by Matisse. Each and every colour in a cut-out will age at a rate dependent on its chemical composition, with the result that an original colour balance might be distorted over time.

The blue pigment that Matisse used was exclusively ultramarine. Quite stable to deterioration due to light exposure, it is, however, seriously degraded in contact with acidic environments. This has caused alteration to many cut-outs, especially those composed entirely of blue. Notable in this regard is the deterioration of *The Swimming Pool*, the largest of the all-blue cut-outs. It was mounted in 1955–6 on burlap to recreate the fabric wall covering in the dining room at the Hôtel Régina for which it was originally created. The acidity of the burlap has caused substantial damage (fig. 70). Other blue cut-outs have been affected by acidity inherent in the manufacture of the white background papers.

The canvas mountings, and the adhesives used during this process, have often been faulted for causing later deterioration. The very large size and complexity of mounting Matisse cut-outs had not been encountered before, and the basic mounting techniques used were, for the period, professional and well carried out. However, the discoloration of the white background papers to which the coloured cut-out shapes are glued has often contributed to an altered overall appearance. One factor is the quality of the mounting paper: S.A.V. Velin is more stable than Canson Lavis B or Barjon Moirans. When two of these papers have been used side by side in one work, such as in *Woman with Amphora and Pomegranates* (no. 123), a colour difference is visible. Many white papers have developed an uneven brownish discoloration over time. The causes of these changes remain unclear, as the location of discoloured areas does not always correspond to a particular set of conditions. The composition of the mounting adhesive has been thought to be a contributing factor. The complex adhesive mixture was tailored to reline canvas paintings, not works on paper. Animal glue, linseed oil and Venice turpentine could all have contributed to colour change over time. Works mounted with an alternative adhesive, a cellulose ether, also exhibit serious discolorations. The moisture introduced into the papers during the original mounting process might have moved components within the paper – sizing, optical brightener and constituents of the adhesive – which did not cause an immediate visual result but would have set the stage for colour change over time. As mentioned earlier the decision made by the Lefebvre-Foinet atelier to paint some of the

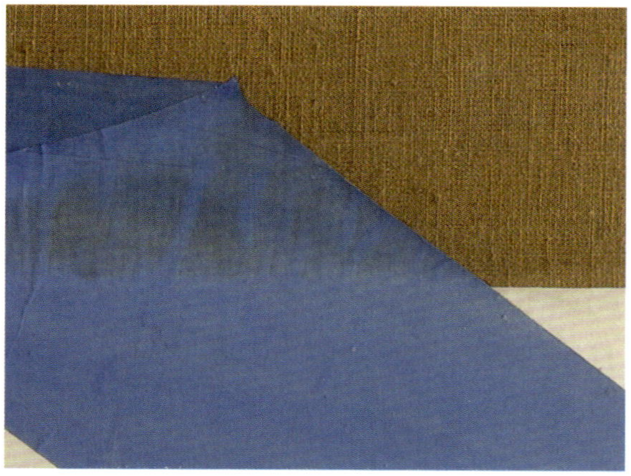

Fig. 70 *The Swimming Pool* (detail). Blue painted paper in contact with acidic burlap has deteriorated more severely than areas mounted onto white paper

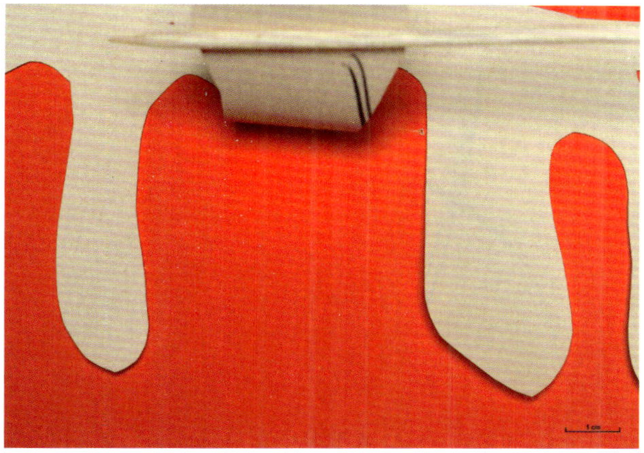

Fig. 71 Colour changes (detail) on *Composition with Red Cross*

background papers white has increased the mottled appearance of these papers, as the white paint only serves to heighten the contrast of the discoloured paper.

A final set of factors are the storage conditions and exhibition conditions – light levels, temperature and relative humidity – that the cut-outs have experienced over time. Light levels and duration of exposure, often under non-museum conditions, have determined the degree of colour alteration. *Blue Nude I* has browned much more noticeably in comparison to the other works in the group of four *Blue Nudes*, as it was exhibited continuously, more in the tradition of a painting than a work on paper, from the 1960s up to 2000. On the reverse and under the red shapes in *White Alga on Red and Green Background* and *Composition with Red Cross* it is clear that the colour and paper have aged at different rates due to the differences in light exposure (fig. 71).

Temperature and relative humidity, two interrelated environmental factors, must certainly have played an important role in the overall deterioration of the cut-outs, especially on the white mounting papers. As moisture migrated through the multi-layer mounting structure, uneven degradation, seen as uneven discoloration, might have been the result.

Transport and exhibition have also contributed to the deterioration of the surface of the cut-outs. Gouache has a very matte surface that is prone to abrasion and dust deposition, especially important for the larger cut-outs, which are difficult to store, transport and exhibit. Framing and glazing is an established method to protect these fragile surfaces.

Conclusion

Matisse's cut-out oeuvre is unique within the artist's total body of work because of the radical interdependence between artist, studio assistants and professional mounters. The interventions of the studio assistants who created the painted paper sheets – however subordinate to Matisse's supervision – remain a key element in the visual materiality of these works. The artistic creation by Matisse – initial choice of colour, cutting the painted papers into shapes, and arranging the compositions – remain the central creative acts of the cut-outs. The subsequent mounting of the cut-outs, some shortly after their making and some posthumously, transformed these works from perceived fragility to permanence, but equally solidified their visual appearance permanently.

In preparation for the first US exhibition of Matisse's cut-outs at a major institution, The Museum of Modern Art, in 1961, the artist's son Pierre Matisse wrote to curator Monroe Wheeler about the proposed title of the exhibition, which initially included the word 'pasted': 'But I do not think it is necessary to refer to the gouaches as PASTED (which is a rather ugly word anyway) as the works were conceived as cut forms, once the artist had cut the paper and decided on the place in his composition he had nothing more to do with the rest of the execution.'[58] Years later, in a letter to MoMA conservators preparing to conserve the newly acquired cut-out, *The Swimming Pool*, Lydia Delectorskaya echoed the same sentiment: 'These three elements – the contour, the composition, the tone of the gouache – are the components of the original work, they come from the art of the painter and must be sacred to the mounters.'[59] Over the subsequent years scholars and casual viewers alike have tried to wrestle with the collaborative nature of the cut-outs, striving to find the true Matisse. For conservators the composite structure, combining both paper and canvas layers, poses the question as to what exactly the long-term preservation goals should be and how best to achieve them. The answer, not always easy to discern immediately, is in the understanding of the creation and myriad details contained within each cut-out. It is these details, artistic and technical, that this essay invites the reader to discover.

Notes

The Studio as Site and Subject

1. André Verdet, *Prestiges de Matisse: Précédé de visite à Matisse, entretiens avec Matisse*, Paris 1952, p.20. 'A large mural composition ...' are Verdet's words. An excerpt is translated in Jack Cowart et al., *Henri Matisse: Paper Cut-Outs*, exh. cat., National Gallery of Art, Washington, DC 1977, p.233; Verdet's interjection that Matisse designated with his hand 'une grande composition murale de papiers découpés' is not included in that translated excerpt.

2. Matisse in 'Interview with Ernst Goldschmidt' (1911) in Jack Flam (ed.), *Matisse on Art*, Berkeley and Los Angeles 1995, p.63.

3. Hilary Spurling quotes Matisse's assistant Lydia Delectorskaya as saying he 'lived in and for it'; see Hilary Spurling, *Matisse the Master: A Life of Henri Matisse, The Conquest of Colour, 1909–1954*, New York 2005, p.428. In a visit to Nice in 1952 Alfred H. Barr, Jr writes in his notebook of 'walls with elaborate découpages of multi-coloured leaves in various brilliant colours and one or two abstract figures'. Alfred H. Barr, Jr, Papers, 9.E.2, The Museum of Modern Art Archives, New York.

4. Verdet 1952, pp. 19–21, as quoted and translated in Spurling 2005, pp.463–4.

5. See the technical essay in this volume (pp.253–65) for an extensive exploration of Matisse's process.

6. Henri Matisse, *Jazz*, Paris 1947, pp.73–4, trans. in Flam 1995, p.172: 'drawing with scissors' and 'cutting directly into vivid color', which 'reminds' him 'of the direct carving of sculptors.' Verdet 1952, p.71, trans. and reprinted in Flam 1995, p.216: 'line with color, contour with surface.'

7. John Elderfield, *Henri Matisse: A Retrospective*, New York 1992, p.413.

8. Letter to André Rouveyre, 22 Feb. 1948, transcribed in Hanne Finsen (ed.), *Matisse, Rouveyre: Correspondance*, Paris 2001, p.486, letter 873: 'l'opération de découpage'.

9. The quotation comes from a letter to André Rouveyre, 25 Dec. 1947, transcribed in Finsen 2001, p.478, letter 860: 'Je suis occupé l'après-midi à faire de nouvelles combinaisons de couleurs avec le système du papier découpé.' There have been debates among observers regarding whether the cut-paper maquette can be considered a finished work. In correspondence between Matisse and Alfred H. Barr, Jr concerning the commission from Nelson Rockefeller for a stained glass window at Union Church in Pocantico Hills, Tarrytown, N.Y., 1954, the artist proposes the maquette (fig. 50) as 'an orginal work' and prices it separately. See letter, 28 Oct. 1954. For Matisse and decoration, see John Hallmark Neff's articles 'Matisse and Decoration: The Schukin Panels', *Art in America* 63, no.4 (July–Aug. 1975), pp.38–48, and the two-part 'Matisse and Decoration', *Arts Magazine* 49, no.9 (May 1975), pp.59–61, and no.10 (June 1975), p.85.

10. For a thorough overview of the chapel project, see Henri Matisse, Marie-Alain Couturier and Louis-Bertrand Rayssiguier, *The Vence Chapel: The Archive of a Creation*, ed. Marcel Billot, trans. Michael Taylor, Turin 1999.

11. For more on Matisse's studios, see Jack Flam, *Matisse: The Man and his Art, 1869–1918*, Ithaca and London 1986, pp.295–322; Pierre Schneider, *Matisse*, trans. Michael Taylor and Bridget Strevens Romer, New York 1984, pp.424–57; John Elderfield, 'The Red Studio', in *Matisse in the Collection of The Museum of Modern Art*, New York 1978, pp.86–9; Alastair Wright, 'Matisse dans l'atelier. La Dialectique de l'espace', in Cécile Debray (ed.) *Matisse: Paires et séries*, exh. cat., Centre Pompidou, Paris 2012, pp.63–8.

12. Isabel Monod-Fontaine, '*Figure décorative* or, A Studio Painting', in Pia Müller-Tamm (ed.), *Henri Matisse: Figure, Color, Space*, exh. cat., K20 Kunstsammlung Nordrhein-Westfalen, Düsseldorf 2005, p.312.

13. Matisse's use of the walls of his studio as a site to work out his ideas has a parallel in the practice of Piet Mondrian. Mondrian hung coloured rectangles on his studio walls, notably in his Manhattan studio at 15 East 59th Street, creating an environment in which his painting schemes seemed to extend into his physical space. See Nancy Troy, 'Piet Mondrian's Atelier', *Arts* 53, no.4 (Dec. 1978), pp.82–7; Nancy Troy, 'Piet Mondrian's Last Thoughts', in Karen Painter and Thomas Crow (eds.), *Late Thoughts: Reflections on Artists and Composers at Work*, Los Angeles 2006, pp.15–35; and *L'Atelier de Mondrian: Récherches et Dessins*, Paris 2007.

14. Spurling (2005, p.463) describes the way Matisse 'filled his white walls with cut-paper leaves, flowers, fronds and fruit from imaginary forests. Blue and white figures – acrobats, dancers, swimmers – looped and plunged into synthetic seas'.

15. The recent conservation of *The Swimming Pool*, 1952, by Karl Buchberg, Senior Conservator, The Museum of Modern Art, both focused our attention on materials and methods – the procedures of the studio – and pointed us towards the importance of Matisse's environmental works.

16. William Kentridge, an artist who often makes the activities of the studio his subject, calls this unspooling of the work's current state to its origin 'the utopian perfectability of the world in reverse'. See his lecture 'Drawing Lesson Four: Practical Epistemology: Life in the Studio', one of six presentations given at Harvard University as part of the Norton Lectures. Lecture Six was delivered on 10 April 2012. For other reflections on the studio, see Brian O'Doherty, *Studio and Cube*, New York 2007, and Daniel Buren, 'The Function of the Studio', *October* 10 (Autumn 1979), pp.51–8.

17. Photographing states of work in progress was already well established by the time of the cut-outs. Consider, for example, Matisse's use of photographs in the development of his *Pink Nude*, 1935. See Jeffrey Weiss's important text on Matisse's use of photographs, 'The Matisse Grid', in Eik Kahng (ed.), *The Repeating Image: Multiples in French Painting from David to Matisse*, exh. cat., Walters Art Museum, Baltimore 2007, pp.173–91. Matisse exhibited photographs of states of his paintings alongside the finished work at Galerie Maeght in Paris in 1945, recently restaged in the exhibition *Matisse: In Search of True Painting* at The Metropolitan Museum of Art, New York. See Dorthe Aagesen, 'Painting as Film', in Aagesen and Rebecca Rabinow (eds.), *Matisse: In Search of True Painting*, exh. cat., The Metropolitan Museum of Art, New York 2012, pp.159–63.

18. Hélène Adant, Lydia Delectorskaya's cousin, carried out the most extensive documentation of Matisse's studio, going as far as restaging for her camera still-life compositions painted by Matisse. For a selection of these photographs, see Marie-France Boyer, *Matisse at Villa le Rêve, 1943–1948*, trans. Anna Bennett, London 2004.

19. Verdet 1952, p.72, trans. in Flam 1995, p.216. In the quotation a slight modification has been made to Flam's translation that changes 'react on' to 'react with.'

20. Éric de Chassey and Émilie Ovaere (eds.), *Ils ont regardé Matisse: Une Réception abstraite, États-Unis/Europe, 1948–1968*, exh. cat., Musée Matisse, Le Cateau-Cambrésis 2009.

21. This thinking about the cut-outs as a wartime practice and Matisse's 'recognition of what catastrophe is' was provoked by T.J. Clark's recent volume *Picasso and Truth: From Cubism to Guernica*, Washington, DC 2013, in which he describes the way the studio is pervaded by 'monsters', the catastrophes of the twentieth century; for recognition, see p.19, and for monsters, p.21, and 'Lecture 4: Monster', pp.147–90. For the war's impact, see Éric de Chassey, 'Une Cohabitation instablé', in Cécile Debray (ed.)

Matisse: Paires et séries, exh. cat., Centre Pompidou, Paris 2012, pp.195–200.

22. Letter to Marguerite Duthuit, June 1940, quoted in Spurling 2005, p.393.

23. For an excellent discussion of this time, see Spurling 2005, ch. 11 ('1939–1945: Paris, Nice, Ciboure, St-Gaudens and Vence'), pp.387–425.

24. For Aragon, see Spurling 2005, p.419. For Tériade, see Rebecca A. Rabinow, 'The Legacy of la Rue Férou: *Livres d'Artiste* Created for Tériade by Rouault, Bonnard, Matisse, Léger, Le Corbusier, Chagall, Giacometti, and Miró', PhD diss., Institute of Fine Arts, New York University, 1995, p.109.

25. Riva Castleman, 'Introduction', to Matisse, *Jazz* facsimilie, New York, 1983, p. x, discussed in Rabinow 1995, pp.110–11; for 'acts of aggression', see Rabinow 1995, p.109.

26. Letter to Pierre Matisse, 3 Nov. 1942, quoted in Spurling 2005, p.402. For Matisse's medical issues, see Spurling 2005, ch.11, pp.387–425. Matisse's 'second life'– the flourishing of his work after his surgery in 1941 and his relationship with André Rouveyre – was the subject of an exhibition at the Louisiana Museum in 2005 organised by Hanne Finsen. See Hanne Finsen (ed.), *Matisse: A Second Life*, exh. cat., Musée du Luxembourg, Paris, 2005.

27. For an investigation into 'late style', see Karen Painter and Thomas Crow (eds.), *Late Thoughts: Reflections on Artists and Composers at Work*, Los Angeles 2006.

28. It was George Salles who described the studio as 'a fantastic laboratory', quoted in Spurling 2005, p.463.

29. Matisse, 'Notes of a Painter' (1908), in Flam 1995, p.38; quoted in Elderfield 1978, p.89.

Inventing a New Operation

1. Letter to André Rouveyre, 22 Feb. 1948, transcribed in Hanne Finsen (ed.), *Matisse, Rouveyre: Correspondance*, Paris 2001, p.486–7, letter 873: 'Les murs de ma chambre sont pleins de découpages'; 'je ne sais encore ce que je ferai de ces nouveaux découpages'; and 'c'est le résultat qui a plus d'importance qu'il n'en a l'air'.

2. The essential resources on the cut-outs remain Jack Cowart et al., *Henri Matisse: Paper Cut-Outs*, exh. cat., National Gallery of Art, Washington, DC 1977, and John Elderfield, *The Cut-Outs of Henri Matisse*, New York 1978. More recent indispensable scholarship includes Anne Coron, 'La Gouache découpée dans l'oeuvre de Henri Matisse: Pratique, esthétique, réception', PhD diss., Université Picardie Jules Verne (Amiens), Faculté des Arts, 2005; Patrice Deparpe (ed.), *Matisse: La Couleur découpée, une donation révélatrice / Cutting into Color, A Revealing Donation*, exh. cat., Musée Matisse, Le Cateau-Cambrésis 2013; Gilles and Xavier-Gilles Néret (eds.), *Henri Matisse: Cut-Outs: Drawing with Scissors*, trans. Pamela Hargreaves and Jonathan Paul Murphy, Cologne 2009. See this volume's bibliography for additional sources.

3. Matisse's closest collaborator, his assistant/secretary/model Madame Lydia Delectorskaya, identifies the cut-outs' 'sacred' features: contour – 'traced with the aid of a scissor is the authentic work of the artist, it has the value of the original line of a drawing'; composition – 'the placement and the axis of each colored form ... to give the desired placement and expression'; and colour – 'chosen by the artist at the moment of its creation'. She uses the word 'sacré': contour – 'tracé à l'aide de ciseaux, est l'oeuvre authentique de l'artiste, il a la valeur du trait original d'un dessin'; composition – 'la place et l'axe de chaque forme colorée ... donner l'emplacement et l'expression voulus'; colour – 'choisi par l'artiste au moment de la création' (Archives Matisse, Paris). Letter to MoMA conservators, 23 July 1976.

4. This film was shot by Adrien Maeght.

5. Letter to André Rouveyre, 22 Feb. 1948, transcribed in Finsen 2001, p.486, letter 873: 'l'opération de découpage'.

6. Matisse quoted in André Verdet, 'Les Papiers découpés', in his *Entretiens, notes et écrits sur la peinture*, Paris 1978, p.130: 'Mais ce n'est plus le pinceau qui s'insinue et glisse sur la toile, ce sont les ciseaux qui taillent dans le papier cartonné et dans la couleur. Les conditions du trajet diffèrent à cent pour cent. Le contour de la figure jaillit donc de la découverte des ciseaux qui lui donnent le mouvement de la vie circulante. Or cet outil ne module pas, il ne brosse pas *sur*, mais il incise *dans*, soulignons-le bien, car les critères d'observation seront tout autres.' (Emphasis as in the original.) An alternative translation is available in Jack Flam (ed.), *Matisse: A Retrospective*, New York 1988, p.380.

7. Patrice Deparpe, 'Une Donation révélatrice / A Revealing Donation', in Deparpe 2013, p.13. This exhibition and catalogue present the recent donation from the Matisse family of forms cut by Matisse that were ultimately not used in his compositions. The range of shapes and their relationships offer important insights into Matisse's work. We are grateful to Patrice Deparpe for sharing his deep knowledge of this collection.

8. Such proliferation and its close relation, pattern, are key elements of the decorative – with which Matisse engaged in composing his cut-outs.

9. Hilary Spurling, 'Material World: Matisse, his Art and his Textiles', in Hilary Spurling et al., *Matisse, his Art and his Textiles: The Fabric of Dreams*, exh. cat., Royal Academy of Arts, London 2004, pp.14–15. For an interesting treatment of the analogies between Picasso's pinning and cutting in his *papiers collés* and contemporary dressmaking and tailoring, see Elizabeth Cowling, 'The Fine Art of Cutting: Picasso's Papiers Collés and Constructions in 1912–14', *Apollo*, vol.142, (Nov. 1995), no.405, pp.10–18.

10. Spurling 2004, p.17 and n.12.

11. Jeffrey Weiss, 'Picasso's Contingent Cubism', lecture at the Frick Collection, 14 Dec. 2011. Weiss's text and our ongoing dialogue have been absolutely essential for my understanding of Matisse's pinning and its implications. Weiss's text also encourages considering the relationship between cubism's *papier collé* and Matisse's cut-outs.

12. Weiss 2011.

13. Weiss 2011.

14. It is interesting that Lydia Delectorskaya expressed sorrow for the pinholes' 'necessary evil'. See letter to The Museum of Modern Art conservators, 23 July 1976, Archives Matisse, Paris: 'Ces petits trous étaient un mal, mais, hélas, inévitable.'

15. Henri Matisse, 'Notes of a Painter' (1908), reprinted and translated in Jack Flam (ed.), *Matisse on Art*, Berkeley and Los Angeles 1995, p.37.

16. Letter from Henri Matisse to Pierre Matisse, 5 April 1948, Pierre Matisse Gallery Archives, Morgan Library, New York, letter 637, box 205: 'Un armateur qui fait un bateau de luxe s'appellant "le génie français" destine à l'orient jusqu'au Japon me propose de me l'acheter pour mettre dans son bateau.'

17. It is interesting to compare La *Négresse* with Picasso's 1913 construction of a guitar player, whose newspaper arms come off the wall into the viewer's space to play an actual guitar, while standing near a real table on which sits a real bottle and a real pipe. See photographs in Anne Umland, *Picasso Guitars, 1912–1914*, exh. cat., The Museum of Modern Art, New York 2011, pp.72–3.

18. Henri Matisse in 'Interview with Georges Charbonnier' (1950) in Flam 1995, p.191.

19. Henri Matisse in 'Letters to Alexander Romm', 14 Feb. 1934, in Flam 1995, pp.115, 116. Matisse elaborates on this concept: 'Architectural painting depends absolutely on the place that has to receive it, and which it animates with a new life ... It must give the space enclosed by the architecture the atmosphere of a wide and beautiful glade filled with sunlight' (Flam 1995, p.116). Yve-Alain Bois discusses Matisse's aspiration toward expansion in 'On Matisse: The Blinding: For Leo Steinberg', trans.

Greg Sims, *October* 68 (Spring 1994), pp.60–121. For Matisse's take on the architectural implications of the Barnes *Dance*, see Dorothy Dudley, 'Notes on Painting: The Matisse Fresco in Merion, Pennsylvania', *Hound and Horn* 7, no.2 (Jan.–March 1934), pp.298–303.

20. Romy Golan, *Muralnomad: The Paradox of Wall Painting, Europe 1927–1957*, New Haven and London 2009.

21. Henri Matisse, 'The Path of Color' (1947), in Flam 1995, p.178 (slightly altered translation in Bois 1994, p.65). For Matisse's interest in the arts of Islam, see Rémi Labrusse, '"What Remains Belongs to God": Henri Matisse, Alois Riegl and the Arts of Islam', in Spurling et al. 2004, pp.46–61, and Rémi Labrusse, 'Decoration Beyond Decoration', in Olivier Berggruen and Max Hollein (eds.), *Henri Matisse: Drawing with Scissors, Masterpieces from the Late Years*, trans. Paul Aston, exh. cat., Schirn Kunsthalle, Frankfurt 2002, pp.67–85. Bois argues that the 'oriental epiphany should not be exaggerated'. See Bois 1994, p.65.

22. Henri Matisse in 'Interview with Georges Charbonnier' (1950) in Flam 1995, p.191.

23. Letter to Matisse, 31 Dec. 1947, transcribed in Finsen 2001, p.479, letter 862: 'Ces papiers découpés ont leur existence très pure alors qu'ils s'échappent de tes mains, de tes ciseaux. Leur matière papier, avec les jeux menus de la lumière sur leur flexibilité, la physique même de cette flexibilité, tout cela concourt à faire une chose miraculeuse et qui perd son essence alors qu'on veut la mettre trop sèchement à plat. Mais ça la garde son essence alors que c'est piqué au mur avec des épingles par Lydia. Car alors cela y garde cette vie du papier dont je parle et subissant des changements incessants.'

24. Letter from Aimé Maeght to Henri Matisse, 17 April 1948, Archives Matisse, Paris.

25. Letter to André Rouveyre, 25 Dec. 1947, transcribed in Finsen 2001, p.478, letter 860: 'Je sais que ces choses doivent rester comme elles sont, des originaux – des gouaches.'

26. Letter to André Rouveyre, 22 Feb. 1948, transcribed in Finsen 2001, pp.486–7, letter 873: 'Pour qui n'a pas vu les originaux ce que donne le livre est le principal.'

27. See 'Lettre à Pierre Berès sur La Perruche et la sirène, 24 June 1954', in Dominique Fourcade (ed.), *Henri Matisse: écrits et propos sur l'art*, Paris 1972, pp.253–4.

28. Henri Matisse in André Verdet, 'Les heures azuréennes', in *Hommage à Henri Matisse, XXe Siècle*, Paris 1970, quoted in Jean Guichard-Meili, *Les Gouaches découpées de Henri Matisse*, Paris 1970, p.57, and in Deparpe 2013, p.15.

An Agreeable Distraction

1. 'A painter ought to have his tongue cut out': Matisse quoted in 'Study Art in America', *The Literary Digest*, 18 Oct. 1930, cited in Jack Flam (ed.), *Matisse on Art*, Berkeley and Los Angeles 1995, p.2.

2. Matisse reiterated this idea over the years in which he worked on the cut-outs: 'I used to say to my young students: "You want to be a painter? First of all you must cut out your tongue because your decision has taken away from you the right to express yourself with anything but your brush."' (Matisse in a radio interview in 1942, cited and trans. in Flam 1995, pp.143–8, esp. p.145.) The first sentence of Matisse's text in *Jazz* begins: 'Why, after having written, "He who wants to dedicate himself to painting should start by cutting out his tongue," do I need to resort to a medium other than my own?' (Henri Matisse, *Jazz*, Paris 1947, cited and trans. in Flam 1995, pp.169–74, esp. p.171.)

3. Lucile Encrevé, 'Chronology: 1948–1968', in Éric de Chassey and Émilie Ovaere (eds.), *Ils ont regardé Matisse: Une Réception abstraite, États-Unis/Europe, 1948–1968*, exh. cat., Musée Matisse, Le Cateau-Cambrésis 2009, pp.14–62. I also draw on the indispensable volume by Catherine C. Bock-Weiss, *Henri Matisse: A Guide to Research*, New York and London, 1996.

4. Christian Zervos, 'À propos de l'exposition Matisse au Musée d'Art Moderne de Paris', *Cahiers d'Art*, vol.24, no.1, 1949, pp.159–70, esp. p.160, cited and trans. in Jack Cowart et al., *Henri Matisse: Paper Cut-Outs*, exh. cat., National Gallery of Art, Washington, DC 1977, p.89.

5. For example, Matisse's design for the *Ascher Squares* were shown in New York at the American British Art Center from 20 October to 1 November 1947 along with other designs by Moore, Derain, Sutherland, Hutchins, Hodgkins, Laurencin and Cocteau. For a review, see Jacques Lassaigne, 'État de la tapisserie', in Jacques Lassaigne et al., *Panorama des Arts 1947*, Paris 1948, pp.250–1.

6. *Exposição do novo libro de Henri Matisse, Jazz, editado per Tériade* at the Galerie Europa, Arte Antiga e Moderna Ltd, Rio de Janeiro.

7. See Claude Roger-Marx, 'Les Découpages de Matisse', in *Le Figaro Littéraire*, 3 Jan. 1948, p.8, and also Jacques Lassaigne, 'Matisse', in Lassaigne et al. 1948, pp.17–18. An article by Claude Morgan was more positive – see Morgan, 'Matisse montre toujours de nouveaux chemins' [on Jazz], in *Les Lettres Françaises*, 8 Jan. 1948.

8. Henri Clifford (ed.), *Henri Matisse: Retrospective Exhibition of Paintings, Drawing and Sculpture Organized in Collaboration with the Artist*, exh. cat., Philadelphia Museum of Art, 1948.

9. Clifford 1948, pp. 10-11.

10. See *Time Magazine*, 5 April 1948, and *Art News* 47 (April 1948), pp.16–54.

11. According to Greenberg, 'Cézanne, Van Gogh, Gauguin, Matisse and the fauves all contributed to the reduction of the easel picture's fictive depth', something that Matisse was then still in the formative stages of dispensing with altogether in the cut-outs: Clement Greenberg, 'The Crisis of the Easel Picture', *Partisan Review* 15, no.4 (April 1948), pp.481–4, reprinted in John O'Brian (ed.), *Clement Greenberg: The Collected Essays and Criticism, Volume 2, Arrogant Purpose, 1945–49*, Chicago and London 1986, pp.221–5.

12. O'Brian 1986, p.222. For more on this, see Pepe Karmel (ed.), *Jackson Pollock: Interviews, Articles, and Reviews*, New York 1999, p.10.

13. O'Brian 1986, p.223.

14. In the spring of 1947, for example, Jackson Pollock's large-scale painting *Mural* of 1943–4 was included in The Museum of Modern Art's exhibition *Large Scale Modern Paintings*, alongside works by Pablo Picasso, Matisse, Fernand Léger, Joan Miró, Max Beckmann and David Alfaro Siqueiros, which ran from 1 April to 4 May 1947 in New York. In his 1947 application for a Guggenheim Fellowship, Pollock wrote: 'I intend to paint large movable pictures which will function between the easel and the mural,' continuing: 'I believe the easel picture to be a dying form, and the tendency of modern feeling is towards the wall picture or mural' (Karmel 1999, p.17). This chimes with Matisse's comments to Verdet five years later in 1952: 'I think that one day easel painting will no longer exist because of changing customs. There will be mural paintings' (cited and trans. in Flam, 1995, p.211). Another important aspect of the reception of Matisse's cut-outs is that they would go on to influence several generations of artists on either side of the Atlantic during the 1950s and 1960s. While a full discussion of this complex web of influence and transmission lies outside the scope of this essay and has already been explored in depth in other studies, just a partial list of these artists would contain figures such as the American Abstract Expressionist painters Barnett Newman, Jackson Pollock and Mark Rothko; a younger generation of American artists including Ellsworth Kelly (who lived

in France during the late 1940s and early 1950s and saw some of Matisse's cut-outs when they were first exhibited), Sam Francis, Morris Louis, Frank Stella, Richard Tuttle and Andy Warhol; and artists in France including the Nouveaux Réalistes *affichistes* Raymond Hains and Jacques Villeglé, along with other French artists such as Daniel Buren, Simon Hantai, Nicolas de Staël and the Support-Surface group and the Swedish artist Öyvind Fahlström. See Gunda Luyken, '"Painting alone remains full of adventure" – Matisse's cut-outs as an inspiration for Nicolas de Staël, Ellsworth Kelly and Andy Warhol', in Olivier Berggruen and Max Hollein (eds.), *Henri Matisse: Drawing with Scissors, Masterpieces from the Late Years*, trans. Paul Aston, exh. cat., Schirn Kunsthalle, Frankfurt 2002, pp.151–9.

15. As Greenberg wrote in *Partisan Review*: 'In Greenwich Village the attempt is being made to create a larger-scale easel art by expanding Matisse's hot color, raised several degrees in intensity, into the bigger more simplified compositional schemes which he himself usually reserved for blacks, grays, and blues' (Clement Greenberg, 'The Situation at the Moment', *Partisan Review*, Jan. 1948, reprinted in O'Brian 1986, pp.194–5).

16. See Marie-Alain Couturier, 'Église d'Assy et la Chapelle de Vence', *L'Art Sacré* 5–6 (May–June 1948), pp.109–10, and 'Un Nouveau projet d'Henri Matisse: La Chapelle de Vence', *Les Amis de l'art* 1, 1948. The following year Matisse's Vence chapel project reached widespread notice with the publication of Rosamond Bernier's illustrated report, 'Matisse Designs a New Church', in *Vogue* 112, 15 Feb. 1949, pp.131–2.

17. See 'Vence, 1944–48', *Verve*, vol.VI, 1948, nos. 21–2.

18. The cut-outs included in the exhibition were *Amphitrite* (1947), *Composition with Red Cross* (1947), *Panel with Mask* (1947), *The Eskimo* (1947), *Two Masks (The Tomato)* (1947), *Azor* (1947), possibly *Negro Boxer* (1947), *White Alga on Orange and Red Background* (1947) and *Bird* (1947). For an excellent survey of the Pierre Matisse's Gallery, see William M. Griswold and Jennifer Tonkovich, *Pierre Matisse and his Artists*, exh. cat., The Pierpont Morgan Library, New York 2002.

19. See, for example 'Exhibition, Pierre Matisse Gallery', *Art News* 47 (Feb. 1949), pp.44–5; and 'Exhibition of Paintings and Drawings at Pierre Matisse Gallery', *Art Digest* 23 (15 Feb. 1949), p.14.

20. Clement Greenberg, 'Art', *The Nation*, 5 March 1949.

21. See the exhibition catalogue (of the same title as the exhibition).

22. See 'Les Oeuvres récentes, Exposition du Musée national d'art moderne', *Art & Decoration* 3, 1949, p.55; Christian Zervos, 'À propos de l'exposition Matisse au Musée d'Art Moderne de Paris', *Cahiers d'Art*, vol.24, no.1, 1949, pp.159–70.

23. See Éric de Chassey, 'Kelly et Matisse. Une Filiation inavouée', *Les Cahiers du Musée national d'art moderne*, no.49, Autumn 1994, pp.41–57, esp. p.47.

24. *XXV Biennale di Venezia*, exh. cat., Venice, 1950.

25. Raymond Cogniat, 'À la Maison de la Pensée Française: la sérenité d'Henri Matisse', in *Arts*, no.271, 14 July 1950.

26. Célia Bertin, 'À Vence: Henri Matisse décore une chapelle', *Arts Plastiques*, 1949, pp.209–14; Paul Bird, 'Matisse's chapel', *Art Digest*, 15 Sept. 1951, vol.25, p.7; Rogers Bordley, 'Matisse's chapel', *Art Digest*, 15 Sept. 1951, vol.25, pp.9, 34.

27. Alfred H. Barr, Jr, *Henri Matisse*, exh. cat., The Museum of Modern Art, New York, 1951.

28. The exhibition toured to Cleveland, Chicago and San Francisco. See, for example, James Fitzsimmons, 'Henri Matisse; the Conflict and Resolution of Opposed Tendencies, Exhibition at Museum of Modern Art', *Art Digest* 26, 1 Dec. 1951, p.9.

29. Barr 1951, esp. p.278. For an excellent appraisal of Barr's monograph, see John Elderfield, 'Alfred H. Barr, Jr's "Matisse: His Art and His Public, 1951"', *Burlington Magazine*, vol.152, no.1282 (Jan. 2010) pp.36–9. In 1953 The Museum of Modern Art acquired its first cut-outs by Matisse – the covers of the catalogue of the 1951 retrospective and Barr's monograph, and the maquette of the *Christmas Eve* window (nos.98, 100, 101).

30 André Verdet, *Prestiges de Matisse: Précédé de visite à Matisse, entretiens avec Matisse*, Paris 1952.

31. For these, see Flam 1995.

32. See Encrevé 2009, p.33.

33. The exhibition was accompanied by a catalogue with an introduction by Tériade. Prior to the Berggruen exhibition opening, Jean Cassou published an illustrated article 'Matisse va présenter au public ses papiers découpés,' *France Illustration* 383, 14 Feb. 1953, pp.234–5.

34. See Léon Degand, 'Les Papiers découpés de Matisse', *Art d'aujourd'hui* 2 (1953), p.28; and R.W.H. [Russell Warren House], 'Events in Paris', in *Apollo*, vol.57, no.338 (April 1953), no.338, p.114.

35. See *Paris Match*, no.294, 13–20 Nov. 1954. The accompanying text on the cover of the magazine stated: 'Nos Envoyés spéciaux dans le maquis de l'Aurès' and 'Quelques semaines avant sa mort, celui qui fut un grand maître de la peinture contemporaine découpe des papiers de couleurs dans son atelier de Cimiez.'

36. Pierre Courthion, 'Papiers découpés d'Henri Matisse', *XXe Siècle*, Jan. 1956, no.6 ('Le papier collé du cubisme à nos jours'), pp.45–6.

37. Jean Cassou, *Henri Matisse: Exposition rétrospective*, exh. cat., Musée national d'art moderne, Paris 1956.

38. See Encrevé 2009, p.41. For reviews, see, for example, Georges Duthuit, 'Material and Spiritual Worlds of Henri Matisse; Retrospective at the Musée d'Art Moderne', Art News 55, no. 484, Oct. 1956, pp.22–5.

39. Georges Duthuit, 'Le tailleur de lumière', in *Dernière oeuvres de Matisse, 1950–1954*, special issue of *Verve*, vol.IX, no. 35–6, July 1958, pp.75–8, 113–14, 119–20, 139–40, 145–6.

40. Franz Meyer, *Henri Matisse, 1950–1954: Les Grandes Gouaches découpées*, exh. cat., Kunsthalle Bern 1959.

41. See Jacques Lassaigne, 'Les Grandes Gouaches découpées d'Henri Matisse; la peinture sans limits', and Jean Leymarie, 'Le Jardin du paradis', *Les Lettres Françaises*, 6 Aug. 1959.

42. Jacques Lassaigne, *Henri Matisse: Les Grandes gouaches découpées*, exh. cat., Musée des Arts Décoratifs, Paris 1961. For the reviews, see, for example, Pierre Schneider, 'Art News from Paris', *Art News* 60, May 1961, p.44.

43. Monroe Wheeler, *The Last Works of Henri Matisse: Large Cut Gouaches*, exh. cat., The Museum of Modern Art, New York 1961.

44. Wheeler 1961, p.7.

45. Edward Said ranked Matisse's cut-outs as one of the supreme examples of an artist's late work in any medium: 'Each of us can readily supply evidence of how it is that late work crowns a lifetime of aesthetic endeavour. Rembrandt and Matisse, Bach and Wagner.' (Edward W. Said, *On Late Style*, London 2006, p.7.)

Avant la Lettre

1. 'Henri Matisse', *Vogue* 91, 15 June 1938, pp.30–1.

2. Dance historian Judith Chazin-Bennahum notes: 'Various newspaper articles indicated that the change acknowledged the fact that the great painter Matisse used to sing a farandole while he painted' (Judith Chazin-Bennahum, *René Blum and the Ballets Russes: In Search of a Lost Life*, New York 2011, p.196). Before the Monte Carlo premiere, however, the ballet was simply referred to as 'La Farandole'; this is how both the 1938 *Vogue* article and the contract between Matisse and the Ballet Russe de Monte Carlo (30 July 1937, Sergei Denham Records of the Ballet Russe de Monte Carlo, c.1936–1978, New York Public Library for the Performing Arts, Jerome Robbins Division) refer to it. This essay will

continue to refer to the ballet as *Rouge et Noir*, which was restored as the title when it came to New York in 1940 and by which it is now more commonly known.

3. 'La Farandole', *Vogue* 91, 15 June 1938, pp.28–9.

4. Henri Matisse with Pierre Courthion, 'Seventh Conversation', in *Chatting with Henri Matisse: The Lost 1941 Interview*, ed. Serge Guilbaut, trans. Chris Miller, Los Angeles 2013, pp.95–106, esp. p.104.

5. Lydia Delectorskaya Scrapbook, unpublished notes for a proposed book on Matisse's cut-outs, Archives Matisse, Paris. See also Matisse & Courthion 2013, p.104.

6. In his essential text on *The Dance* Jack Flam provides an authoritative titling convention for the mural project's three versions. *Unfinished Dance Mural* refers to the original canvases on which Matisse began work in charcoal and paint in April 1931, rediscovered only in 1992. *Paris Dance Mural* denotes the composition Matisse began to build up in cut paper on top of *Unfinished Dance Mural* in the autumn of 1931, and whose incorrect dimensions were discovered in February 1932, but which was nonetheless subsequently completed in oil on canvas. Both of these now belong to the Musée d'Art Moderne de la Ville de Paris. *Merion Dance Mural* designates the mural's final version, begun in July 1932 after the mistake was discovered, completed in April 1933 and now residing in the Barnes Foundation (Jack Flam, *Matisse: 'The Dance'*, Washington, DC 1993, p.10).

7. See, for example, letter from Henri Matisse to Albert Barnes, Nice, 24 April 1931: 'Je vous envoie par ce courrier une série de photos qui je l'espère, vous amuseront. Mais gardez vous de prendre rien de ce qui s'y trouve comme définitif' [In this letter I'm sending you a series of photographs that I hope will amuse you. But don't consider anything you find there to be definitive] (Barnes Foundation Archives, Merion, PA. AR.ABC.1931.399 2/3).

8. According to Flam's titling convention, this is *Unfinished Dance Mural*.

9. This is the version that would become (per Flam) *Paris Dance Mural*.

10. Jane Simone Bussy, 'A Great Man', *Burlington Magazine*, vol.128, no.995 (Feb. 1986), p.82. The author was the daughter of Simon Bussy, the French painter and a close friend of Matisse's.

11. The version that would become (per Flam) *Merion Dance Mural*.

12. Letter from Henri Matisse to Pierre Matisse, 29 Nov. 1931 (Pierre Matisse Gallery Archives, Morgan Library, New York, letter 182, box 195; trans. from Flam 1993, p.45).

13. Letter from Pierre Matisse to Henri and Amélie Matisse, 26 Feb. 1932 (Pierre Matisse Gallery Archives, Morgan Library, letter 189, box 196; trans. from Flam 1993, p.48).

14. See Flam 1993, p.26., fig.9.

15. *Le Chant de Rossignol* was created for Serge Diaghilev's Ballets Russes (1909–29), of which the Ballet Russe de Monte Carlo was one successor. For more on the designs for this ballet, see Rémi Labrusse's article 'Matisse's Second Visit to London and His Collaboration with the "Ballets Russes"', *Burlington Magazine*, vol.139, no.1134 (Sept. 1997), pp.588–99.

16. Pierre Schneider, *Matisse*, trans. Michael Taylor and Bridget Strevens Romer, New York 1984, p.624 n.81 ('Recorded by Pierre Courthion'). See also Matisse & Courthion 2013, p.99, where Matisse recounts: 'I made a little maquette: a box-shaped scale model of the stage with my whole set and props and my characters represented by little pieces of paper in different colors moving about inside it'.

17. Vladimir Polunin, *The Continental Method of Scene Painting: Seven Years with the Diaghileff Company*, ed. Cyril W. Beaumont, New York 1979, p.61.

18. Fig.15 shows *Unfinished Dance Mural*.

19. No.3 represents stages of *Paris Dance Mural*.

20. Flam (1993, p.75) notes that 'although in the past [Matisse] had sometimes photographed his works while they were in progress, with the Barnes murals he did this more systematically than ever before' and attributes this thoroughness to 'a new self-consciousness about the act of creation'. Matisse began work on the first set of full-size canvases in April 1931 and completed the final version of the mural in April 1933.

21. The version in progress in these photographs is the *Paris Dance Mural*.

22. *Verve*, vol.I, no.1, Dec. 1937, and *Verve,* vol.II, no.8, June 1940; see nos.11 and 13 for maquettes. Among the artist's other, non-cover contributions to early issues of *Verve* was a cut-out version of his 1910 painting *The Dance* (no.12), specifically made to be reproduced in *Verve,* vol.I, no.4, Nov. 1938.

23. 'I dream of a book on "Matisse's colour" which would contain all your previously expressed and new thoughts on colour and would be illustrated by large plates (much larger than in *Verve*) in the style of the "chromatic symphony" and *Dance*. It would be very exciting if you talked about all the potential development of colour with the utmost freedom, since the reproduction of the coloured collages could be absolutely faithful.' (Letter from Tériade to Matisse, 20 Aug. 1940, H. Matisse Archives, Paris, quoted and trans. in Gilles and Xavier-Gilles Néret, (eds.), *Henri Matisse: Cut-Outs: Drawing with Scissors*, trans. Pamela Hargreaves and Jonathan Paul Murphy, Cologne 2009, p.91.)

24. 'H.M. m'a fait apporter les deux compositions inachevées, tirées des éléments restés dans ses cartons depuis son travail pour le ballet, (ce qui – parachevé – devint part la suite dans le JAZZ, Le Clown et Le Tobaggan). Le projet d'un album de reproduction de 20 "gouaches découpées", composées par H.M. spécialement à la dimension du volume et reproduites en facsimile, est né là' (Lydia Delectorskaya Scrapbook).

25. 'Seuls les deux sujets déjà existants, n'était pas au format, ont du être l'un réduit, l'autre agrandi mécaniquement' (ibid.).

26. This connection is pointed out by Jack Cowart et al., *Henri Matisse: Paper Cut-Outs*, exh. cat., National Gallery of Art, Washington, DC 1977, p.103.

27. 'H. Matisse annonça alors que tous ses costumes ne seront que des collants, mais de couleurs différentes par groupes de danseurs (blanc, noir, rouge, bleu, gris?, jaune?) rehaussées d'applications de la même couleur, mais brilliant sur mat – grandes formes d'algues épousant le corps' (Lydia Delectorskaya Scrapbook).

28. Matisse, in André Verdet, 'Azure Hours', *Hommage to Henri Matisse* (*XXe Siècle* special issue), ed. G. di San Lazzaro, New York 1970, p.114.

29. See Cowart et al. 1977, cat. no.13. The green and white version was a printing sample for the multi-coloured design. According to Pierre Schneider, Albert Marquet saw this version and felt that 'that was all that was needed', and Matisse agreed; see Schneider 1984, p.709 n.15.

30. 'Henri Matisse acquired a reproduction of the *Hercule et Antée* by Del Pollaiolo and kept it by him as a symbol of his own principles and convictions. And he redrew it himself repeatedly over the years.' (Lydia Delectorskaya, *With Apparent Ease … Henri Matisse: Paintings from 1935–1939* trans. Olga Tourkoff, Paris 1988, p.89.) A line drawing version of this composition also appears on the cover of the 1939 programme for the ballet; see Delectorskaya 1988, p.272.

31. This cut-out would later appear as part of a larger arrangement on the wall of Villa le Rêve, Vence; see p.39 in this volume.

32. 3 May 1938: 'collé la maquette du rideau' (Matisse's diary, Archives Matisse, Paris). I am grateful to Wanda de Guébriant for bringing this note to my attention and for a thoughtful conversation about its ramifications regarding the identity of the maquette in Schall's photograph. Especially because the Pompidou's maquette (fig.20) did not figure in the comprehensive catalogue, Cowart et al. 1977 (it was donated to Pompidou from Pierre Matisse's estate in

1991), I had initially suspected that it may be a somewhat deconstructed state of the work seen in the photograph. But because Matisse specifies that the final maquette for the curtain was 'glued', this still-tacked cut-out must be something else; perhaps, as Wanda suggests, it was used in the process of realising the related lithograph. The present location of the final glued curtain maquette remains unknown.

33. 'Le panneau retravaillé ensuite à plusieurs reprises, non seulement place Charles-Félix mais aussi au Régina, a été donc achevé, au plus tôt, dans la deuxième moitié de 1938' (Lydia Delectorskaya, letter to Pierre Matisse, 29 Dec. 1985, Pierre Matisse Gallery Archives, Morgan Library, letter 185, box 30). Matisse moved to the Régina in autumn 1938.

34. 'C'est donc une oeuvre qui avait découlé du travail de H. Matisse pour le ballet en tant que sujet, mais déjà une oeuvre indépendante, qui a été travaillée pour elle-même et longuement, comme un tableau de chevalet ... En somme, votre panneau de 1938 est une "gouache découpée" avant la lettre' (Lydia Delectorskaya, letter to Pierre Matisse, 29 Dec. 1985, Pierre Matisse Gallery Archives, Morgan Library, letter 185, box 30).

35. 'C'était un matériau pour application simplement' (interview between Claude Duthuit and Lydia Delectorskaya, Archives Matisse, Paris).

36. 'Ce n'est pas de la gouache découpée, c'est un système d'aide technique' (ibid.). See Cowart et al. 1977, fig.23, p.88.

37. Lydia Delectorskaya, annotations to Cowart et al. 1977, p.98 (Archives Matisse, Paris).

38. 'Pour moi ce n'est pas encore du papier découpé ... il imaginait des sujets, il les traduisait en couleurs, il illustrait son image, son idée' (interview between Claude Duthuit and Lydia Delectorskaya, Archives Matisse, Paris).

39. 'Ce travail lui donne l'idée que des papiers gouachés assemblés on peut tirer des choses expressives. C'est en 1944–45, il faisait des compositions très, très simple qu'il mettait au mur. Il passait beaucoup de temps à les regarder, il meditait en cherchant quelle serait la possibilité de s'exprimer' (ibid.).

40. 'Finalement, il a fait un découpage "La Harpe" une petite chose bleu sur blanc, il a dit "c'est mon premier découpage", c'est à dire une oeuvre conçue, il a réussi à donner une émotion dedans. Ça, c'est le départ' (ibid.).

41. 'Le décor du ballet ~~Rouge et noir~~ *Étrange farandole* n'a pas de rapport avec les "gouaches découpées" dans l'oeuvre de Matisse' (Lydia Delectorskaya Scrapbook).

42. 'Ils cheminaient depuis loin, en secret.' (Matisse, in André Verdet, *Entretiens, notes et écrits sur la peinture*, Paris 1978, p.131; trans. in Jack Flam, 'Jazz', in *Matisse on Art*, Berkeley and Los Angeles 1995, p.293 n.6.)

Game and Endgame

1. 'J'ai parfait mon mur de découpages' (letter from Henri Matisse to Pierre Matisse, 5 April 1948, Pierre Matisse Gallery Archives, Morgan Library, New York, letter 637, box 205).

2. Some elements seen in this photograph were never incorporated into finished compositions, and some move and merge to combine with others.

3. 'This panel, printed on linen – white for the motifs and beige for the background – forms, together with a second panel, a wall tapestry composed during reveries that came fifteen years after a voyage to Oceania ... It is only now that these wonders have returned to me, with tenderness and clarity, and have permitted me, with protracted pleasure, to execute these two panels.' (Matisse, 'Océanie', *Labyrinthe*, nos.22–3, Dec. 1946, reprinted as 'Oceania' in Jack Flam (ed.), *Matisse on Art*, Berkeley and Los Angeles 1995, p.169.)

4. Note from Lydia Delectorskaya to the Musée Matisse, Le Cateau-Cambrésis, Oct. 1997, cited and trans. in Patrice Deparpe, 'Matisse: L'Inspiration Polynesienne / Matisse: His Polynesian Inspiration', in Patrice Deparpe (ed.), *Matisse: La Couleur découpée, une donation rélévatrice / Cutting into Color, A Revealing Donation*, exh. cat., Musée Matisse, Le Cateau-Cambrésis 2013, p.65 n.22.

5. Brassaï, *Conversations with Picasso*, trans. Jane Marie Todd, Chicago and London 1999, p.293.

6. See Valerie D. Mendes and Frances Hinchcliffe, *Ascher: Fabric, Art, Fashion*, London 1987, p.36: 'Matisse indicated the wall and asked if Zika could reproduce the design which was almost complete. Ascher replied without hesitation that he could.'

7. Louis Aragon, 'Matisse-en-France', in *Henri Matisse: Thèmes et variations*, Paris 1943, p.27. The interview took place in 1942 but was published the following year.

8. Clement Greenberg, 'The Situation at the Moment', *Partisan Review* (Jan. 1948), reprinted in John O'Brian (ed.) *Clement Greenberg: The Collected Essays and Criticism, Volume 2, Arrogant Purpose, 1945–49*, Chicago and London 1986, pp.194–5. For a larger discussion of the 'quasi-mural' as a register of 'twentieth-century doubts about the identity and meaning of art', see Romy Golan, *Muralnomad: The Paradox of Wall Painting, Europe 1927–1957*, New Haven and London 2009.

9. It is worth noting that Matisse was accustomed to papering the walls of his studio with works in progress even when they lacked mural-size ambition. For example, visiting Nice-Cimiez in 1941, the poet and novelist Francis Carco observed: 'Arranged in several rows, one above the other, a series of drawings executed after an initial study covered the walls.' Matisse referred to this sequential presentation as 'the cinema of my sensibility.' See 'Interview with Francis Carco', in Flam 1995, p.135.

10. 'Les murs de ma chambre sont pleins de découpages': Henri Matisse to André Rouveyre, 22 Feb. 1948, letter 873, in Hanne Finsen (ed.), *Matisse, Rouveyre: Correspondance*, Paris 2001, p.487.

11. 'Je ne sais encore ce que je ferai de ces nouveaux découpages certainement pas un *Jazz*' (ibid.).

12. 'Si tu peux y passer ton impression m'interessera' (Henri Matisse to André Rouveyre, 13 Dec. 1947, letter 854, in Finsen 2001, p.475). In letter 858, 20 Dec. 1947 (Finsen 2001, p.477), Rouveyre mentions that he 'was curious to see what his impression [of the book] would be after more than 2 years where I saw them [the cut-outs] in Vence escape from the hands of the prestidigitator'.

13. 'C'est sec et froid. Juste exactement le contraire de ce qui est ton génie ... On a l'impression d'être devant, tu sais, de ces boîtes où, en manière de jouets, sont des plaques de bois recouvertes de scènes coloriées et qui sont découpées en morceaux qu'il faut brouiller et remettre dans leur ordre chacun.' (Letter 858, in Finsen 2001, p.477.)

14. 'Tes planches très bien présentées ... Je les ai revues avec une affectueuse émotion' and 'Dis que je suis bête et que je ne comprends rien ... que tu as bien le droit de t'amuser, de tailler à ta fantasie' (André Rouveyre to Henri Matisse, 20 Dec. 1947, letter 858, in Finsen 2001, pp.476–7); 'intimement chagrin de t'avoir écrit avec cette extreme liberté à propos de ton Jazz' (André Rouveyre to Henri Matisse, 25 Dec. 1947, letter 859, in Finsen 2001, p.477).

15. 'C'est la *matière* qui n'y est plus. Quand tu fixes tes papiers découpés ça reflète ta flamme, c'est vraiment du papier découpé par toi. Travail de prestidigitateur ... du moment où ton travail passe par des intermédiaries le feu se trouve perdu en route' (André Rouveyre to Henri Matisse, 25 Dec. 1947, letter 859, in Finsen 2001, pp.477–78).

16. 'Je te remercie de ta franchise au sujet de Jazz. *Je suis absolument de ton avis* ... C'est absolument *un raté*' (Henri Matisse to André Rouveyre, 28 Dec. 1947, letter 860, in Finsen 2001, p.478).

17. '... et pourquoi ces découpés lorsque je les fais, que je les vois au mur me sont-ils sympathiques et sans le caractère de pulzts [puzzle] que je leur trouve dans Jazz. Je crois que ce qui les gâte absolument est la transposition qui leur enlève la sensibilité' (ibid.).

18. 'Note que je ne m'en trouve nullement découragé, puisque je suis occupé l'après-midi à faire de nouvelles combinaisons de couleurs avec le système du papier découpé' (ibid.).

19. 'Mais je sais que ces choses doivent rester comme elle sont, des originaux – des gouaches tout simplement' (ibid.).

20. 'Ce parfum de tes découpages participe aussi de la grâce infinie qui émane d'une chose exceptionelle mais d'une existence précaire, fragile, telle qu'est celle de tes papiers quand ils tombent dans tes doigts sous tes ciseaux' (André Rouveyre to Henri Matisse, Tuesday evening, 10pm, 17 Feb. 1948, letter 872, Finsen 2001, p.486).

21. 'Tu as raison, je crois, et c'est aussi mon avis, ces papiers découpés ont leur existence très pure alors qu'ils s'échappent de tes mains, de tes ciseaux. Leur matière papier, avec les jeux menus de la lumière sur leur flexibilité, la physique même de cette flexibilité, tout cela concourt à faire une chose miraculeuse et qui perd son essence alors qu'on veut la mettre trop sèchement à plat. Mais ça la garde son essence alors que c'est piqué au mur avec les épingles par Lydia. Car alors cela y garde cette vie du papier dont je parle et subissant des changement incessants. Vouloir mettre à plat sèchement cela, c'est imaginer de vouloir tendre la surface de la peau d'une belle fille à plat, comme une peau de lapin qu'on veut faire sécher. Tu me comprends, parbleu!' (André Rouveyre to Henri Matisse, 31 Dec. 1947, letter 862, in Finsen 2001, p.479.)

22. Others have used the metaphor of the puzzle in describing the cut-outs without this negative association. See, for example, Jane Simone Bussy, 'A Great Man', *Burlington Magazine*, vol.128, no.995 (Feb. 1986), p.82, in which she notes that the in-progress Barnes mural was 'ingeniously composed of bits of coloured paper. These were pinned to the wall and could be shifted about like a gigantic jigsaw puzzle.'

23. *Merriam-Webster's Collegiate Dictionary*, 11th edn, Springfield, MA 2012, p.1269.

24. Henri Matisse, 'On Modernism and Tradition', *The Studio*, vol.9, no.50 (May 1935), p.238, trans. in Flam 1995, p.72.

25. Henri Matisse, 'Repertoire 6', c.1946, quoted in Flam 1993, p.43 n.82.

26. Henri Matisse, in Maria Luz, 'Témoignages: Henri Matisse', *XXe Siècle*, n.s. 2 (Jan. 1952), pp.66–7: 'Testimonial', 1951, trans. in Flam 1995, p.137.

27. See Jack Cowart et al., *Henri Matisse: Paper Cut-Outs*, exh. cat., National Gallery of Art, Washington, DC 1977, cat. no.63.

28. See Cowart et al. 1977, cat. no.81.

29. See Cowart et al. 1977, cat. no.78.

30. See Cowart et al. 1977, cat. no.75.

31. See Cowart et al. 1977, cat. no.74.

32. An extraordinary gift comprising those gouached elements cut out by Matisse but ultimately unused in finished compositions was recently presented by the Matisse family to the Musées Matisse, Nice and Le Cateau-Cambrésis. This discarded shape represents inv. no. 487, held by the former. For more on the donation, see the latter's exhibition catalogue, Deparpe 2013, in which a selection of these unused elements are reproduced.

33. 'Un armateur qui fait un bateau de luxe s'appellant "le génie français" destiné à l'orient jusqu'au Japon ma proposé de me l'acheter pour mettre dans son bateau dans un cadre serieux et sous glace – J'ai dit que je réflecherai.' (Letter from Henri Matisse to Pierre Matisse, 5 April 1948, Pierre Matisse Gallery Archives, Morgan Library, letter 637, box 205.)

34. '... mais un gros obstacle – dans ce pays d'humidité excessive toutes mes gouaches moississaient' (ibid.).

35. 'J'aime mieux les garder ou bien les encadrer pour motifs' (ibid.).

36. 'Les oeuvres pour une exposition sont toutes rassemblées et mises dans un coin' (Henri Matisse to Pierre Matisse, 13 Oct. 1948, Pierre Matisse Gallery Archives, Morgan Library, letter 659, box 205).

37. 'Les papiers découpés, 22 motifs (assez fragiles)' (ibid.).

Chapel Factory

1. Letter from Henri Matisse to Father Couturier, 7 May 1949, in Henri Matisse, Marie-Alain Couturier and Louis-Bertrand Rayssiguier, *The Vence Chapel: The Archive of a Creation*, ed. Marcel Billot, trans. Michael Taylor, Turin 1999, p.183.

2. 'Go next door (to the big studio), go take a look at the factory', remarks by Matisse reported by Brother Rayssiguier, 15 Feb. 1950: Matisse et al. 1999, p.294.

3. Reverend Father Couturier, 'Church Full of Joy', *Vogue*, Dec. 1951, p.129.

4. For more on Father Couturier's ideas about the revival of religious art, see Marcel Billot, 'Le Père Couturier et l'Art Sacré', in *Paris-Paris/1937–1957*, exh. cat. Centre Georges Pompidou, Paris, 1981, pp.196–200. See also Sarah Wilson, *Henri Matisse*, Barcelona 2009, esp. pp.78–82.

5. For more on Léger's Assy mosaic, see Yvonne Brunhammer (ed.), *Fernand Léger: L'Opera monumentale*, Milan 2005, pp.95–9.

6. 'Le jour où Dufy, Segonzac, Picasso, Derain, Matisse, Bonnard auront des commandes pour Saint-Sulpice, pour Notre-Dame ou pour le faubourg Saint-Honoré, le jour où Perret, Le Corbusier, Mallet-Stevens auront à bâtir dans les Chantiers du Cardinal, autant d'églises que M. Barbier ou M. Tartempion, une grande partie de notre tâche sera faite. Non point qu'à notre avis, cela suffise à assurer la renaissance de l'art chrétien (ni même que nous soyons très sûr que les oeuvres sorties de ces mains illustres soient toutes très religieuses) mais une chose essentielle sera restaurée: l'Église aura retrouvé dans ce domaine le sens de la grandeur, l'habitude de s'adresser aux plus grands, aux véritables maîtres et non plus à des médiocres plus ou moins spécialisés' (Father Couturier quoted in Billot 1981, p.198).

7. 'Ce n'est pas un travail que j'ai choisi mais bien un travail pour lequel j'ai été choisi par le destin sur la fin de ma route, que je continue selon mes recherches, la chapelle me donnant l'occasion de les fixer en les réunissant' (Henri Matisse, *Chapelle du Rosaire des Dominicaines de Vence*, Vence, 1951, np., trans. in Jack Flam [ed.], *Matisse on Art*, Berkeley and Los Angeles 1995, p.128).

8. Matisse quoted in Jack Cowart et al., *Henri Matisse: Paper Cut-Outs*, exh. cat., National Gallery of Art, Washington, DC 1977, p.149.

9. Remarks by Henri Matisse reported by Brother Rayssiguier in Matisse et al. 1999, p.39.

10. Matisse et al. 1999, p.42.

11. Cowart et al. 1977, p.151.

12. Letter from Henri Matisse to Brother Rayssiguier, 12 May 1948, in Matisse et al. 1999, p.66.

13. Alfred H. Barr, Jr, *Henri Matisse*, exh. cat., The Museum of Modern Art, New York 1951, p.280.

14. Remarks from Father Couturier's diary, 9 Aug. 1948, in Matisse et al. 1999, p.82.

15. Matisse et al. 1999, p.82.

16. Barr, Jr, p.281.

17. See Wilson 2009, p.78; and Françoise Gilot, *Matisse and Picasso: A Friendship in Art*, London 1990, p.206.

18. Interiors of Vence are Matisse's last fully realised paintings, and he would make two more in 1951, but they were both left unfinished. For more on the Interiors of Vence, see Marie-Thérèse Pulvenis de Séligny et al., *Henri Matisse – Vence, l'espace d'un atelier: Nature morte aux grenades*, exh. cat., Musée Matisse, Nice, 2007; and Dorthe Aagesen and Rebecca Rabinow (eds.), *Matisse: In Search*

of True Painting, exh. cat., The Metropolitan Museum of Art, New York 2013.

19. Letter from Henri Matisse to Father Couturier, 14 Nov. 1948, in Matisse et al. 1999, p.102.

20. Matisse had an upholstered armchair with special support made, which allowed him to work in bed for hours without extensive exertion.

21. Remarks by Henri Matisse reported by Brother Rayssiguier, 24 Jan. 1949, in Matisse et al. 1999, p.137.

22. Remarks by Brother Rayssiguier, 18 Nov. 1948, in Matisse et al. 1999, p.108.

23. Letter from Henri Matisse to Father Couturier, 27 Feb. 1950, in Matisse et al. 1999, p.303.

24. Matisse et al. 1999, p.303.

25. Father Couturier quoted in Wilson 2009, p.83.

26. Studio assistant Paule Caen-Martin refers to the long pole with a charcoal, which allowed Matisse to draw from a distance, as a bamboo wand. See Paule Caen-Martin, 'Chez Henri Matisse, témoignage / At Home with Henri Matisse, a Personal Account', in Patrice Deparpe (ed.), *Matisse: La Couleur découpée, une donation révélatrice/Cutting into Color, A Revealing Donation*, exh. cat., Musée Matisse, Le Cateau-Cambrésis 2013, p.48.

27. Letter from Henri Matisse to Father Couturier, 7 April 1949, in Matisse et al. 1999, p.171.

28. Transferring the drawings of the *Stations of the Cross*, *St Dominic* and the *Virgin and Child* onto the ceramic tiles turned out to be one of the most technically challenging endeavours. Both finding a way of painting in pure black on the white panels and securing sufficiently large and resistant tiles proved a draining exercise for Matisse, who had to pay regular visits to the Ramies workshop in Vallauris, where Picasso also made his ceramics. Picasso, whose knowledge of ceramics was unrivalled, followed Matisse's ceramics' saga from its outset, offering support as the process became increasingly demanding. For more, see Gilot 1990, p.196.

29. Henri Matisse, 'The Chapel of the Rosary, 1951', in Flam 1995, p.130.

30. Remarks by Henri Matisse to Brother Rayssiguier and Milon de Peillon, 27 April 1949, in Matisse et al. 1999, p.178. Lydia Delectorskaya, Matisse's long-time assistant, suggested that the image was inspired by Françoise Gilot, Picasso's wife, who had recently given birth to their daughter Paloma. Matisse was amused by the idea that Picasso had had to be reassured by Gilot that there was no reason for jealousy – especially as Matisse was aiming for universality rather than subjectivity: Gilot 1990, pp.200–5.

31. Remarks by Henri Matisse to Brother Rayssiguier, 5 Feb. 1949, in Matisse et al. 1999, p.142.

32. Matisse et al. 1999, p.142.

33. Letter from Father Couturier to Henri Matisse, 5 May 1949, in Matisse et al. 1999, p.181.

34. Remarks by Henri Matisse to Brother Rayssiguier, 12 July 1950, in Matisse et al. 1999, p.342.

35. For more, see remarks by Henri Matisse to Brother Rayssiguier, 19 June 1950, in Matisse et al. 1999, p.337.

36. For more on Matisse's relationship with dance, see Marie Thérèse Pulvenis de Séligny, '"Danseuse créole", 1950. L'éxubérance d'une composition', / "Creole Dancer", 1950. The Exuberance of a Composition' in Deparpe 2013, pp.54–9, and for a mention of Katherine Dunham's influence on Matisse see Cowart et al. 1977, p.165.

37. John Russell, *Matisse: Father & Son*, New York 1999, pp.362–3.

38. Letter from Father Couturier to Henri Matisse, 24 May 1950, in Matisse et al. 1999, trans. Pamela Hargreaves and Jonathan Paul Murphy, p.329.

39. Tériade quoted in Gilles and Xavier-Gilles Néret (eds.), *Henri Matisse: Cut-Outs: Drawing with Scissors*, trans. Pamela Hargreaves and Jonathan Paul Murphy, Cologne 2009, p.272.

40. Paule Caen-Martin in Deparpe 2013, p.49.

41. Cowart et al. 1977, p.181.

42. Letter from Henri Matisse to Monsignor Rémond, Bishop of Nice, in Néret 2009, p.235.

Bodies and Waves

1. See, for example, Jack Cowart et al., *Henri Matisse: Paper Cut-Outs*, exh. cat., National Gallery of Art, Washington, DC 1977, pp.233–4; André Verdet, *Prestiges de Matisse: Précédé de visite à Matisse, entretiens avec Matisse*, Paris 1952, pp.64–5, trans. in Jack Flam (ed.), *Matisse on Art*, Berkeley and Los Angeles 1995, p.215.

2. For a detailed chronology of 1952, see John Elderfield, 'Appendix', in *The Cut-Outs of Henri Matisse*, New York 1978, pp.42–3, and his overview of the making of the *Blue Nudes*, pp.26–9.

3. Paule Caen-Martin, 'Chez Henri Matisse, témoignage/At Home with Henri Matisse, a Personal Account', in Patrice Deparpe (ed.), *Matisse: La Couleur découpée, une donation révélatrice / Cutting into Color, A Revealing Donation*, exh. cat., Musée Matisse, Le Cateau-Cambrésis 2013, p.53.

4. Lydia Delectorskaya, annotations to Cowart et al. 1977, Archives Matisse, Paris: 'Avec maestria. Chacun à un jour différent, ils ont été découpés d'un trait, d'un seul coup des ciseaux, en 10 minutes ou 15 au maximum.'

5. Louis Aragon, *Henri Matisse: A Novel*, trans. Jean Stewart, New York 1972, p.308.

6. One of Matisse's assistants, Jacqueline Duhême, explained how Matisse made 'rough sketches' and then 'used the scissors to continue with his idea of the drawing': see 'Entretien avec Jacqueline Duhême, 12 décembre 2012 / Conversation with Jacqueline Duhême, December 12, 2012', in Deparpe 2013, p.39.

7. A facsimile of the sketchbook: Henri Matisse, *Carnet de dessins*, text by Jean Cassou, Paris 1955.

8. For a thorough discussion of the making of the Barnes *Dance*, see Jack Flam, *Matisse: 'The Dance'*, Washington, DC 1993, and Karen Butler's entry on *The Dance* and Yve-Alain Bois, 'Matisse's Awakening', in Yve-Alain Bois, Barbara Buckley, Karen Butler, Claudine Grammont and Jennifer Maas, *Matisse in the Barnes Foundation*, forthcoming.

9. William Tucker, 'Matisse's Sculpture: The Grasped and the Seen', *Art in America* 63, no.4 (July–Aug. 1975), p.87. See also Dorothy Kosinski et al., *Matisse: Painter as Sculptor*, exh. cat., Dallas Museum of Art 2007.

10. For a discussion of the importance of what she calls the 'void' in Matisse's cut-outs, see Anne Coron, 'La Gouache découpée dans l'oeuvre de Henri Matisse: Pratique, esthétique, réception', PhD diss., Université Picardie Jules Verne (Amiens), Faculté des Arts, 2005, Section III, 2.4.

11. Fatimah Tobing Rony, *The Third Eye: Race, Cinema, and Ethnographic Spectacle*, Durham and London 1996, p.199.

12. Alicja Sowinska, 'Dialectics of the Banana Skirt: The Ambiguities of Josephine Baker's Self-Presentation', *Michigan Feminist Studies* 19 (Fall 2005 – Spring 2006).

13. Verdet 1952, pp.31–2: 'Les attaches sont sensibles, concentrées et simplifiées à l'extrême. Il y a des vides rapides entre certaines parties du corps. Par ces vides, l'air glisse, court, augmentant ainsi la sensation du mouvement de l'ensemble. Vide entre le buste et le ventre, vide entre le ventre et les jambes.'

14. Baker in Rony 1996, p.200. Verdet 1952, p.32: 'Le ventre ainsi isolé est un merveilleux ballon où vibre l'âme de la danse.'

15. *The Swimming Pool* is described in the 1958 issue of *Verve* as a maquette for a ceramic. The Musée Matisse in Nice has recently installed a ceramic version of *The Swimming Pool*.

16. Lydia Delectorskaya, 'Histoire de la PISCINE', Archives Matisse, Paris: 'Un

matin il annonça qu'il avait envie de voir des plongeuses. On convoqua la voiture de louage habituelle et il est parti à Palm-Beach de Cannes. Nous y sommes arrivés juste à midi. Un soleil de plomb! Et pas un baigneur ou baigneuse à la piscine de l'établissement! H.M. rit et, ayant fait à peine quelques pas le long de la piscine (aux dimensions plutôt modestes), il me souffla: 'Partons vite: avec ce soleil, je vais y attraper la crève!' Rentré à la maison, il dit: 'Je vais me faire une piscine à moi.' Et il me fit placer sur les murs tout autour de la pièce où il vivait, une bande de papier blanc de 70 cms de large, à une hauteur qu'il me désigna.'

17. Ibid.: 'Ensuite, au cours des semaines qui suivirent, quelquefois le jour d'autres fois me faisant appeler au milieu de la nuit; il y plaça une à une les formes humaines – plongeuses ou nageuses – mais pas aux emplacements successifs, les jetant tantôt ci tantôt là. La plupart des corps naissaient d'une façon spontanée, comme si, avant de demander du papier bleu et les ciseaux, il avait longuement médité sur la silhouette à créer et son emplacement.'

18. Matisse quoted in Carolyn Lanchner, *Henri Matisse*, New York 2008, p.37, and John Elderfield, *Matisse in the Collection of The Museum of Modern Art*, New York 1978, p.162. The quotation was recorded in September 1952 by Margaret Scolari Barr during a visit with her husband to Matisse's studio (Alfred H. Barr, Jr, Papers 11.III.S.2, The Museum of Modern Art Archives, New York).

19. Lanchner 2008, p.40.

20. Henri Matisse in Maria Luz, 'Testimonial' (1951), in Flam 1995, p.209.

21. Lydia Delectorskaya (annotations to Cowart et al. 1977, Archives Matisse, Paris) explains the circumstances of making the *Acrobats*: 'On the request of H. Matisse, a model clothed in black tights had executed some acrobatic dance for him. He then made large drawings of this subject, in brush and ink. Shortly thereafter he cut a Blue Acrobat. As opposed to the drawings that he found very good, this blue form left him unsatisfied. He therefore set himself to reworking it, modeling it like a clay sculpture: sometimes adding, sometimes removing these volumes. During the weeks of this work, he cut a second blue Acrobat, but of a totally different expression.'

22. Roger Benjamin, 'The Decorative Landscape, Fauvism, and the Arabesque of Observation', *Art Bulletin* 75, no. 2 (June 1993), pp. 295–316, esp. p. 310.

23. Henri Matisse in 'Interview with André Verdet', in Flam 1995, p. 211.

24. Verdet 1952, p.63; the present translation modifies that in Flam 1995, p.214, which reads 'is amplified by imagination'.

25. Matisse in Verdet 1952, pp.51–2: 'Observez cette grande composition: feuillage, fruits, ciseaux; un jardin. Le blanc intermédiaire est déterminé par l'arabesque du papier-couleur découpé qui donne à ce *blanc-ambiant* une qualité rare et impalpable. Cette qualité est celle du contraste. Chaque groupe particulier de couleurs a en lui-même une atmosphère particulière. C'est ce que j'appellerai *l'ambiance expressive*.' (Emphasis as in original.) An alternative translation is available in Flam 1995, p.212. Matisse's interest in exploiting whiteness is rooted, at least in part, in his interest in the work of Paul Cézanne, especially in the way he leaves the paper in reserve in his watercolours or allows areas of his oil paintings to remain unfinished. Matisse's interest in Stephane Mallarmé's use of the white sheet in his poetry might also be considered here – Matisse made prints to illustrate Mallarmé's *Poésies*, published in 1932. See John Elderfield, *The Cut-Outs of Henri Matisse*, New York 1978, p.31. Elderfield writes that Matisse understood that 'the white surface of a picture can be made pictorial even when not covered with paint'. See also Yve-Alain Bois, 'Cézanne and Matisse: From Apprenticeship to Creative Misreading', in Joseph Rishel and Katherine Sachs (eds.), *Cézanne and Beyond*, exh. cat., Philadelphia Museum of Art 2009, pp.103–20.

26. Henri Matisse's 'Réponses à un questionnaire de Gaston Diehl' (1949), reprinted in Dominique Fourcade (ed.), *Henri Matisse: Écrits et propos sur l'art*, Paris 1972, p.244, trans. in Yve-Alain Bois, 'On Matisse: The Blinding: For Leo Steinberg', trans. Greg Sims, *October* 68 (Spring 1994) 1994, pp.60–121, esp. p.121; Henri Matisse in 'Interview with Georges Charbonnier' (1950) in Flam 1995, p.191.

27. Bois 1994, p.64.

28. Rémi Labrusse, 'Decoration Beyond Decoration', in Olivier Berggruen and Max Hollein (eds.), *Henri Matisse: Drawing with Scissors, Masterpieces from the Late Years*, trans. Paul Aston, exh. cat., Schirn Kunsthalle, Frankfurt 2002, pp.78, 80.

29. Bois 1994, p.105; Labrusse 2002, 75.

30. Aragon 1972, p.208.

31. Henri Matisse in 'Interview with André Verdet', in Deparpe 2013, p.64 (which alters translation in Flam 1995, p.241); in this excellent text Deparpe discusses the importance of the Tahiti trip for Matisse's cut-outs.

32. Henri Matisse in André Verdet, 'Les heures azuréennes', in *Hommage à Henri Matisse, XXe Siècle*, Paris 1970, as quoted and translated in Deparpe 2013, pp.66–7.

Chromatic Composition

1. The role of the charcoal or crayon lines in later works such as *La Négresse*, *Memory of Oceania* and *Acanthuses*, where they come to the fore, is still unclear. In part they extend the arabesque silhouettes of coloured and shaped pieces of card against a white background, which Matisse allowed to assume more prominence in such spare and often asymmetric late compositions as *Acanthuses*, *La Négresse* and *The Sheaf*. Matisse explained this to André Verdet in spring 1952 with reference to *The Parakeet and the Mermaid*, but in terms that would foreshadow the works from the next (and last) two years of his career: 'The white intermediary is determined by the arabesque of the cutout coloured paper which gives this *white-atmosphere* a rare and impalpable quality. This quality is that of contrast. Each particular group of colours has a particular atmosphere. It is what I will call the *expressive atmosphere*.' See André Verdet, *Prestiges de Matisse: Précédé de visite à Matisse, entretiens avec Matisse*, Paris 1952, p.52, trans. in Jack Flam (ed.), *Matisse on Art*, Berkeley and Los Angeles 1995, p.212.

2. This was confirmed in an unpublished interview with Matisse's assistant Paule Martin, Paris, Jan. 2012, conducted by the present author.

3. The multicoloured quatrefoils that are distributed over the finished versions of *La Négresse* and *Large Decoration with Masks* employ the same shades of blue, orange, green, red and pink.

4. That the cut-outs from this period went through multiple states was confirmed by Lydia Delectorskaya in interview with Claude Duthuit, Archives Matisse, Paris.

5. As Lydia Delectorskaya recollected: 'Ensuite je vais disposer à peu près chronologiquement, mais c'est très difficile car il menait en même temps plusieurs choses, dans son atelier, sur les deux murs, et dans sa chambre encore autre chose.' (Interview between Claude Duthuit and Lydia Delectorskaya [with some handwritten notes by Françoise Garnaud, secretary to Claude Duthuit] recorded on a typewritten insert in the unpublished scrapbook compiled by Lydia Delectorskaya now in the possession of the Archives Matisse, Paris, hand-copied and translated by Karl Buchberg at the Archives in November 2011.)

6. Duhême recalled that this 'made Matisse very happy. She danced for him in Vence. It was quite impressive I must say because when we look at dancers, it always seems so aerial and light but when they stand just three meters away, you realise all the work it requires. You hear the noise of the feet and pointed toes. Matisse was very, very interested in this. He would say,

"You see Jacqueline: everything is an effort. Even when one looks so light, it is still hard. Everything is hard!'" (Unpublished interview with Jacqueline Duhême, Paris, May 2013.)

7. Louis Aragon, *Henri Matisse, Roman*, 2 vols., Paris 1971, vol.2, p.305, and Jack Cowart et al., *Henri Matisse: Paper Cut-Outs*, exh. cat., National Gallery of Art, Washington, DC 1977, pp.84–271, esp. p.165.

8. John Hallmark Neff, 'Matisse, his cut-outs and the ultimate method', in Cowart et al. 1977, pp.21–35, esp. p.35 n.29.

9. This photograph (reproduced in John Elderfield, *The Cut-Outs of Henri Matisse*, New York 1978, p.121) also seems to show the charcoal markings around *La Négresse* drawn directly onto the studio wall.

10. This *Gesamtkunstwerk* aspect of Matisse's studio was also echoed by Françoise Gilot, a frequent visitor to Matisse's studio with Picasso during these years: 'It was very funny, because even though he was many times receiving us, and he was in bed, he always had a very nice colour of sweater – green, et cetera – and then behind him there was a dark purple Chinese drape of some kind, or something else. It was always very well organised. That's why my son said, "Ha, he is a real painter! Mother, that one is a real painter, because he lives in the things he does"' (unpublished interview with Françoise Gilot, New York, Jan. 2012, conducted by Karl Buchberg, Nicholas Cullinan and Jodi Hauptman).

11. Verdet 1952 (a photograph of *La Négresse* is reproduced on p.33).

12. As John Elderfield (1978, p.42) writes: 'Although illustrations for Verdet's book could easily have been collected later in 1952 (its date of publication), it is certain that the work was in this state at the time of the Verdet interviews because Verdet reports seeing the seated *Blue Nudes* and the women of *Women of Monkeys* [sic] all of which were made after *La Négresse* reached its initial state. It seems likely, therefore, that after just beginning *The Parakeet and the Mermaid* in his bedroom in March, Matisse turned to *La Négresse* in his studio and brought it to its early state by about the end of that month.'

13. Another photograph shows a later stage of *La Négresse* with some of the blue, pink red and green quatrefoil embellishments fixed in their final positions, across from a seemingly complete version of *The Wild Poppies* of 1953 on the facing wall, rather than the earlier *Blue Nude* that occupied the same spot – demonstrating how Matisse's compositions reached fruition at different rhythms and tempos, depending on their scale and complexity, period of gestation, and how forms and motifs tumbled and migrated across the walls from one idea to another.

14. Matisse cited in Pierre Schneider, *Matisse*, trans. Michael Taylor and Bridget Strevens Romer, New York and London 1984, p.739.

15. *Amis de l'Art*, n.s. 2, Oct. 1951.

16. Verdet 1952, p.64–5, cited and trans. in Cowart et al. 1977, p.231.

17. Verdet 1952, p.32.

18. Verdet 1952, pp.64–5, cited and trans. in Cowart et al. 1977, p.231.

19. Verdet 1952, pp.64–5.

20. Though one of Matisse's most abstract compositions, *The Snail* is not completely abstract: David Fraser Jenkins has argued that it is based on earlier figurative drawings. See David Fraser Jenkins, '*Baigneuses* and *Demoiselles*: "Bathers" in Cézanne, Picasso and Matisse', *Apollo*, vol.145, no. 421 (March 1997), pp.39–44.

21. Here I am reminded of Theodor Adorno's classic account of Beethoven's last compositional phase, which speaks of 'the irascible gesture [of] the hand of the master [which] sets free the masses of material that he used to form its tears and fissures' in order to create 'fractured landscapes ... [torn] apart in time' (Theodor W. Adorno, 'Late Style in Beethoven', in *Essays on Music*, ed. Richard Leppert, with new translations by Susan H. Gillespie, Berkeley, Los Angeles and London 2002, pp.564–8, esp. pp.566–7).

22. 'For Matisse the volution was a metaphor which embodied universal movement' (Cowart et al. 1977, p.244).

23. Lydia continued: '*The Snail* was made in the Hôtel Régina at Nice. H. Matisse had at his disposal sheets of paper painted in gouache by assistants, in all the colours he used for the "papiers découpés". A background of white paper – of the dimensions indicated by H.M. – was put on the wall and the assistant pinned onto it the pieces of gouached paper which H.M. passed to him indicating exactly where they should be placed. When H.M. decided that his composition was finished, it was lightly stuck to the background. The panel was taken down when H.M. needed the wall for a further work. When later on it was sent to Lefebvre-Foinet [in Paris] to be pasted down, before anything was moved, an extremely precise tracing was made to ensure that no changes were made in the composition, not even by so much as a millimetre.' (Letter from Lydia Delectorskaya to Ronald Alley, 30 March 1976, Tate Archives.)

24. Lefebvre-Foinet continued: 'Entrusted personally with the completion of the collages by M. Henri Matisse, we had the work pinned onto paper – two very exact tracings were made. We used raw canvas which had been sponged over twice and attached to a temporary stretcher. Thin paper was pasted onto this canvas to serve as a support and a means of attachment. Next the paper of the background was pasted down, then the work itself was fixed ... This work was done by me with the help of M. Matisse's secretary, and completed and approved by the artist and Madame Duthuit.' (Letter from Maurice Lefebvre-Foinet to Ronald Alley, 19 Feb. 1976, Tate Archives).

25. Two more photographs show *The Snail*, now with a few tweaks and signed, and with, above it, the top part of *Large Decoration with Masks* – the green leaves on the right-hand side and blue on the left (though Matisse tried both arrangements).

26. Around this time Matisse also returned to work on *La Négresse*. A photograph dating from around February 1953 (Elderfield 1978, p.122) shows it in exactly the same state and position on the studio wall, next to the radiator, as the photograph from April 1952, but now with *Large Decoration with Masks* in an advanced state of development directly next to it on the adjoining wall, which, as John Elderfield argued, 'dates this photograph as no earlier than February 1953'. Elderfield (1978, p.43) continued: 'The *Large Decoration with Masks* is seen in an earlier state in the photograph on p.124, surrounded by cut-outs that had been made before the end of June 1952 (c.f. p.114). Only after virtually completing *Large Decoration with Masks*, then, did Matisse return to work on *La Négresse*. Later in-progress photographs of *La Négresse* (p.123) definitely confirm that Matisse only arrived at the final configuration of this work by introducing square sheets containing four-leaf patterns such as he had used in the *Large Decoration with Masks*. Since *Large Decoration with Masks* and *Decoration, Fruits* preceded *Apollo*, which was completed by May 1953, all these large decorative works were finalized in the early spring of 1953. All of Matisse's great environmental cut-outs were therefore produced between the spring of 1952 and the spring of 1953, in the space of a single astonishingly productive year.'

27. Sigmund Freud, *Civilisation and its Discontents*, in *The Standard Edition of the Complete Psychological Works of Sigmund Freud*, vol. 21, London 2001, pp.64–145.

28. Matisse recalled the island and lagoons of Tahiti at length in conversation with André Verdet, just before embarking on *Memory of Oceania* that summer: 'The light of the Pacific, of the Islands [is] a deep golden goblet into which you look' (Verdet 1952, p.60, cited and trans. in Cowart et al. 1977, p.247.

29. '*Souvenir d'Oceanie* [*Memory of Oceania*] appears to have developed from these earlier works. The view is

once again out over the beach; the yellow shape at upper left apparently refers to a banana tree and the yellow shape at lower right to the native pirogue Matisse had sketched over 20 years before (*Cahiers d'Art*, 1936, ill. p.15). The large green diagonal rectangle suggests the Papeete, and the thin, straight fuschia shape superimposed over the "ship" suggests a mast. (Matisse had reduced the details of this ship to a similar geometric scheme as early as 1936 in his painting *La Chemise verte* (Copenhagen, Statens Museum for Kunst), in which *Fenêtre à Tahiti* is represented in the background.) The direction of the "ship" in the cut-out – from lower right to upper left – corresponds to the placement of the ship in Matisse's original photograph, the etching, and the tapestry. The distant horizon is implied by the deep yellow and orange rectangles at the center and upper right, evoking the sky and sea, respectively. The orange border, like the roseate border in the tapestry cartoon, suggests a window' (Cowart et al. 1977, p.247).

30. 'Il faudrait l'accompagner d'un dessin de Tahiti. Pas celui du bateau avec la balustrade, mais le dessin du Lagon avec l'arbre penché au dessus, comme ça' (interview between Claude Duthuit and Lydia Delectorskaya, as n.5).

31. 'This view through the trees to the harbor with the sailing ship Papeete moored to the dock below was Matisse's first large scale work on a Tahitian theme, although Aragon had noted (1971, I, p.205) that the source of the balustrade in the composition was not Tahiti, but Nice' (Cowart et al. 1977, p.247).

32. Unpublished interview with Jacqueline Duhême, Paris, May 2013.

33. There are forty-four documents in the correspondence between Sidney Brody and Matisse and his representatives in the Archives Matisse in Paris, including plans and photographs of Mr Brody's house. The first letter from Mrs Brody to Marguerite Duthuit, dated 5 August 1952, enquires about the possibility of Matisse making a ceramic mural to decorate their home and includes photographs and plans of their home with measurements of the living area where it is envisaged the mural will be displayed.

34. Tetsuo Abe's photograph of 28 September 1952 showing *The Wild Poppies* of 1953 in its very early stages next to the right-hand section of *The Parakeet and the Mermaid* and superimposed on various large-scale line drawings for the Vence chapel demonstrates how much he was using his crowded studio walls as both sketchbook and canvas. Jacqueline Duhême also made an important point about the works of this period: 'Matisse had three houses. He still had Paris at the time: Paris, Vence and Nice. Later on, he spent more time in Nice because the walls were higher there and because there were better doctors who could help him' (unpublished interview with Jacqueline Duhême, Paris, May 2013). All of the late large-scale works correspond to the floor-to-ceiling heights of the rooms in Villa le Rêve.

35. Cowart et al. 1977, p.3.

36. The Cowart et al. 1977 catalogue incorrectly dates the beginning of Matisse's work on *Large Decoration with Masks* to January 1953: see p.253.

37. Pierre Matisse Gallery Archives, Morgan Library, New York, box 185, Folder 9.

38. John Russell, *Matisse: Father & Son*, New York 1999, p.365.

39. Russell 1999, p.366.

40. Russell 1999, p.367.

41. Photographs of the work in progress show that it originally began bookended by the two blue fluted columns that also appear in the corners of *Large Decoration with Masks* and *Decoration Fruits*, providing a device with which to frame and enclose the overall composition. An early state includes the lines of axes used by Matisse to structure this symmetrical design. The sun at the top centre of the work originally had a swirling yellow pattern. Under this were scattered some multicoloured slivers of arrow-shaped works. The next stage shows the mask of Apollo added, with the sun above modified to its present and final state. Matisse then replaced the arrow-shaped cut-outs with the foliate designs that proliferate across the work today. The three lozenges that feature in the final version were added next, along with the tendril-like line drawing. Photographs of Matisse propped up in bed and talking on the telephone in front of the work show a bouquet of flowers next to it, similar to the one next to *La Négresse*, which indicates that these may have been an inspiration. Presumably all of these photographs were taken in the early part of 1953, before the Brodys saw the finished work that May.

42. Russell 1999, pp.365–6.

43. Russell 1999, p.366.

44. Photographs of the work in progress show that it was originally constructed from the bottom right-hand corner outwards and was set against a plain white background. The blue and green leaves were then gradually built up with the small sections of (then) blue 'berries' that are interspersed among the leaves. At some point Matisse substituted this background for the orange-yellow, 'tobacco' one of the final version and inserted a grid of overlaid lines dividing it into nine smaller squares. In the final stage Matisse swapped the blue berries for the red ones, which provide chromatic contrast to the blue and green leaves and yellow background, and gradually increased their numbers (see no.133).

45. For more on this, see Rebecca Daniels, 'Henri Matisse's stained-glass window "La Rosace" (1954)', *Burlington Magazine*, vol. 155, no. 1326 (Sept. 2013), pp.612–20.

46. In the same letter d'Harnoncourt described and drew *Large Decoration with Masks*, which was evidently still pinned to the wall of Matisse's studio almost two years after it was begun. Because the work was not wanted by the Brodys, Matisse's retort to their rejection of it on their visit to his studio in May 1953 that 'if they didn't want it, that was of no importance, because I would keep it for myself' was no idle threat. D'Harnoncourt wrote: 'He now has a huge panel laid out in his studio ... It has great charm but is (unquestionably?) on the "decorative" side.' (Rockefeller Archive Center, New York, Nelson A. Rockefeller, Personal Activities. III.4.A. Box 156/1714.)

47. Ibid.

48. Ibid.

49. Hilary Spurling, *Matisse the Master: A Life of Henri Matisse: The Conquest of Colour, 1909–1954*, New York 2005, p.466.

50. As Françoise Gilot observed: 'And also, remember, when you are not in a very good health, I don't think you can ... worry about the future at all. You want to do something in the present. And also ... with Matisse, who was, who had not been so gifted at the start – who had, who had been even, you might say, a late bloomer as a painter, it took him from the age of twenty to aged thirty-one at least to become himself. So it was pure joy to be able in ten minutes to do something that was of now, now, now.' (Unpublished interview with Françoise Gilot, New York, 2012.)

Materials and Techniques

1. Antoinette King, 'Technical Appendix', in Jack Cowart et al., *Henri Matisse: Paper Cut-Outs*, exh. cat., National Gallery of Art, Washington, DC 1977, pp.272–7.

2. Paul Vermeulen, 'An investigation into the discoloration of the background paper of Matisse's *La Perruche et la sirène*', *Paper Conservator*, vol.21, 1997, pp.15–25; Calvin Winner, 'Installation of *L'Escargot* by Henri Matisse', in Sally Woodcock (ed.), *Big Pictures: Problems and Solutions for Treating Outsize Paintings*, London 2005, 33–9; Dominique Royer (ed.), *Musée Matisse Nice. Conservation, restauration, pour l'avenir d'une collection*, exh. cat., Musée Matisse, Nice 2003.

3. During the course of the three-year research project *Fondation Beyeler – National Suisse Conservation Project*

Henri Matisse 'Acanthes', which was completed in 2012, Markus Gross and Stephan Lohrengel conducted extensive investigations into *Acanthuses*, other works in the Fondation Beyeler Collection and a further fifty cut-outs; see Markus Gross, Gerhard Mack, Stephan Lohrengel, *Fondation Beyeler – National Suisse Conservation Project Henri Matisse 'Acanthes' 2009–2012*, Riehen/Basel 2012. This work was carried out with the generous support of the Swiss insurance group Nationale Suisse, the international art insurer based in Basel (Switzerland).

4. In 2008 The Museum of Modern Art (hereafter MoMA) embarked on two related projects: the conservation of the room-sized cut-out *The Swimming Pool* and an exhibition of Matisse cut-outs. Research for both of these initiatives formed the basis for information incorporated into this essay.

5. In the early 1940s Matisse experimented with commercial coloured printers' papers to facilitate the translation from cut-out to actual printed covers and illustrations. In correspondence between Matisse and Tériade in June–July 1941 Matisse asked for coloured printers' papers, indeed specifying particular colours. Tériade responded that he would attempt to procure them, but also suggested that any gouache colour that Lydia Delecktorskaya could paint out could be accurately reproduced in printed form. This brief period is the only time that commercial coloured papers were used. (Tériade correspondence, Archives Matisse, Paris.)

6. 'Entretien avec Jacqueline Duhême, 12 décembre 2012/Conversation with Jacqueline Duhême, December 12, 2012, in Patrice Deparpe (ed.), *Matisse: La Couleur découpée, une donation révélatrice / Cutting into Color, A Revealing Donation*, exh. cat., Musée Matisse, Le Cateau-Cambrésis 2013, p.39. Jacqueline Duhême, studio assistant from July 1948 to August 1949 remembers: 'He used all sorts of paper, from white or blue wrapping paper to inexpensive, ordinary paper. Canson paper can stand on its own where you cut it, whereas wrapping paper is soft and difficult to cut. He also used paper in different shades of blue that I would buy for him. It was paper for wrapping books.'

7. See also King 1977, pp.272–3, on the subject of the chemical analysis of the papers used. For more on the paper used for drawings, see Thomas Primeau and Kimberly Schenck, 'Matisse's drawings and prints. Materials and techniques', in *Matisse: Drawing Life*, exh. cat., Queensland Art Gallery, Gallery of Modern Art, Brisbane, 2011, pp.323–4.

8. Olivier Berggruen and Max Hollein (eds.), *Henri Matisse: Drawing with Scissors, Masterpieces from the Late Years*, trans. Paul Aston, exh. cat. Schirn Kunsthalle, Frankfurt 2002, pl.41., p.96.

9. S.A.V. = Société Anonyme des Papeteries de Vidalon, Ancienne Manufacture Royale/Ancienne manufacture Canson & Montgolfier; see King 1977, p.273.

10. Letter from Lydia Delectorskaya to MoMA, 23 July 1976.

11. The sample set, donated by Georges Matisse, was selected to represent the colour range used by Matisse as determined by visual comparisons to actual cut-outs. The exact date of actual fabrication in the Matisse studio of each sample is unknown.

12. Analysis carried out by Ana Martins, Associate Research Scientist at MoMA, with the assistance of Caitlin Breare and Melissa Tan, graduate students at the Conservation Center of the Institute of Fine Arts, New York University. Analytical techniques used were micro-FTIR (Fourier Transform Infrared Spectroscopy), XRF (X-ray Fluorescence Spectroscopy), UV (Ultraviolet light) examination, Microscopy (UV and visible light under magnification) and Microfading.

13. The analysis of *White Alga on Red and Green Background* (no.59), *Blue Nude I* (no.109), *Blue Nude, the Frog* (no.116) and *Acanthuses* (no.135) was carried out by Stefan Zumbühl and Nadim Scherrer, Bern University of Applied Sciences Department Conservation HKB, Art Technology Laboratory. The analytical techniques used were FTIR and EDX (Energy-Dispersive X-Ray Spectroscopy.)

14. The green shades of *Acanthuses*, for example, contain phtalocyanine green (PG 7), both pure and mixed with Hansa yellow (PY 3) in two different proportions and possible added chrome green. For analytical techniques, see n.13.

15. 'Yes, gouache paint. Linel, sometimes Sennelier. There [in Paris] were Sennelier shops nearby: one on the quays and another one near his former house in Montparnasse.' (Unpublished interview with Jacqueline Duhême, Paris, May 2013.)

16. Ibid.

17. Unpublished interview with Paule Caen-Martin, 2012, conducted by Nicholas Cullinan and Wanda de Guébriant.

18. Lydia Delectorskaya (quoted in King 1977, p.274) recounts that any such minimal differences in texture were of no interest to Matisse.

19. Personal communication between Claude Duthuit and Karl Buchberg.

20. The brushes were between 5 and 8 cm wide; Paule Caen-Martin mentions a 'huge Japanese brush' (Paule Caen-Martin, 'Chez Henri Matisse, témoignage/ At Home with Henri Matisse, a Personal Account', in Deparpe 2013, p.47).

21. Deparpe 2013, p.47: 'Il me fallait passer une première couche de haut en bas puis, la feuille encore mouillée, disposer cette dernière en travers et recommencer la même operation dans l'autre sens. Moi, j'aimais les couleurs assez dense mais d'autres personnes, avant ou après moi, laissaient plus de transparence. Ainsi, nous intervenions, à notre manière, dans la création.'

22. There are finger marks at the edges and corners of the pieces of paper in *Composition Green Background* (no.148), *Creole Dancer* (no.85) and *The Snail* (no.129).

23. This was done when the paper was not itself pure white, or in order to prevent it from darkening. 'In the very early days of his studies and researches into the range of possibilities that were achievable in a considered juxtaposition of colours in "gouaches découpées", he used ordinary drawing paper or even writing paper. As soon as he had made up his mind and was sure that his studies could stand as finished, powerfully expressive works, he had the white fragments painted with white gouache, so that the gradually yellowing paper would not detract from the relationship between the colours that he had sought to create in a composition.' (Lydia Delectorskaya to MoMA, 23 July 1976.)

24. 'Dessiner avec des ciseaux. Découper à vif dans la couleur me rapelle la taille directe des sculpteurs' [Cutting directly into vivid colour reminds me of the direct carving of sculptors] (Henri Matisse, *Jazz*, Paris 1947, pp.73–4, trans. Jack Flam (ed.), *Matisse on Art*, Berkeley and Los Angeles 1995, p.172).

25. Unpublished interview with Jacqueline Duhême, Paris, May 2013.

26. Deparpe 2013, pp.40 (conversation with Jaqueline Duhême), 48.

27. The sizes of the pinholes that remain in the cut-outs indicate the size of the pin or nail. The strength needed for attachment, as well as work surface, dictated the choice and thickness of either pin or nail. The term pin will be used exclusively in this essay. Drawing pins (thumb tacks) were sometimes used for the small-format works attached to board.

28. Around 1,000 pinholes were counted in *Acanthuses*, indicating various working steps.

29. Deparpe 2013, pp.130, 167, 174–5.

30. Lydia Delectorskaya, *L'Apparente facilité – Henri Matisse: Peintures de 1935–1939*, Paris, 1986, p.274.

31. Matisse used exactly the same method in *The Eskimo* (no.57), where there

traces of a head shape, which he replaced with an Inuit head.

32. Lydia Delectorskaya quoted in Anne Coron, 'Un Thème, trois variations?', in Cécile Debray (ed.), *Matisse: Paires et séries*, exh. cat., Centre Pompidou, Paris, 2012, pp.245–53, esp. pp.251–2, and Deparpe 2013, p.53.

33. See Cowart et al. 1977, cat no.200.

34. See Cowart et al. 1977, cat no.204.

35. 'Une question m'inquiète, c'est le collage des différents éléments. Il faut que ça soit bien fait ou bien ça se décolle' (One thing bothers me, it's how to glue the different elements. It has to be well done or they will become unstuck): Matisse to Tériade, 27 Oct. 1943, Vence, quoted in Pierre Schneider, *Matisse*, trans. Michael Taylor and Bridget Strevens Romer, New York 1984, p.709 n.14.

36. It was not until later that the *Jazz* sheets were glued more comprehensively or mounted in their entirety on canvas. The technique of attaching cut-out elements with localised spots of adhesive is called spot-gluing.

37. In Cowart et al. 1977, p.141, the entry for *Composition, Violet and Blue* states: 'This work and no.66 (*Panel with Mask)* are some of the very few which have not been mounted or pasted flat. The result is that the paper elements here are extraordinarily tactile and "alive" and communicate a strong sense of their actual material. Matisse is known to have been especially aware of the particular physical characteristics of his *unpasted* paper cut-outs, but his desire to protect and preserve the works eventually led him to recognize the necessity of pasting them down.'

38. Quoted in King 1977, p.275.

39. Letter from Gloria de Herrera to Lydia Delectorskaya, 1 May 1985, and Lydia Delectorskaya to Gloria de Herrera, 7 May 1985 (Gloria de Herrera papers, Getty Research Institute, Research Library, accession no.980024, box 1, folder 18).

40. This traditional French technique (*rentoilage*), dating back to the seventeenth century, was used to reline paintings on a new canvas (Èmile Rostain, *Rentoilage et transposition des tableaux*, Paris 1981).

41. 'Après des années de recherches des spécialistes [Lefebvre-Foinet à Paris] ont finalement trouvé le moyen de coller mes gouaches en plein d'une façon impeccable ce qui est important pour leur présentation ainsi que, et surtout, pour leur conservation' (After some years of research the specialists [Lefebvre-Foinet in Paris] have at last found a way to glue my gouaches, in their entirety, in an impeccable manner, which is important for their presentation as it also is, above all, for their conservation): letter from Henri Matisse to J. Rubow, 6 June 1954 (Cowart et al. 1977, p.281).

42. There are two detailed descriptions of the mounting process by Lydia Delectorskaya (letter from Lydia Delectorskaya to Edy de Wilde, Stedelijk Museum Amsterdam, 28 Sept. 1976, Paper Conservation Files, Stedelijk Museum Amsterdam).

43. Gloria Claire de Herrera (1929–85) was first employed at LACMA in 1949, where she also received training in the conservation department. Around 1953 Herrera was hired by Maurice Lefebvre-Foinet and restored paintings by Mondrian and Chagall, before starting work mounting cut-outs, which she did from 1953 to 1959 (Gloria de Herrera papers, Getty Research Institute, Research Library, accession no.980024).

44. In view of the great importance of this step, it is likely that it was done by Lydia Delectorskaya.

45. The density of the weave in the examined works is between 9–14 warp threads and 12–19 weft threads per sq. cm.

46. 'La colle employée se compose de farine de seigle, farine de froment (graine de lin bouillie et tamisée) et un peu de colle de nerfs et très peu de térébenthine de Venise' (letter from Maurice Lefebvre-Foinet to Pierre Matisse, 19 Jan. 1973, Pierre Matisse Gallery Archives, Morgan Library, New York, box 77, folder 50).

47. *Venus*: Analysis Report, Science Department, National Gallery of Art, Washington, DC, 4 Feb. 1988, Paper Conservation Files. Adhesive on *The Swimming Pool* analysed by Chris McGlinchey, Conservation Scientist, MoMA. Analysis of the four works owned by the Fondation Beyeler showed no clear result due to the very small amount of test material.

48. André Verdet, *Prestiges de Matisse: Précédé de visite à Matisse, entretiens avec Matisse*, Paris 1952, pp.51–2: 'Observez cette grande composition [*The Parakeet and the Mermaid*]: feuillage, fruits, ciseaux; un jardin. Le blanc intermédiaire est déterminé par l'arabesque du papier-couleur découpé qui donne à ce "blanc-ambiant" une qualité rare et impalpable. Cette qualité est celle du contraste. Chaque groupe particulier de couleurs a en lui-même une atmosphère particulière. C'est ce que j'appellerai "l'ambiance expressive".' (Flam 1995, p.212: 'Observe this big composition [*The Parakeet and the Mermaid*]: foliage, fruit, scissors; a garden. The white intermediary is determined by the arabesque of the cutout colored paper which gives this "white-atmosphere" a rare and impalpable quality. This quality is that of contrast. Each particular group of colors has a particular atmosphere. It is what I will call the "expressive atmosphere".')

49. *Woman with Amphora and Pomegranates*, 1952 (XRF-Report of Analysis, Science Department, NGA, 22 Sept. 1987, Paper Conservation Files, NGA). Laboratory analyses have shown that the paint used was a zinc white or a mixture of zinc white and barium sulphate.

50. 'D'autre part je tiens à vous signaler que j'ai décidé la division de la grande composition par panneaux. En cas de besoin vous pourrez la placer sur deux murs formant un angle de deux façons suivantes.' [On the other hand, I do want to inform you that I decided on the division of the large composition into panels. If necessary, you can place it on two walls, forming an angle in the following two ways.] (Letter from Matisse to Pierre Berès, 20 Jan. 1953: Cowart et. al. 1977, p.281.)

51. See Cowart et al. 1977, cat no.205.

52. Lydia Delectorskaya, quoted in King 1977, p.274.

53. 'Cher Monsieur Berès, Depuis votre dernière visite chez moi je suis très préoccupé et redoute un excès persistant de lumière dans la pièce où vous désirez placer provisoirement "La Perruche". Si la gouache n'a pas la fragilité de l'aquarelle, elle n'est pourtant pas, vous le savez, comme la céramique insensible à la lumière en excès. Je serais, vous n'en doutez pas, tout à fait navré si cette gouache, que je mets en très bonne place dans l'ensemble de mon oeuvre, devait perdre certaine de ses qualités. La douce intensité de son harmonie par exemple. Tous mes efforts tendent à obtenir sans brutalité le maximum de force colorée. Ce serait donc porter à celle-ci un préjudice énorme que de laisser atténuer ses valeurs. J'ai alors pensé vous demander s'il vous serait possible de faire installer dès maintenant un système de rideaux qui sans changer la qualité de la lumière en réduirait la brutalité. Peut-être des jalousies, dites à l'Italienne, qui tamisent la lumière de si jolie façon (en les laissant blanches bien entendu) ou tout autre mode d'écran qui vous conviendra et répondra à ce que nous cherchons. Je ne doute pas que vous serez de mon avis pour éviter des forces destructives à cette oeuvre que nous sommes au moins deux à aimer ... Soyez assez aimable pour me faire savoir de quelle façon vous avez pu solutionner la question lumière.' [Dear Mr. Berès, Since your last visit, I have been very worried and fear a persistent excess of light in the room where you would like to temporarily place 'The Parakeet'. If gouache is not as fragile as watercolour, it is not, you understand, insensitive to excessive light, like ceramic. I would be, you do not doubt, very upset if this gouache, which I hold in high esteem within my body of work, should lose some of its qualities. The sweet intensity of its

harmony, for example. All my efforts aim towards obtaining, without brutality, the maximum force of colour. It would therefore be an enormous loss to this work to let its values diminish. I therefore thought of asking you if you could now install a system of curtains that, without changing the quality of light, would reduce its brutality. Perhaps *jalousies*, in the Italian style, which filter the light in such a pretty way (of course leaving the whites) or any other kind of screen which suits you and provides what we are looking for. I have no doubt you will agree with me to avoid forces which could destroy this work, which is loved at least by the two of us ... Be kind enough to let me know in which way you are able to solve the light issue.] (Matisse to Pierre Berès, 24 June 1954, in Dominique Fourcade (ed.), *Henri Matisse: Écrits et propos sur l'art*, Paris 1972, pp. 253–4.)

54. A spectrophotometer analyses the spectrum of visible light; it measures the reflectance of the sample and returns the measured data as a chromatic 'fingerprint'. Microfading is an accelerated method for assessing the vulnerability of individual museum objects to light-fading. The microfader supplies data that is compared to the Blue Wool Scale, a set of eight standards (0–8) that each fade at a known rate.

55. Measurements were at an interval of seven years (2000–7) at five monitoring points on a range of coloured papers (CIE Lab* Spectrophotometrie, Minolta CM-2022).

56. The light-fastness of all the analysed colour samples is greater than Blue Wool Standard 3: report by Rebecca Lange, Haida Liang, 11 June 2012.

57. Extremely light sensitive: below Blue Wool Standard 2; moderately light sensitive: between Blue Wool Standards 2 and 3; stable: Blue Wool Standard 3 or above.

58. Letter from Pierre Matisse to Monroe Wheeler, 12 Aug. 1961, MoMA Archives. The exhibition was entitled *The Last Works of Henri Matisse: Large Cut Gouaches*.

59. Letter from Lydia Delectorskaya to MoMA Conservation Department, 23 July 1976.

Selected Bibliography

This selection highlights sources that feature Matisse's cut-outs. It is divided into three sections: books, articles and essays, and exhibition catalogues. The first two parts are sorted alphabetically by authors' last names, while the third is arranged chronologically. In some cases, exhibition reviews have been listed without a corresponding catalogue entry, and several exhibition catalogues that address the cut-outs, although cut-outs were not shown in the exhibition itself, have also been included. Preference has been given to English editions of works, when available. For a bibliography that spans Matisse's career, see Catherine Bock-Weiss's *Henri Matisse: A Guide to Research* (New York and London: Garland, 1996).

Books

Alliez, Éric, and Jean-Claude Bonne. *La Pensée-Matisse: Portrait de l'artiste en hyperfauve*. Paris: Passage, 2005.

Anthonioz, Michel. *'Verve': The Ultimate Review of Art and Literature (1937–1960)*, translated by I. Mark Paris. New York: Harry N. Abrams, 1988.

Aragon, Louis. *Henri Matisse: A Novel*, translated by Jean Stewart. New York: Harcourt Brace Jovanovich, 1972, 2 vols.

Barr, Alfred H. Jr, *Matisse: His Art and his Public*. New York: The Museum of Modern Art, 1951.

Bock-Weiss, Catherine. *Henri Matisse: A Guide to Research*. New York and London: Garland, 1996.

Bock-Weiss, Catherine. *Henri Matisse: Modernist Against the Grain*. University Park: Pennsylvania State University Press, 2009.

Bois, Yve-Alain. *Matisse and Picasso*. Paris: Flammarion, 1998.

Boyer, Marie-France. *Matisse at Villa le Rêve 1943–1948*, translated by Anna Bennett. London: Thames and Hudson, 2004.

Brassaï. *The Artists of my Life*, translated by Richard Miller. New York: Viking Press, 1982.

Brassaï. *Conversations with Picasso*, translated by Jane Marie Todd. Chicago and London: The University of Chicago Press, 1999.

Brauner, Haidrun. *"Natürlich ist das Dekoration": Perspektiven eines Begriffes in der Kunst des 20. Jahrhunderts ausgehend von Henri Matisse*. Frankfurt: Peter Lang, 1992.

Coron, Anne. *Henri Matisse: Les Nus bleus: Illustrations au pochoir à la gouache*. Paris: Bernard Chauveau, 2004–6, 3 vols.

Coron, Anne. 'La Gouache découpée dans l'oeuvre de Henri Matisse: Pratique, esthétique, réception'. Ph.D. diss., Université Picardie Jules Verne (Amiens), Faculté des Arts, 2005, 3 vols.

Coron, Anne. *Henri Matisse: 'La Piscine': Illustrations au pochoir à la gouache*. Paris: Bernard Chauveau, 2005.

Coron, Anne. *Henri Matisse: 'La Polynésie': Illustrations au pochoir à la gouache*. Paris: Bernard Chauveau, 2006.

Couturier, Marie-Alain. *Sacred Art*, translated by Granger Ryan. Austin: University of Texas Press, 1989.

Delectorskaya, Lydia. *With Apparent Ease ...: Henri Matisse: Paintings from 1935–1939*, translated by Olga Tourkoff. Paris: Adrien Maeght, 1988.

Delectorskaya, Lydia. *Henri Matisse: Contre vents et marées: Peinture et livres illustrés de 1939 à 1943*. Paris: Éditions Irus et Vincent Hansma, 1996.

Durozoi, Gérard. *Matisse*, translated by John Greaves. London: Studio Editions, 1993.

Duthuit, Claude, with Françoise Garnaud. *Henri Matisse: Catalogue raisonné des ouvrages illustrés*. Paris: Union, 1988.

Elderfield, John. *The Cut-Outs of Henri Matisse*. New York: George Braziller, 1978.

Elderfield, John, with William S. Lieberman and Riva Castleman. *Matisse in the Collection of The Museum of Modern Art*. New York: The Museum of Modern Art, 1978.

Elsen, Albert E. *The Sculpture of Henri Matisse*. New York: Harry N. Abrams, 1972.

Finsen, Hanne (ed.). *Matisse, Rouveyre: Correspondance*. Paris: Flammarion, 2001.

Flam, Jack (ed.). *Matisse: A Retrospective*. New York: Hugh Lauter Levin; Macmillan, 1988.

Flam, Jack. *Matisse: 'The Dance'*. Washington DC: National Gallery of Art, 1993.

Flam, Jack (ed.). *Matisse on Art*. Revised edition, Berkeley and Los Angeles: University of California Press, 1995.

Fourcade, Dominique. *Henri Matisse: Écrits et propos sur l'art*. Paris: Hermann, 1972.

Gilot, Françoise. *Matisse and Picasso: A Friendship in Art*. New York: Doubleday, 1990.

Girard, Xavier. *La Chapelle du Rosaire 1948–1951*. Paris: Réunion des Musées Nationaux, 1992.

Girard, Xavier. *Matisse in Nice, 1917–1954*, translated by Saron Hughes. London: Thames and Hudson; New York: Universe/Vendome, 1996.

Golan, Romy. *Muralnomad: The Paradox of Wall Painting, Europe 1927–1957.* New Haven and London: Yale University Press, 2009.
Gross, Markus, Gerhard Mack, Stephan Lohrengel. *Fondation Beyeler – Nationale Suisse Conservation Project Henri Matisse 'Acanthes' 2009–2012.* Riehen/Basel: Beyeler Museum, 2012.
Guichard-Meili, Jean. *Matisse, Paper Cutouts*, translated by David Macey. London and New York: Thames and Hudson, 1984.
Jedlicka, Gotthard. *Die Matisse Kapelle in Vence: Rosenkranzkapelle der Dominikanerinnen*. Frankfurt: Suhrkamp, 1955.
Klein, John. *Matisse's Late Decorations and the Essential Quality of Art*. New Haven: Yale University Press, forthcoming 2016.
Lavarini, Beatrice. *Henri Matisse: 'Jazz' (1943–1947): ein Malerbuch als Selbstbekenntnis*. Munich: Scaneg, 2000.
Laudon, Paule. *Matisse in Tahiti*, translated by Michael Taylor. Paris: Vilo International, 2001.
Liberman, Alexander. *The Artist in his Studio*. New York: Viking Press, 1960; expanded edition, New York: Random House, 1988.
Matisse, Henri. *Jazz*. Paris: Tériade, 1947.
Matisse, Henri. *Chapelle du Rosaire des Dominicaines de Vence*. Paris: Mourlot, 1951.
Matisse, Henri. *Carnet de dessins*. Paris: Huguette Berès; Berggruen, 1955. Facsimile with text by Jean Cassou.
Matisse, Henri. *Jazz*. Munich: R. Piper, 1957. Translated by Monroe Wheeler and reprinted on the occasion of an exhibition at The Museum of Modern Art, New York, 1960.
Matisse, Henri. *Jazz*. New York: George Braziller, 1983. Full-sized facsimile with introduction by Riva Castleman and translation of the text into English by Sophie Hawkes.
Matisse, Henri. *Jazz*. Munich, London, New York: Prestel, 2001. Reduced-size facsimile with introduction by Egbert Baqué, text by Katrin Wiethege, and translation of the text into English by Christopher Wynne. Full-sized facsimile; Munich, Berlin, London, New York: Prestel, 2009.
Matisse, Henri. *Les Gouaches découpées de La Chapelle de Vence*. Paris: Bernard Chauveau, 2003–5.
Matisse, Henri, Marie-Alain Couturier, Louis-Bertrand Rayssiguier. *The Vence Chapel: The Archive of a Creation,* edited and introduced by Marcel Billot with foreword by Dominique de Menil, translated by Michael Taylor. Turin: Skira, 1999.
Matisse, Henri, with Pierre Courthion. *Chatting with Henri Matisse: The Lost 1941 Interview,* Serge Guilbaut (ed.), translated by Chris Miller. Los Angeles: Getty Research Institute, 2013.
Monod-Fontaine, Isabelle. *Matisse: Le Rêve ou les belles endormies*. Paris: Adam Brio, 1989.
Monod-Fontaine, Isabelle, Anne Baldassari, and Claude Laugier. *Matisse 1869–1954: Oeuvres de Henri Matisse: Catalogue*. Paris: Éditions du Centre Pompidou, 1989.
Moulin, Raoul Jean. *Henri Matisse: Drawings and Paper Cut-Outs*, translated by Michael Ross. London: Thames and Hudson, 1969.
Nelck, Annelies. *L'Olivier du rêve. Matisse à Vence: Témoinage*. Nice: Imprimix, 1999.
Néret, Gilles. *Matisse*, translated by Lisa Davidson. London: Cromwell Editions, 1993.
Néret, Gilles. *Henri Matisse: Cut-Outs.* Cologne: Benedikt Taschen, 1994.
Néret, Gilles and Xavier-Gilles (eds.). *Henri Matisse: Cut-Outs: Drawing with Scissors*, translated by Pamela Hargreaves and Jonathan Paul Murphy. Cologne: Taschen, 2009, 2 vols.
O'Brian, John. *Ruthless Hedonism: The American Reception of Matisse.* Chicago and London: The University of Chicago Press, 1999.
Percheron, René, and Christian Brouder. *Matisse: From Color to Architecture*, translated by Deke Dusinberre. New York: Harry N. Abrams, 2003.
Rabinow, Rebecca A. 'The Legacy of la Rue Férou: *Livres d'Artiste* Created for Tériade by Rouault, Bonnard, Matisse, Léger, Le Corbusier, Chagall, Giacometti, and Miró'. Ph.D. diss., Institute of Fine Arts, New York University, 1995, 3 vols.
Rodari, Florian. *Le Collage: Papiers collés, Papiers déchirés, Papiers découpés*. Geneva: Skira, 1988.
Russell, John. *The Meanings of Modern Art*. New York: The Museum of Modern Art; Harper and Row; London: Thames and Hudson, 1981.
Russell, John. *Matisse: Father and Son*. New York: Harry N. Abrams, 1999.
Schiebler, Ralf. *Henri Matisse: Scherenschnitte.* Munich: Schirmer/Mosel, 1994.
Schneider, Pierre. *Matisse*, translated by Michael Taylor and Bridget Strevens Romer. New York: Rizzoli, 1984. Revised edition, Paris: Flammarion, 1992.
Spurling, Hilary. *Matisse the Master: A Life of Henri Matisse: The Conquest of Colour, 1909–1954*. New York: Alfred A. Knopf, 2005.
Verdet, André. *Prestiges de Matisse: Précédé de visite à Matisse, entretiens avec Matisse*. Paris: Émile-Paul, 1952.
Verdet, André. *Entretiens, notes et écrits sur la peinture – Braque, Léger, Matisse, Picasso*. Paris: Galilée, 1978.
Watkins, Nicholas. *Matisse*. Oxford: Phaidon, 1984; New York: Oxford University Press, 1985.
Wescher, Herta. *Collage*, translated by Robert E. Wolf, New York: Harry N. Abrams, 1971.

Articles and Essays

Arikha, Avigdor. 'Matisse et l'*Apocalypse de Saint-Sever. Beatus* et *Jazz*', in *Peinture et regard: Écrits sur l'art 1965–1990.* Paris: Hermann, 1991; pp.193–205.
Baker, Kenneth. 'Performing Forms: Notes on Matisse's Cutouts', in *Artforum*, vol.16 no.5, Jan. 1978, pp.60–3.
Barron, Stephanie, and Larry Rosing. 'Matisse and Contemporary Art', in *Arts Magazine*, vol.49 no. 9, May 1975, pp.66–9.
Bernier, Rosamond. 'Matisse Designs a New Church', in *Vogue*, 15 Feb. 1949, pp.76–8, 131–2.
Bernier, Rosamond. 'Le Musée Matisse à Nice', in *L'Oeil*, no.105, Sept. 1963, pp.20–9, 66.
Bernier, Rosamond. 'Visits to Matisse', in *Some of my Lives: A Scrapbook Memoir*. New York: Farrar, Straus and Giroux, 2011; pp.90–9.
Bertin, Célia. 'Visite à Henri Matisse', in *Le Figaro Littéraire*, 24 April 1948, p.5.
Bertin, Célia. 'À Vence: Henri Matisse décore une chapelle', in *Arts Plastiques*, 1949, pp.209–14.
B.K. 'Henri Matisse' [review of New York exhib.], in *Art News*, vol.47 no.10, Feb. 1949, pp.44–5.
Bougault, Valérie. 'Les Papiers découpés de Matisse', in *Connaissance des arts*, no.623, 2005, pp.6–15.
Broude, Norma. 'Miriam Schapiro and "Femmage": Reflections on the Conflict between Decoration and Abstraction in Twentieth-Century Art', in *Feminism and Art History, Questioning the Litany*, edited by Norma Broude and Mary D. Garrard. New York: Harper and Row, 1982; pp.314–29.
Buchanan, Donald W. 'Interview in Montparnasse', in *Canadian Art*, vol.8 no.2, 1950, pp.61–5.
Cassou, Jean. 'Travel to France' [incl. review of Paris exhib.], in *Art News*, vol.48 no.4 June–Aug. 1949, pp.19, 65.
Cassou, Jean, and Georges Salles. 'Matisse va présenter au public ses papiers découpés', in *France Illustration*, no.383, 14 Feb. 1953, pp.234–5.
Chassey, Éric de. 'Kelly et Matisse: Une Filiation Inavouée', in *Les Cahiers du Musée national d'art moderne*, no.49, Autumn 1994, pp.41–57.
Chastel, André. 'La "Peinture au ciseau" de Matisse' [review of Paris exhib.], in *Le Monde*, 6 March 1953, p.7.

Cork, Richard. 'A Sensual paradise' [review of Hayward exhib.], in *The Listener*, vol.112 no.2879, 11 Oct. 1984, pp.32–3.

Coron, Anne. 'Les Tapisseries et tentures décoratives de Matisse, *Océanie*, *Polynésie*: enjeux esthétiques d'un projet "décoratif"', in *Histoire de l'art*, no.61, Oct. 2007, pp.61–71.

Coural, Jean. 'Matisse et les manufactures des Gobelins et de Beauvais. Notes et documents', in *Bulletin de la société de l'histoire de l'art français*, 1994, pp.253–71.

Courthion, Pierre. 'Papiers découpés d'Henri Matisse', in *XXe Siècle*, no.6, Jan. 1956, pp.45–6.

Couturier, Marie-Alain. 'Religious Art and the Modern Artist', in *Magazine of Art*, vol.44 no.7, Nov. 1951, pp.268–72.

Cowart, Jack. 'Matisse's Artistic Probe: The Collage', in *Arts Magazine*, vol.49 no.9, May 1975, pp.53–5.

Cowart, Jack. 'Travailler avec des ciseaux dans ce papier est pour moi une occupation dans laquelle je peux me perdre', in *Connaissance des arts*, no.307, Sept. 1977, pp.60–7.

Cullinan, Nicholas. 'Henri Matisse. Cut-Outs. Drawing with scissors' [review of 2009 Néret book], in *Burlington Magazine*, vol.153 no.1298, May 2011, pp.337–8.

Daniels, Rebecca. 'Henri Matisse's Stained-Glass Window "La Rosace" (1954)', in *Burlington Magazine*, vol.155 no.1326, Sept. 2013, pp.612–20.

Degand, Léon. 'Les Papiers découpés de Matisse' [review of Paris exhib.], in *Art d'aujourd'hui*, vol.4 no.2 , March 1953, p.28.

Devree, Howard. 'Romantic to Modern: Works by Samuel Palmer, Matisse and Knaths' [review of New York exhib.], in *New York Times*, 6 Feb. 1949, p.9.

Diehl, Gaston. 'Henri Matisse: Contributions à l'art décoratif', in *Art et décoration*, no.6, Autumn 1947, pp.2–10.

Duthuit, Georges. 'The Material and Spiritual Worlds of Henri Matisse', in *Art News*, vol.55 no.6, Oct. 1956, pp.22–5, 67.

Duthuit, Georges. 'Matisse's Illuminations', in *Portfolio & ARTnews Annual*, no.5, 1962, pp.84–99.

Elgar, Frank. 'Triomphe de Matisse', in *Carrefour*, 7 Jan. 1948, p.6.

Forgey, Benjamin. 'The Matisse Cutouts', in *Art News*, vol.76 no.10, Dec. 1977, pp.66–9.

Glueck, Grace. 'Modern Gets Huge Matisse Cutout in $1 Million Trade', *New York Times*, 10 March 1976.

Goldin, Amy. 'Matisse and Decoration: The Late Cut-Outs', in *Art in America*, vol.63 no.4 July–Aug. 1975, pp.49–59.

Goldin, Amy. 'The Body Language of Pictures', in *Artforum*, vol.16 no.7, March 1978, pp.54–9.

Gosling, Nigel. 'Decoration in the Basement', in *Observer*, 14 Aug. 1966, p.17.

Greenberg, Clement. 'Art' [review of New York exhib.], in *The Nation*, 5 March 1949, pp.284–5.

Greenberg, Clement. 'Feeling is All', in *Partisan Review* (Jan.– Feb. 1952); slightly revised, '*Partisan Review* "Art Chronicle", 1952', in *Art and Culture: Critical Essays*. Boston: Beacon Press, 1961, pp.146–53.

[Hess, Thomas B.] T.B.H. 'Matisse at his Best' [review of New York exhib.], in *Art News*, vol.50 no.8, Dec. 1951, pp.40–1, 55.

[House, Russell Warren] R.W.H. 'Events in Paris' [incl. review of Berggruen exhib.], in *Apollo*, vol.57 no.338, April 1953, p.114.

Hudson, Andrew. 'Washington: Matisse's Influence' [review of exhib.], in *Artmagazine*, Dec. 1977 – Feb. 1978, pp.12–17.

Humbert, Agnès. 'Recent Acquisitions of the Musée national d'art moderne Paris', in *The Studio*, vol.148 no.736, July 1954, pp.10–17.

J.C. 'Henri Matisse Paper Cut-Outs' [review of St Louis exhib.], in *St. Louis Art Museum Bulletin*, vol.14 no.1, Jan. – March 1978, pp.2–5.

Jenkins, David Fraser. '*Baigneuses* and *Demoiselles:* "Bathers" in Cézanne, Picasso and Matisse', in *Apollo*, vol.145 no.421, March 1997, pp.39–44.

Kéry, Bert-Alan. '"Apollon" och det mytologiska hos Matisse', in *Konsthistorisk tidskrift*, vol.56 no.4, 1987, pp.157–68.

Klein, John. 'Inventing Mediterranean Harmony in Matisse's Paper Cut-Outs', in *Modern Art and the Idea of the Mediterranean*, edited by Vojtěch Jirat-Wasiutyński, with the assistance of Anne Dymond. Toronto, Buffalo, London: University of Toronto Press, 2007; pp.146–60.

Kuenzi, André. 'Henri Matisse' [review of Bern exhib.], in *Gazette de Lausanne*, 8 Aug. 1959, p.12.

Labrusse, Rémi. 'Matisse's Second Visit to London and his Collaboration with the "Ballets Russes"', in *Burlington Magazine*, vol.139 no.1134, Sept. 1997, pp.588–99.

Langdon, Gabrielle. '"A Spiritual Space": Matisse's Chapel of the Dominicans at Vence', in *Zeitschrift für Kunstgeschichte*, vol.51 no.4, 1988, pp.542–73.

Lebensztejn, Jean-Claude. 'Eight Interviews/Statements: Roy Lichtenstein, Paul Sharits, Tom Wesselmann, Carl Andre, Frank Stella, Brice Marden, Donald Judd, Andy Warhol', in *Art in America*, vol.63 no.4, July – Aug. 1975, pp.67–75.

Lemoine, Colin. 'Matisse: Ils ont regardé le maître [review of Le Cateau-Cambrésis exhib.], in *L'Oeil*, no.612, April 2009, pp.76–80.

Leymarie, Jean. 'Les Grandes gouaches découpées de Matisse à la Kunsthalle de Berne', in *Quadrum*, no.7, 1959, pp.103–14, with English summary on p.192.

Lieberman, William S. 'Illustrations by Henri Matisse', in *Magazine of Art*, vol.44 no.8, Dec. 1951, pp.308–14.

Linker, Kate. 'Matisse and the Language of Signs', in *Arts Magazine*, vol.49 no.9, May 1975, pp.76–8.

Marchiori, Giuseppe. 'Papiers découpés', in *La Biennale di Venezia*, no.26, 1955, pp.28–30.

Marmer, Nancy. 'Matisse and the Strategy of Decoration' [review of Los Angeles exhib.], in *Artforum*, vol.4 no.7, March 1966, pp.28–33.

Marshall, Neil. 'Patterning', in *Arts Magazine*, vol.55 no.1, Sept. 1980, pp 120–1.

Mathey, François. 'Situation du vitrail en France', in *Quadrum*, no.4, 1957, pp.84–98.

Matisse, Henri. 'Océanie', in *Labyrinthe*, nos.22–3, Dec.1946

'Matisse's Last Tile Mural', in *Art News*, vol.55 no.4, Summer 1956, pp.30–1, 67.

Medley, Robert. 'Matisse's "L'Escargot"', in *The Listener*, vol.71 no.1824, 12 March 1964, pp.438–9.

Millard, Charles W. 'The Matisse Cut-Outs', in *The Hudson Review*, vol.31 no.2, Summer 1978, pp.321–7.

Morgan, Claude. 'Matisse montre toujours de nouveaux chemins', in *Les Lettres Françaises*, 8 Jan. 1948, p.4.

Motherwell, Robert. 'Words of the Painter' [review of *Matisse on Art* by Flam and Washington, Detroit, Saint Louis exhib. cat.], in *New York Times Book Review*, 4 June 1978, pp.12, 42–3.

'Les Papiers découpés de Matisse' [review of Salon de Mai], in *Art et décoration*, no.35, 1953, p.40.

Paris-Match, no.294, 20 Nov. 1954, pp.30–5.

Roger-Marx, Claude. 'Les Découpages de Matisse', in *Le Figaro Littéraire*, 3 Jan. 1948, p.8.

Russell, John. 'Processes of Renewal', in *Sunday Times*, 7 Aug. 1966, p.29.

[San Lazzaro, Gualtieri di.] S.L. 'Découpages de Henri Matisse', in *XXe Siècle*, no.4, Jan. 1954, p.73.

Schneider, Pierre. 'Art News from Paris' [incl. review of Paris exhib.], in *Art News*, vol.60 no.3, May 1961, p.44.

Slivka, Rose. 'The Matisse Chasubles', in *Craft Horizons*, vol.16 no.1, Jan–Feb. 1956, pp.22–5.

Spies, Werner. 'Mit der Schere gezeichnet: eine amerikanische Wanderausstellung mit dem Spätwerk von Henri Matisse' [review of Detroit exhib.], in *Frankfurter Allgemeine Zeitung*, 13 Jan. 1978.

'Une Tapisserie de Matisse', in *Art et décoration*, no.8, 1948, p.55.

Verve, vol.9 no.35–6, 1958 (Special Issue: 'The last works of Matisse, 1950–1954').

Watkins, Nicholas. [Review of 1978 Elderfield books], in *Burlington Magazine*, vol.122 no.923, Feb. 1980, pp.136–7.
Watkins, Nicholas. 'Henri Matisse: Paper Cut-Outs' [review of Frankfurt/Berlin exhibition], in *Apollo*, vol.158 no.500, Oct. 2003, pp.49–50.
Watt, Alexander. 'Paris Commentary' [incl. review of Paris exhib.], in *The Studio*, vol.162 no.819, July 1961, pp.22–5.
Welters, Linda. 'Matisse: The Fabric of Dreams' [review of New York exhib.], in *Textile*, vol.4 no.3, Fall 2006, pp.376–82.
Wescher, Herta. 'Collages: Figuration transposée', in *Art d'aujourd'hui*, vol.5 nos.2–3, March–April 1954, pp.40–1.
Wind, Edgar. 'Traditional Religion and Modern Art', in *Art News*, vol.52 no.3, May 1953, pp.18–22, 60, 63.
Wood, William. 'Boudoir Scissorhands: Matisse, the Cut-Outs and the Canon', in *RACAR: Revue d'art canadienne/Canadian Art Review*, vol.18 nos.1–2, 1991, pp.5–17.
Wright, Martha. 'Washington Letter' [incl. review of Washington exhib.], in *Art International*, vol.21 no.5, Oct. – Nov. 1977, pp.51–5.
Wullschlager, Jackie. 'Dazzling Fruits of an Exuberant Old Age' [review of Paris exhib.], in *Financial Times*, 20 April 2005, p.13.
XXe Siècle, 1970, no.3 ('Hommage à Henri Matisse'); English edition: *XXe Siècle: Homage to Henri Matisse*. New York: Tudor, 1970.
Zervos, Christian. 'À propos de l'exposition Matisse au Musée d'Art Moderne de Paris', in *Cahiers d'Art*, vol.24 no.1, 1949, pp.159–70.
Zervos, Christian. 'Les Expositions à Paris et ailleurs: Henri Matisse' [incl. review of Paris exhib.], in *Cahiers d'Art*, vol.25 no.2, 1950, pp.387–8.

Exhibition catalogues

Cassou, Jean. *Henri Matisse: Oeuvres récentes, 1947–1948*. Musée national d'art moderne, Paris, June – Sept. 1949.
Troller, Aloïs, Jean Cassou, Hanspeter Landolt. *Henri Matisse*. Musée des Beaux-Arts Lucerne, 9 July – 2 Oct. 1949.
Salon de mai. Paris, 9–31 May 1950.
Aragon. *Henri Matisse: Chapelle, peintures, dessins, sculptures*. Maison de la Pensée Française, Paris, 5 July – 24 Sept. 1950.
Henri Matisse. National Museum, Tokyo, 3 March – 6 June 1951.
Barr, Alfred H. Jr, *Henri Matisse*. The Museum of Modern Art, New York, 13 Nov. 1951 – 13 Jan. 1952; Cleveland Museum of Art, 5 Feb. – 16 March 1952; The Art Institute of Chicago, 1 April – 4 May 1952; San Francisco Museum of Art, 22 May – 6 July 1952.
Henri Matisse: Thèmes et variations, Le Rêve – La Chapelle. Galerie Samlaren, Stockholm, 31 Dec. 1951 – 31 Jan. 1952.
Salon de mai. Paris, 9–29 May 1952.
Tériade, E. *Henri Matisse: Papiers découpés*. Berggruen et Cie., Paris, 27 Feb. – 28 March 1953.
Rostrup, Haavard, and Jean Cassou. *Henri Matisse: Skulpturer, Malerier, Farveklip*. Ny Carlsberg Glyptotek, Copenhagen, 6 Nov. – 6 Dec. 1953.
Salon de mai. Paris, 7–31 May 1954.
Cassou, Jean. *Henri Matisse: Exposition rétrospective*. Musée national d'art moderne, Paris, 28 July – 18 Nov. 1956.
Wennberg, Bo. *Henri Matisse: Apollon*. Nationalmuseum, Stockholm, 4–23 Sept. 1957.
Meyer, Franz. *Henri Matisse, 1950–1954: Les Grandes gouaches découpées*. Kunsthalle Bern, 25 July – 20 Sept. 1959; Stedelijk Museum, Amsterdam, 29 April – 20 June 1960.
Lassaigne, Jacques. *Henri Matisse: Les Grandes gouaches découpées*. Musée des Arts Décoratifs, Paris, 22 March – 15 May 1961.
Wheeler, Monroe. *The Last Works of Henri Matisse: Large Cut Gouaches*. The Museum of Modern Art, New York, 17 Oct. – 3 Dec. 1961; The Art Institute of Chicago, 10 Jan. – 13 Feb. 1962; San Francisco Museum of Art, 12 March – 22 April 1962.
Gowing, Lawrence. *Henri Matisse: 64 Paintings*. The Museum of Modern Art, New York, 1966.
Leymarie, Jean, Herbert Read, William S. Lieberman. *Henri Matisse: Retrospective 1966*. UCLA Art Galleries, Los Angeles, 5 Jan. – 27 Feb. 1966; The Art Institute of Chicago, 11 March – 24 April 1966; Museum of Fine Arts, Boston, 11 May – 26 June 1966.
Buchmann, Mark, and Erika Billeter. *Collagen: Die Technik der Collage in der angewandten Kunst*. Kunstgewerbemuseum, Zurich, 8 June – 18 Aug. 1968.
Gowing, Lawrence. *Matisse, 1869–1954: A Retrospective Exhibition*. Hayward Gallery, London, 11 July – 8 Sept. 1968.
Schneider, Pierre. *Henri Matisse: Exposition du Centenaire*. Grand Palais, Paris, April–Sept. 1970.
Colt, Priscilla. *Color and Field 1890–1970*. Albright-Knox Art Gallery, Buffalo, 15 Sept. – 1 Nov. 1970; Dayton Art Institute, 20 Nov. 1970 – 10 Jan. 1971; Cleveland Museum of Art, 4 Feb. – 28 March 1971.
Finsen, Hanne. *Matisse: en retrospektiv Udstilling*. Statens Museum for Kunst, Copenhagen, 10 Oct. – 29 Nov. 1970.
Elderfield, John. *European Master Paintings from Swiss Collections: Post-Impressionism to World War II*. The Museum of Modern Art, New York, 7 Dec. 1976 – 1 March 1977.
Cowart, Jack, Jack D. Flam, Dominique Fourcade, John Hallmark Neff. *Henri Matisse: Paper Cut-Outs*. National Gallery of Art, Washington DC, 10 Sept. – 23 Oct. 1977; Detroit Institute of Arts, 23 Nov. 1977 – 8 Jan. 1978; Saint Louis Art Museum, 29 Jan. – 12 March 1978.
Hoet, Jan, and Catherine Millet. *Henri Matisse en de Hedendaagse Franse Kunst*. Museum van Hedendaagse Kunst, Ghent, 7 Oct. – 20 Nov. 1978.
Hirschland, Ellen B. *Henri Matisse, Jazz and Other Illustrated Books*. Heckscher Museum, Huntington, NY, 12 Jan. – 18 Feb. 1979.
Weisner, Ulrich. *Matisse: Das Goldene Zeitalter*. Kunsthalle Bielefeld, 18 Oct. – 13 Dec. 1981.
Baumann, Felix (ed.). *Henri Matisse*. Kunsthaus, Zurich, 15 Oct. 1982 – 16 Jan. 1983; Städtische Kunsthalle, Düsseldorf, 29 Jan. – 4 April 1983.
Rubin, William (ed.). *'Primitivism' in 20th Century Art: Affinity of the Tribal and the Modern*. The Museum of Modern Art, New York, 27 Sept. 1984 – 15 Jan. 1985; Detroit Institute of Arts, 27 Feb. – 19 May 1985; Dallas Museum of Art, 23 June – 1 Sept. 1985.
Elderfield, John. *The Drawings of Henri Matisse*. Hayward Gallery, London, 4 Oct. 1984 – 6 Jan. 1985; The Museum of Modern Art, New York, 27 Feb. – 14 May 1985.
Russell, John, Pierre Schneider, Ulf Linde et al. *Henri Matisse*. Louisiana, Humlebaek, 19 Jan. – 14 April 1985; catalogue published in *Louisiana Revy*, Jan. 1985, vol.25 no.2.
Bell, Tiffany, Dore Ashton, Irving Sandler. *After Matisse*. Independent Curators Inc. Queens Museum, Flushing, NY, 30 March – 25 May 1986; Chrysler Museum, Norfolk, VA, 11 Sept. – 9 Nov. 1986; Portland Museum of Art, Portland, ME, 9 Dec. 1986 – 9 Feb. 1987; Bass Museum of Art, Miami Beach, FL, 17 March – 17 May 1987; Phillips Collection, Washington DC, 19 June – 14 Aug. 1987; Dayton Art Institute, Dayton, OH, 12 Sept. – 8 Nov. 1987; Worcester Art Museum, Worcester, MA, 9 Dec. 1987 – 7 Feb. 1988.
Girard, Xavier, Youri Roussakov, Jérôme Peignot, Christian Arthaud. *Henri Matisse: L'Art du livre*. Musée Matisse, Nice, 4 July – 30 Sept. 1986.
Mendes, Valerie D., and Frances M. Hinchcliffe. *Ascher: Fabric, Art, Fashion*. Victoria and Albert Museum, London, 15 April – 14 June 1987.
Schneider, Pierre (ed.). *Henri Matisse: Matisse et l'Italie*. Ala Napoleonica e Museo Correr, Venice, 30 May – 18 Oct. 1987.
Girard, Xavier. *Les Chefs-d'oeuvre du Musée Matisse, Nice, Cimiez*. Musée des Beaux-Arts de Dijon, 6 July – 6 Oct. 1991.
Monod-Fontaine, Isabelle, and Claude Laugier. *Dation Pierre Matisse*. Musée

national d'art moderne, Paris, 18 June – 13 Sept. 1992.
Elderfield, John. *Henri Matisse: A Retrospective*. The Museum of Modern Art, New York, 24 Sept. 1992 – 12 Jan. 1993.
Finsen, Hanne, and Mikael Wivel. *Matisse: Kapellet i Vence / Matisse: Chapelle du Rosaire des Dominicaines de Vence*. Ordrupgaard, Copenhagen, 12 Feb. – 2 May 1993.
Flam, Jack. *Matisse: Image into Sign*. Saint Louis Art Museum, 19 Feb. – 25 April 1993.
Pagé, Suzanne, Richard H. Glanton, Jack Flam et al. *Autour d'un chef-d'oeuvre de Matisse: Les Trois versions de La Dance Barnes (1930–1933)*. Musée d'Art Moderne de la Ville de Paris, 18 Nov. 1993 – 6 March 1994.
Delectorskaya, Lydia, Ortrud Dreyer, Jack Flam et al. *Henri Matisse: Zeichnungen und Gouaches découpées*. Staatsgalerie Stuttgart, 11 Dec. 1993 – 20 Feb. 1994.
Turner, Caroline, and Roger Benjamin (eds.). *Matisse*. Queensland Art Gallery, Brisbane, 29 March – 16 May 1995; National Gallery of Australia, Canberra, 27 May – 9 July 1995; National Gallery of Victoria, Melbourne, 19 July – 3 Sept. 1995.
Baum, Peter. *Henri Matisse (1869–1954)*. Neue Galerie der Stadt Linz, 16 Nov. 1995 – 18 Feb. 1996.
Schneider, Pierre, Claude Duthuit, Jackie Matisse Monnier, Paul Matisse. *Matisse: Visages découverts, 1945–1954.* Mona Bismarck Foundation, Paris, 1996.
Flam, Jack, Jean Leymarie, Dominique Szymusiak et al. *Matisse et Tériade*. Palazzo Medici Riccardi, Museo Mediceo, Florence, 20 Sept. – 8 Dec. 1996; Musée Matisse, Le Cateau-Cambrésis, 14 Dec. 1996 – 2 March 1997.
Szymusiak, Dominique. *Les Chasubles de Matisse*. Musée Matisse, Le Cateau-Cambrésis, 15 March – 15 June 1997.
Di Crescenzo, Casimiro. *Matisse and Tériade: Collaborative Works by the Artist and Art Publisher from 'Verve' (1937–1960), 'Lettres portugaises', 1946*. Yoshii Gallery, New York, 1 May – 28 June 1997.
Thom, Ian M., and John O'Brian. *Matisse Illustrates.* Vancouver Art Gallery, 26 June – 19 Oct. 1997.
Duthuit, Claude, Albert Kostenevich, Rémi Labrusse, Jean Leymarie. *Matisse: 'La Révélation m'est venue de l'Orient'*. Musei Capitolini, Palazzo dei Conservatori, Rome, 20 Sept. 1997 – 20 Jan. 1998.
Szymusiak, Dominique, Rémi Labrusse, Paule Laudon, John Klein. *Matisse et l'Océanie: Le Voyage à Tahiti*. Musée Matisse, Le Cateau-Cambrésis, 28 March – 28 June 1998.
Durey, Philippe, Isabelle Monod-Fontaine, Dominique Brachlianoff, Claude Laugier. *Matisse: La Collection du Centre Georges Pompidou, Musée national d'art moderne*. Musée des Beaux-Arts de Lyon, 4 April – 28 June 1998.
Pulvenis de Séligny, Marie-Thérèse, Danièle Mouchot, Paul-Louis Rinuy. *Matisse et l'antiquité*. Musée Matisse, Nice, 30 April – 30 Aug. 1999.
Alaoui, Brahim, Claude Duthuit, Rémi Labrusse et al. *Le Maroc de Matisse*. Institut du monde arabe, Paris, 19 Oct. 1999 – 30 Jan. 2000.
Pulvenis de Séligny, Marie-Thérèse. *Matisse, un siècle de couleurs: Le Bleu de l'été*. Musée Matisse, Nice, 8 July – 25 Sept. 2000.
Solana, Guillermo, and Marie-Thérèse Pulvenis de Séligny. *Matisse: Espíritu y sentido: Obra sobre papel*. Fundación Juan March, Madrid, 5 Oct. 2001 – 20 Jan. 2002.
Cowling, Elizabeth, Anne Baldassari, John Elderfield et al. *Matisse Picasso*. Tate Modern, London, 11 May – 18 Aug. 2002; Les Galeries Nationales du Grand Palais, Paris, 25 Sept. 2002 – 6 Jan. 2003; The Museum of Modern Art, New York, 13 Feb. – 19 May 2003.
Berggruen, Olivier, and Max Hollein (eds.). *Henri Matisse: Drawing with Scissors, Masterpieces from the Late Years*, translated by Paul Aston. Schirn Kunsthalle, Frankfurt, 20 Dec. 2002 – 2 March 2003; Nationalgalerie, Sammlung Berggruen, Berlin, 13 March – 25 May 2003.
Szymusiak, Dominique, Nicolas Surlapierre, Claudine Grammont et al. *Matisse et l'arbre*. Musée Matisse, Le Cateau-Cambrésis, 11 Oct. 2003 – 11 Jan. 2004.
Amano, Chika, Isabelle Monod-Fontaine, Masayuki Tanaka. *Henri Matisse: Processus/variation*. National Museum of Western Art, Tokyo, 10 Sept. – 12 Dec. 2004.
Spurling, Hilary, Jack Flam, Rémi Labrusse et al. *Matisse, His Art and His Textiles: The Fabric of Dreams*. Musée Matisse, Le Cateau-Cambrésis, 23 Oct. 2004 – 25 Jan. 2005; Royal Academy of Arts, London, 5 March – 30 May 2005; The Metropolitan Museum of Art, New York, 23 June – 25 Sept. 2005.
Finsen, Hanne (ed.). *Matisse: A Second Life*. Musée du Luxembourg, Paris, 16 March – 17 July 2005; Louisiana Museum of Modern Art, Humlebaek, 12 Aug. – 4 Dec. 2005.
Müller-Tamm, Pia (ed.). *Henri Matisse: Figure, Color, Space*. K20 Kunstsammlung Nordrhein Westfalen, Düsseldorf, 29 Oct. 2005 – 19 Feb. 2006.
Beyeler, Ernst, Christoph Vitali, Ulf Küster et al. *Matisse: Figure, couleur, espace*. Fondation Beyeler, Riehen/Basel, 19 March – 9 July 2006.
Kosinski, Dorothy, Jay McKean Fisher, Steven Nash. *Matisse: Painter as Sculptor*. Dallas Museum of Art and Nasher Sculpture Center, 21 Jan. – 29 April 2007; San Francisco Museum of Modern Art, 9 June – 16 Sept. 2007; Baltimore Museum of Art, 28 Oct. 2007 – 3 Feb. 2008.
Pulvenis de Séligny, Marie-Thérèse, Annelies Nelck, Peter Kropmanns, Isabelle Monod-Fontaine. *Henri Matisse: Vence: L'Espace d'un atelier: Nature morte aux grenades*. Musée Matisse, Nice, 7 July – 30 Sept. 2007.
Chassey, Éric de, and Émilie Ovaere (eds.). *Ils ont regardé Matisse: Une Réception abstraite: Etats-Unis/Europe 1948–1968*. Musée Matisse, Le Cateau-Cambrésis, 15 March – 14 June 2009.
Rajakaruna, C., Claude Duthuit, Pierre Schneider, Nicholas Zmelty. *Une Autre langue: Matisse et la gravure*. Mona Bismarck Foundation, Paris, 1 Dec. 2010 – 15 Feb. 2011.
Beltramo Ceppi Zevi, Claudia (ed.). *Matisse: La Seduzione di Michelangelo*. Museo di Santa Giulia, Brescia, 11 Feb. – 12 June 2011.
Pulvenis de Séligny, Marie-Thérèse, Peter Kropmanns, Isabelle Monod-Fontaine. *Henri Matisse: La Dissolution du trait et de la couleur, autour de la donation de la céramique 'La Piscine'*. Musée Matisse, Nice, 1 July – 2 Oct. 2011.
Szymusiak, Dominique, Anne Coron, Émilie Ovaere-Corthay et al. *Les Dessins au pinceau de Matisse*. Musée Matisse, Le Cateau-Cambrésis, 15 Oct. 2011 – 19 Feb. 2012.
Debray, Cécile (ed.). *Matisse: Paires et séries*. Centre Pompidou, Paris, 7 March – 18 June 2012.
Deparpe, Patrice (ed.). *Matisse: La Couleur découpée, une donation révélatrice/Cutting into Color, A Revealing donation*. Musée Matisse, Le Cateau-Cambrésis, 9 March – 9 June 2013.
Aagesen, Dorthe, and Rebecca Rabinow (eds.). *Matisse: In Search of True Painting*. Statens Museum for Kunst, Copenhagen, 14 July – 28 Oct. 2012; The Metropolitan Museum of Art, New York, 4 Dec. 2012 – 17 March 2013.
McCully, Marilyn, Tara Reddi, Sarah Bertalan, Michael Raeburn. *Matisse, The Essence of Line: Selected Prints, 1900–1950*. Marlborough Gallery, New York, 12 Sept. – 12 Oct. 2013, Marlborough Fine Art, London, 4 Dec. 2013 – 11 Jan. 2014, Galeria Marlborough, Madrid, Feb. – March 2014.

List of Exhibited Works

Measurements are given in centimetres followed by inches, and height precedes width. Works that appear in Jack Cowart et al., *Henri Matisse: Paper Cut-Outs*, exh. cat., National Gallery of Art, Washington 1977, are identified by a 'C' number for reference. The catalogue or figure number of the work is given in brackets after this 'C' number. French titles are given when applicable, and reflect how works are best known in that language.

Reclining Nude II
(*Nu couché II*) 1927
Bronze, 28.3 × 49.5 × 14.9
(11⅛ × 19½ × 5⅞)
Tate. Purchased 1953
Not in C (no. 125)
Tate only

Reclining Nude III
(*Nu couché III*) 1929
Bronze, 18.7 × 46.5 × 15.1
(7⅜ × 18⅜ × 6)
Hirshhorn Museum and Sculpture Garden, Smithsonian Institution, Washington, DC. Gift of Joseph H. Hirshhorn, 1966
Not in C (no. 126)
Tate only

Venus in a Shell I
(*Vénus à la coquille I*) 1930
Bronze, 31.1 × 18.2 × 20.2
(12¼ × 7⅛ × 8)
Private collection
Not in C (no. 127)
Tate only

The Dance (*La Danse*) 1931
Study for the Barnes mural (Paris version; recto and verso)
Gouache and pencil on paper (recto); pencil and ink on paper (verso), 14 × 40 (5½ × 15¾)
Private collection
Not in C (no. 1)
MoMA only

The Dance (*La Danse*) 1931–3
Study for the Barnes mural (Paris version)
Gouache and pencil on paper
27.9 × 75.9 (11 × 29⅞)
The Metropolitan Museum of Art, New York. The Pierre and Maria-Gaetana Matisse Collection, 2002, 2002.456.43
Not in C (no. 2)
MoMA only

Unknown photographer
Photographs of the Barnes mural in progress 1931–3
27 gelatin silver prints
dimensions variable
Barnes Foundation Archives, Merion, PA
Not in C (no. 3)
MoMA only

Venus in a Shell II
(*Vénus à la coquille II*) 1932
Bronze, 32.4 × 20.3 × 23.2
(12¾ × 8 × 9⅛)
Hirshhorn Museum and Sculpture Garden, Smithsonian Institution, Washington, DC. Gift of Joseph H. Hirshhorn, 1966
Not in C (no. 128)
Tate only

Cover maquette for the journal *Cahiers d'Art*, nos. 3–5 (1936) 1936
Gouache on paper, cut and pasted, 32.8 × 54 (12⅞ × 21¼)
Staatliche Museen zu Berlin, Nationalgalerie, Museum Berggruen
C 2 (no. 10)
MoMA only

Présages, cover maquette for the journal *Verve*, vol. I, no. 1 (1937) 1937
Gouache on paper, cut and pasted, and ink
36.5 × 55.5 (14⅜ × 21⅞)
Hilti Art Foundation, Schaan, Liechtenstein
C 3 (no. 11)

Verve, vol. I, no. 1 1937 (not illus.)
The Museum of Modern Art Library, New York
MoMA only

Verve, vol. I, no. 1 1937
(not illus.)
Louisa Riley-Smith, 20th Century Art Archives
Tate only

Two Dancers (*Deux Danseurs*) 1937–8
Stage curtain design for the ballet *Rouge et Noir*
Gouache on paper, cut and pasted, notebook papers, pencil and drawing pins (thumb tacks)
80.2 × 64.5 (31⅝ × 25⅜)
Centre Pompidou, Paris. Musée national d'art moderne / Centre de création industrielle. *Dation*, 1991
C 4 (no. 7)

Small Dancer on Red Background (*Petit Danseur sur fond rouge*) 1937–8
Gouache on paper, cut and pasted, 59.7 × 46.4 (23½ × 18¼)
Private collection, Houston
C 5 (no. 4)

Dancer (*Le Danseur*) 1937–8
Gouache and pencil on paper, cut and pasted
74.9 × 62.2 (29½ × 24⅜)
Private collection
C 6 (no. 5)

Two Dancers
(*Deux Danseurs*) 1937–8
Stage curtain design for the ballet *Rouge et Noir*
Gouache on paper, cut and pasted, mounted on board
63 × 64.5 (24⅞ × 25⅜)
Private collection
C 8 (no. 6)

The Dance (*La Danse*) 1938
Maquette for a lithographic reproduction for the journal *Verve*, vol. I, no. 4, 1938
Gouache on paper, cut and pasted, and ink
48.5 × 61.5 (19⅛ × 24¼)
The Perl Collection
C 9 (no. 12)

Symphonie chromatique, cover maquette for the journal *Verve*, vol. II, no. 8 (1940) 1939
Coloured papers, cut and pasted, 35.2 × 55.3 (13⅞ × 21¾)
Hilti Art Foundation, Schaan, Liechtenstein
C 10 (no. 13)

Verve, vol. II, no. 8 1939
(not illus.)
The Museum of Modern Art Library, New York
MoMA only

Verve, vol. II, no. 8 1939
(not illus.)
Louisa Riley-Smith, 20th Century Art Archives
Tate only

Still Life with Shell (*Nature morte au coquillage*) 1940
Gouache, coloured pencil and charcoal on cut paper, and string, pinned to canvas
83.5 × 115 (32⅞ × 45¼)
Private collection
C 11 (no. 8)

Still Life with Shell (*Nature morte au coquillage*) 1940
Oil on canvas
54 × 81 (21¼ × 31⅞)
The State Pushkin Museum of Fine Arts, Moscow
Not in C (no. 9)
Tate only

Cover maquette for the journal *Verve*, vol. IV, no. 13 (1945) 1943
Gouache on paper, cut and pasted, mounted on canvas
38.1 × 56.8 (15 × 22⅜)
Staatliche Museen zu Berlin, Nationalgalerie, Museum Berggruen
C 12 (no. 15)

The Fall of Icarus
(*La Chute d'Icare*) 1943
Gouache on paper, cut and pasted, and pins
35 × 27 (13¾ × 10⅝)
Private collection
C 14 (no. 17)

The Clown (*Le Clown*) 1943
Maquette for plate I from the illustrated book *Jazz* (1947)
Gouache on paper, cut and pasted, mounted on canvas
67.2 × 50.7 (26½ × 20)
Centre Pompidou, Paris. Musée national d'art moderne / Centre de création industrielle. *Dation*, 1985
C 16 (no. 18)

The Toboggan
(*Le Toboggan*) 1943
Maquette for plate XX from the illustrated book *Jazz* (1947)
Gouache on paper, cut and pasted, mounted on canvas
63.2 × 53.3 (24⅞ × 21)
Centre Pompidou, Paris. Musée national d'art moderne / Centre de création industrielle. *Dation*, 1985
C 17 (no. 39)

The Circus (*Le Cirque*) 1943
Maquette for plate II from the illustrated book *Jazz* (1947)
Gouache on paper, cut and pasted, mounted on canvas
45.2 × 67.1 (17¾ × 26⅜)
Centre Pompidou, Paris. Musée national d'art moderne / Centre de création industrielle. *Dation*, 1985
C 18 (no. 19)

Monsieur Loyal 1943
Maquette for plate III from the illustrated book *Jazz* (1947)
Gouache on paper, cut and pasted, mounted on canvas
54.7 × 42.7 (21½ × 16¾)
Centre Pompidou, Paris. Musée national d'art moderne / Centre de création industrielle. *Dation*, 1985
C 19 (no. 20)

Circus Scene (*Scène de cirque*) 1943
Drawing for the illustrated book *Jazz* (1947)
Pencil on paper
27.9 × 38.1 (11 × 15)
Pierre and Tana Matisse Foundation, New York
Not in C (no. 22)
MoMA only

Circus Scene (*Scène de cirque*) 1943
Drawing for the illustrated book *Jazz* (1947)
Pencil on paper
28.3 × 38.4 (11⅛ × 15⅛)
Private collection
Not in C (no. 23)
MoMA only

The Nightmare of the White Elephant (*Le Cauchemar de l'éléphant blanc*) 1943
Maquette for plate IV from the illustrated book *Jazz* (1947)
Gouache on paper, cut and pasted, mounted on canvas
43.9 × 66.7 (17¼ × 26¼)
Centre Pompidou, Paris. Musée national d'art moderne / Centre de création industrielle. *Dation*, 1985
C 20 (no. 21)

The Horse, the Rider and the Clown (*Le Cheval, l'écuyère et le clown*) 1943
Maquette for plate V from the illustrated book *Jazz* (1947)
Gouache on paper, cut and pasted, mounted on canvas
42.5 × 65.6 (16¾ × 25⅞)
Centre Pompidou, Paris. Musée national d'art moderne / Centre de création industrielle. *Dation*, 1985
C 21 (no. 24)

The Heart (*Le Coeur*) 1943
Maquette for plate VII from the illustrated book *Jazz* (1947)
Gouache on paper, cut and pasted, mounted on canvas
44.5 × 67.3 (17½ × 26½)
Centre Pompidou, Paris. Musée national d'art moderne / Centre de création industrielle. *Dation*, 1985
C 23 (no. 26)

The Codomas (*Les Codomas*) 1943
Maquette for plate XI from the illustrated book *Jazz* (1947)
Gouache on paper, cut and pasted, mounted on canvas
43.5 × 67.1 (17⅛ × 26⅜)
Centre Pompidou, Paris. Musée national d'art moderne / Centre de création industrielle. *Dation*, 1985
C 27 (no. 30)

The Sword Swallower (*L'Avaleur de sabres*) 1943
Maquette for plate XIII from the illustrated book *Jazz* (1947)
Gouache on paper, cut and pasted, mounted on canvas
43.3 × 34.3 (17 × 13½)
Centre Pompidou, Paris. Musée national d'art moderne / Centre de création industrielle. *Dation*, 1985
C 29 (no. 32)

The Cowboy (*Le Cow-Boy*) 1943
Maquette for plate XIV from the illustrated book *Jazz* (1947)
Gouache on paper, cut and pasted, mounted on canvas
43 × 68 (16⅞ × 26¾)
Centre Pompidou, Paris. Musée national d'art moderne / Centre de création industrielle. *Dation*, 1985
C 30 (no. 33)

Icarus (*Icare*) 1943(?)–4
Maquette for plate VIII from the illustrated book *Jazz* (1947)
Gouache on paper, cut and pasted, mounted on canvas
43.4 × 34.1 (17⅛ × 13⅜)
Centre Pompidou, Paris. Musée national d'art moderne / Centre de création industrielle. *Dation*, 1985
C 24 (no. 27)

Pierrot's Funeral (*L'Enterrement de Pierrot*) 1943–4(?)
Maquette for plate X from the illustrated book *Jazz* (1947)
Gouache on paper, cut and pasted, mounted on canvas
44.5 × 66 (17½ × 26)
Centre Pompidou, Paris. Musée national d'art moderne / Centre de création industrielle. *Dation*, 1985
C 26 (no. 29)

The Knife Thrower (*Le Lanceur de couteaux*) 1943–4
Maquette for plate XV from the illustrated book *Jazz* (1947)
Gouache on paper, cut and pasted, mounted on canvas
43.3 × 67.5 (17 × 26⅝)
Centre Pompidou, Paris. Musée national d'art moderne / Centre de création industrielle. *Dation*, 1985
C 31 (no. 34)

The Dragon (*Le Dragon*) 1943–4
Gouache on paper, cut and pasted
42.5 × 65.5 (16¾ × 25¾)
Staatliche Museen zu Berlin, Nationalgalerie, Museum Berggruen
C 37 (no. 40)
Tate only

The Wolf (*Le Loup*) 1944
Maquette for plate VI from the illustrated book *Jazz* (1947)
Gouache on paper, cut and pasted, mounted on canvas
45 × 67.1 (17¾ × 26⅜)
Centre Pompidou, Paris. Musée national d'art moderne / Centre de création industrielle. *Dation*, 1985
C 22 (no. 25)

Forms (*Formes*) 1944
Maquette for plate IX from the illustrated book *Jazz* (1947)
Gouache on paper, cut and pasted, mounted on canvas
44.3 × 67.1 (17½ × 26⅜)
Centre Pompidou, Paris. Musée national d'art moderne / Centre de création industrielle. *Dation*, 1985
C 25 (no. 28)

The Swimmer in the Tank (*La Nageuse dans l'aquarium*) 1944
Maquette for plate XII from the illustrated book *Jazz* (1947)
Gouache on paper, cut and pasted, mounted on canvas
44.2 × 66 (17⅜ × 26)
Centre Pompidou, Paris. Musée national d'art moderne / Centre de création industrielle. *Dation*, 1985
C 28 (no. 31)

Destiny (*Le Destin*) 1944
Maquette for plate XVI from the illustrated book *Jazz* (1947)
Gouache on paper, cut and pasted, mounted on canvas
44.6 × 67.1 (17½ × 26⅜)
Centre Pompidou, Paris. Musée national d'art moderne / Centre de création industrielle. *Dation*, 1985
C 32 (no. 35)

The Lagoon (*Le Lagon*) 1944
Maquette for plate XVII from the illustrated book *Jazz* (1947)
Gouache on paper, cut and pasted, mounted on canvas
44 × 66.3 (17⅜ × 26⅛)
Centre Pompidou, Paris Musée national d'art moderne / Centre de création industrielle. *Dation*, 1985
C 33 (no. 36)

The Lagoon (*Le Lagon*) 1944
Maquette for plate XVIII from the illustrated book *Jazz* (1947)
Gouache on paper, cut and pasted, mounted on canvas
43.6 × 67.1 (17⅛ × 26⅜)
Centre Pompidou, Paris. Musée national d'art moderne / Centre de création industrielle. *Dation*, 1985
C 34 (no. 37)

The Lagoon (*Le Lagon*) 1944
Maquette for plate XIX from the illustrated book *Jazz* (1947)
Gouache on paper, cut and pasted, mounted on canvas
44 × 67.1 (17⅜ × 26⅜)
Centre Pompidou, Paris. Musée national d'art moderne / Centre de création industrielle. *Dation*, 1985
C 35 (no. 38)

Drawing for *Pierre à feu* 1945
Pencil on paper, 27 × 21.1 (10⅝ × 8¼)
Private collection
Not in C (no. 41)
MoMA only

Pierre à feu, unrealised cover maquette for the book *Les Miroirs profonds* (1947) 1945
Gouache on paper, cut and pasted, and pencil
24.8 × 42.5 (9¾ × 16¾)
Private collection
Not in C (no. 43)
MoMA only

Pierre à feu, cover maquette for the book *Les Miroirs profonds* (1947) 1945
Gouache on paper, cut and pasted, and ink
25 × 41 (9⅞ × 16⅛)
Fondation Marguerite et Aimé Maeght, Saint-Paul, France
C 41 (no. 42)

The Propeller (*Motif – L'Hélice*) 1945
Gouache on paper, cut and pasted, and ink
52.5 × 40.5 (20⅝ × 16)
Pierre and Tana Matisse Foundation, New York
C 49 (no. 46)

Verve, vol. IV, no. 13 1945 (not illus.)
The Museum of Modern Art Library, New York
MoMA only

Verve, vol. IV, no. 13 1945 (not illus.)
Louisa Riley-Smith, 20th Century Art Archives
Tate only

Composition (Tahitian Harmony) (*Composition [Harmonie tahitienne]*) 1945–6
Gouache on paper, cut and pasted
56.5 × 36.5 (22¼ × 14⅜)
Private collection
C 44 (no. 44)

Composition (Red Circle with Four Black Triangles on Green Background) (*Composition [cercle rouge aux quatre triangles noirs sur fond vert]*) 1945–6
Gouache on paper, cut and pasted
52.5 × 40.5 (20⅝ × 16)
Private collection
C 48 (no. 47)

Ace of Clubs (*As de trèfle*) 1945–6
Gouache on paper, cut and pasted, 53.7 × 41.4 (21⅛ × 16¼)
Private collection
C 52 (no. 48)
MoMA only

The Sails (*Les Voiles*) 1945–6
Gouache on paper, cut and pasted, 52.7 × 40.4 (20¾ × 15⅞)
Private collection
C 53 (no. 45)
MoMA only

The Lyre (*La Lyre*) 1946
Gouache on paper, cut and pasted
31.6 × 23.3 (12½ × 9⅛)
Private collection
C 38 (no. 49)

Oceania, the Sky (*Océanie, le ciel*) summer 1946 (realised as silkscreen 1946)
Gouache on paper, cut and pasted, on paper, mounted on canvas, 178.3 × 369.7 (70⅛ × 145½)
Musée départemental Matisse, Le Cateau-Cambrésis. Gift of the Matisse family, 2004
C 55 (no. 52)

Oceania, the Sea (*Océanie, la mer*) summer 1946 (realised as silkscreen 1946)
Gouache on paper, cut and pasted, on paper, mounted on canvas, 178.5 × 392.8 (70¼ × 154⅝)
Musée départemental Matisse, Le Cateau-Cambrésis. Gift of the Matisse family, 2004
C 56 (no. 53)

Calligraphic studies for *Jazz* c. 1946 (not illus.)
Four sheets, ink on paper
Dimensions variable
Pierre and Tana Matisse Foundation, New York
Not in C
MoMA only

Ascher Square A 1947
Printed blue silk
91.44 × 91.44 (36 × 36)
Produced in an edition of 275 in collaboration with Zika Ascher (Czech, 1910–83) for Ascher Studio
The Ascher Family Collection
Not in C (no. 50)

Ascher Square B 1947
Printed grey silk
91.44 × 91.44 (36 × 36)
Produced in an edition of 275 in collaboration with Zika Ascher (Czech, 1910–83) for Ascher Studio
Ascher Family Collection
Not in C (no.51)

Amphitrite 1947
Gouache on paper, cut and pasted
85.5 × 70 (33⅝ × 27½)
Private collection
C 61 (no.55)

Composition with Red Cross (*Composition à la croix rouge*) 1947
Gouache on paper, cut and pasted
74.1 × 52.4 (29⅛ × 20⅝)
Private collection
C 62 (no.54)

Composition Green Background (*Composition fond vert*) 1947
Gouache on paper, cut and pasted, and pencil
104.1 × 40.3 (41 × 15⅞)
The Menil Collection, Houston
C 64 (no.66)

Composition (The Velvets) (*Composition [Les Velours]*) 1947
Gouache on paper, cut and pasted
51.5 × 217.5 (20¼ × 85⅝)
Kunstmuseum Basel. Acquired with support from Dr Richard Doetsch-Benziger, Basel, and Marguerite Hagenbach, Basel, 1954
C 65 (no.65)

Panel with Mask (*Le Panneau au masque*) 1947
Gouache on paper, cut and pasted, 110 × 53 (43¾ × 20⅞)
Designmuseum Danmark
C 66 (no.56)

The Eskimo (*L'Esquimau*) 1947
Gouache on paper, cut and pasted, 40.5 × 86 (16 × 33⅞)
Designmuseum Danmark
C 67 (no.57)

Composition, Black and Red (*Composition, noir et rouge*) 1947
Gouache on paper, cut and pasted, 40.6 × 52.7 (16 × 20¾)
Davis Museum and Cultural Center, Wellesley College, Wellesley, MA. Gift of Professor and Mrs John McAndrew
C 69 (no.64)
MoMA only

Two Masks (The Tomato) (*Deux Masques [La Tomate]*) 1947
Gouache on paper, cut and pasted
47.7 × 51.8 (18¾ × 20⅜)
Mr and Mrs Donald B. Marron, New York
C 71 (no.62)

Negro Boxer (*Boxeur nègre*) 1947
Gouache on paper, cut and pasted, 32 × 25.5 (12⅝ × 10)
Private collection, New York
C 73 (no.63)

Composition, Yellow, Blue and Black (*Composition, jaune, bleu et noir*) 1947
Gouache on paper, cut and pasted, 47 × 34 (18½ × 13⅜)
Private collection
C 76 (no.58)

White Alga on Red and Green Background (*Algue blanche sur fond rouge et vert*) 1947
Gouache on paper, cut and pasted
52.5 × 40.5 (20¾ × 16)
Fondation Beyeler, Riehen/Basel, Beyeler Collection
C 77 (no.59)

White Alga on Orange and Red Background (*Algue blanche sur fond orange et rouge*) 1947
Gouache on paper, cut and pasted, 52.5 × 40.5 (20⅝ × 16)
Mr and Mrs Donald B. Marron, New York
C 79 (no.60)

Alga on Green Background
(*Algue sur fond vert*) 1947
Gouache on paper, cut and
pasted, 24.8 × 14.6 (9¾ × 5¾)
Pierre and Tana Matisse
Foundation, New York
C 80 (no.70)

Black and Violet Arabesques
on Orange Background
(*Arabesques noires et violettes*
sur fond orange) 1947
Gouache on paper,
cut and pasted
40 × 26.5 (15¾ × 10⅜)
Collection Howard
and Nancy Marks
C 82 (no.68)

Screen Panel, Beige
Background (*Feuille de*
paravent, fond beige) 1947
Gouache on paper,
cut and pasted
162 × 53.5 (63¾ × 21)
Private collection
C 83 (no.67)
MoMA only

Red Interior: Still Life on a Blue
Table (*Intérieur rouge, nature*
morte sur table bleue) 1947
Oil on canvas
116 × 89 (45⅝ × 35)
Kunstsammlung Nordrhein-
Westfalen, Düsseldorf
Not in C (no.73)
Tate only

Jazz 1947 (not illus.)
Illustrated book with
20 *pochoir* plates
Overall: 42.4 × 33 × 4.4
(16⅝ × 13 × 1¾)
Published by Tériade, Paris
Printed in an edition of 250
by Edmond Vairel and
Draeger Frères, Paris
The Museum of Modern Art,
New York. The Louis E. Stern
Collection, 1964
Not in C

Jazz 1947 (not illus.)
Illustrated book with
20 *pochoir* plates
42 × 32.2 (16⅝ × 12⅝)
Scottish National Gallery
of Modern Art, Edinburgh
Not in C
Tate only

Jazz 1947 (not illus.)
Portfolio of 20 *pochoir* plates
Each sheet: 42.5 × 65.3
(16¾ × 25¾)
Published by Tériade, Paris
Printed in an edition of 100
by Edmond Vairel and
Draeger Frères, Paris
The Museum of Modern Art,
New York. Gift of the artist,
1948
Not in C
MoMA only

Pierre à feu. Les Miroirs
profonds 1947 (not illus.)
Fondation Marguerite et Aimé
Maeght, Saint-Paul, France

Palmette (*Feuille violet sur*
fond orange) c.1947
Gouache on paper, cut and
pasted, 71.1 × 53.3 (28 × 21)
Mr and Mrs Donald B. Marron,
New York
Not in C (no.71)

Interior with Black Fern
(*Intérieur à la fougère noire*)
1948
Oil on canvas
116.5 × 89.5 (45⅞ × 35¼)
Fondation Beyeler, Riehen /
Basel, Beyeler Collection
Not in C (no.72)
Tate only

Celestial Jerusalem
(*Jerusalem céleste*) early 1948
First maquette for the apse
window of the Chapel of
the Rosary, Vence
Gouache on paper, cut and
pasted, on paper, mounted
on canvas, 265.5 × 130
(104½ × 51⅛)
Centre Pompidou, Paris.
Musée national d'art moderne/
Centre de création industrielle.
Gift of Madame Claude
Duthuit in memory of Claude
Duthuit, 2013
C 89 (no.75)

The Bees (*Les Abeilles*)
summer 1948
Preliminary maquette for
the side windows of the
Chapel of the Rosary, Vence
(realised 1955 for H. Matisse
primary school, Le Cateau-
Cambrésis)
Gouache on paper, cut and
pasted, mounted on canvas
101 × 241 (39¾ × 94⅞)
Musée Matisse, Nice.
Gift of the artist's family, 1963
C 90 (no.74)
Tate only

Flowering Tree (*Mural Scroll*)
(*Arbre en fleur*) 1948
Maquette for silkscreen
(realised 1949)
Gouache on paper,
cut and pasted
51.2 × 63.7 (20⅛ × 25⅛)
Private collection
C 91 (no.61)

Cover maquette for the
journal *Verve*, vol. VI,
nos. 21–2 (1948) 1948
Gouache on paper, cut and
pasted, 36 × 54 (14⅛ × 21¼)
Private collection
C 92 (no.14)
MoMA only

Verve, vol. VI, no. 21/22 1948
(not illus.)
The Museum of Modern
Art Library, New York
MoMA only

Study for the hands
of *St Dominic*
(*Saint Dominique*) 1948
Ink on paper
21.5 × 17 (8½ × 6⅔)
Private collection
Not in C (fig.31)
MoMA only

Leaf Motif (*Motif – Feuille*)
c.1948
Maquette for scarf
(realised c.1948)
Gouache on paper,
cut and pasted, and ink
34 × 19.5 (13⅜ × 7⅝)
Pierre and Tana Matisse
Foundation, New York
Not in C (no.69)

Pale Blue Window
(*Vitrail bleu pâle*)
November 1948 – January 1949
Second maquette for the
apse window for the Chapel
of the Rosary, Vence
Two-part panel: gouache on
paper, cut and pasted, on kraft
paper, mounted on canvas
509.8 × 252.3 (200¾ × 99⅜)
Centre Pompidou, Paris.
Musée national d'art
moderne / Centre de création
industrielle. Gift of Mme Jean
Matisse and Gérard Matisse,
1982
C 94 (no.77)

Study for *Virgin and Child*
(*Vierge à l'enfant*) 1949
Ink on paper
16.8 × 25.1 (6⅝ × 9⅞)
Private collection
Not in C (fig.34)
MoMA only

Study for *St Dominic*
(*Saint Dominique*) 1949
Ink on paper
22.1 × 14.8 (8⅝ × 5⅞)
Private collection
Not in C (fig.29)
MoMA only

Study for *Virgin and Child*
(*Vierge à l'enfant*) 1949
Ink and pencil on paper
16.5 × 30.2 (6½ × 11⅞)
Private collection
Not in C (fig.33)
MoMA only

Simon of Cyrene Helps Jesus
to Carry the Cross (*Simon de*
Cyrène aidant Jésus) 1949
Study for the Fifth
Station of the Cross
Ink on paper
26.7 × 20.3 (10½ × 8)
Private collection
Not in C (no.79a)
MoMA only

Veronica Wipes the
Face of Jesus (*La Voile*
de Véronique) 1949
Study for the Sixth
Station of the Cross
Ink on paper
26.3 × 20.3 (10⅜ × 8)
Private collection
Not in C (no.79b)
MoMA only

Christ on the Cross
(*Le Christ en croix*) 1949
Study for the Twelfth
Station of the Cross
Ink on paper
26.7 × 20.3 (10½ × 8)
Private collection
Not in C (no.79c)
MoMA only

Cover maquette for the book
Les Fauves by Georges Duthuit
(1949) 1949
Gouache on paper, cut and
pasted, 32.3 × 50.8 (12¾ × 20)
Private collection
C 100 (no.99)

Les Fauves, by Georges
Duthuit 1949 (not illus.)
Louisa Riley-Smith,
20th Century Art Archives
Tate only

Study for *The Tree of Life*
(*L'Arbre de vie*) c.1949
Ink on paper
27 × 21 (10⅝ × 8¼)
Private collection
Not in C (fig.35)
MoMA only

Maquettes for the
tabernacle of the Chapel
of the Rosary, Vence c.1949
(related design realised 1951)
Gouache on paper,
cut and pasted
20.3 × 24.8 (8 × 9¾) (a)
19.7 × 24.8 (7¾ × 9¾) (b)
20.3 × 25.4 (8 × 10) (c)
Private collection
Not in C (no.78)
MoMA only

The Four Rosettes with Blue Motifs (*Les Quatres Rosaces aux motifs bleus*) 1949–50
Gouache on paper, cut and
pasted, 38 × 54 (15 × 21¼)
Collection of Mr Julian
Robertson
C 103 (no.90)

Mimosa 1949–51
Maquette for rug
(realised 1951)
Gouache on paper, cut and
pasted, mounted on canvas
148 × 98 (58¼ × 38⅝)
Ikeda Museum of 20th
Century Art, Ito, Japan
C 158 (no.91)

Zulma early 1950
Gouache on paper, cut and
pasted, 238 × 133 (93¾ × 52⅜)
Statens Museum for Kunst,
Copenhagen
C 109 (no.84)

Creole Dancer (*Danseuse créole*) June 1950
Gouache on paper, cut and
pasted, on paper, mounted
on canvas, 205.1 × 120
(80¾ × 47¼)
Musée Matisse, Nice.
Gift of Henri Matisse, 1953
C 110 (no.85)

The Thousand and One Nights
(*Les Mille et Une Nuits*)
June 1950
Gouache on paper, cut and
pasted, 139 × 374 (54¾ × 147¼)
Carnegie Museum of Art,
Pittsburgh. Acquired through
the generosity of the Sarah
Mellon Scaife Family, 71.23
C 111 (no.86)

The Japanese Mask (*Le Masque japonais*) early 1950
Gouache on paper, cut and
pasted, 79.5 × 49.5 (31¼ × 19½)
Private collection
C 112 (no.88)
MoMA only

Study for the stained-glass
window *The Tree of Life*
(*L'Arbre de vie*) 1950
Frosted coloured glass,
set with lead, 62.3 × 85 × 2
(24½ × 33½ × ¾)
Produced in collaboration with
Paul Bony (French, 1911–82)
Musée Matisse, Nice. Bequest
of Madame Henri Matisse,
1960
Not in C (fig.36)
MoMA only

Fish (*Poissons*) 1950 (not illus.)
Study for the embroidery
on the altar cloth
Ink on three sheets of paper,
joined, 79.1 × 20.8 (31⅛ × 8 ¼)
Private collection
MoMA only

The Virgin and Child (*La Grande Vierge à l'enfant*) c.1950
Charcoal on paper
330 × 610 (130 × 240¼)
Skissernas Museum –
Museum of Artistic Process
and Public Art, Lund, Sweden
Not in C (no.76)
Tate only

Maquette for *Red Chasuble*
(front) 1950–2
(realised 1952)
Gouache on paper,
cut and pasted
133.4 × 198.4 (52½ × 78⅛)
The Museum of Modern Art,
New York. Acquired through
the Lillie P. Bliss Bequest, 1953
C 145 (no.82)

Maquette for *Red Chasuble*
(back) 1950–2
(realised 1952)
Gouache on paper,
cut and pasted
128.2 × 199.4 (50½ × 78½)
The Museum of Modern Art,
New York. Acquired through
the Lillie P. Bliss Bequest, 1953
C 146 (no.83)

Maquettes for a set of
red and yellow liturgical
vestments c.1950
(realised 1952)
Gouache on paper, cut and
pasted, mounted on paper
Stole: 124.5 × 19 (49 × 7½)
Maniple: 43.2 × 21.3 (17 × 8⅜)
Chalice veil: 51.4 × 51.4
(20¼ × 20¼)
Burse: 25.4 × 22.2 (10 × 8¾)
The Museum of Modern Art,
New York. Acquired through
the Lillie P. Bliss Bequest, 1953
C 147
MoMA only

Maquette for *Black Chasuble*
(front: *'Esperlucat'*) 1950–2
Gouache on paper, cut and
pasted, mounted on canvas
125.6 × 197.6 (49½ × 77¾)
Centre Pompidou, Paris.
Musée national d'art
moderne / Centre de création
industrielle. On loan to Musée
départemental Matisse,
Le Cateau-Cambrésis, 1986
C 154 (no.80)
Tate only

Maquette for *Black Chasuble*
(back) 1950–2
Gouache on paper, cut and
pasted, mounted on canvas
132 × 197 (52 × 77⅝)
Centre Pompidou, Paris.
Musée national d'art
moderne / Centre de création
industrielle. On loan to Musée
départemental Matisse, Le
Cateau-Cambrésis, 1986
C 155 (no.81)
Tate only

Snow Flowers
(*Fleurs de neige*) 1951
Gouache on paper,
cut and pasted, on paper,
mounted on canvas
174 × 80.6 (68 ½ × 31 ¾)
The Metropolitan Museum
of Art, New York. Jacques
and Natasha Gelman
Collection, 1998, 1999.363.46
C 117 (no.94)

Cover maquette for the book
Matisse: His Art and his Public
by Alfred H. Barr, Jr (1951)
1951
Gouache on paper, cut and
pasted, 27 × 42.9 (10⅝ × 16⅞)
The Museum of Modern Art,
New York. Transferred from
The Museum of Modern Art
Publications Department, 1953
C 122 (no.101)

Matisse: His Art and his Public,
by Alfred H. Barr, Jr 1951
(not illus.)
The Museum of Modern
Art Archives, New York
MoMA only

Cover maquette for
the exhibition catalogue
Henri Matisse (1951) 1951
Gouache on paper, cut and
pasted, 27 × 40 (10⅝ × 15¾)
The Museum of Modern Art,
New York. Transferred from
The Museum of Modern Art
Publications Department, 1953
C 123 (no.100)

Chinese Fish
(*Poissons chinois*) 1951
Maquette for stained-glass
window (realised 1951)
Gouache on paper, cut and
pasted, and charcoal on white
paper, mounted on canvas
189.9 × 90.2 (74¾ × 35½)
Colección Patricia Phelps
de Cisneros
C 127 (no.93)

The Bell (*La Cloche*) 1951
Gouache on paper, cut and pasted, and watercolour, mounted on canvas
122 × 48.5 (48 × 19⅛)
Private collection
C 156 (no.89)

Tree (*L'Arbre*) December 1951
Ink, gouache, and charcoal on paper, mounted on canvas
177.8 × 152.4 (70 × 60)
The Metropolitan Museum of Art, New York. The Pierre and Maria-Gaetana Matisse Collection, 2002, 2002.456.58
Not in C (no.92)

Vegetables (*Végétaux*) c.1951
Gouache on paper, cut and pasted, 175 × 81 (68⅞ × 31⅞)
Private collection
C 118 (no 95)

Cover maquette for the book *Apollinaire* by André Rouveyre (1952) 1951–2
Gouache on paper, cut and pasted, 32.7 × 25.4 (12⅞ × 10)
The Mourlot Archives
C 189 (no.103)

Black Leaf on Red Background (*Feuille noire sur fond rouge*) 1952
Gouache on paper, cut and pasted, 50 × 40 (19¾ × 15¾)
Private collection
C 118 (no.97)

Black Leaf on Green Background (*Feuille noire sur fond vert*) 1952
Gouache on paper, cut and pasted, 60 × 39 (23⅝ × 15⅜)
The Menil Collection, Houston
C 159 (no.96)

Christmas Eve (*Nuit de Noël*) 1952 (realised 1952)
Maquette for stained-glass window
Gouache on paper, cut and pasted, mounted on board
322.8 × 135.9 (127 × 53½)
The Museum of Modern Art, New York. Gift of Time Inc., 1953
C 162 (no.98)

Blue Nude I (*Nu bleu I*) spring 1952
Gouache on paper, cut and pasted, mounted on canvas
106 × 78 (41¾ × 30¾)
Fondation Beyeler, Riehen / Basel, Beyeler Collection
C 167 (no.109)

Blue Nude II (*Nu bleu II*) spring 1952
Gouache on paper, cut and pasted, on white paper, mounted on canvas
116.2 × 88.9 (45¾ × 35)
Centre Pompidou, Paris. Musée national d'art moderne / Centre de création industrielle. Purchase, 1984
C 168 (no.110)

Blue Nude III (*Nu bleu III*) spring 1952
Gouache on paper, cut and pasted, on white paper, mounted on canvas,
112 × 73.5 (44⅛ × 29)
Centre Pompidou, Paris. Musée national d'art moderne / Centre de création industrielle. Purchase, 1982
C 169 (no.111)

Blue Nude IV (*Nu bleu IV*) spring 1952
Gouache on paper, cut and pasted, and charcoal on white paper, mounted on canvas
102.9 × 76.8 (40½ × 30¼)
Musée d'Orsay, Paris, on long-term loan to the Musée Matisse, Nice. Gift of Mme Jean Matisse, 1979
C 170 (no.107)

The Parakeet and the Mermaid (*La Perruche et la sirène*) 1952
Gouache on paper, cut and pasted, and charcoal on white paper, 337 × 768.5 (132⅝ × 302½)
Collection Stedelijk Museum, Amsterdam, acquired with the generous support of the Vereniging Rembrandt and the Prins Bernhard Cultuurfonds
C 172 (no.118)

Blue Nude with Green Stockings (*Nu bleu aux bas verts*) 1952
Gouache on paper, cut and pasted, 260 × 168 (102⅜ × 66⅛)
Fondation Louis Vuitton, Paris
C 173 (no.117)

Acrobat (*Acrobate*) 1952
Ink on paper, 105.5 × 74.5 (41½ × 29⅜)
Private collection
Not in C (fig.45)
MoMA only

Acrobats (*Acrobates*) spring – summer 1952
Gouache on paper, cut and pasted, and charcoal on white paper, mounted on canvas
213 × 208.3 (83⅞ × 82)
Private collection
C 175 (no.113)

Women and Monkeys (*Femmes et singes*) 1952
Gouache on paper, cut and pasted, and charcoal on white paper
71.7 × 286.2 (28¼ × 112⅝)
Museum Ludwig, Köln / Sammlung Ludwig
C 176 (no.120)

The Swimming Pool (*La Piscine*) late summer 1952
Maquette for ceramic (realised 1999 and 2005)
Gouache on paper, cut and pasted, on painted paper, overall
185.4 × 1643.3 (73 × 647)
Installed as nine panels in two parts on burlap-covered walls 345.4 (136) high. Frieze installed at a height of 165 (65)
The Museum of Modern Art, New York. Mrs. Bernard F. Gimbel Fund, 1975
C 177 (no.121)
MoMA only

Standing Blue Nude (*Nu bleu debout*) 1952
Gouache on paper, cut and pasted, 112.7 × 73.7 (44⅜ × 29)
The Metropolitan Museum of Art, New York. The Pierre and Maria-Gaetana Matisse Collection, 2002, 2002.456.58
C 179 (no.114)

Blue Nude, the Frog (*Nu bleu, la grenouille*) 1952
Gouache on paper, cut and pasted, mounted on canvas
141 × 134 (55½ × 52¾)
Fondation Beyeler, Riehen / Basel, Beyeler Collection
C 180 (no.116)
MoMA only

Venus (*Vénus*) 1952
Gouache on paper, cut and pasted, on white paper, mounted on paper panel
101.2 × 76.5 (39⅞ × 30⅛)
National Gallery of Art, Washington. Ailsa Mellor Bruce Fund, 1973.18.2
C 181 (no.115)

Cover maquette for the book *The Decisive Moment* (*Images à la sauvette*) by Henri Cartier-Bresson (1952) 1952
Gouache on paper, cut and pasted, and ink
36 × 57 (14⅛ × 22½)
Musée départemental Matisse, Le Cateau-Cambrésis. Gift of Mme Marie Matisse, 1995
C 187 (no.102)

Cover maquette for the exhibition catalogue *Henri Matisse: papiers découpés* (1953) 1952
Gouache on paper, cut and pasted
23.2 × 12.2 (9⅛ × 4¾)
Private collection
C 197 (no.104)
Tate only

Henri Matisse 1952 (not illus.)
The Museum of Modern Art Library, New York
MoMA only

Apollinaire, by André Rouveyre, 1952 (not illus.)
Louisa Riley-Smith, 20th Century Art Archives
Tate only

Christmas Eve (*Nuit de Noël*) summer – fall 1952 (not illus.)
Stained glass
322.8 × 135.9 (127 × 53½)
Produced in collaboration with Paul Bony (French, 1911–82)
The Museum of Modern Art, New York. Gift of Time, Inc., 1953
Not in C

Little Girl (*La Fillette*) c.1952
Gouache on paper, cut and pasted, 152.4 × 117.5 (60 × 46¼)
Private collection
C 165 (no.87)
MoMA only

Untitled (study for *Blue Nude* [*Nu bleu*]) c. 1952
Coloured pencil on paper
27 × 21 (10⅝ × 8¼)
Indianapolis Museum of Art. Gift of Mr and Mrs J.W. Alsdorf
Not in C (no.108a)
MoMA only

Untitled (study for *Blue Nude* [*Nu bleu*]) c. 1952
Coloured pencil on paper
27 × 21 (10⅝ × 8¼)
Indianapolis Museum of Art. Gift of Mr and Mrs J.W. Alsdorf
Not in C (no.108b)
MoMA only

Untitled (study for *Blue Nude* [*Nu bleu*]) c.1952
Pencil on paper
27 × 21 (10⅝ × 8¼)
The Detroit Institute of Arts. Gift of John S. Newberry
Not in C (no.108c)
MoMA only

Untitled (study for *Blue Nude* [*Nu bleu*]) c.1952
Pencil on paper
27 × 21 (10⅝ × 8¼)
Private collection
Not in C (no.108d)
MoMA only

Untitled (study for *Blue Nude* [*Nu bleu*]) c. 1952
Ink on paper
27 × 21 (10⅝ × 8¼)
Rhode Island School of Design. Gift of Mr and Mrs Barnet Fain
Not in C (no.108e)
MoMA only

Ten drawings of *Acrobats* (*Acrobates*) c. 1952
Ink on paper, each (vertical or horizontal) 27 × 21 (8¼ × 10⅝)
Private collection
Not in C (no.112)
MoMA only

The Wave (*La Vague*) c. 1952
Gouache on paper, cut and pasted
51.1 × 158.4 (20⅛ × 62⅜)
Musée Matisse, Nice. Gift of the artist's estate, 1963
C 163 (no.122)
MoMA only

Memory of Oceania (*Souvenir d'Océanie*) summer 1952 – early 1953
Gouache on paper, cut and pasted, and charcoal on paper, mounted on canvas
284.4 × 286.4 (112 × 112⅞)
The Museum of Modern Art, New York. Mrs Simon Guggenheim Fund, 1968
C 199 (no.130)

The Snail (*L'Escargot*) 1953
Gouache on paper, cut and pasted, on paper, mounted on canvas
286.4 × 287 (112¾ × 113)
Tate. Purchased with assistance from the Friends of the Tate Gallery, 1962
C 198 (no.129)

Woman with Amphora and Pomegranates (*Femme à l'amphore et grenades*) 1953
Gouache on paper, cut and pasted, mounted on canvas
243.8 × 96.2 (95⅞ × 37⅞)
National Gallery of Art, Washington. Ailsa Mellon Bruce Fund, 1973.18.3
C 201 (no.123)

Woman with Amphora (*Femme à l'amphore*) 1953
Gouache on paper, cut and pasted, mounted on canvas
168.5 × 48 (66⅜ × 18⅞)
Centre Pompidou, Paris. Musée national d'art moderne / Centre de création industrielle, on long-term loan to the Musée Matisse, Nice
C 202 (no.124)

Large Decoration with Masks (*Grande Décoration aux masques*) 1953
Preliminary maquette for ceramic
Gouache on paper, cut and pasted, and ink on white paper, mounted on canvas
353.6 × 996.4 (139¼ × 392¼)
National Gallery of Art, Washington. Ailsa Mellon Bruce Fund, 1973.17.1
C 203 (no.131)

The Sheaf (*La Gerbe*) 1953
Maquette for ceramic (realised 1953)
Gouache on paper, cut and pasted, on paper, mounted on canvas
294 × 350 (115¾ × 137¾)
Collection University of California, Los Angeles. Hammer Museum. Gift of Mr and Mrs Sidney F. Brody
C 206 (no.136)

Coloured samples for *The Sheaf* 1953 (not illus.)
Nine sheets, gouache on paper, dimensions variable
Los Angeles County Museum of Art. Gift of Frances L. Brody
Not in C

Green Alga on Black Background (The Swan) (*Algue verte sur fond noir [La Cygne]*) 1953 (not illus.)
Gouache on paper, cut and pasted, 81 × 65 (31⅞ × 25⅝)
Private collection
MoMA only
C 211

Ivy in Flower (*Lierre en fleur*) 1953
Maquette for stained-glass window (realised 1956)
Gouache on paper, cut and pasted, and pencil on coloured paper
284.2 × 286.1 (111⅞ × 112⅝)
Dallas Museum of Art, Foundation for the Arts Collection. Gift of the Albert and Mary Lasker Foundation
C 212 (no. 134)

Acanthuses (*Les Acanthes*) 1953
Maquette for ceramic (realised 1953)
Gouache on paper, cut and pasted, and charcoal on white painted paper, mounted on canvas
311.7 × 351.8 (122¾ × 138½)
Fondation Beyeler, Riehen / Basel, Beyeler Collection
C 213 (no. 135)

Cover maquette for the exhibition catalogue *Henri Matisse: Lithographies Rares* (1954) c. 1954
Gouache on paper, cut and pasted, 22.1 × 23.6 (8¾ × 9¼)
Courtesy of Frederick Mulder Ltd
C 214 (no. 105)
Tate only

Cover maquette for the journal *Verve*, vol. IX, nos. 35–6 (1958) c. 1954
Gouache on paper, cut and pasted, 35.9 × 54.9 (14⅛ × 21⅝)
Private collection
C 215 (no.16)
MoMA only

Works not by Matisse

Frédéric Rossif (French, 1922–90; not illus.)
[Matisse], rushes 1950
Film, 16 mm (transferred to DVD at The Museum of Modern Art), colour, and silent, 8 min
La Cinémathèque française

Paul Bony (French, 1911–82; not illus.)
Tracings for the stained-glass window *Christmas Eve* (*Nuit de Noël*) 1951
Pencil on tracing paper
A: 134 × 147 (52¾ × 57⅞)
B: 85 × 148 (33½ × 58¼)
C: 58 × 150 (22⅞ × 59)
D: 73 × 149 (28¾ × 58⅝)
Fonds atelier Bony, Paris
Not in C

Paul Bony (French, 1911–82; not illus.)
Colour samples for the stained-glass window *Christmas Eve* (*Nuit de Noël*) 1951
Glass
Dimensions variable
Fonds atelier Bony, Paris
Not in C

Adrien Maeght (French, b. 1930; not illus.)
Matisse Making Cut-Outs (*Matisse faisant des papiers découpés*) 1945
Film, 16 mm (transferred to DVD at The Museum of Modern Art), black and white, and silent, 1 min
Galerie Maeght, Paris
© Maeght 2014

Photo Credits

All images by Henri Matisse © Succession H. Matisse / DACS 2014

Plates

Image courtesy Aquavella Galleries 95
© 2014 The Barnes Foundation Archives 3
Photo: Robert Bayer, Basel 54, 59, 72, 109, 116, 135
bpk / Nationalgalerie, Museum Berggruen, SMB / Jens Ziehe 15, 40
Photo Philip Bernard 102
The Bridgeman Art Library 108c
Photo: Cathy Carver ID186
Photo: Christopher Burke frontispiece, 14, 16, 22, 23, 41, 43, 45, 46, 48, 50, 51, 69, 70, 78, 87, 108d, 112, 113
© Centre Pompidou, MNAM-CCI, Dist. RMN-Grand Palais / Philippe Migeat 7, 18, 19, 20, 21, 25, 26, 27, 28, 29, 30, 31, 32, 33, 34, 35, 36, 37, 38, 39, 75, 124
© Centre Pompidou, MNAM-CCI, Dist. RMN-Grand Palais / Droits reserves 80, 81, 110, 111, front cover
© Christie's Images / The Bridgeman Art Library 44, 68
© Christie's Images Limited 2014, 12, 46
Dallas Museum of Art, Foundation for the Arts Collection 134
Davis Museum and Culture Center, Wellesley College, Wellesley, MA 64
Photo: Marc Domage courtesy Fondation Louis Vuitton 117
Photo: Mike Fear 127
Photo: François Fernandez 74, 85, 107, 122, 128
© 2014. Photo Fine Art Images / Heritage Images / Scala, Florence 9
Photo: Fondation Beyeler, Riehen / Basel 72
© Photo Claude Germain – Archives Fondation Maeght, Saint-Paul de Vence (France) 42
Photography by Erik Gould, courtesy of the Museum of Art, Rhode Island School of Design, Providence 108e
Photo: Hickey-Robertson, Houston 66, 96
Courtesy Hilti Foundation 11
Ikeda Museeum of Twentieth Century Art, Ito City, Japan 91
Photographer: Alex Jamison 1, 55
Photo: Pernille Klemp 56, 57
Kunstsammlung Nordrhein-Westfalen, Dusseldorf, Germany / The Bridgeman Art Library 73
Kunstmuseum Basel, Photo: Martin P. Bühler 65
Private Collection, courtesy of Lefevre Fine Art, London 61
Photo by Eric Lubrick, courtesy of the IMA 108a–b
Courtesy Henri Matisse Archives 4, 8, 10, 13, 24, 47, 49, 63, 67, 77, 86, 89, 100, 101, 106, 119, 125, 132, 133, 135
Photo: Claude Mercier Photography 99
© 2014 Digital image. The Metropolitan Museum of Art / Art Resource / Scala Florence 2, 92, 94, 114
Courtesy Mourlot Archives 103
Photo by: Mark Morosse 93
Courtesy of Frederick Mulder Ltd 105
Image courtesy Museum of Modern Art, New York 79a–c, 82, 83, 88, 98, 121
© 2014 Digital image The Museum of Modern Art, New York / Scala Florence 130
© National Gallery of Art, Washington 115, 123, 131
© Rheinisches Bildarchiv Köln, rba_d016269 120
Photo Alberto Ricci 17
Photo: Skissernas Museum 76
© SMK Photo 84
Courtesy of Sotheby's Picture Library 97
Photo © Stedelijk 118
© 2014 Tate Photography 104, 126, 129
Photo J.-F. Tomasian 52, 53

Photo essay

Photo: © Tetsuo Abe. Courtesy Tsutomu Abe (Japan) pp. 68–9, pp. 80–1, back cover
© Hélène Adant courtesy Matisse Archives p.47, p.71, p.73, p.79, p.82
© M. Bérard p.46
© Henri Cartier-Bresson / Magnum Photos p.36
"Centre Pompidou – MnamCci – Bibliothèque Kandinsky" Photo by Hélène Adant pp.32–5, pp.52–3, p.56, p.58, p.62, p.66, p.74, p.77
© Clifford Coffin p.43, p.45
© Lucien Hervé pp.48–9, pp.54–5
© Dimitri Kessel, Paris p.70
Courtesy Henri Matisse Archives pp.40–1, p.57, p.59, p.61, pp.63–5, p.67, p.72, pp.75–6, p.78, p.83
© Paris Match / Getty Images pp.50–1,
The Pierpont Morgan Library, New York. MA 5020. Gift of the Pierre Matisse Foundation, 1997 p.37
© John Rewald, NY p.60
© Michel Sima / Rue des Archives pp.38–9, p.42, p.44,

Essay comparatives

akg / Archivio Cameraphoto Epoche fig.22
© 2014 The Barnes Foundation Archives fig.6, figs.12–13, fig.15
Photo Philip Bernard fig.4, fig.24, fig.61
Photo: Christopher Burke fig.35, fig.45
© Centre Pompidou, MNAM-CCI, Dist. RMN-Grand Palais / Philippe Migeat fig.20, fig.40
"Centre Pompidou – MnamCci – Bibliothèque Kandinsky" Photo by Hélène Adant fig.28, fig.30, fig.50
© Conde Nast fig.11
Foto: Lydia Delectorskaya fig.47, fig.63
Photo: François Fernandez fig.36
© J. Paul Getty Trust Foto: Alexander Liberman fig.60
Foto: Fondation Beyeler, Riehen / Basel figs.53–9, figs.67–9, fig.71
Graphic: Fondation Beyeler fig.62, figs.64–5
© Getty Images fig.8
Photo by Interfoto (Venice) fig.3
© Felix H. Mann fig.27
Courtesy Henri Matisse Archives fig.2, fig.5, figs.7–8, fig.14, figs.16–19, fig.23, fig.25, figs.37–9, figs.42–4, fig.46, figs.48–9, fig.52, fig.66
The Morgan Library & Museum, New York fig.26
Image courtesy Museum of Modern Art, New York fig.29, fig.31, figs.33–4, fig.41
© Paris Match / Getty Images fig.1
Photo Roger Schall © Collection Schall figs.9-10, fig.21
Photo: Skissernas Museum fig.32

Index

Page numbers in *italic* type refer to illustrated works.

Supporting Tate

Tate relies on a large number of supporters – individuals, foundations, companies and public sector sources – to enable it to deliver its programme of activities, both on and off its gallery sites. This support is essential in order for Tate to acquire works of art for the Collection, run education, outreach and exhibition programmes, care for the Collection in storage and enable art to be displayed, both digitally and physically inside and outside Tate. Your donation will make a real difference and enable others to enjoy Tate and its Collection both now and in the future. There are a variety of ways in which you can help support Tate and also benefit as a UK or US taxpayer. Please contact us at:

Development Office
Tate
Millbank
London SWIP 4RG
Tel: 020 7887 4900
Fax: 020 7887 8098

Tate Americas Foundation
520 West 27 Street Unit 404
New York, NY 10001
USA
Tel: 001 212 643 2818
Fax: 001 212 643 1001

Donations, no matter the size, are gratefully received, either to support particular areas of interest, or to contribute to general activity costs.

Tate Trustees
Tomma Abts
Lionel Barber
Tom Bloxham, MBE
The Lord Browne of Madingley, FRS, FREng (Chairman)
Mala Gaonkar
Maja Hoffmann
Lisa Milroy
Elisabeth Murdoch
Franck Petitgas
Dame Seona Reid DBE
Hannah Rothschild
Monisha Shah
Gareth Thomas
Wolfgang Tillmans

Tate Foundation Trustees and Honorary Members
Victoria Barnsley
John C Botts, CBE*
Mrs James Brice
The Lord Browne of Madingley, FRS, FREng
Susan Burns
Christina Chandris
Melanie Clore
Sir Howard Davies
Dame Vivien Duffield
George Economou
Noam Gottesman
Oliver Haarmann
Peter Kellner
Mr Ronald and the Hon Mrs Rita McAulay
Scott Mead*
Mandy Moross
Elisabeth Murdoch
Marilyn Ofer
Simon Palley*
Franck Petitgas (Chairman)*
John Porter
Sir John and Lady Ritblat
Emmanuel Roman*
Dame Theresa Sackler
The Rt Hon Sir Timothy Sainsbury
Sir Anthony Salz*
Sir Nicholas Serota*
Peter Simon
Jon Snow
Lord Stevenson of Coddenham, CBE*
Mercedes Stoutzker
John J Studzinski, CBE
Ian Taylor
Anita Zabludowicz

* Executive Trustee

Tate Americas Foundation Trustees
Frances Bowes
Estrellita Brodsky
James Chanos
Henry Christensen III
Ella Fontanals-Cisneros
Tiqui Atencio Demirdjian (Ex-officio)
Jeanne Donovan Fisher (Chair)
Noam Gottesman
Robert Rennie (Ex-officio)
John J Studzinski, CBE
Juan Carlos Verme

Tate Modern Donors to the Founding Capital Campaign
29th May 1961 Charitable Trust
AMP
The Annenberg Foundation
Arts Council England
The Asprey Family Charitable Foundation
Lord and Lady Attenborough
The Baring Foundation
Ron Beller and Jennifer Moses
Alex and Angela Bernstein
David and Janice Blackburn
Mr and Mrs Anthony Bloom
BNP Paribas
Mr and Mrs Pontus Bonnier
Lauren and Mark Booth
Mr and Mrs John Botts
Frances and John Bowes
Ivor Braka
Mr and Mrs James Brice
The British Land Company plc
Donald L Bryant Jr Family
Melva Bucksbaum
Cazenove & Co
The Clore Duffield Foundation
CGU plc
Clifford Chance
Edwin C Cohen
The John S. Cohen Foundation
Ronald and Sharon Cohen
Sadie Coles
Carole and Neville Conrad
Giles and Sonia Coode-Adams
Douglas Cramer
Alan Cristea Gallery
Thomas Dane
Michel and Hélène David-Weill
Julia W Dayton
Gilbert de Botton
Pauline Denyer-Smith and Paul Smith
Sir Harry and Lady Djanogly
The Drapers' Company
Energis Communications
English Heritage
English Partnerships
The Eranda Foundation
Esmée Fairbairn Charitable Trust
Donald and Doris Fisher
Richard B. and Jeanne Donovan Fisher
The Fishmongers' Company
Freshfields Bruckhaus Deringer
Friends of the Tate Gallery
Bob and Kate Gavron
Giancarlo Giammetti
Alan Gibbs
Mr and Mrs Edward Gilhuly
GKR
GLG Partners
Helyn and Ralph Goldenberg
Goldman Sachs
The Horace W Goldsmith Foundation
The Worshipful Company of Goldsmiths
Lydia and Manfred Gorvy
Noam and Geraldine Gottesman
Pehr and Christina Gyllenhammar
Mimi and Peter Haas
The Worshipful Company of Haberdashers
Hanover Acceptances Limited
The Headley Trust
Mr and Mrs André Hoffmann
Anthony and Evelyn Jacobs
Jay Jopling
Mr and Mrs Karpidas
Howard and Lynda Karshan
Peter and Maria Kellner
Madeleine Kleinwort
Brian and Lesley Knox
Pamela and C Richard Kramlich
Mr and Mrs Henry R Kravis
Irene and Hyman Kreitman
The Kresge Foundation
Catherine and Pierre Lagrange
The Lauder Foundation – Leonard and Evelyn Lauder Fund
Lazard Brothers & Co., Limited
Leathersellers' Company Charitable Fund
Edward and Agnès Lee
Lex Service Plc
Lehman Brothers
Ruth and Stuart Lipton
Anders and Ulla Ljungh
The Frank Lloyd Family Trusts
London & Cambridge Properties Limited
London Electricity plc, EDF Group
Mr and Mrs George Loudon
Mayer, Brown, Rowe & Maw
Viviane and James Mayor
Ronald and Rita McAulay
The Mercers' Company
The Meyer Foundation
The Millennium Commission
Anthony and Deirdre Montagu
The Monument Trust
Mori Building, Ltd
Mr and Mrs M D Moross
Guy and Marion Naggar
Peter and Eileen Norton, The Peter Norton Family Foundation
Maja Oeri and Hans Bodenmann
Sir Peter and Lady Osborne
William A Palmer
Mr Frederik Paulsen
Pearson plc
The Pet Shop Boys
The Nyda and Oliver Prenn Foundation
Prudential plc
Railtrack plc
The Rayne Foundation
Reuters
Sir John and Lady Ritblat
Rolls-Royce plc
Barrie and Emmanuel Roman
Lord and Lady Rothschild
The Dr Mortimer and Theresa Sackler Foundation
J. Sainsbury plc
Ruth and Stephan Schmidheiny
Schroders
Mr and Mrs Charles Schwab
David and Sophie Shalit
Belle Shenkman Estate
William Sieghart
Peter Simon
Mr and Mrs Sven Skarendahl
London Borough of Southwark
The Foundation for Sports and the Arts
Mr and Mrs Nicholas Stanley
The Starr Foundation
The Jack Steinberg Charitable Trust
Charlotte Stevenson
Hugh and Catherine Stevenson
John J Studzinski, CBE
David and Linda Supino
The Government of Switzerland
Carter and Mary Thacher
Insinger Townsley
UBS
UBS Warburg
David and Emma Verey
Dinah Verey
The Vintners' Company
Clodagh and Leslie Waddington
Robert and Felicity Waley-Cohen
Wasserstein, Perella & Co., Inc.
Gordon D Watson
The Weston Family
Mr and Mrs Stephen Wilberding
Michael S Wilson
Poju and Anita Zabludowicz
and those who wish to remain anonymous

Donors to The Tate Modern Project
The Blavatnik Family Foundation
Lauren and Mark Booth
The Deborah Loeb Brice Foundation
The Lord Browne of Madingley, FRS, FREng
John and Christina Chandris
James Chanos
Paul Cooke
Ago Demirdjian and Tiqui Atencio Demirdjian
Department for Culture, Media and Sport
George Economou
English Partnerships
Jeanne Donovan Fisher
Mala Gaonkar
The Ghandehari Foundation
Thomas Gibson in memory of Anthea Gibson
Lydia and Manfred Gorvy
Noam Gottesman
The Hayden Family Foundation
Maja Hoffmann/LUMA Foundation
Peter and Maria Kellner
Madeleine Kleinwort
Catherine Lagrange
Pierre Lagrange
London Development Agency
Allison and Howard W. Lutnick
Donald B. Marron
Anthony and Deirdre Montagu
Elisabeth Murdoch
Eyal Ofer Family Foundation
Maureen Paley
Midge and Simon Palley
Daniel and Elizabeth Peltz
Catherine and Franck Petitgas
Barrie and Emmanuel Roman
The Dr Mortimer and Theresa Sackler Foundation
John J Studzinski, CBE
Tate Americas Foundation
Tate Members
Nina and Graham Williams
The Wolfson Foundation
and those who wish to remain anonymous

Tate Modern Benefactors and Major Donors
We would like to acknowledge and thank the following benefactors who have supported Tate Modern prior to 1 November 2013.

29th May 1961 Charitable Trust
The Ampersand Foundation
Annenberg Foundation
The Art Fund
Art Mentor Foundation Lucerne
Arts Council England
Arts & Humanities Research Council
Charles Asprey
Marwan T Assaf
David and Liane Aukin
averda
Gillian Ayres
John Baldessari
Miroslaw Balka
Pedro Barbosa
The Estate of Peter and Caroline Barker-Mill
The Barns-Graham Charitable Trust
Veronica and Jeffrey Berman
Barbara Bertozzi Castelli

Anne Best
Big Lottery Fund
Billstone Foundation
Maria Rus Bojan
The Charlotte Bonham-Carter Charitable Trust
Pontus Bonnier
Charles Booth-Clibborn
John C Botts, CBE
Louise Bourgeois
Frances Bowes
Sir Alan and Sarah Bowness
Bowness, Hepworth Estate
Pierre Brahm
The Estate of Dr Marcella Louis Brenner
British Council
The Broad Art Foundation
The Estate of Joseph and Ruth Bromberg
Elizabeth and Rory Brooks
The Estate of Mrs Kathleen Bush
Lucy Carter
The Trustees of the Chantrey Bequest
Henry Christensen III
Patricia Phelps de Cisneros
Toby Clarke
The Clore Duffield Foundation
The Clothworkers' Foundation
Contemporary Art Society
Isabelle and John Corbani
Paul Coulon
Douglas S Cramer
Alan Cristea Gallery
The Estate of William Crozier
Thomas Dane Ltd
Dimitris Daskalopoulos
Julia W Dayton
Ago Demirdjian and Tiqui Atencio Demirdjian
Department for Business, Innovation and Skills
Department for Culture, Media and Sport
Anthony and Anne d'Offay
Peter Doig
Jytte Dresing, The Merla Art Foundation, Dresing Collection
EDP – Energias de Portugal, S.A.
Maryam and Edward Eisler
The John Ellerman Foundation
Ibrahim El-Salahi
European Commission
Esmée Fairbairn Collections Fund
Fares and Tania Fares
The Estate of Maurice Farquharson
Dan Fauci
HRH Princess Firyal of Jordan
Wendy Fisher
The Fisher Family
Jeanne Donovan Fisher
David Fitzsimons
Lady Lynn Forester de Rothschild
Eric and Louise Franck
Froehlich Foundation, Stuttgart
Glenn and Amanda Fuhrman
William Furlong
Gagosian Gallery
Johanna and Leslie J. Garfield
The Getty Foundation
Thomas Gibson
Milly and Arne Glimcher
Goethe-Institut
Nicholas and Judith Goodison
Goodman Gallery, Johannesburg and Cape Town
Douglas Gordon and Artangel
Margot and George Greig
Konstantin Grigorishin
Guaranty Trust Bank Plc
Calouste Gulbenkian Foundation
The Haberdashers' Company
Paul Hamlyn Foundation
Viscount and Viscountess Hampden and Family
Heritage Lottery Fund
Friends of Heritage Preservation
Damien Hirst
Robert Hiscox
David Hockney
The Estate of Mrs Mimi Hodgkin
Maja Hoffmann/LUMA Foundation
Vicky Hughes and John A Smith
The Idlewild Trust
Cristina Iglesias
Iran Heritage Foundation
Fady Jameel
Amrita Jhaveri
Karpidas Family
J. Patrick Kennedy and Patricia A. Kennedy
Kirby Laing Foundation
Jack Kirkland
James and Clare Kirkman
Leon Kossoff
Samuel H. Kress Foundation, administered by the Foundation of the American Institute for Conservation
David and Amanda Leathers
The Leche Trust
Agnes and Edward Lee
Simon and Carine Lee
Legacy Trust UK
The Leathersellers' Company Charitable Fund
The Leverhulme Trust
Gemma Levine
London Organising Committee of the Olympic and Paralympic Games
The Henry Luce Foundation
Peter and Susan MacGill
Christopher Eykyn and Nicholas Maclean
The Estate of Sir Edwin Manton
The Manton Foundation
Fernanda Feitosa and Heitor Martins
Lord McAlpine of West Green
Mark McCain
The Andrew W Mellon Foundation
Mikati Foundation
Sir Geoffroy Millais
Jean-Yves Mock
Mondriaan Foundation, Amsterdam
The Henry Moore Foundation
Peter Moores Foundation
Daido Moriyama
The Estate of Mrs Jenifer Ann Murray
NADFAS
National Heritage Memorial Fund
Embassy of the Kingdom of the Netherlands
The Netherlands Organisation for Scientific Research (NWO)
New Art Trust
Mr Sean O'Connor
Tony Oursler and Artangel
Outset Contemporary Art Fund
Irene Panagopoulos
The Paolozzi Foundation
The Estate of Mr Brian and Mrs Nancy Pattenden
Stephen and Yana Peel
Andrea and José Olympio Pereira
Slavica Perkovic
Catherine Petitgas
Clive Phillpot
Stanley Picker Trust
PINTA Museum Acquisition Program
The Porter Foundation
Gilberto Pozzi
Isabella Prata and Idel Arcuschin
Glenstone Foundation, Emily and Mitchell Rales
The Reed Foundation
Frances Reynolds
Sir John Richardson
Yvonne Robinson
Barrie and Emmanuel Roman
Edward Ruscha
Keith and Kathy Sachs
The Estate of Simon Sainsbury
Sally and Anthony Salz
The Sandra Charitable Trust
Fondation Saradar
James Scott
Robert Scott
The Search Foundation
Candida and Rebecca Smith
Clive K Smith, OBE in memory of his wife, Ann Moya Smith
Susana and Ricardo Steinbruch
Mercedes and Ian Stoutzker
Luisa Strina
Ambassador Louis and Marjorie Susman
Swiss Arts Council Pro Helvetia
The Estate of Jiro Takamatsu
Tate Africa Acquisitions Committee
Tate Americas Foundation
Tate Asia-Pacific Acquisitions Committee
Tate International Council
Tate Latin American Acquisitions Committee
Tate Members
Tate Middle East and North Africa Acquisitions Committee
Tate North American Acquisitions Committee
Tate Patrons
Tate Photography Acquisitions Committee
Tate Russia and Eastern Europe Acquisitions Committee
Tate South Asia Acquisitions Committee
Taylor Family Foundation
Melissa Tecklenberg
Terra Foundation for American Art
The Estate of Mr Nicholas Themans
Tishman Speyer
The Tretyakov Family Collection
US Embassy, London
Petri and Jolana Vainio
The Vandervell Foundation
The Wellcome Trust
The Estate of Fred Williams
Jane and Michael Wilson
Ivan and Manuela Wirth
Samuel and Nina Wisnia
The Lord Leonard and Lady Estelle Wolfson Foundation
Poju and Anita Zabludowicz
Ms Silke Ziehl
and those who wish to remain anonymous

Platinum Patrons

Mr Alireza Abrishamchi
Ghazwa Mayassi Abu-Suud
Mr Shane Akeroyd
Basil Alkazzi
Ryan Allen and Caleb Kramer
Mr and Mrs Edward Atkin CBE
Rhona Beck
Beecroft Charitable Trust
Mr Harry Blain
Rory and Elizabeth Brooks (Chair)
The Lord Browne of Madingley, FRS, FREng
Karen Cawthorn Argenio
Mr Stephane Custot
Ms Miel de Botton
Ms Sophie Diedrichs-Cox
Elizabeth Esteve
Mr David Fitzsimons
The Flow Foundation
Mr Michael Foster
Edwin Fox Foundation
Mrs Lisa Garrison
Hugh Gibson
The Goss-Michael Foundation
Ms Nathalie Guiot
Mr and Mrs Yan Huo
Mr Phillip Hylander
Anne-Marie and Geoffrey Isaac
Mrs Gabrielle Jungels-Winkler
Maria and Peter Kellner
Esperanza Koren
Mr and Mrs Eskandar Maleki
Scott and Suling Mead
Gabriela Mendoza and Rodrigo Marquez
Pierre Tollis and Alexandra Mollof
Mr Donald Moore
Mary Moore
Mr and Mrs Paul Phillips
Mariela Pissioti
Maya and Ramzy Rasamny
Frances Reynolds
Simon and Virginia Robertson
Mr and Mrs Richard Rose
Claudia Ruimy
Vipin Sareen and Rebecca Mitchell
Hakon Runer and Ulrike Schwarz-Runer
Mr and Mrs J Shafran
Mrs Andrée Shore
Maria and Malek Sukkar
Mr Vladimir Tsarenkov and Ms Irina Kargina
Mr and Mrs Petri Vainio
Michael and Jane Wilson
Poju and Anita Zabludowicz
and those who wish to remain anonymous

Gold Patrons

Eric Abraham
The Anson Charitable Trust
Katrina Barter
Jenny and Robert Borgerhoff Mulder
Elena Bowes
Broeksmit Family Foundation
Ben and Louisa Brown
Nicolò Cardi
Melanie Clore
Beth and Michele Colocci
Bilge Ogut-Cumbusyan and Haro Cumbusyan
Mr Dónall Curtin
Mrs Robin D'Alessandro
Harry G. David
Mr Frank Destribats
Mrs Maryam Eisler
Mala Gaonkar
Kate Groes
Mrs Helene Guerin-Llamas
Ms Natascha Jakobs
Tiina Lee
Paul and Alison Myners
Reem Nassar
Mr Francis Outred
Simon and Midge Palley
Mathew Prichard
Valerie Rademacher
Carol Sellars
Mrs Dana Sheves
Mr and Mrs Stanley S. Tollman
Emily Tsingou and Henry Bond
Mrs Celia Forner Venturi
Rebecca Wang
Manuela and Iwan Wirth
Barbara Yerolemou
and those who wish to remain anonymous

Silver Patrons

Allahyar Afshar
Agnew's
Sharis Alexandrian
Ms Maria Allen
Mrs Malgosia Alterman
Toby and Kate Anstruther
Mr and Mrs Zeev Aram
Mrs Charlotte Artus
Tim Attias
Miss Silvia Badiali
Mrs Jane Barker
Mr Edward Barlow
Victoria Barnsley, OBE
Jim Bartos
Alex Beard
Mrs Cynthia Lewis Beck
Mr Harold Berg
Lady Angela Bernstein
Madeleine Bessborough
Ms Karen Bizon
Janice Blackburn
Shoshana Bloch
David Blood and Beth Bisso
Mrs Sofia Bogolyubov
Nathalie and Daniel Boulakia
Helen Boyan
Mr Brian Boylan
Ivor Braka
Alex Branczik
Viscountess Bridgeman
The Broere Charitable Foundation
Mr Dan Brooke
Michael Burrell
Mrs Marlene Burston
Mrs Aisha Caan
Timothy and Elizabeth Capon
Mr Francis Carnwath and Ms Caroline Wiseman
Lord and Lady Charles Cecil
Dr Peter Chocian
Frank Cohen
Nicola Collard
Mrs Jane Collins
Dr Judith Collins
Terrence Collis
Mr and Mrs Oliver Colman
Carole and Neville Conrad
Giles and Sonia Coode-Adams
Alastair Cookson
Cynthia Corbett
Mark and Cathy Corbett
Tommaso Corvi-Mora
Mr and Mrs Bertrand Coste
Kathleen Crook and James Penturn
James Curtis
Loraine da Costa
Sir Howard Davies
Mr and Mrs Roger de Haan
Giles de la Mare
Maria de Madariaga
Mr Jean-Evrard Dominicé and Mrs Stephanie de Preux Dominicé
Anne Chantal Defay Sheridan
Marco di Cesaria
Simon C Dickinson Ltd
James Diner
Liz and Simon Dingemans
Ms Charlotte Ransom and Mr Tim Dye
Rafe Eddington
Joan Edlis
Lord and Lady Egremont
Jeffrey and Jennifer Eldredge
John Erle-Drax
Dr Nigel Evans
Stuart and Margaret Evans
Eykyn Maclean LLC
Gerard Faggionato
Ms Rose Fajardo
Richard Farleigh
Mrs Heather Farrar

David Fawkes
Mrs Margy Fenwick
Mr Bryan Ferry, CBE
The Sylvie Fleming Collection
Mrs Jean Fletcher
Lt Commander Paul Fletcher
Steve Fletcher
Katherine Francey Stables
Elizabeth Freeman
Stephen Friedman
Mr Mark Glatman
Ms Emily Goldner and
Mr Michael Humphries
Mr Jonathan Goodman
Kate Gordon
Mr and Mrs Paul Goswell
Penelope Govett
Martyn Gregory
Sir Ronald Grierson
Mrs Kate Grimond
Richard and Odile Grogan
Michael and Morven Heller
Richard and Sophia Herman
Mrs Patsy Hickman
Robert Holden
James Holland-Hibbert
Lady Hollick, OBE
Holtermann Fine Art
John Huntingford
Mr Alex Ionides
Maxine Isaacs
Helen Janecek
Sarah Jennings
Mr Haydn John
Mr Michael Johnson
Jay Jopling
Mrs Marcelle Joseph and
Mr Paolo Cicchiné
Mrs Brenda Josephs
Tracey Josephs
Mr Joseph Kaempfer
Andrew Kalman
Ghislaine Kane
Jag-Preet Kaur
Dr Martin Kenig
Simon and Jeannette Kenny
Mr David Ker
Nicola Kerr
Mr and Mrs Simon Keswick
Richard and Helen Keys
Mrs Mae Khouri
David Killick
Mr and Mrs James Kirkman
Brian and Lesley Knox
The Kotick Family
Kowitz Trust
Mr and Mrs Herbert Kretzmer
Linda Lakhdhir
Mrs Julie Lee
Simon Lee
Mr Gerald Levin
Leonard Lewis
Sophia and Mark Lewisohn
Mr Gilbert Lloyd
George Loudon
Mrs Elizabeth Louis
Mark and Liza Loveday
Catherine Lovell
Daniella Luxembourg Art
Kate MacGarry
Anthony Mackintosh
Fiona Mactaggart
The Mactaggart Third Fund
Mrs Jane Maitland Hudson
Lord and Lady Marks
Marsh Christian Trust
David McCleave
Mrs Anne-Sophie McGrath
Ms Fiona Mellish
Mr Martin Mellish
Mrs R W P Mellish
Professor Rob Melville
Mr Alfred Mignano
Victoria Miro
Ms Milica Mitrovich
Jan Mol
Lulette Monbiot
Mrs Bona Montagu
Mr Ricardo Mora
Mrs William Morrison
Richard Nagy
Julian Opie
Pilar Ordovás
Isabelle Paagman
Desmond Page
Maureen Paley
Dominic Palfreyman
Michael Palin
Mrs Adelaida Palm
Stephen and Clare Pardy
Mrs Véronique Parke
Mr Sanjay Parthasarathy
Frans Pettinga
Trevor Pickett
Mr Oliver Prenn
Susan Prevezer QC
Mr Adam Prideaux
Mr and Mrs Ryan Prince
James Pyner
Ivetta Rabinovich
Patricia Ranken
Mrs Phyllis Rapp
Ms Victoria Reanney
Dr Laurence Reed
The Reuben Foundation
Sir Tim Rice
Lady Ritblat
Ms Chao Roberts
David Rocklin
Frankie Rossi
Mr David V Rouch
Mr James Roundell
Mr Charles Roxburgh
Naomi Russell
Mr Alex Sainsbury and
Ms Elinor Jansz
Mr Richard Saltoun
Mrs Amanda Sater
Mrs Cecilia Scarpa
Cherrill and Ian Scheer
Sylvia Scheuer
The Schneer Foundation
Mrs Cara Schulze
Deborah Scott
The Hon Richard Sharp
Neville Shulman, CBE
Ms Julia Simmonds
Paul and Marcia Soldatos
Mr George Soros
Louise Spence
Mr and Mrs Nicholas Stanley
Mr Nicos Steratzias
Mrs Patricia Swannell
Mr James Swartz
The Lady Juliet Tadgell
Tot Taylor
Christopher and Sally Tennant
Anthony Thornton
Britt Tidelius
Mr Henry Tinsley
Karen Townshend
Andrew Tseng
Melissa Ulfane
Mrs Cecilia Versteegh
Mr Jorge Villon
Gisela von Sanden
Audrey Wallrock
Sam Walsh AO
Stephen and Linda Waterhouse
Offer Waterman
Terry Watkins
Lisa West
Miss Cheyenne Westphal
Walter H. White, Jnr.
Sue Whiteley
Mr David Wood
Mr Douglas Woolf
Anthony Zboralski
and those who wish to remain anonymous

Young Patrons
Vinita Agarwal
Stephanie Alameida
HH Princess Nauf AlBendar Al-Saud
Jonathan Algar
Miss Noor Al-Rahim
HRH Princess Alia Al-Senussi (Chair, Young Patrons Ambassador Group)
Miss Sharifa Alsudairi
Sigurdur Arngrimsson
Miss Katharine Arnold
Maria and Errikos Arones
Miss Joy Asfar
Ms Mila Askarova
Miss Olivia Aubry
Flavie Audi
Sarah Bejerano
Josh Bell and Jsen Wintle
Miss Marisa Bellani
Mr Erik Belz
Mr Edouard Benveniste-Schuler
Miss Margherita Berloni
William Bertagna
Mrs Sofia Bocca
Roberto Boghossian
Alina Boyko
Johan Bryssinck
Miss Verena Butt
Miss May Calil
Miss Sarah Calodney
Matt Carey-Williams and
Donnie Roark
Georgina Casals
Alexandra and Kabir Chhatwani
Miss Katya Chitova
Arthur Chow
Bianca Chu
Mrs Mona Collins
Mrs Laura Comfort
Alicia Corbin
Thamara Corm
Daphné Cramer
Miss Amanda C Cronin
Mr Theo Danjuma
Mr Joshua Davis
Ms Lora de Felice
Countess Charlotte de la Rochefoucauld
Emilie De Pauw
Agnes de Royere
Federico Martin Castro Debernardi
Carine Decroi
Mira Dimitrova
Ms Michelle D'Souza
Indira Dyussebayeva
Alexandra Economou
Miss Roxanna Farboud
Emilie Faure
Jane and Richard Found
Mr Andreas Gegner
Mrs Benedetta Ghione-Webb
Miss Dori Gilinski
Georgia Griffiths
Jessica Grosman
Olga Grotova and Oleksiy Osnach
Mr Nick Hackworth
Alex Haidas
Ms Michelle Harari
Sara Harrison
Kira Allegra Heller
Christoph Hett
Mrs Samantha Heyworth
Andrew Honan
Katherine Ireland
Miss Eloise Isaac
Kamel Jaber
Scott Jacobson
Mr Christopher Jones
Ms Melek Huma Kabakci
Sophie Kainradl
Miss Meruyert Kaliyeva
Efe and Aysun Kapanci
Nicole Karlisch
Philipp Keller
Miss Tamila Kerimova
Ms Chloe Kinsman
Ms Marijana Kolak
Zeynep Korutürk
Alkistis Koukouliou
Miss Marina Kurikhina
Mr Jimmy Lahoud
Ms Aliki Lampropoulos
Ms Anna Lapshina
Isabella Lauder-Frost
Mrs Julie Lawson
Lin Lei
Karen Levy
Miss MC Llamas
Mr Justin Lobo
Alex Logsdail
Mr John Madden
Ms Sonia Mak
Mr Jean-David Malat
Kamiar Maleki
Zoe Marden
Rebecca Marques
Dr F. Mattison Thompson
Ms Clémence Mauchamp
Miss Nina Moaddel
Mr Fernando Moncho Lobo
Ms Michelle Morphew
Erin Morris
Ali Munir
Katia Nounou
Mrs Annette Nygren
Katharina Ottmann
Christine Chungwon Park
Ms Camilla Paul
Alexander V. Petalas
Mrs Stephanie Petit
The Piper Gallery
Mr Eugenio Re Rebaudengo
Mr Bruce Ritchie and
Mrs Shadi Ritchie
Mr Simon Sakhai
Miss Tatiana Sapegina
Olga Savchenko
Elena Scarpa
Franz Schwarz
Alex Seddon
Count Indoo Sella Di Monteluce
James Sevier
Robert Sheffield
Henrietta Shields
Mr Paul Shin
Ms Marie-Anya Shriro
Laura Simkins
Jag Singh
Tammy Smulders
Miss Jelena Spasojevic
Thomas Stauffer and Katya Garcia-Anton
Alexandra Sterling
Gemma Stewart-Richardson
Mr Dominic Stolerman
Gerald Tan
Mr Edward Tang
Nayrouz Tatanaki
Miss Georgiana Teodorescu
Miss Inge Theron
Soren S K Tholstrup
Hannah Tjaden
Mr Giancarlo Trinca
Mrs Padideh Trojanow
Mr Philippos Tsangrides
Ms Navann Ty
Angus Walker
Mr Neil Wenman
Ms Hailey Widrig Ritcheson
Lars N. Wogen
Miss Julia Wright
Ms Seda Yalcinkaya
Arani Yogadeva
Daniel Zarchan
Alma Zevi
and those who wish to remain anonymous

International Council Members
Mr Segun Agbaje
Staffan Ahrenberg, Editions Cahiers d'Art
Doris Ammann
Mr Plácido Arango
Gabrielle Bacon
Anne H Bass
Cristina Bechtler
Nicolas Berggruen
Olivier and Desiree Berggruen
Baron Berghmans
Mr Pontus Bonnier
Frances Bowes
Ivor Braka
The Deborah Loeb Brice Foundation
The Broad Art Foundation
Bettina and Donald L Bryant Jr
Melva Bucksbaum and
Raymond Learsy
Andrew Cameron AM
Fondation Cartier pour l'art contemporain
Nicolas and Celia Cattelain
Mrs Christina Chandris
Richard Chang
Pierre TM Chen, Yageo Foundation, Taiwan
Lord Cholmondeley
Mr Kemal Has Cingillioglu
Mr and Mrs Attilio Codognato
Sir Ronald Cohen and
Lady Sharon Harel-Cohen
Mr Douglas S Cramer and
Mr Hubert S Bush III
Mr Dimitris Daskalopoulos
Mr and Mrs Michel David-Weill
Julia W Dayton
Ms Miel de Botton
Tiqui Atencio Demirdjian and
Ago Demirdjian
Joseph and Marie Donnelly
Mrs Olga Dreesmann
Mrs Jytte Dresing
Barney A Ebsworth
Füsun and Faruk Eczacibaşi
Stefan Edlis and Gael Neeson
Mr and Mrs Edward Eisler
Carla Emil and Rich Silverstein
Alan Faena
Harald Falckenberg
Fares and Tania Fares
HRH Princess Firyal of Jordan
Mrs Doris Fisher
Mrs Wendy Fisher
Dr Corinne M Flick
Amanda and Glenn Fuhrman
Candida and Zak Gertler
Alan Gibbs
Lydia and Manfred Gorvy
Kenny Goss
Mr Laurence Graff
Ms Esther Grether
Konstantin Grigorishin
Mr Xavier Guerrand-Hermès
Mimi and Peter Haas Fund
Margrit and Paul Hahnloser
Andy and Christine Hall
Mr Toshio Hara
Paul Harris
Mrs Susan Hayden
Ms Ydessa Hendeles
Marlene Hess and James D. Zirin
André and Rosalie Hoffmann
Ms Maja Hoffmann (Chair)
Vicky Hughes
ITYS, Athens
Dakis and Lietta Joannou
Sir Elton John and
Mr David Furnish
Pamela J. Joyner
Mr Chang-Il Kim
Jack Kirkland
C Richard and Pamela Kramlich

Bert Kreuk
Catherine Lagrange
Mr Pierre Lagrange and
Mr Roubi L'Roubi
Bernard Lambilliotte
Agnès and Edward Lee
Mme RaHee Hong Lee
Jacqueline and Marc Leland
Mr and Mrs Sylvain Levy
Mr Eugenio Lopez
Mrs Fatima Maleki
Panos and Sandra Marinopoulos
Mr and Mrs Donald B Marron
Andreas and Marina Martinos
Mr Ronald and The Hon
Mrs McAulay
Angela Westwater and
David Meitus
Mr Leonid Mikhelson
Simon and Catriona Mordant
Mrs Yoshiko Mori
Mr Guy and The Hon Mrs Naggar
Mr and Mrs Takeo Obayashi
Hideyuki Osawa
Irene Panagopoulos
Young-Ju Park
Yana and Stephen Peel
Daniel and Elizabeth Peltz
Andrea and José Olympio Pereira
Catherine and Franck Petitgas
Sydney Picasso
Mr and Mrs Jürgen Pierburg
Jean Pigozzi
Lekha Poddar
Ms Miuccia Prada and
Mr Patrizio Bertelli
Laura Rapp and Jay Smith
Maya and Ramzy Rasamny
Patrizia Sandretto Re Rebaudengo
and Agostino Re Rebaudengo
Robert Rennie and Carey Fouks
Mr John Richardson
Michael Ringier
Lady Ritblat
Dame Theresa Sackler
Mrs Lily Safra
Muriel and Freddy Salem
Dasha Shenkman
Uli and Rita Sigg
Michael S Smith
Norah and Norman Stone
Julia Stoschek
John J Studzinski, CBE
Maria and Malek Sukkar
Mrs Marjorie Susman
David Teiger
Mr Budi Tek, The Yuz Foundation
Mr Robert Tomei
The Hon Robert H Tuttle and
Mrs Maria Hummer-Tuttle
Mr and Mrs Guy Ullens
Mrs Ninetta Vafeia
Corinne and Alexandre Van
Damme
Paulo A W Vieira
Robert and Felicity Waley-Cohen
Diana Widmaier Picasso
Christen and Derek Wilson
Michael G Wilson
Mrs Sylvie Winckler
The Hon Dame Janet Wolfson
de Botton, DBE
Anita and Poju Zabludowicz
Michael Zilkha
and those who wish to remain anonymous

Africa Acquisitions Committee
Tutu Agyare (Co-Chair)
Bolanle Austen-Peters
Mrs Nwakaego Boyo
Lavinia Calza
Priti Chandaria Shah
Mrs Kavita Chellaram
Salim Currimjee
Harry G. David
Mr and Mrs Michel David-Weill
Robert Devereux (Co-Chair)
Hamish Dewar
Mrs Wendy Fisher
Kari Gahiga
Andrea Kerzner
Samallie Kiyingi
Matthias and Gervanne Leridon
Nicholas Logsdail
Caro Macdonald
Dr Kenneth Montague
Miles Morland
Alain F. Nkontchou
Professor Oba Nsugbe QC
Pascale Revert Wheeler
Kathryn Jane Robins
Emile Stipp
Roelof Petrus van Wyk
Varnavas A. Varnava
Mercedes Vilardell
Tony Wainaina
and those who wish to remain anonymous

Asia-Pacific Acquisitions Committee
Bonnie and R Derek Bandeen
Andrew Cameron AM
Mr and Mrs John Carrafiell
Mrs Christina Chandris
Richard Chang
Pierre TM Chen, Yageo
Foundation, Taiwan
Adrian Cheng
Mr and Mrs Yan d'Auriol
Katie de Tilly
Mr Hyung-Teh Do
Ms Mareva Grabowski
Reade and Elizabeth Griffith
Louisa Guinness
Kyoko Hattori
Cees Hendrikse
Mr Yongsoo Huh
Tessa Keswick
Shareen Khattar Harrison
Mr Chang-Il Kim
Ms Yung Hee Kim
Alan Lau
Woong Yeul Lee
Mr William Lim
Ms Dina Liu
Ms Kai-Yin Lo
Anne Louis-Dreyfus
Mrs Geraldine Elaine Marden
The Red Mansion Foundation
Mr Jackson See
Mr Paul Serfaty
Dr Gene Sherman AM
Leo Shih
Mr Robert Shum
Sir David Tang (Chair)
Mr Budi Tek, The Yuz Foundation
Rudy Tseng (Taiwan)
and those who wish to remain anonymous

Latin American Acquisitions Committee
Monica and Robert Aguirre
Karen and Leon Amitai
Luis Benshimol
Billy Bickford, Jr. and
Oscar Cuellar
Estrellita and Daniel Brodsky
Trudy and Paul Cejas
Patricia Phelps de Cisneros
Gerard Cohen
David Cohen Sitton
HSH the Prince Pierre d'Arenberg
Tiqui Atencio Demirdjian (Chair)
Patricia Druck
Angelica Fuentes de Vergara
Mauro Herlitzka
Rocio and Boris Hirmas Said
Anne Marie and Geoffrey Isaac
Nicole Junkermann
Jack Kirkland
Fatima and Eskander Maleki
Becky and Jimmy Mayer
Solita and Steven Mishaan
Catherine and Michel Pastor
Catherine Petitgas
Frances Reynolds
Erica Roberts
Judko Rosenstock and
Oscar Hernandez
Guillermo Rozenblum
Alin Ryan Lobo
Lilly Scarpetta and Roberto
Pumarejo
Norma Smith
Juan Carlos Verme
Tania and Arnoldo Wald
Juan Yarur Torres
and those who wish to remain anonymous

Middle East and North Africa Acquisitions Committee
HRH Princess Alia Al-Senussi
Abdullah Al Turki
Mehves Ariburnu
Sule Arinc
Marwan T Assaf
Perihan Bassatne
Boghossian Foundation
Ms Isabelle de la Bruyère
Füsun Eczacibaşi
Maryam Eisler (Co-Chair)
Shirley Elghanian
Delfina Entrecanales, CBE
Noor Fares
Taymour Grahne
Maha and Kasim Kutay
Nina Mahdavi
Mrs Fatima Maleki
Fayeeza Naqvi
Dina Nasser-Khadivi
Ebru Özdemir
Mrs Edwina Özyegin
Ramzy and Maya Rasamny
(Co-Chair)
Mrs Karen Ruimy
Dania Debs-Sakka
Sherine Magar-Sawiris
Miss Yassi Sohrabi
Maria and Malek Sukkar
Ana Luiza and Luiz Augusto
Teixeira de Freitas
Berna Tuglular
and those who wish to remain anonymous

North American Acquisitions Committee
Carol and David Appel
Jackie Appel
Dorothy Berwin and
Dominique Levy
Paul Britton
Dillon Cohen
Matt Cohler
Beth Rudin De Woody
James Diner
Wendy Fisher
Glenn Fuhrman
Victoria Gelfand-Magalhaes
Pamela Joyner
Monica Kalpakian
Elisabeth and Panos Karpidas
Christian K Keese
Anne Simone Kleinman
and Thomas Wong
Celine and Jacques Lamarre
Marjorie and Michael Levine
James Lindon
Massimo Marcucci
Lillian and Billy Mauer
Liza Mauer and Andrew Sheiner
Nancy McCain
Della and Stuart McLaughlin
Marjorie and Marc McMorris
Stavros Merjos
Gregory R. Miller
Shabin and Nadir Mohamed
Jenny Mullen
Elisa Nuyten and David Dime
Amy and John Phelan
Nathalie Pratte
Melinda B and Paul Pressler
Liz Gerring Radke and
Kirk Radke
Laura Rapp and Jay Smith
Robert Rennie (Chair) and
Carey Fouks
Kimberly Richter
Amie Rocket and
Anthony Munk
Donald R Sobey
Robert Sobey
Beth Swofford
Dr Diane Vachon
Christen and Derek Wilson
and those who wish to remain anonymous

Photography Acquisitions Committee
Ryan Allen
Sheikha Fatima Bint Hazza'
Bin Zayed Al Nahyan
Artworkers Retirement Society
Joumana Lati Asseily
Mr Nicholas Barker
Marisa Bellani
Veronica and Jeffrey Berman
Pierre Brahm (Chair)
William and Alla Broeksmit
Elizabeth and Rory Brooks
Marcel and Gabrielle Cassard
Nicolas and Celia Cattelain
Beth and Michele Colocci
Fares and Tania Fares
David Fitzsimons
Louise Baring Franck
Lisa Garrison
Ms Emily Goldner and
Mr Michael Humphries
George and Margot Greig
Alexandra Hess
Michael Hoppen
Bernard Huppert
Tim Jefferies, Hamiltons Gallery
Dede Johnston
Jack Kirkland
Cynthia Lewis Beck
Mr Scott Mead
Sebastien Montabonel
Mr Donald Moore
Mr Axel Nordin
Ellen and Dan Shapiro
Saadi Soudavar
Maria and Malek Sukkar
Mrs Caroline Trausch
Michael and Jane Wilson
and those who wish to remain anonymous

Russia and Eastern Europe Acquisitions Committee
Dilyara Allakhverdova
David Birnbaum
Maria Rus Bojan
Maria Bukhtoyarova
Mark Čuček
Mr Pavel Erochkine
Dr Kira Flanzraich (Chair)
Lyuba Galkina
Konstantin Grigorishin
Cees Hendrikse
Carl Kostyál
Arina Kowner
Mrs Grażyna Kulczyk
Peter Kulloi
Ms Nonna Materkova
Teresa Mavica
Neil K. Rector
Ovidiu Sandor
Zsolt Somlói
Tretyakov Family Collection
Igor Tsukanov
Mrs Alina Uspenskaya
and those who wish to remain anonymous

South Asia Acquisitions Committee
Dr Amin Jaffer
Darashaw K Mehta
Yamini Mehta
Mr Rohan Mirchandani
Shalini Misra
Amna and Ali Naqvi
Fayeeza Naqvi
Mrs Chandrika Pathak
Puja and Uday Patnaik
Lekha Poddar (Chair)
Mrs Mehreen Rizvi-Khursheed
Rajeeb Samdani
Tarana Sawhney
Mrs Faiza Seth
Azad Shivdasani
Dinesh and Minal Vazirani,
Saffronart
Iwan Wirth
and those who wish to remain anonymous

Tate Modern Corporate Supporters
Bank of America Merrill Lynch
Bloomberg
BMW
BP
Christie's
EY
Hanjin Shipping
Hildon Limited
Hyundai Motor
Itaú
Le Méridien
Sotheby's
Vodafone Group
and those who wish to remain anonymous

Tate Modern Corporate Members
AIG
Baker & McKenzie
Bank of America Merrill Lynch
Christie's
Citi
Clifford Chance LLP
Deloitte LLP
Deutsche Bank
EY
GAM (UK) Limited
HSBC
JATO Dynamics
JCA Group
The John Lewis Partnership
Kingfisher plc
Linklaters
Mace
Mazars
Morgan Stanley
Native Land and Grosvenor
Oliver Wyman
Pearson
Saatchi & Saatchi
The Brooklyn Brothers
Tishman Speyer
Unilever
Vodafone
Wolff Olins
and those who wish to remain anonymous

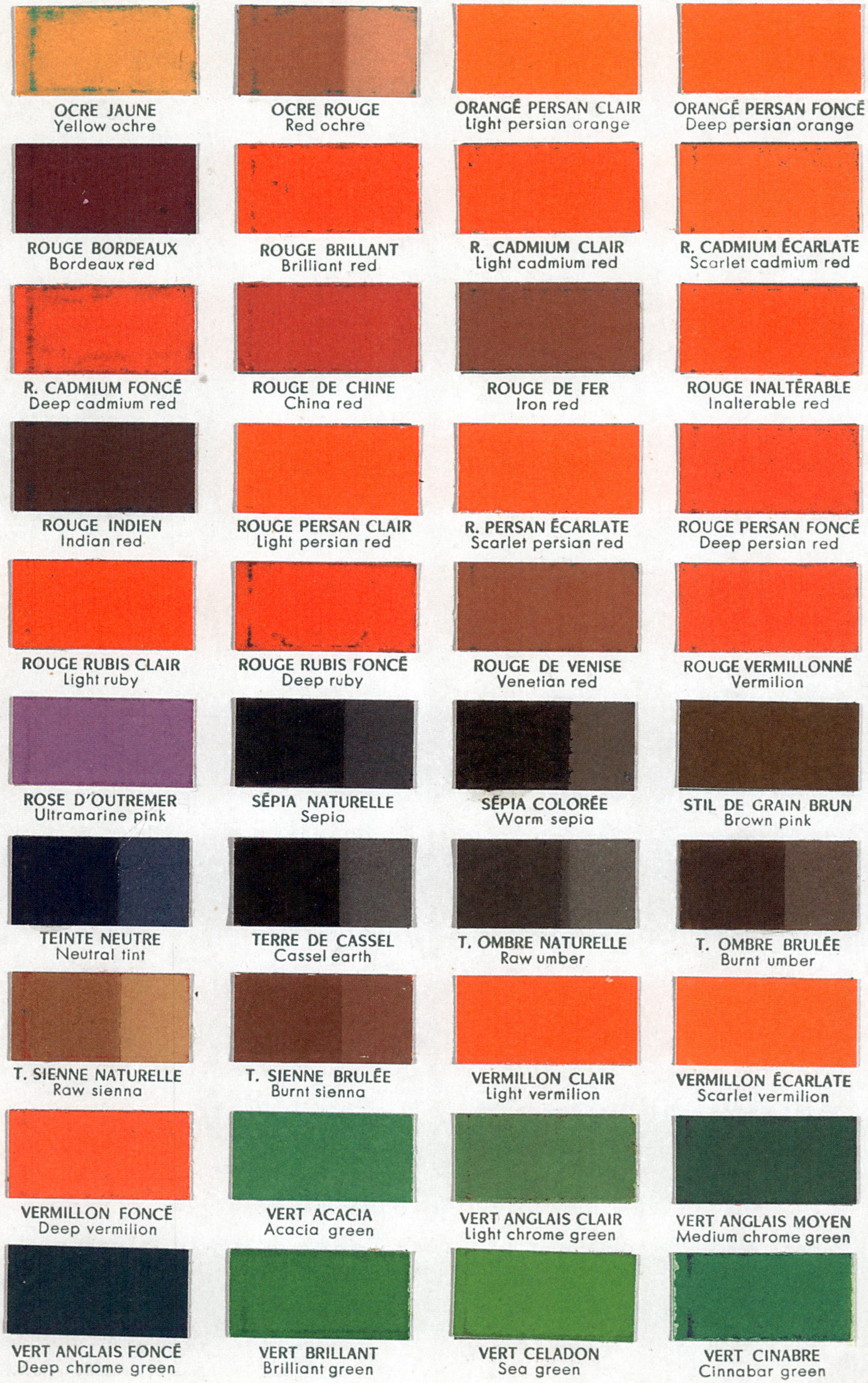
OCRE JAUNE
Yellow ochre
OCRE ROUGE
Red ochre
ORANGÉ PERSAN CLAIR
Light persian orange
ORANGÉ PERSAN FONCÉ
Deep persian orange
ROUGE BORDEAUX
Bordeaux red
ROUGE BRILLANT
Brilliant red
R. CADMIUM CLAIR
Light cadmium red
R. CADMIUM ÉCARLATE
Scarlet cadmium red
R. CADMIUM FONCÉ
Deep cadmium red
ROUGE DE CHINE
China red
ROUGE DE FER
Iron red
ROUGE INALTÉRABLE
Inalterable red
ROUGE INDIEN
Indian red
ROUGE PERSAN CLAIR
Light persian red
R. PERSAN ÉCARLATE
Scarlet persian red
ROUGE PERSAN FONCÉ
Deep persian red
ROUGE RUBIS CLAIR
Light ruby
ROUGE RUBIS FONCÉ
Deep ruby
ROUGE DE VENISE
Venetian red
ROUGE VERMILLONNÉ
Vermilion
ROSE D'OUTREMER
Ultramarine pink
SÉPIA NATURELLE
Sepia
SÉPIA COLORÉE
Warm sepia
STIL DE GRAIN BRUN
Brown pink
TEINTE NEUTRE
Neutral tint
TERRE DE CASSEL
Cassel earth
T. OMBRE NATURELLE
Raw umber
T. OMBRE BRULÉE
Burnt umber
T. SIENNE NATURELLE
Raw sienna
T. SIENNE BRULÉE
Burnt sienna
VERMILLON CLAIR
Light vermilion
VERMILLON ÉCARLATE
Scarlet vermilion
VERMILLON FONCÉ
Deep vermilion
VERT ACACIA
Acacia green
VERT ANGLAIS CLAIR
Light chrome green
VERT ANGLAIS MOYEN
Medium chrome green
VERT ANGLAIS FONCÉ
Deep chrome green
VERT BRILLANT
Brilliant green
VERT CELADON
Sea green
VERT CINABRE
Cinnabar green